T0335474

Examining Information Retrieval and Image Processing Paradigms in Multidisciplinary Contexts

Joan Lu
University of Huddersfield, UK

Qiang Xu
University of Huddersfield, UK

A volume in the Advances in Information Quality and Management (AIQM) Book Series

www.igi-global.com

Published in the United States of America by
IGI Global
Information Science Reference (an imprint of IGI Global)
701 E. Chocolate Avenue
Hershey PA, USA 17033
Tel: 717-533-8845
Fax: 717-533-8661
E-mail: cust@igi-global.com
Web site: http://www.igi-global.com

Library of Congress Cataloging-in-Publication Data

Names: Lu, Zhongyu, 1955- editor. | Xu, Qiang, 1963- editor.
Title: Examining information retrieval and image processing paradigms in
  multidisciplinary contexts / Joan Lu, Qiang Xu, [editors].
Description: Hershey, PA : Information Science Reference, [2017] | Series:
  Advances in information quality and management | Includes bibliographical
  references and index.
Identifiers: LCCN 2016048128| ISBN 9781522518846 (hardcover) | ISBN
  9781522518853 (ebook)
Subjects: LCSH: Information retrieval. | Image processing--Digital
  techniques. | Electronic books. | Reading, Psychology of. | Multiagent
  systems.
Classification: LCC ZA3075 .E97 2017 | DDC 025.5/24--dc23 LC record available at https://lccn.loc.gov/2016048128

This book is published in the IGI Global book series Advances in Information Quality and Management (AIQM) (ISSN: 2331-7701; eISSN: 2331-771X)

British Cataloguing in Publication Data
A Cataloguing in Publication record for this book is available from the British Library.

All work contributed to this book is new, previously-unpublished material. The views expressed in this book are those of the authors, but not necessarily of the publisher.

For electronic access to this publication, please contact: eresources@igi-global.com.

Advances in Information Quality and Management (AIQM) Book Series

Siddhartha Bhattacharyya
RCC Institute of Information Technology, India

ISSN:2331-7701
EISSN:2331-771X

MISSION

Acquiring and managing quality information is essential to an organization's success and profitability. Innovation in information technology provides managers, researchers, and practitioners with the tools and techniques needed to create and adapt new policies, strategies, and solutions for information management.

The **Advances in Information Quality and Management (AIQM) Book Series** provides emerging research principals in knowledge society for the advancement of future technological development. This series aims to increase available research publications and emphasize the global response within the discipline and allow for audiences to benefit from the comprehensive collection of this knowledge.

COVERAGE

- Supply Chain Management
- Knowledge Management
- Mobile Commerce
- Human and Societal Issue
- Web services and technologies
- Emerging Technologies Management
- IT Management in Public Organizations
- Decision Support and Group Decision Support Systems
- Business Process Management and Modeling
- IT Innovation and Diffusion

IGI Global is currently accepting manuscripts for publication within this series. To submit a proposal for a volume in this series, please contact our Acquisition Editors at Acquisitions@igi-global.com or visit: http://www.igi-global.com/publish/.

Titles in this Series

For a list of additional titles in this series, please visit: www.igi-global.com

Handbook of Research on Information Architecture and Management in Modern Organizations
George Leal Jamil (Informações em Rede, Brazil) José Poças Rascão (Polytechnic Institute of Setúbal, Portugal)
Fernanda Ribeiro (Porto University, Portugal) and Armando Malheiro da Silva (Porto University, Portugal)
Information Science Reference • copyright 2016 • 625pp • H/C (ISBN: 9781466686373) • US $325.00 (our price)

Inventive Approaches for Technology Integration and Information Resources Management
Mehdi Khosrow-Pour (Information Resources Management Association, USA)
Information Science Reference • copyright 2014 • 315pp • H/C (ISBN: 9781466662568) • US $205.00 (our price)

Quality Innovation Knowledge, Theory, and Practices
Latif Al-Hakim (University of Southern Queensland, Australia) and Chen Jin (Zhejiang University, China)
Information Science Reference • copyright 2014 • 640pp • H/C (ISBN: 9781466647695) • US $245.00 (our price)

Rethinking the Conceptual Base for New Practical Applications in Information Value and Quality
George Leal Jamil (FUMEC University, Brazil) Armando Malheiro (Universidade do Porto, Portugal) and Fernanda
Ribeiro (Universidade do Porto, Portugal)
Information Science Reference • copyright 2014 • 345pp • H/C (ISBN: 9781466645622) • US $175.00 (our price)

Cases on Electronic Records and Resource Management Implementation in Diverse Environments
Janice Krueger (Clarion University of Pennsylvania, USA)
Information Science Reference • copyright 2014 • 467pp • H/C (ISBN: 9781466644663) • US $175.00 (our price)

www.igi-global.com

701 E. Chocolate Ave., Hershey, PA 17033
Order online at www.igi-global.com or call 717-533-8845 x100
To place a standing order for titles released in this series, contact: cust@igi-global.com
Mon-Fri 8:00 am - 5:00 pm (est) or fax 24 hours a day 717-533-8661

Table of Contents

Section 1
Data Mining Approaches and Image Data Processing and Applications

Section 2
Factors Influence Reading from Screen of Arabic Textbook for Learning by Children Aged 9 to 13

Section 3
Neural Trust Model for Multi-Agent Systems

Chapter 21

Final Remarks on The Investigation in Neural Trust in Multi-Agent Systems and Possible Future

Gehao Lu, Yunnan University, China
Joan Lu, University of Huddersfield, UK

Detailed Table of Contents

Section 1
Data Mining Approaches and Image Data Processing and Applications

Chapter 1

QingE Wu, Zhengzhou University of Light Industry, China
Weidong Yang, Fudan University, China

In order to complete an online, real-time and effective aging detection to software, this paper studies a local approach that is also called a fuzzy incomplete and a statistical data mining approaches, and gives their algorithm implementation in the software system fault diagnosis. The application comparison of the two data mining approaches with four classical data mining approaches in software system fault diagnosis is discussed. The performance of each approach is evaluated from the sensitivity, specificity, accuracy rate, error classified rate, missed classified rate, and run-time. An optimum approach is chosen from several approaches to do comparative study. On the data of 1020 samples, the operating results show that the fuzzy incomplete approach has the highest sensitivity, the forecast accuracy that are 96.13% and 94.71%, respectively, which is higher than those of other approaches. It has also the relatively less error classified rate is or so 4.12%, the least missed classified rate is or so 1.18%, and the least runtime is 0.35s, which all are less than those of the other approaches. After the performance, indices are all evaluated and synthesized, the results indicate the performance of the fuzzy incomplete approach is best. Moreover, from the test analysis known, the fuzzy incomplete approach has also some advantages, such as it has the faster detection speed, the lower storage capacity, and does not need any prior information in addition to data processing. These results indicate that the mining approach is more effective and feasible than the old data mining approaches in software aging detection.

Chapter 2

QingE Wu, Zhengzhou University of Light Industry, China
Weidong Yang, Fudan University, China

The existing image processing algorithms mainly studied on feature extraction of gray image with one-dimensional parameter, such as edges, corners. However, the extraction of some characteristic points to color image with three-dimensional parameters, such as the extraction of color edge, corner points, inflection points, etc., is an image problem to be urgently solved. In order to carry out a fast and accurate feature extraction on color image, this paper proposes two types of extraction algorithms to color edge and corner points of color image, i.e., similar color segment algorithm and pixel probabilistic algorithm, compares with the two algorithms, gives the two algorithms are used to different color distribution situations, as well as shows the extraction effect of color by the combination of the two algorithms, moreover, gives the contrast experiment and effect analysis of the two algorithms. To compare the similar color segment algorithm with the probabilistic algorithm, experimental results show that the similar color segment algorithm is better than the pixel probabilistic algorithm under the more obvious color edge, because it has the better edge detection, stronger anti-noise ability, faster processing speed and other advantages. Under the transition phase of color edge is gentle or color edge is no clear, the image detection effect of the pixel probabilistic algorithm is better than that of the similar color segment algorithm. But the combinative effect of the two algorithms is the best in this case, which is more close to the color effect of original image. Moreover, this paper analyzes the performance of the similar color segment algorithm, and gives the comparison of the proposed two algorithms and existing classical algorithms used usually to feature extraction of color image. The two algorithms proposed and these researches development in this paper have not only enriched the contents of image processing algorithms, but also provide a solution tool for image segmentation, feature extraction to target, precise positioning, etc., such as extraction of complexion, physiological color photographs processing, feature extraction of ionosphere, detection and extraction of biological composition of oceans, to be applied to a lots of departments, such as the police, hospital departments, surgery, polar department, and so on, as well as provide a way of thinking for the rapid, accurate detection of case, surgery, scientific research information search.

Chapter 3

QingE Wu, Zhengzhou University of Light Industry, China
Weidong Yang, Fudan University, China

Image segmentation is an important research direction in pattern recognition and image understanding, but existing texture segmentation algorithms cannot take full advantage of some texture information of texture image, such as the direction, width, density of ridge line, and so on, and can also not effectively carry out the segmentation of various texture image quality. In order to efficiently implement the texture image segmentation, strengthen the amassing of region segmentation, improve the accuracy of segmentation, achieve more accurate target recognition, this paper defines the direction of the texture, calculates the width of ridge line, gives the distance characteristics between textures, and establishes the mathematical model of the texture border, accordingly presents a new texture segmentation algorithm and compares with other texture segmentation algorithms. The simulation results show that the segmentation algorithm has some advantages to texture segmentation, such as has higher segmentation precision, faster segmentation speed, stronger anti-noise capability, less lost information of target, and so on. The segmented regions hardly contain other texture regions and background region. Moreover, this paper extracts the characteristic points and characteristic parameters in various segmented regions for texture image to obtain the characteristic vector, compares the characteristic vector with the standard template vectors, and identifies the type of target in a range of threshold value. Experimental results show that the proposed target recognition approach has higher recognition rate, faster recognition speed, and stronger anti-noise characteristics than the existing target recognition approaches.

Chapter 4

QingE Wu, Zhengzhou University of Light Industry, China
Weidong Yang, Fudan University, China

To carry out an effective recognition for palmprint, this paper presents an algorithm of image segmentation of region of interest (ROI), extracts the ROI of a palmprint image and studies the composing features of palmprint. This paper constructs coordinates by making use of characteristic points in the palm geometric contour, improves the algorithm of ROI extraction, and provides a positioning method of ROI. Moreover, this paper uses the wavelet transform to divide up ROI, extracts the energy feature of wavelet, gives an approach of matching and recognition to improve the correctness and efficiency of existing main recognition approaches, and compares it with existing main approaches of palmprint recognition by experiments. The experiment results show that the approach in this paper has the better recognition effect, the faster matching speed, and the higher recognition rate which is improved averagely by 2.69% than those of the main recognition approaches.

Chapter 5

QingE Wu, Zhengzhou University of Light Industry, China
Weidong Yang, Fudan University, China

In order to provide an accurate and rapid target recognition method for some military affairs, public security, finance and other departments, this paper studies firstly a variety of fuzzy signal, analyzes the uncertainties classification and their influence, eliminates fuzziness processing, presents some methods and algorithms for fuzzy signal processing, and compares with other methods on image processing. Moreover, this paper uses the wavelet packet analysis to carry out feature extraction of target for the first time, extracts the coefficient feature and energy feature of wavelet transformation, gives the matching and recognition methods, compares with the existing target recognition methods by experiment, and presents the hierarchical recognition method. In target feature extraction process, the more detailed and rich texture feature of target can be obtained by wavelet packet to image decomposition to compare with the wavelet decomposition. In the process of matching and recognition, the hierarchical recognition method is presented to improve the recognition speed and accuracy. The wavelet packet transformation is used to carry out the image decomposition. Through experiment results, the proposed recognition method has the high precision, fast speed, and its correct recognition rate is improved by an average 6.13% than that of existing recognition methods. These researches development in this paper can provide an important theoretical reference and practical significance to improve the real-time and accuracy on fuzzy target recognition.

Section 2
Factors Influence Reading from Screen of Arabic Textbook for Learning by Children Aged 9 to 13

Chapter 6

Azza A Abubaker, Benghazi University, Libya & University of Huddersfield, UK
Joan Lu, University of Huddersfield, UK

The research aims to identify the problems and seek for possible solutions in e-reading context from a systematic discussion that is supported by more than 50 relevant references. The definitions of the problem have been presented. Numbers of research questions are asked prior to the methodologies. The importance and differences of qualitative and quantitative methods are addressed. Meanwhile, ethical issues and their benefits and risks are discussed and explained. Finally, the research framework is proposed as guidance for the near future research actions.

Chapter 7

Reading from Screen: Theoretical and Empirical Background 123

Azza A Abubaker, Benghazi University, Libya
Joan Lu, University of Huddersfield, UK

This research aims to deliver the fundamental, theoretical and empirical background surrounding electronic reading. It is structured into five sections starting with a reading definition, reading process, and a comparison between reading from paper and from an electronic format. The fourth section discusses the variables that influence reading electronic texts. These variables are classified into three categories: the individual or user variables (age, gender, experience and educational level); the text layout variables (font type and size, line length, spaces between lines of text, colour); and the applied technology (hardware and software). In the fifth section, a summary of previous studies is given and a framework for these variables is suggested based on the previous surveys.

Chapter 8

Theoretical and Empirical Background to the eBook 150

Azza A Abubaker, Benghazi University, Libya & University of Huddersfield, UK
Joan Lu, University of Huddersfield, UK

A textbook in any e-educational system is an important element that requires a closer look at its components and structure, as well as identifying the barriers that affect the level of learning. This can be achieved in different aspects such as the analysis of textual content or sentence structure which is one of the concerns of linguists. On the other hand, examining the textual content can determine the appropriateness of the education level for students. This type of assessment is part of educators' concerns and by examining and defining the factors that could affect reading a text on screen, this is usually related to the way of displaying text such as font size, colour, background colour, amount of text and the location of the text on the screen. This is a key focus of this research. In this chapter, the concern will be to define the concepts and the structure of an e- document as a starting point to investigate the usability of e-texts as it covers the following: definition of e-document; history of eBook; structure of e-textbook; contribution of e-textbook for education; comparison between reading electronic and paper book; young people and the use of the internet and computer; statistical data for using the internet in Arabic countries; designing an e-textbook.

Chapter 9

Access and Use of the Internet among Libyan Primary School Students: Analysis of
Questionnaire Data.. 173

Azza A Abubaker, Benghazi University, Libya & University of Huddersfield, UK
Joan Lu, University of Huddersfield, UK

This chapter aims to examine the use of the internet and eBook among students in public primary schools in Libya. The literature showed a lack of research that examines access to the Internet, students' awareness of eBook, and using the computer for learning at school. However, this type of research has been important in providing a better understanding of eBook usage and helping designers to create eBooks that meet user needs. Thus, the number of netizens determines the causes of use as a starting point for understanding and determining e- reading stages in order to investigate the factors that affect e- text reading among young people. This chapter presents the questionnaire data as analysed by the Statistical Package for the Social Sciences (SPSS) software for analysis and focuses on collecting quantitative data that can help build a clear understanding of current user behaviour. At the end of this chapter, these two objectives should be met: examining the use of Internet among students aged 9 to 13, and defining the awareness and aim of using eBook among students.

Chapter 10
Azza A Abubaker, Benghazi University, Libya
Joan Lu, University of Huddersfield, UK

In order to be sure that the level of e-text usability in early education can be improved, the following questions should be answered by the end of this chapter: RQ1: What are the existing prototypes (structure) of schoolbooks in primary education (PE)? RQ2: How are students interacting with schoolbooks in the electronic and printed version? RQ3: Is there a difference in the reading process between e-school textbook and p-school text-book? Quantitative and qualitative data were used in order to answer these three questions. The outcome was two flow charts which explain the interactions among students when reading e- schoolbook and paper schoolbook. In addition, it draws a clear picture of the design and structure of schoolbooks in Libya which are similar to schoolbooks used in other Arabic countries at the same educational level. The chapter comprises two main sections. The first section presents the data collection methods and research type. The second section displays the results of the observation. The chapter ends with a conclusion highlighting the main points that has discussed in the chapter.

Chapter 11
Azza A Abubaker, Benghazi University, Libya
Joan Lu, University of Huddersfield, UK

The outcomes for the previous experiment in this research indicated that students' attitudes differ according to the way of presenting the text and text layout. As the aim of the study was to investigate the three main typographic variables [font size, font type and line length] we will start by font size and font type. Much research has highlighted the character size as a factor in visual display, and reported that font size has a significant effect on readability of texts in both versions. Therefore, defining a readable font size for the Arabic language is the main focus of this experiment, taking into account the effect of one dependent variable, four controlled variables and two independent variables: content length and font type. Students were required to make different judgments of letter pairs, thus indicating which letters were distinguishable. Based on the findings of this experiment, subsequent experiments were designed. In addition, the findings of this experiment will be able to address the issues related to reading Arabic text from screen by children in relation to the following: RQ1: In which font size is the Arabic text read most effectively? RQ2: Is there any correlation between age of the reader and font size? RQ3: Which font type is more readable?

Chapter 12

Although experimental studies have shown a strong impact of text layout on the legibility of e- text, many digital texts appearing in eBook or the Internet use different designs, so that there is no straightforward answer in the literature over which one to follow when designing e- material. Therefore, in this chapter we shall focus on the text layout, particularly the influence of line length. This experiment is divided into two parts. The first part focuses on the factor of line length by studying its effect on reading speed and accuracy using various columns [one column and two columns] with each page having the same amount of information. The second part tests a new approach which basically assumes that by using different colours for the first and last word of each line, it will improve students' reading level. This hypothesis was based on pervious findings over the difficulty of being able to immediately locate the following line (Chan and Lee 2005). In addition, this approach was based on explanation of the eye movement which, in the reading process, does not scan a line but stops for about ¼ of a second before jumping to new place such as at the end of the line when the eye goes back to the beginning of the new line.

Chapter 13

Selecting an optimal layout of academic text for display on screen was affected by several factors such as; type of material, subject or readers` age. In this study researcher assumed that each reading strategy requires a specific layout. Thus, the study starts with an understanding of the way that students interact with the text in both formats [electronic and paper]. Findings from this phase were linked with three common typography variables to provide standards for optimal design. In this chapter, the findings of this research are interpreted in the light of the theoretical perspective of the study by linking it with the objectives of the study already set out in chapter one. The first section is devoted to debating the outcomes related to the use of the Internet and eBooks by children at school and at home. This is identified as the first layer of the children's usability of online text, suggesting a further analysis of the children's experience of the e- text with a focus on the reading processes of the schoolbook in both versions [paper and online]. The third section is devoted to discussing the results related to readable Arabic font size and type. Section four is concerned with the findings from testing the effect of line length on reading speed and comprehension of Arabic text; whereas, the fifth section is devoted to debating the outcomes related to the new method for presenting Arabic texts.

Chapter 14

This research is an attempt to examine the effect of reading processes on designing e-texts for children using Arabic script. In addition, it aims to develop a model for designing acceptance that will have the power to demonstrate acceptance and usage behaviour of the e-school text using a schoolbook for primary schools in Libya. Alternatively, dealing with the research problem led to the specification of the following research objectives, which were achieved through four inter- related surveys: to build an e-reading strategy for a schoolbook based on users' cognitive and behaviour processes, to define the typographical variables that affect reading Arabic texts from the screen such as font size, font type, background color, line length and text format from a literature survey, to provide a standard that can help keep children's concentration on the text, to create a guideline that could help designers when designing e-Arabic texts for children, to examine in-depth the challenges of reading Arabic e-texts, to study the efficiency of Arabic text reading and the factors impacting the efficiency of reading and comprehension, to understand children's behaviour when reading from a screen. The aim of this chapter is to discuss the study's contribution to knowledge and provide recommendations for future research.

Section 3
Neural Trust Model for Multi-Agent Systems

Chapter 15

Gehao Lu, Yunnan University, China
Joan Lu, University of Huddersfield, UK

Introducing trust and reputation into multi-agent systems can significantly improve the quality and efficiency of the systems. The computational trust and reputation also creates an environment of survival of the fittest to help agents recognize and eliminate malevolent agents in the virtual society. The research redefines the computational trust and analyzes its features from different aspects. A systematic model called Neural Trust Model for Multi-agent Systems is proposed to support trust learning, trust estimating, reputation generation, and reputation propagation. In this model, the research innovates the traditional Self Organizing Map (SOM) and creates a SOM based Trust Learning (STL) algorithm and SOM based Trust Estimation (STE) algorithm. The STL algorithm solves the problem of learning trust from agents' past interactions and the STE solve the problem of estimating the trustworthiness with the help of the previous patterns. The research also proposes a multi-agent reputation mechanism for generating and propagating the reputations. The mechanism exploits the patterns learned from STL algorithm and generates the reputation of the specific agent. Three propagation methods are also designed as part of the mechanism to guide path selection of the reputation. For evaluation, the research designs and implements a test bed to evaluate the model in a simulated electronic commerce scenario. The proposed model is compared with a traditional arithmetic based trust model and it is also compared to itself in situations where there is no reputation mechanism. The results state that the model can significantly improve the quality and efficacy of the test bed based scenario. Some design considerations and rationale behind the algorithms are also discussed based on the results.

Chapter 16

Gehao Lu, University of Huddersfield, UK & Yunnan University, China
Joan Lu, University of Huddersfield, UK

This chapter provides a systematic background study in the neural trust and multi-agent system. Theoretic models are discussed in details. The concepts are explained. The existing systems are analyzed. The limitations and strength of previous research are discussed. About 59 references are cited to support the study for the investigation. The study did address the research importance and significance and finally, proposed the future directions for the research undertaken.

Gehao Lu, University of Huddersfield, UK & Yunnan University, China
Joan Lu, University of Huddersfield, UK

The problems found in the existing models push the researcher to look for a better solution for computational trust and computational reputation. According the problem exposed earlier, the newly proposed model should be a systematic model which supports both trust and reputation. The model should also take the learning capability for agents into consideration because agents cannot quickly adapt to the changes without learning. The model also needs to have the ability to make decisions according to its recognition of trust. Before actually building the model, it is necessary to analyze the concept of trust. Usually when people say trust they mean human trust, however, in this research trust refers to computational trust. How human trust is different from computational trust is a very interesting question. The answers to the question helped the researcher recover many features of computational trust and built a solid theoretical foundation for the proposed model. The definitions of trust in different disciplines such as economy, sociology and psychology will be compared. A possible definition of computational trust will be made and such trust from several different perspectives will be analyzed. The description of the model is important. As a whole, it is represented as a framework that defines components and component relationships. As the concrete components, the purposes and responsibilities of the specific component are explained. This is to illustrate the static structure of the model. The dynamic structure of the model is described as the process of executing the model.

Gehao Lu, Yunnan University, China
Joan Lu, University of Huddersfield, UK

Predict uncertainty is critic in decision making process, especially for the complex systems. This chapter aims to discuss the theory involved in Self-Organizing Map (SOM) and its learning process, SOM based Trust Learning Algorithm (STL), SOM based Trust Estimation Algorithm (STL) as well as features of generated trust patterns. Several patterns are discussed within context. Both algorithms and how they are processed have been described in detail. It is found that SOM based Trust Estimation algorithm is the core algorithm that help agent make trustworthy or untrustworthy decisions.

Gehao Lu, Yunnan University, China
Joan Lu, University of Huddersfield, UK

Reputation plays an important role in multi-agent system. It is a socialized form of trust which makes agent cooperate with each other and reduces the cost of agents' interaction. In a world with only computational trust, the agent can only perceive its own interactions. Its learned trust pattern can only be used by itself. There is no socialized mechanism to magnify the trustworthiness that has been learned. To introduce reputation is the solution to efficiently exploit the trust patterns. If the NTR algorithm is designed for intelligent agents, then the reputation propagation models and reputation generation mechanism are designed for multi-agent systems. Introducing reputation into multi-agent systems brings many benefits: the agent can greatly extend its range of influence to cover other agents. The agent also can share the interaction experience with others. Such sharing will accelerate the washing out of malevolent agents and increase the possibility of transactions for benevolent agents. The reputation will improve the executive efficiency of agents by avoiding unnecessary communication and transactions. In general, reputation is the key to form a tight coupling agent society. There is no acknowledged or standard definition for computational reputation. But it is possible to describe it from five facets: interaction experience, intention of propagation, range of propagation, path of propagation, content of reputation. Interaction experience explains the reputation from the view of information source; intention of propagation explains from the view of agents' motivation; range of propagation explains from the view of spatial consideration; path of propagation explains from the view of network; content of reputation explains from the expression of the reputation. The author builds three models of reputation propagation. Point-to-point based inquiry allows an initiative agent start an inquiry request to its acquaintance. If the middle agent has intention to transfer the inquiry, then the request can be propagated far from the initiative agent and thus form a reputation network. Broadcasting based propagation is to let agent broadcast its experience about every interaction or transaction so that every other agents in the society can learn what happened.

Chapter 20

This chapter focuses on the testing for a complete systematic neural trust model developed previously based on the trust learning algorithms, trust estimation algorithm and reputation mechanisms. The focus is to describe the detailed design of the model and explain the rationales behind the model design. The purpose is to evaluate the proposed neural trust model from different aspects and analyze the results of the evaluations. Experiments have been conducted. Results are presented and discussed. Finally, based on the analysis and comparison of acquired results, conclusions are drawn.

Chapter 21

This chapter provides the book's summary and conclusion on the neural trust in multi-agent systems. It also discusses possible future research directions in the field. The other chapters that make up this book collectively discuss ontology and big data.

Preface

OVERVIEW

Information retrieval is a classical topic. Most existing books in the area are textbooks, which go back to 1963's *Natural Language and Computer* (Garvin, 1963). A number of books were published in 1990s. The books were mainly focused on document engineering, as addressed in *Text-Based Intelligent Systems: Current Research and Practice in Information Extraction and Retrieval* (Jacobs, 1992), *Lexical Acquisition: Exploiting On-Line Resources to Build a Lexicon* (Zernik, 1991), and *From Documentation to Information Science: The Beginnings and Early Development of the American Documentation Institute* (Farkas-Conn, 1990), and rarely extended to interdisciplinary and multiple disciplinary collaborations.

In 2008, a book titled *An Introduction to Information Retrieval* by Christopher D. Manning, Prabhakar Raghavan, and Hinrich Schütze was published. The book introduced some theories and technology, such as Web, Internet, and XML into the topic area. However, the focus of the book is still on the publishing area.

In 2010, Stefan Büttcher, Charles L. A. Clarke, and Gordon V. Cormack published a book titled *Information Retrieval: Implementing and Evaluating Search Engines*. This textbook provided detailed materials for the students at both theoretic and practical levels mainly in the search engines that were used in IR.

In 1999 a textbook titled *Modern Information Retrieval* by Ricardo Baeza-Yates and Berthier Ribeiro-Neto was published by Anderson Wesley Longman. This chapter-based book was written by leading researchers, each chapter for one topic in the subject area. However, powerful environments like distributed systems (e.g. Grid, Cloud, etc.) for IR were still in laboratory-based investigations at that time, or were not developed at all. Thus, this knowledge introduced in this book certainly needs to be updated.

Likewise, in 2015, Springer published a research-based book titled *Advances in Information Retrieval* (Hanbury, Kazai, Rauber, & Fuhr, 2015). This book is the conference proceedings that revealed there is no systematically serious research approach as the contents are a collection of short papers. Table 1 shows a summery for the requested information, although they are not completely presented.

In the light of above, Information Retrieval (IR) is experiencing a challenge moving forward from traditional technology to emerging technologies. Today's IR needs the support from Web services, distributed systems (e.g. Cloud storage), security measures, big data science, including static text message passing and dynamic imaging processing, dynamic data streaming, and data visualization. Single technology, single topic and discipline are insufficient to cope with the fast increase of data/document exchanging and transferring speed and volume, variety of resources, and maintaining the quality of data.

Table 1. Published books on information retrieval

Titles	Authors	Publisher	Price	Year	Pages
Natural Language and the Computer	Paul L. Garvin	McGraw-Hill	Not found	1963	420
Text-Based Intelligent Systems: Current Research and Practice in Information Extraction and Retrieval	Paul S. Jacobs	Lawrence Erlbaum Associates	£61.6	1992	300
From Documentation to Information Science: The Beginnings and Early Development of the American Documentation Institute	Irene S. Farkas-Conn	Greenwood Press	£74 (Amazon)	1990	248
Lexical Acquisition: Exploiting On-Line Resources to Build a Lexicon	Uri Zernik	Lawrence Erlbaum Associates	Hardcover, £95 Paper cover, £51.59 (Amazon)	1991	216
Modern Information Retrieval	Ricardo Baeza-Yates and Berthier Ribeiro-Neto	Addison Wesley Longman	£24.99 (Amazon)	1999	544
Introduction to Information Retrieval	Christopher D. Manning, Prabhakar Raghavan, and Hinrich Schütze	Cambridge University Press	£39.99 (Amazon)	2008	506
Information Retrieval: Implementing and Evaluating Search Engines	Stefan Büttcher, Charles L. A. Clarke, and Gordon V. Cormack	MIT Press	£44.95 (Amazon)	2010	632
Advances in Information Retrieval	Hanbury, Kazai, Rauber, and Fuhr	37th European Conference on IR Research, ECIR 2015, Vienna, Austria, March 29 - April 2, 2015. Proceedings, Series: Lecture Notes in Computer Science, Vol. 9022, Subseries: Information Systems and Applications, incl. Internet/Web, and HCI	£74	2015	894

HOW THE TOPIC FITS INTO TODAY'S WORLD

The proposed book integrates emerging technologies into the IR domain. The organisation of the book is a research-based structure that differs from other existing textbooks and from chapter-based short paper collections. The topics are uniquely presented in retrieval and extraction, such as ontology, e-reading, particularly related to the education for the children, XML security, a sensitive topic in modern document retrieval, data transferring in distributed systems, image processing, which involves large data process and is always debated in the latest research topic of big data science, and the contributions of distributed systems to IR. Each section is a complete piece of research consisting of several chapters. Researchers, students, professors, lecturers, and professionals at different levels can benefit from the materials provided in the book. The authors of this book are from international communities from countries in Europe (the UK), the Middle East (Jordan, Libya), and the Far East (China) that may provide a good marketing opportunity to promote the book in the near future.

THE TARGET AUDIENCE

Immediate audiences for this book are from the area of information retrieval around world. The book targets the readers who are interested in the latest theories, methods, technologies, and tools for IR in interdisciplinary and multidisciplinary research and applications; researchers who are working in higher education, industrial companies, and professional bodies can also benefit from the book; professors, lectures, and teachers from a wide range of subject areas can benefit from the book if they are interested in IR. The book can be an inspiration for research initiatives, reading material for educators and students, and a library collection for this fast-developing subject area with emerging cutting-edge technologies.

THE IMPORTANCE OF EACH OF THE CHAPTERS

This book is organized in three sections with 21 chapters. Section one is about Data Mining Approaches and Image Data Processing and Applications. Section two is about Factors Influence Reading from Screen of Arabic Textbook for Learning by Children Aged 9 to 13. Section 3 is about Neural Trust Model for Multi-agent Systems. The importance of each section will be introduced as follows.

Section one includes 5 chapters in the investigation of the data mining into the image data processing and applications. As the aerospace, polar environments, software systems and its operating environment have become increasingly complex, types of events are an increasingly more, the complexity is increasing, there are many uncertainties leading to the equipment aging and affecting the survivability of a variety of systems. For extracting related properties that affect system stability, there is considerable fuzziness and incompleteness. In order to effectively real time apply in engineering and present a multidimensional stability measurement model that can reflect a running state and an adaptive ability of the system, how to mine potential, useful data from the mass, fuzzy and complex data, and effectively classify data, is an urgent in-depth research subject.

Section two includes seven chapters that research into the factors that influence reading from screen of Arabic textbook for learning by children aged 9 to 13. The problems with e-texts are related to the way texts are displayed on a screen, with multiple and different aspects that affect legibility, making readers prefer to read a paper format rather than e-resources. This research describes the factors that affect the legibility of online texts aimed at obtaining a better understanding of the usability of electronic Arabic texts for learning purposes within the field of electronic reading; mainly reading Arabic texts for students aged 9 to 13. This study sets out three particular aims: (1) building a reading strategy for Arabic schoolbook in both formats electronic and paper format based on users' cognitive and behavioral processes; (2) defining the influence of three typographical variables that affect reading Arabic texts on a screen (font size, font-type and line length); and (3) studying the efficiency of reading Arabic texts and the related factors impacting the efficiency of reading and comprehension.

The study has made a significant contribution to the understanding of electronic reading of Arabic language. This contribution addressed five aspects: (1) Two models of reading process for schoolbook using Arabic language were built according to users' interaction with the school textbook in two formats (electronic and paper). These models will not only help define the interaction amongst users and e-books, but will also help designers to understand user behavior of e-books and thereby to establish the most appropriate functions/features when building an e-book interface. (2) Identify the optimal font size for reading an Arabic script from screen by children aged 9 to 13. (3) Based on collecting data from experiments (2) and (3) and comparing this date with other researches that have done in the same field, new model explains the interaction between three topographical variables [font size, font type and line length] and their relationships with independent variables were provided. (4) Test a new display technique to improve the legibility of reading Arabic online texts by using color to increase the ability to focus vision when moving from one line to another so as to improve the screen display. And (5) according to quantitative and qualitative several of the rules were recommended for designers and educators to follow when designing and presenting Arabic text on screen.

Section three includes 7 chapters that present a piece of research work in neural trust model for multi-agent systems. Introducing trust and reputation into multi-agent systems can significantly improve the quality and efficiency of the systems. The computational trust and reputation also creates an environment of survival of the fittest to help agents recognize and eliminate malevolent agents in the virtual society. The research redefines the computational trust and analyzes its features from different aspects. A systematic model called Neural Trust Model for Multi-agent Systems is proposed to support trust learning, trust estimating, reputation generation, and reputation propagation. In this model, the research innovates the traditional Self Organizing Map (SOM) and creates a SOM based Trust Learning (STL) algorithm and SOM based Trust Estimation (STE) algorithm. The STL algorithm solves the problem of learning trust from agents' past interactions and the STE solve the problem of estimating the trustworthiness with the help of the previous patterns. The research also proposes a multi-agent reputation mechanism for generating and propagating the reputations. The mechanism exploits the patterns learned from STL algorithm and generates the reputation of the specific agent. Three propagation methods are also designed as part of the mechanism to guide path selection of the reputation. For evaluation, the research designs and implements a test bed to evaluate the model in a simulated electronic commerce scenario. The proposed model is compared with a traditional arithmetic based trust model and it is also compared to itself in situations where there is no reputation mechanism. The results state that the model can significantly improve the quality and efficacy of the test bed based scenario. Some design considerations and rationale behind the algorithms are also discussed based on the results.

CONCLUSION

This book opens a set of discussions into today's information retrieval paradigm. The concepts and the state-of-the-art technology in the information retrieval and approaches are addressed. It covers:

1. Contributions of key technologies in IR (i.e., spatial data mining, ontology, big data analytic tool, spatial data mining, XML security, distributed systems, web mining, text mining, etc.);
2. Contributions of key application areas to IR (i.e., multimedia, social media, e-banking, information science, etc.); and
3. New challenges in the research into retrieval efficiency, accuracy, and correctness for a wide range of disciplines.

REFERENCES

Baeza-Yates, R., & Ribeiro-Neto, B. (1999). *Modern information retrieval*. Reading, MA: Addison Wesley Longman.

Büttcher, S., Clarke, C. L. A., & Cormack, G. V. (2010). *Information retrieval: Implementing and evaluating search engines*. Cambridge, MA: MIT Press.

Farkas-Conn, I. S. (1990). *From documentation to information science: The beginnings and early development of the American Documentation Institute*. Westport, CT: Greenwood Press.

Garvin, P. L. (1963). *Natural language and the computer*. New York: McGraw-Hill.

Hanbury, A., Kazai, G., Rauber, A., & Fuhr, N. (Eds.). (2015). *Proceedings of the advances in information retrieval, 37th European conference on IR research*, Vienna, Austria. Springer.

Jacobs, P. S. (1992). *Text-based intelligent systems: Current research and practice in information extraction and retrieval*. Hoboken, NJ: Lawrence Erlbaum Associates.

Manning, C. D., Raghavan, P., & Schütze, H. (2008). *Introduction to information retrieval*. Cambridge, UK: Cambridge University Press. doi:10.1017/CBO9780511809071

Zernik, U. (1991). *Lexical acquisition: Exploiting on-line resources to build a lexicon*. Hoboken, NJ: Lawrence Erlbaum Associates.

Section 1
Data Mining Approaches and Image Data Processing and Applications

Chapter 1
A Local Approach and Comparison with Other Data Mining Approaches in Software Application

QingE Wu
Zhengzhou University of Light Industry, China

Weidong Yang
Fudan University, China

ABSTRACT

In order to complete an online, real-time and effective aging detection to software, this paper studies a local approach that is also called a fuzzy incomplete and a statistical data mining approaches, and gives their algorithm implementation in the software system fault diagnosis. The application comparison of the two data mining approaches with four classical data mining approaches in software system fault diagnosis is discussed. The performance of each approach is evaluated from the sensitivity, specificity, accuracy rate, error classified rate, missed classified rate, and run-time. An optimum approach is chosen from several approaches to do comparative study. On the data of 1020 samples, the operating results show that the fuzzy incomplete approach has the highest sensitivity, the forecast accuracy that are 96.13% and 94.71%, respectively, which is higher than those of other approaches. It has also the relatively less error classified rate is or so 4.12%, the least missed classified rate is or so 1.18%, and the least runtime is 0.35s, which all are less than those of the other approaches. After the performance, indices are all evaluated and synthesized, the results indicate the performance of the fuzzy incomplete approach is best. Moreover, from the test analysis known, the fuzzy incomplete approach has also some advantages, such as it has the faster detection speed, the lower storage capacity, and does not need any prior information in addition to data processing. These results indicate that the mining approach is more effective and feasible than the old data mining approaches in software aging detection.

DOI: 10.4018/978-1-5225-1884-6.ch001

INTRODUCTION

Because of the rapid increase of measurement data in engineering application and the participation of human, the uncertainty of information in data is more prominent, and the relationship among data is more complex. How to mine some potential and useful information from plentiful, fuzzy, disorderly and unsystematic, strong interferential data, so as to perform real-time and effective engineering applications, this is a problem needs to be urgently further study.

Data mining is a process of selection, exploration and modeling to a mass of data for discovering beforehand unknown rules and relations, whose purpose is to get some clear and useful results for the owner of the database (Giudici et al., 2004).

The spread speed of data mining was very fast, and its application scope was widespread day by day (Giudici et al., 2004, Liang 2006, Zhang et al., 2008, Hu et al., 2008, Liao and Yang, 2009, Chen et al., 2008). The literatures provided several data mining algorithms and some applications in engineering, and introduced three data mining algorithms in medicine applications. However, the data mining industry was still in the initial stage of development in China, the domestic industries basically didn't have their own data mining systems.

In 1989 (Arai, 1989), at the 11th International symposium on Artificial Intelligence, scholars first proposed the conception of knowledge discovery in database (KDD). At the United States' annual meeting on Computer in 1995, some scholars began to regard data mining as a fundamental step in knowledge discovery in databases, or discussed the two as synonyms.

Now, some algorithms on data mining have been relatively mature (Arai, 1989), (Farzanyar, Kangavari et al., 2012), (Qiu and Tamhane, 2007), (Wolff, Bhaduri et al., 2009), (Balzano and Del Sorbo, 2007), (Alp, Büyükbebeci et al., 2011). The decision Tree algorithm based on CHAID, some rules generated by Scenario could be applied to the unclassified data set to predict which records would have promising results. Scenario's decision tree algorithm is very flexible, which gives the user the choice to split any variable, or the choice of splitting with statistical significance. He carried out the graphical analysis to the crude data by using the fold line chart, histogram and scatter plot. Liang Xun listed several main software developers on data mining (Liang, 2006).

This paper introduces two new approaches on data mining, uses them and other four classical supervised learning data mining technologies to learn and classify 1020 data, validates the feasibility and effectiveness for the new data mining approaches, and compares the performance of each approach with each other, so as to hope that can select an optimum mining approach for fault diagnosis in software system. The neural network (NN), support vector machine (SVM), decision tree and logistic regression are the best approaches to depict the nonlinearity of data in the data mining, moreover, the fuzzy incomplete and statistical approaches can also depict the nonlinearity of data, so they are very suitable for the characteristic of data of fault diagnosis in software system. This paper evaluates the performance of each approach from sensitivity, specificity, accuracy, error classified rate, missed classified rate, respectively, and also records the running time on the Pentium 4, 2.66GHz, 1GB memory machine, uses the 6 indexes as standards to evaluate the advantages and disadvantages of each approach, and selects an approach with optimal performance from these approaches as the approach of fault diagnosis in software system.

Local Approach

Basic Knowledge

An important characteristic of data mining using rough set (Pawlak, 1982) approach is to use a positive region to perform the reduction of data or attribute. The definitions of the positive region and the reduction are as follows:

Definition 1.1: Assume Ω is a universal set, P and Q are two equivalence relation clusters defined on Ω and $Q \subseteq P$, the P positive region of Q is defined as $POS_P(Q) = \bigcup\limits_{X \in \Omega/Q} P_\sim(X)$. Where $P_\sim(X)$ is the lower approximation of X, that is $P_\sim\left(X\right) = \bigcup\limits_{Y \in \Omega/P, Y \subseteq X} Y$, Ω/P expresses the set constituted by all equivalence classes of P.

Definition 1.2: Assume Ω is a universal set, P and Q are two equivalence relation clusters defined on Ω, if the Q independent subset of P is $S \subset P$, and $POS_S(Q) = POS_P(Q)$, then S is called Q reduction of P.

Label all the Q reduction relation clusters of P as $RED_Q(P)$.

Definition 1.3: Assume Ω is a universal set, P and Q are two equivalence relation clusters defined on Ω, all the Q not omitted relation clusters of P are called the Q core of P, labeled as $CORE_Q(P)$.

An important means of reduction is the relation between the reduction set and the core set. According to the above definition 1.2 and definition 1.3, there is the following theorem.

Theorem 1.1: Assume Ω is a universal set, P and Q are two equivalence relation clusters defined on Ω, $RED_Q(P)$ is all the Q reduction relation clusters of P, $CORE_Q(P)$ is Q core of P, then $CORE_Q\left(P\right) = \cap RED_Q(P)$.

From theorem 1.1 seen, the core is the intersection of all reductions. Its effect has two aspects: First, it can be used as the computable basis of all reductions, because the core is included in all reductions and the calculation can be immediately carried out. Second, it can be explained that it is the set of knowledge characteristic which cannot be eliminated in knowledge reduction. Therefore, the attribute reduction can be started from the core attribute, and then other attributes can be analyzed one by one.

The reduction for the information system of decision table is a reduction problem for a condition attribute C to relative to decision attributes. That is, some necessary condition attributes are found from the set of conditional attributes, so as to make the classification formed by this part condition attributes to relative to the decision attributes and the classification formed by all the condition attributes to relative to the decision attributes are consistent, i.e., the necessary condition attributes have the same classification ability with all the condition attributes to relative to the decision attribute D.

Local Approach

The local approach that is also called a fuzzy incomplete approach is defined by satisfying the following conditions:

Reduction Algorithm

A common reduction algorithm is as follows:

Input: A set of condition attribute is $C=\{a_1, a_2, ..., a_n\}$, and a set of decision attribute is $D=\{d\}$.
Output: A set of attribute reduction is $RED(\Omega)$.
Step 1: Compute the C positive region of D is $POS_C(D)$.
Step 2: For an attribute $a_i \in C$, after it is removed, the obtained subset of condition attribute is $C\backslash\{a_i\}$.
   Then compute the $C\backslash\{a_i\}$ positive region of D is $POS_{(C\backslash\{a_i\})}(D)$.
Step 3: If $POS_{(C\backslash\{a_i\})}(D) = POS_C(D)$, then it indicates the attribute a_i to relative to the decision attribute
   D is unnecessary. Assign $C= C\backslash\{a_i\}$ and go to the step 2. Otherwise, the attribute reduction
   $RED(\Omega)=C$ is output.

In addition to the approach of calculating reduction in accordance with the definition of reduction, there is a heuristic reduction algorithm based on the importance of attribute.

The heuristic reduction algorithm uses the core as the starting point of calculating reduction, which calculates a best or a specified minimum reduction by user. The algorithm uses the importance of attribute as a heuristic rule. First, the algorithm adds an attribute to the attribute set according to the importance of attribute from big to small one by one, until the set is a reduction. Then the algorithm checks every attribute in the set, and judges whether removing this attribute will change the dependence of the set to decision attributes. If not affecting, then delete it. The worst-case complexity of this algorithm is $O((k+|C|)|C||U|)$, because the max number of execution cycle is $|C|$. The complexity of the dependence degree among the attributes is the same as that of the positive region.

The heuristic reduction algorithm based on the importance of attribute is shown as follows:

Initialize the candidate set Red as the core attribute: Red=Core.

Calculate the dependence degree of the entire conditional attribute set, labeled as *f*max.

Max=0.

When max<*f*max.

Try to add a new attribute in Red every time. Calculate the dependent coefficient of the set Red, and then find an attribute *i* which makes the dependent coefficient of Red is maximal.

$$\text{Red} = \text{Red} \cup \{i\}.$$

Calculate the dependence degree of max=Red.

For each non-core attribute of Red, try to remove it and view whether it influences the dependent coefficient of Red. If not, then delete it.

Return Red, end.

By the similarity degree d between the measured attribute value and the necessary attribute of the above-mentioned core set, and according to the cut set, we do the attribute or data reduction. The similarity degree is bigger, the deviation between the measured attribute and the necessary attribute is smaller, which shows the measured attribute is a necessary attribute, otherwise, this measured attribute is a unnecessary attribute.

Similarity Measure

Define $\alpha_i(k)$ is the deviation between the measured attribute and the necessary attribute, for example, it is a norm or a covariance of error.

If we choose the normal membership function, the similar degree of the deviation under the normal operating condition at the moment k is

$$d_i\left(k\right) = e^{-b\alpha_i\left(k\right)}$$

where the $0 < b \leq 1$ is a pending constant. Obviously, there is $0 \leq d_i(k) \leq 1$.

When $\forall k \in \{1,2,\ldots,l\}$, after the $d_i(k)$ is obtained, the similarity vector between the standard value of the necessary attribute and the measured value of the real state in the normal operating condition is also obtained, and labeled as $M_i(l)$, i.e.,

$$M_i\left(l\right) = \left(d_i\left(1\right), d_i\left(2\right), \cdots, d_i\left(l\right)\right)'$$

where $M_i(l) \in [0,1]^l$.

Based on the definition of fuzzy synthetic function, define the synthetic similar degree of the deviation from time 1 to time l is

$$\beta_i\left(l\right) \underset{=}{\triangle} S_l\left(M_i\left(l\right)\right) = S_l\left[\left(d_i\left(1\right), d_i\left(2\right), \cdots, d_i\left(l\right)\right)'\right]$$

where the $\underset{=}{\triangle}$ is a definition operator.

So $\beta_i(l)$ is a fusion result after the $d_i(1)$, $d_i(2)$,…,$d_i(l)$ are synthesized.

Here, the fuzzy synthetic functions S_l may be selected as follows

$$S_l\left(M_i\left(l\right)\right) = \left(\frac{1}{l}\sum_{k=1}^{l} d_i^q\left(k\right)\right)^{\frac{1}{q}}, q > 0$$

$$S_l\left(M_i\left(l\right)\right) = \left(\prod_{k=1}^{l} d_i\left(k\right)\right)^{\frac{1}{l}},$$

Attribute Mining

In order to give the similarity judgment between the standard value and the measured value, we assume H_0 and H_1 are the following event:

H_0: If the similar degree is bigger than a certain threshold value, a certain attribute is a necessary attribute;
H_1: If the similar degree is not bigger than a certain threshold value, a certain attribute is an unnecessary attribute.

Assume the threshold parameter is ξ. According to the experience and the test, there is $0.5 \leq \xi \leq 1$. If

$$\beta_i(l) > \xi \quad (1\text{-}1)$$

Then H_0 is accepted, i.e., a certain attribute is a necessary attribute; otherwise H_1 is accepted. Therefore, some data of the test similarity that satisfy the formula (1-1) are required. Otherwise some unsatisfactory data are removed.

Case 1.1: Assume $\Omega = \{1,2,\dots,8\}$ is a universe of discourse. Define C is a condition attribute set and $C = \{p_1, p_2, p_3, p_4\}$, D is a decision-making attribute set and $D = \{d\}$. According to the historical measured data of software system, the initial decision-making information systems can be obtained, such shown in Table 1 In Table 1, the p_1 denotes the design aging (DE), p_2 denotes the memory leak (EM), p_3 denotes the aging caused by some base course causes, such as OS or network (OS), and so on, and p_4 denotes the aging caused by external environment changes of the whole system (EC).

Then there are the following equivalence class and the "positive region (*POS*)":

$\Omega/C = \{\{1\}, \{2\}, \{3\}, \{4\}, \{5\}, \{6\}. \{7\}, \{8\}\}$;

$\Omega/D = \{\{1,2,6\}, \{3,4,5,7,8\}\}$;

Table 1. Decision-making information systems

Ω	Condition Attributes				Decision Attributes (Aging State)
	DE	**EM**	**OS**	**EC**	
1	DE_1	EM_2	OS_3	EC_2	No
2	DE_1	EM_3	OS_2	EC_1	No
3	DE_2	EM_2	OS_3	EC_2	Yes
4	DE_2	EM_2	OS_3	EC_1	Yes
5	DE_2	EM_2	OS_1	EC_1	Yes
6	DE_3	EM_1	OS_1	EC_1	No
7	DE_1	EM_1	OS_3	EC_2	Yes
8	DE_3	EM_1	OS_2	EC_2	Yes

$POS_C(D) = \Omega;$

$\Omega / (C \backslash p_1) = \{\{1,3\}, \{2\}, \{4\}, \{5\}, \{6\}, \{7\}, \{8\}\};$

$\Omega / (C \backslash p_2) = \{\{1,7\}, \{2\}, \{3\}, \{4\}, \{5\}, \{6\}, \{8\}\};$

$\Omega / (C \backslash p_3) = \{\{1\}, \{2\}, \{3\}, \{4,5\}, \{6\}, \{7\}, \{8\}\};$

$\Omega / (C \backslash p_4) = \{\{1\}, \{2\}, \{3,4\}, \{5\}, \{6\}, \{7\}, \{8\}\}.$

Then there are

$$POS_{(C \backslash p_1)}(D) = \{2,4,5,6,7,8\},$$

$$POS_{(C \backslash p_2)}(D) = \{2,3,4,5,6,8\},$$

$$POS_{(C \backslash p_3)}(D) = \Omega = POS_C(D),$$

$$POS_{(C \backslash p_4)}(D) = \Omega = POS_C(D).$$

However,

$\Omega / (C \backslash (p_3, p_4)) = \{\{1\}, \{2\}, \{3,4,5\}, \{6,8\}, \{7\}\},$

then $POS_{(C \backslash (p_3, p_4))}(D) = \{1,2,3,4,5,7\}.$

Therefore, all D reductions of C are

$$RED_D(C) = \{\{p_1, p_2, p_4\}, \{p_1, p_2, p_3\}\} = \{S_1, S_2\}.$$

The D core of C is

$$CORE_D(C) = \cap RED_D(C) = \bigcap_i S_i = \{p_1, p_2\}.$$

For the attribute DE, we use the above section (1.2.1) and (1.2.2), a result that H_0 is rejected is obtained under the test level $\xi = 0.6$, i.e., we may think that the attribute DE is an unnecessary attribute. According to the same method, we calculate other attributes, and know if the fault of attribute EM or OS appears, then the fault of software system will appear, but the fault of attribute DE or EC appears, the fault of software system will not always appear. So the attribute EM or OS is the necessary attribute.

Statistical Approach

This paper implements the data mining to the unknown parameters by the characteristics of statistical distribution. Because many random variables in practice problems obey (or approximately obey) a normal distribution, this paper focuses on the introduction of the mining of unknown parameters about the normal population.

Let $X_1, X_2, \ldots, X_n$ be a sample with n capacities from a normal population $N(a, \sigma^2)$.

Here give an Instance whether a mean is equal to the mining of known value.

This mining problem is

$H_0: a=a$
$H_1: a \neq a_0$

Here, a_0 is a known mean. The σ^2 is an unknown. The σ^2 is discussed as follows:

When the H_0 comes into existence, $\dfrac{\bar{X} - a_0}{\sigma / \sqrt{n}}$ contains an unknown parameter σ, but

$$S^{*2} = \frac{1}{n-1} \sum_{i=1}^{n} \left(X_i - \bar{X} \right)^2 = \frac{n}{n-1} S^2$$

approximates to σ^2 better, so we think naturally that we may use the $S^* = \sqrt{S^{*2}} = \sqrt{\dfrac{n}{n-1}} S$ to replace

the parameter σ in $\dfrac{\bar{X} - a_0}{\sigma / \sqrt{n}}$. Thus, the statistic

$$\frac{\bar{X} - a_0}{\sqrt{\dfrac{n}{n-1}} S / \sqrt{n}} = \frac{\bar{X} - a_0}{S} \bullet \sqrt{n-1}$$

is obtained. According to the statistical theory, when the H_0 comes into existence, there is $\dfrac{\bar{X} - a_0}{S} \sqrt{n-1} \triangleq T \sim t(n-1)$. So, for a given significant level $\alpha (0 < \alpha < 1)$, the critical value t_α of the distribution with the freedom degree $n-1$ can be obtained by the t-distribution table so as to make $P(|T| > t_\alpha) = \alpha$, which is shown in Figure 1.

For a given sample observed value $x_1, \ldots, x_n$, we calculate the value of $T = \dfrac{\bar{X} - a_0}{S} \sqrt{n-1}$ is $t = \dfrac{\bar{x} - a_0}{s} \sqrt{n-1}$. The mining method is:

If $|t| > t_\alpha$, then H_0 is rejected, otherwise H_0 is accepted. The mining method is called the T-mining method.

Figure 1. Critical value t_α

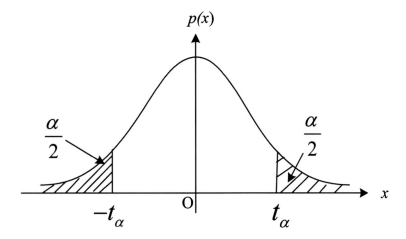

Example 1.1: For the above case 1.1, the system parameters (condition attributes) of the software historical data are some parameters that may cause the software aging, that is the design aging, the memory leak, aging caused by some base course causes, such as OS or network, and aging caused by external environment changes of the whole system, etc. Assume that the running lifetime of the OS parameter in software system is $\xi \sim N(a,\sigma^2)$. The normal running time is $a=2000$ hours. After measuring 8 historical data of the software system, we obtain the measured mean of the parameter is $\bar{x} = 1832$ and the deviation is $s=498$. Whether is the parameter normal? Where the test level $\alpha=0.05$ is given.

Solution: The statistical assumptions of the above problem are

$$H_0 : a = 2000 \triangleq a_0,$$
$$H_1 : a \neq a_0.$$

This is a mining problem whether a normal population mean is equal to the known value, and σ^2 is unknown. So we use the *T*-mining method

For the given significant level $\alpha=0.05$, the critical value $t_{0.05}=2.37$ of the distribution with the freedom degree 7 is obtained by the *t*-distribution table. However, according to the calculated result, there is

$$|t| = \frac{\left|\bar{x} - a_0\right|}{s} \cdot \sqrt{n-1} = \frac{\left|1832 - 2000\right|}{498}\sqrt{7} \approx 0.893 < 2.37.$$

Therefore, under the significant level $\alpha=0.05$, H_0 is accepted. So we may think the parameter is normal.

By using this approach to calculate the parameters that may cause the software aging, from the calculated result known, the fault of the parameter EM or OS occurs, then the fault of the decision attribute occurs, namely the software system must appear to be fault, but when the DE or EC is fault, the software system is not always fault, so the EM and OS are the necessary attributes.

For the above problem, we again present a following problem:

The aging degree of the parameter EM in software system is $\xi \sim N(a,\sigma^2)$, and the aging degree is $\sigma^2 \leq 0.18$ under running normally. After running a period of time, whether is the parameter still keeping the original aging degree? It needs to be examined. After observing 8 historical data of the software system, the measured aging degree of the parameter is obtained to be $s^2 = 0.326$.

By the above known, if the $\sigma^2 \leq 0.18$ comes into existence, it means that the parameter still keep the earlier aging degree, otherwise, the aging degree breaks up. In fact, the problem is the following single-sided mining:

$$H_0 : \sigma^2 \leq \sigma_0^2 \triangleq 0.18,$$
$$H_1 : \sigma^2 > \sigma_0^2.$$

Assume $X_1, \ldots, X_n$ are from the samples of known normal population $N(a,\sigma^2)$. Some obvious conclusions are easy to be obtained. If H_0 exists, then the possibility that the $S^{*2} \leq \sigma_0^2$ comes into existence should be high. Inversely, the possibility that the $\dfrac{S^{*2}}{\sigma_0^2}$ is too large should be small. Therefore, if the $\dfrac{S^{*2}}{\sigma_0^2}$ is too large, or the $\dfrac{S^{*2}}{\sigma_0^2/(n-1)} = \dfrac{nS^2}{\sigma_0^2}$ is larger than a certain critical value, then H_0 should be rejected.

When H_0 comes into existence, the distribution of $\dfrac{nS^2}{\sigma_0^2}$ can be not known, so the problem must be transformed. Through observing these known conditions, if H_0 comes into existence, then $\dfrac{nS^2}{\sigma_0^2} \leq \dfrac{nS^2}{\sigma^2} \sim \chi^2 (n-1)$. Where the $\chi^2(n-1)$ is a χ^2 distribution with freedom degree $n-1$. Thus, for $\forall \sigma^2 \leq \sigma_0^2$, there is

$$P\left(\frac{nS^2}{\sigma_0^2} > \chi_\alpha^2 \right) \leq P\left(\frac{nS^2}{\sigma^2} > \chi_\alpha^2 \right).$$

For a given significant level α, the critical value χ_α^2 can be obtained by χ^2- distribution table so as to make $P\left(\dfrac{nS^2}{\sigma^2} > \chi_\alpha^2 \right) = \alpha$ exist. Where the α is a small positive number. This means that the H_0 exists, the $\left\{ \dfrac{nS^2}{\sigma^2} > \chi_\alpha^2 \right\}$ and further $\left\{ \dfrac{nS^2}{\sigma_0^2} > \chi_\alpha^2 \right\}$ are a small probability event, respectively. Let

$$C = \left\{ (x_1 \cdots, x_n) : \frac{nS^2}{\sigma_0^2} > \chi_\alpha^2 \right\}$$

be the critical region of the mining problem. So the mining method is obtained as follows:

According to the sample observed value $x_1, \ldots, x_n$, if $\dfrac{nS^2}{\sigma_0^2} > \chi_\alpha^2$ comes into existence by the calculation, i.e., or $(x_1, \ldots, x_n) \in C$, then H_0 is rejected, otherwise H_0 is accepted.

In the above concrete case, for a given significant level α=0.05, the critical value $\chi_{0.05}^2 = 14.07$ of the distribution with the freedom degree 7 is obtained by the χ^2-distribution table. Calculate

$$\frac{nS^2}{\sigma_0^2} = \frac{\sum\limits_{i=1}^{7} v_i \left(x_i - \overline{x} \right)^2}{0.18} \approx 14.5 > 14.07 .$$

So, under the given significant level α=0.05, H_0 is rejected, i.e., the aging degree breaks up after the parameter runs a period of time.

SEVERAL EXISTING DATA MINING APPROACHES

Neural Network Approach

This paper only introduces the Kohonen self-organizing feature map (SOFM) data mining algorithm.

By the above case, the attribute parameter values in a historical data observation are shown in Table 2. Using the trained SOFM network, the basic steps of data mining for the above example are as follows:

P1 - Initialization: The dimension of output grid is fixed, here the chosen dimension is a 5 × 5, the input layer is a four-order network, and the weights connecting with the input neurons and the output neurons are initialized randomly. Let t denote the number of iterations of algorithm, and $t=0$.

P2 - Select Winners: The parameter values of the above table are input to the input neurons of the network. For each input neuron value x_j, the winning output neuron i^* is chosen, namely the output value S_i^t of the node in competition layer is minimized.

P3 - Update the Weights: Let $N(i^*)$ be a near neighbor of the winning output neuron i^*, which is designated by the distance between the output neurons. For each output neuron $i \in \{N(i^*), i^*\}$, the weight is adjusted and updated by the expression

Table 2. The aging degree of the attribute parameter values

Attributes	DE (Aging Degree)			EM (Aging Degree)			OS (Aging Degree)			EC (Aging Degree)	
Parameter values	1.2	1.5	1.8	10.1	10.3	10.6	11.22	12.58	22.00	6.01	1.23

$$\omega_{kj}(t+1) = \begin{cases} \omega_{kj}(t) + \eta(t)\left(x_k - \omega_{kj}(t)\right) & if \ j \in N(i) \\ 0 & otherwise \end{cases}$$

where the $\eta(t)=\eta$ has been determined in advance. This rule only updates the near neighbor of the winning output neuron.

P4 - Standardize the Weights: Standardize the updated weights so as to make them be consonant with the input measure standards.

P5 - Continue to Cycle: Repeat the steps from 1 to 4. The number of iterations is set to $t=t+1$, until the stop criteria is satisfied. Where the stop criteria is $\|x_j-\omega_{ji}(t)\|<\varepsilon$, take $\varepsilon=0.5$, or stop until the maximum number of cycles is exceeded.

The four condition attributes in the above case are input to the neural network. By using the above steps to mine, finally, the reduction attribute is a set of neighborhood $N(i)=\{EM,OS\}$.

Support Vector Machine Approach

The support vector machine is an approach based on statistical learning, which has a very solid theoretical foundations and excellent characteristics. The support vector machine carries out mainly a continuous data processing. The literature (Liang 2006) introduced the support vector machine approach, here we omit it.

Assume the above case can be expressed as (x_i,y_i). Where the x_i is a 11-dimension vector, which denotes all attribute parameter values of the case in the data set, as shown in Table 2. Because the decision attributes only have two kinds of cases, let the decision attribute y be a two types. Take $y_i=1$ and -1 respectively. According to Table 2, after solving the above problem, the optimal decision plane can be calculated by

$$f(x) = \text{sgn}\left(\sum_{i \ is \ a \ support \ vector} y_i \alpha_i^* \langle x_i,x \rangle + b^* \right)$$

Due to all the α_i corresponding to non-support vectors are 0, and all the α_i that are not 0 corresponds to the support vector, so the summation of the above formula actually only carries out that of the support vectors. From Table 1 and the measured value known, the $y_i = (-1, -1, -1, 1, 1, 1, 1, -1, 1, 1, 1)$ is obtained. By calculating, there are $\alpha^*= (0.202, -0.125, 0, 1, 0, 0, 1.212, -1, 0, 0, 0)$, and $b^*=-1$.

According to the optimal decision hyperplane, the data classification mining can be obtained.

Decision Tree

In the process of data mining, by data fitting and learning, we automatically learn a decision tree from the training data. The decision tree repeats cutting on the data set through the hyperplane formed by attribute values, until the decision category can be separated, the cutting process forms a decision tree. The decision tree can be used for the regression analysis or the classification.

The decision tree itself not only embodies the inferential process, but also is the expression form of knowledge. The top layer of its structure is the root node, which is also an internal node or is called as a non-leaf node. Each internal node is used for testing a certain characteristic attribute of the data and the branches are come into being by the test results. If another characteristic attribute of the data needs to be test in the branch, the branch is connecting with another internal node; otherwise it connects with a terminal node that is called a leaf node. In here, the leaf node signifies the value or the category of the measured characteristic attribute, as shown in Figure 2.

Example 1.2: According to the test results of the tested data in the software system, we determine whether the subject appears to a fault, a weak or a serious fault. Now there are some actual recommendation cases, according to these cases, the law of judging fault needs to be discovered. In this problem, the response variable is the "judging fault" whose value is no, weak fault and serious fault. The test items as independent variables are the "design aging parameter" (denoted with DE), the "aging caused by some base course causes, such as OS or network" (denoted with OS), the "memory leak" (denoted with EM) and the "aging caused by external environment changes of the whole system" (denoted with EC). Let DE_1, DE_2, DE_3 denote three kinds of values of the measured data DE, respectively; OS_1, OS_2 denote two kinds of values of measured data OS, respectively; EM_1, EM_2 denote two kinds of values of measured data EM, respectively; EC_1, EC_2 denote two kinds of values of measured data EC, respectively. We discuss the historical measured data with 34 instances of the software system in the following, namely we discuss the universe of discourse is $\Omega=\{1,2,\ldots,34\}$. According to the historical measured data of the software system, the initial decision information system is obtained, i.e., the actual data of the sample is shown in Table 3.

The following 34 original data are placed in the root node. In the root node, the forking norm is determined based on the characteristic attribute "the aging caused by external environment changes of the whole system". The value of any tested data in an instance that is the aging caused by external environment changes of the whole system is EC_1 (a total of 13 cases), which are partitioned to a left-branch, please see Figure 2. Any tested data which value is EC_2 (a total of 21 cases) are partitioned to a right-branch, please see Figure 2.

Figure 2. Schematic diagram of decision tree

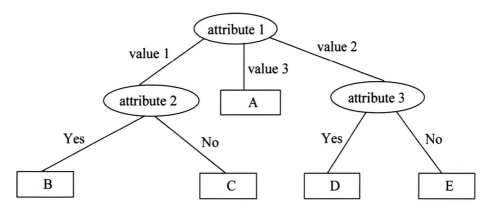

Table 3. The tested data of the subject in the software system

Ω	Condition Attributes				Decision Attributes (Fault State)
	EM	**OS**	**DE**	**EC**	
1	EM_1	OS_1	DE_1	EC_1	no
2	EM_1	OS_1	DE_1	EC_2	serious
3	EM_2	OS_1	DE_1	EC_2	weak
4	EM_1	OS_1	DE_1	EC_1	no
5	EM_2	OS_1	DE_1	EC_2	weak
6	EM_1	OS_1	DE_1	EC_2	serious
7	EM_1	OS_1	DE_1	EC_2	weak
8	EM_1	OS_2	DE_1	EC_2	serious
9	EM_1	OS_2	DE_1	EC_1	no
10	EM_2	OS_2	DE_1	EC_1	no
11	EM_2	OS_2	DE_1	EC_2	weak
12	EM_1	OS_2	DE_1	EC_2	serious
13	EM_1	OS_2	DE_1	EC_1	no
14	EM_1	OS_1	DE_2	EC_1	no
15	EM_1	OS_1	DE_2	EC_2	serious
16	EM_2	OS_1	DE_2	EC_1	no
17	EM_1	OS_1	DE_2	EC_2	serious
18	EM_1	OS_2	DE_2	EC_2	no
19	EM_2	OS_2	DE_2	EC_2	weak
20	EM_2	OS_2	DE_2	EC_1	no
21	EM_1	OS_2	DE_2	EC_1	no
22	EM_1	OS_2	DE_2	EC_2	no
23	EM_1	OS_2	DE_2	EC_2	no
24	EM_2	OS_1	DE_3	EC_1	no
25	EM_2	OS_1	DE_3	EC_2	no
26	EM_1	OS_1	DE_3	EC_2	serious
27	EM_1	OS_1	DE_3	EC_1	no
28	EM_2	OS_2	DE_3	EC_2	weak
29	EM_1	OS_1	DE_3	EC_2	serious
30	EM_2	OS_2	DE_3	EC_2	weak
31	EM_2	OS_2	DE_3	EC_1	no
32	EM_1	OS_2	DE_3	EC_2	no
33	EM_2	OS_2	DE_3	EC_2	weak
34	EM_1	OS_2	DE_3	EC_1	no

All the 13 cases in the left-branch are judged to be a trouble-free, high consistency and no bifurcation, so they are set to the leaf nodes, no longer are continued to subdivide. The 5 cases of the 21 cases in the right-branch are judged to be no fault, 8 cases are judged to be a weak fault and 8 cases are judged to be a serious fault, and the consistency is not high, so they are set to the internal nodes, and are continued to subdivide by the "design aging parameter" as a forking norm. The value of any tested data under design aging parameter is DE_2 (a total of 8 cases), which are partitioned to a left-branch. Any tested data of design aging parameter which value is DE_1 (a total of 13 cases) are partitioned to a right-branch. The 7 cases of the 8 cases in the left-branch are judged to be a weak fault, only one case is judged to be no fault, and the consistency is relatively higher, so they are set to the leaf nodes, no longer are continued to subdivide.

The 8 cases of the 13 cases in right-branch are judged to be a serious fault, the 1 case is a weak fault and the 4 cases are no fault, and the consistency is not high enough, so they are set to the internal nodes, and are continued to subdivide by the "aging caused by some base course causes, such as OS or network" as a forking norm. The value of tested data of 7 cases in the 13 cases caused by some base course causes, such as OS or network, is OS_1, including 6 cases are judged to be a serious fault, only one case is judged to be a weak fault, and the consistency is relatively higher, so they are set to the leaf nodes and no longer are continued to subdivide.

The value of tested data of other 6 cases in the 13 cases caused by some base course causes, such as OS or network, is OS_2, including 2 cases are judged to be a serious fault, 4 cases are judged to be no fault, and the consistency is not high enough, so they are set to the internal nodes, and are continued to subdivide with the "memory leak" as a forking norm. As a result, the 2 leaf nodes are obtained. The one has two cases that both are EM_1 and are judged to be a serious fault. The other has 4 cases, including 3 cases are EM_2 and one case is EM_3, all are judged to be no fault. Thus, the decision tree is completed, as shown in Figure.3.

This regression analysis approach also has its problems, such as the regression tree analysis is not too stable, that is the process of structuring tree is not stable. The slightest change of the learning samples may affect the choice of every internal node to the characteristic attributes, and this influence may be passed to the whole next generation nodes. In addition, the regression tree generated by the numerical learning sample data may be quite complex, etc.

Regression Analysis

The effect of the regression analysis is to reveal the law that the response variable responds with the changes of one or several independent variables, and expresses this response law in a certain appropriate form such as a function. In data mining, there also exists a phenomenon that some factors may affect a certain factor among some characteristic attributes of data. So, the regression analysis can also be used for describing this influence effect.

The Confusion Matrix

The confusion matrix is used for calculating the classification accuracy. To the classification of 3 categories as an example, the confusion matrix is shown in Table 4.

Figure 3. The decision tree of judging fault

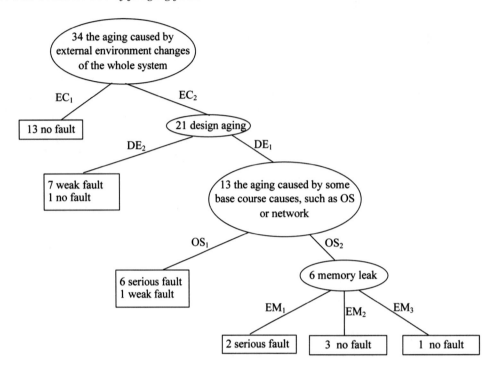

Table 4. The confusion matrix of classification of 3 categories

	Actually Belong to C_1 Category	Actually Belong to C_2 Category	Actually Belong to C_3 Category
Classified as C_1 category	C_{11}	C_{12}	C_{13}
Classified as C_2 category	C_{21}	C_{22}	C_{23}
Classified as C_3 category	C_{31}	C_{32}	C_{33}

That is, the matrix is $\begin{pmatrix} C_{11} & C_{12} & C_{13} \\ C_{21} & C_{22} & C_{23} \\ C_{31} & C_{32} & C_{33} \end{pmatrix}$.

According to the definition of the confusion matrix, the C_{11} denotes the number of the data that should belong to C_1 category, and are actually also classified as C_1 category. The C_{12} denotes the number of the data that should belong to C_2 category, but are actually classified as C_1 category. The C_{13} denotes the number of the data that should belong to C_3 category, but are actually classified as C_1 category, and so on. Therefore, the numbers on the diagonal of the matrix all denote the number of the data classified as the correct category. In general, the correct rate A and the misclassification rate R_e of a N categories classification can be calculated respectively as follows:

$$A = \frac{\sum_{k=1}^{N} C_{kk}}{\sum_{i=1}^{N} \sum_{j=1}^{N} C_{ij}}$$

$$R_e = 1 - A$$

In practical applications, the classification accuracy is not the only and absolute evaluation criteria. According to the specific requirements, sometimes it also needs to consider the cost factor of data mining, and then we can make a comprehensive judgment for its performance. For example, we usually use other two evaluation criteria, i.e., sensitivity and specificity.

The sensitivity is calculated by

$$N_1 = \frac{N_{c1}}{N_{c1} + N_m}$$

The specificity is calculated by

$$N_2 = \frac{N_{c2}}{N_{c2} + N_e}$$

The classification or prediction accuracy is calculated by

$$A = \frac{N_{c1} + N_{c2}}{N_{c1} + N_m + N_{c2} + N_e}$$

Assume $N = N_{c1} + N_m + N_{c2} + N_e$ and $N_c = N_{c1} + N_{c2}$. The correct classified rate, the error classified rate and the missed classified rate are defined as follows:

$$P_c = \frac{N_c}{N}, \quad P_e = \frac{N_e}{N}, \quad P_m = \frac{N_m}{N}$$

where the N_{c1} is the number of samples for the first kind correct classification, i.e., denotes the number of the samples that actually belong to the correct, and are also classified as the correct. The N_m is the number of samples for the missed classification, i.e., denotes the number of the samples that actually belong to the correct, but classified as the error. The N_{c2} is the number of samples for the second kind correct classification, i.e., denotes the number of the samples that actually belong to the error and are also classified as the error. The N_e is the number of samples for the error classification, i.e., denotes the number of the samples that actually belong to the error but classified as the correct. The above variables can be shown in Table 5. The N denotes the total number of samples. The N_c is the number of samples for the correct classification. The P_c denotes the correct classified rate. The P_e denotes the error classified rate. The P_m denotes the missed classified rate. Then, obviously, there exists $P_c+P_e+P_m=1$. We usually use their relative frequency instead of their probability in simulation.

That is, the confusion matrix is $C_M = \begin{pmatrix} N_{c1} & N_e \\ N_m & N_{c2} \end{pmatrix}$.

The above parameters all can reflect the performance of data mining scheme. In the practical applications of data mining, these parameters (such as sensitivity and specificity) may restrict each other. Therefore, the suitable performance standard is designed according to the actual conditions and the specific requirements. In order to show the restrictive relationship between the sensitivity and the specificity, sometimes we can adopt the receiver operating characteristics (ROC) to evaluate their comprehensive performance.

Generally, the value of the area covered under the ROC curve can be used for measuring the performance. The value of area is closer to 0.5, indicating that the performance is worse. The ideal value should be 1.

The Logistic Regression

We determine the nature of the prediction model of response variable. A qualitative response problem is usually broken down into a binary response problem (such as Agresti, 1990). The basic element of most qualitative variable response models is the logistic regression model, which is one of the very important data mining prediction approaches. Assume the $y_i(i=1,2,...,n)$ is the observed value of binary response variable, only value 0 or 1. The value 1 denotes an interested event occurs, which is called the success. The logistic regression model is defined by a fitted value, and is interpreted as the probability of event occurred in different subspace:

$\pi_i=P(Y_i=1)$, $(i=1,2,...,n)$.

In practical applications, the values of some variables only have two states. Such variable is called a binary variable. The linear regression model applied to numerical data cannot directly describe the response law of such binary variable, but the logistic regression model is applicable to this type of problem. In the logistic regression model, the response variable is the ratio between the occurrence probability of the specific event and the nonoccurrence probability of this event. The value of the response variable of logistic regression is always between the closed interval [0,1]. The logistic regression is a nonlinear model, sometimes by transformation, calculated with a linear model.

The logistic regression model has many forms. The common form, i.e., the multi- element linear regression equation, is shown as follows:

Table 5. The confusion matrix of performance index

	Actually Belong to the Correct	Actually Belong to the Error
Classified as the correct samples	N_{c1}	N_e
Classified as the error samples	N_m	N_{c2}

$$\ln \frac{p}{1-p} = \sum_{j=1}^{M} a_j x_j + b + \varepsilon$$

$$p = \frac{e^{\sum_{j=1}^{M} a_j x_j + b + \varepsilon}}{1 + e^{\sum_{j=1}^{M} a_j x_j + b + \varepsilon}}$$

where the p is the occurrence probability of the specific event. The 1–p is the nonoccurrence probability of this event.

In accordance with the approaches and criteria that are similar to the linear regression analysis, the coefficient a_j and b are solved to complete the logistic regression analysis, this solving is usually an iterative process.

APPLICATION COMPARISONS OF SEVERAL DATA MINING APPROACHES IN THE DIAGNOSIS OF SOFTWARE AGING

Experiment and Comparison

The test results of three approaches on data mining are given in experiment in here, i.e., the test results of performance of the fuzzy incomplete, statistical and decision tree approaches for 10-group samples, which are shown in Table 6, Table 7 and Table 8. Similarly, the test results of other approaches can also be given. Here they are omitted.

In Table 8, the Fin denotes the fuzzy incomplete approach. The St denotes the statistical approach. The Dt denotes the decision tree approach. The l denotes the sequence number. The P denotes the classified rate.

We experiment with 10-group data, but for simplicity, the test results of only one sample set here are given, as shown in Table 9.

In the previous literatures (Zhang et al., 2008, Chen et al., 2008), (Aburrous, Hossain et al. 2010), (Khalifelu and Gharehchopogh 2012), the forecast accuracy of the decision tree approach is higher than the corresponding value of other approaches, and its standard deviation is less than that of other approaches. But by experimental validation, these performances of the fuzzy incomplete approach introduced in this paper are better than those of the decision tree approach. Moreover, from the experimental analysis known, the fuzzy incomplete approach has also some advantages, such as it has the faster detection speed, the lower storage capacity, and does not need any prior information in addition to data processing.

In this study, we use six indexes which are sensitivity, specificity, forecast accuracy, error classified rate, missed classified rate and runtime to compare the performances of six data mining approaches. From Figure 4~ Figure 7 and Table 9 known, the fuzzy incomplete approach has the highest sensitivity, the forecast accuracy for every group measured data, which is higher than those of other approaches. The average forecast accuracy of fuzzy incomplete approach is also slightly higher than that of the other approaches, and its runtime is least. Moreover, in the test of small sample set, the standard deviation of the forecast accuracy, sensitivity and specificity of fuzzy incomplete approach in the 10 groups, mean of

Table 6. Test results of performance of fuzzy incomplete and statistical approaches

Group No.	Total Samples	Fuzzy Incomplete					Statistical Approach				
	Sample No.	Confusion Matrix		Sensitivity	Specificity	Accuracy	Confusion Matrix		Sensitivity	Specificity	Accuracy
1	172	102	4	0.9107	0.9333	0.9186	93	15	0.8378	0.7541	0.8081
		10	56				18	46			
2	286	185	7	0.9343	0.9205	0.9301	170	22	0.8543	0.7471	0.8217
		13	81				29	65			
3	396	247	8	0.9114	0.9360	0.9192	223	29	0.8383	0.7769	0.8182
		24	117				43	101			
4	499	339	10	0.9313	0.9259	0.9299	268	36	0.8701	0.8115	0.8477
		25	125				40	155			
5	506	324	12	0.9231	0.9226	0.9229	300	29	0.8108	0.8014	0.8081
		27	143				70	117			
6	607	372	12	0.9007	0.9381	0.9127	345	26	0.8175	0.8595	0.8303
		41	182				77	159			
7	712	457	20	0.9327	0.9099	0.9256	422	47	0.8810	0.7983	0.8539
		33	202				57	186			
8	813	507	19	0.9286	0.9288	0.9287	470	42	0.8672	0.8450	0.8598
		39	248				72	229			
9	919	587	17	0.9143	0.9386	0.9217	550	33	0.8475	0.8778	0.8564
		55	260				99	237			
10	1020	298	42	0.9613	0.9408	0.9471	266	70	0.9110	0.9038	0.9059
		12	668				26	658			
Mean				0.9248	0.9295	0.9256			0.8536	0.8175	0.8410
St.Dev.				0.0162	0.0093	0.0089			0.0285	0.0499	0.0286

error classified rate and missed classified rate all are less than those of the other approaches, it indicates its forecast results are relatively stable. Therefore, the performance of the forecast model established by the fuzzy incomplete approach is better than that of other models on the whole. So, the fuzzy incomplete approach is a preferred approach, secondly, followed by decision tree and support vector machine is better, and then followed by Logistic regression, statistical approach and the neural networks in turn.

Applicable Conditions of Various Approaches

1. When the prior probability and the conditional probability are unknown, we use the fuzzy incomplete approach, because it does not need to provide any prior information in addition to data processing. However, according to the known conditions, the upper and lower approximation of the set composed by problem or the positive region, fuzzy degree, synthetic function of its subset, and so on, can be known. The processing speed of this approach is faster.

Table 7. Test results of performance of fuzzy incomplete and decision tree approaches

Group No.	Total Samples	Fuzzy Incomplete					Decision Tree Induction				
	Sample No.	Confusion Matrix		Sensitivity	Specificity	Accuracy	Confusion Matrix		Sensitivity	Specificity	Accuracy
1	172	102	4	0.9107	0.9333	0.9186	98	7	0.8829	0.8852	0.8837
		10	56				13	54			
2	286	185	7	0.9343	0.9205	0.9301	179	9	0.9086	0.8989	0.9056
		13	81				18	80			
3	396	247	8	0.9114	0.9360	0.9192	239	16	0.8885	0.8740	0.8838
		24	117				30	111			
4	499	339	10	0.9313	0.9259	0.9299	279	25	0.8971	0.8670	0.8858
		25	125				32	163			
5	506	324	12	0.9231	0.9226	0.9229	312	15	0.8643	0.8966	0.8735
		27	143				49	130			
6	607	372	12	0.9007	0.9381	0.9127	355	15	0.8513	0.9211	0.8731
		41	182				62	175			
7	712	457	20	0.9327	0.9099	0.9256	446	23	0.9065	0.8955	0.9031
		33	202				46	197			
8	813	507	19	0.9286	0.9288	0.9287	492	27	0.9077	0.9004	0.9053
		39	248				50	244			
9	919	587	17	0.9143	0.9386	0.9217	583	8	0.8847	0.9692	0.9086
		55	260				76	252			
10	1020	298	42	0.9613	0.9408	0.9471	288	52	0.9231	0.9266	0.9255
		12	668				24	656			
Mean				0.9248	0.9295	0.9256			0.8915	0.9034	0.8948
St.Dev.				0.0162	0.0093	0.0089			0.0207	0.0280	0.0164

Table 8. The test results of correct, error and missed classified rate

P	P_c			P_e			P_m			N
l	Fin	St	Dt	Fin	St	Dt	Fin	St	Dt	
1	0.9186	0.8081	0.8837	0.0233	0.0872	0.0407	0.0581	0.1047	0.0756	172
2	0.9301	0.8217	0.9056	0.0245	0.0769	0.0315	0.0455	0.1014	0.0629	286
3	0.9192	0.8182	0.8838	0.0202	0.0732	0.0404	0.0606	0.1086	0.0758	396
4	0.9299	0.8477	0.8858	0.0200	0.0721	0.0501	0.0501	0.0802	0.0641	499
5	0.9229	0.8081	0.8735	0.0237	0.0562	0.0296	0.0534	0.1357	0.0968	506
6	0.9127	0.8303	0.8731	0.0198	0.0428	0.0247	0.0675	0.1269	0.1021	607
7	0.9256	0.8539	0.9031	0.0281	0.0660	0.0323	0.0463	0.0801	0.0646	712
8	0.9287	0.8598	0.9053	0.0234	0.0542	0.0332	0.0480	0.0929	0.0615	813
9	0.9217	0.8564	0.9086	0.0185	0.0374	0.0087	0.0598	0.1122	0.0827	919
10	0.9471	0.9059	0.9255	0.0412	0.0686	0.0510	0.0118	0.0255	0.0235	1020

Table 9. The performance indexes of each approach

Performance Indexes	Fuzzy Incomplete		Statistic		Neural Networks		Support Vector		Decision Tree		Logistic Regress	
Confusion Matrix	298	42	266	70	246	40	247	34	288	52	258	41
	12	668	26	658	42	692	37	702	24	656	35	686
Sensitivity	96.13%		91.10%		85.42%		86.97%		92.31%		88.05%	
Specificity	94.08%		90.38%		94.54%		95.38%		92.66%		94.36%	
Accuracy	94.71%		90.59%		91.96%		93.04%		92.55%		92.55%	
Error rate	4.12%		6.86%		3.92%		3.33%		5.10%		4.02%	
Missed rate	1.18%		2.55%		4.12%		3.63%		2.35%		3.43%	
runtime/s	0.35		0.51		1. 01		2.39		2.28		0.95	

By the experiment of 10-group data, the results of correct performance to every approach are shown in Figure 4~Figure 7.

Figure 4. The accuracy and the mean of 6 approaches

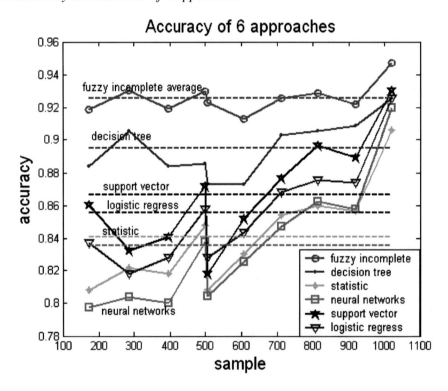

2. When the prior probability, conditional probability and statistical distribution of the condition item are known, sometimes every probability that is required to be independent is also known, we use the probability statistical approach. The classified effect of this approach is more precise.

3. When every data type is dense and tends to a bunch, we use the SOFM neural network approach. When the amount of original data are large and influenced by larger noise interference, or the dependence relation of response variables to independent variables presents complex nonlinear, the artificial neural network is an appropriate approach for processing and analysis. The neural network

Figure 5. Standard deviations of accuracy of 6 approaches

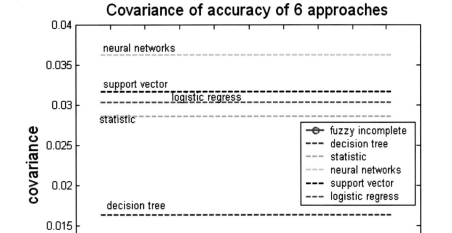

Figure 6. The missed classified rate of 6 approaches

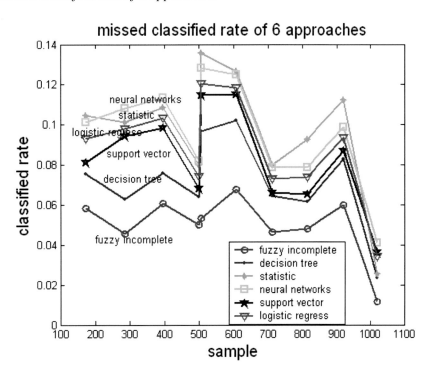

Figure 7. The error classified rate of 6 approaches

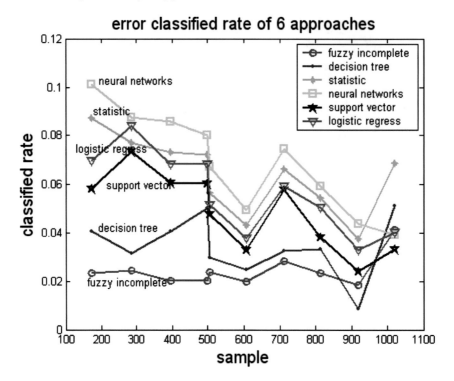

can be used to analyze the numerical and classified data. But when dealing with the classified data, it needs to convert the form of original data, which is its inconvenience.

4. When the data is continuous value, and the partial derivatives of the constructed Lagrangian function to the parameters *w*, *b* exist, we use the support vector machine approach.
5. When the data have obvious attributes or attribute value, we use the decision tree approach.
6. When revealing the law that the response variable responds with changes of one or several independent variables, and expresses this response law with a certain appropriate form such as a certain function, we use the regression analysis approach to describe this effect. The regression analysis is applied to both the classified data and also the numerical data.

Therefore, based on the collected data, we choose an appropriate approach or a combination of several approaches to adapt to the complexity of measured data in software and the diversification of software aging.

CONCLUSION

This paper uses the six data mining approaches to test 10-group data whose number of samples is 286, 499, 607, 712, 919, 1020, and so on, respectively. A best performance is selected from every approach based on the sensitivity, specificity, accuracy, error classified rate, missed classified rate and running time to compare with each other, in order to discover a suitable approach for fault characteristic research of software system. The test results show that the fuzzy incomplete approach is the best, the next is the decision tree, followed by the support vector machine, Logistic regression and statistical approach, the worst is the neural network. Through the contrast research discovered, the fuzzy incomplete approach is more suitable for the research of characteristic discrimination of the fault diagnosis in software system.

REFERENCES

Aburrous, M., Hossain, M. A., Keshav, D., & Fadi, T. (2010). Intelligent phishing detection system for e-banking using fuzzy data mining. *Expert Systems with Applications*, *37*(12), 7913–7921. doi:10.1016/j. eswa.2010.04.044

Agresti, A. (1990). Categorical data analysis.New York. Statistics and Application, 2(4), 2013-12-24.

Alp, Ö. S., Büyükbebeci, E., & İşcanog, A. (2011). CMARS and GAM & CQP—modern optimization methods applied to international credit default prediction. *Journal of Computational and Applied Mathematics*, *235*(16), 4639–4651. doi:10.1016/j.cam.2010.04.039

Arai, M. (1989). Mapping abilities of three-layer neural networks. *Proceedings of the International Joint Conference on IEEE Neural Networks*, New York (pp. 419-423). doi:10.1109/IJCNN.1989.118598

Balzano, W., & Del Sorbo, M. R. (2007). Genomic comparison using data mining techniques based on a possibilistic fuzzy sets model. *Bio Systems*, *88*(3), 343–349. doi:10.1016/j.biosystems.2006.07.014 PMID:17204362

Chen, J. X., Xi, G. C., Wang, W., Zhao, H. H., & Chen, J. (2008). A comparison study of data mining algorithms in coronary heart disease clinical application. *Beijing Biomedical Engineering*, *27*(3), 249–252.

Farzanyar, Z., Kangavari, M., & Cercone, N. (2012). Max-FISM: Mining (recently) maximal frequent itemsets over data streams using the sliding window model. *Computers & Mathematics with Applications (Oxford, England)*, *64*(6), 1706–1718. doi:10.1016/j.camwa.2012.01.045

Giudici P., Yuan F., Wang Y., & Wang L.J. (2004). *Applied Data Mining Statistical Methods for Business and Industry*. Electronics industry Press.

Khalifelu, Z. A., & Gharehchopogh, F. S. (2012). Comparison and evaluation of data mining techniques with algorithmic models in software cost estimation. *Procedia Technology*, *1*, 65–71. doi:10.1016/j. protcy.2012.02.013

Liang, X. (2006). Data mining algorithm and its application. Beijing University Press.

Liao, Z. M., & Yang, W. L. (1990). Probability theory and mathematical statistics. Beijing Normal University Press.

Pawlak, Z. (1982). Rough sets. *International Journal of Computer & Information Sciences*, *11*(5), 341–356. doi:10.1007/BF01001956

Qiu, D., & Tamhane, A. C. (2007). A comparative study of the K-means algorithm and the normal mixture model for clustering: Univariate case. *Journal of Statistical Planning and Inference, 137*(11), 3722–3740. doi:10.1016/j.jspi.2007.03.045

Wolff, R., Bhaduri, K., & Kargupta, H. (2009). A generic local algorithm for mining data streams in large distributed systems. *IEEE Transactions on Knowledge and Data Engineering, 21*(4), 465–478. doi:10.1109/TKDE.2008.169

Zhang, L., Gong, Z. L, Chen, Y., & Gu, S. D. (2008). *Biomedical data mining.* Shanghai Science and technology press.

Chapter 2
Feature Extraction Algorithms to Color Image

QingE Wu
Zhengzhou University of Light Industry, China

Weidong Yang
Fudan University, China

ABSTRACT

The existing image processing algorithms mainly studied on feature extraction of gray image with one-dimensional parameter, such as edges, corners. However, the extraction of some characteristic points to color image with three-dimensional parameters, such as the extraction of color edge, corner points, inflection points, etc., is an image problem to be urgently solved. In order to carry out a fast and accurate feature extraction on color image, this paper proposes two types of extraction algorithms to color edge and corner points of color image, i.e., similar color segment algorithm and pixel probabilistic algorithm, compares with the two algorithms, gives the two algorithms are used to different color distribution situations, as well as shows the extraction effect of color by the combination of the two algorithms, moreover, gives the contrast experiment and effect analysis of the two algorithms. To compare the similar color segment algorithm with the probabilistic algorithm, experimental results show that the similar color segment algorithm is better than the pixel probabilistic algorithm under the more obvious color edge, because it has the better edge detection, stronger anti-noise ability, faster processing speed and other advantages. Under the transition phase of color edge is gentle or color edge is no clear, the image detection effect of the pixel probabilistic algorithm is better than that of the similar color segment algorithm. But the combinative effect of the two algorithms is the best in this case, which is more close to the color effect of original image. Moreover, this paper analyzes the performance of the similar color segment algorithm, and gives the comparison of the proposed two algorithms and existing classical algorithms used usually to feature extraction of color image. The two algorithms proposed and these researches development in this paper have not only enriched the contents of image processing algorithms, but also provide a solution tool for image segmentation, feature extraction to target, precise positioning, etc., such as extraction of complexion, physiological color photographs processing, feature extraction of ionosphere, detection and extraction of biological composition of oceans, to be applied to a lots of departments, such as the police, hospital departments, surgery, polar department, and so on, as well as provide a way of thinking for the rapid, accurate detection of case, surgery, scientific research information search.

DOI: 10.4018/978-1-5225-1884-6.ch002

INTRODUCTION

At present, the data of color image is more and more. Because of the feature of color image that the amount of information is larger, its use was widespread concerned and used, for example, when the surgeon was operating some surgeries to implement operation positioning with the help of images often. But a few years ago, most of them were using a gray scale image, thus the success rate of a number of key operations is not too high. In recent years, most of surgeons operate the surgery by means of color Doppler ultrasound, color images, such as color picture or projection, the surgery success rates are improved a lot. To further improve surgical success rates, some image processing algorithms on feature extraction for edges and corner points of color image should be developed, and the developed algorithms should have some good features, such as fast speed, small operation, easy programming, etc. In addition, when the public security system implemented some detection of cases, it required to a fast and accurate extraction for some features, such as complexion, color video, texture of pictures, and searched for valuable information as soon as possible, all these needed urgently to provide a powerful tool. According to some acquired data of color images, such as aurora, ionosphere, geomagnetism, ocean, biology and meteorological data, the polar scientific research departments need to carry out the effective feature extraction, fine classification, and establish a rational database for some scientific researches, such as the environmental control of northern and southern polar, resource conservation, rational exploitation of resources, as well as renewable resources. These issues require the development of feature extraction methods or algorithms of color image for edges, corners, etc.

In image retrieval, calibration, classification, clustering, the effective feature extraction from the image is an important requirement. However, the color feature is one of the most widely used visual features. The color histogram is the most common method to denote the color characteristics. In the paper (Alamdar and Keyvanpour, 2011), it presented the feature extraction of color based on the square histograms. It prescribed for images with different sizes and quadtree decomposition of homogeneous wood, and extracted the color histogram of wood with the same size and skin feature of surface. In contrast to global color histogram, the image retrieval results demonstrated the feasibility and effectiveness of this approach. (Ilbeygi and Shah-Hosseini, 2012) gave a fuzzy recognition systems of facial expression, and carried out the facial recognition for color facial expression. (Aydın and Uğur, 2011) introduced a ant colony optimization method, as a general color clustering analysis method, and used the method to implement a classification and extraction for area of flower in color image. At the same time, it also presented an image segmentation method for flower image. According to flame color and vibrational frequency analysis, (Chen and Bao, 2012) presented digital image processing for the color of flame. For color image processing, (Lissner and Urban, 2012) implemented a unified color space based on perceptual image processing, (Bhuiyan, Khan et al., 2010) proposed a two dimensional empirical mode decomposition method, (Marques, 2011) discussed the actual image and video processing by using MATLAB tools. According to some examples of clinical application of medicine, (Galigekere, 2010) described the importance of applications of color images.

The edge is the most basic feature of image, and is the first step of image segmentation. Some classical edge detection methods and algorithms, such as, Roberts, Sobel, Prewitt, canny, Kirsch, Laplace, and other methods and algorithms (Bayro-Corrochano and Eklundh, 2011), all were almost to construct an edge detection operator for a small neighborhood of pixels in the original image, implemented the first order differential or second-order differential operation, sought a maximum gradient or zero-cross point of the second derivative, and finally select the appropriate thresholds to extract edge. Since these algorithms involved the operation to gradient, there are sensitive to noise, compute-intensive and other disadvantages. In practice, we found the Susan algorithm (Smith and Brady, 1997) was only based on the comparison of gray scale of surrounding pixels, did not involve any calculations on gradient, so its anti-noise ability is very strong, and its computation is relatively small. But these algorithms are to carry out the image processing of gray scale for one-dimensional parameter. However, during surgery and diagnosis (Galigekere, 2010), (Jukić, Kopriva et al., 2013), doctors need to pinpoint the color image; the polar department want to establish a rational database, it requires to carry out the fine classification of data for various types of mass data, but the classification of data need to process effectively color pictures (Xie, Wu et al., 2013), (Lo, Pickering et al., 2011), (Gonçalves and Bruno, 2013). For the feature extraction of color images, it requires developing some new extraction algorithms.

To search for valuable information from color image as soon as possible, this paper presents two extraction algorithms of three dimensional parameter of color image for extraction of edges and corner points, which is the similar color segment algorithm and pixel probabilistic algorithm, and gives the comparison and experiment of different color distribution of the two algorithms. Finally, the two algorithms are applied to the classification and recognition of aurora image.

STRUCTURE OF COLOR IMAGE

True Color Image

The common used model of color is RGB and HIS model in image processing. When processing true color images, the combination of RGB and HIS models is often used. Three components R, G, B represent a pixel's colors. If we want to read the pixel value of the position (100, 50) in the image, we may view tri-data (100, 50, 1:3).

True color image can be stored by using double precision, and the brightness value range is [0, 1]. More customary method of storage is uint8, and the luminance value range is [0,255]. The color intensity of palette in the MATLAB is [0, 1], and 0 represents the darkest, 1 is the lightest.

In actual read data in color image, the red, green and blue values are in the range [0,255], but when implementing the algorithm of R, G, B, the values of R, G, B are usually done a normalization processing, so as to make their values are in the range [0,1]. After doing normalization processing to the R, G, B values, here we give RGB values of 12 kinds of common used color in Table 1.

In the RGB model, each color appears in the spectral components of primary colors of red, green and blue, this model is based on the Cartesian coordinate system. In order to draw simple geometric

Table 1. RGB values of 12 common used colors

Color R G B	Color R G B
Black 0 0 0	Magenta 1 0 1
White 1 1 1	Cyanine 0 1 1
Red 1 0 0	Deep red 0.5 0 0
Green 0 1 0	Orange yellow 1 0.5 0
Blue 0 0 1	Sky blue 0.67 0 1
Yellow 1 1 0	Grey 0.5 0.5 0.5

figures of color subspace, R, G, B values are normalized, and then the color subspace is obtained to be a color cube as shown in Figure 1. In Figure 8, R, G, B lie in the 3 corner angles, the black lies in origin, and the white is in the corner angle far away from the origin. In this model, the gray level distribution is along the lines between two points of the black and white. The different colors locate on the cube or its interior, and can be defined by the vector of distribution from the origin.

HSI Color Model

RGB system can be a very good match with the eyes feeling very strong primary colors of red, green and blue. But RGB and other similar color models cannot adapt well to the color that the human actually explain, because it does not cover the percentage of each original color composition that is formed. Usually, one color is distinguished with another color by the color characteristics, which the characteristics have the illuminance, hue, saturation.

HSI model is based on human's feeling to color. HSI model describes three fundamental characteristics of color, i.e., hue, saturation, luminance.

The hue is the color that is reflected from an object or permeated and transmitted via the objects. On the standard color wheel with the 0~360°, the hue is measured by position. Under normal use, the hue is marked and identified by a color name, such as red, orange, yellow, green, blue, indigo, and violet. The saturation sometimes is also called chroma and is the intensity or purity of the color, which it reflects a measurement that a solid color is diluted by white. The saturation denotes the proportion of ingredients of the grey in hue, and is measured by a percentage from 0% (grey) to 100% (full saturation). On the standard color wheel, the saturation gradually increases from the center to the edge. The illuminance is the relative degrees of bright and dark of color, and is usually measured by a percentage from 0% (black) to 100% (white), as shown in Figure 2.

According to the cube in Figure 1, a regular tetrahedron with the white as a vertex can be obtained, and a regular triangular pyramid with the black as a vertex is also obtained, as shown in Figure 3. The

Figure 1. RGB space model

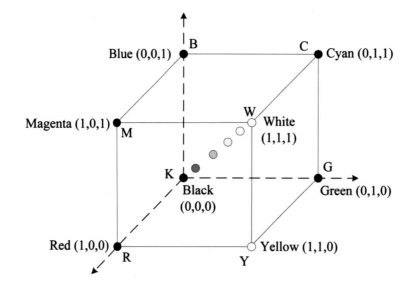

Figure 2. HSI color model

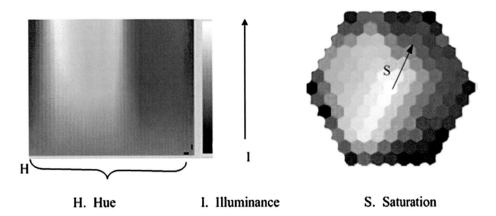

H. Hue   **I. Illuminance**   **S. Saturation**

definitions of the hue and the saturation that are the color component of HSI color model colors have to do with the triangle RGB as shown in Figure 3. In three-dimensional color spaces, the combination of hue, saturation and illuminance is carried out, and then two regular triangular pyramid structure with the same underside can be generated as shown in Figure 3. For any color point P on the surface of this structure or its interior, assume the hue H of the point P is the shaft angle between the vector $\overrightarrow{KP}$ and the red axis $\overrightarrow{KR}$. When $H=0°$, the point P is red. When $H=45°$, the point P is yellow, and so on. The saturation S of color point P represents a degree that a color is diluted by white, and it is proportional to the distance between the point P and the midpoint M of the connected line KW. The more far from the midpoint M the point P is, the greater the saturation of this color is. The measurement of illuminance has to do with the straight line KW that is perpendicular to the triangle RGB and passes through the center of the triangle. Pass through the point P do a straight line to be perpendicular to the straight line KW, then a perpendicular point P' on the straight line KW is obtained. According to the position of

Figure 3. Regular triangular pyramid

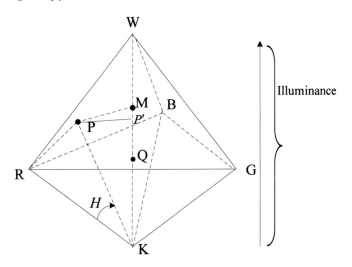

P' on the straight line KW, the illuminance of pixels P is determined. The more far from the point K the point P' is, the greater the illuminance of the point P. That is, along the WK direction, the illuminance gradually darkens to be black. On the contrary, along the KW direction, the illuminance becomes bright to white.

To solve the polyhedron W-RGB-K, assume the coordinate of the point P is $P(R,G,B)$. By the coordinates $R(1,0,0)$ and $K(0,0,0)$ of the points R and K, solving the triangle KRP, the hue H is obtained as follows:

$$H = \arccos \frac{R}{\sqrt{R^2 + G^2 + B^2}} \tag{1}$$

By the coordinate $M\left(\frac{1}{2}, \frac{1}{2}, \frac{1}{2}\right)$ of the midpoint M of line segment KW, the saturations from the center M of the cube to the furthest point on the surface of the cube and the maximum saturation is 1, the saturation should be $S = \dfrac{|PM|}{|MW|}$ based on the analysis, further it is calculated as follows:

$$S = \frac{2\sqrt{3\left[\left(R - \frac{1}{2}\right)^2 + \left(G - \frac{1}{2}\right)^2 + \left(B - \frac{1}{2}\right)^2\right]}}{3} \tag{2}$$

The illuminance I of the point P is proportional to the length of the line segment KP', so the length of the line segment KP' need to be solved for achieving I. Firstly, the angle PKM or its cosine of the triangle KPM is solved, and then the right triangle KPP' is also solved. According to the length of KP, the length of KP' can be obtained to be $\left|KP'\right| = \dfrac{R+G+B}{\sqrt{3}}$. $R \leq 1, G \leq 1,$ and $B \leq 1$ exist, so $\left|KP'\right| \leq \sqrt{3}$, but $\left|KW\right| = \sqrt{3}$, therefore it accords with the objective reality. The luminance of W is 1, so the illuminance of the point P is $I = \dfrac{\left|KP'\right|}{\left|KW\right|}$, that is,

$$I = \frac{R+G+B}{3} \tag{3}$$

According to the calculation process to H, S and I, when the range of R, G and B values is [0, 255], R, G and B are inversely normalized, then the equations (1)-(3) come into being all the same.

The definition of color of HSI color model has also something to do with the normalized R, G and B values. According to R, G and B values, the values *r,g,b* of red, green and blue to HSI model are calculated as follows:

$$r = \frac{R}{R+G+B} \tag{4}$$

$$g = \frac{G}{R+G+B} \tag{5}$$

$$b = \frac{B}{R+G+B} \tag{6}$$

The equations (4)-(6) indicate that the values of *r,g,b* are also in the range [0, 1], and *r,g,b* satisfy *r+g+b=1*.

Pixel Probabilistic Algorithm

For extraction of color edges and corner points to color image, this section proposes a pixel probabilistic algorithm, i.e., the probability that color of homochromy pixel possesses in the entire region of interest (ROI) is calculated. It specific definition is as follows:

Definition 2.1: Divide up the ROI of a color image. Calculate the number of pixels in ROI is *n*, and the number of pixels of a single color is *m*. Then the calculation of percentage of the single color in the ROI is called pixel probabilistic algorithm, i.e.,

$$\Pr = \frac{m}{n} \tag{7}$$

This algorithm is to use the proportion that the pixel occurs in ROI. The ROI is chosen by the requirements of target or testing. The ROI can be manually chosen, and can be also automatically chosen. For ROI of color, this paper gives the selection of a ROI through the value of hue. The selection algorithm of ROI is as follows:

Statistic Algorithm

If the composition of color of image is clear, the luminance value of each pixel is counted. The number of pixels of some colors can be computed by the luminance value. The counted pixels of each color are marked, respectively, and then the ROI can be marked out. In simulation, we select the range of luminance value of the pixel is [220, 240], and use the "red" to mark the pixel. The simulation result is shown in Figure 4, which the red region is the delineated ROI.

Figure 4. ROI chosen by computing the number of pixels of some colors

Hue Algorithm

If the hue and illuminance of the color of image gradually change, i.e., the color information is not clear, any pixel X is chosen in the region of pixels where the color information is uncertain, and then again a pixel $\{A_1, A_2, \ldots, A_{12}\}$ is randomly chosen in the region of pixels from the each determinate color. By calculating and comparing the hue value $H(X)$ of the pixel X and the hue value $H(A_i)$, we find the absolute value of the difference $|H(X)-H(A_i)|$ is minimum, i.e., solve the

$$\left| H\left(X\right) - H\left(A_{i_0}\right) \right| = \min_i \left\{ \left| H\left(X\right) - H\left(A_i\right) \right| \right\},$$

then we determine the color of the pixel X is i_0, and make the color marking to i_0. After classifying pixels, we determine some colors $j \in \{1,2,\ldots,N\}$ that we are ready to discuss. Where $N \leq 12$, and $i=1,2,\ldots,12$ represents the 12 colors. The boundary of region that consists of this several colors j is identified by the hue value H_j, then the region surrounded by the boundary is the ROI. Through this method, the ROI determined by the simulation is shown in Figure 5, i.e., the region that contains the red square surrounded by the red border is the chosen ROI. In simulation, the values of hue and illuminance are taken from the top, bottom, the most left and right of images at the beginning, and these pixels that their values of hue and illuminance all are greater than 0 compose the boundary of ROI.

Figure 5. ROI chosen by the hue dividing up border

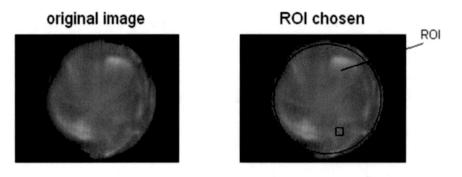

SIMILAR COLOR SEGMENT ALGORITHM

Because the integration that the hue combines with the saturation is called the color, this section gives the similar color segment algorithm, is to use the compared difference between the hue, saturation and illuminance of the center of the chosen color and those of its similar color pixels, and by the given appropriate threshold values of edge and corner points, carries out the extraction of characteristic points, i.e., edge and corner points extraction. The detection algorithm to edge and corner points is as follows:

A point of interest or a characteristic point in ROI is chosen, which the point is called the core O. (1) If $R_0>0$ exists, and the circle ΘO, which the point O is the center of circle and R_0 is the radius, contains only the pixels of one color, then this point O is not a edge point or a corner point, is a point in the flat region, as shown in Figure 6 (a), (d)-(h). (2) For any length $R>0$, if the circle ΘO, which the point O is the center of circle and R is the radius, all contain the pixels of two and more colors, then this point O is not a edge point or a corner point or a bifurcation point, as shown in Figure 13 (b), (c), (i). Figure 6 is the feature point detection to a color image based on the above described method. In Figure 6, the center of circle O is denoted by the symbol *, the original image is a colour pattern with a white rectangular background, and Figure 7 shows nine instances that the circle O lies in different positions.

The hue value H, saturation value S and illuminance value I of each pixel within the circle O are compared with those of the core point O. If the corresponding differences between the hue value, saturation value and illuminance value of the pixels within the circle O and those of the core point O all are less than the corresponding given thresholds, then this point within the circle and the core point O are the same or similar, and some pixels that satisfy such conditions make up of a region, which the region is called a similar color segment (SCS).

By SCS algorithm detection, some detected characteristic points cannot be distinguished from whether they are an edge point, a corner point or a bifurcation point. We take these characteristic points as the center of circle to do a series of concentric circle rings, respectively. We view a circle along the clockwise

Figure 6. Feature point detection of color image

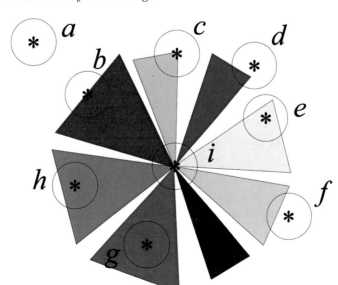

Figure 7. Color extractions by the pixel probabilistic algorithm to ambiguous color boundary

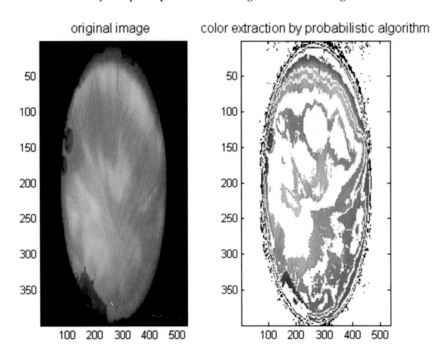

or counter clockwise direction ring, so as to find the number of change of hue. The center of circle that the number of change is more than 2 is a bifurcation point. The specific approach is: For some pixels in the neighborhood of the point O, their red hue value, saturation value and illuminance value are the same or similar to those of this point O, we label these pixels as 1. According to the same method, we label the pixels with the same or similar blue as 2, label the pixels with green as 3, black pixels as 0, white pixels as 12, and so on. The different colors are labeled by different number, respectively. From the beginning of a certain point on circle ring, we view the distribution of pixels of any a circle ring along the clockwise or counter clockwise direction, and record a change color of pixels from "1" to "2", or from "2" to "3", or from "0" to "1" and so on as a times jump of color. The center of circle that the times of color jump is equal to 2 is marked as an edge point or a corner point, however, the center of circle that the times of color jump is more than 2 is marked as a bifurcation point. Then the center of circle that the times of color jump is n ($n>2$) is marked as a n bifurcation point.

By the times of color jump, the edge point and the corner point cannot be distinguished. To distinguish between the two types of characteristic points, it needs further to extract the edge point and the corner point by the hue value, saturation value and illuminance value of the pixels, the given thresholds. The analysis for the edge point and the corner point is given as follows:

In Figure 7, the white regions in the circle (a), the circle (d) and the circle (f) are the SCS, respectively. Similarly, the red region in the circle (b), the green region in the (c), the yellow region in the (e), the purple region in the (g), and the sky blue region in the (h) are the SCS, respectively. It can be seen from Figure 7, when the circle O is completely in the background or completely in the target, the area of SCS is the largest, i.e., SCS is the largest in the flat region, as shown in Figure 7 (a) and (g). However, the area of SCS gradually diminishes when the core point is near the edge or corner points of target. When the core point is on edge of target, the size of SCS reduces to half, such as the circle (b) shown. When the core point lies in the corner point of target, SCS is the smallest, as shown in the circle (c). The basic principle of extraction algorithm for edge and corner points by using SCS can be obtained. That is, the SCS is smaller at the edge and SCS is the smallest at the corner point. The SCS algorithm is based on different area of SCS at each point to distinguish the current point is the interior point, border points or corner points of the studied region. The size of SCS of each point in the image is acted as the distinctive measurement of the feature on this point, and then the feature of point that its SCS is the smaller is remarkable. This algorithm can quick detect the corner points, intersections, edge points once, and no directional requirement. The specific algorithms are given as follows:

Edge Detection Algorithm of SCS

The edge detection algorithm by SCS is to calculate the pixel points within the circle O of the given size in the image so as to produce the initial response of edge, then to process the initial edge response so as to obtain the final edge.

The hue value H, saturation value S and illuminance value I of each point within the circle O and those of the core point O are compared by the following similar comparison function.

$$C_1\left(\vec{r}_0,\vec{r}\right) = \begin{cases} 1, & \left|H\left(\vec{r}\right)-H\left(\vec{r}_0\right)\right| \leq g_1 \\ 0, & \left|H\left(\vec{r}\right)-H\left(\vec{r}_0\right)\right| > g_1 \end{cases} \tag{8}$$

$$C_2\left(\vec{r}_0,\vec{r}\right) = \begin{cases} 1, & \left|S\left(\vec{r}\right)-S\left(\vec{r}_0\right)\right| \leq g_2 \\ 0, & \left|S\left(\vec{r}\right)-S\left(\vec{r}_0\right)\right| > g_2 \end{cases} \tag{9}$$

$$C_3\left(\vec{r}_0,\vec{r}\right) = \begin{cases} 1, & \left|I\left(\vec{r}\right)-I\left(\vec{r}_0\right)\right| \leq g_3 \\ 0, & \left|I\left(\vec{r}\right)-I\left(\vec{r}_0\right)\right| > g_3 \end{cases} \tag{10}$$

In the formula, g_1, g_2 and g_3 are the difference thresholds of the hue, saturation and illuminance, respectively, which are the threshold values to determine the degree of similarity. The selection of g_i is determined by the comparative degree between the color and the background in an image. $\vec{r}_0$ is the position (x_0,y_0) of the current core point. $\vec{r}$ is the position (x,y) of other any point in the circle O. $H\left(\vec{r}_0\right)$ and $H\left(\vec{r}\right)$, $S\left(\vec{r}_0\right)$ and $S\left(\vec{r}\right)$, $I\left(\vec{r}_0\right)$ and $I\left(\vec{r}\right)$ are the hue values, saturation values and illuminance values of the core point and other points in the circle O, respectively. $C_i\left(\vec{r}_0,\vec{r}\right)$ is the discriminant function of pixels that belong to SCS in the circle O, and it is an output. Where $i=1,2,3$.

By the comparison of the hue, the size of SCS can be calculated by the following equation:

$$n_1\left(\vec{r}_0\right) = \sum_{\vec{r}\in c(\vec{r}_0)} C_1\left(\vec{r},\vec{r}_0\right) \tag{11}$$

By comparing the saturation, the size of SCS can be calculated by the following equation:

$$n_2\left(\vec{r}_0\right) = \sum_{\vec{r}\in c(\vec{r}_0)} C_2\left(\vec{r},\vec{r}_0\right) \tag{12}$$

By comparing the illuminance, the size of SCS can be calculated by the following equation:

$$n_3\left(\vec{r}_0\right) = \sum_{\vec{r}\in c(\vec{r}_0)} C_3\left(\vec{r},\vec{r}_0\right) \tag{13}$$

Finally, the size of SCS can be determined by the following formula:

$$n\left(\vec{r}_0\right) = \min_i \left\{n_1\left(\vec{r}_0\right), n_2\left(\vec{r}_0\right), n_3\left(\vec{r}_0\right)\right\} \tag{14}$$

In the formulae, $n\left(\vec{r}_0\right)$ is the size of SCS of the core point $\vec{r}_0$, and $c\left(\vec{r}_0\right)$ is the circular region with $\vec{r}_0$ as the center of circle.

According to the experimental analysis, in a real image with noise, if the core point is near the edge, n is not generally greater than the value $3n_{max}/4$. The initial edge response is produced by the following formula:

$$R\left(\vec{r}_0\right) = \begin{cases} n_0 - n\left(\vec{r}_0\right) & if\ n\left(\vec{r}_0\right) < n_0 \\ 0 & otherwise \end{cases} \tag{15}$$

In the formula, n_0 is a threshold. $R\left(\vec{r}_0\right)$ is the response function.

Under the noise exists, it can be seen by calculating the mean value of $n\left(\vec{r}\right)$, the mean value is close to 0.7 but less than 0.7. Therefore, the threshold can be defined to be $n_0=2n_{max}/3$, where n_{max} is the maximum that $n\left(\vec{r}_0\right)$ can attain.

The size of initial edge response obtained by the formula (11) accords with a rule, i.e., "the smaller the SCS is, the greater the initial edge response is."

To determine the edge direction, the edge is divided into two different cases. The first case is that SCS is a region of symmetry of axis about pixels, i.e., there are definite distance between the position of gravity center of the pixels in SCS and the position of the core. The second case is that the position of gravity center of the pixels in SCS and the position of the core are coincident or are close to superposition. The edge direction is determined in the following.

For the first case of edge, the vector direction between the position of center of gravity and position of core is perpendicular to the edge direction. The center of gravity is calculated by the following equation:

$$\vec{g}\left(\vec{r_0}\right) = \frac{\sum_{\vec{r}} \vec{r} C\left(\vec{r_0}, \vec{r}\right)}{\sum_{\vec{r}} C\left(\vec{r_0}, \vec{r}\right)} = \left(x_g, y_g\right)$$

Then, the edge direction is $k_1 = \dfrac{x_0 - x_g}{y_g - y_0}$

For the second case of edge, the edge direction can be determined by looking for the longest axis of the symmetric part of all pixels in the SCS. By the results of theoretical and experimental analysis found, the connective line between the center of gravity and the core point O is the longest axis of symmetric part in the SCS.

For any point $\left(x, y\right) = \vec{r}$ within the SCS, its symmetric point about the core $O(x_0, y_0)$ is $\vec{r}' = \left(2x_0 - x, 2y_0 - y\right)$, and then the connective line between $\vec{r}$ and $\vec{r}'$ is the edge direction, that is

$k_2 = \dfrac{y - y_0}{x - x_0}$, where $\left(x, y\right) = \vec{r}$, $\left(x_0, y_0\right) = \vec{r_0}$.

According to the above discussion, the specific calculation process is as follows:

1. Make a circle O on each pixel of the image.
2. In the circle O, using the equations (8)~(10) to calculate the hue value, saturation value and illuminance value of pixels that are similar to those of the core, and then, using the equations (11)~(14) to calculate the number of these pixels. The number of these pixels is defined as the SCS.
3. Use the equation (15) to generate the image of edge response.
4. After achieving the initial edge response, make use of center of gravity of the SCS and the longest axis of symmetry to determine the local edge direction.
5. At the local edge vertical direction, take the position of the point of local maximum of initial response as the edge point. Then, select a wavelet function $\psi(t)$ to make $\psi_{j,k}(t) = 2^{j/2}\psi(2^j t - k)$ and make it with this local edge implement the inner product so as to carry out some image processing, such as, refine, smooth, connect the discontinuous edge points, eliminate the pseudo edge points, remove small branches of edge, and so on, in order to obtain a single, continuous, smooth output of the edge.

Corner Point Detection Algorithm of SCS

As shown in Figure 7, when the core lies in a certain corner point of target, the SCS is the minimum, such as the circle (c) shown.

The corner detection algorithm is the same to the edge detection algorithm, which its calculation formula is also the above formula (8)-(15). But only in the formula (15), its geometric threshold n_0 is different to the threshold value of edge detection. The n_0 to extract the corner point is smaller, in general $n_0 = 2n_{max}/5$. While the value n_0 to extract the edge is larger, usually $n_0 = 2n_{max}/3$. n_0 mainly affects the sharpness of feature points, i.e., the smaller the n_0 is, the more sharp the corner point is.

According to the definition of SCS, n must be smaller than the half of its largest possible value at the corner point. In other words, if the corner point exists, the area of SCS is less than half of the area of the circle O, and this value should be a local minimum at the corner point. Accordingly, an initial response of corner point can be obtained by using the equation (2-15′) as follows:

$$R\left(\vec{r}_0\right) = \begin{cases} n_{angle} - n\left(\vec{r}_0\right) & if\ n\left(\vec{r}_0\right) < n_{angle} \\ 0 & otherwise \end{cases} \tag{15}$$

where n_{angle} is the threshold of corner point detection.

Finally, search for the local maximum value of the initial corner response, and label its corresponding pixel points as the corner points.

When implementing the corner detection, because the borders of color region are fuzzy, it will lead to some pseudo corner points. In order to remove the pseudo corner points, the center of gravity of SCS needs to be calculated, and then the distance between the center of gravity and the center of circle O is calculated. If the distance is smaller, the corner point is not a correct corner point. On the other hand, there is the other method to remove the pseudo corner points. The method is to judge whether the pixels that the connective line between the center of gravity of SCS and the center of circle O passes through all are belong to the SCS. If the answer is positive, the detected corner point is probably the correct; otherwise, this detected corner point is definitely pseudo. The latter method enhances the coherence of SCS, which it is very necessary in the actual image, particularly in the image with noise.

Finally, the maximum method is used, that is, an edge point is taken as the center of the circle O, and it is compared with the points of its neighborhood. If the values of the hue, saturation and illuminance of this edge point all are the maximum, the edge point holds, thus, it is the right corner point obtained. The response functions of region near the corner point all are likely to have a larger value. However, the position that its response function has only the local maximum is the correct position of the corner point. Therefore, the local non-maximization is inhibited to obtain the final correct results.

The specific calculation steps (1)-(3) of the corner point detection algorithm is the same that of edge detection algorithm. The other two steps are as follows:

6. By calculating and finding the distance or connective line between the center of gravity of SCS and the center of circle O, the pseudo corner point is tested.
7. The maximum method is used to find the correct corner points.

Performance Analysis of SCS Algorithm

1. **The Effect of Edge Detection Is Good:** Whether to the straight line or the curve edge, SCS algorithms can basically detect all the edges, and the detection results are better. Although the one-pixel accuracy is achieved in experiment, it is mainly because both sides of the edge have been applied the SCS algorithm. For a concrete practical application, SCS algorithm may be applied to background

no longer. Thus, the edge can be not only thinned, but also the computational complexity is greatly reduced. However, Robert operator, Sobel operator and Prewitt operator could not detect the edges of some straight lines, and also partly leaved out the edges of circle. Gauss-Laplace operator and Canny operator could basically detect all the edges, but their positioning effect was relatively poor, and the edge pixels detected by them was wider.

2. **The Anti-Noise Ability of Algorithm Is Strong:** The sum to SCS is equivalent to the quadrature, so this algorithm is insensitive to noise. Moreover, SCS algorithms do not involve the calculation of gradient, so this algorithm has a good anti-noise performance. Obviously, if the independent identically distributed Gaussian noise is considered, as long as the thresholds of the similar hue, saturation and illuminance of the noise are less than those of the SCS function, respectively, then the noise can be ignored. For local mutation isolated noise, even if the hue, saturation and illuminance of noise is similar to those of the core, as long as the local hue, saturation and illuminance values of SCS are less than the corresponding thresholds, respectively, it cannot either lead to an impact on edge detection. Therefore, the edge detection algorithm by SCS can be applied to the edge detection of the image polluted by noise. However, other edge detection algorithms, such as Robert operator, Prewitt operator, Gauss-Laplace operator, as well as the widely used Canny operator, because these algorithms are related to the calculation of first order gradient, or even second-order gradient, their anti-noise ability is relatively poor.

3. **The Use of Algorithm Is Flexible:** The threshold parameters g_i, $i=1,2,3$, n_0 and n_{angle} can be used to control the detection and recognition of characteristic points in an image. That is, the detection and recognition of characteristic points can easily carried out by setting the appropriate thresholds g_1, n_0 and n_{angle} for the image with different contrast degree and different shape based on the specific situations. For example, if the contrast degree of the image is larger, we can choose a larger value g_i. If the contrast of the image is smaller, we can choose a smaller value g_i. Therefore, this algorithm is very applied to some low contrast images or target recognition.

4. **The Computational Complexity of Algorithm Is Small, and Its Processing Speed Is Fast:** For a color image with the size 256×256, SCS algorithm is used to carry out some calculations on the image. For every point, 13 times addition operations and 3 times division operations are carried out, i.e., there are a total of 256×256×13 times addition, 256×256×3 times division need to be done. However, for other classical edge detection algorithms to carry out color feature extraction, if Euclid's distance is used as the gradient operator, Sobel operator used two 3×3 templates, for every point, 27 times addition, 18 times multiplication and 3 times square root operations needed to be done, then there was a total of 256×256×27 times addition, 256×256×6 times multiplication, and 256×256 square root operations needed to be done. For Gauss-Laplace operator, Priwitt operator and Canny operator, the amount of calculation is greater.

5. **The Algorithm Can Detect the Edge Direction Information:** In fact, SCS algorithm can detect the edge direction information. This specific algorithm is: for each test point, calculate the center of gravity of a set of pixels in the circle *O*, which the hue, saturation or illuminance of these pixels are similar to those of the test point, the connective line vector between this test point and this center of gravity is perpendicular to the edge.

EXPERIMENTAL RESULTS ANALYSIS AND COMPARISON OF THE PROPOSED AND EXISTING ALGORITHMS

Color Extraction by Pixel Probabilistic Algorithm and Similar Color Segment Algorithm

1.   For a color image, which the hue and illuminance of the color border gradually change, as shown in Figure 8 (left), the probability that different color occurs in ROI is calculated by pixel probabilistic algorithm, and then some colors are extracted. Simulation result is shown in Figure 8 (right).

When the similar color segment algorithm is used to carry out some color extraction, the threshold values of similarity comparison function to detect edges and corner points are set to $g_1=9$, $g_2=11$ and $g_3=10$, respectively. The threshold of initial edge response function is set to $n_0=2382$. The threshold to detect the corner points is set to $n_{angle}=1413$. Simulation results are shown in Figure 9 (a) and (b). Figure 9 (a) is the extraction of color edge and corner points, Figure 9 (b) is the extraction of color.

It can be seen from Figure 8 and Figure 9, for color extraction by using the two algorithms to ambiguous color boundary, the extraction effect of the pixel probabilistic algorithm is better than that of the similar color segment algorithm, which it can extract the different order color classes. However, the similar color segment algorithm regards the unclear borderline color as a flat region to extract it, so it cannot well extract the different order color classes.

2.   For a color image, which the color boundary is obvious, as shown in Figure 10 (a). The probability that different color occurs in ROI is calculated by the pixel probabilistic algorithm, and then some colors are extracted. The simulation result is shown in Figure 10 (b).

Figure 8. Color extractions by the similar color segment algorithm to ambiguous color boundary

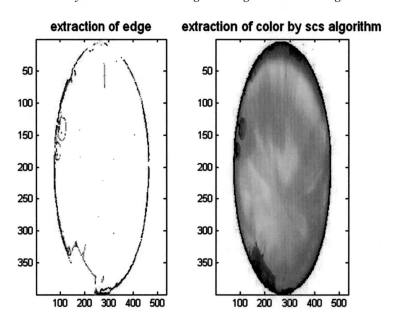

Figure 9. Color extractions by the pixel probabilistic algorithm to obvious color boundary

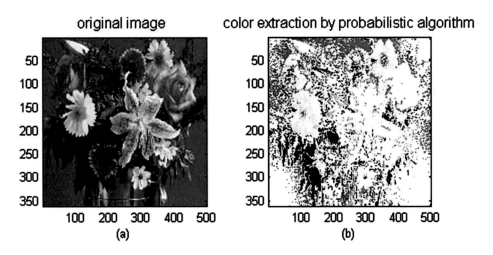

Figure 10. Color extractions by similar color segment algorithm to obvious color boundary

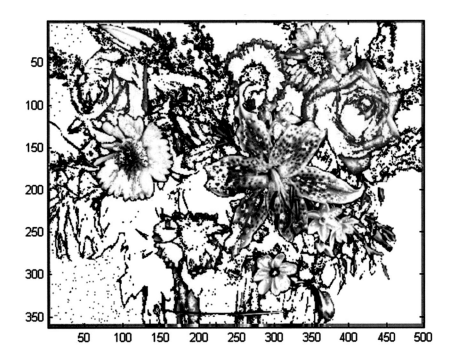

However, for this color image with obvious color boundary, the similar color segment algorithm is used to carry out the its feature extraction, the threshold values of similarity comparison function to detect edges and corner points are still set to g_1=9, g_2=11 and g_3=10, respectively. The threshold of initial edge response function is still set to n_0=2382. The threshold to detect the corner points is still set to n_{angle}=1413. The simulation result is shown in Figure 11.

Figure 11. Smoothing to color edge extracted by similar color segment algorithm

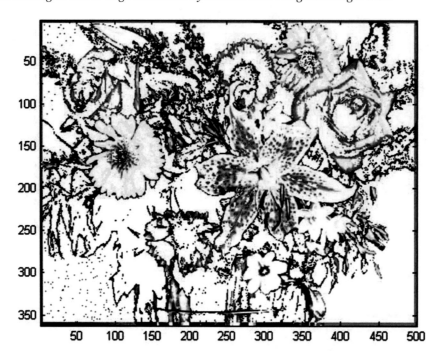

From Figure 10 and Figure 11 seen, for the color extraction that the color boundary is obvious, the extraction effect of the pixel probabilistic algorithm is not better than that of the similar color segment algorithm. The features such as edge, corner points, color, and so on, extracted by the similar color segment algorithm is more distinct, and the effect of noise filtering is good.

It can be also seen from Figure 8 to Figure 11, the effect of pixel probabilistic algorithm to the color extraction that the color boundary is not obvious is better than its effect to the color extraction that the color boundary is obvious. For the extraction results to the color image that the color boundary is obvious, there is more noise. However, the effect of similar color segment algorithm to the color extraction that the color boundary is obvious is better than its effect to the color extraction that the color boundary is not obvious, and its anti-noise ability is strong.

Further, the smoothing to local edge in Figure 12 is again carried out by using two-dimensional Gabor function, i.e., the convolution product of Gabor function $g(x,y)$ with two-dimensional image $p(x,y)$ is carried out to be $f(x,y) = g(x,y) \otimes p(x,y)$. A fairly good result of edge can be obtained, as shown in Figure 18. Where the chosen Gabor function is

$$g(x,y) = \frac{1}{2\pi\delta_x\delta_y} \cdot e^{-\frac{1}{2}\left[\left(\frac{x}{\delta_x}\right)^2 + \left(\frac{y}{\delta_y}\right)^2\right] + j(ux+vy)},$$

and assume the $\delta_x = \delta_y = 4$, $u = v = \frac{\pi}{8}$.

Figure 12. Extraction of edges and corners of color by combination of two proposed algorithms

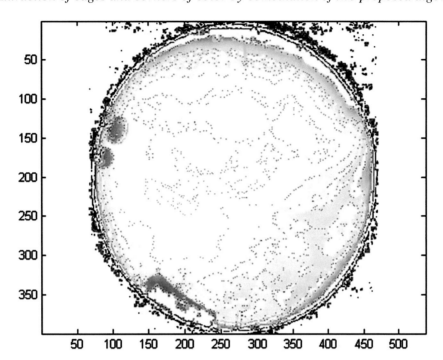

Extraction of Color by the Combination of Two Algorithms

If the pixel probabilistic algorithm and the similar color segment algorithm are combined with, for a color image that the color boundary is not obvious, as shown in Figure 8 (a), the extraction effect of color by the combined method is better than that of the two algorithms, because the extraction effect of color not only is more obvious, but also the detection rate to characteristic points such as edges, corner points, etc, is higher, as well as the anti-noise ability is strong. The extraction result of edge and corner points of color is shown in Figure 13.

Comparison of the Proposed Two and Several Existing Algorithms for Color Extraction

For feature extraction of color images, the extraction results which are given by two color feature extraction algorithms proposed in this paper and existing relevant extraction algorithms to edge and corner of color image are compared. The simulation results show that the extraction effect of the pixel probabilistic algorithm to the color with ambiguous boundary is good, and its processing speed is fast. For a color image with size 362×500, the pixel probabilistic algorithm to the image processing is used, its processing time is 0.516s, but its eliminating noise ability is relatively weak. However, the similar color segment algorithm is used to extract features of color, such as edges, corners, bifurcation points, and so on. The results show that its extraction effect is not only good, but also it can detect the edge direction information, as well as its eliminating noise ability is strong, and its processing speed is faster. For a color image with 362×500, its processing times are only 0.157s. Moreover, this algorithm in use is flexible,

Figure 13. Feature extractions by 5 existing image processing algorithms to color image

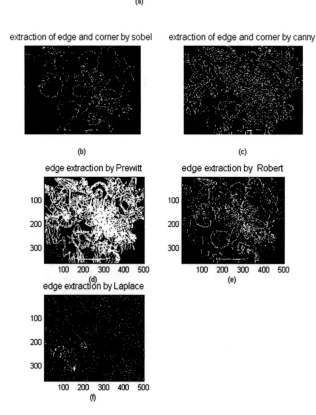

which it is because some thresholds, such as threshold of the comparison function, threshold of edge response, threshold of corner response, can be differently set in simulation based on actual situation and experimental analysis. The experiment and simulation for the two algorithms are given in Section 2.5.1. Please refer to the simulation results shown in this section.

However, Robert, Sobel and Prewitt operators could not detect the edges of some straight lines, and either could not detect the part edges of circle. Though Gauss-Laplace and Canny operators could basically detect all the edges, but their positioning effect was relatively poor, the edge pixels detected by them was wider, and the edges and corners extracted by them all were gray scale pixels. Their processing speed was slightly slow. For a color image with 362×500, an average processing time of Robert, Laplace and Prewitt operators was about 13.969s, that of Sobel was 0.75s, that of Canny was 21.61s. Moreover, their eliminating noise ability was weak. Simulation results are shown in Figure 14 (b)-(f), and Figure 14 (a) is the original image.

Moreover, there was an equilibrium compensating algorithm by using a multi-band color of image (Ma, Wang et al. 2011). It is used to extract the color, as shown in Figure 15. Its extraction effect is not as that of the above Figure 8-Figure 14 as shown. Its extraction efficiency to edge and corner is poor, and some color information is loss.

Feature Extraction by Similar Color Segment Algorithm to ROI

According to the partition algorithms to ROI in Section 2.3, and feature extraction by similar color segment algorithm to color images, the simulation is carried out in here. The extraction of characteristic points in ROI is achieved, as shown in Figure 16.

It can be seen from Figure 16, using this algorithm, the characteristic points of target in ROI can be detected or extracted. However, the features of targets and background outside of ROI cannot be extracted. In this way, some desired features can be designedly extracted. Some unnecessary calculations are reduced. Some resources and time are saved. The detection rate and the extraction speed are improved. More real-time target tracking and target recognition can be achieved.

Figure 14. Feature extractions by equilibrium compensating algorithm to color image

Figure 15. Extraction of edge and corner points of ROI by similar color segment algorithm

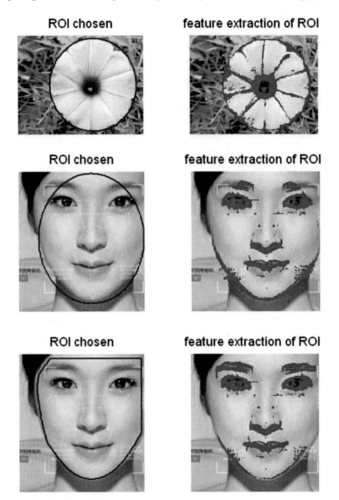

CONCLUSION

This paper studies the features of color images, presents the feature extraction of three-dimensional parameter color images, gives the extraction algorithms of edges and corners, i.e., the pixel probabilistic algorithm and the similar color segment algorithm, as well as gives the comparison and experiment of the two algorithms under different color distribution. Finally, for feature extraction of color images, the extraction results which are given by the two proposed algorithms and existing extraction algorithms to edge and corner of color image are compared. For the similar color segment algorithm to extract the features of color image, such as edges, corners, bifurcation points, and so on, the simulation results indicate that it has the better extraction effect, stronger anti-noise ability, faster processing speed, more flexible use, as well as can detect the edge direction information.

The next task is how to make the two algorithms proposed in this paper be applied to the classification and recognition of aurora image. In the future research work, it needs to strengthen the various applications of color extraction algorithms in engineering, particularly in some fields of applied research of some departments, such as, the polar region, medicine, aerospace, military, public security departments, and so on. Moreover, in different applications, how to choose flexibly some threshold values needs to carry out the debugging and learning in the test. How to give effectively the appropriate threshold values is an issue to be further studied.

REFERENCES

Alamdar, F., & Keyvanpour, M. (2011). A new color feature extraction method based on QuadHistogram. *Procedia Environmental Sciences, 10*(1), 777–783. doi:10.1016/j.proenv.2011.09.126

Aydın, D., & Uğur, A. (2011). Extraction of flower regions in color images using ant colony optimization. *Procedia Computer Science, 3*, 530–536. doi:10.1016/j.procs.2010.12.088

Bayro, C. E., & Eklundh, J. O. (2011). Advances in theory and applications of pattern recognition, image processing and computer vision. *Pattern Recognition Letters, 32*(16), 2143–2144. doi:10.1016/j.patrec.2011.10.008

Bhuiyan, S. M., Khan, J. F., & Adhami, R. R. (2010). A bidimensional empirical mode decomposition method for color image processing.*Proceedings of the 2010 IEEE Workshop On Signal Processing Systems*, Guangzhou (pp. 272 – 277). doi:10.1109/SIPS.2010.5624802

Chen, J., & Bao, Q. (2012). Digital image processing based fire flame color and oscillation frequency analysis. *Procedia Engineering, 45*, 595–601. doi:10.1016/j.proeng.2012.08.209

Galigekere, R. R. (2010). Color-image processing: An introduction with some medical application-examples. *Proceedings of the2010 IEEE International Conference on Systems in Medicine and Biology*, Washington (pp. 3-9). doi:10.1109/ICSMB.2010.5735331

Gonçalves, W. N., & Bruno, O. M. (2013). Dynamic texture segmentation based on deterministic partially self-avoiding walks. *Computer Vision and Image Understanding, 117*(9), 1163–1174. doi:10.1016/j.cviu.2013.04.006

Ilbeygi, M., & Hamed, S. H. (2012). A novel fuzzy facial expression recognition system based on facial feature extraction from color face images. *Engineering Applications of Artificial Intelligence, 25*(1), 130–146. doi:10.1016/j.engappai.2011.07.004

Jukić, A., Kopriva, I., & Cichocki, A. (2013). Noninvasive diagnosis of melanoma with tensor decomposition-based feature extraction from clinical color image. *Biomedical Signal Processing and Control, 8*(6), 755–763. doi:10.1016/j.bspc.2013.07.001

Lissner, I., & Urban, P. (2012). Toward a unified color space for perception-based image processing. *IEEE Transactions on Image Processing, 21*(3), 1153–1168. doi:10.1109/TIP.2011.2163522 PMID:21824846

Lo, J. T. H. (2012). A cortex-like learning machine for temporal hierarchical pattern clustering, detection, and recognition. *Neurocomputing, 78*(1), 89–103. doi:10.1016/j.neucom.2011.04.046

Marques, O. (2011). Color Image Processing, Practical image and video processing using MATLAB. John Wiley & Sons.

Smith, S. M., & Brady, J. M. (1997). SUSAN—a new approach to low level image processing. *International Journal of Computer Vision, 23*(1), 45–78. doi:10.1023/A:1007963824710

Wu, Q., An, J., & Lin, B. (2012). A texture segmentation algorithm based on PCA and global minimization active contour model for aerial insulator images. *IEEE Journal of Selected Topics in Applied Earth Observations and Remote Sensing, 5*(5), 1509–1518. doi:10.1109/JSTARS.2012.2197672

Xie, X. Z., Wu, J. T., & Jing, M. G. (2013). Fast two-stage segmentation via non-local active contours in multiscale texture feature space. *Pattern Recognition Letters, 34*(11), 1230–1239. doi:10.1016/j.patrec.2013.04.016

Chapter 3
A Texture Segmentation Algorithm and Its Application to Target Recognition

QingE Wu
Zhengzhou University of Light Industry, China

Weidong Yang
Fudan University, China

ABSTRACT

Image segmentation is an important research direction in pattern recognition and image understanding, but existing texture segmentation algorithms cannot take full advantage of some texture information of texture image, such as the direction, width, density of ridge line, and so on, and can also not effectively carry out the segmentation of various texture image quality. In order to efficiently implement the texture image segmentation, strengthen the amassing of region segmentation, improve the accuracy of segmentation, achieve more accurate target recognition, this paper defines the direction of the texture, calculates the width of ridge line, gives the distance characteristics between textures, and establishes the mathematical model of the texture border, accordingly presents a new texture segmentation algorithm and compares with other texture segmentation algorithms. The simulation results show that the segmentation algorithm has some advantages to texture segmentation, such as has higher segmentation precision, faster segmentation speed, stronger anti-noise capability, less lost information of target, and so on. The segmented regions hardly contain other texture regions and background region. Moreover, this paper extracts the characteristic points and characteristic parameters in various segmented regions for texture image to obtain the characteristic vector, compares the characteristic vector with the standard template vectors, and identifies the type of target in a range of threshold value. Experimental results show that the proposed target recognition approach has higher recognition rate, faster recognition speed, and stronger anti-noise characteristics than the existing target recognition approaches.

DOI: 10.4018/978-1-5225-1884-6.ch003

INTRODUCTION

In recent years, texture image segmentation is an important topic in the fields of computer vision, pattern recognition, and image processing (Wu et al. 2012). At present, it is widely used in many fields, such as fingerprint identification in the public security system, surgical image processing in medicine, textile testing and image retrieval. Therefore, the technology research in texture image segmentation is of important theoretical and practical significance.

At present, there were a lot of image texture segmentation algorithms. However, these algorithms all had some disadvantages. The histogram threshold value division algorithm did not need any prior information of image and had smaller calculation, but it did not take into account local spatial information, it is difficult to ensure the continuity of the divided region, also had lower reliability when a complex image was divided (Rachidi, Chappard et al., 2008). The basic ideas of region growing for image segmentation was to collect some pixels with similar attributes together to constitute a region, its segmentation effect relied on the seed selection and the growth order, its relative parameter selection was more difficult, and its calculation accuracy to noise was sensitive (Nikou, Galatsanos et al., 2007). The segmentation algorithm based on edge detection could achieve the borderline, but the edge outline was required a follow-up action in order to keep its continuum. It was difficult to determine the region at the not obvious border zone (Evans and Liu, 2006). The segmentation algorithm based on neural network had good results, but the category of its segmentation was too much, and its computational complexity was also larger (Ong, Yeo et al., 2002). The traditional Markov random field (MRF) (Long and Younan, 2013) had the better segmentation effect to micro-texture, but the segmentation result to macro-texture was not good because there were often a lot of islands or small areas, which was contrary to the result of subjective perception and effect of expectation.

In Fuzzy clustering segmentation algorithms, the fuzzy c-means (FCM) (Yu, 2011) clustering was most widely used, because it had some good characteristics, such as it accorded with human cognitive characteristics, its description was the simple and clear, it was easy to be implemented, and so on. But this algorithm also had some disadvantages, such as its performance depended on the initial clustering centers, anti-noise capacity was insufficient, its convergence speed was slow, etc. In 1973, Haralick (Haralick and Shanmugam, 1973) presented the famous GLCM. Soh and Tsataoulis presented an average algorithm by different scales and directions to reduce the computation of GLCM (Soh and Tsatsoulis, 1999). GLCM in texture analysis was a good way, widely used to translate the gray values into the texture information. Yu gave a texture extraction method of WGLCP, but its operation speed was slow (Yu et al., 2012).

From comprehensive analysis known, the existing texture segmentation algorithms could not reflect very well texture characteristic of texture image, could not make full use of texture direction information images of texture image, and could not very effectively carry out the segmentation of various texture image quality. It will not be able to effectively carry out the segmentation for texture image if the gray mean values and mean-square deviation of gray corresponding to the region are only considered. Therefore, other attributes need to be further in-depth studied in corresponding region, in order to obtain more desirable segmentation indexes. The effective region of texture image has good texture characteristic, but the background region as relatively smooth region does not have good texture characteristic. This paper takes fully into account some good texture characteristics of effective texture region which are the direction, width and distance of ridge line, etc. Moreover, based on the gray mean value and the mean-square deviation of gray, respectively, five different segmentation indexes are obtained to constitute a characteristic vector, then the characteristic vector is used to achieve the effective segmentation of texture image. Experimental results show that the proposed texture segmentation algorithm has higher segmentation precision, stronger anti-noise capability and faster convergence speed to compare with the non-oriented segmentation algorithm.

To propose a more effective, rational texture segmentation algorithm, the overall performance of algorithm must be better. Firstly, the algorithm has to more accurately describe the texture characteristic, and achieves the mathematical modeling of textures which should be also a major consideration. On the basis of more precise mathematical descriptions of texture images, some correlation analysis and extraction of the texture image can be carried out more accurately. Secondly, the algorithm should have the stronger anti-interference ability for all kinds of noises. The algorithm can be implemented an appropriate and flexible adjustment for noise of different image so as to better fit for the adaptive capacity of texture segmentation algorithm to the noise. Finally, the algorithm should have good keeping capability to minutiae features and the faster processing speed.

Analysis of Texture Images

At present, how to extract the accurate and reliable characteristic information from low quality texture image, so as to effectively improve the performance and adaptability of automatic texture recognition system on texture image quality is currently a research focus in the area of automatic texture recognition.

The uniformity of region pixel doesn't exist in natural texture image. The texture of the image is often arranged by the repeated texture primitive element according to certain rules. The texture is not dependent on a single pixel. In fact, a single pixel in the texture image is meaningless. So the selection of characteristic parameters is a key step on texture segmentation algorithm, which it directly affects the recognition ability of algorithm to texture.

In usual texture images, they mostly contain background and texture regions. If the whole image that contains the background region is processed, the time of image preprocessing and feature extraction is not only greatly extended, but also a large number of false characteristic information is extracted from the background region, thus it seriously affects the recognition results. In the case of noise interference is not serious, as shown in Figure 1, then the algorithm based on the mean value and variance of gray can achieve the segmentation of texture region and background region, as shown in Figure 2.

Figure 1. Means and variances of background and target is 5.5206 and 169.2567, 9.1400 and 21.4727, respectively

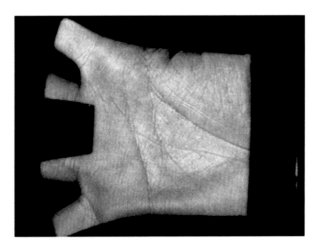

Figure 2. Texture segmentation based on mean and variance of gray

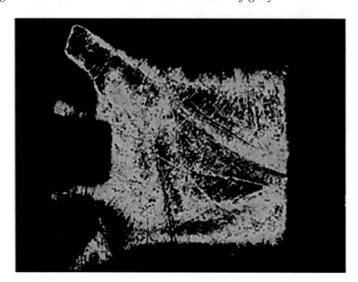

The existing segmentation algorithms are designed mainly based on statistical characteristics of texture images for texture regions and the background regions, such as variance and mean (Nikou, Galatsanos et al., 2007), (Melendez, Garcia et al., 2011). On the premise of good texture images quality, this algorithm can achieve very good texture segmentation, which is able to meet the basic needs of subsequent image processing. However, under strong noise interference, because the noise has seriously disrupted the statistical characteristics of the original texture image, the obtained statistical characteristics cannot truly portray the image it should have the characteristic information. Therefore, the judgement algorithm based on variance and mean cannot achieve very well the accurate segmentation to low quality texture image. Although some existing algorithms (Mailing and Cernuschi-Frías, 2011), (Han, Tao et al., 2011), (Goncalves and Bruno, 2013) considered the texture characteristics of texture, and used the direction information, but they only took into account the consistency of direction in the local texture region, and used it as a criterion index to achieve the texture image segmentation. From comprehensive analysis known, the existing texture segmentation algorithms could not reflect very well the texture characteristic of the texture image, could not make full use of texture direction information of texture image, and could not very effectively carry out the segmentation of various texture image quality.

To compare with the background region, the effective texture region has better direction selectivity, which it shows good anisotropy, but the background region shows the isotropy in relative character. The stronger direction selectivity of texture region shows completely different characteristics on the horizontal, vertical and 45° direction from the grey scale difference. According to this regularity of direction, the texture segmentation can effectively be achieved for texture image.

For the image as shown in Figure 3, the grey scale of each pixel in the texture region and the background region is different, which shows in different energy diagram as shown in Figure 4. Figure 4 is the model of a valid texture region and a background region in three dimensions. It can be very clearly found from the diagram that the texture characteristic is very prominent in valid texture region image, which shows good energy jump. However, the energy characteristics of the background region levels off, its jump is not obvious.

Figure 3. Low-noise image

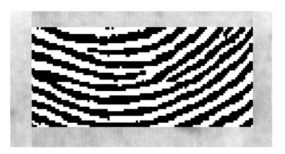

Figure 4. Energy characteristics of texture image: 3-dimension energy of background region (left); 3-dimension energy of target region (right)

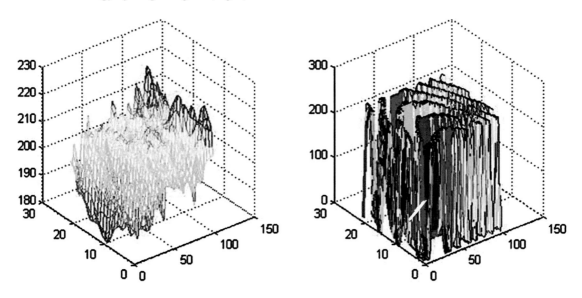

If the texture region can be accurately and reliably divided up from background region in the case of strong noise interference, so that the only effective texture region is processed in subsequent processes, then to shorten the time of image preprocessing and to increase accuracy of feature extraction are of great significance. For the image of texture and background regions with noise interference, as shown in Figure 5, the texture segmentation cannot be achieved by only using mean value and variance of gray scale. In Figure 5, the A region denotes the target region while the B region is the background region. The existing texture segmentation algorithms also had introduced the position characteristic vectors (Mailing and Cernuschi-Frías, 2011), (Han, Tao et al., 2011), (Goncalves and Bruno, 2013). The algorithm introduced three directions which is the horizontal position v_x, vertical position v_y and the center radial distance v_r, and implemented the segmentation of texture and background regions with a strong noise interference, as shown in Figure 6. The segmentation results are some texture information in the target region are lost. The segmentation effect of this position algorithm to Figure 5 and Figure 7 (a4) is not ideal, because its error segmentation rate and missing segmentation rate all are larger.

Figure 5. Mean and variance of target and background regions: (a) mean and variance of A region: 177.3, 14.18, mean and variance of B region: 229.3, 11.96; (b) mean and variance of A region: 202.8, 8.57, mean and variance of B region: 239.0, 11.02

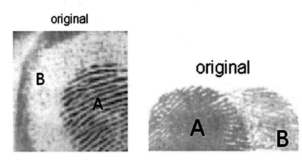

The mean-square deviation and mean value of gray scale of B region in Figure 5 (b) all are approximately equal to those of A region, which directly leads to the invalidation of segmentation index. Thus, the texture segmentation cannot effectively be carried out if the mean value and mean-square deviation of gray scale corresponding to the region are considered only. Therefore, other attributes need to be studied further, in order to obtain more desirable segmentation index. Here, the character of distance orientation is given to divide up the texture regions of the above image. This segmentation algorithm is given as follows:

The distance orientation algorithm introduces a position character that is the distance v_r from a pixel to vertex of edge, as one-dimensional characteristic vector of image, and it is given as follows:

$$v_r(x,y) = \sqrt{(x - width)^2 + (y - height)^2}$$

where width and height are the width and height of image, according to the experiment and $r = \sqrt{\left(\dfrac{width}{2}\right)^2 + \left(\dfrac{height}{2}\right)^2}$, the threshold value r_0 of $v_r(x,y)$ is given. A 5-dimensional characteristic vector $V=[\mu,\sigma,x,y,v_r]$ consists of the x, y, v_r and a 2-dimensional mean value and variance of gray scale, and it is used to describe the characteristics of different textures, then the texture segmentation of effective region based on the characteristic vector can be achieved. This algorithm is simple, but the selection of threshold value is crucial, and it is also easy to lose some effective image information.

According to the distance orientation, the extraction of target region to Figure 5 is shown in Figure 6, and the processing time is 0.343s and 1.344s, respectively. From Figure 6 known, a good segmentation to target and background regions is obtained, but some texture information in target region will lose.

The existing algorithm introduced also the tangent direction and normal direction. It requires implementing an accurate positioning to tangent and normal direction, or giving accurately the texture model. However, to give accurately the random diverse texture models are more difficult, because the establishment of a unified model to diverse textures is hard, each texture region also cannot be completely accurately divided up for different textures in an image. For implementing an accurate segmentation to

Figure 6. Texture segmentation by distance orientation

segmentation by distance orientation

segmentation by distance orientation

each different texture, this paper defines another direction, width and distance of ridge line, and takes the mean value and variance of gray scale, direction, width and distance of ridge line as the characteristic parameters to divide up the texture.

TEXTURE SEGMENTATION ALGORITHM BASED ON GRAY SCALE JUMP

Algorithm Proposed

This paper uses the jump characteristic of gray scale to determine the direction, the distance and the width of ridge lines in the horizontal direction, vertical direction, 1/4 arc direction. Take the pixel point i as a vertex to open a size $r \times r$ window in its neighborhood. Calculate the mean μ_i and variance σ_i of gray scale of the window as two characteristic parameters of the pixels i. Take the pixel point i as a center of circle and r as a radius of a circle to draw a 1/4 circle, labeled as $\Theta_i(1/4)$. Find the jump number of the gray scale, c_h, c_v and $c_{1/4}$, along the radius direction of image width, the radius direction of image height, and 1/4 arc direction, respectively. Define three parameters as a direction characteristic vector of the pixel i, labeled as $\text{dir}_i = \left(c_{ih}, c_{iv}, c_{i,1/4} \right)$. Along the 1/4 arc direction again, label the gray level jump positions $Q_{kl}(x_k, y_l)$, $k,l \in N$. Calculate the distance between two adjacent consecutive jump points, $d_{Q_{kl}}$, $k,l = 1,2,\ldots$. Simultaneously, calculate the gray scale values of any one point between two adjacent jump points, G, G'. Further, calculate the average value $\bar{d}_{i1}$ and $\bar{d}_{i2}$ of distance $d_{Q_{kl}}$ between similar gray scale values, then the width of the wave crest and wave valley can be defined as $\bar{d}_{i1}$ and $\bar{d}_{i2}$, i.e., as the distance and the width of ridge line, respectively. In conclusion, the characteristic vector of segmentation to pixel i is

$$V_i = \left[\mu_i, \sigma_i, \text{dir}_i, \bar{d}_{i1}, \bar{d}_{i2} \right] \tag{1}$$

When the gray scale jump is calculated based on the original image, the relatively large threshold value is used, which its range is usually [50, 200]. If the original image is preprocessed to binarization image, the threshold value is 1 to calculate the number of jumps. The segmentation algorithm to image by using the gray scale jump on the horizontal direction and vertical direction is given as follows:

Assume the sizes of image height and image width are m and n, respectively. On the one hand, when the image height is at a fixed point, that is, $height = m_i$, the number of gray level jump, c_i, $i=1,\ldots,m$, is sought along the image width direction. According to the experimental result to texture and background regions, the number of gray scale jump of texture region is more than that of background region. Further, according to the jump number c_i, a threshold value M_1 can be given. For any jump number is greater than this threshold, i.e., $c_i > M_1$, at this time, the height and width are recorded, which represented as y_{k_1} and x_{k_1}, respectively, $k_1 \in N$, and a set of ordered pairs is acquired as equation (2).

$$I_1 = \left\{ \left(x_{k_1}, y_{k_1} \right) \middle| c_i > M_1 \right\} \tag{2}$$

On the other hand, under a given fixed point along image width direction, i.e., $width = n_j$, the number of gray scale jump, d_j, $j=1,\ldots,n$, is sought along the image height direction. Then according to the jump number d_j, another threshold value M_2 can be given. Similarly, for any jump number is greater than this threshold, i.e., $d_j > M_2$, at this time, the width and height are recorded, which represented as x_{k_2} and y_{k_2}, respectively, $k_2 \in N$, and a set of ordered pairs is obtained as equation (3).

$$I_2 = \left\{ \left(x_{k_2}, y_{k_2} \right) \middle| d_j > M_2 \right\} \tag{3}$$

According to equations (2) and (3), the set of ordered pairs

$$I = I_1 \cup I_2 = \left\{ \left(x_k, y_k \right), k \in N \right\}$$

can be obtained. Based on (x_k, y_k), the fitting curve that x_k and y_k satisfy can be obtained. Then the edge line of target region can be obtained by carrying out borderline modeling of texture. This algorithm of texture segmentation is called the gray scale jump algorithm.

The minimal values and maximum values are calculated as follows:

$$x_{\min} = \min_k \left\{ x_k \right\}, \quad x_{\max} = \max_k \left\{ x_k \right\}, \quad y_{\min} = \min_k \left\{ y_k \right\}, \quad y_{\max} = \max_k \left\{ y_k \right\}$$

Under $x_{\min}$ are satisfied, according to the ordered pair (x_k, y_k) in I, the

$$y_{up1} = \min_k \left\{ y_k \middle| x_{\min}, \left(x_{\min}, y_k \right) \in I \right\} \text{ and } y_{down1} = \max_k \left\{ y_k \middle| x_{\min}, \left(x_{\min}, y_k \right) \in I \right\}$$

can be obtained.

Similarly, the following expression can also be obtained.

$$y_{up2} = \min_k \left\{ y_k \middle| x_{\max}, \left(x_{\max}, y_k \right) \in I \right\} \text{ and } y_{down2} = \max_k \left\{ y_k \middle| x_{\max}, \left(x_{\max}, y_k \right) \in I \right\}$$

$$x_{left1} = \min_{k}\left\{x_k \left| y_{\min} , \left(x_k, y_{\min}\right) \in I\right.\right\} \text{ and } x_{right1} = \max_{k}\left\{x_k \left| y_{\min}, \left(x_k, y_{\min}\right) \in I\right.\right\}$$

$$x_{left2} = \min_{k}\left\{x_k \left| y_{\max} , \left(x_k, y_{\max}\right) \in I\right.\right\} \text{ and } x_{right2} = \max_{k}\left\{x_k \left| y_{\max}, \left(x_k, y_{\max}\right) \in I\right.\right\}$$

In this way, the eight different points $P_1\left(x_{\min}, y_{up1}\right)$, $P_2\left(x_{\min}, y_{down1}\right)$, $P_3\left(x_{\max}, y_{up2}\right)$, $P_4\left(x_{\max}, y_{down2}\right)$, $P_5\left(x_{left1}, y_{\min}\right)$, $P_6\left(x_{right1}, y_{\min}\right)$, $P_7\left(x_{left2}, y_{\max}\right)$, $P_8\left(x_{right2}, y_{\max}\right)$ are obtained. The point $P_1 P_5 P_6 P_3 P_4 P_8 P_7 P_2$ are connected in turn, thus the enclosing dividing line of texture region is achieved. Or according to the target requirement or experiment, the part points are connected to achieve local dividing line. The more segmentation points are obtained by using linear interpolation. The more the interpolation points are, the more accurate the segmentation positioning is.

In addition, the segmentation algorithm can also be given by using the following method:

Calculate the midpoint $P_{M1}(x_{\min}, y_{M1})$ of P_1 and P_2, the midpoint $P_{M2}(x_{\max}, y_{M2})$ of P_3 and P_4, the midpoint $P_{N1}(x_{N1}, y_{\min})$ of P_5 and P_6, the midpoint $P_{N2}(x_{N2}, y_{maz})$ of P_7 and P_8. The linear equation l_1 of P_{M1} and P_{M2} can be obtained as follows: $y = k_1 x + b_1$, where

$$k_1 = \frac{y_{M2} - y_{M1}}{x_{\max} - x_{\min}}, \quad b_1 = \frac{x_{\max} y_{M1} - x_{\min} y_{M2}}{x_{\max} - x_{\min}}$$

The linear equation l_2 of P_{N1} and P_{N2} is: $y = k_2 x + b_2$, where

$$k_2 = \frac{y_{\max} - y_{\min}}{x_{N2} - x_{N1}}, \quad b_2 = \frac{x_{N2} y_{\min} - x_{N1} y_{\max}}{x_{N2} - x_{N1}}$$

Calculate the intersection point $O(x_0, y_0)$ of l_1 and l_2. According to several distances from the points P_{M1}, P_{M2}, P_{N1} and P_{N2} to the point O, respectively, as well as the coordinates of 8 points $P_1, P_2, P_3, P_4, P_5, P_6, P_7, P_8$ obtained by above, the model of the dividing line can be established. The model may be the line, circle, ellipse, etc., or a combination of several curves. For example, if we use the smooth curves as the dividing line, the following instances are usually used:

1. If these distances from the points P_{M1}, P_{M2}, P_{N1} and P_{N2} to the point O within a certain range of error are equal, then the dividing line is circle $(x-x_0)^2 + (y-y_0)^2 = r^2$, which the center of circle is $O(x_0, y_0)$, and the radius r is the distance from the point P_{M1} to the point O.
2. If these distances from the points P_{M1}, P_{M2}, P_{N1} and P_{N2} to the point O within a certain range of error are not equal, but the midpoint M_{10} of P_{M1} and P_{M2}, the midpoint M_{20} of P_{N1} and P_{N2} within a given tolerance are coincident to the point O, then the smooth dividing line may be established to be the ellipse $(x-x_0)^2/a^2 + (y-y_0)^2/b^2 = 1$, where the $a = |P_{M1} M_{10}|$, $b = |P_{N1} M_{20}|$.

Take count of gray scale jump on the 1/4 arc direction, then carry out the calculation of image segmentation, which the method is similar to the calculation of the horizontal and vertical directions.

Experimental Results and Conclusions

In order to verify the actual performance of the proposed segmentation algorithm for texture image, several different texture images are chosen to implement the simulation of segmentation. The segmentation line and the segmentation effect of the simulation results are shown in Figure 7.

According to the proposed algorithm on gray scale jump, the different texture regions to image are carried out the texture segmentation, and the extracted results of different textures are shown in Figure 8. By using this jump algorithm, the segmentation results that the texture images with strong noise are carried out are shown in Figure 7 (b2), and the texture extraction results are shown in Figure 7 (d2).

To evaluate the good and bad of a texture segmentation algorithm, it is mainly to validate the overall performance index of the algorithm is good, such as it has the better holding capability to detailed features of texture, faster processing speed, and stronger anti-noise capability.

In order to compare the performance of proposed segmentation algorithm and the existing segmentation algorithm, the main image data selected here is the palmprint Database and more difficult segmentation B library of open fingerprints database-BVC2004 at biometric identification research center of Hong Kong Polytechnic University. The image segmentation is carried out by using the proposed segmentation algorithm and the classical algorithms based on variance of gray scale, k-means, tangent and normal directions, respectively. Figure 8, Figure 9 and Figure 10 are the actual results of segmentation that the four algorithms to different textures and texture with noise carry out the image segmentation. From the segmentation results found, the segmentation result of the proposed algorithm to noise region is more accurate, and its anti-noise interference capability is stronger than those of the variance based on gray scale, k-means, tangent and normal directions. By analysis known, the local noise can cause the variance cumulation of corresponding texture region, so as to form the larger value of variance and mean in local region. Thus, the feature of variance and mean in noise region is consistent to that of effective texture region, and the positioning of tangent and normal direction to texture is not accurate, consequently, it leads to the texture segmentation algorithms based on variance, k-means, tangent and normal direction fail, so that these algorithms cannot accurately divide up the background region and different texture regions from region of interest of texture image. However, neither the local noise forms different effective texture, nor exhibits the consistent feature of texture as texture region of interest. The algorithm in this paper uses the different exhibition of textures in different texture region and background region to carry out the texture segmentation.

By Figures 8, 9, to compare with the segmentation algorithms to Figure 7 (b5), Figure 8 and Figure 7 (b2, d2), the segmentation results to Figure 7 and Figure 8 are better than those to Figure 9. The image information loses little by using the segmentation algorithms for Figure 6 and Figure 8, but the information loses more by using other algorithms in the segmentation process. From Figure 10 known, the segmentation accuracy of jump algorithm of gray scale to image with strong noise is also very high, this is better than the segmentation effect of other segmentation algorithms. The processing time of different segmentation algorithm to image is different. For Figures 7 (a2), the processing time of this proposed algorithm is 0.516s, but that of existing algorithms is as follows: that of the algorithm based on mean and variance is 0.308s, that of k-means is 3.01s, that of distance orientation is 3.44s.

Through the comprehensive analysis, to compare with the existing texture segmentation algorithms, the proposed jump algorithm of gray scale in this paper has some advantages, such as its segmentation accuracy is higher, its anti-noise capability is stronger, its segmentation speed is faster, the image information loses less, and so on. So, it is an ideal texture segmentation algorithm at present.

Figure 7. Texture segmentation line and its effect

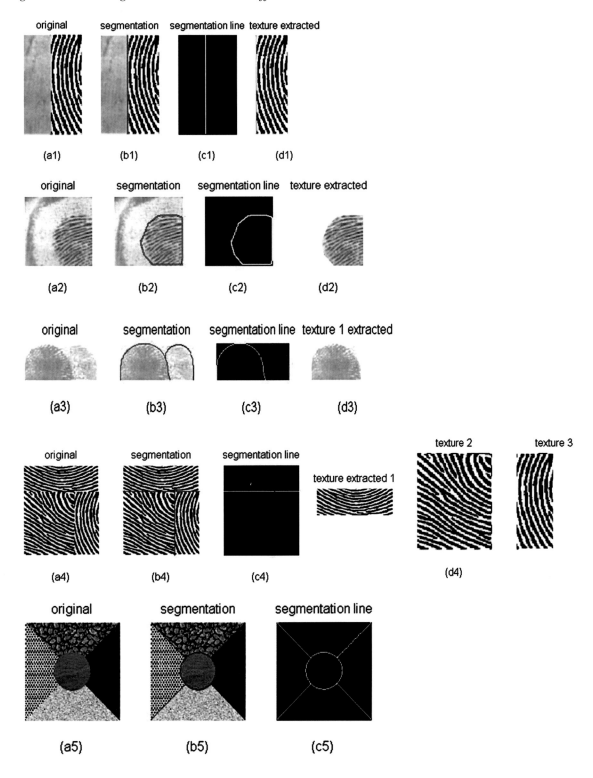

Figure 8. Texture segmentation and extraction by using proposed jump algorithm of gray scale

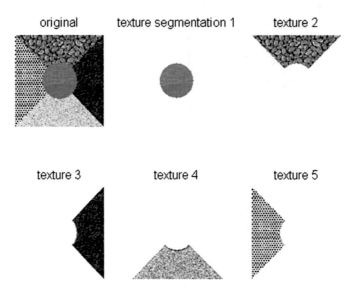

Figure 9. Comparison of the proposed and existing texture segmentation algorithms to texture image with multi-regions: (a) texture segmentation by mean-variance; (b) texture segmentation by k-means; (c) texture segmentation by distance orientation; (d) segmentation by proposed gray scale jump

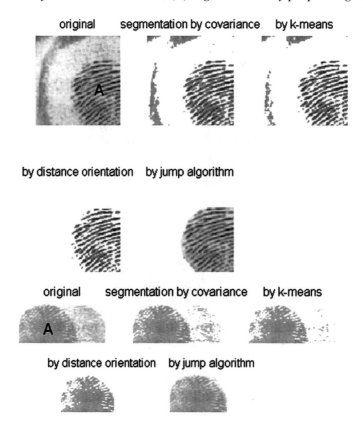

Figure 10. Comparison of the proposed and existing texture segmentation algorithms to images with noise

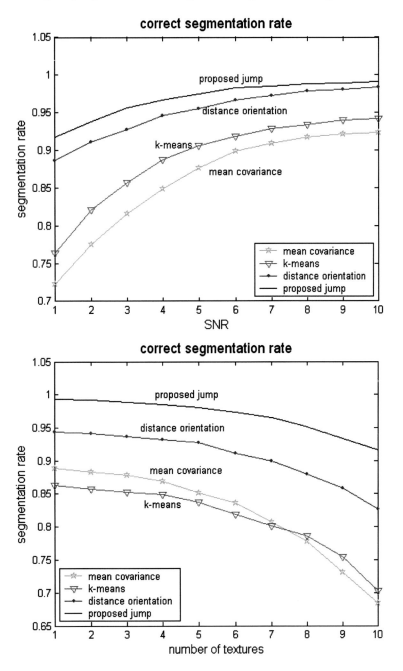

Performance Analysis of Segmentation Algorithm

Performance Analysis

To evaluate the segmentation effect, we here consider three types of ratio: the first type is the correct segmentation rate is the ratio which the marked image can be completely exactly divided up. For given samples, the area S_0 of the actual target region can be measured by optical instruments. The area S of target region can be obtained after the image is divided up by using texture segmentation algorithm, then the correct segmentation rate can be defined:

$$R_c = 1 - \frac{\left| S - S_0 \right|}{S_0} \text{ or } R_c = \frac{N_c}{N_l} \tag{4}$$

The second type is the error segmentation rate is the ratio which other texture regions or background region are incorrectly divided up the effective texture regions, and it is defined as:

$$R_e = \frac{N_e}{N_l} \tag{5}$$

The third type is the missed segmentation rate is the ratio which the effective texture region is incorrectly divided up other texture regions or background region, it is defined as

$$R_m = \frac{N_m}{N_l} \tag{6}$$

where M_l is the number of pixels within the target region of marked samples which the signal to noise ratio is l. N_c is the number of pixels for the correct segmentation. N_e is the number of pixels to the error segmentation. N_m is the number of pixels to missed segmentation.

Obviously, there exists $R_c + R_e + R_m = 1$. For different signal to noise ratio l, the above results are different, but R_c, R_e and R_m will approximate to a certain stable value with the increase l. The conclusion may be confirmed by the following simulation.

In experiment, the window size is chosen to be 3×3 on image segmentation, and 100 samples are tested. Under given different signal to noise ratio l, the comparison of the proposed and existing segmentation algorithms is implemented. For the texture image with noise, as shown in Figure 7 (a3), the correct average segmentation rate of the proposed algorithm is 96.89%, that of the algorithm based on the mean and variance is 86.1%, that of k-means is 88.99%, that of distance orientation algorithm is 95.11%. As the signal to noise ratio increases, the correct segmentation rates of different algorithms also increase. The comparisons of correct segmentation rates with change of signal to noise ratio are shown in Figure 11 (a).

For an image with different number $N=1,2,\ldots,10$ of texture regions, the comparison of the proposed and existing segmentation algorithms is also carried out. For multi-texture image, as shown in Figure 7 (a5), the correct average segmentation rate of the proposed segmentation algorithm is 96.79%, that of the algorithm based on the mean and variance is 82.08%, that of k-means is 81.24%, that of distance orientation algorithm is 90.6%. As the number of texture regions increases, the correct segmentation rate of different algorithms decreases, but that of the jump algorithm of gray scale decreases slowly. The comparisons that the correct segmentation rates vary with the number of texture regions are shown in Figure 11 (b).

Figure 11. Comparisons of correct segmentation rate of the proposed and existing segmentation algorithms: (a) change of signal to noise ratio; (b) change of the number of texture regions

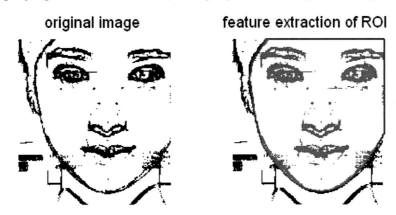

From Figure 11 known, the correct segmentation rate of the proposed segmentation algorithm to texture is higher than that of existing algorithms, and the robustness of the algorithm is well.

Because the variance and mean of noise region are approximately consistent to those of target region, the segmentation algorithm based on the mean and variance cannot properly implement the segmentation to regions, so that the residual background formed by segmentation is a lot. At the same time, the texture segmentation algorithm based on directional consistency (Mailing and Cernuschi-Frías, 2011), (Han, Tao et al., 2011), (Goncalves and Bruno, 2013), because there were the part conglutination in the target region, and the residual ridge structure in the background existed, led directly to the directional consistency in target region was not strong, but the directional consistency in other texture regions and background region was relatively higher, consequently, the algorithm could not effectively carry out the texture image segmentation, its error segmentation rate and missed segmentation rate were larger. Through in-depth research on features of texture region, seven categories of segmentation index here are considered comprehensively, i.e., the seven indexes are the mean and variance of gray scale, horizontal direction, vertical direction, 1/4 arc direction, ridge line width, and ridge line distance, and then the texture segmentation algorithm based on gray scale jump achieves the segmentation to image. In order to verify the performance of the segmentation algorithm, this paper uses several segmentation algorithms based on mean and variance of gray scale, k-means, distance orientation and gray scale jump, respectively, to carry out the texture segmentation to the multi-texture image and the texture image with noise, and compares with these segmentation algorithms to original image processing. Moreover, to describe effectively the actual segmentation results of four algorithms, this paper defines three types of performance indexes: (1) correct segmentation rate R_c, (2) error segmentation rate R_e, (3) missed segmentation rate R_m. For the original texture image of Figure 7 (a3, a5), the actual performance indexes are shown in Table 1.

To compare the proposed segmentation algorithm with the traditional texture segmentation algorithms based on mean and variance of gray scale, k-means, distance orientation, the experimental results show that the proposed algorithm based on gray scale jump can more accurately carry out texture segmentation. For texture images with more complex background, the proposed segmentation algorithm has better robustness.

Table 1. Segmentation results of four algorithms to two typical multi-texture and noise texture images

Algorithm	Noise Texture Image with Different SNR, as Shown in Figure 7 (a3)			Multi-Texture with Change of the Number of Texture Region, as Shown in Figure 7 (a5)		
	$\bar{R}_c$ (%)	$\bar{R}_e$ (%)	$\bar{R}_m$ (%)	$\bar{R}_c$ (%)	$\bar{R}_e$ (%)	$\bar{R}_m$ (%)
Mean variance	86.1	10.6	3.3	82.08	12.77	5.15
k- means	88.99	5.02	5.99	81.24	9.86	8.9
Distance orientation	95.11	0.33	4.56	90.6	7.51	1.89
Gray scale jump	96.89	2.99	0.12	96.79	3.06	0.15

Comprehensive Analysis and Comparison

In order to evaluate the overall performance of each algorithm, we adopt the combination of quantitative analysis and qualitative analysis method, and synthesize comparison based on several factors such as the correct segmentation rate, computing speed, anti-noise capability, loss of information, acclimation, and so on. We evaluate the merits and demerits of the proposed algorithm and existing algorithms. The Table 2 gives the results of a comprehensive comparison.

In Table 2, the computing speed is the mean time obtained by the mean computing time of 10 times repeating test of these algorithms at each step in two cases simulation environment, which the computing time is only the computing time of algorithm itself. In simulation, the computer used is the Pentium 4 and 2G memory, and the programming language is MATLAB. The anti-noise capability and the loss of information are estimated approximately based on the simulation course and simulation results of every algorithm. The acclimation is the environment that these algorithms adapt to image with a complex background, such as the difference of texture and background region, the level of noise interference, the

Table 2. Comprehensive comparison of several segmentation algorithms for different SNR

Algorithm	Average Correct Segmentation Rate $\bar{R}_c$ (2 Kinds SNR)		Computing Speed (2 Kinds SNR)		Anti-Noise Capability	Loss of Information	Acclimation
	Figure 7(a3)	Figure 7(a5)	Figure 7(a3)	Figure 7(a5)			
variance	0.861	0.8208	0.031s	0.422s	weak	Much	low noise & less regions
k-means	0.8899	0.8124	0.062s	1.406s	weak	More	low noise & less regions
distance	0.9511	0.906	3.4252s	5.8184s	little strong	Little	little complex
Jump	0.9689	0.9679	0.499s	2.687s	strong	Less	complex

number of texture regions, and so on. From the results of Table 2 seen, the average correct segmentation rates are the average of two stages which are an average of 50 times simulations and then taking an average of 10 time-steps for every algorithm under the given simulation environment case 1 and case 2. In fact, they are the average of the correct segmentation rates in space and time, so they are an overall average of the correct segmentation rates.

FEATURE EXTRACTION TO TARGET

The target region can be divided up by using the proposed algorithm of gray scale jump, and then some feature detections, such as edge, corner point, etc., can be achieved in divided region. The detection algorithm is given as follows:

Place a size $w \times w$ estimated window at each pixel position s. The center pixel of the window is called nucleus. The gray values of each point in the window and the nucleus point are compared. If the difference value between the gray scale of pixels in the window and that of nucleus pixel is less than a given threshold value, the point in the window is considered to be equal to or be similar to the nucleus point, and which a region consists of pixels to satisfy this condition is called similar segment nucleus (SSN).

Make the window move over the image. The gray values of each point in the window and the nucleus point are compared by using the following comparison function.

$$C(x,y) = \begin{cases} 1, if \left| I(x,y) - I(x_0, y_0) \right| \leq h \\ 0, if \left| I(x,y) - I(x_0, y_0) \right| > h \end{cases} \tag{7}$$

In the formula, h is the threshold value of difference of gray scales, i.e., the threshold value is to determine the similarity. The selection of h is determined according to the comparative degree of target and background in the image. The (x_0, y_0) is the position of the current nucleus point. The (x,y) is the position of other any point in the window. $I(x_0, y_0)$ and $I(x,y)$ are the gray values of nucleus and other points in the window, respectively. $C(x,y)$ is the discriminant function of pixels in the window belonging to the SSN.

Next, calculate the size of the SSN. The size of the SSN can be calculated by the following formula:

$$n(x_0, y_0) = \sum_{(x,y) \in c(x_0, y_0), (x,y) \neq (x_0, y_0)} C(x,y) \tag{8}$$

where $n(x_0, y_0)$ is the size of the SSN of the point (x_0, y_0). The $c(x_0, y_0)$ is the window to take (x_0, y_0) as the center.

When the window locates in different position, the size of the SSN is different. According to the experimental analysis, if the nucleus point is in neighbour of the edges in actual noise image, the n is generally not greater than $3n_{max}/4$. However, If the nucleus point is at the corner point, the SSN region is the smallest, thus the corner point can be detected. The value g to extract the corner point is smaller, generally $g = n_{max}/2$. The n_{max} is the maximum value that $n(x_0, y_0)$ can arrive. The value g affects mainly the sharpness of characteristic points. The smaller the g is, the sharper the obtained corner points are.

The initial response of edges and corner points can be created by the following formula:

$$R(x_0, y_0) = \begin{cases} g - n(x_0, y_0), & n(x_0, y_0) < g \\ 0, & n(x_0, y_0) \geq g \end{cases} \tag{9}$$

where g is the geometry threshold of response. The $R(x_0, y_0)$ is the response function.

To determine the edge direction, there are two edge cases. The first case is that the SSN is the axis of symmetry between pixels. The second case is that the position of center of gravity of pixels is close to or overlaps to the position of nucleus. The edge direction is determined respectively as follows:

In the first case, the vector direction between center of gravity and position of nuclear is perpendicular to the edge direction. The center of gravity can be calculated:

$$\begin{cases} \overline{g}_x = \dfrac{\sum_x xC(x, y)}{\sum_x C(x, y)} \\ \overline{g}_y = \dfrac{\sum_y yC(x, y)}{\sum_y C(x, y)} \end{cases}$$

In the second edge case, the SSN region is the thin lines of edge direction, and then the edge direction can be determined by looking for the long axis of symmetric part, that is,

$$\overline{x} = \sum_x \left| x - x_0 \right| C(x, y) \tag{10}$$

$$\overline{y} = \sum_y \left| y - y_0 \right| C(x, y) \tag{11}$$

$$\overline{xy} = \sum_{x,y} (x - x_0)(y - y_0)C(x, y) \tag{12}$$

The ratio of $\overline{y}$ and $\overline{x}$ determines the edge direction. The symbol of $\overline{xy}$ are used to determine the positive or negative of the diagonal edge gradient direction. To the detailed implementation of edge and corner, please refer to (Smith and Brady, 1997).

According to the above detection algorithm for edge and corner point, the feature detection of target to region of interest (ROI) is shown in Figure 12.

In Figure 12, the red region is ROI. The pink lines or pink points are the extracted features. From Figure 13 seen, the features in ROI are only extracted, but the features outside ROI are not extracted, so that it reduces unnecessary feature detection. Thus, the speed of feature detection is not only improved, but also the effective characteristic points are obtained, consequently, the detection efficiency is improved.

Figure 12. Feature detection to target in ROI

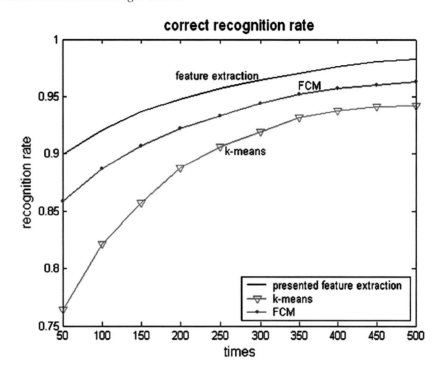

Target Recognition Based on Feature Extraction

Based on the extracted characteristic vector of image, we perform the target recognition, as it is a typical problem of pattern matching. For a given standard template of image library, the known characteristic vector consists of characteristic parameters of the target. We compare the characteristic vectors of unknown target image with the characteristic vectors of known classificatory target image that has been trained and stored in the retrieval system. Based on the minimum difference principle, if and only if the difference value between the characteristic vector of unknown target image and the characteristic vector of given i_0th target image is minimal, we judge that the unknown target belongs to the i_0th category. The recognition algorithm based on the principle for image feature detection is given in the following section.

Assume there are n categories of target image. For simplifying the discussion, the 'target image' is called the 'target' for short in the following. The characteristic vector of every target consists of k characteristic parameters, for example, the characteristic vector of the face image consists of the eyes, eyebrows, nose and the edge contour, corner points, vertex of mouth, etc. The parameter value of characteristic points is defined to be the relative position x_i, y_i to the center of the image, the distance v_{ir} to the center of image, gray values μ_i, and so on, for example, the canthus (left canthus1, 2 and right canthus 1, 2), a total of 4*4. We assume the ith category target has n_{ij} values on the jth characteristic parameter, X_{ij}^m denotes the mth number of the ith category target on the jth characteristic parameter; $\tilde{X}_j$ is the detection value of the unknown target on the jth characteristic parameter, where $i=1, 2,\ldots, n, j=1, 2,\ldots, k$, $m=1,\ldots, n_{ij}$.

In order to determine the type of the unknown target, we need to make certain the difference degree d_{ij}^m between $\tilde{X}_j$ and X_{ij}^m, i.e.,

$$d_{ij}^m = \left| \tilde{X}_j - X_{ij}^m \right| \tag{13}$$

So, we obtain the difference vector between the unknown $\tilde{X}_j$ and j^{th} the parameter of the ith category target is $d_{ij} = \left[d_{ij}^1, d_{ij}^2, \cdots, d_{ij}^{n_{ij}} \right]$. As long as d_{ij} the norm of is less than a given threshold, i.e., $\left\| d_{ij} \right\| = \sum_{m=1}^{n_{ij}} d_{ij}^m < \varepsilon$ then we judge that the unknown $\tilde{X}_j$ and the jth characteristic parameter of the i_0^{th} category target is similar or same. Where ε is a given arbitrary small positive number. $\left\| \bullet \right\|$ is a vector norm. So, we obtain the difference vector between the characteristic vector of identified target image and the characteristic vector of the ith category target image is

$$D_i = \left[d_{i1}, d_{i2}, \cdots, d_{ik} \right], \ \forall i \in \left\{ 1, 2, \cdots, n \right\} \tag{14}$$

If $\exists i_0 \in \left\{ 1, 2, \cdots, n \right\}$, subject to

$$i_0 = \arg \min_{i \in \left\{ 1,2,\cdots,n \right\}} \left\{ \left\| D_i \right\| \right\} \tag{15}$$

Then based on the minimum difference principle, we judge that the target to be identified belongs to the i_0th category, that is, the target image is judged which standard template categories it belongs to.

In simulation, we assume there are 40 known target image categories that have been trained, and select three characteristic parameters to construct the characteristic vector of the target. We choose randomly 120 characteristic parameters according to the uniform distribution, normal distribution and logarithmic normal distribution respectively, and distribute randomly and equiprobably to 40 target categories. Assume the measurement error of the unknown target obeys the Gaussian distribution, and the standard variance of measurement error is 2 percent of corresponding known characteristic parameter. We choose the 1-norm of vector as the discriminant function for target recognition in simulation, and then after the simulation is carried out to be 500 times, we obtain the correct recognition rate of the proposed target recognition approach based on feature extraction to image is 95.36%, that of conventional k-means is 89.07%, that of fuzzy c-means (FCM) (Yu, 2011) is 92.85%, respectively, and the obtained recognition time of these approaches is 0.406s, 0.92s, 0.465s, respectively. Because we only calculate the norm of the vector difference in the simulation, the storage capacity required is low. Figure 13 shows the comparison curves of correct recognition rate. From simulation results known, the proposed recognition approach based on feature extraction to image not only has the faster processing speed, the lower storage capacity, but also has better recognition effect.

CONCLUSION

The texture image segmentation includes mainly two processes which is the feature extraction and feature classification. The feature extraction is a critical step, and its purpose is to find out a set of parameters that can reflect the texture characteristics of image to constitute a characteristic vector, so as to satisfy

Figure 13. Comparison of correct recognition rates of the proposed recognition approach based on feature extraction and the traditional approaches

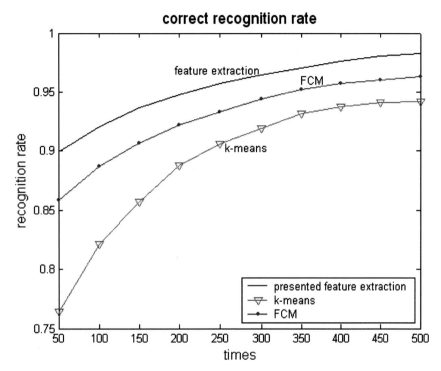

the aggregation within texture class and the dispersion between texture classes (Rachidi, Chappard et al., 2008). It overcame the shortcomings of traditional evolutionary algorithms to some extent, but also it could implement a rational partition to the solved questions and effectively jump out of a local optimum.

For any observed image g, place a size $w \times w$ estimated window at each pixel position s. This paper presents the texture segmentation algorithm based on the gray scale jump to carry out image texture segmentation, an area response to carry out the feature extraction, and the recognition approach based on gray scale jump to achieve the target identification, classification. The example and simulation experiment results prove the feasibility and effectiveness of all proposed algorithms or approaches in each stage.

Whether the proposed algorithm based on gray scale jump in this paper is applied to the color jump of color images, as well as which features the color jump needs to use, so that the segmentation to color target is more precise, it is a question which needs further study in the future.

REFERENCES

Evans, A. N., & Liu, X. U. (2006). A morphological gradient approach to color edge detection. *IEEE Transactions on Image Processing*, *15*(6), 1454–1463.

Gonçalves, W. N., & Bruno, O. M. (2013). Dynamic texture segmentation based on deterministic partially self-avoiding walks. *Computer Vision and Image Understanding*, *117*(9), 1163–1174.

Goncalves, W. N., & Bruno, O. M. (2013). Dynamic texture analysis and segmentation using deterministic partially self-avoiding walks. *Expert Systems with Applications*, *40*(11), 4283–4300.

Han, S., Tao, W. B., & Wu, X. L. (2011). Texture segmentation using independent-scale component-wise Riemannian-covariance Gaussian mixture model in KL measure based multi-scale nonlinear structure tensor space. *Pattern Recognition*, *44*(3), 503–518.

Haralick, R. M., & Shanmugam, K. (1973). Textural features for image classification. *IEEE Transactions on Systems, Man, and Cybernetics*, *3*(6), 610–621.

Long, Z., & Younan, N. H. (2013). Multiscale texture segmentation via a contourlet contextual hidden Markov model. *Digital Signal Processing*, *23*(3), 859–869.

Mailing, A., & Cernuschi-Frías, B. (2011). A method for mixed states texture segmentation with simultaneous parameter estimation. *Pattern Recognition Letters*, *32*(15), 1982–1989.

Melendez, J., Miguel, A. G., Domenec, P., & Maria, P. (2011). Unsupervised texture-based image segmentation through pattern discovery. *Computer Vision and Image Understanding*, *115*(8), 1121–1133.

Nikou, C., Nikolaos, G., & Aristidis, L. (2007). A class-adaptive spatially variant mixture model for image segmentation. *IEEE Transactions on Image Processing*, *16*(4), 1121–1130.

Ong, S. H., Yea, N. C., & Lee, K. H. (2002). Segmentation of color images using a two-stage self-organizing network. *Image and Vision Computing*, *20*(4), 279–289.

Rachidi, M., Chappard, C., & Marchadier, C. (2008). Application of Laws' masks to bone texture analysis: An innovative image analysis tool in osteoporosis. *Proceedings of the 2008 5th IEEE International Symposium on Biomedical Imaging: From Nano to Macro* (pp. 1191-1194).

Soh, L. K., & Tsatsoulis, C. (1999). Texture analysis of SAR sea ice imagery using gray level co-occurrence matrices. *IEEE Transactions on Geoscience and Remote Sensing*, *37*(2), 780–795.

Wu, Q., An, J., & Lin, B. (2012). A texture segmentation algorithm based on PCA and global minimization active contour model for aerial insulator images. *IEEE Journal of Selected Topics in Applied Earth Observations and Remote Sensing*, *5*(5), 1509–1518.

Yu, J. (2011). Texture segmentation based on FCM algorithm combined with GLCM and space information. *Proceedings of the 2011 International Conference on Electric Information and Control Engineering*, Beijing (pp. 4569 – 4572).

Yu, P., Qin, A. K., & Clausi, D. A. (2012). Unsupervised polarimetric SAR image segmentation and classification using region growing with edge penalty. *IEEE Transactions on Geoscience and Remote Sensing*, *50*(4), 1302–1317.

Chapter 4
Palmprint Recognition Based on Image Segmentation of Region of Interest

QingE Wu
Zhengzhou University of Light Industry, China

Weidong Yang
Fudan University, China

ABSTRACT

To carry out an effective recognition for palmprint, this paper presents an algorithm of image segmentation of region of interest (ROI), extracts the ROI of a palmprint image and studies the composing features of palmprint. This paper constructs coordinates by making use of characteristic points in the palm geometric contour, improves the algorithm of ROI extraction, and provides a positioning method of ROI. Moreover, this paper uses the wavelet transform to divide up ROI, extracts the energy feature of wavelet, gives an approach of matching and recognition to improve the correctness and efficiency of existing main recognition approaches, and compares it with existing main approaches of palmprint recognition by experiments. The experiment results show that the approach in this paper has the better recognition effect, the faster matching speed, and the higher recognition rate which is improved averagely by 2.69% than those of the main recognition approaches.

INTRODUCTION

Rapid development of information technology has prompted the society progress, and the society gives a renewal and a further demand to the information technology. The occurrence of computer has prompted the development of network and society informationization. On the other hand, the networked and informationized society demands a higher security for the information and systems (Janarthanam, Ramalingam et al., 2010). The body biometric recognition technology is to use the biological characteristics owned by the human body to carry out an automatic identification, biology recognition technique for

DOI: 10.4018/978-1-5225-1884-6.ch004

short, which is one of fundamental methods which are used for enhancing the security of information and systems. The palmprint recognition technology is an important part of the biology recognition ones (Yue and Zuo, 2010). Since the palmprint has a fine uniqueness and stability, as well as a wealth of texture information, the palmprint recognition technique has got a rapid development and been widely used in the field of information security. Currently, the palmprint recognition technique has been widely used in police department, military branch and so on. Therefore, the research on palmprint recognition technique is of important theoretical and practical significance.

Although the research of palmprint recognition started relatively late, it has also experienced stages of emergence, development and maturation during its development of more than ten years. Now it is experiencing the deeper and more detailed development.

In 1985, Matsumoto introduced the application of palmprint recognition in the field of identification firstly, however, without deeper research (Matsumoto, 1985). In 1991, Kovesip and Shiono gave an experimental result of identification using the comprehensive features of palmprint (Kovesip and Shiono, 1991). They proposed an identification method in combination with the palm shape and the texture of palmprint. In 1998, the idea of automatic identification by using palm recognition was described systematically and comprehensively by Hong-Kong Polytechnic University and Tsinghua University (Shu and Zhang, 1998), which summarized comprehensively the characteristic of palm and the palmprint and opened up the research areas of palmprint recognition technology. Based on high resolution palmprint images, Jane You et al used the point of interest in the palmprint to carry out identification (You, Li et al., 2002). Duta et al utilized the binarization and resampling approach to extract 300-400 characteristic points from a palmprint image, and implemented the palmprint recognition based on the location and direction of these points (Duta, Jain et al., 2002). Ze Zhang et al put forward the method of palmprint classification based on the triangular points formed by the papillary ridge in the area of lower part of finger roots (Zhang, Shu et al. 2002). In 2004 and 2006, Kong and Zhang D improved the Palmcode method by using 2-dimension Gabor filters (Kong and Zhang, 2004), (Kong, Zhang et al., 2006), and formed a new kind of palmprint feature code called Fusioncode. However, both Palmcode and Fusioncode do not contain the direction information of every point in palmprint, which reduces their distinguishing performance. Additionally, some fruitful researches had been implemented by many universities and institutes in the world.

Among algorithms of image segmentation (Xie, Wu et al., 2013), (Lo, Pickering et al., 2011), (Long and Younan, 2013), the Fuzzy C-Means clustering (Yu 2011) that was one of algorithms has some better features which can meet the human cognition pattern, be described concisely and clearly, be easy to implement and so on. However, this algorithm has some disadvantages such as its performance depends on the initial clustering center, poor antinoise capability, and slow convergence and so on. From the research of traditional Markov Random Field (MRF) known, the segmentation effect of MRF to micro texture was better, but the segmentation result to macro texture had many isolated islands or small areas.

The palmprint recognition approach proposed in this paper mainly focuses on the segmentation and extraction of region of Interest (ROI) of a palmprint image, and the concrete algorithm of segmentation and extraction is given. In the stage of feature extraction, this paper extracts the features of texture principal lines, papilla ridges and bifurcation points of ROI. At the same time, this paper divides up the ROI of palmprint image by wavelet transform, extracts the energy feature of palmprint and constructs characteristic vectors. In the stage of matching and identification, this paper calculates the distance between the characteristic vector of identified palmprint and that of known palmprint, and estimates the similar degree between the two vectors by the distance. Finally, the comparison of the calculated distance and an experimental threshold value is given. According to the minimum distance, the recognition result can be obtained.

Feature Analysis of Palmprint

The main research object of palmprint recognition is the whole human palm excluding fingers, i.e., the part between the finger roots and the wrist. There is a plenty of texture information in this area including several obvious principal lines, irregular wrinkles, trivial papillary ridges and a number of bifurcation points (Shu and Zhang, 1998), which can be used as the features of palm and extracted by different methods to carry out an identification. In recent years, some researches on palmprint recognition had been attracted special attention, and some progress had been obtained, but further researches are to be made.

In palmprint image, the gray level of pixels in the target region and ones in the background are different, as shown in the energy diagrams of Figure 1. Figure 1 is the 3-dimension energy model of palmprint region and background region. From the Figure found clearly, the texture feature in the palmprint region is very prominent, which shows a fine feature of energy mutation, but the energy feature diagram of background region almost levels off and the mutation is not obvious.

The various features of palmprint are introduced respectively as follows:

1. **Features of Principal Lines:** There are several principal textures with obvious and thick lines in each human palm, which are usually called lifeline, career line, emotions line and so on. The patterns of those principal lines vary with each individual and remain unchanged in one's lifetime. The principal lines are unique for each person, and have the fine stability and the uniqueness. Therefore, it has become one of the mainstreams of palmprint recognition researches by utilizing the features of principal lines to carry out identification.
2. **Features of Wrinkles:** Besides the principal lines, there are a lot of wrinkles with shallow texture and thin lines in a palm. The distribution of these wrinkles is irregular and their patterns are fairly complicated. In the same way, those wrinkles as features of palmprint may be used to carry out

Figure 1. Energy feature of palmprint image

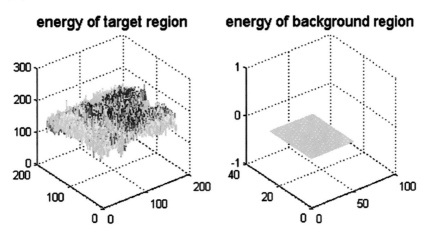

identification. However, the extraction of their features is difficult due to the irregularity of their distribution. So, there is no deep study to identification based on those wrinkles, and then the further study and breakthrough are expected in the future research.

3. **Features of Papillary Ridges:** There are also widespread papillary ridges in a palm, which are similar to the fingerprints and spread over the lower part of finger root and the center part of palm. These papillary ridges have various shapes such as the triangular point in the lower part of finger root. However, they are too trivial and the clear pictures can only be obtained by high resolution camera, thus which limits their application.

4. **Features of Bifurcation Points:** In a palm, there are plenty of dermal lines spreading over a palm, which have different direction, length, width and depth. Due to the existence of so many dermal lines, they are bound to cross and form a lot of intersection points. The types of these intersection points are different, including bifurcated points, trident points, four bifurcation points, and so on. The position and amount of these bifurcation points are unique in one's palm, which can be used to carry out identification as the precise features.

There are a plenty of papillary ridges in a palm, which are analogous to the fingerprints. However, compared with fingerprints, the geometric regularity of papillary ridges is not so evident. Through a large number of observations, these papillary ridges show some certain regularity in specific region of palm exclude fingers. As shown in Figure 2, in the lower part of index finger root, middle finger root, ring finger root and little finger root, there are four convergent points called as triangular points, which are formed by the corresponding papillary ridges. Since these triangular points are innate and not susceptible to being damaged, and their positions are very fixed, a palmprint image can be divided up by the positions of these triangular points.

In comparison with most recognition approaches, the palmprint recognition suffers fewer disturbances because of the shape of palm and the acquirement of palmprint image is stable. Thus, a relatively fixed

Figure 2. Triangular point in a palm

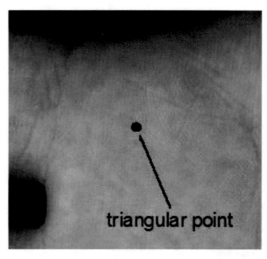

palmprint image can be obtained no matter in when and where, and what state. In a concrete extraction, either the one of those features of palmprint may be extracted such as the one of principal lines and bifurcation points, or all features are extracted by high resolution acquisition equipment and fuse them together to construct a high precision palmprint recognition system.

SEGMENTATION AND EXTRACTION OF ROI OF PALMPRINT IMAGE

In a gathered palmprint image, besides the noise in the data of palm and background, the translation and rotation of palm can influence the quality of image. All these factors do not make against the extraction and matching of palmprint features. Therefore, some preprocessing such as segmentation, calibration and normalization must be implemented before the features extraction of palmprint is carried out.

Segmentation and Extraction of ROI Based on Palm Edge Contour

1. **Extraction of Palmprint Edge Contour:** The image border is the discontinuous reflection of local characteristics of an image, such as the mutation of gray level, colors and texture, which marks the end of a region and the beginning of another region. For the calculation simplicity, the first order derivative or the second derivative is usually used to check the border of an image. It can be easy to detect the discontinuity of gray level by taking advantage of the derivative. The detection of border can be realized by the convolution based on the spatial differential operators. Some smoothness and binarization processing should be done before the extraction of border is implemented.

Assume the original palmprint image is $f'(x, y)$, the smooth filtering to $f'(x, y)$ in a spatial domain can be carried out by using a low-pass filter H and the output image is $g(u,v)$, as shown in equation (1).

$$g(u, v) = \sum_x \sum_y f'(x, y) H(u - x + 1, v - y + 1) \tag{1}$$

A relative complete image of palm edge can be obtained after filtering. Then a binarization processing for image $g(u,v)$ is carried out by choosing a proper threshold value h. As shown in equation (2), the processed image is $f(x,y)$.

$$f(x, y) = \begin{cases} 1 \\ 0 \end{cases} \begin{cases} 1, & g(u, v) > h \\ 0, & g(u, v) \le h \end{cases} \tag{2}$$

Then the edge detection for the binarization image can be carried out in image width and image height directions by making use of gray-level mutation. The algorithm is as follows:

Assume the sizes of image height and image width are m and n, respectively. The number of gray-level change, c_i, $i=1,\ldots,m$, is sought along the image width direction. According to the experimental result to texture and background regions, the number of gray change of texture region is more than that of background region. Further, according to the change number c_i, a threshold value M_1 can be given.

For any change number is greater than this threshold, i.e., $c_i > M_1$, at this time, the height and width are recorded, which represented as y_{k_1} and x_{k_1}, respectively, $k_1 \in N$, and the set of ordered pairs is acquired as equation (3).

$$I_1 = \left\{ \left(x_{k_1}, y_{k_1} \right) \middle| c_i > M_1 \right\} \tag{3}$$

On the other hand, at a given fixed point along image width direction, i.e., *width=n_j*, the number of gray-level change, d_j, *j=1,…,n*, is sought along the image height direction. Then according to the change number d_j, another threshold value M_2 can be given. Similarly, for any change number is greater than this threshold, i.e., $d_j > M_2$, at this time, the width and height are recorded, which represented as x_{k_2} and y_{k_2}, respectively, $k_2 \in N$, and the set of ordered pairs is obtained as equation (4).

$$I_2 = \left\{ \left(x_{k_2}, y_{k_2} \right) \middle| d_j > M_2 \right\} \tag{4}$$

According to equations (3) and (4), the set of ordered pairs $I = I_1 \cup I_2 = \left\{ \left(x_k, y_k \right), k \in N \right\}$ can be obtained. Based on (x_k, y_k), the fitting curve that x_k and y_k satisfy can be obtained. The edge line of palmprint region can be obtained by carrying out borderline modeling of texture. This algorithm of texture segmentation is called the gray-level mutation algorithm. The extraction process of palmprint edge based on the mutation algorithm is shown in Figure 3.

2. **Construction of Coordinate System:** Tracking the acquired palmprint edge, taking the center of gravity of palmprint contour as a reference point, calculating the distance between each point on the edge and the center of gravity, and searching the minimum distance between the convergence points of index finger and middle finger and the center of gravity, represented as K_1, can be extracted. In the same way, the minimum distance between the convergence point of ring finger and little finger and the center of gravity, represented as K_2, can be extracted.

Assume the straight line L passing through the point $K_1(x_1, y_1)$ and the point $K_2(x_2, y_2)$ is *y=kx+b*, which is the tangent passing through vertexes of the edge line between fingers and plamprint, as shown in Figure 4(a). Then the midpoint $K_0(x_0, y_0)$ between point K_1 and K_2 on line L can be obtained by equation (5), and satisfies $y_0 = kx_0 + b$.

$$x_0 = \frac{x_1 + x_2}{2}, \quad y_0 = \frac{y_1 + y_2}{2} \tag{5}$$

Do the vertical line L' of L passing through point K_0, and the line L' with the contour edge of palmprint-end intersects with the point P. A coordinate system is constructed by using L as *y* axis and L' as *x* axis, respectively, and using the point K_0 as an original point O, then again it is adjusted by rotating, as shown in Figure 4(b).

Figure 3. Extraction of palmprint edge contour based on gray-level mutation algorithm

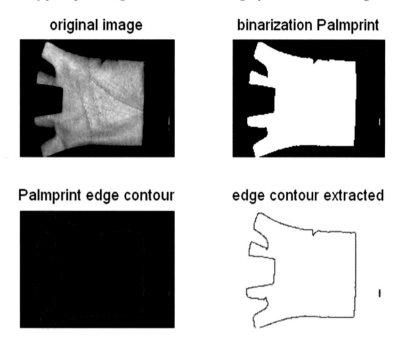

Figure 4. Construction of a coordinate system

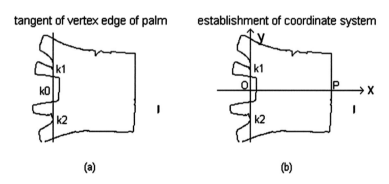

3. **Extraction of ROI:** In the coordinate system shown in Figure 4, how to divide up a palmprint image and get the Region of Interest (ROI) that contains the abundant information and simplicity of operation, this paper gives a fast and convenient approach. That is to say, firstly, in the OP direction along x axis, searches a sharp growth value h_1 and a sharp reduction value h_2 in the gray-level mutation, then the left boundary l_1 and right boundary l_2 of ROI can be obtained. Secondly, in the $k_1 k_2$ direction along y axis, searches a sharp growth value w_1 and a sharp reduction value w_2 in the gray-level mutation, then the upper boundary l_3 and lower boundary l_4 of ROI are obtained. Where, the sharp growth and sharp reduction in the gray-level have something to do with the amount of pixel of edge width and edge height of palmprint, as well as the position of edge between fingers and palm, i.e., the mutation case of gray-level is decided by the two factors. The numbers of pixel on edge width and edge height are shown in Figure 5, and the coordinates of edge between fingers and palm are shown in Figure 6.

Figure 5. Numbers of pixel on edge width and height

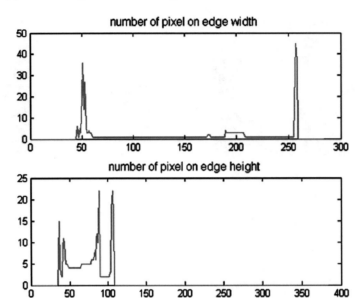

Figure 6. Coordinates of edge between fingers and palm

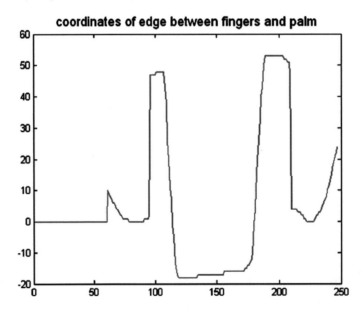

A rectangle is formed by the four straight lines l_1, l_2, l_3, l_4, as shown in Figure 7. The area of image falling within this rectangle is then extracted as the ROI, as shown in Figure 8. The ROI obtained in this way has eliminated the influence of noise, rotation, translation and so on. Experiment proved that the ROI extracted in this way is more beneficial to the subsequent feature extraction of palmprint.

Figure 7. Divided up ROI

information-rich rectangle region of palm

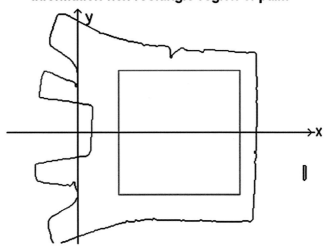

Figure 8. Palmprint extraction in ROI

palmprint in rectangle region   **palmprint extracted in rectangle region**

Segment and Extraction of ROI Based on Distance-Orientation Algorithm

A 5-dimension characteristic vector $V=[\mu,\sigma,x,y,v_r]$ can be constructed by given gray-level mean, gray-level mean square deviation, pixel position x and y, distance v_r between a pixel and the edge vertex. This characteristic vector can be used to carry out the segmentation of ROI of palmprint image. This algorithm based on this characteristic vector is called the distance-orientation algorithm. With the help of this algorithm, a ROI of palmprint image can be extracted, as shown in Figure 9.

Here, the calculation of μ,σ,x,y,v_r is as follows:

$$\mu\left(i,j\right) = \frac{1}{\left(2n+1\right)^2} \sum_{k=i-n}^{i+n} \sum_{l=j-n}^{j+n} I\left(k,l\right) \tag{6}$$

Figure 9. Segmentation and extraction of ROI based on distance-orientation algorithm

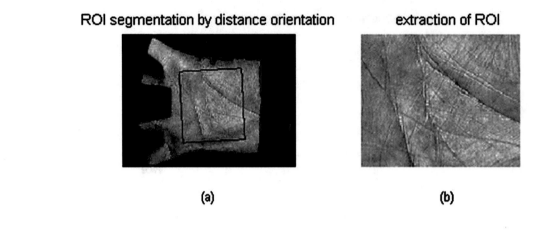

ROI segmentation by distance orientation   extraction of ROI

(a)   (b)

$$\sigma\left(i,j\right) = \frac{1}{\left(2n+1\right)^2} \sum_{k=i-n}^{i+n} \sum_{l=j-n}^{j+n} \left|I\left(k,l\right) - \mu\left(i,j\right)\right| \tag{7}$$

$$v_r\left(x,y\right) = \sqrt{\left(x - width\right)^2 + \left(y - height\right)^2} \tag{8}$$

where $2n+1$ is the window size, $\mu(i,j)$ is the mean of gray-level $I(k,l)$ in the window, $\sigma(i,j)$ is the mean square deviation of gray-level $I(k,l)$ in the window, x and y are the position of pixel in the window, v_r is the distance between a pixel and the edge vertex, width and height are the width and height of palmprint image, respectively.

Feature Extraction of Palmprint

Here two algorithms on feature extraction are given. The first one, i.e., the gray-level mutation algorithm mentioned above not only can carry out the edge detection of image, but also can implement the characteristic points detection such as corner points, end points, bifurcation points and so on. To acquire these characteristic points, the numbers of gray-level change c_i and d_j are searched along the image width and image height direction of a palmprint, respectively. If there is $c_i > M_1$ or $d_j > M_2$, the detected pixel points are the characteristic points such as edge points, corner points, bifurcation points and so on. Where M_1 and M_2 are the two given thresholds. So, the characteristic vector that every detected characteristic point is corresponding to is $V=[c_i, d_j]$. The detection of characteristic points in ROI by gray-level change is shown in Figure 10.

The second algorithm is to carry out the feature extraction of palmprint by wavelet transform. Choose a function $\psi\left(\vec{t}\right)$ to construct $\psi_{\vec{j},\vec{k}}\left(\vec{t}\right) = 2^{\vec{j}/2} \psi\left(2^{\vec{j}}\vec{t} - \vec{k}\right)$, and make it do inner product with image $p(x,y)$, which can carry out some processing for a palmprint image such as smoothing, denoising, enhancing, compressing and so on. Where, $\vec{t} = (x,y)$, $\vec{j} = \left(j_1, j_2\right)$, $\vec{k} = \left(k_1, k_2\right)$. An alternative way is usually to choose a two-dimension Gabor function as a wavelet as follows:

Figure 10. Detection of characteristic points in ROI by gray-level change

characteristic points detection in ROI by gray change

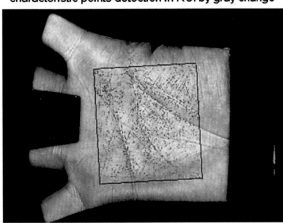

$$g\left(x,y\right) = \frac{1}{2\pi\delta_x \delta_y} \cdot e^{-\frac{1}{2}\left[\left(\frac{x}{\delta_x}\right)^2 + \left(\frac{y}{\delta_y}\right)^2\right] + j\left(ux+vy\right)}$$ (9)

Make it process the image $p(x,y)$, then the concrete algorithm is $W_{j,\bar{k}} = \left\langle \psi_{j,\bar{k}}(\vec{t}), p\left(x,y\right)\right\rangle$, which can carry out a decomposition and extraction of energy coefficient features of image $p(x,y)$. For a region of texture with rich features, it shows that the energy is denser, the difference in amplitude is little, and the distribution of energy is regular as the decomposition levels increase. For a region with sparse texture, the energy takes on the form of jumping, sparse rendering as the decomposition levels increase.

From the decomposition calculation of wavelet known, the ith level energy feature of ripple is calculated by the ith level decomposition coefficient of wavelet, which shows the texture feature of a palmprint image in the 2^{-i} scale, in different directions and different positions.

The palmprint image passes through n-level two-dimensional discrete wavelet transform, the detail image of each level in horizontal (H_i), vertical (V_i) and diagonal (D_i) directions can be obtained, respectively, as shown in Figure 11, where $i=1,2,…,n$.

Assume the size of the detail image in each direction by ith level wavelet transform is $M \times N$, then the ith level wavelet energy in the corresponding direction is defined as follows:

$$WE_{i,h} = \sum_{j=1}^{M}\sum_{k=1}^{N}\left[H_i\left(j,k\right)\right]^2$$ (10)

$$WE_{i,v} = \sum_{j=1}^{M}\sum_{k=1}^{N}\left[V_i\left(j,k\right)\right]^2$$ (11)

Figure 11. 3-level wavelet decomposition of haar

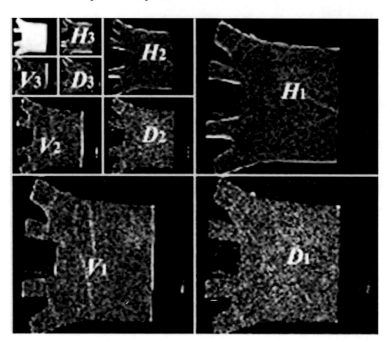

$$WE_{i,d} = \sum_{j=1}^{M} \sum_{k=1}^{N} \left[D_i \left(j, k \right) \right]^2 \tag{12}$$

where $WE_{i,h}$, $WE_{i,v}$ and $WE_{i,d}$ represent the edge intensity of texture of a palmprint image in various directions. In the texture image of palmprint, the edges of image are to form the fundamental components of palmprint texture, i.e., the wrinkles, papillary ridges of palmprint and so on. Therefore, the equations (10)~(12) represent the intensity of these fundamental components in all directions under the ith level wavelet decomposition. Since the wavelet coefficients of non-oscillating signal increase as the wavelet decomposition level increases, but through comparing the oscillating signal with the non-oscillating signal in the same oscillating frequency, the wavelet decomposition coefficients of oscillating signal are much less than those of non-oscillating signal at a higher level decomposition, thus the energy of non-oscillating wrinkles of palmprint mainly concentrates on the detail image of large-scale wavelet decomposition. However, the energy of oscillating papillary ridge mainly concentrates on the detail image of small-scale wavelet decomposition. Therefore, after n-level wavelet transform is carried out, the texture characteristic vector that consists of different level energy is

$$V' = \left(WE_{1,h}, WE_{1,v}, WE_{1,d}, WE_{2,h}, WE_{2,v}, WE_{2,d}, \cdots, WE_{n,h}, WE_{n,v}, WE_{n,d} \right) \tag{13}$$

Then V' can be normalized as follows,

$$V = \frac{1}{\sum_{i=1}^{n}\left(WE_{i,h} + WE_{i,v} + WE_{i,d}\right)} V' = \left(V_{1,h}, V_{1,v}, V_{1,d}, V_{2,h}V_{2,v}V_{2,d}, \cdots, V_{n,h}V_{n,v}V_{n,d}\right) \tag{14}$$

Assume the energy feature V_i of ith level wrinkles is $V_i = (V_{i,h}, V_{iv}, V_{i,d})$, then the comprehensive characteristic vector of wrinkles is obtained as follows:

$$V = (V_1, V_2, \ldots, V_n) \tag{15}$$

From the equation (15) known, the energy feature V of wrinkles consists of every level energy feature of wrinkles, so it shows the detail texture characteristic of a palmprint image in different directions, different positions and different resolutions.

The different level energy features of an image can be obtained by different level wavelet decompositions to the image, as shown in Figure 12.

MATCHING AND RECOGNITION

Algorithm of Matching and Recognition

According to the above approach of feature extraction, different sample sets of palmprint are trained and learnt, and the energy characteristic vectors in different level can be acquired. Use these characteristic

Figure 12. Different level energy features with different level wavelet decompositions

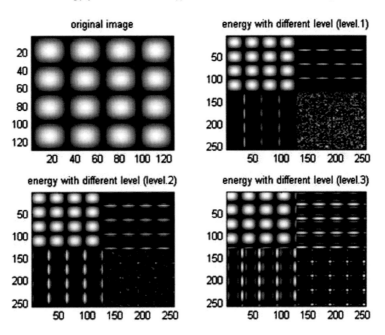

vectors as a standard template is stored in the system. We compare the characteristic vectors of unknown palmprint image with the characteristic vectors of known classificatory palmprint image that has been trained and stored in the retrieval system. Based on the minimum difference principle, if and only if the difference value between the characteristic vector of unknown palmprint image and the characteristic vector of given i_0th palmprint image is minimal, we judge that the unknown palmprint belongs to the i_0th category. The feature matching of palmprint is to judge whether two palmprint images are from the same one hand. If the matched result is positive, the system will output the information of the hand. If the matched result is negative, the system continues to match with other standard templates. Therefore, the identification can be achieved.

For the first algorithm of feature extraction, the matching system compares the characteristic vector V of every detected characteristic point with the corresponding characteristic vectors of palmprint image in the standard template database, and calculates the difference values. The matching recognition results are obtained based on the principle of minimum distance.

Here, mainly take the second algorithm of feature extraction as an example, the matching algorithm is described as follows:

If W_l is the known characteristic vector in the retrieval system, V is the characteristic vector to be identified. Where $l=1,2,\ldots,Q$ and Q is the number of known characteristic vectors. The following distance is defined to estimate the distance between the energy characteristic vectors V and W_l of two wrinkles.

$$d_l = \left\| V - W_l \right\| = \sum_{i=1}^{n} \left| V_i - W_{li} \right| \tag{16}$$

where

$$\left| V_i - W_{li} \right| = \left[\left(WE_{i,h}^{V} - WE_{i,h}^{W_l} \right)^2 + \left(WE_{i,v}^{V} - WE_{i,v}^{W_l} \right)^2 + \left(WE_{i,d}^{V} - WE_{i,d}^{W_l} \right)^2 \right]^{1/2}.$$

The distance d_l represents the degree of variance between the characteristic vector V and the characteristic vector W_l of the lth category. The recognition principle is described as follows:

- When Q is finite and quite small, we use the minimum distance principle to judge the category of the target to be identified. This recognition approach is as follows:

If $\exists l_0 \in \{1, 2, \cdots, Q\}$, satisfy

$$l_0 = \arg \min_{l \in \{1,2,\cdots,Q\}} \{d_l\} \tag{17}$$

Then based on the minimum distance principle, we judge that the target to be identified belongs to the l_0th category, that is, the palmprint is judged which standard template categories it belongs to.

- When Q is relatively larger, we use the threshold value to judge the category of the target to be identified. That is, if $d_l < \varepsilon$, the identified palmprint is considered to be belong to the lth category. Conversely, if $d_l > \varepsilon$, the palmprint to be identified does not belong to the lth category. Where ε is a threshold value which is decided by experiment, as described in simulation section.

Experiment and Analysis

The main palmprint database used here is the Polytechnic University (PolyU) palmprint Database (The second version), which is constructed in biometric identification research center of Hongkong Polytechnic University. The experimental basic steps are given as follows:

P1: 100 different palms are chosen from PolyU Palmprint Database, and 6 palmprint images sampled in different time are selected for each palm. These palmprint images are divided into two groups randomly, where the first group consists of 100 different images that are from 100 palms and is taken as the learning samples database, and the other group is consist of the remaining 500 images and is taken as the test samples database.

P2: The first group images are carried out a preprocessing and feature extraction by 3-level Haar wavelet decomposition. The energy characteristic vectors WE_i of 3-level wavelet decomposition of 100 palms are acquired, which are archived as training samples.

P3: The second group images are used as the test samples to be identified. Firstly, a palmprint image from the second group is chosen randomly, and is carried out the preprocessing and feature extraction with 3-level Haar wavelet decomposition. Then the obtained characteristic vectors are matched with those samples in palmprint archive. The energy characteristic vector to be identified with all energy characteristic vectors WE_i in palmprint archive is matched. The random selections and matching recognitions in 500 times are implemented based on the recognition principle (1). The most similar characteristic vector is chosen as the recognition result which has the maximum energy similarity with the vector to be identified. In a similar way, the test can be implemented according to the recognition principle (2) and the threshold value is determined based on experiments.

P4: For each image in the test sample database, after 500 times recognition are done according to the step P3, the times of the correct recognition and error recognition are recorded respectively, and the correct recognition rates are obtained by calculating.

For each palmprint image, 10 times repeating experiments are carried out by the step P1 to step P4 based on Haar wavelet basis function in simulation. The number of samples is different in each experiment. The proposed ROI approach compares with those currently usually used approaches such as Gabor (Pan and Ruan, 2009), Fourier transform (Li, Zhang et al., 2002) and PCA (Connie, Teoh et al., 2003). The experimental results show that the average correct recognition rates of these approaches are 95.14%, 92.45%, 88.17% and 83.51% in simulation of 500 times, respectively. The simulation results are shown in Figure 13.

From Figure 13 concluded, the average correct recognition rate of the recognition approach based on ROI feature extraction is the highest among all referred approaches. In experiment, the average correct recognition rate increases constantly with the increasing recognition samples, and the curve of average correct recognition rate gradually levels off as the samples increase when the number of samples reaches a certain value.

Figure 13. Comparison of correct recognition rate for the proposed ROI and other approaches

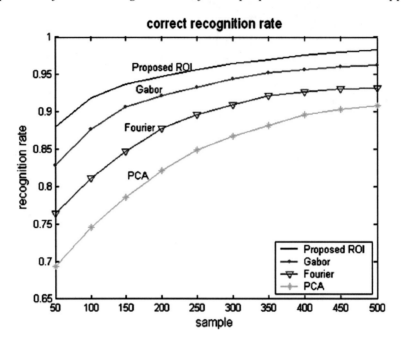

To evaluate the comprehensive performance of these approaches, we adopt the combination of quantitative analysis and qualitative analysis method, and synthesize comparison based on factors such as the computing speed, memory capacity, communications traffic and correct recognition rate. We evaluate the merits and demerits of different recognition approaches for palmprint. Table 1 gives the results of a comprehensive comparison.

In Table 1, the computing speed is the mean time obtained by the mean computing time of 10 times repeating test of these approaches at each step in simulation environment, which the computing time is only the computing time of algorithm itself. In simulation, the computer used is the Pentium 4 and 2G memory, and the programming language is MATLAB. The memory capacity and the communications traffic are estimated approximately based on the computing course and complexity of every approach. From the results of Table 1 seen, the memory capacity and communications traffic are close related. The average correct recognition rates are the average of two stages which are an average of 500 times

Table 1. Comprehensive comparison of different recognition approaches for palmprint

Approaches	Average Correct Recognition Rate $\bar{R}_c$	Computing Speed	Memory Capacity	Communications Traffic
PCA	0.8351	0. 546s	Middle	Middle
Fourier	0.8817	0.82s	Middle	Middle
Gabor	0.9245	0.49s	Lower	Lower
Proposed ROI	0.9514	0.426s	Low	Low

simulations and then taking an average of 10 time-steps for every approach under the given simulation environment. In fact, they are the average of the correct recognition rates in space and time, so they are an overall average of the correct recognition rates.

On the basis of the simulation results, the recognition approach based on feature extraction of ROI not only has the faster processing speed, the lower memory capacity and communications traffic, but also has better recognition effect.

CONCLUSION

Firstly, this paper analyzes the features of a palmprint image such as wrinkles, principal ridges, papillary ridges, triangular points and so on. Then, this paper presents two segmentation algorithms of ROI, which the one is based on the palm edge contour and the other is based on the distance and direction. Moreover, this paper gives the feature extraction algorithm of ROI, the matching and recognition approach of target image, and carries out the simulation test. Finally, the simulation results prove the feasibility and effectiveness of all proposed algorithms or approaches in each stage.

REFERENCES

Duta, N., Jain, A. K., & Mardia, K. (2002). Matching of palmprints. *Pattern Recognition Letters*, *23*(4), 477–485. doi:10.1016/S0167-8655(01)00179-9

Janarthanam, S., Ramalingam, M., & Narendran, P. (2010). Texture analysis on low resolution images using unsupervised segmentation algorithm with multichannel local frequency analysis. *Proceedings of the2010 IEEE International Conference on Communication and Computational Intelligence*, New York (pp. 260 – 265).

Kong, A. W.-K., & Zhang, D. (2004). Feature-level fusion for effective palmprint authentication. In Biometric Authentication (pp. 761-767). Springer.

Kong, W., Zhang, D., & Kame, M. (2006). Palmprint identification using feature-level fusion. *Pattern Recognition*, *39*(3), 478–487. doi:10.1016/j.patcog.2005.08.014

Kovesip, P., & Shiono, E. (1991). Image features from phase on gruene. *Video Journal of Computer Vision Research*, *1*(3), 1-27.

Lo, E. H., Mark, R. P., Michael, R. F., & John, F. A. (2011). Image segmentation from scale and rotation invariant texture features from the double dyadic dual-tree complex wavelet transform. *Image and Vision Computing*, *29*(1), 15–28. doi:10.1016/j.imavis.2010.08.004

Long, Z., & Younan, N. H. (2013). Multiscale texture segmentation via a contourlet contextual hidden Markov model. *Digital Signal Processing*, *23*(3), 859–869. doi:10.1016/j.dsp.2012.11.009

Matsumoto, K. (1985). Palm-recognition systems: An ideal means of restricting access to high security areas. *Mitsubishi Electric Advance*, *131*, 31–32.

Shu, W., & Zhang, D. (1998). Automated personal identification by palmprint. *Optical Engineering (Redondo Beach, Calif.)*, *37*(8), 2359–2362. doi:10.1117/1.601756

Shu, W., & Zhang, D. (1998). Automated personal identification by palmprint. *Optical Engineering (Redondo Beach, Calif.)*, *37*(8), 2359–2362. doi:10.1117/1.601756

You, J., Li, W. X., & Zhang, D. (2002). Hierarchical palmprint identification via multiple feature extraction. *Pattern Recognition*, *35*(4), 847–859. doi:10.1016/S0031-3203(01)00100-5

Yu, J. (2011). Texture segmentation based on FCM algorithm combined with GLCM and space information.*Proceedings of the 2011 International Conference on Electric Information and Control Engineering*, Beijing (pp. 4569 – 4572).

Yue, F., Zuo, W. M., & Zhang, D. P. (2010). Survey of palm print recognition algorithms. *Acta Automatica Sinica*, *36*(3), 353–365. doi:10.3724/SP.J.1004.2010.00353

Zhang, Z., Shu, W., & Rong, G. (2002). Automatic palmprint classification method based on the orientation of ridges. *Journal Tsinghua University*, *42*(9), 1222–1224.

Chapter 5
A Hierarchical Target Recognition Method Based on Image Processing

QingE Wu
Zhengzhou University of Light Industry, China

Weidong Yang
Fudan University, China

ABSTRACT

In order to provide an accurate and rapid target recognition method for some military affairs, public security, finance and other departments, this paper studies firstly a variety of fuzzy signal, analyzes the uncertainties classification and their influence, eliminates fuzziness processing, presents some methods and algorithms for fuzzy signal processing, and compares with other methods on image processing. Moreover, this paper uses the wavelet packet analysis to carry out feature extraction of target for the first time, extracts the coefficient feature and energy feature of wavelet transformation, gives the matching and recognition methods, compares with the existing target recognition methods by experiment, and presents the hierarchical recognition method. In target feature extraction process, the more detailed and rich texture feature of target can be obtained by wavelet packet to image decomposition to compare with the wavelet decomposition. In the process of matching and recognition, the hierarchical recognition method is presented to improve the recognition speed and accuracy. The wavelet packet transformation is used to carry out the image decomposition. Through experiment results, the proposed recognition method has the high precision, fast speed, and its correct recognition rate is improved by an average 6.13% than that of existing recognition methods. These researches development in this paper can provide an important theoretical reference and practical significance to improve the real-time and accuracy on fuzzy target recognition.

DOI: 10.4018/978-1-5225-1884-6.ch005

INTRODUCTION

In the modern society of higher information age, target recognition and identity validation become more and more important in our life, and have infiltrated every aspect of everyday life. For instance, finance, security, network, digital electric business, etc. Due to the requirement of confidentiality on traffic, communications and military, the rapid development of network technology, as well as the increasingly complex signal environment, the characteristic parameters of the characteristic vector that is constituted have a certain ambiguity. Thus, the difficulty and importance to target recognition or identity validation have become more and more prominent. Therefore, the signal processing to fuzzy image is an urgent solved problem in many departments now.

For carrying out the target recognition, the literature (Biswal, Dash et al., 2009) studied uncertain power signal processing method. (Ji, Sun et al., 2011) used the fuzzy lifting wavelet packet transform to solve the noise suppression of magnetic flux leakage signal. On the basis of analyzing fast convolution and fast Fourier transform of digital signal processing, (Liu and Kreinovich, 2010) proposed a kind of asymptotic range of convolution to process uncertain signals. The literature (Lo 2012) presented a learning machine which was called clustering instructions possibility associative memory (CIPAM). The CIPAM consisted of clustering equipment and an annotator. The clustering equipment was a feedback neural network of unsupervised processing units (UPUs). The annotator was many supervisory processing units (SPUs) from the clustering equipment to branch. Through using the novel and efficient parallel computing platform of CIPAM to carry out the signal processing, to process temporary and hierarchy pattern clustering, the detection and recognition of digital signal carried out.

But in order to process the fuzzy, incomplete and uncertain signals, people have developed various mathematical theories and methods, for example, fuzzy mathematics, rough set, fuzzy automata, probability theory and Dempster-Shafer (D-S) evidence-based reasoning. In order to scientifically solve the universal fuzzy phenomena in the objective world, the concept of fuzzy set was introduced (Zadeh, 1965), and the fuzzy theory were widely used in civil, military and many other aspects (Kılıç and Leblebicioğlu, 2012), (Xuebing, Wei et al., 2011), (Ji, Massanari et al., 2007).

In order to better target identification, this paper will implement the signal processing of fuzzy images by using the rich fuzzy set theory and fuzzy technology. However, that these technologies are only used is difficult to achieve accurate recognition and multi-dimensional parameter extraction of fuzzy signal to image. This will require developing new theories and methods. To solve the accurate recognition of fuzzy signal to achieve finally accurate image understanding, this paper studies how to solve a large number of fuzzy and incomplete signal problems exist in the reality, and further studies fuzzy target recognition methods. For reducing signal processing costs, lowering personnel's labor intensity to target recognition, these researches in this paper have a special practical significance and broad practical application prospects.

SIGNAL PROCESSING METHOD TO FUZZY IMAGE

Because of image acquisition system, different physical phenomena such as illumination cannot be completely evenly distributed, and many other reasons, the obtained edge intensity of image is different. Moreover, in real-world situations, image data is often contaminated by noise. While the scenery features mixed together so that it makes subsequent interpretation very difficult. To achieve the accurate grasp of the picture intent, it needs to study a target recognition method that can not only detect the non-continuity of intensity, but also can determine their exact position. It needs to develop new uncertainty processing methods and algorithms to solve such problems.

In some cases, the acquired most of images are fuzzy. In addition to objective reasons, there are also some subjective reasons to cause the images are fuzzy, such as images were dissevered, soiled, etc. For the fuzziness in these images, this paper uses the threshold approach to process fuzzy signal on the basis of uncertainty factor classification and influence analysis, and presents fuzzy signal processing method and algorithm that can improve the image quality, as shown in Figure 1.

The threshold value is used to smooth image processing and eliminate the fuzziness of image. The basic algorithm is given as follows:

Fuzzy Processing by Using the Threshold Value

After the wavelet transform is used for the signal with noise, the correlation of wavelet coefficients between adjacent scales is calculated. According to the correlative degree, the type of wavelet coefficient is distinguished, chosen and given up, and then the wavelet coefficient is reconstructed.

The traditional denoising methods are to make the signal by noise interference pass through a filter, so as to filter out the frequency component of noise. However, for pulse signal, white noise, non-stationary signals, and so on, the traditional methods have certain limitations. For these types of signals, after they are filtered in low signal to noise ratio situations, the signal to noise ratio not only cannot be greatly improved, but also the position information of signals has been blurred.

The denoising method based on wavelet transform uses variable scale characteristic of wavelet transform so that it has a "concentration" capability for sure signal. If a signal's energy focuses on a small number of wavelet coefficients in wavelet transform domain, so their values must be greater than values of wavelet coefficients of the energy-dispersive many signals and noise in the wavelet transform domain. For this case, this threshold method can be used.

For a given threshold value δ, the wavelet coefficients that all absolute values are less than δ are classified as "noise", and their values are replaced by 0. But the wavelet coefficients that are more than the threshold value δ are got values again after they are reduced, and the symbols of the obtained coefficients

Figure 1. Fuzzy image pre-processing

| image with noise | fuzzy processing by proposed method |

are the symbols of the original wavelet coefficients. This approach means that the threshold removes minor extent noises or undesired signals. The desired signal can be obtained by wavelet inverse transform.

1. **Threshold Value:** The soft threshold method and the hard threshold method are two main methods to the wavelet coefficient that is more than the threshold value is reduced.

    The soft threshold method is

$$W_\delta = \begin{cases} \mathrm{sgn}\,(W)(|W| - \delta), & |W| \geq \delta \\ 0, & |W| < \delta \end{cases}$$

    The hard threshold method is

$$W_\delta = \begin{cases} W, & |W| \geq \delta \\ 0, & |W| < \delta \end{cases}$$

    The two threshold methods are different. The former has the continuity, and it is easy to be processed in mathematics. However, the latter is closer to the practical situation. The key of the threshold method are the choice of threshold value. If the threshold value is too small, the noise remains after the image is denoised, but if the threshold value is too big, some important signals and characteristics of image will be filtered out, which it causes the deviation.

2. **Choice of Threshold Value:** Intuitively say, for the obtained wavelet coefficient, the more the noise is, the greater the threshold value should also be. The selection chosen process of the majority threshold value is for a group of wavelet coefficients, according to the statistical properties of this group of wavelet coefficients, a threshold value δ can be obtained by calculating.

    Donoho presented a typical threshold selection method which are given and proved in theory, and the threshold value δ is direct proportional to the covariance σ of the noise. The relationship between the two is

$$\delta = \sigma\sqrt{2\log n}$$

where n is the number of layers of wavelet decomposition.

In fact, for finite length signal, the formula is only the upper bound of optimization of threshold value. The optimization formula of threshold value is gradual change with signal length. When the length of signal is infinite, the threshold value is accord to the above formula. Therefore, when the signal is enough long, the denoising effect is obvious.

3. **De-Noising Step of Wavelet Threshold:** The step of threshold denoising method based on wavelet transform is outlined as follows:

a. The appropriate wavelet function is chosen to carry out wavelet decomposition transform to a given signal, and then the wavelet transform coefficient *W* is obtained.

b. The wavelet threshold value δ is calculated, and the appropriate threshold method is chosen, such as soft threshold or hard threshold, to choose and give up for the wavelet coefficients. Thus, the new wavelet coefficients *Wb* are obtained;

c. The obtained wavelet coefficients *Wb* are carried out the inverse wavelet transform, i.e., the wavelet coefficients are reconstructed, and then the denoised images are acquired.

In denoising, assume the variance of the noise is estimated, and then the problem has been resolved. In practice, how to determine the type of noise and its variance is a very important problem.

Simulation and Analysis

1. **Denoising by Threshold:** In simulation, we use the original image and the image after adding noise. The added noise is the Gauss white noise with the covariance σ = 0.1, as shown in Figure 2.

Based on the above given denoising method, the image after adding noise is denoised by using the soft and hard threshold. The results are shown in Table 1 and Figure 3.

From Table 1 and Figure 3 known, after the images are denoised via the Haar and the db4 filters, the mean-square variances of the noise in the image all decrease, while the signal to noise ratios all increase. Moreover, for the same filter, the denoising effect of soft threshold is better than that of hard

Figure 2. Original image and image after adding noise

Table 1. Comparison of image denoising effect by wavelet in n=2 to image after adding noise

Denoising Method	Noise and Denoising	Mean-Square Variance	Signal to Noise Ratio
	Image of Adding Noise	**0.11**	**20.2235**
haar filter	denoising by soft threshold	0.0556	25.5648
	denoising by hard threshold	0.0758	25.136
db4 filter	denoising by soft threshold	0.0539	25.3606
	denoising by hard threshold	0.0651	25.0667

Figure 3. Denoising effect by using soft and hard threshold based on haar and db4

denoising with soft threshold (haar)

denoising with hard threshold (haar)

denoising with soft threshold (db4)

denoising with hard threshold (db4)

threshold, i.e., the image denoised by soft threshold is clearer and smoother. The effect by using db4 is better than that using Haar.

Then, the images with noise are carried out by different layers decomposition for denoising. The comparison of denoising effect by different levels is shown in Table 2 and Figure 4

From Table 2 and Figure 4, at different decomposition level, the mean-square variances of the noise in the image all are reduced, all SNR are also improved. But for image polluted seriously by noise, as shown in Figure 4, the more the number of decomposition layers is, the better the denoising effect is. However, the mean-square variance of denoising based on soft threshold at $n=2$ is less than that at $n=3$,

Table 2. Comparison of different decomposition layers for image denoising

Layers for Denoising	Noise and Denoising	Mean-Square Variance	Signal To Noise Ratio
	Image of Adding Noise	**0.1**	**20.0205**
$n=2$	denoising by soft threshold	0.0508	26.0069
	denoising by hard threshold	0.0714	22.9239
$n=3$	denoising by soft threshold	0.0588	24.6059
	denoising by hard threshold	0.0711	22.9654
$n=4$	denoising by soft threshold	0.0482	26.3345
	denoising by hard threshold	0.0586	24.6401
$n=6$	denoising by soft threshold	0.0457	26.8088
	denoising by hard threshold	0.0485	26.2789

Figure 4. Image denoising in different decomposition levels for n=3, n=6

denoising with soft threshold (n=3)

denoising with hard threshold (n=3)

denoising with soft threshold (n=6)

denoising with hard threshold (n=6)

and the signal to noise ratio of denoising based on soft threshold at $n=2$ is higher than that at $n=3$. These simulation results also show that the denoising effect is best when the number of decomposition layer reaches a certain fixed value. The number of decomposition layers is too small or too large, thus the effects all are not good.

2. **Fuzzy Processing by Weight Adjustment:** No matter the soft threshold or the hard threshold are used for image denoising, if a public threshold value is shared in all directions, then the denoising method is called a public threshold denoising. If the different threshold value is used in different direction, the denoising method is called an alone threshold denoising.

The weighting function $\omega = [1, 0.9, 1; 0.8, -7.1, 1; 0.85, 0.9, 1.1]$ is used to adjust the image I, and the image is adjusted as follows:

$$G = \omega \otimes I$$

Then, the image smoothing is carried out by the 3 layers coefficient decomposition of the wavelet haar, and then the fuzziness of image is eliminated by using the threshold to sharpen it. By this signal processing method for image processing, the quality of fuzzy image is improved, and its clarity degree is also improved.

To compare the proposed fuzzy image processing method with the existing image processing methods, the proposed fuzzy processing method has the faster processing speed and the better effect than other processing methods for image, as is shown in Figure 5.

Figure 5. Comparison of the proposed fuzzy image processing method and existing image processing methods

original image

image with noise

denoising with public threshold

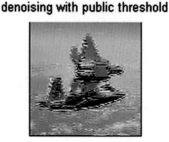

denoising with alone threshold

Gauss denoising

denoising with proposed weight

IMAGE PROCESSING

Image Processing by Wavelet Packet

Choose a function $\psi(\vec{t})$ to construct $\psi_{\vec{j},\vec{k}}\left(\vec{t}\right) = 2^{\vec{j}/2}\psi\left(2^{\vec{j}}\vec{t} - \vec{k}\right)$, and make it do inner product with image $p(x,y)$, i.e. $\left\langle \psi_{\vec{j},\vec{k}}(\vec{t}), p\left(x, y\right) \right\rangle$, which can carry out some processing for an image such as smoothing, denoising, enhancing, compressing and so on, where, $\vec{t} = (x, y)$, $\vec{j} = \left(j_1, j_2\right)$, $\vec{k} = \left(k_1, k_2\right)$.

To implement the processing to the image $p(x,y)$, the concrete algorithm is $W_{\vec{j},\vec{k}} = \left\langle \psi_{\vec{j},\vec{k}}(\vec{t}), p\left(x, y\right) \right\rangle$, which can carry out a decomposition and feature extraction to energy coefficient of image $p(x,y)$. From the decomposition calculation of wavelet known, the *i*th level energy feature of ripple is calculated by the *i*th level decomposition coefficient of wavelet, which shows the energy feature of an image in the 2^{-i} scale, in different directions and different positions.

In order to further carry out the subdivision to the decomposed frequency band, that is, to further carry out the localization of time-frequency, the definition of wavelet packet is introduced.

To wavelet packet, we here give a one-dimensional wavelet packet transform. Assume the $\phi(t)$ is the orthogonal scaling function of wavelet decomposition, and the $\psi(t)$ is the wavelet basis generated by scaling functions. Again, assume $\psi_0(t)=\phi(t)$ and $\psi_1(t)=\psi(t)$, if the two satisfy the following progression, respectively

$$\begin{cases} \psi_0(t) = \sum_k p_k \psi_0(2t-k) \\ \psi_1(t) = \sum_k q_k \psi_0(2t-k) \end{cases} \tag{1}$$

Then, a wavelet packet can be defined. Because the wavelet $\psi(t)$ is an orthogonal, there is $q_n = (-1)^{n-1} \overline{p}_{-n+1}$. Where $\overline{p}_{-n+1}$ is the conjugation of p_{-n+1}. The wavelet packet can be defined as follows:

Definition 1: A function sequence $\psi_n(t)$ is defined by $\begin{cases} \psi_{2l}(t) = \sum_k p_k \psi_l(2t-k) \\ \psi_{2l+1}(t) = \sum_k q_k \psi_l(2t-k) \end{cases}$, which is called a

wavelet packet about orthogonal scaling function $\phi(t)$. Where $n=2l$ or $2l+1$, $l=0,1,\ldots$.

The $\{2^{j/2}\psi(2^j t - l) : l \in Z\}$ is the normal orthogonal basis of wavelet subspace W_j. The wavelet packet can further subdivide each wavelet subspace W_j.

Use the $\{\psi_n\}$ to generate a family of subspaces

$$U_j^n := clos_{L^2(R)} \langle 2^{j/2} \psi_n(2^j \cdot -k) : k \in Z \rangle, j \in Z, n \in Z^+.$$

For each $j=1,2,\ldots$, the wavelet subspace W_j can be further subdivided into

$$\begin{cases} W_j = U_{j-1}^2 \oplus U_{j-1}^3 \\ \quad W_j = U_{j-2}^4 \oplus U_{j-2}^5 \oplus U_{j-2}^6 \oplus U_{j-2}^7 \\ \qquad \cdots\cdots \\ \quad W_j = U_{j-k}^{2^k} \oplus U_{j-k}^{2^k+1} \oplus \cdots \oplus U_{j-k}^{2^{k+1}-1} \\ \qquad \cdots\cdots \\ \quad W_j = U_0^{2^j} \oplus U_0^{2^j+1} \oplus \cdots \oplus U_0^{2^{j+1}-1} \end{cases} \tag{2}$$

Then, for each $m=0,1,\ldots,2^k-1$, $k=1,2,\ldots$, and the family of functions $\left\{2^{\frac{j-k}{2}} \psi_{2^k+m}\left(2^{j-k}t - l\right) : l \in Z\right\}$ is an orthogonal basis of $U_{j-k}^{2^k+m}$.

The multiresolution analysis of image decomposes the original image into low-frequency approximate detail images in three directions, i.e., horizontal, vertical, diagonal directions, further decomposes each low frequency approximate image into four images step by step. In addition to the decomposition of low frequency approximate image, the wavelet packet analysis of image decomposes also the high frequency detail image, which the decomposition process is represented as a full quad-tree. Figure 6 and Figure 7 give the quad-tree representation method of wavelet packet and the instance of 2-level image decomposition, respectively. The first parameter of brackets in Figure 6 denotes the scale, and the second parameter is the decomposition parameter of wavelet packet.

Figure 6. Quad-tree of wavelet packet to image decomposition

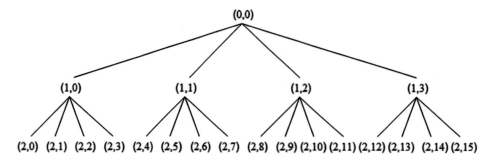

Figure 7. 2-level image decomposition by using wavelet packet

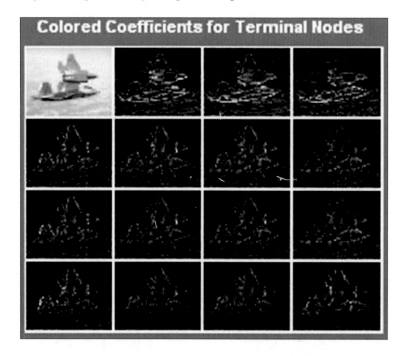

Feature Extraction of Target

Feature Extraction of Decomposition Coefficient to Image

Assume $g_j^n(t) \in U_j^n$, it can be expressed as $g_j^n(t) = \sum_l d_l^{j,n} \psi_n(2^j t - l)$. According to the calculation of wavelet packet decomposition, the decomposition coefficient is

$$
\begin{cases}
d_l^{j,2n} = \sum_k a_{k-2l} d_k^{j+1,n} \\
d_l^{j,2n+1} = \sum_k b_{k-2l} d_k^{j+1,n}
\end{cases}
\tag{3}
$$

where $a_n = \frac{1}{2}\bar{p}_n$ and $b_n = \frac{1}{2}\bar{q}_n$, $\bar{p}_n$ and $\bar{q}_n$ are the conjugation of p_n and q_n, respectively.

By the calculation of wavelet package reconstruction, the reconstruction coefficient is

$$d_l^{j+1,n} = \sum_k \left[p_{l-2k} d_k^{j,2n} + q_{l-2k} d_k^{j,2n+1} \right] \tag{4}$$

Firstly, the 2-level image decomposition to preprocessed images is carried out by using wavelet packet function $\psi(t)$. The decomposition results based on Haar wavelet basis are shown in Figure 8. The function $\psi_n(t)$ returns the tree structure of wavelet packet decomposition. It is an image user interface. The detailed images of the corresponding node are obtained by clicking at each node. Secondly, the wavelet packet coefficients of each node can be calculated by using the reconstruction coefficient function $d_l^{j+1,n}(t)$ at each decomposition layer, and the result is shown in Figure 9. Finally, all the coefficients are normalized to compose the characteristic vectors. Assume the characteristic vector of wavelet packet decomposition coefficient at the ith layer is V_i, then there is

$$V_i = \left(c_{i0}, c_{i1}, c_{i2}, \cdots, c_{i2^{2i}-1} \right) \tag{5}$$

where i denotes the number of layers of wavelet packet decomposition, c_j denotes the normalization coefficient values of wavelet packet at each layer.

Feature Extraction of Energy to Image Decomposition

The energy feature can be calculated by using the decomposition results of wavelet packet to image. According to the algorithm described in this paper, the energy of image decomposed by wavelet packet is defined as follows:

$$E_{(i,j)} = \sum_{x=1}^{n \times 2^{-i}} \sum_{y=1}^{m \times 2^{-i}} \left[H_{(i,j)}(x,y) \right]^2 \tag{6}$$

Figure 8. Nodes of wavelet packet and the detailed image at node (1,2)

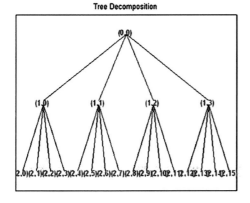
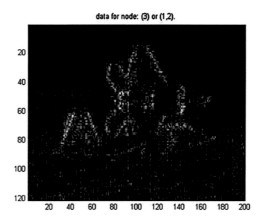

Figure 9. Reconstruction coefficients at different nodes

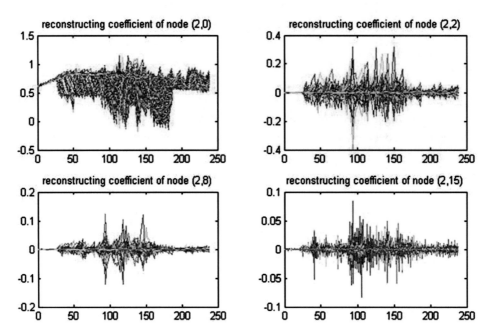

where, $E_{(i,j)}$ is the energy of image at each node, and (i,j) denotes different nodes in a quad-tree of wavelet packet decomposition. Under the 2-level wavelet packet decomposition, there are $i \in \{0,1,2\}$ and $j \in \{0,1,2,...,15\}$. $H_{(i,j)}(x,y)$ is the energy of detailed image on each node. m and n are the height and width of the image, respectively. To extract the energy of detailed image on each layer, the energy feature of the image decomposed by the wavelet packet can be established as follows:

$$E_i = \left(E_{(i,0)}, E_{(i,1)}, E_{(i,2)}, \cdots, E_{(i,2^{2i}-1)} \right) \tag{7}$$

Therefore, the E_i is called the energy feature of image decomposition at the ith layer. It is normalized as follows:

$$E_j = \frac{E_{(i,j)}}{\sum_{x=1}^{n}\sum_{y=1}^{m}\left[H_{(0,0)}(x,y) \right]^2} \tag{8}$$

where $j \in \{0,1,2,...,2^{2i}-1\}$. The further simplification can be obtained:

$$E_i = \left(E_0, E_1, E_2, \cdots, E_{2^{2i}-1} \right) \tag{9}$$

MATCHING AND RECOGNITION METHODS

Matching and Recognition

The feature matching is to carry out the judgment of the similarity between the two characteristic vectors. The two targets are judged whether they are from the same target by calculating the similarity of two characteristic vectors. The similarity is expressed by the similar degree of the distance between characteristics.

We compare the characteristic vectors of unknown target image with the characteristic vectors of known classificatory target image that has been trained and stored in the retrieval system. If and only if the similarity between the characteristic vector of unknown target image and the characteristic vector of given i_0th target image is maximum, we judge that the unknown target belongs to the i_0th category based on the maximum membership principle. The matching algorithm is given as follows:

If W_l is the known characteristic vector in the retrieval system, V is the characteristic vector to be identified. Where $l=1,2,\ldots,Q$ and Q is the number of known characteristic vectors. The similarity between the characteristic vectors V and W_l of two targets is defined as follows:

$$d_l = e^{-\|V-W_l\|} = e^{-\sum_{i=1}^{n}|V_i-W_{li}|} \tag{10}$$

where, $\left|V_i - W_{li}\right| = \dfrac{1}{2^{2i}} \displaystyle\sum_{j=0}^{2^{2i}-1} \left|c_{ij}^{V_i} - c_{ij}^{W_{li}}\right|$ represents the similarity between the characteristic vectors of coefficient for image, or $\left|V_i - W_{li}\right| = \dfrac{1}{2^{2i}} \displaystyle\sum_{j=0}^{2^{2i}-1} \left|E_{ij}^{V_i} - E_{ij}^{W_{li}}\right|$ is the similarity between the characteristic vectors of energy of the image decomposed by wavelet packet. $c_{ij}^{V_i} \in V_i$, $c_{ij}^{W_{li}} \in W_{li}$, $E_{ij}^{V_i} \in E_i^{V_i}$, $E_{ij}^{W_{li}} \in E_i^{W_{li}}$, i is the number of layers of the wavelet packet to the image decomposition.

The similarity d_l represents the degree of similarity between the characteristic vector V and the characteristic vector W_l of the lth category. The recognition principle is as follows:

If $\exists l_0 \in \{1,2,\ldots,Q\}$, subject to

$$l_0 = \arg\max_{l \in \{1,2,\cdots,Q\}} \{d_l\} \tag{11}$$

Then based on the maximum membership principle, we judge that the target to be identified belongs to the l_0th category.

Hierarchical Recognition Method

In the recognition process, it needs to search for all the samples in the database, so as to find the sample which it and the identified target image are from the same target, and then the target recognition is achieved. In order to improve the accuracy and efficiency of recognition, the hierarchical recognition method is introduced for searching. After preprocessing and feature extraction to each target image, the target image is determined by two kinds of characteristics. Firstly, the database is searched by the feature of image decomposition coefficient for the first time, and then the candidate set that consists of the target images of similar features of coefficient is obtained. Then, in the candidate set, the second search is carried out by using the energy feature of image decomposition achieved by wavelet packet, and then the final recognition results are obtained. In the recognition process, we use the feature of image decomposition coefficient to search for the first time is because of its computational complexity is relatively small, which increases the speed of recognition. To implement the search for the second time to the candidate set, because the number of samples in candidate set is less than that of in the database, similarly, the overall recognition efficiency is also improved. Figure 10 shows the flow chart of hierarchical recognition.

Experiment and Results Analysis

1. **Establish a Standard Template Database:** The target image database used in experimental test and the sample database are established as follows:
   a. 100 different samples are chosen randomly from image database, and 3 images are chosen randomly from 10 images of each target. Thus, a total of 300 target images are obtained.
   b. An image is chosen randomly from 3 images of each target, which the total is 100 images to compose experimental database of target image. The remaining 200 target images compose the test samples database.
   c. The established 100 target images are carried out a preprocessing and feature extraction by 5-level Daubechies-4 wavelet packet decomposition. The 100 characteristic vector sets P of decomposition coefficient and 100 characteristic vector sets Q of energy of image decomposition are acquired, respectively. Each characteristic set contains 100 characteristic vectors.
2. **Matching:** The basic step of the target matching recognition is as follows:
   a. **P1:** The target images in test database are carried out a preprocessing by 5-level Daubechies-4 wavelet packet and the feature extraction of 2-level decomposition. The coefficient features V and the energy features E based on 2-level image decomposition by using wavelet packet are obtained.
   b. **P2:** According to the hierarchical recognition process as shown in Figure 10, the test coefficient feature V is carried out the first matching with all characteristic vectors of decomposition coefficient feature sets P in the standard database. The candidate set is composed by the corresponding energy features which correspond to the matched similarity coefficient features.

Figure 10. Flow chart of hierarchical recognition

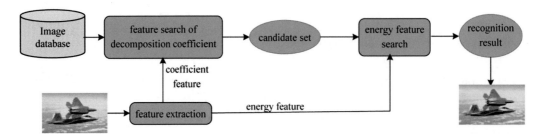

The test energy feature E is carried out the second matching with the characteristic vectors in the candidate set. The corresponding target image which corresponds to the maximum similarity of energy features is the recognition result after the matching is finished.

c. **P3:** For each image in the test sample database, after 300 times recognition are done according to the steps P1~P2, the times of the correct recognition and the error recognition are recorded respectively, and the correct recognition rates are obtained by calculating.

3. **Results Analysis:** For each target image, 12 times repeating experiments are carried out by the step P1 to step P3 based on Daubechies-4 wavelet basis function in simulation. The number of samples is different in each experiment. The proposed hierarchical recognition method compares with those currently usually used recognition methods such as Gabor (Pan and Ruan, 2009), statistical method (Yang, Adelstein et al., 2009). The experimental results show that the average correct recognition rates of these methods are 96.82%, 89.93%, 85.98% in simulation of 300 times, respectively. The simulation results are shown in Figure 11.

From Figure 11 known, the average correct recognition rate based on the hierarchical recognition method is the maximum among all referred methods. In experiment, the average correct recognition rate increases constantly with the increasing number of samples, and the curve of average correct recognition rate gradually levels off as the samples increase when the number of samples reaches a certain value.

The proposed hierarchical recognition method and the usual used recognition methods (Pan and Ruan, 2009), (Yang, Adelstein et al., 2009) are compared from two aspects that are the computing speed and the correct recognition rate. Table 3 gives the results of a comprehensive comparison. From the comparison seen, the proposed hierarchical recognition method has better recognition effect than other methods.

Figure 11. Comparison of correct recognition rate of the proposed and existing recognition methods

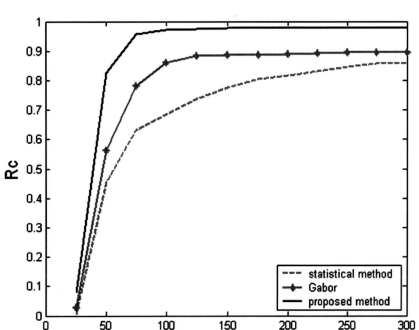

Table 3. Comparison of different target recognition methods

Recognition Methods	Statistical Method	Gabor	Proposed Method
Average correct recognition rate	0.8598	0.8993	0.9682
Computing speed	0.141 s	0.171 s	0.167 s

In Table 3 the computing speed is the mean time obtained by the mean computing time of 12 times repeating test of these methods at each step in simulation environment, which the computing time is only the computing time of algorithm itself. In simulation, the computer used is the Pentium 4 and 2G memory, and the programming language is MATLAB. The average correct recognition rates are the average of two stages which are an average of 300 times simulations and then taking an average of 12 time steps for every method under the given simulation environment. In fact, they are the average of the correct recognition rates in space and time, so they are an overall average of the correct recognition rates.

From the simulation results known, the hierarchical recognition method not only has the faster processing speed, but also has better recognition effect.

CONCLUSION

This paper uses the wavelet packet analysis to carry out feature extraction of target for the first time, and presents the hierarchical recognition method. In target feature extraction process, the more detailed and rich texture feature of target can be obtained by wavelet packet to image decomposition to compare with the wavelet decomposition. In the process of matching and recognition, the hierarchical recognition method is used to improve the recognition speed and accuracy. Therefore, this method provides a new way of thinking for target recognition.

How to choose or construct a proper wavelet basis function, and how many levels of decomposition can be carried out to obtain the best recognition effect, are some questions which need further study in the future.

ACKNOWLEDGMENT

This work is supported by Henan Province Outstanding Youth on Science and Technology Innovation (No. 164100510017), and National 973 Program (No. 613237), respectively.

REFERENCES

An, X. B., Zhang, W., & Yang, J. (2011). Research on Evaluation of Banks Ecological Culture Based on Fuzzy Mathematics. *Energy Procedia*, *5*, 302–306. doi:10.1016/j.egypro.2011.03.052

Biswal, B., Dash, B. K., & Panigrahi, B. K. (2009). Non-stationary power signal processing for pattern recognition using HS-transform. *Applied Soft Computing*, *9*(1), 107–117. doi:10.1016/j.asoc.2008.03.004

Ji, F.Z., Sun, S.Y., Wang, C.L., Zuo, X.Z., & Wang, J. (2011). Applications of Fuzzy Lifting Wavelet Packet Transform in MFL Signal Processing. *Nondestructive Testing*, *33*(5), 22–25.

Ji, Y., Massanari, R. M., Ager, J., Yen, J., Miller, R. E., & Ying, H. (2007). A fuzzy logic-based computational recognition-primed decision model. *Information Sciences*, *177*(20), 4338–4353. doi:10.1016/j.ins.2007.02.026

Kılıç, E., & Leblebicioğlu, K. (2012). From classic observability to a simple fuzzy observability for fuzzy discrete-event systems. *Information Sciences*, *187*(15), 224–232. doi:10.1016/j.ins.2011.11.008

Liu, G., & Kreinovich, V. (2010). Fast convolution and fast Fourier transform under interval and fuzzy uncertainty. *Journal of Computer and System Sciences*, *76*(1), 63–76. doi:10.1016/j.jcss.2009.05.006

Lo, J. T. H. (2012). A cortex-like learning machine for temporal hierarchical pattern clustering, detection, and recognition. *Neurocomputing*, *78*(1), 89–103. doi:10.1016/j.neucom.2011.04.046

Pan, X., & Ruan, Q. Q. (2009). Palmprint recognition using Gabor-based local invariant features. *Neurocomputing*, *72*(7), 2040–2045. doi:10.1016/j.neucom.2008.11.019

Yang, Y. L., James, A. S., & Amin, I. K. (2009). Target discovery from data mining approaches. *Drug Discovery Today*, *14*(3), 147–154. doi:10.1016/j.drudis.2008.12.005 PMID:19135549

Zadeh, L. A. (1965). Fuzzy sets. *Information and Control*, *8*(3), 338–353. doi:10.1016/S0019-9958(65)90241-X

Section 2

Factors Influence Reading from Screen of Arabic Textbook for Learning by Children Aged 9 to 13

Chapter 6
Introduction to E-Reading Context

Azza A Abubaker
Benghazi University, Libya & University of Huddersfield, UK

Joan Lu
University of Huddersfield, UK

ABSTRACT

The research aims to identify the problems and seek for possible solutions in e-reading context from a systematic discussion that is supported by more than 50 relevant references. The definitions of the problem have been presented. Numbers of research questions are asked prior to the methodologies. The importance and differences of qualitative and quantitative methods are addressed. Meanwhile, ethical issues and their benefits and risks are discussed and explained. Finally, the research framework is proposed as guidance for the near future research actions.

1. INTRODUCTION

Day after day, interest in the way of displaying data on screen has continued to increase, especially with the rise in the number of people who now use electronic texts for learning purposes. So, this requires more focus on factors that affect legibility on screen such as text format and user requirements. In addition, the numbers of previous attempts such as (Lee, Shieh, Jeng & Shen, 2008; Huang, Rau, & Liu, 2009) that cover all these factors affecting electronic reading are notably limited. One likely reason is that many researchers have concentrated their work on designing issues more than the analysis of the impact of these factors on display and reading electronic texts by children for learning. Another reason is that much of the research has focused on the effect of reading electronic text by examining the factors without grading or defining the relationship between these factors (Hartley & Burnhill, 1977; Dillon, Richardson & McKnight, 1990; Lee, et al, 2008; Huang et al. 2009).

In addition, most of these researchers have focused merely on multimedia features such as sounds, animation and dictionary option, with little focus on the format of electronic texts. Moreover, most of

DOI: 10.4018/978-1-5225-1884-6.ch006

the reading theories are merely concerned with paper texts, without examining if they are suitable also as e- texts.

Additionally, the reading topic has become more interesting for many researchers in different areas of research such as information science, computing science, and human science. Thus, there are three categories of digital reading studies:

1. Researchers focused on the usability of e-texts, e.g. comparing reading electronic to paper reading; measuring the legibility and comprehension of texts (Dillon, 1994; Noorhidawati & Forbes, 2008; Davis, Tierney & Chang, 2005); and examining user behaviours in digital environments.
2. Researchers presented a 'new approach using technologies to support reading electronic that concentrates on new software and hardware, hypertext, and interface design such as (Anonymous, 2003; Godoy, Schiaffino & Amandi, 2004; Thissen, 2004; White, 2007).
3. Finally, researchers focused on the phenomenology of reading, as in studying human interaction with e-resources and reading process in both linear texts and hypertexts such as (Huang, 2005).

This research could not be included within any of these classifications to avoid falling into the same shortcomings of other research but aim to connect different aspects from different areas to provide a model that encompasses all the factors that affect legibility of e- texts according to the qualitative data and statistical analysis from several experiments.

However, the critical issues of how to increase usage of e- text are national concerns in developing countries. Although some Arabic countries have various national plans and policies to increase the use of e- text among children such as the 'Report and Recommendations of the Fifteenth Meeting of the Group' to develop a strategy of Arab telecommunications and information (2005) which aims to activate the role of communication technology, and to employ such technology in the Arab world. But unfortunately, the average reading of electronic text is still low; therefore, there are questions to be dealt with such as the following: (1) how to motivate more children to read e- text; (2) how to stimulate teachers to use online material in class; (3) how to motivate readers to modify their reading behaviour, from reading paper to reading e- text; (4) how to stimulate designers to display e-texts on screen in a way that encourages readers to read online. Part of these questions will be answered in this research thorough following different methods.

Thus, this research will focus on the text as the main tool for learning and addressing the effect of the reading process in the design online academic text by developing a model that explains the relationship between the variables. It will also show the average effect by using students from primary schools in Libya as subjects. In addition, the results of this study have the potential to impact the future of web-based testing; online publications, e- learning, and other electronic document formats.

2. PROBLEM DEFINITION

Text is still an important means of communicating with a learner and in many ways it is the most powerful. Furthermore, applying technology in education brings new issues related to visual display and how it affects the readability and legibility of e- text. In particular, when developing teaching material, it is very important to cover all these factors that may affect legibility of e- text, define the correlation between typographic variables, and see how it affects the reading process.

However, the difficulty of reading electronic texts is caused by several factors as previously reported such as display context (Wiggins, 1977; American National Standard, 1988; Wright & Lickorish, 1988; Dillon, et al. 1990; Dyson & Kipping 1997; Youngman & Scharff 1998; Dyson, 2004; Abdullah, 2007; Leeuw & Rydin 2007; Lee, et al. 2008, Muter & Maurutto, 1991; Marchionini, 1995; Foltz, 1996; Grainger & Jacobs, 1996; Singhal, 1999; Sun, 2003; Sun 2007; Wastlund, Norlander & Archer, 2008).

Alternatively, empirical findings show poor reading performance compared to reading from paper. For instance, Tenopir et al. (2009) indicated that 54.4% of college students prefer reading printed articles. Also, the majority of university students are still not keen on electronic books (Rogers & Roncevic, 2002; Mash, 2003) because reading from screen was slower and less accurate. These findings encourage researchers to investigate the reasons behind poor reading from screen. Otherwise, the average reading from screen has increased in contrast to reading printed material especially among younger readers who are more familiar with the new technology.

Moreover, there are factors that affect the legibility of e- text, which may be classified into five elements: machine aspects, designing aspects, reading behaviour, personal characteristics, and motivation of use. There is another factor that can be added to the above factors - language. As revealed by several researchers, there are differences in the way of reading and moving from one language to another, which has led to defining the effect of these variables on each language instead of using the findings of research done in different languages.

The problem that needs to be addressed in this research can be defined in two dimensions as outlined below.

First Dimension: How Students Read E-Text for Learning Purposes

With the growing number of pupils who read e- context for pleasure or learning, there are still deficiencies in studies that seek to understand how digital texts are read, as previous studies have shown that what have been done in the area of e- reading simply focused on comparing issues without having a clear idea of how the reader deals with e- text or whether this technology has affected the way the e-text is read. Kol & Schcolink (2000) argued that understanding the reading strategy and teaching students how to deal with e- text could help them read effectively from screen. Moreover, Terras (2005) suggested a model of how experts read an ancient text by understanding a complex process in humanities. This study reported that the reading process is linear and also based on the interaction of different facets in the expert's knowledge. These findings help implement a computer system that can work in several approaches.

Alternatively, the reading process differs according to the purpose of reading and the type of the material, as Dillon (1994) and Terras (2005) have reported. Also, the hypertext brings radical changes to the way of reading, e.g. hypertext linking allows reader to control the reading process rather than the author, and to interact dynamically with other texts. Importantly, theories and models on displaying text and reading have been developed mostly for adults and in Western languages (such as English and French). For instance, Dillon (1994) built two models of the reading process, one for reading academic journals and the second manual. These models cannot be applied to children because of differences in their aims, skills and requirements. Most importantly, most of the research in this area have focused on the English language in higher education and only a limited number of researchers have concentrated on the Arabic language (Elgohary, 2008; Asmaa & Asma 2009). This makes it difficult to deal with the Arabic text, which is totally different.

Second Dimension: Focusing on the Variables that Affect the Display and Reading of E- Text by Learners Aged 9 to 13

In the early stages of the e- book, designers and writers attempted to create eBook using the metaphor of a paper book, while the capabilities of e- book have led to changes in the way of reading. In the same context, Coyle (2008) defined the reason behind failure of e- book to render the print book electronically rather than developing new standards as a guide for designers and writers to use when designing e- text. This idea was supported in many studies that examined the display of e- text; for example, Lonsdale et al (2006), DeStefano & LeFevre (2007) examined the effect of the layout of questions and answer sheet for the English language (Lonsdale, Dyson & Reynolds, 2006). Study findings show that text layout affects reading performance significantly.

Otherwise, searching in-depth into the reading process and usability of e- text raises new factors related to language structure, which makes comparison between English and Arabic unfair for several reasons such as the fact that these two languages have different morphological structures, e.g. English has a concatenative morphological structure, while Arabic is non-concatenative. On the other hand, 15 letters of the Arabic alphabet have dots in them, and a large number of the letters differ depending on the number of dots or where the dots are put, while in English only two letters have dots (Shirali-shahreza & Shirali-shahreza, 2006). For example, in Figure (1) the first letter ثـ and the second one تـ differ in the number of dots, making it difficult to differentiate between them especially by children and when the font size is small. Also, when one word containing two letters have dots and are conjoined, it becomes difficult to differentiate between them. This problem does not exist in the English language [EL] which makes applying the criteria based on EL to other languages such as Arabic [AL] difficult.

In addition, Arabic letters have up to four different shapes depending on its relative position in the text. Amin (2000) highlighted certain facts related to Arabic characters which are summarised in Table 1, and compared it to Latin. These differences have to do with the characters' width, position and morphological structure.

In additional, a comparison of the Arabic system to Chinese shows that the first one belongs to an alphabetic system where words are written in units, and there are salient spaces between words. Whereas, the Chinese language belongs to a logographic system, where words are written in units, and there are no salient spaces between words (Huang et al. 2009; Shu & Zhuo, 2010). Thus, this research will focus on the language factor to determine the extent of its impact on reading, taking into account the factors that have previously been identified.

Figure 1. Dots in some Arabic letters

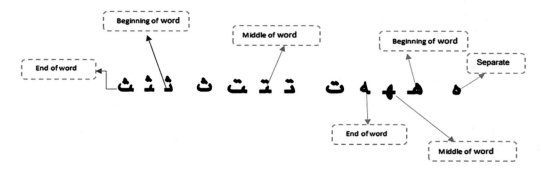

Table 1. Similarities and differences between Arabic characters and Latin characters

Arabic Language	Latin Language
Arabic language is written from right to left.	Latin language is written from left to right.
Use letters and vowel. In some cases, the absence of vowel diacritics dictates a different meaning.	Use letters.
Words are separated by spaces.	Words are separated by spaces.
Some word can be divided into smaller units called sub words.	
Some characters of the same font have different sizes.	
Combine seven vowels.	
15 letters have dots; these dots can be at the top or bottom of the letters.	Two letters have dot.
The shapes of the letters differ based on their position in the word (e.g. medial, final, and isolated).	
Vowels are placed above the characters.	
Six letters (ا د ذ ر ز و) have only an isolated or final form.	
Some letters look almost the same in all four forms	

Some researchers combined a number of variables and compare these layouts with a control condition; this method is known as the "kitchen sink" method (Muter, 1996) which begins by recognizing the effect of individual typographic factors and then test the effect of one variable depending on another using systematic relations. In addition, most researchers (Muter, 1991; Bruljn, Mul & Oostendorp, 1992) used a well-structured text as the method to test the effect of those variables and investigate the relationship between those variables. Researchers in this field of Arabic literature are limited. A critical attempt was provided by Asmaa & Asma (2009) when they opened the door towards further investigating the typographical variables that effect the readability of Arabic script. They asked 35 children aged 7 to 9 to read an e- story of ten pages. Each page of the e-story was written with various font types and sizes. Then, participants were invited to respond to 4 questions to measure their level of satisfaction regarding font type and size. According to the findings, Simplified Arabic or Unicode MS with size 14 are the most readable for Arab children. On the other hand, children were able to read faster with 2/3 screen line length. Although this study may shed light on some factors related to the readability of Arabic texts, it was not able to provide adequate answers to cover all these factors. Thus, we may consider this study as a springboard to further research in this topic for the following reasons:

- Did not address all the variables that effect e-reading of Arabic texts nor define the relationship between these variables.
- Did not measure the impact of these factors on the reading process.

Moreover, Abdullah (2007) investigated the effect of two Arabic fonts [Times New Roman, and Courier] matching to three print font size on reading performance. Each sentence contains 16 words which were printed with black letters on white-background A4 sheets. 100 participants who were studying at university and had a distance visual of (6/6)[1] volunteered to do the experiment. The study shows that there was an effect on the reading speed from using two different fonts, simulated and visual impairment. For instance, the print size increases the reading speed and the rate was enhanced significantly with Times New Roman. Therefore, this study focused on the use of large print size, which is different to the screen size font. Thus, further investigation is needed for the Arabic language with variables that affect reading from a screen. In addition, both researchers did not consider the effect of all these factors on Arabic reading efficiency. Furthermore, determining the effect of the reading skills is important and has a great effect on the process of reading.

3. RESEARCH AIMS

This research is an attempt to examine the three factors that affect reading and designing of e-texts for children using Arabic script. In addition, it aims to develop a model for designing acceptance that will have the power to demonstrate acceptance and usage behaviour of the e-school text using a schoolbook for primary schools in Libya. Alternatively, dealing with the research problem led to the specification of the following research objectives, which were achieved through four inter- related surveys:

- To build an e-reading strategy for a schoolbook based on users' cognitive and behaviour processes.
- To test the effect of three typographical variables that affect reading electronic Arabic texts (font size, font type, and line length). These three factors were defended by the majority of researchers as the most influential.
- To provide a standard that can help keep children`s concentration on the e- text.
- To create a guideline that could help designers when designing e-academic Arabic texts for children.
- To examine in-depth the challenges of reading Arabic e-texts.
- To study the efficiency of Arabic text reading and the factors impacting the efficiency of reading and comprehension.
- To understand children's behaviour when reading Arabic electronic text.

4. RESEARCH QUESTIONS

In order to investigate the effect of using e-resources, we need to develop a model which can present a user reading strategy and help define the behavioural processes of users. However, answering the following questions was needed in order to be sure that the level of legibility of e-texts in early education can be improved. Questions were divided into three groups based on research objectives:

- **First Group: "Using Internet and E-Book":**
  ◦ Do students in primary schools in Libya use the internet and eBooks?
  ◦ For what purpose do students in Libya school use the Internet and eBooks?
  ◦ Which factors affect the use of the Internet and eBooks among Libyan primary school children?
- **Second Group: "Reading Process":**
  ◦ Is there a difference in the reading process between e-school textbook and p-school text-book?
  ◦ What are the existing prototypes of schoolbooks in primary education (PE)?

- ◦ How are students interacting with schoolbooks in two formats (electronic and printed format)?
- ◦ Is there a significant relationship between human information processing and text layout?
- **Third Group: "Typology Factors":**
  - ◦ Is there a statistically significant difference between the means in the reading speed and word errors for each font size?
  - ◦ Does the difference between the Arabic written system and other languages have an effect on designing standards?
  - ◦ In which font size is the Arabic text read most effectively?
  - ◦ Is there any correlation between age of the reader and font size?
  - ◦ Which font type is more readable?
  - ◦ Which Line Length is more readable for Reading Schoolbook on Screen?

5. METHODOLOGY

It is important to determine a research paradigm that is dependent on the principles of methodology before constructing a research design (Collis & Hussey, 2009). In this context, several researchers such as (Easterby-Smith M, Thorpe & Lowe, 2002; Eldabi, Irani, Paul & Love, 2002) consider it essential to have a proper understanding of the philosophical issues behind any methodology, because it can assist in defining research designs, recognising which designs will and will not be produced, showing designs that may be beyond one's past experience, and finally, being able to indicate the limitations of the research.

Furthermore, building a research philosophy should be based on the way the researcher thinks about the development of knowledge. Usually, research philosophy points to the way the researcher thinks about the improvement of knowledge which falls within one of two classifications: positivism or phenomenology. Selecting the more suitable one will be made in terms of the research questions and objectives.

In addition, Hausenblas et al draw up a clear picture on how to distinguish between these two philosophies (Hausenblas, Carron & Mack, 1997). The phenomenological approach deals with the measuring of social phenomena by focusing on the subjective aspects of human activity (Saunders, Lewis & Thornhill, 2007), whereas, positivism can be described as quantitative, objectivistic, scientific, experimental or traditional. From researcher point of view, each approach works effectively when connected to the appropriate variables. Therefore, the investigator must be aware of the need to select an approach that can achieve the research objectives and provide accurate data. For example, researchers such as Collis & Hussey (2009) see quantitative research as unconvincing for recognising the context or setting in which people talk; whereas, a qualitative approach allows researchers to understand people`s meaning. This may not be a weak point if the researcher is not looking to investigate or understand human performance.

Based on the nature of the research questions and objectives, positivism and phenomenology philosophies have been selected as a research philosophy for this study. The rationale for this combination is that each philosophy works successfully under specific circumstances. Thus, using a combination of philosophies would take advantage of their strengths and make up for their disadvantages. E.g., using a phenomenological philosophy will allow us to investigate in-depth the reader's behaviour and its relationship to text structure; on the other hand, a positivist philosophy will be able to deal with a larger sample. For a long time, researchers simply make use of quantitative and qualitative research approaches when doing research, but they also note that there are a weakness in both approaches as has been outlined above. Therefore, a multi-faceted methodology (quantitative and qualitative) has been used in this study in order to meet its main objectives and to highlight different aspects related to the effects of usability of electronic Arabic texts in Primary education (PE). In addition, multi-faceted methodology focuses on collecting, analysing, and mixing both quantitative and qualitative data into a single whole which should provide a better understanding of research problems than either approach alone (Creswell & Clark, 2007; Saunders, et al. 2007). Figure 2 shows the strategy of mixing quantitative and qualitative approach in this research, starting with the quantitative approach to collect data for the next stage of building on the qualitative data.

Due to the aim and objectives of this research, this study is divided into three stages, with each stage requiring different tools and techniques. The following are some of the justifications for selecting a mixed-methodology for this research:

- A quantitative research philosophy is adopted for this study in the first stage in order to expand on the general statement about the phenomenon being researched (i.e. "Using computer and accessing the internet in Libyan primary schools") which should be based on data collected from a large number of students over a short period of time.

- Because a quantitative approach cannot consider the manner that humans interact with a phenomenon and it is not very effective in understanding processes of significance that people attach to actions, therefore, a qualitative approach was applied in the second and third stage of the research to define the manner of reading a school textbook in electronic and paper formats in order to build an e- reading strategy model for Arabic language that will support the designing of eBook and to examine students' behaviour and attitudes towards the phenomenon through the use of different techniques.

- For measuring the factors that affect reading electronic texts, the phenomenological paradigm was applied to examine students' behaviour and attitudes towards the phenomenon using different techniques.

- A mixed-methodology will offer a better understanding of the topic under examination, where statistical analysis of the quantitative data will make abstracts, evaluations and generalisations easy

Figure 2. Mixing both quantitative and qualitative data

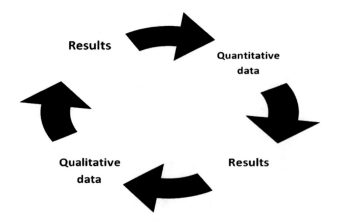

and accurate, whereas qualitative records will offer a method for explanation, justification and description of measures, actions, approaches, and behaviour. This would lead to more meaningful philosophies from the standpoint of the subjects being explored.

- An exploratory design was applied to acquire quantitative participant characteristics so as to guide a purposeful sampling for the qualitative phase. In addition, an exploratory design does not require a guiding framework or theory which commensurate with the nature of this research, especially with the lack of comprehensive theories in the field of e-reading.
- As mentioned in this s, there are a few empirical studies (Reimer, Brimhall, Cao & O'Reilly, 2009; Asmaa & Asma, 2009; Nicholas, Huntington, Hamid, Rowlands, Dobrowolski & Tenopir, 2008; Lee et al., 2008) which have been conducted in the field of electronic reading, designing electronic Arabic texts, and the lack of studies examining the factors that affect the reading of an Arabic script. But generally, these studies only applied one approach [either quantitative or qualitative] which is a clear limitation of these studies.

Alternatively, an inductive approach was used in this research as a strategy, because it provides more flexibility to weaving back and forth between theory and data for linking theory to the research. The process is different in each strategy. E.g., a deductive process starts by investigating the existing theory via observations to derive a set of propositions, whereas, an induction process starts with observing any phoneme to find material for building a new theory.

6. ETHICAL ISSUES

In this research, ethical issues have been taken into account at all research stages since the beginning, as Silverman has recommended (Seale & Gobo, 2006). In addition, because the research deals mainly with children and teachers during teaching hours, ethical issues should be a concern in all research stages. Those who volunteered to take part in the collection of data were made aware that they had a right to withdraw from the research process at any time. Particularly in this study, due regard was given to protecting the identity of those involved and all efforts were made to ensure that their taking part would not adversely affect in any way their sense of privacy. Some of these concerns are noted and debated below.

6.1 Benefit and Risk

This research will be beneficial to education in schools with its contribution to knowledge. In addition, this research offers opportunities for participants to discover a new learning style [eBook]. Students showed great interest in eBook through the questions they raised after finishing the observation. When they asked about the change that could happen in the way of learning, special students made complaints about this way of learning, with some describing it as boring while others found it difficult.

Furthermore, students taking part in the observation learned how to use the e- content available in the skoool.com website, which presents the Libya schoolbook and starts comparing differences in each format. In addition, students get a list of the useful websites that support learning as an initial step in assisting them, especially in the absence of direction from the teacher.

As for the risks, it is clear that there would be no health and safety risks. But at the same time, this research was concerned at the beginning about wasting the students' time. And so, tests were done in class to reduce this risk and lessons were taken from the schoolbook. In the third and fourth experiments, students were tested outside school time.

7. PROPOSED RESEARCH FRAMEWORK

Finally, Figure 3 presents a research framework where the research was divided into five phases. In the first and the second phases, the aims and research questions were confirmed through reviewing research on the topic of electronic reading, eBook and usability. The third phase includes survey design and

Figure 3. Research framework

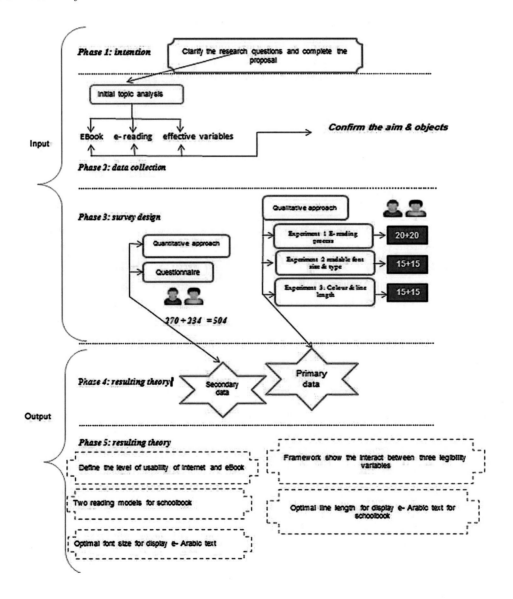

implementation. The output of the early three phases is two types of data [secondary and primary data]. The secondary data used to clarify some issues is not addressed in previous research, while the primary data provide answers to research questions. The last phase provides the contribution of the research which comes in four main areas.

8. CONCLUSION

This research approaches a popular topic, i.e. E-reading, especially its impact is significantly on the digital age. The target group is focused on the children. The following achievements are demonstrated so far:

- The research problems are defined into two dimensions;
- Seven research aims are set up;
- Thirteen research questions are asked;
- A model for Methodologies is presented, and especially discussed in qualitative and quantitative approaches;
- Ethic issues are addressed, particularly mentioned in the benefits and risks;
- Research framework is proposed.

Above achievements can also be acting as guidance for further research activities.

REFERENCES

Abdullah, Z. A. (2007). A Study into Usability of Tools for Searching and Browsing E-books with Particular Reference to Back-of-the-Book Index (PhD Dissertation). Department of Computer and Information Sciences, Strathclyde.

Amin, A. (2000). Recognition of printed Arabic text based on global features and decision tree learning techniques. *Pattern Recognition, 33*, 1309-1323.

Asmaa, A., & Asma, A. O. (2009). Arab children are reading preferences for e-learning programs. *Proceedings of the 2009 conference on Information Science, Technology and Applications.*

Tenopir, C., Edwards, S., King, D. W., & Wu, L. (2009). Electronic journals and changes in scholarly article seeking and reading patterns. *Aslib Proceedings, 61*(1), 5–32. doi:10.1108/00012530910932267

Collis, J. & Hussey, R. (2009). *Business research: A practical guide for undergraduate & postgraduate students.* Academic Press.

Coyle, K. (2008). E-Reading. *Journal of Academic Librarianship, 34*(2), 160–163. doi:10.1016/j.acalib.2008.01.001

Nicholas, D., Huntington, P., Hamid, R. J., Rowlands, I., Dobrowolski, T., & Tenopir, C. (2008). Viewing and reading behaviour in a virtual environment: the full- text download and what can be read into it. *ASLP Proceedings, 60*(3), 185-198.

Davis, J., Tierney, A., & Chang, E. (2005). A user adaptable user interface model to support ubiquitous user access to EIS style applications. *Computer Software and Applications Conference, 2005, COMPSAC 2005, 29th Annual International.*

Bruljn, D., Mul, S., & Oostendorp, H. (1992). The influence of screen size and text layout on the study of text. *Behaviour & Information Technology, 11*(2), 71–78. doi:10.1080/01449299208924322

Leeuw, S.D., & Rydin, I. (2007). Migrant children's digital stories. *Identity Formation and Self-Representation Through Media Production, 10*(4), 447.

DeStefano, D., & LeFevre, J. A. (2007). Cognitive load in hypertext reading: A review. *Computers in Human Behavior, 23*(3), 1616–1641. doi:10.1016/j.chb.2005.08.012

Dillon, A., Richardson, J., & McKnight, C. (1990). The effects of display size and text splitting on reading lengthy text from screen. *Behaviour & Information Technology, 9*(3), 215–227. doi:10.1080/01449299008924238

Dillon, A. (1994). *Designing usable electronic text: ergonomic aspects of human information usage.* Philadelphia, PA: Taylor & Francis. doi:10.4324/9780203470343

Dyson, M. C., & Kipping, G. J. (1997). The legibility of screen formats: Are three columns better than one? *Computers & Graphics, 21*(6), 703–712. doi:10.1016/S0097-8493(97)00048-4

Easterby-Smith, M., Thorpe, R., & Lowe, A. (2002). *Management research: an introduction.* London: SAGE.

Elgohary, A. (2008). Arab universities on the web: A webometric study. *The Electronic Library, 26*(3), 374–386. doi:10.1108/02640470810879518

Foltz, P. W. (1996). *Comprehension, Coherence and Strategies in Hypertext and Linear Text.* Hypertext and Cognition. Retrieved from http://www-psych.nmsu.edu/~pfoltz/reprints/Ht-Cognition.html

Godoy, D., Schiaffino, S., & Amandi, A. (2004). Interface agents personalizing web-based tasks – special issue on intelligent agents and data mining for cognitive systems. *Cognitive Systems Research, 5*(3), 207–222. doi:10.1016/j.cogsys.2004.03.003

Grainger, J., & Jacobs, A. M. (1996). Orthographic processing in visual word recognition: A multiple read-out model. *Psychological Review, 103*(3), 228–244. doi:10.1037/0033-295X.103.3.518 PMID:8759046

Hartley, J., & Burnhill, P. (1977). Fifty guide-lines for improving instructional text. *Programmed Learning and Educational Technology Research and Development, 14*(1), 65–73.

Hausenblas, H. A., Carron, A. V., & Mack, D. E. (1997). Application of the theories of reasoned action and planned behavior to exercise behavior: A meta-analysis. *Journal of Sport & Exercise Psychology, 19*(1), 36–51. doi:10.1123/jsep.19.1.36

Huang, D., Rau, P. P., & Liu, Y. (2009). Effects of font size, display resolution and task type on reading Chinese fonts from mobile devices. *International Journal of Industrial Ergonomics, 39*(1), 81–89. doi:10.1016/j.ergon.2008.09.004

Information. (2005). *Report and recommendations of the Eighteenth Meeting of the Arab team in charge of preparations for the World Summit on the Information Society.* Author.

Creswell, J. W., & Clark, V. P. (2007). *Designing & conducting mixed methods research.* London: Sage Publications.

Kol, S., & Schcolink, M. (2000). Enhancing Screen Reading Strategies. *CALICO Journal, 18*(1), 67–80.

Korat, O. (2010). Reading electronic books as a support for vocabulary, story comprehension and word reading in kindergarten and first grade. *Computers & Education, 55*(1), 24–31. doi:10.1016/j.compedu.2009.11.014

Lee, D., Shieh, K., Jeng, S., & Shen, I. (2008). Effect of character size and lighting on legibility of electronic papers. *Displays, 29*(1), 10–17. doi:10.1016/j.displa.2007.06.007

Mash, S. D. (2003). Libraries, books, and academic freedom. *Academe, 89*(3), 50–55. doi:10.2307/40252470

Marchionini, G. (1995). *Information seeking in electronic environment.* New York: Cambridge University Press. doi:10.1017/CBO9780511626388

Lonsdale, M.D.S., Dyson, M. C., & Reynolds, L. (2006). Reading in examination- type situations: the effects of text layout on performance. *Research in Reading, 29*(4), 433-453.

Muter, P. (1996). *Interface design and optimization of reading of continuous text.* Cognitive Aspects of Electronic Text Processing.

Muter, P., & Maurutto, P. (1991). Reading and skimming form computer screen and books: The paperless office revisited? *Behaviour & Information Technology, 10*, 257–266. doi:10.1080/01449299108924288

American National Standard. (1988). *Human Factors Engineering of Visual Display Terminal Workstations A. H. S. N. 100-1988.* Santa Monica, CA: Author.

Noorhidawati, A., & Forbes, G. (2008). Students attitudes towards e-books in a Scottish higher education institute: Part 1. *Library Review, 57*(8), 593–605. doi:10.1108/00242530810899577

Lam, P., Lam, S. L., & McNaught, C. (2009). Usability and usefulness of ebooks on PPCs. *Australasian Journal of Educational Technology, 25*(1), 30–44. doi:10.14742/ajet.1179

Rogers, M., & Roncevic, M. (2002). E-book aftermath: Three more publishers fold electronic imprints. *Library Journal, 127*(1), 4.

Saunders, M., Lewis, P., & Thornhill, A. (2007). *Research Methods for Business Students.* Prentice Hall.

Seale, C., & Gobo, G. (Eds.). (2006). *Ethical issues.* London: SAGE.

Shirali-shahreza, M. H., & Shirali-shahreza, S. (2006). Persian/ Arabic text font estimation using dots. *IEEE International Symposium on Signal Processing and Information Technology,* 420-425. doi:10.1109/ISSPIT.2006.270838

Shu, H., Zhou, W., Yan, M., & Kliegl, R. (2010). Font size modulates saccade- target selection in Chinese reading. *Attention, Perception & Psychophysics, 73*(2), 482–490. doi:10.3758/s13414-010-0029-y PMID:21264735

Singhal, M. (1999). *The effects of reading strategy instruction on the reading comprehension, reading process and strategy use of adult SL readers* (PhD Thesis).

Sun, Y. (2007). *Using the organizational and narrative thread structures in an E- book to support comprehension* (PhD Dissertation). Computing, The Robert Gordon University.

Terras, M. (2005). Reading the Readers: Modelling Complex Humanities Processes to Build cognitive System. *Literary and Linguistic Computing, 20*(1), 41–59. doi:10.1093/llc/fqh042

Thissen, F., (2004). *Screen design manual: Communicating effectively through multimedia.* Springer.

Eldabi, T., Irani, Z., Paul, J., & Love, P. E. D. (2002). Quantitative and qualitative decision-making methods in simulation modelling. *Management Decision, 40*(1), 64–73. doi:10.1108/00251740210413370

Wastlund, E., Norlander, T., & Archer, T. (2008). The effect of page layout on mental workload: A dual-task experiment. *Computers in Human Behavior, 24*(3), 1229–1245. doi:10.1016/j.chb.2007.05.001

White, A. (2007). Understanding hypertext cognition: Developing mental models to aid users' comprehension. *First Monday, 1.*

Dyson, M. C. (2004). How physical text layout affects reading from screen. *Behaviour & Information Technology, 23*(6), 377–393. doi:10.1080/01449290410001715714

Wiggins, R. H. (1977). Effects of three typographical variables on speed of reading. *Visible Language, 1*, 5–18.

Wright, P., & Lickorish, A. (1988). Colour cues as location aids in lengthy texts on screen and paper. *Behaviour & Information Technology, 7*(1), 11–30. doi:10.1080/01449298808901860

Sun, Y. C. (2003). Extensive reading online: An overview and evaluation. *Journal of Computer Assisted Learning, 19*(4), 438–446. doi:10.1046/j.0266-4909.2003.00048.x

Reimer, Y. J., Brimhall, E., Cao, C., & OReilly, K. (2009). Empirical user studies inform the design of an e- note taking and information assimilation system for students in higher education. *Computers & Education, 52*(4), 893–913. doi:10.1016/j.compedu.2008.12.013

Youngman, M., & Scharff, L. (1998). *Text width and margin width influences.* South Western Psychological Association.

ENDNOTE

[1]   The standard definition of normal visual acuity.

Chapter 7
Reading from Screen:
Theoretical and Empirical Background

Azza A Abubaker
Benghazi University, Libya

Joan Lu
University of Huddersfield, UK

ABSTRACT

This research aims to deliver the fundamental, theoretical and empirical background surrounding electronic reading. It is structured into five sections starting with a reading definition, reading process, and a comparison between reading from paper and from an electronic format. The fourth section discusses the variables that influence reading electronic texts. These variables are classified into three categories: the individual or user variables (age, gender, experience and educational level); the text layout variables (font type and size, line length, spaces between lines of text, colour); and the applied technology (hardware and software). In the fifth section, a summary of previous studies is given and a framework for these variables is suggested based on the previous surveys.

READING DEFINITION

From the history of research on the topic of reading, researchers put forward a set of definitions, but it is to be noted that the majority of them focused on one concept without providing a clear definition of the concept of reading to make it incomprehensible to all elements that related to reading. One of these definitions classified reading as an active process, self-directed by the reader in many ways and for different purposes (Gibson & Levin 1976). Others believe it is a complex, rule-based system that must be imposed on biological structures that were designed or evolved for other reasons (Malicky & Norman, 1989). Still, others consider reading as extracting information from the text. Furthermore, children's reading is usually defined according to the brain structure (Frey & Fisher 2010), where the brain is divided into three areas in the early stages of learning: the prefrontal cortex, the parietal cortex, and the cerebellum (Kosslyn & Rosenberg, 2004). Therefore, reading occurs only through the intentional appropriation of existing structures within the brain.

DOI: 10.4018/978-1-5225-1884-6.ch007

Generally, reading aims to create a comprehensive understanding of the text. This requires from the designer of the text a good organised text, with a clear structure and clear links between words (Malicky G., & Norman C.A., 1989). In addition, Kenneth Moorman and Ashwin Ram (1994) defined reading as the cognitive task of understanding a text.

Based on the above, reading is both a bodily and mental process, and it is difficult to describe it because it is one of those deep and complex phenomena involving the human brain. Moreover, it is a complex interaction between the text and the reader, shaped by the reader's prior knowledge, experiences, attitude, and language community which is culturally and socially determined. The complexity of the process of reading can be attributed to the absence of a comprehensive definition and that each definition focuses only on one side, perhaps because of the complexity of the reading process.

In addition, Harrison (2000) classified reading into six types:

1. Skimming through the content,
2. Reading to answer a specific question,
3. Reading to learn,
4. Reading to critique,
5. Reading to cross-reference,
6. Reading to support listening.

From the above, it can be concluded that the reading process goes through several stages, making it difficult to narrow it down to a single definition or model of reading, as we shall see in the next section.

READING PROCESS

Before describing and discussing the process of reading, it is important to give a brief definition of the reading process by referring to it as a manner of reciting or acting with the text. In other words, it is a method that the reader follows when reading any type of material. However, the reading process varies according to the type of information and other factors such as the text size, organization, and search tools. For example, the organization of an article is different from that of a book, conference paper, or report. Therefore, we must investigate the reading process for each type and genre of information by defining the differences between them, which will help outline the requirements of each type.

On the other hand, many would think that reading online is similar to reading from paper but looking at it more deeply from a transactional perspective, electronic reading is actually more complex as it imposes on readers to learn reading skills such as decoding, fluency and synthesizing.

Discussing the reading process can have two dimensions. The first dimension focuses on investigating how readers create sense when reading electronic or a paper text, where in researchers apply different theories such as the cueing system theory or the transactional theory to define reading strategies and good reading skills. In the second dimension, which is applied in this research, the reading process is examined to define how readers deal with the physical entity of information (Eagleton and Dobler, 2006).

In addition, asking questions like "why, what and how people read a document" have been made by several researchers in different fields of research such as psychology and education whose concern is building theories on how a child learns to read and develop cognitive and linguistic skills; whereas, linguistics has been concerned principally with the analysis of speed and only give passing mention of writing systems and reading. Meanwhile, researchers in the field of usability are focused on addressing these questions which are used in the first stage of any research into the reading generally and e-reading specifically. Moreover, focusing attention on cognitive and behavioural aspects of the reader by asking why and how the reader reads a text brings forth issues related to the context which affects the presentation. From previous research, there are different reading processes which will be classified into:

- Reading process according to the type of sources.
- Reading process according to ways of designing and presenting the text.

Reading Process According to the Type of Sources

The reading process differs on the basis of the type of information resources as mentioned by many researchers. For example, Andrew (Dillon 2001) investigated the reasons for people wanting to access journals, and the author reported that students access journals for numerous reasons such as: answering a particular question (73%), keeping up with developments in an area (46%), or for personal interest (20%). Moreover, Figures 1 and 2 present the reading process in two different types of material, providing clear evidence that the reading process changes according to the type of reading material. For example,

Figure 1. Generic model of journal usage
Dillon, 2001.

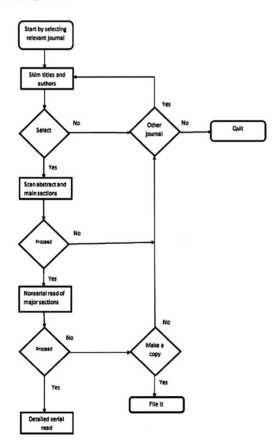

Figure 2. Generic model of manual usage

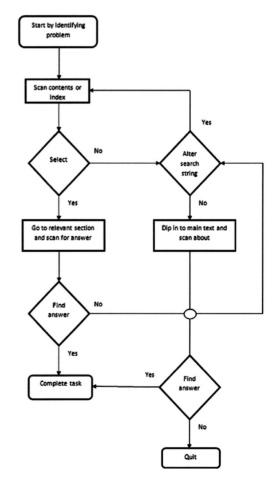

readers only skim through the titles when reading journals, while they scan the contents or index to get a general idea of the work rather than select related sections and scan for answer.

Alternatively, Meliss Terras (2005) provided a model to explain how experts read ancient texts, using a qualitative method [content analysis, focused interviews and think aloud protocols] to build their model. Researcher found that three experts use different methods to examine the document; they also spent a long time checking the text and the word in a different order. In addition, they deal with visual features and then build up knowledge about the document (see Figure 3).

These two studies provided strong evidence that the reading process differs according to the type of information resources and the reading's aim. To be sure, the reading process is quite different, from a child who reads a picture book to the mature reader who extracts information from highly specialized texts in mathematics, logic or physics. Thus, the researcher expects that the reading process for a schoolbook should also be different (Dillon 2001; Terras 2005; Abubaker and Lu 2011).

The Reading Process through Linear and Non-Linear Design

The other issue that drew the attention of researchers in the field of e-reading is the reading process in terms of the text design which may be classified into two categories: linear and non-linear (hypertext) design. Presenting text using linear design allows reader starting at the beginning and reading to the end while nonlinear design (hypertext) design allows reader browse through the sections of the text, jumping from one text section to another and so on.

Figure 3. A model that explains how experts read ancient texts
(Terras, 2005)

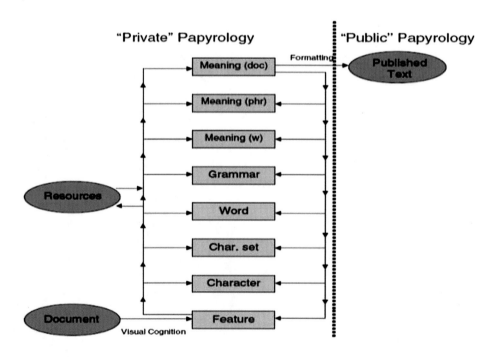

For example, D. DeStefano (2005) presented a model showing the steps followed by the reader when reading a hypertext as seen in Figure 3 where the amount of nodes and the reading process are distinct when reading a hypertext structure. As can be noted, the reading process in this format is not under control and can change according to the readers' prior knowledge and skills.

There are different types of hypertext: (1) Hierarchical hypertext (2) Additional links; (3) Semantic links and (4) Networked hypertext. Each type has a different effect depending on the type of text and the purpose of reading. For example, hierarchical is better for the readers' memory than network.

In addition, researchers on non-liner structure have focused on the effect of the reader's navigation path by exploring the relationship between reading method and comprehension, and reported different strategies of navigation used by readers according to users, knowledge seekers, features, and apathetic hypertext (Dillon 2001). In addition, changing the order of the text could influence comprehension in a liner text which is affected by different criteria such as the logical order versus random. More research needs to be done to cover this area in order to determine the difference as well as the negative and positive impacts.

However, the debate about factors affecting the reading process is extended to investigate the readers' cognitive process. For instance, Panayiota et al., (2007) examined the impact of epistemic beliefs and on-line text structure by reading refutation and non-refutation scientific text using the think-aloud method. They reported a significant impact of text structure on reading comprehension. On the other hand, there is no difference in the total amount of information recalled between students who have more or less prior knowledge.

In addition, numerous studies in visual research that investigate the effect of the number of links on the process of browsing, reading and learning by measuring the speed of the search for information or word such as (Cress and Knabel 2003; Lin 2004; DeStefano and LeFevre 2007) concluded that there is an inverse relationship between the number of links and cognitive.

Moreover, the construction integration model has received much attention among researchers on hypertext comprehension. The model pointed to several elements that affect text comprehension, with an

Figure 4. Process model of hypertext reading
(De Stefano and LeFevre, 2005)

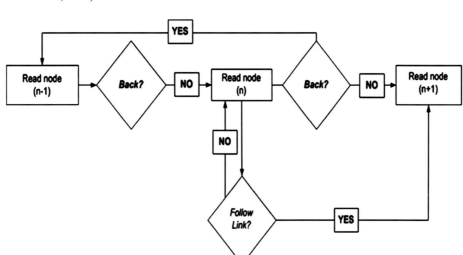

emphasis on prior knowledge and coherence as a key element affecting comprehension (Yoh, Damhorst et al., 2003). However, most research used these two models to define reading stages on hypertext by analysing the navigation path, order of reading, and the number of nodes that the reader followed to access the information. These reported a significant effect of prior knowledge, reader skills and education level on the path of reading (W Kintsch 2004. Ajzen 2011).

Alternatively, in the case of reading to learn learners are more positive with fewer nodes in comprehension reading (Ajzen 2011). On the other hand, the reading time is not affected by the number of links. Such findings assist designers to create the tool that commensurate with the requirements of readers, for instance, create a map illustrating the path of the reader in the text or determine the strength of the relationship between text and links.

THEORIES BEING APPLIED IN THE READING FIELD

Examining previous studies shows a mixture of theories being applied by researchers and are related to using technology such as the eBook and the Internet. These theories could be classified according to the aspects that deal with it or even by the methods used to achieve their goals. In this context, it can be classified into three perspectives;

Theoretical Perspectives on (Dealing with) Human Behaviour

This type of theories is for the reader in the sociology and psychology field which focused on understanding and analysing user behaviour and attitudes generally. It focuses attention on the behavioural aspects of the reader and studies its interaction with the different types of information technology. Looking at previous research shows that there are three theories that have been used before in the analysis of human behaviour in terms of using information technology (e.g. using the Internet).

We may begin with the social cognitive theory (SCT) which was provided by Bandura (A. 1986). It is used in different fields such as psychology, education and communication. It focused on three aspects: behavioural, personal, and environmental factors. It stemmed from the area of social learning. Alternatively, according to this theory, human behaviour has an impact on the environment and thus must be studied and understood in order to determine the extent of its impact on the environment. This can help create a synergy (balance) between the user and the product, and can also deliver a product that takes into account the nature of human behaviour. In the same context, the theory proves that a large part of human behaviour is acquired. On the other hand, some have argued that the theory is always applied to studying self-efficiency.

From our standpoint, it is difficult to accept that only this theory can activate the use of electronic texts. And that is because there are various aspects affecting the reading process such as language, text structure, technology, and so on. In addition, the theory refers to human behaviour without providing explanations as to the effect of the product on user behaviour. This could be adjusted or linked to other theories that could be used in determining the student's interaction with the text in a hard or e-copy. Defining this interaction will differ depending on the type of reading media as well as the factors that caused those differences.

The second is the Reasoned Action Theory (RAT) which concerns understanding and explaining human behaviour in different areas, where it is assumed that behaviour is affected by other opinions either negatively or positively. In addition, it is based on two aspects: attitudes and norms (to predict behavioural intent) (Hausenblas, Carron et al., 1997). Theoretical perspectives illustrate that research connected to IT begins with this theory to understand the effect of the opinion of others who are considered as part of the users' surrounding. In this study, the student is usually influenced by the information types and education system. Each one requires different skills, abilities and influence.

Davis first proposed the technology acceptance model based on (RAT). The model has been applied to expound or inspect individual behaviours by focusing on two theoretical constructs: perceived usefulness and perceived ease of use. It is provided with strong behavioural elements and allows the person to act without limitation. Venkatesh and Davis then developed the model and introduced it for the first time into management science (Venkatesh and Davis 2000). It covers extra strategic elements that concern social influence and cognitive instrumental processes for recognizing their effect on the target system.

Because of the limitations of the reasoned action theory (RAT) in dealing with behaviour, Ajzen (1991) proposed a planned behaviour theory (PBT) by introducing a third independent determinant of intention. According to the PBT, human activities are dictated by three types of attitude: behavioural beliefs, normative beliefs, and control beliefs. These three elements give additional opportunity to the person for more action and thus will increase the person's chance of delivering a desired action.

However, several researchers have effectively applied this theory in IT acceptance, e.g. (Bobbitt and Dabholkar, 2001, Yoh et al., 2003)(Truong 2009). These theories all agree on being designed to study human behaviour, but they differ in the comprehensiveness of certain elements; for example, the theory of reasoned action focused only on two elements; attitude [*the main predictor of behavioural intention when self- influence is stronger than perceived subjective norm*] and subjective norm [*the main predictor of a behavioural intention for behaviours in which normative implications are dominant*], while the planned behaviour theory adds a third element: perceived behavioural control (Icek Ajzen 1991). In addition, the decomposed theory of planned behaviour adds a new branch for each element of the preceding ones; for instance, it defines three antecedents of attitude, namely, perceived ease of use, perceived usefulness, and compatibility.

Text-Focused, Theoretical Perspectives Classified into Two Categories

The first category consists of theories that emphasise on structure of the text such as rhetorical structure theory (RST), computational or natural language generational. These types of theories are usually built on the perspective of linguists who are not considered in this research. The second category focuses on the text format such as the linear and non- linear system theory (see reading process section).

The visual attention theory (VAT) aimed to understand and explain the visual process and identify the factors that affect visibility. It was first presented in 1990 by Bundesen (Bundesen 1990); according to this theory, it aims to analyse two aspects (recognition and access), an any object recognized at the same time was picked or selected. This is contrary to the previously reported theory by Broadbent (1958) who thought that selection occurs prior to recognition, while J.A. Deutsch & D. Deutsch (1963) provided just the opposite. It is notable that the theory did not address the factors associated with visual recognition, while Vidyasagar (TR and K 1999) highlighted part of these factors such as colour, texture and form but it concerned with determining the visual process without addressing the factors that impact visibility. In spite of many barriers to online reading, the visibility problem is defined as an initial hypothesis for reading difficulty. This thought was based on several experimental researches concerning the reasons that cause visual deficit. These agreed that unstable visual display of words or characters is one of many reasons that causes reading difficulty such as a dorsal stream deficit (de Boer-Schellekens and Vroomen 2005).

Theoretical Perspectives Dealing with the Reading Process

Previous studies show that there is limitation in the studies that focused on explaining the reading process. Ingrid Fontanni (2004) provides a good and clear overview of reading theories that aim to explain the transformation of information. The study concluded that reading is a complex cognitive process that goes through various steps such as reorganizing a text and linking information. These processes are influenced by several factors related to the reader and text. In addition, Gernsbacher provided a framework (structure building) that describes the cognitive process. The model considers the new input as a fundamental stage where the reader in this stage may slow down but then in the next stage the memory maps it (Fontanini 2004).

In addition, the landscape model was used to provide a conceptual framework of the reading process, as it helps to understand the complex factors that impact the reading process. This model is just focused on the cognitive process that occurs during reading and directs readers' attention to specific textual content and their effect on memory without considering the effect of typographic factors in reading such as font type and size (Linderholm 2004) because of their ability to show the readers` purpose for reading and their background knowledge during the reading process. Information processing theory suggested that the human mind works as a computer system through following logical rules and strategies when processing information. The theory confirmed that changes made in the hardware will improve the computer's processing of information, so, changing the reading rules and strategies they have learned will lead to improving the reading of online texts (Swanson 1987). On the other hand, the reader response theory (RRT) has been applied in several studies to understand the action of the reader, showing clearly the relationship between three elements that are basic to any reading process: text, author and reader, as seen in Figure 5 (Swanson 1987).

In addition, the related literature shows that there are two approaches to (RRT): the phenomenological approach and epistemological approach. According into Fish (Hirvela 1996), the theory is focused on the reader's response where the readers control their reactions to the text, while Iser (1978) thinks that the reader is free to make a response based on the text where there is no right or wrong way.

Figure 5. The element of the reading process based on Reader Response Theory
(Swanson, 1987)

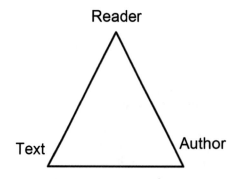

Applying this theory to explain the reading process of a schoolbook shows the missing elements that play a significant role in reading schoolbooks. Where two elements should be added [teacher and parent] when dealing with schoolbook. These two elements cannot ignore in this study where students usually get support from their parents at home and teachers at school; therefore, modification has been made on the basic theory (RRT) in this research by adding two elements: teachers and parents, as seen in Figure 6. Data Collected on experiment (1) conformed the importance of the role of these two.

In this model, the text is presented in the middle of the reading process wherein all the other elements deal with the text at different levels with different methods. However, the reader comes in at the top of the diamond shape while parents and teachers are found at the same level.

FACTORS THAT AFFECT THE READING PERFORMANCE

Based on analysis of more than 89 studies concerned, an investigation into the variables affecting usability of electronic content framework was suggested. 67.5% of these studies were carried out in the 1990s. An overview of these studies shows a good number of factors that affect reading generally. The average effect of these factors differs, however. For example, Dillon (1992) at the end of an empirical research that investigates differences between reading electronic text and paper text concluded that no one variable is likely responsible for the difference in reading performance between the two formats, and identifying a single factor without identifying all the relevant issues will only lead to misunderstanding. Dyson (2004) defines the text layout variables in terms of line length, columns, window size, and inter-linear spacing. This attempt cannot be considered as an integrated variable that covers all the factors for it neglected other variables as font size that was considered very influential, whereas the study confirmed the relation between variables through reviewing other works such as (LUND 1999).

From our standpoint, the factors could be classified into two groups: factors related to the usability of e-content, and legibility factors related to reading online texts. A third group is related to users or readers included in demographic characteristics, educational levels and experiences.

Figure 6. The relationship between the fie elements in the reading process of school textbook

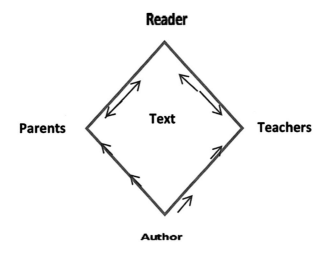

Individual Variables

Firstly, age has been reported in most usability empirical studies than any other demographic variable. Although more research are related to age difference in using e- content have reported mixed results, other studies have also shown that older users are expected to deal with electronic text more effectively than younger users (Cheyne 2005). Unfortunately, differences in age have not been theoretically discussed to clarify causes of such differences. Alternatively, understanding age difference in reading from a screen will help define difficulties, requirements and the nature of the use which will lead to an enhanced higher level of usability of e-content than ever before. There are 132 studies in reading from screen which could be classified into different categories such as factors affecting reading, reading process and application. These studies did not focus on the relationship between the reader's age and reading from a screen. In the same perspective, some studies revealed that age had a significant impact on the usability of e-text. The significant differences concern types of material, text format, line length and window size. Therefore, more research still needs to be done to clarify the effect of this variable on reading online. Generally speaking, findings of empirical studies across many countries clearly show that age is the most researched variable more than any other demographic variables (12 studies). This clearly indicates that age ought to be considered as a key demographic variable (e.g. Miller and Gagne 2008).

Secondly, the relationship between gender and reading from screen has been investigated in the literature on human-computer interaction by many researchers such as (Cheyne 2005). Mixed results have shown that while some (Liu and Huang 2007) have indicated that gender is positively and significantly correlated with reading from screen, others have found no such significant relationship. For example, 3 studies (Sellen and Harpter 2002, Liu 2006, Liu and Huang 2007) reported few significant results as to the effect of gender on online reading, whereas three other researchers indicated significant findings. Overall, empirical studies regarding the role of gender in reading from screen have continued to produce inconsistent and mixed results. Of the 123 studies reviewed, none or few pointed to any significant impacts or relationship.

In addition, the educational level and use of e-text have been studied in the literature on human computer interface to define their influence on reading from screen. In early research, some researchers argued that educational level does not appear to have an impact on reading online, whereas others have suggested that a significant relationship between the two exists. On the other hand, some researchers found online reading to be positively impacted by educational level and these researchers argued that educational level is one of the crucial variables. Some did not consider educational level at all such as Noorhidawati (2008). Finally, in the current review, it is clear that educational level had no significant relationship with reading online. The remaining three showed some statistical difference in reading from screen based on educational level.

Usability Factors Affecting the Use of E-Content

Several researches try to address the factors that affect the usability of electronic Book by comparing it with paper book using different theories and methods, some of which merely focus on general aspects while others go into it more thoroughly. For example, the main web design guidelines (Powell 2000) classify usability factors into six categories (as seen in Figure 7), where the logical structure and navigation were outlined as important factors affecting usability with more emphasis on navigation as the

Figure 7. Powell's factors of Web usability
(Powell, 2000)

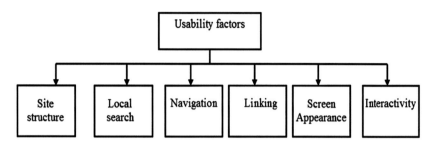

main factor that affects the content structure. These six factors could be accepted as general factors, but defining the elements of each factor is needed.

Moreover, according to Nielsen (2000) there are two main factors that affect using e- content (as seen in Figure 8): page design and content design. However, there is a certain deficiency in this classification which ignores elements related to page design such as font size, margin, spaces between lines, colour and location of the text. Moreover, it included elements not strongly related to this factor such as page linking which was defined as part of page design and the speed of reading access which usually depends on the type of technology being used. In addition, content design concerns elements such as the number of words per line, sentence structure, and headings.

In the same context, IBM web guide emphasises four elements: structure, navigation, visual layout, and content (IBM 2005). The guide recommends using different structures depending on the type of information. Alternatively, the guide focused on access to technologies that use screen resolution and size. Moreover, IBM differs from previous guides in how it implements media in different content types and sizes.

Generally, these models and usability guidelines are concerned with explaining the factors that affect the usability of websites more than reading eBook and have been applied by researchers to evaluate websites such as (Chau, Au et al., 2000; Agarwal and Venkatesh 2002; First 2005; Robert, Paul et al., 2008; Nathan and Yeow 2011). Whereas, examining the usability area shows a lacuna in the literature that examines the usability and legibility of electronic texts.

Figure 8. Nielsen's factors of Web usability
(Nielsen, 2000)

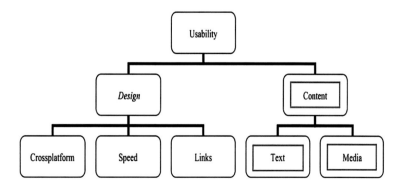

The studies on technology usability models show the insufficiency in these models, although there are several studies that focused on investigating the factors that influence using e-content through various technologies. Table 1 displays five models that are applied in the majority of usability research. As can be noted, each model focuses on one aspect. Therefore, a comprehensive model that covers all the influential factors is needed.

Most researchers who are interested in reading agree that there are several factors that influence reading speed, accuracy, and comprehension. In addition, there are a number of empirical studies that provide strong evidence about the effect of these factors on reading from paper media. On the other hand, there is limited research addressing all the aspects related to reading from screen. For example, the findings of Kruk and Muter (Kruk and Muter 1984) drew attention to differences between displaying a text on screen and paper, by presenting the text using the same structure of a paper book. The findings also show the difficulty of reading online texts that are presented using a paper structure. No wonder, the number of empirical studies in the field of human computer interface with focus on displaying text on screen has increased (Nai-Shing, Jie-Li et al., 2011). But at the same time, the relationship between optimising reading from screen and text layout is still unclear (MUTER 1996). Even though there are many studies that measure the average influence of layout text on reading from screen, the picture is still relatively underdeveloped because of the limited evidence over the effect of text layout on the different methods of reading (Dyson 2004).

Table 1. Factors influencing the use of e- content based on five usability models

Factors	WUM	TAM	UTAUT	MOPTAM (Kotzé 2007)
Site structure	Yes	No	No	No
Local search	Yes	No	No	No
Navigation	Yes	No	No	No
Linking	Yes	No	No	No
Content	No	No	No	No
Visual layout	No	No	No	No
Screen appearance	Yes	No	No	No
Interactivity	Yes	Yes	Yes	Yes
Social influence	No	Yes	Yes	Yes
Behavioural intention	No	Yes	Yes	Yes
Easy to use	No	Yes	Yes	Yes
Attitude	No	Yes	No	Yes
Actual system use		Yes	No	Yes
Personal factors	No	No	No	No
Facilitating conditions	No	Yes	No	No
Perceived usefulness	Yes	Yes	No	No
Demographic	No	Yes	No	Yes
Learning influence	No	No	No	No
Content language	No	No	No	No

Legibility Factors

Several studies that focused on investigating typographical factors such as (Alotaibi 2007; Zhang, Shu et al., 2007; Der-Song Lee, Kong-King Shieh et al., 2008; Wastlund, Norlander et al., 2008; Huang, Patrick Rau et al., 2009; Shu, Zhou et al., 2010; Nai-Shing, Jie-Li et al., 2011) emphasise different factors such as font size, line length, margin, font and background colour, and line space. The majority of these researches applied using Latin or China script while in this research, three factor [font size, font type and line length] have been studied in detail using Arabic script. Selecting these three typographical factors set depend on the findings of previous research that confirmed it as the most influential as can be noted during the presentation in the next section (Der-Song Lee, Kong-King Shieh et al., 2008; Shu, Zhou et al., 2010).

Font Type and Size

Font size is one of the typographical factors that have received considerable attention by researchers interested in studying displaying texts on screen through investigating their effect on reading speed and accuracy. The findings of these researchers could be classified into three groups. The first group reported a significant impact of font size and type on electronic reading (Bernard 2002; Hedrick 2002; Bernard, Chaparro et al., 2003; Maria dos santos Lonsdale 2006). The second group reported a limited effect. The third group reported no effect (Chen and Chien 2005; Shu, Zhou et al., 2010). However, the points usually used to measure the size of the letters include the cap high of the letters plus a small interval of space above and below the letters. Points are also used to measure the distance between lines.

In the same perspective, the studies that confirmed the effect of font size and type did not agree on the optimal size and type that could be considered as standards for designing e-text. For example, Bernard et al., (2002) tested three different font sizes (10, 12, and 14 points) with 8 font types using a sample of 20 participants aged 18 to 55. They were asked to read passages of over 1000 words. The study reported that speed and accuracy were affected by font size, and font size at 12 point size was read faster than at 10 point and posited a relationship between speed reading and font size. This finding goes in the same line as Shurtleff (1967) and the National findings (National 1988). Furthermore, the findings of research by Smith (1996) indicated that characters' height has a significant effect on search time and accuracy, e.g. the average accuracy rate was about 91% in 2.2 mm. This average decreased to 81% in size 1.4 mm, and in 3.3 mm the search speed increased but decreased when the characters' height was up to 3.3m. Consequently, Jayeeta et al., (Banerjee, Majumdar et al., 2011) reported that there was no statistical difference in the reading speed between font size 10 and 12, while some researchers pointed out that the readable font size starts from 14 point such as (Banerjee et al., 2011).

Furthermore, few researchers such as Chien and Chen (2005) argued that increasing the size did not necessarily improve the perception of legibility. Kolers & Duchnicky (1981) debated whether smaller characters with more characters per line are read faster. Also, font type was reported as influential variables but this impact is not as strong as the font size reported as the main factor affecting a reading from screen. Vrinda font size 14 was reported as the most readable font followed by Arial in the same size, while Times New Roman was the worst (JE, MV et al., 2005; Banerjee, Majumdar et al., 2011). This finding was rejected by Banerjee (2011) who pointed out that Times New Roman font size 10 and 12 are like size 14 of Courier New font.

Overall, it is notable that most of the studies compared just two font types (RW, HL et al., 1993; Banerjee, Majumdar et al., 2011) which makes drawing conclusion difficult and in some cases researchers did not justify their selection. A justified text can be very readable if the designer ensures that the spacing between letters and words is consistent. Italics reduced the legibility of characterise and words (Sheedy, Subbaram et al., 2005). Otherwise, other researchers in typographic literature (e.g.Banerjee et al, 2011) believed that serifs have a significant impact on the readability of texts on screen because they reckoned serifs increased letter discriminability.

In general, the findings of empirical studies across several conditions show that font size is the main typographical factor affecting the display of texts on screen. What is more, this factor is affected by other variables such as font type and line length but to draw a clearer conclusion, more research should be done to consider such relationships. Table 2 provides summary to the main findings of research that have been done in this area.

Line Length

The line length of the text was considered to be one of several typographical factors that affected reading speed and comprehension. Line length is measured in typographic units (picas), which are used to increase or reduce the amount of space between letters. Other researchers used units of inch and centimetre, while resent studies attempted to measure line length using a totally number of characters. In addition, eye movement, reading speed and average of errors are common methods used to identify optimal line length which may explain the difference in the findings. (Randolph and Anuj 2005) divided the factors affected by line length according to the analysis by several previous studies as follows: (1) subjective factors such as ease of reading and user preference and satisfaction; (2) objective factors such as comprehension and reading rate.

Looking at the related research did not provide a clear answer on this issue, upon which mix findings were reported (Randolph and Anuj 2005). For example, according to Creed et al., (1987), one column

Table 2. Summary the main findings related to font size

	Findings
Font size	• Use a serif for the main text (Maria dos Santos Lonsdale, 2006)(Russell-Minda, Jutai et al., 2007). • Increasing size did not necessarily improve the perception of legibility (BERNARD 2002). • 10, 11 & 12 points are readable size for Latin alphabet (Wijnholds 1997; Maria dos santos Lonsdale 2006). • Smaller characters with more characters per line are read faster. • Size 14 point is more comfortable, ease for reading and reading fatigue than size 10 (Chan and Lee, 2005, Nai-Shing et al., 2011) (Chinese language). • Size 10 and 12 are readable size for reading Arabic print text (Alotaibi, 2007, Bernard, 2002). • Font size had no effect on reading efficiency (BERNARD 2002; Chen and Chien 2005). • Most international standards suggest 16 & 22 as minimum size for good reading of Latin alphabet (Smith 1996). • Creating spaces between words is more useful than increased font size of the words (Shu, Zhou et al., 2010).
Font type	• Times New Roman was read faster in Arabic print text (Alotaibi 2007). • Arab children's performance improve when using Simplified Arabic font with font size 12 point or Arial Unicode with font size 14 point (Asmaa and Asma 2009). • There was no difference between Arial and TNR (M, B et al., 2003). • Arial sans serif to be preferred over TNR serif, serif font in size 10, 12 & 14 point, TNR is less time in size 10 & 12 similar in size 14 Courier New (Banerjee, Majumdar et al., 2011).

was read faster among younger readers (18-24 year olds), while there was no influence of column format on older readers (over 25 years old) and the reading rate was affected by the column format. This finding was also supported by Dyson and Kipping (1997) when they measured the effect of a three-column format on the reading rate and comprehension using texts from online magazines in which 18 participants read text in two situations (single column, about 80 characters per line; two columns; and three columns, about 25 characters per line). They also reported that comprehension was better for faster readers in the three-column page format. This means that a faster reader may be able to scan a short column easily. In the same context, Dillon et al., (1990) measured the comprehension and reading rate on screen using different sizes of screen [20 & 60 line]. They pointed out that there was no difference in the performance of readers. According to Duchnicky and Kolers (1983), whose experiment investigated the reading speed of text on screen, a text with 80 characters were read faster than one with 40 characters.

In addition, Youngman and Scharff (1998) calculated the optimised line length to be 100 letters and is unlikely to be as long as 123 letters. On the other hand, Dyson and Haselgrove (2001) estimated that the line length with 55 characters produces better comprehension scores than the longest line in the case of multiple choice questions. This finding was rejected by Chaparro, Shaikh et al. (2005) who claimed no significant effect of text layout on comprehension performance. And when using a comparison method between screens to measure readers' perceptions, they reported that the line length with 55 characters reads easily but were not the fastest.

Moreover, Landoni and Diaz. (2003) provide different outcomes from reading online. Based on designing two difference models, 15 inches display 60 lines and 12 inches display 23 lines. 56 participants were asked to read a "legal-sociological discourse" of around 1900 words and remember the text. They pointed out that the screen containing 23 lines were better for learning time than the one with 60 lines. Moreover, Landoni and Gibb (2000) compared three situations, two in print and one on screen. To explore reasons for the slower reading of text from screen, the survey indicated that 40 lines were read faster than 20 lines in both print and on screen. Some researchers downplayed the significance of this study because its main focus was on the print text, and is therefore not suitable for collecting empirical evidence for reading online (Dyson, 2004).

Furthermore, Yi, Park et al. (2011) surveyed the affected number of columns in the readability, comprehension and satisfaction of e-book. English is a second language for participants (22- 26-year-olds). They were asked to read a text with 400 words (2000 to 2010 characters) and answer five questions in one minute. The survey reported that participants prefer reading one column. Table 3 summarised the main findings for line length.

Randolph and Anuj (2005) provided a guideline according to the distilled studies. The guide provides general recommendations without providing explanations that show if these principles are concerned with all the differences that affect reading the text.

On the other hand, In the Chinese language, some researchers such as Nai-Shing et al., (2011) reported that double columns and double line spacing are read more comfortably than the single column. While in Arabic language, there is no study providing empirical evidence for optimal line length for reading online text.

Thus, the effect of the column format still requires more thinking to cover these aspects. Most of these surveys prove the effect of scrolling on reading. And they were limited to showing just the favourite display format without providing any explanations as to why the reader prefers this and why he/she dislikes the other format. Also, could this decision be affected by the type of reading? This type of question should be asked by researchers when doing this kind of research.

Table 3. Summary of the main recommendations of studies that focused on line length

Line Length	• Between 60- 70 characters and additional interlinear space of 1 to 4 points (Maria dos santos Lonsdale, 2006). • Long line lengths need more interlinear spacing to ensure that the eyes locate the next line down accurately (Bouma, 1980). • 132 characters per line give faster reaction time (Youngman and Scharff, 1998). • Using 2/3 screen line length improves reading speed for Arab children (Asmaa and Asma, 2009). • If the text requires headings, a single column is advisable (Hartley, 1977; Southall, 1984). • For scientific journals, a single column layout with wide margins is read more quickly (Simmonds 1994). • More target words are located with a double column (Foster, 1970; Hartley, 1978), a speed- accuracy trade- off with double columns (Creed, 1987). • People over 25 years old show no differences in reading rate across the three columns, while people aged 18-24-year-olds are faster when reading a single page column (Dyson and Kipping 1997). • No difference between single column and double column (Creed, 1987). • Single or long column read faster. (Duchnicky and Kolers, 1983; Creed, 1987; Dyson and Kipping, 1997; Youngman and Scharff, 1998; Yi, Park et al., 2011). • No influence of column format on reader over 25 year (Creed, 1987). • No influence of column format on reader (Chaparro, Shaikh et al., 2005). • Short column easy to scan by faster reader. (three column) (Dyson and Haselgrove, 2001) • Long line was preferred for reading from printed material (Landoni and Gibb, 2000).

Colour

The other variable is colour, which has been examined to define its effect on the reading process by several researchers such as (Singleton and Henderson 2006). When colour and font are combined, the visual as well as the emotional attributes of the font are enhanced. At the same time, changing the colour of the font or background can significantly affect legibility. As defined by Alan Clarke (2001), hue is what we usually call colour. Saturation is an approach that describes the cleanliness of a colour and how it varies from grey to its most pure bright form. And intensity is a measure of the lightness of a colour.

In addition, the same colour can appear very different when placed on different backgrounds, and that different colours can appear nearly the same when juxtaposed with different backgrounds. Moreover, when working with colour and type, it is important to be aware of all the ways in which colour contrasts can be accomplished. Table 4 provides some examples showing how colours interact. E.g. using solid and contrasting colours for backgrounds behind text is more acceptable for avoiding textures which may

Table 4. Contrast and legibility of text beads on colour theory

Best	Better	Good
• Black text (T) on a white background (BG). • Kashmir green T on a white BG. • Midnight blue T on a white BG. • Burnt umber T on a white BG. • Peruvian turquoise T on a BG. • Raw umber T on a white BG. • Forest green T on a white BG. • Viridian green T on a BG. • Yellow T on a black BG. • Green T on a black BG. • Cyan T on a black BG. • Magenta T on a black BG.	• Charcoal Gray T on a white BG. • Slate T on a white BG. • Navy blue T on a white BG. • Deep burnt sienna T on a BG. • Indigo Blue T on a white BG. • Prussian blue T on a white BG. • Deep burgundy T on a white BG. • Black T on a cyan BG. • Black T on a pale halo yellow green BG. • White T on a blue BG.	• Indigo blue T on an indigo blue BG. • Dark grey T on a charcoal gray BG. • Medium grey T on a charcoal gray BG. • Medium gray T on an indigo blue BG. • Goldenrod T on an indigo blue BG. • Blue T on an indigo blue BG.

Gabriel-Petit 2007.

make letterforms difficult to distinguish, while a black text on a white background offers optimal readability for texts (Gabriel-Petit 2007). In addition, according to Xue-min et al., (2007), using white with black and deep blue and blue with yellow and white were the better options for displaying Chinese text.

However, some degree of colour blindness affects about 8% of people; e.g. they cannot distinguish between red and green. Random use of colour is not going to achieve the reader's goals. It is likely to have the opposite effect, e.g. it can cause eye strain after they have completed using the reading material. Thus, to gain the positive advantages from using colour, it must be used in a systematic way to achieve a distinct objective. Moreover, the colour theory explains the relation between colour and how they work effectively together.

In addition, there are two studies (Bobbitt and Dabholkar 2001; Yoh, Damhorst et al., 2003) that have highlighted the important implications of colour on designing e-texts. These studies and others made it clear that a better background and font colour matching will enhance the text processing efficiency. But still, more research needs to cover issues such as the relationship between font colour, size, and type, or the relationship between the user's age and background colour. Research like that may help designers improve the reading from screen. On the other hand, according to Xue-min (Terras, 2005), a survey that examined 3-level background colours with 5 font colours, using white as a background was more effective with black and deep blue. And a blue background works more effetely with font colour yellow, white, and red green. Black should be avoided as a background. On the other hand, some researchers (Nes, 1986; Rubin, 1988) see that using colour may be useful in the case of emphasis or highlighting. In designing e- learning materials, text colour is normally used in (Alan, 2001).

Proposal Model

Based on the literature overview in section 2.5, it is clear that there is a range of factors control and affect display electronic text. The factors that most relevant to dealing with electronic text are collected according their relationships and interactions with each other. Then a factor affect interact with the electronic text model [FAIWETM] is proposed in Figure 8. The model is described by discussion the individual variables in section 2.5.1, usability variables in section 2.5.2 and legibility variables in section 2.5.3. These factors were divided into three groups; user, legibility and usability factors. Each group contains a number of elements which differ in their level of influence.

- **User Factors:** It is divided into two levels the first level contains four individual factors; age, gender, education level and experience which affect the intention of reading and usage behaviour. While, cognitive component set on a second level. In this research number of three of the user`s factors were considered; age, gender and education level.

- **Legibility Factors:** As illustrated in Figure 9, a number of factors have been identified as influencing legibility of electronic text. It was classified into two groups; factors related to text format and other related to text layout. In this research, the focus will be on the three factor [font size, font type and line length] which is related to text format. These three factors were addressed by most of the researchers as the most influential in reading. In addition, language was considered within this category, at the time that some researchers who deal with text format proved differences such as in defining the optimal font size or line length this difference go back into different in the writing system.

- **Usability Factors:** this group was synthesised from the factors of the web usability model by Powell (2000) and Nielsen (2000) and refined by integrating the findings of other studies on usability of electronic text that is discussed in section 2.

5. METHOD FOR EXAMINING TEXT LAYOUT

Exam the methods that used in previous studies to measure and determine the optimal design to display electronic text, showed that there are several of aspects that must be taken into account when obtaining data such as; type of collecting data, the purpose of collecting data and size of the data. Which categorizes to two parts; objective and subjective measurements as illustrated in section 1.3 (Rivera-Nivar and Pomales-García, 2010).

Most of the studies expended reading performance to measure and determine optimal layout through applying several criteria such as; reading speed, comprehension, satisfaction and behaviour. Table 5 provides a summary for the methods that applied in pervious researches. It is notably that attend between researchers to define reading performance was through two criteria; reading time and error rate when testing learning material.

In addition, selecting a suitable method should related to natural of investigating variables, e.g. studies that investigate the effect of font type and size in recall information usually operate searching time as tool to determine reading speed and comprehension used (i.e., Liu and Huang,2007; Lee, Shieh et al., 2008; Wastlund, Norlander et al., 2008; Asmaa and Asma, 2009; Korat, 2010), While, satisfaction was achieved via a satisfaction questionnaire.

On the other hand, the majority of researches used eye movement to investigate readers` behaviour when reading text (e.g. Miller & Gagne, 2008; Yen et al., 2008). Other studies operated observation to

Figure 9. Framework of factors that affect reading an e-text based on theoretical perspective

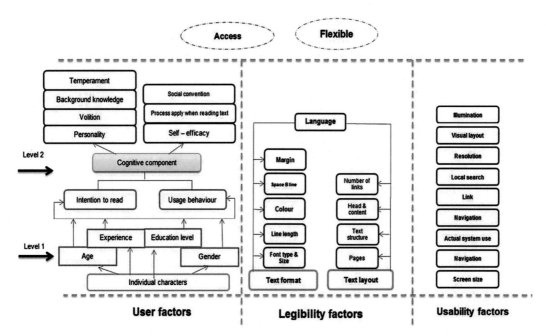

exam reading process and interactive (e.g. Fisch, 2002). Because the target population in this research are students and the testing text was used for learning purpose the reading speed and accuracy have been used to measure the reading performance. While eye movement was not considered although, it is referred to how the reader navigates through the text but mainly focus on investigating cognitive processes. Thus, the study measurements produced two types of data; objective data, which resulted from observation method, and subjective data with resulted from the questionnaire to measure the satisfaction.

Table 5. Provide a summary to the methods and tools that used

Reading Performance	Tools Collecting Data	Text Layout			Reading Process
		Font Size	Font Type	Line Length	
		References			
Reading speed	Eye movement				(Ashby & Rayner 2004; Laarnia, et al., 2004; Siegenthaler, et al., 2011)
	number of correct responses			(Ling & Schaik 2006; Yi, et al., 2011)	(Miller & Gagne 2008)
	Time to read task	(Bernard, Frank et al., 2001; Russell and Chaparro 2001; Feely, Rubin et al., 2005; Sheedy, Subbaram et al., 2005; Alotaibi 2007; AYAMA, et al., 2007; Huang, et al., 2009)	(Bernard, et al., 2001; Dillon, et al., 2004; Poole 2005; Sheedy, Subbaram et al., 2005; Alotaibi 2007)	(Shaikh 2005; Sheedy, et al., 2005; Ling & Schaik 2006; Walker, et al., 2007; Yi, et al., 2011)	(Liu & Huang 2007; Miller & Gagne 2008; 2011)
	searching time	(Huang, et al., 2009; Rivera-Nivar and Pomales-García 2010)	(Gasser & Boeke 2005; Rivera-Nivar & Pomales-García 2010)	(Rivera-Nivar & Pomales-García 2010)	
Comprehension	Eye movement	(Rello, 2011)			(Nel, et al., 2004; Rello, et al., 2011)
	Number of error	(Alotaibi 2007)	(Alotaibi 2007)	(Dillon, Kleinman et al., 2004; Yi, Park et al., 2011)	(Miller & Gagne 2008; 2011)
	Time to read task	(Russell & Chaparro 2001)		(Shaikh 2005; Walker, et al., 2007; Yi, et al., 2011)	
	searching time		(Chaparro, et al., 2005)		
Satisfaction	Questionnaire	(Bernard, et al., 2001; Russell & Chaparro 2001; F 2007; Rivera-Nivar & Pomales-García 2010)	(Bernard, et al., 2001; Chaparro, et al., 2005; Rivera-Nivar & Pomales-García 2010)	(Rivera-Nivar & Pomales-García 2010)	
behaviour	Eye movement				
	Observation				(Fisch, et al., 2002)

6. CONCLUSION

This chapter provides a systematic discussion in definition, process, theories, factors and methods for reading. It is found the majority of definitions without providing a clear definition explaining the concept of reading; the reading process was classified into two types, i.e. linear and nonlinear design, based on the type of sources and the design of information; theories are divided into three categories:

1. Theoretical perspectives concerning human behaviour;
2. Theoretical perspectives focusing on the text which were further classified into two categories; and
3. Theoretical perspectives dealing with the reading process; a key method called Reader Response theory (RRT) has been modified to address the two elements: teachers and parents.
4. Finally the proposed model presents three main factors [user factors, legibility factors and usability factors] each one is divided into several sub factors.

REFERENCES

Abubaker, A., & Lu, J. (2011). Model of E-Reading Process for E-School Book in Libya. *International Journal of Information Retrieval Research, 1*(3), 35–53. Retrieved from http://www.irma-international.org/viewtitle/64170/ doi:10.4018/ijirr.2011070103

Agarwal, R., & Venkatesh, V. (2002). Assessing a firm's web presence: A heuristic evaluation procedure for the measurement of usability. *Information Systems Research, 13*(2), 168–186. doi:10.1287/isre.13.2.168.84

Ajzen, I. (2011). The theory of planned behaviour: Reactions and reflections. *Psychology & Health, 26*(9), 1113–1127. doi:10.1080/08870446.2011.613995 PMID:21929476

Alan, C. (2001). designing computer- based learning materials, Gower Publishing Limited.

Alotaibi, A. Z. (2007). The effect of font size and type on reading performance with Arabic words in normally sighted and simulated cataract subjects. *Clinical & Experimental Optometry, 90*(3), 203–203. doi:10.1111/j.1444-0938.2007.00123.x PMID:17425766

Ashby, J., & Rayner, K. (2004). Representing syllable information during silent reading: Evidence from eye movements. *Language and Cognitive Processes, 19*(3), 391–426. doi:10.1080/01690960344000233

Asmaa, A., & Asma, A. O. (2009). Arab children's reading preferences for e-learning programs.*Proceedings of the 2009 conference on Information Science, Technology and Applications*, Kuwait. ACM.

Ayama, M., Ujike, H., Iwai, W., Funakawa, M., & Okajima, K. (2007). Effects of Contrast and Character Size upon Legibility of Japanese Text Stimuli Presented on Visual Display Terminal. *Optical Review, 14*(1), 48–56. doi:10.1007/s10043-007-0048-7

Bandura, A. (1986). *Social Foundations of Thought and Action: A Social Cognitive Theory. NJ.* Englewood Cliffs: Prentice Hall.

Banerjee, J., & Majumdar, D. et al.. (2011). "Readability, Subjective Preference and Mental Workload Studies on Young Indian Adults for Selection of Optimum Font Type and Size during Onscreen Reading." Al Ame en J. *Medical Science*, *4*(2), 131–143.

Bernard, M., Lida, B., Riley, S., Hackler, T., & Janzen, K (2002). A comparison of popular online fonts: which size and type is best? *UsabilityNews.org*.

Bernard, M. L., Chaparro, B. S., Mills, M. M., & Halcomb, C. G. (2003). Comparing the effects of text size and format on the readability of computer-displayed Times New Roman and Arial text. *International Journal of Human-Computer Studies*, *59*(6), 823–835. doi:10.1016/S1071-5819(03)00121-6

Bobbitt, L. M., & Dabholkar, P. A. (2001). Integrating attitudinal theories to understand and predict use of technology-based self-service: The internet as an illustration. *International Journal of Service Industry Management*, *12*(5), 423–450. doi:10.1108/EUM0000000006092

Bouma, H. (1980). Visual reading processes and the quality of text displays. *IPO Annual Progress Report.*, *15*, 83–90.

Broadbent, D. E. (1958). *Perception and communication.* London: Pergamon Press. doi:10.1037/10037-000

Bundesen, C. (1990). A Theory of Visual Attention. *Psychological Review*, *97*(4), 523–547. doi:10.1037/0033-295X.97.4.523 PMID:2247540

Chaparro, B. S., & Shaikh, A. D. et al.. (2005). Reading Online Text with a Poor Layout: Is Performance Worse? *Usability News*.org.

Chau, P. Y. K., & Au, G. et al.. (2000). Impact of information presentation modes on online shopping: An empirical evaluation of broadband interactive shopping service. *Journal of Organizational Computing and Electronic Commerce*, *10*, 1–22.

Chen, C.-H., & Chien, Y.-H. (2005). Effect of dynamic display and speed of display movement on reading Chinese text presented on a small screen. *Perceptual and Motor Skills*, *100*(3), 865–873. doi:10.2466/PMS.100.3.865-873 PMID:16060457

Cheyne, S. M. E. (2005). can electronic textbook help children to learn. *The Electronic Library*, *23*(1), 103–115. doi:10.1108/02640470510582781

Creed, A., Dennis, I., & Newstead, S. (1987). Proof-reading on VDUs. *Behaviour & Information Technology*, *6*(1), 3–13. doi:10.1080/01449298708901814

Cress, U., & Knabel, O. B. (2003). Previews in hypertexts: Effects on navigation and knowledge acquisition. *Journal of Computer Assisted Learning*, *19*(4), 517–527. doi:10.1046/j.0266-4909.2003.00054.x

De Boer-Schellekens, L., & Vroomen, J. (2005). Sound can improve visual search in developmental dyslexia. *Experimental Brain Research*, *216*(2), 243–248. doi:10.1007/s00221-011-2926-2 PMID:22064932

DeStefano, D., & LeFevre, J.-A. (2007). Cognitive load in hypertext reading: A review. *Computers in Human Behavior*, *23*(3), 1616–1641. doi:10.1016/j.chb.2005.08.012

Deutsch, J. A., & Deutsch, D. (1963). Attention: Some theoretical considerations. *Psychological Review*, *70*(1), 80–90. doi:10.1037/h0039515 PMID:14027390

Dillon, A. (1992). Designing usable electronic text. New York: CRC PRESS.

Dillon, A. (2001). designing usable electronic text: ergonomic aspects of human information usage. London: Taylor & Francis Inc.

Dillon, A., & Kleinman, L. et al.. (2004). *Visual Search and Reading Tasks Using ClearType and Regular Screen Displays: Two Experiments.* University of Texas at Austin/ School of Information.

Dillon, A., Richardson, J., & McKnight, C. (1990). The effects of display size and text splitting on reading lengthy text from screen. *Behaviour & Information Technology*, *9*(3), 215–227. doi:10.1080/01449299008924238

dos Santos Lonsdale, M., & Reynolds, L. (2006). Reading in examination-type situations: the effects of text layout on performance. *Research in reading*, *29*(4), 433- 453.

Duchnicky, J., & Kolers, P. (1983). Readability of text scrolled on visual display terminals as a function of window size. *Human Factors*, *25*, 683–692. PMID:6671649

Dyson, M. C. (2004). How physical text layout affects reading from screen. *Behaviour & Information Technology*, *23*(6), 377–393. doi:10.1080/01449290410001715714

Dyson, M. C., & Haselgrove, M. (2001). The influence of reading speed and line length on the effectiveness of reading from screen. *International Journal of Human-Computer Studies*, *54*(4), 585–612. doi:10.1006/ijhc.2001.0458

Dyson, M. C., & Kipping, G. J. (1997). The legibility of screen formats: Are three columns better than one? *Computers & Graphics*, *21*(6), 703–712. doi:10.1016/S0097-8493(97)00048-4

Eagleton, M. B., & Dobler, E. (2006). *Reading the Web: Strategies for Internet Inquiry.* New York, NY, USA: Guilford Press.

Yen, N.-S., Tsai, J.-L., Chen, P.-L., Lin, H.-Y., & Chen, A.L.P. (2011). Effects of typographic variables on eye-movement measures in reading Chinese from a screen. *Behaviour & Information Technology*, *30*(6), 797–808. doi:10.1080/0144929X.2010.523900

Feely, M., Rubin, G. S., Ekstrom, K., & Perera, S. (2005). Investigation into font characteristics for optimum reading fluency in readers with sight problems. *International Congress Series*, *1282*, 530–533. doi:10.1016/j.ics.2005.05.121

First, U. (2005). *Usability in website and software design.* Usability First.

Fisch, S. M., Shulman, J. S., Akerman, A., & Levin, G. A. (2002). Reading Between The Pixels: Parent-Child Interaction While Reading Online Storybooks. *Early Education and Development*, *13*(4), 435–451. doi:10.1207/s15566935eed1304_7

Fontanini, I. (2004). Reading theories and some implications for the processing of linear texts and hypertexts. *Linguagem & Ensino*, *7*(2), 165–184.

Foster, J. J. (1970). A study of the legibility of one- and two-column layouts for BPS publications. *Bulletin of the British Psychological Society*, (23): 113–114.

Frey, N., & Fisher, D. (2010). Identifying instructional moves during guided learning: Expert teachers use a four-part process to scaffold student understanding during small-group guided instruction. *The Reading Teacher, 64*(2), 84–95. doi:10.1598/RT.64.2.1

Gabriel-Petit, P. (2007). Applying Color Theory to Digital Displays. Retrieved from http://www.uxmatters.com/mt/archives/2007/01/applying-color-theory-to-digital-displays.phpApplying

Gibson, E. J., & Levin, H. (1976). *The Psychology of Reading The Colonial Press Inc.*

Harrison, B.L. (2000). E-books and the future of reading. *IEEE Computer Graphics and Applications, 20*(3), 32-39.

Hartley, J. B. P. (1977). Fifty guide-lines for improving instructional text. *Programmed Learning and Educational Technology Research and Development, 14*(1), 65–73.

Hausenblas, H. A., Carron, A. V., & Mack, D. E. (1997). Application of the theories of reasoned action and planned behavior to exercise behavior: A meta-analysis. *Journal of Sport & Exercise Psychology, 19*(1), 36–51. doi:10.1123/jsep.19.1.36

Hirvela, A. (1996). Reader-response theory and ELT. *ELT, 50*(2), 127–134. doi:10.1093/elt/50.2.127

Huang, D.-L., Patrick Rau, P.-L., & Liu, Y. (2009). Effects of font size, display resolution and task type on reading Chinese fonts from mobile devices. *International Journal of Industrial Ergonomics, 39*(1), 81–89. doi:10.1016/j.ergon.2008.09.004

IBM (2005). Design basics.

Iser, W. (1978). The act of reading: a theory of aesthetic response. London: Routledge and Kegan Paul.

Kintsch, W. (2004) The construction-integration model of text comprehension and its implications for instruction.

Kolers, P. A., Duchnicky, R. L., & Ferguson, D. C. (1981). Eye movement measurement of readability of CRT displays. *Human Factors, 23*, 517–527. PMID:7319497

Kosslyn, S. M., & Rosenberg, R. S. (2004). The Brain, The Person, The World. *Psychology (Savannah, Ga.).*

Kotzé, J. B. P. (2007). Modelling the Factors that Influence Mobile Phone Adoption. ACM: 152- 161.

Kruk, R. S., & Muter, P. (1984). Reading of continuous text on video screens. *Human Factors, 26*, 339–345.

Kudik, C. (2007). Effects of Font Size and Paper Color on Resume Review Decisions. *Stephen F. Austin State University.*

Laarnia, J., & Simolaa, J. et al. (2004). Reading vertical text from a computer screen. *Behaviour & Information Technology, 23*(2), 75–82. doi:10.1080/01449290310001648260

Landoni, M., & Diaz, P. (2003). E-education: Design and evaluation for teaching and learning. *Journal of Digital Information, 3*(4).

Landoni, M., & Gibb, F. (2000). The role of visual rhetoric in the design and production of electronic books: The visual book. *The Electronic Library*, *18*(3), 190–201. doi:10.1108/02640470010337490

Lee, D.-S., Shieh, K.-K., Jeng, S.-C., & Shen, I.-H. (2008). Effect of character size and lighting on legibility of electronic papers. *Displays*, *29*(1), 10–17. doi:10.1016/j.displa.2007.06.007

Lee, D.-S., Shieh, K.-K., Jeng, S.-C., & Shen, I.-H. (2008). Effect of character size and lighting on legibility of electronic papers. *Displays*, *29*(1), 10–17. doi:10.1016/j.displa.2007.06.007

Lin, D. M. (2004). Evaluating older adults' retention in hypertext perusal: Impacts of presentation media as a function of text topology. *Computers in Human Behavior*, *20*(4), 491–503. doi:10.1016/j.chb.2003.10.024

Linderholm, T., Virtue, S., Tzeng, Y., & van den Broek, P. (2004). Fluctuations in the availability of information during reading: Capturing cognitive processes using the landscape model. *Discourse Processes*, *37*(2), 165–186. doi:10.1207/s15326950dp3702_5

Ling, J., & Schaik, P. (2006). The influence of font type and line length on visual search and information retrieval in web pages. *International Journal of Human-Computer Studies*, *64*(5), 395–404. doi:10.1016/j.ijhcs.2005.08.015

Liu, Z., & Huang, X. (2007). Gender differences in the online reading environment. *The Journal of Documentation*, *64*(4), 616–626. doi:10.1108/00220410810884101

Liu, Z. (2005). Reading behaviour in the digital environment. *Journal of Documentation*, *61*(6), 700-712.

Lund, O. (1999). Knowledge Construction in Typography: the Case of Legibility Research and the Legibility of Sans Serif Typefaces [PhD]. Reading University, UK.

M, B., C. B, et al., (2003). Comparing the effects of text size and format on the readability of computer-displayed Times New Roman and Arial text. *Int. J. Human-Computer Studies*, *59*(6), 823-835.

Miller, L. M. S., & Gagne, D. D. (2008). Adult age differences in reading and rereading processes associated with problem solving. *International Journal of Behavioral Development*, *32*(1), 34–45. doi:10.1177/0165025407084050

Moorman, K., & Ram, A. (1994). *A Functional Theory of Creative Reading. Technical Report. G. I. o.* Georgia: Technology.

Muter, P. (1996). *Interface design and optimization of reading of continuous text. In Cognitive Aspects of Electronic Text Processing.*

Nathan, R. J., & Yeow, P. H. P. (2011). Crucial web usability factors of 36 industries forÂ students: A large-scale empirical study. *Electronic Commerce Research*, *11*(2), 151–180. doi:10.1007/s10660-010-9054-0

National, A. (1988). *American National Standard for Human Factors Engineering of Visual Display Terminal Workstations.*

Nel, C., & Dreyer, C. et al. (2004). An analysis of the reading profiles of first-year students at Potchefstroom University: A cross-sectional study and a case study. *South African Journal of Education*, *24*(1), 95–103.

Nes, F. L. V. (1986). Space, colour and typography on visual display terminals. *Behaviour & Information Technology*, *5*(2), 99–118. doi:10.1080/01449298608914504

Nielsen, J. (2000). *Designing Web Usability: The Practice of Simplicity*. New York: New Riders.

Noorhidawati, A., & Forbes, G. (2008). Students attitudes towards e-books in a Scottish higher education institute: Part 1. *Library Review*, *57*(8), 593–605. doi:10.1108/00242530810899577

Panayiota, K., & Broek, P. V. E. (2007). The effects of prior knowledge and text structure on comprehension processes during reading of scientific texts. *Memory & Cognition*, *35*(7), 1567–1577. doi:10.3758/BF03193491 PMID:18062535

Poole, A. (2005). *Literature Review: Which Are More Legible: Serif or Sans Serif Typefaces? Alexpoole. info*.

Powell, T. A. (2000). *Web Design: the Complete Reference*. California: McGraw Hill.

Randolph, G. B., & Anuj, A. N. (2005). Optimal Line Length in Reading - A Literature Review. *Visible Language*, *39*(2), 120–125.

Randolph, G. B., & Anuj, A. N. (2005). Optimal Line Length in Reading - A Literature Review. *Visible Language*, *39*(2), 120–125.

Rello, L., Kanvinde, G., & Baeza-Yates, R. (2011). Layout Guidelines for Web Text and a Web Service to Improve Accessibility for Dyslexics. *Proceedings of the 21st International World Wide Web Conference*.

Rivera-Nivar, M., & Pomales-García, C. (2010). E-training: Can young and older users be accommodated with the same interface? *Computers & Education*, *55*(3), 949–960. doi:10.1016/j.compedu.2010.04.006

Robert, J. N., & Paul, H. P. Y. et al.. (2008). Key usability factors of service-oriented web sites for students: An empirical study. *Online Information Review*, *32*(3), 302–324. doi:10.1108/14684520810889646

Russell, M. C., & Chaparro, B. S. (2001). exploring effects of speed and font size with RSVP. Human factors and ergonimics society 45th Annual meeting.

Russell-Minda, E., & Jutai, J. W., Strong, J.G., Campbell, K.A., Gold, D., Pretty, L., & Wilmot, L. (2007). The Legibility of Typefaces for Readers with Low Vision: A Research Review. *Journal of Visual Impairment & Blindness*, *101*(7), 402–415.

RW, D. L., E. HL, et al., (1993). Performance differences between Times and Helvetica in a reading task. *Electronic Publishing*, *6*(3), 241–248.

Shaikh, A. D. (2005). The Effects of Line Length on Reading Online News. *Usability News*, *7*(2), 2–4.

Sheedy, J. E., Subbaram, M.V., Zimmerman, A.B., & Hayes, J.R. (2005). Text legibility and the letter superiority effect. *Human Factors*, *47*(4), 797- 815.

Sheedy, J. E., Subbaram, M. V., Zimmerman, A. B., & Hayes, J. R.JE. (2005). Text legibility and the letter superiority effect. *Human Factors*, *47*(4), 797–815. doi:10.1518/0018720057755570998 PMID:16553067

Shu, H., Zhou, W., Yan, M., & Kliegl, R. (2010). Font size modulates saccade- target selection in Chinese reading. *Attention, Perception & Psychophysics, 73*(2), 482–490. doi:10.3758/s13414-010-0029-y PMID:21264735

Shurtleff, D. (1967). Studies in television legibility: A review of the literature. *Information Display, 4*, 40–45.

Siegenthaler, E., Wurtz, P., Bergamin, P., & Groner, R. (2011). Comparing reading processes on e-ink displays and print. *Displays, 32*(5), 268–273. doi:10.1016/j.displa.2011.05.005

Simmonds, D. R. L. (1994). *Data presentation and visual literacy in medicine and science.* Oxford: Butterworth-Heinemann.

Singleton, C., & Henderson, L.-M. (2006). Visual factors in reading. *London Review of Education, 4*(1), 89- 98.

Smith, W. J. (1996). *ISO and ANSI Ergonomic standards for computer products: a guide to implementation and compliance.* Prentice Hall.

Southall, R. (1984). First principles of typographic design for document production. *TUGboat, 5*(2), 79–91.

Swanson, H. L. (1987). Information Processing Theory and Learning Disabilities: A Commentary and Future Perspective. *Journal of Learning Disabilities, 20*(3), 155–166. doi:10.1177/002221948702000303 PMID:3549949

Terras, M. (2005). Reading the Readers: Modelling Complex Humanities Processes to Build cognitive System. *Literary and Linguistic Computing, 20*(1), 41–59. doi:10.1093/llc/fqh042

Truong, Y. (2009). An Evaluation of the Theory of Planned Behaviour in Consumer Acceptance of Online Video and Television Services. *The Electronic Journal Information Systems Evaluation, 12*(2), 177–186.

Venkatesh, V., & Davis, F. D. (2000). A theoretical extension of the technology acceptance model: Four longitudinal field studies. *Management Science, 46*(2), 186–204. doi:10.1287/mnsc.46.2.186.11926

Vidyasagar, T. R., & Pammer, K. (1999). Impaired visual search in dyslexia relates to the role of the magnocellular pathway in attention. *Neuroreport, 10*(6), 1283-1287.

Walker, R., Schloss, P., & Vogel, C. A. (2007). *Visual-Syntactic Text Formatting: Theoretical Basis and Empirical Evidence for Impact on Human Reading.*

Wastlund, E., Norlander, T., & Archer, T. (2008). The effect of page layout on mental workload: A dual-task experiment. *Computers in Human Behavior, 24*(3), 1229–1245. doi:10.1016/j.chb.2007.05.001

Wijnholds, A. D. B. (1997). *Using type: The typographer's craftsmanship and the ergonomist's research.* The Netherlands: Utrecht University.

Yen, M., Tsai, J., Tzeng, O. J. L., & Hung, D. L. (2008). Eye movements and parafoveal word processing in reading Chinese. *Memory & Cognition, 36*(5), 1033–1045. doi:10.3758/MC.36.5.1033 PMID:18630209

Yi, W., Park, E., & Cho, K. (2011). E-Book Readability, Comprehensibility and Satisfaction. Proceedings of ICUMC`11, Seoul, Korea.

Yoh, E., Damhorst, M. L., Sapp, S., & Laczniak, R. (2003). Consumer adoption of the internet: The case of apparel shopping. *Psychology and Marketing*, *20*(12), 1095–1118. doi:10.1002/mar.10110

Youngman, M., & Scharff, L. (1998). *Text width and margin width influences*. South Western Psychological Association.

Zhang, X.-m., Shu, H., & Ran, T. (2007). Effect of computer screen back and font color on Chinese reading comprehension. *Proceedings of theInternational Conference on Intelligent Pervasive Computing*. IEEE.

Chapter 8
Theoretical and Empirical Background to the eBook

Azza A Abubaker
Benghazi University, Libya & University of Huddersfield, UK

Joan Lu
University of Huddersfield, UK

ABSTRACT

A textbook in any e-educational system is an important element that requires a closer look at its components and structure, as well as identifying the barriers that affect the level of learning. This can be achieved in different aspects such as the analysis of textual content or sentence structure which is one of the concerns of linguists. On the other hand, examining the textual content can determine the appropriateness of the education level for students. This type of assessment is part of educators' concerns and by examining and defining the factors that could affect reading a text on screen, this is usually related to the way of displaying text such as font size, colour, background colour, amount of text and the location of the text on the screen. This is a key focus of this research. In this chapter, the concern will be to define the concepts and the structure of an e- document as a starting point to investigate the usability of e-texts as it covers the following: definition of e-document; history of eBook; structure of e-textbook; contribution of e-textbook for education; comparison between reading electronic and paper book; young people and the use of the internet and computer; statistical data for using the internet in Arabic countries; designing an e-textbook.

1. DEFINITION OF E-DOCUMENT

Before discussing the factors that impact electronic display, it is important to give a brief look at the definition of digital document; this should help clarify the difference between paper documents and the electronic format, which is difficult to recognize and the underlying concept less clear.

However, the examination of knowledgeable production showed the use of multiple terms by researchers, such as visual book (Landoni, 1997; Wilson, Landoni & Gibb, 2003; Crestani, Landoni & Melucci,

DOI: 10.4018/978-1-5225-1884-6.ch008

2006; Landoni, 2000), CD- ROM book e.g. Maynard & McKnight, 2001), eBook (Ismail & Zainab, 2005; Anuradha & Usha, 2006; Martínez-Prieto, Fuente, Vegas, Adiego & Cuesta, 2008; Landoni, 2010), e – paper (Jeng, Lin, Liu, Liao, Wen, Chao & Shieh, 2005) e- work (Martínez-Prieto, Fuente, Vegas, Adiego & Cuesta, 2008), digital book (Cavanaugh, 2006; Leeuw & Rydin, 2007), web book (Kleeck, 2003), and electronic text book (Landoni, 2002; Cheyne, 2005).

At the same time, the studies focusing on eBook emphasize that the terms eBook and digital book are more used than other terms. For example, Vassiliou & Rowley (2008) in their study reported that 19 definitions used the term 'digital', while 20 definitions used 'electronic' and 12 others used the term 'online'. However, using different terms when providing a definition to eBook could be attributed to the type of e- book that is used in the same period.

Alternatively, various attempts have been made to introduce different concepts to eBook according to several perspectives, such as format (Lynch, 2001; Lam, et al., 2009), media (Landoni & Diaz 2003; Cheyne, 2005), goal of delivery, or benefits of use (Anuradha & Usha 2005; Connaway, 2007). In this study, the focus was on attempts to define eBook within the period from 1990 to 2011, wherein the majority of definitions had become out-dated due to rapid changes in the field of ICT.

In chronological order, Martin (1990) focused on the hyperlink and how this function changes the concept of eBook and made it different from a paper book. In the same line Hamilton, et al (2001), Wilson et al (2002) focused on the power of an eBook compared to the paper version. In addition, Wilson and Landoni (2001) provided three definitions to an eBook according to different perspectives: (1) hardware devices used to read e- content such as HI eBook; (2) software such as Microsoft Reader and Adobe Acrobat Reader; and (3) web book that can be accessed online. In addition, Barker (2005) categorized eBook into 10 types based on three aspects (publication medium, functions, and facilities), while Hawkine (2000) divided eBook into four types.

Moreover, Noorhidawati (2007) defined the eBook as a package of elements. Generally, Noorhidawati's definition is acceptable to a large extent compared to previous definitions, which as noted previously, focused only on one side. And yet, we cannot say that it is a comprehensive definition that covers all aspects of the e-book even though it summarises all the elements addressed in the previous definitions without any attempt to cover the gaps in these definitions.

In 2008, Vassiliou and Rowley (2008) proposed a definition combined from two parts; the first part focused on the content of the e- book while the second focused on the functionality aspect. Lam et al. (2009) defined eBook as e- formats of books that can be viewed on a computer screen or hand-held devices. On the other hand, according to the user's perspective, an eBook was known as dedicated reading.

Generally, there is no universal standard definition for eBook in the literature according to the survey of the eBook field (Bennett, 2005). In this research, e-textbook has been used to refer to educational materials that have been electronically published to assist with both teaching and learning. It may take different forms depending on the technology used to store content, e.g. it has an open structure which is divided into a hierarchy of physical components such as pages, columns, paragraphs, text lines, words, tables, and figures, as well as logical components such as titles, authors, affiliations, and abstracts. From Table 1, we may note that there are differences between an e-book and a website. These differences could be summarized in terms of three aspects: components, dimensions, and boundaries.

Table 1. Differences between e-books and websites

Information Architecture	Books	Web sites
Components	Cover, title, author, chapters, sections, pages, page numbers, table of contents, index.	Main page, navigation, links, content pages sitemap, site index, searches.
Dimensions	Two- dimensional pages presented in a linear, sequential order.	Multidimensional information space with hyper textual navigation.
Boundaries	Tangible & finite with a clear beginning & ending.	Fairly intangible with fuzzy borders that "bleed" information into other sites.

Johnston & Huczynski, 2006.

2. BRIEF HISTORY OF EBOOK

E-text has a shorter history compared to the paper. Its history is also less clear compared with the paper document or physical environment. The concept of eBook can be traced back to Memex and Dynabook. Memex was envisioned by Vannevar Busk in 1945 to use as an information workstation in the first stage before applying it as a device to store books (as seen in Figure 1) and then used for reading and retrieving them. Dynabook was created by Alan Kay in 1986 which was envisaged for notebook PCs and laptops.

In 1971, the Michael Hart Project [Gutenberg Project] is seen as the first significant attempt at developing an eBook, a project that freely offers access to read and retrieve on screen currently more than 20,000 titles. In addition, in 1976, FRESS was used by Brown University students to read poems and other critical materials on a computer. These two attempts are seen as the first significant effort in e-book development (Abdullah, 2007).

In 1985, an eBook called *Superbook* was presented by the Bellcare Laboratory; the eBook was built according to a user- centre design model where the e-book has a similar structure to the paper book as in a table of contents in addition to computer-based features such as examining words. On the other hand,

Figure 1. Drawing of Bush's Theoretical Memex Machine[1]

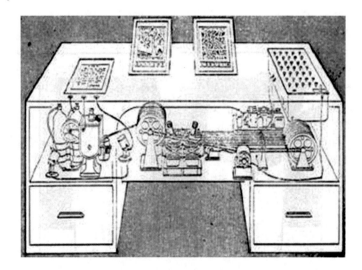

present reference materials such as encyclopaedias and dictionaries began to be published in digital versions during the 1980s and 1990s on CD- ROM (Egan, et al. 1989).

In 1998, NuvoMedia (Anonymous, 1999) introduced the Rocket eBook for reading an eBook. The number of dedicated eBook readers in the market increased after that date. For example, each year Sony introduced a number of eBook portable readers such as PRS500 in 2006, PRS- 600 and PRS900 in 2009, PRS- 350, PRS-650 and PRS- 950 in 2010, and Wi-Fi PRS-T1 in 2011. Figure 2 shows examples of eBook readers that have been produced by Sony.

Moreover, in 2007, Amazon.com developed Amazon Kindle [eBook reader], which enables readers to download, browse, and read news and books. Each device-generation used different file formats, e.g. first generation used plain text file (TXT), Topaz formats books (TPZ), and Amazon's proprietary DRM-restricted format (AZW), while the second generation insert Portable Document Format (PDF). The fourth generation (Kindle, Kindle Touch and Kindle Touch 3G) is able to display Kindle (AZW), TXT, PDF, unprotected MOBI, and PRC files natively. HTML, DOC, DOCX, JPEG, GIF, PNG, and BMP are usable through conversion. In addition, the Touch and Touch 3G versions are also able to play Audible (Audible Enhanced (AA, AAX) and MP3 files (as see in Figure 3) (Murray, 2012).

3. CONTRIBUTION OF E- TEXTBOOK FOR EDUCATION

The use of electronic information has increased in various spheres of life such as the military, commercial, medical, and educational fields. In the field of education, the eBook was firstly used in higher education widely before it became popular. Limited use of eBook at the beginning could be due to the use of just a linear format of printed documents which led librarians and educators to slow down the

Figure 2. Example of the latest eBook portable readers from Sony[2]

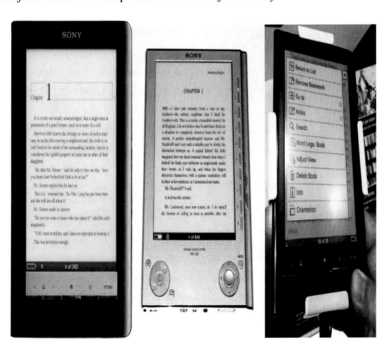

Figure 3. First generation of the Amazon Kindle[3]

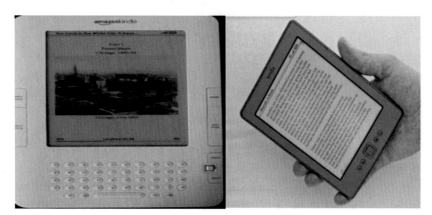

turnout into eBooks. But with the rapid development in eBook technology such as addition of interactive features and dynamic tools, it has led to the widespread use of eBook for educational purposes. In addition, comparing the use of p- version and eBook showed that there were multiple factors affecting the choice of reading materials, as will be explained later in detail.

Moreover, every day new findings in the research into using eBook to develop children's learning have shown promising results in several aspects such as enhancing children's phonological awareness (Chera & Wood, 2003), word recognition skills (Miller, 1994) and extending verbal knowledge (Segers, 2002).

On the other hand, using eBook, computer and internet in schools bring several with it several challenges to educators (Shaffer & Clinton, 2006), where simply setting up computers in schools is not enough to enhance learning but suitable pedagogical tools and materials must be designed, in addition to modifying the goals of schools in keeping with the digital age (Ben-David & Kolikant 2009). For example, computer students in developed countries such as USA used to get high scores on regular quizzes (OECD 2005). Maybe this occurs because teachers do not use anymore pedagogical tools that were developed for use in traditional education.

Furthermore, educators still face the problem related to slower reading from text on screen. Part of this problem is related to screen quality and the other is related to the text format such as font size, line length, background colour, line colour, text segment, and links. For instance, Park (2009) points out that reading eBook can be uncomfortable due to reading from a screen. In addition, adding new functions such as multimedia features may further lead to several difficulties associated with usability (Landoni, et al. 2000; Shiratuddin, et al. 2003).

However, there have recently been a certain number of research into using e- textbook among children, with the main concern being the functionality issues such as investigating reading comprehension (Greenlee-Moore & Smith 1996; Maynard & McKnight, 2001), addressing the beneficial outcome for pupils' reading, examining pupils' recall (Trushell, et al. 2001; Segal-Drori, et al. 2009), exploring the impact of e- textbook on reading speed (Maynard & McKnight 2001). Still, a limited number of studies were more concerned with how young readers learn from textbooks and how they deal with information in the e- format. One of these studies by Maynard and Cheyne (2005) involved children aged 11- 12 in England. The study aimed to compare children's reading and learning from eBook which combined hypertext, glossary, background music, and web links. The findings of this research showed a positive effect on learning as it helped these pupils to work effectively, making teaching and learning more fun and interactive. It also showed difficulty with navigating e- textbooks and students were more familiar with print navigating tools. But they failed to mention how students followed when dealing with e- text or define a legible format for e- educational text.

Moreover, Shin (2011) has also attempted to understand the concept of e- book usability by using an empirical perspective to explore the use of gratification and expectation confirmation theory to explain the development in reader-behaviour through understanding emotional and cognitive factors. The study recorded two important elements affecting the usability of eBook: (1) ease of use and usefulness; and (2) difficulty of reading texts online. The study confirms that the most significant weakness of e-books is the lack of content.

Consistent with prior research, it is notable that these researchers were unable to provide answers to many questions such as: how children read and use the e- textbook; what affective factors are impacting e- reading; and how do children feel about e-textbook. Such questions will be considered in this research and we will examine e- reading strategies for reading e- textbook in a Libyan school so as to build an e-reading model and to investigate the format factors that impact reading an Arabic text on screen by examining the effect of font size and type on accuracy and reading speed. It will also define a readable font size in order to build a guideline as it were that can help designers come up with effective e-learning materials in the Arabic language that can enhance the reading of an e-textbook.

On the other hand, with the increase in studies that emphasize the importance of applying eBooks in early education since the 1990s, we must also address other aspects associated with the rates of using eBooks and related problems. Analysing the usability of the eBook within the last ten years does not resolve the situation for eBook but leave the door open to more research to clarify the situation. Table 2 provides some examples of research that addressed students' awareness of eBook in higher education. It is notable that the average use of e- materials among university students in the U.S.A. increased from 33% in 2003 to 51% in 2006.

Moreover, Jamali et al (2009) looked at 16,000 students and listed several advantages that encourage students to use eBook such as portability, cost, search ability, and so on (Jamali, Nicholas & Rowlands, 2009). In addition, the same study indicated that 7.6% of respondents do not prefer using an eBook because of screen reading, while 6% of participants point out that they prefer reading printed books because of the difficulty of browsing and scrolling the text on screen.

Table 2. Some examples of research that addressed students' awareness of eBook in higher education

Studies	Had Not Used eBook	Country
Chu (2003)	67%	US
Ismail & Zainab (2005)	61%	Malaysia
Bennett & Landoni (2005)	61%	
Anuradha & Usha (2006)	66%	Indian
Levine-Clark (2006)	49%	US
Noorhidawati & Forbes (2008)	60%	UK
Wu & Chen (2011)	Use both version	Taiwan

4. COMPARISON BETWEEN READING ELECTRONIC AND PAPER TEXT

There are two thoughts on the field of reading. The first is that paper will never be replaced by e- text. This might be due to the ease and flexibility of using paper format. For instance, manipulating paper is achieved by manual dexterity, using fingers to turn pages, keeping one finger in a section as a location aid, or flicking through tens of pages, while browsing the contents of a document is either difficult or impossible to support electronically.

Although browsing through the electronic document might involve using a mouse and scroll bar in one application, one might require menu selection and page numbers, whilst another supports touch-sensitive buttons and screens. Hypertext manipulation of large electronic texts can be rapid and simple while other systems might take several seconds to refresh the screen after the execution of another page (Dillon, 1994).

Alternatively, the second thought concerns those who believe that eBook will replace paper format, and build such thought on several advantages of the eBook such as ease of storage and retrieval (Liu, 2005; Tenopir, 2009). Also, it has the ability to use several features such as sounds, animations, less cost, ability to download and use hotspots (Polding, Nunes & Kingston, 2008). In addition, Shiratuddin et al. (2003) compared eBook with paper format based on previous studies; the summary of the comparison is found in Table 3. From the table, it can be noted that paper content is more legible than e- content.

Table 3. Comparison of p-book and eBook

Features	pContent	eContent
Tactile	Yes	No
Portable	Yes	Yes & No
Access without devices	Yes	No
Easy random access*	No	Yes
Multiple access at one time	Yes	Yes
Customisable (font size, annotations etc.)	No	Yes
Hyperlinks	No	Yes
Text	Yes	Yes
Pictures	Yes	Yes
Audio	No	Yes
Animation/video	No	Yes
Instant search facility	No	Yes
Easily and conveniently read	Yes	No
Easily damaged (i.e. tear)	Yes	No
Content updated easily	No	Yes
Go out of print	Yes	No
Highly interactive	No	Yes
Good legibility	Yes	No
Easily reproduced with the same quality	No	Yes

Shiratuddin, et al. 2003.

However, it can be observed that the arguments provided by each team to support their point of view differ; for instance, defenders of paper book consider it better in terms of ease of handling and taking notes, but is not as good when it comes to search or capacity for storage like eBook. Moreover, the other hand, supporters of the eBook see it as easy to navigate especially for academic purposes. Therefore, there must be a third approach, which, while knowing that eBook would not replace the p-book, considers the two formats as complementing each other in order to satisfy the needs of readers. The evidence behind this belief is numerous, e.g. when university students search for specific information they prefer using e- text while they still prefer to read it as a p-version (Nicholas, et al, 2008). But, we should be working to improve the way of displaying text on screen by defining the barriers that effect legibility on screen.

Dillon (1994) sets a clear mark in the field by providing a comprehensive view of the empirical literature on reading from paper against electronic. This was followed by Dyson (2004) who examined the relation between layout of the paper format and reading electronic text. The study reported that typographic factors have a significant impact on reading speed of electronic texts and characters per line were reported as an essential factor.

Even though reading electronically offers clear advantages to readers, there are still a lot of challenges facing the reader when using e- media. Studies comparing reading in both versions show mixed results. Most research findings from the period 1980s to 1990s (Landoni, 1997; Wilson, et al. 2003; Crestani, et al. 2006) show that reading from screen takes more time, without giving any explanations about the reasons behind it.

Consequently, the electronic environment has specific characteristics that make it different from paper reading. Some researchers such as Alan (2001) reported that presenting an electronic text is broadly similar to displaying it on the page with a number of differences such as quality, size, and orientation. This might account for the poor reading on screen.

Additionally, the other hand, reviewing empirical evidence and theory on reading from screen shows there are distinctions to be made between paper and PC reading processes (Wright, 1988; Dillon, 1994). In addition, the study on the optimization of reading has been done with paper and then circulated on the electronic format (Frenckner, 1990). On the other hand, comparison between a conventional view of the text and e- text has been used as a starting point to examine reading on screen (Dyson, 2004). These researchers focused on comparisons in their research without investigating the variables that affect reading on screen. At the same time, Dyson (2004) focused on the typographic variables related to text formats on paper and screen such as line length, columns, and window size.

5. YOUNG PEOPLE AND USE THE INTERNET AND COMPUTER

With the increased access to the Internet at home and at school, especially in developed countries, there arises the need to investigate several issues related to users' attitudes toward ICT and their effect on people's lives. On the other hand, searching topics by using the Internet and computer from children's perspectives seems limited, although several researchers have suggested doing more examinations at different levels of using the Internet and computer among young users (Perse & Dunn, 1998; Ma, 2005).

Most studies reported that children used the Internet more for entertainment and social interaction. Staflerd, Kline and Dimmich (1999) reported in their survey, which examined the purposes of using the Internet, that 61% of responders used the internet for communication by e-mail. In addition, Papacharissi and Rubin (2000) explored motives of internet usage among students in college [279 students]. The study reported several motivations for using the internet such as seeking information and entertainment.

In the same perspective, the US Census Bureau (2012) reported that 24.7% of children aged 6 to 11 in the USA use the Internet, 64% have a computer at home, while 47.9% of children aged 12 to 17 use the Internet and 69% have access at home. In the Silicon Valley in the USA, the average access to the Internet was high among children aged 10- 17, where 79% have internet access, 39% have access to more than one computer at home. The same study found that schools provide access to the Internet for students. 95% of participants have access to the Internet from lab, library or their desk in the classroom (News & Foundation, 2003).

In 2001, 71% of US students in public schools depended on web materials, while in 2005 95% of American public schools have access to the Internet (Eagleton & Dobler, 2006). In addition, 99% of students aged 9 to 13 in Canada use the Internet at home regularly (Gunn & Hepburn, 2003).

From the same perspective, Valkensburg and Soeters (2001) did their investigation by examining 194 children aged 8-13. They found that there is not much difference between younger and older children in using the internet, where both use it for entertainment except older children who use the internet for finding information about sport. Ma (2005) investigated using the internet at home and at school among students in middle schools in Ohio. The survey reported that Internet is used for entertainment and learning, and is used at home for doing homework, satisfy personal interest, do shopping, listen to music or watch movie clips. Still, using the internet at school was limited.

Moreover, some studies have confirmed that there is a difference between males and females in their concept of using the Internet (Tapscott, 1998; Miller, 2001; Harcourt, 2004), while others reported little difference in their attitudes toward the Internet (Weiser, 2002). These differences could point to two aspects: type of websites, and tools. For example, Shaw and Gant (2002) found that women mainly used the Internet for interpersonal communication while men used the Internet to collect different types of information (Shaw & Gant, 2002). This finding is similar to a finding that was reported by the Technology Student Association (2003). The study surveyed 675 students from middle schools and high schools which showed that boys tended to use the internet to check up on sport information while girls mainly used the Internet for communicating socially. Moreover, Valkensburg (2001) found that boys enjoy sensational content like violence and pornography while girls love cartoon sites such as Disney.

The contribution of employing internet in education could be summarized in three aspects:

- **Easy to Access:** Students can access lessons anytime and anywhere.
- **Communication Needs:** Internet plays a major role in communication between students and teachers by allowing teachers to provide lessons online and to link to different classes at the same time.
- **Abundance and Diversity of Content:** Despite the lack of accurate statistics on the level of intellectual achievement, it is notable that searching the Internet it is not something small especially when presented in various visual and textual formats.

Finally, Tsai (2004), Chou, et al. (2007) and Chon, et al. (2009) provided the 4T and 5T frameworks for using the computer and internet, which may be summarised as follows:

- **Tool:** Help students in doing tasks such as homework and learning.
- **Toy:** Enable users to play online games.

- **Telephone:** Allow users to communicate with other users.
- **Territory:** Assist users to present their interests and hobbies.
- **Treasure:** Ability to browse and access a huge collection of online information.

Statistic Data of Internet Use in Arabic Counties

Arabic users understand the importance of using the Internet in their daily lives as a medium for both formal and informal communication. Comparing the use of the internet in Arabic countries to the total average use in the world showed a much lower use rate in the former.

Utilization rates of the Internet vary among Arabic countries according to various factors (such as political, economic, social and cultural); however, the political and economic factors are more influential than others. This is seen in Table 4 which displays the latest statistics of the number of subscribers to the Internet in Arabic countries in 2010, compared to the population of each country. It is notable that Bahrain comes in first place with 3,777,900 users who represent 88% of the population, while Iraq comes in at the last place with only 325,000 users (1.1%) (Tadoz, 2010).

The use of the Internet in Libya dates back to 1998, where it was confined to only a limited segment of society. In 2000, the Internet became available for public use, which could be seen as the first real use of the Internet in Libya. At the beginning, connection was only available via telephone, but in 2005 users were able to use ADSL servers and then WiMax (Khatkar, 2014). In addition, Al Bayan UAE (2004) reported that the number of public centres and private Internet cafes increased to about 3000 centres throughout Libyan cities.

Table 4. Statistics on the number of subscribers to the Internet in Arabic countries in 2010

Countries	No. of Internet Users	Percentage to Total Number of Population
Bahrain	649.300	88%
Emirates	3.777.900	75%
Qatar	436.000	50%
Amman	1.236.700	41%
Kuwait	1.100.000	39%
Tunisia	3.600.000	34%
Saudi Arabia	9.800.000	33%
Lebanon	1,000.000	24.2%
Jordan	1.741.9000	24%
Egypt	17.060.000	21.2%
Syria	3.935.500	17.7%
Sudan	4.700.000	13.6%
Libya	353.900	5.5%
Yemen	420.000	1.8%
Iraq	325.000	1.1%

Tadoz, 2010.

Alternatively, the limited number of resources shows that there is a dramatic increase in the number of Internet users despite the high costs of subscribing. A monthly subscription fee was relatively high given the low level salaries where subscribers would have to pay $400 (700 LYD) annually to access the internet.

In addition, the average Internet use in Libya differs from year to year. For example, in 2001 the average Internet use was 300,000 users; this number increased to 850,000 then decreased again to 205,000 users in 2006. Identifying the cause(s) of this declined is yet to be made (as can be seen in Table 5) (Elmabruk, 2009).

Table 6 summarizes the studies that have addressed the use of the eBook and the Internet. Studies with vague approaches were excluded to filter findings to be considered in this research. These studies show mixed results which make drawing up conclusions fairly difficult.

6. DESIGNING E-TEXTBOOK [ETB] FOR YOUNG STUDENTS

When discussing designing issues concerning e- textbook, two aspects ought to be looked at, structure of the text and typographical factors, both of which have a significant impact on the reading level. The structure of e- text may lead to changes in the fundamental relationship between readers and author, where the reader has control over travelling back and forth between horizontal and vertical texts. For example, using non-linear format will allow readers to control their path which is not the same in the case of a linear format that is used to design a paper text) Foltz, 1996).

In addition, it is used in at least three individual perspectives by different researchers and writers in the reading field. The first perspective determines the structure of what the reader will build through knowledge gained (conklin, 1987). The second perspective defines structure as a convention representation of text which occurs according to the expected rules that a writer follows during document production (Suchman, 1988). The final perspective refers to the structure based on the nature of each scientific area (Hammond & Allinson, 1989). Furthermore, the concept of structure for designers refers to breaking the text down into chunks or viewed as a whole content.

A paper book`s layout generally includes front and back cover, table of contents, introductions, main body which is normally numbered sequentially and separated into sections, as well as additional material such as appendix, index or glossary, references and spine. Employing information technology has led to the advent of several types of eBooks which may be classified into 10 types according to Barker`s classifications (Barker, 1992).

Table 5. The number of Internet users in Libya

Year	
1998	Did not exceed one hundred
2001	300000
2003	850000
2006	205000
2009	3539000

Elmabruk, 2009.

Table 6. Studies that addressed the use of the eBook and Internet

Authors and Year	Sample, File and Country	Method and Statistical Tests	Research Focus	Material	Findings
CNN, USA Today, National Science Foundation & Gallup	740 children aged 13 through 17/ middle & high school	Telephone interviews	Children's familiarity with computer & Internet		• 55% had the opportunity to use the Internet • 67% have computer at home.
Perse & Dunn (Perse & Dunn 1998)	Adult/ 1071		Motivations for internet use		People mostly use Internet at home for entertainment.
Stafford, et al. (Stafford, Lline et al. 1999)		Interviews			• 61% use the Internet for communication • 25% business reasons.
National Public Radio	Aged 10- 17		Internet use		Children are more positive than adults in accessing modern technology at school.
Valkenburg & Soetcrs (Valkensburg & Soeters 2001)	194 children aged 8- 13/	MANOVA/	Examine motives for using the Internet & their positive and negative aspects/ use for entertainment & social interaction.		• There is not much difference between younger & older children. • Older children use Internet for finding information about sport and cited email more than younger children • 73% have negative experience with internet.
Sally & Cliff (Maynard & McKnight 2001)	161 participants aged 18- 56+/ Leicestershire area in the UK/ public libraries.	Postal questionnaire	Investigate users about eBook. Awareness of eBook.		96.3% considered eBook as multimedia CD-ROM book & 68.9% thought all texts available in the internet were eBook.
US Bureau of the census (2012)	children aged 6- 11	Questionnaire			• 64.1% have computer access at home • 47.7% using internet.
San Jose Mercury news et al. (Annonymous, 2003)	USA / Silicon Valley/ aged 10- 17/ 804	Randomly selected/ questionnaire	Using computer & Internet		• 79% have Internet access at home • 39% have Internet access from more than one computer at home • 95% having access to Internet at school [lab or library or their desk]
Sally & Emily (Cheyne 2005)	60 pupils/ 12 groups/ aged 11- 12/ local schools in UK.	Experimental/ observations/ qualitative/ ANOVA test.	Comparing reading and learning from paper with reading similar electronic version.	Paper textbook & CD-ROM	Using e-textbook in learning has significant effect on pupils' learning and understanding.

continued on next page

Table 6. Continued

Authors and Year	Sample, File and Country	Method and Statistical Tests	Research Focus	Material	Findings
Buzzetto-More, N., R. Sweat-Guy et al. (Buzzetto-More, Sweat-Guy et al. 2007)	261 students/ 62.2% female (157)/ nearly 74% between the ages of 17-19/ the University of Maryland Eastern Shore USA/	One- way ANOVA test/ questionnaire	• Home internet access. • Use the Internet to gather news and information. • Comfortable reading off a computer screen.		• 92.7% have Internet access at their local residence. • 98% feel comfortable reading off a computer screen. • 22% had read an eBook. • 80% prefer to purchase their textbooks at the bookstore. • 54.8% prefer hardcopy to a digital format. • 58.6% print out a copy from digital format.
Ian Rowlands et al. (Rowlands, Nicholas et al. 2007)			Investigate academic users' awareness, perceptions and existing levels of use of eBooks.		
Grimshaw, S et al. (Grimshaw, Dungworth et al. 2007)	132 children from different primary schools in UK. Aged 9 to 11. From different ethnic and social backgrounds.	Comprehension test/ one- way ANOVA.	Comparing between reading from paper and electronic format.	Story book, in two formats, e & paper format.	Comprehension reading affected by type of materials.
Wood (Wood et al. 2009)	80 participants/ Children aged 5 & 6. 40 males & 40 females. UK	Experimental / read aloud / x^2test/	Investigate the effect of talking book on children reading strategy	4 styles of Talking books/	Talking book has a positive effect on children's performance.
Okon E. Ani (Okon, Margaret et al. 2010)	Undergraduate students in public universities in Nigeria	Questionnaire			• Using for academic purpose • 75% for email
Curtis, Polly et al. (Polly 2009)	five- to 16-year-olds/ UK/	Questionnaire	Address what has been dubbed the "toxic childhood" of children living under intense media influence.		• 62% have profile on social networks. • The number of children aged 5- 16 who read books decreased from 82% in 2006, 80% in 2007and down to 74% in 2009. • 1 in 6 use the Internet 6 hours a day • Average use of the Internet: 1,7 hour a day. • Use less at school.

Generally there is not any particular order or rules to follow when designing e-text which usually depends on the subject, purpose of the text, age of reader, amount of text and screen size. Alternatively, the structure of e- learning material usually depends on what education system is aiming to achieve. In many cases, learning material may be presented as a package which relies mainly on itself to transmit understanding and knowledge to the learner. This special structure of educational material requires from designers a method for displaying content that can help learner to access and define the content of such a learning package (Westwood, 2000).

In addition, two options are available for designers of e- learning material: a deep or shallow structure. A deep structure has several levels, and complex navigation and learners have many options and potentials for full interactions. However, the user with limited experience could be disoriented and lost within this structure. Where, a shallow structure is a simple design. It is also basic and provides the lowest selection.

In the same context, Martin (1990) suggested many conceptual models of eBook such as envelope model, hierarchy model, and the network model. Selecting the most suitable model requires a thorough understanding of the learners' needs and age. The first model ("envelope model") is where information is divided into chunks and then structured before each chunk is then viewed by title. A single envelope can contain other envelopes. This model is easy to index and create; the problem with this model is the lack of links between contents within the envelopes. The second model ("hierarchy model") is similar to the envelope model except that in this model the context is organized in a hierarchical structure using Microsoft Word and World Wide Web. This model allows for connecting cross-links, seeing the structure clearly, but at the same time it lacks the flexibility of navigation. The network structure model has the ability to navigate through an e- text and access the user's needs. The idea of this model is based on adding a navigational structure to the hierarchical content, so that this model can help develop a website based on eBook.

Reviewing this variety of e-educational material shows that there are two designing styles being used:

- **Hypertext Book or Non- Linear:** This type of structure allows the reader to access information by linking many texts to the other. This type takes advantage of e- data processing to organize itself. Thus, it increases the ability of the readers to navigate a complex search structure, helps them to make large quantities of information accessible, and gives the reader the ability not just to read the text from beginning to the end but also to offer choices to select from among many links. Figure 4 is a diagram showing the basic structure of hypertext.

However, in several cases, a hypertext can confuse the reader, especially where readers need to know where they are and where to go next. Thus, some designers suggest using tools that help readers define their path in the text such as a dynamic table of contents, map of contents, or list of chapters. The effect of these tools is the focus of discussion among many researchers interested in online reading by younger pupils, and they argued that understanding navigation search when reading hypertext will provide optimal use to e- text provided in the hypertext format (Salmerón & García, 2011; Lawless et al., 2002; Amadieu, et al. 2009).

- **Linear Format:** Linear refers to the text that is presented in a straight line and read from beginning to end. This is usually done by using portable document format (PDF) which offers several advantages to readers and designers such as the ability to download it install it on every PC network, and security to the text. Figure 5 presents some examples of text presented in the PDF format.

Figure 4. The basic structure of hypertext
Palmer, 1993.

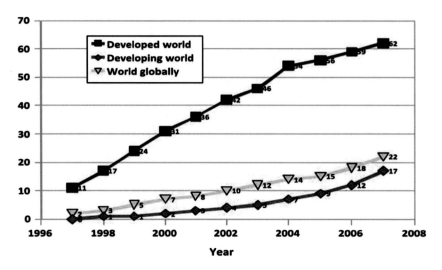

Figure 5. Example of a PDF book[4]

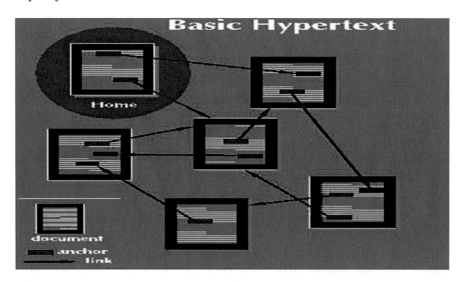

However, the impact of this style in reading for learning is not clear, and that is because most studies conducted in this regard has only focused on the designing issues. Also, the number of comparative studies is not enough. Extensively, eBook for children is used in Arabic countries due to the PDF file and its ability to be downloaded.

In addition, Walker et al (2007) suggested the Visual-Syntactic Text Formatting Theoretical (VSTF) method for increasing reading comprehension as shown in Figure (6). The method has been tested with adults and students in classroom of year 10 and 11 according to UK education (age 15 to 16). The study

Figure 6. Electronic textbooks used in VSTF
Technologies, 2001.

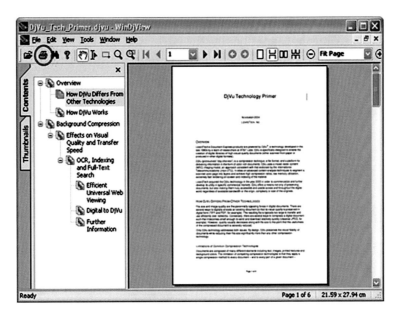

reported a significant improvement in reading comprehension, and score of the quizzes and retention. For example, the mean reading comprehension for control group (reading black text) was 0.225, while it was 0.235 for students who read a VSTF text.

7. EBOOK GUIDELINE

Searching for an eBook guideline has unveiled that only simple and limited attempts have been made, only offering general advice without going into detail or provide any standard for use. For instance, electronic books on screen interface (EBONI) is meant to advise designers when designing material for higher education in an electronic format (Wilson & Monica 2002). The guideline is divided into 22 parts, with each part focusing on one element such as hypertext, text format or eBook technologies. Another guideline ("design typographical aspects carefully") provided suggestions to enhance readability such as using white spaces justify the text to the left side and use line lengths of 10 to 15 words. This guide cannot be accepted as comprehension reference for designing Arabic text for a number of reasons (Haboubi, et al. 2006):

- Different morphological structure to Latin.
- Difference in character width and position.
- Combination of seven vowels.

In the same context, W3C provided in 1999 Web Content Accessibility Guideline 1.0 (Chisholm, 1999), which aims to improve the accessibility of e- content to a wide range of people with disabilities. The last version of the guideline, 2.0, contains four principles, with the third principle intended to "make text content readable and understandable", while the section is divided into three levels. Although the guidelines deal with elements which have an effect on accessibility such as line lengths, page format, and links, there are shortcomings in these principles, e.g. the guideline does not mention the optimal size of a web page and only recommends dividing the page into parts. In addition, it does not solve the problem of using links by defining the optimal number of links.

8. CONCLUSION

This chapter provided a review of the literature in relation to the theoretical and empirical background of eBook and the internet. Generally, there is no universal standard definition for eBook in the literature according to the survey of the eBook field. The review found that the term eBook is still unclear even though several terms have been used in the field such as CD-Room book, visual book, e- paper, web book, electronic text book, and digital book. . The majority of research mentioned in this chapter focused on the application aspects but with limited focus on the conception aspect.

Generally, there is no particular order or rules to follow when designing e-text which is usually dependent on the subject, the purpose of the text, age of the reader, the amount of the text and screen size. Alternatively, the structure of e- learning material usually depends on whatever the education system is aiming to achieve.

The contribution of eBook and the Internet in education has been proven by many studies and experiments that have illustrated the advantages of applying the eBook such as using it to enhance students' phonological awareness, word recognition skills, or extending their verbal knowledge. The average use of the Internet in the developing world is quite high compared to the developing world. In Libya, the average use of the Internet differs from year to year, from the very beginning when it was only available via telephone to the enormous improvement in Internet technology which has seen the number of Internet users dramatically increased.

REFERENCES

W3C. (1999). *Web Content Accessibility Guidelines 1.0*. Retrieved from http://www.w3.org/TR/WCAG10/

Abdullah, N. (2007). *A Study into Usability of Tools for Searching and Browsing E-books with Particular Reference to Back-of-the-Book Index* (PhD Dissertation). Department of Computer and Information Sciences, Strathclyde.

Alan, C. (2001). *Designing computer- based learning materials*. Gower Publishing Limited.

Amadieu, F., Tricot, A., & Marine, C. (2009). Prior knowledge in learning from a nonlinear electronic document: Disorientation and coherence of the reading sequences. *Computers in Human Behavior*, *25*(2), 381–388. doi:10.1016/j.chb.2008.12.017

Ani, O. E., Edem, M. B., & Ottong, E. J. (2010). Analysis of internet access and use by academic staff in the University of Calabar, Calabar, Nigeria. *Library Management*, *31*(7), 535–545. doi:10.1108/01435121011071229

Anonymous, . (1999). NuvoMedia eRocket. *Information Today*, *16*(9), 45.

Anonymous. (2012). *Computer and Internet*. U.S. Department of Commerce. Retrieved from http://census.gov/topics/population/computer-internet.html

Anonymous. (2012). *Access to computer and internet use by U.S.* Retrieved from https://www.census.gov/

Anuradha, K., & Usha, H. S. (2006). Use of e-books in an academic and research environment: A case study from the Indian Institute of Science. *Program*, *40*(1), 48–62. doi:10.1108/00330330610646807

Association, T. T. S. (2003). *Technology update. Techniques*. Author.

Barker, P. (1992). Electronic book and libraries of the future. *The Electronic Library*, *10*(3), 139–149. doi:10.1108/eb045143

Barker, P. (2005). Using e-books for knowledge management. *The Electronic Library*, 5–8.

Bennett, L., & Landoni, M. (2005). E-books in academic libraries. *The Electronic Library*, *23*(1), 9–16. doi:10.1108/02640470510582709

Buzzetto-More, N. R., Sweat-Guy, R., & Elobaid, M. (2007). Reading in A Digital Age: e-Books Are Students Ready For This Learning Object? *Interdisciplinary Journal of Knowledge and Learning Objects*, *3*, 239–250.

Cavanaugh, T. W. (2006). *The Digital Reader: Using E-books in K–12 Education*. Eugene, OR: International Society for Technology in Education.

Chera, P., & Wood, C. (2003). Animated multimedia talking books can promote phonological awareness in children beginning to read. *Learning and Instruction*, *13*(1), 33–52. doi:10.1016/S0959-4752(01)00035-4

Cheyne, S. M. E. (2005). Can electronic textbook help children to learn. *The Electronic Library*, *23*(1), 103–115. doi:10.1108/02640470510582781

Chien, C., Chen, C. H., & Wu, H. C. (2007). *Tool, toy, telephone, or information: Children' perceptions of the Internet*. San Francisco: APA.

Chou, C., Yu, S., Chen, C., & Wu, H. (2009). Tool, Toy, Telephone, Territory, or Treasure of information: Elementary school students attitudes toward the internet. *Computers & Education*, *53*(2), 308–319. doi:10.1016/j.compedu.2009.02.003

Conklin, J. (1987). Hypertext: An introduction and survey. *Computers & Education*, 17–41.

Connaway, L. S. (2007). *The future of e- book*. New York: Marcel Dekker.

Crestani, F., Landoni, M., & Melucci, M. (2006). Appearance and functionality of electronic books. *International Journal on Digital Libraries*, *6*(2), 192–209. doi:10.1007/s00799-004-0113-9

Dillon, A. (1994). *Designing usable electronic text: ergonomic aspects of human information usage*. Philadelphia, PA: Taylor & Francis. doi:10.4324/9780203470343

Dyson, M. C. (2004). How physical text layout affects reading from screen. *Behaviour & Information Technology*, *23*(6), 377–393. doi:10.1080/01449290410001715714

Egan, D. E., Remde, J. R., Gomez, L. M., Landauer, T. K., Eberhardt, J., & Lochbaum, C. C. (1989). Formative design evaluation of super book. *ACM Transactions on Information Systems*, *7*(1), 30–57. doi:10.1145/64789.64790

Elmabruk, R. (2009). *Using the Internet to support Libyan in-service EFL teachers' professional development* (PhD Dissertation). University of Nottingham.

Foltz, P. W. (1996). *Comprehension, Coherence and Strategies in Hypertext and Linear Text*. Hypertext and Cognition. Retrieved from http://www-psych.nmsu.edu/~pfoltz/reprints/Ht-Cognition.html

Frenckner, K. (1990). *Legibility of continuous text on computer screens -- a guide to the literature*. TRITA-NA.

Greenlee-Moore, M., & Smith, L. (1996). Interactive computer software: The effects on young childrens reading achievement. *Reading Psychology*, *17*(1), 43–64. doi:10.1080/0270271960170102

Gunn, H., & Hepburn, G. (2003). Seeking information for school purposes on the Internet. *Canadian Journal of Learning and Technology*, *29*(1).

Haboubi, S., Maddouri, S., & Amiri, H. (2006). *Identification of Arabic word from bilingual text using character features: Case of structural features*. Retrieved from https://arxiv.org/ftp/arxiv/papers/1103/1103.3430.pdf

Hamilton, R., Richards, C., & Sharp, C. (2001). *An examination of E- learning and E- books. SocBytes Journal*.

Hammond, N., & Allinson, L. (1989). Extending Hypertext for Learning: an Investigation of Access and Guidance Tools People and Computers. Cambridge University Press.

Harcourt, W. (2004). The personal and political: Women using the internet. *Cyberpsychology & Behavior*, *3*(5), 693–697. doi:10.1089/10949310050191692

Hawkins, D. T. (2000). Electronic books: A major publishing revolution (part 1). *Online*, *24*(4), 14–28.

Ismail, R., & Zainab, A. N. (2005). The pattern of e-book use amongst undergraduates in Malaysia: A case of to know is to use. *Malaysian Journal of Library and Information Science*, *10*(2), 1–23.

Jamali, H.R., Nicholas, D. & Rowlands, I. (2009). Scholarly ebooks: the views of 16,000 academics. *New Information Perspectives, 61*(1), 33-47.

Jeng, S. C., Lin, Y. R., Liu, K. H., Liao, C. C., Wen, C. H., Chao, C. Y., & Shieh, K. K. (2005). *Legibility of electronic paper*. The 5th International Meeting on Information Display. Seoul, Korea.

Johnston, S. P., & Huczynski, A. (2006). Textbook publishers website objective question banks: Does their use improve students examination performance? *Active Learning in Higher Education*, *7*(3), 257–271. doi:10.1177/1469787406069057

Khatkar, A., (2014). A Comprehensive Review on WiMAX Networks. *International Journal of Innovations in Engineering and Technology, 3*(3).

Kleeck, A. V. (2003). *Research on book-sharing: another critical look.* Mahwah, NJ: Lawrence Erlbaum Associates.

Kolikant, Y. B. D. (2009). Digital Students in a Book-Oriented School: Students' Perceptions of School and the Usability of Digital Technology in Schools. *Journal of Educational Technology & Society*, *12*(2), 131–143.

Lam, P., Lam, S. L., Lam, J., & McNaught, C. (2009). Usability and usefulness of ebooks on PPCs. *Australasian Journal of Educational Technology*, *25*(1), 30–44. doi:10.14742/ajet.1179

Landoni, M. (1997). *The Visual Book system: a study of the use of visual rhetoric in the design of electronic books.* Glasgow, UK: University of Strathclyde.

Landoni, M. (2010). Ebooks children would want to read and engage with.*Proceedings of the third workshop on Research advances in large digital book repositories and complementary media,25*-28. doi:10.1145/1871854.1871862

Landoni, M., & Diaz, P. (2003). E-education: Design and evaluation for teaching and learning. *Journal of Digital Information*, *3*(4).

Landoni, M., & Gibb, F. (2000). The role of visual rhetoric in the design and production of electronic books: The visual book. *The Electronic Library*, *18*(3), 190–201. doi:10.1108/02640470010337490

Landoni, M., & Wilson, R. (2002). *EBONI: Electronic Textbook Design Guidelines.* University of Strathclyde.

Landoni, M., Wilson, R., & Gibb, F. (2000). From the visual book to the web book: The importance of design. *The Electronic Library*, *18*(6), 407–419. doi:10.1108/02640470010361169

Leeuw, S.D., & Rydin, I. (2007). Migrant children's digital stories. *Identity Formation and Self-Representation Through Media Production, 10*(4), 447.

Liu, Z. (2005). Reading behaviour in the digital environment: changes in reading behaviour over the past ten years. *Journal of Documentation, 61*(6), 700- 712.

Ma, H. (2005). Interpreting middle school students` online experiences a phenological approach. colloge of education. Ohio, Ohio university. PhD: 237.

Martin, J. (1990). *Hyperdocuments and how to create them.* Prentice Hall.

Martínez-Prieto, M. A., Fuente, P. D. L., Vegas, J. M., Adiego, J., & Cuesta, C. E. (2008). Enhancing literary electronic books with logical structure: Electronic work. *The Electronic Library*, *26*(4), 490–504. doi:10.1108/02640470810893747

Maynard, S., & McKnight, C. (2001). Childrens comprehension of electronic books: An empirical study. *The New Review of Childrens Literature and Librarianship, 7*(1), 29–53. doi:10.1080/13614540109510643

Maynard, S., & McKnight, C. (2001). electronic book for children in the UK public libraries. *The Electronic Library*, *19*(6), 405–423. doi:10.1108/02640470110412026

Maynard, S. & McKnight, C. (2001). *Electronic books for children in UK public libraries.* Academic Press.

Miller, L., Blackstock, J., & Miller, R. (1994). An exploratory study into the use of CD-ROM storybooks. *Computers & Education*, 22(1-2), 187–204. doi:10.1016/0360-1315(94)90087-6

Miller, L. M. (2001). middle school students` technology practices and preferences: Reexamine gender difference. *Journal of Educational Multimedia and Hypermedia*, 10(2), 125–140.

Murray, M. (2012). Amazon kindle.Back Stage, 53(39), 17.

Nathan, R. J., Yeow, P. P., & Murugesan, S. (2008). Key usability factors of service-oriented web sites for students: An empirical study. *Online Information Review*, 32(3), 302–324. doi:10.1108/14684520810889646

News, S. J. M. & Foundation, K.F. (2003). *Growing Up Wired: Survey on Youth and the Internet in the Silicon Valley*. Academic Press.

Nicholas, D., Hamid, P. H., Rowlands, J. I., Dobrowolski, T., & Tenopir, C. (2008). Viewing and reading behaviour in a virtual environment: The full- text download and what can be read into it. *Aslib Proceedings*, 60(3), 185–198. doi:10.1108/00012530810879079

Noorhidawati, A., & Forbes, G. (2008). Students attitudes towards e-books in a Scottish higher education institute: Part 1. *Library Review*, 57(8), 593–605. doi:10.1108/00242530810899577

OECD. (2005). *Are students ready for a technology-rich world? What PISA studies tell us*. Paris: OECD.

Palmer, S. B. (1993). *Proto HTML*. Retrieved 20-10-2011, from http://infomesh.net/stuff/proto

Papacharissi, Z., & Rubin, A. M. (2000). Predictors of internet use. *Journal of Broadcasting & Electronic Media*, 44(2), 175–197. doi:10.1207/s15506878jobem4402_2

Park, W. H. (2009). Academic internet use in Korea: Issues and lessons in e- research. WebSci09: Society on-line, Athens, Greece.

Perse, E. M., & Dunn, D. G. (1998). The utility of home computers and media use: Implications of multimedia and connectivity. *Journal of Broadcasting & Electronic Media*, 42(4), 435–456. doi:10.1080/08838159809364461

Polding, R., Nunes, J. M. B., & Kingston, B. (2008). Assessing e-book model sustainability. *Journal of Librarianship and Information Science*, 40(4), 255–268. doi:10.1177/0961000608096715

Polly, C. (2009). National: Internet generation leave parents behind: Change in communication creating divide, says study: Children spend six hours a day in front of screens. *The Guardian*.

Rowlands, I., Nicholas, D., Jamali, H. R., & Huntington, P. (2007). What do faculty and students really think about e-books? *Aslib Proceedings: New Information Perspectives*, 59(6), 489–511. doi:10.1108/00012530710839588

Salmerón, L., & García, V. (2011). Reading skills and childrens navigation strategies in hypertext. *Computers in Human Behavior*, 27(3), 1143–1151. doi:10.1016/j.chb.2010.12.008

Segers, E., & Verhoven, L. (2002). Multimedia support of early literacy learning. *Computers & Education*, 39(3), 207–221. doi:10.1016/S0360-1315(02)00034-9

Shaffer, D. W., & Clinton, K. A. (2006). Tool for thoughts: Re-examining thinking in the digital age. *Mind, Culture, and Activity, 13*(4), 283–300. doi:10.1207/s15327884mca1304_2

Shaw, L. H., & Gant, L. M. (2002). users divided? use. *Cyberpsychology & Behavior, 5*(6), 517–527. doi:10.1089/109493102321018150 PMID:12556114

Shin, D.H. (2011). Understanding e-book users: Uses and gratification expectancy model. *New Media & Society, 13*(2), 260-278.

Shiratuddin, N., Landoni, M., Gibb, F., & Hassan, H. (2003). E-book technology and its potential applications in distant education. *Journal of Digital Information, 3*(4).

Stafford, L., Kline, S. L., & Dimmick, J. (1999). Home e-mail: Relational maintenance and gratification opportunities. *Journal of Broadcasting & Electronic Media, 43*(4), 659–669. doi:10.1080/08838159909364515

Suchman, L. (1988). *Plans and Situated Action.* Cambridge, UK: Cambridge University Press.

Tadoz. (2010). *What the Arab state in Internet use.* Tadoz Technical Arabic.

Tapscott, D. (1998). Educating in digital world. *Education Canada, 41*(1), 4–7.

Tenopir, C., King, D. W., Edwards, S., & Wu, L. (2009). Electronic journal and changes in scholarly article seeking and reading patterns. *Aslib Proceedings, 61*(1), 5–32. doi:10.1108/00012530910932267

Trushell, J., Burrell, C., & Maitland, A. (2001). Year 5 pupils reading an Interactive Storybook on CD-ROM: Losing the plot? *British Journal of Educational Technology, 32*(4), 389–401. doi:10.1111/1467-8535.00209

Valkensburg, P. M. & Soeters, K.E., (2001). Children`s positive and negative experience with the internet: an exploratory survey. *Communication Research, 28*(5), 652- 675.

Vassiliou, M. & Rowley, J., (2008). Theme article progressing the definition of "e- book". *Library Hi Tech, 26*(3), 355-368.

Walker, R. C., Gordon, A. S., & Schloss, P. (2007). Visual-Syntactic Text-Formatting: Theoretical Basis and Empirical Evidence for Impact on Human Reading. *IEEE International Professional Communication Conference Engineering the Future of Human Communication.* doi:10.1109/IPCC.2007.4464068

Weiser, E. B. (2002). Gender differences in internet usepatterns and internet application preferences: A two sample comparison. *Cyberpsychology & Behavior, 3*(2), 167–178. doi:10.1089/109493100316012

Wilson, R., Landoni, M., & Gibb, F. (2002). A user-centred approach to Ebook design. *The Electronic Library, 20*(4), 30–32. doi:10.1108/02640470210438865

Wilson, R., Landoni, M., & Gibb, F. (2003). The WEB Book experiments in electronic textbook design. *The Journal of Documentation, 59*(4), 454–476. doi:10.1108/00220410310485721

Wright, P., & Lickorish, A. (1988). Colour cues as location aids in lengthy texts on screen and paper. *Behaviour & Information Technology, 7*(1), 11–30. doi:10.1080/01449298808901860

ENDNOTES

[1]   http://www.kerryr.net/pioneers/gallery/ns_bush8.htm

[2]   http://en.wikipedia.org/wiki/Sony_Reader#2006_Model_.28Discontinued_late_2007.29

[4]   http://www.hd-videoconverter.com/convert-djvu-to-pdf.html.

Chapter 9

Access and Use of the Internet among Libyan Primary School Students:
Analysis of Questionnaire Data

Azza A Abubaker
Benghazi University, Libya & University of Huddersfield, UK

Joan Lu
University of Huddersfield, UK

ABSTRACT

This chapter aims to examine the use of the internet and eBook among students in public primary schools in Libya. The literature showed a lack of research that examines access to the Internet, students' aware- ness of eBook, and using the computer for learning at school. However, this type of research has been important in providing a better understanding of eBook usage and helping designers to create eBooks that meet user needs. Thus, the number of netizens determines the causes of use as a starting point for understanding and determining e- reading stages in order to investigate the factors that affect e- text reading among young people. This chapter presents the questionnaire data as analysed by the Statistical Package for the Social Sciences (SPSS) software for analysis and focuses on collecting quantitative data that can help build a clear understanding of current user behaviour. At the end of this chapter, these two objectives should be met: examining the use of Internet among students aged 9 to 13, and defining the awareness and aim of using eBook among students.

DATA COLLECTION METHODS AND RESEARCH TYPE

In phase one, a quantitative approach is employed to collect numerical data. Research questions one, two and three were concerned with determining the use of the Internet, eBook and computer among students in primary schools in Libya. Data can be collected by employing different methods such as interviews, questionnaire, observations, etc. The choice between these techniques depends on the research philosophy

DOI: 10.4018/978-1-5225-1884-6.ch009

and the aim of the study or research questions; thus, questionnaire was selected as the collecting method in this phase which is defined as a list of carefully structured questions (Collis, 2009).

The most appropriate questionnaire type to use was a collective administration questionnaire (Kumar, 2011). Collective administration questionnaire was used because it has been widely used as a primary data collecting method in usability research and applying the Internet in education process studies in particular. The opportunity to analyse a large amount of information, the limited time and resource available to the researcher, allows for personal contact with the study population. This in turn makes it easy to explain the purpose and difficult terms, to collect the completed questionnaires within a short time, and get a very high response rate wherein no one refuses to participate.

1.1 Questionnaire Design

The design of the questionnaire can have a huge impact on many aspects of the research conducted. It provides a framework for the collection and analysis of data, while a poor design will fail to provide accurate answers to questions under investigation. Thus, several researchers recommend a number of considerations that should be taken into account when building a questionnaire such as the questions' order, type, and length (Boynton & Greenhalgh 2004; Bell, 2007).

Therefore, careful attention was given in this study to improving the questionnaire through focusing on the principles of questionnaire design that are effective in the case of paper questionnaires (Phillips, 2008). In addition, it was crucial to ensure that the format of the questionnaire was clear, with the use of sub-headings, clearly defined sections, and bold text where appropriate, and the use of simple language to facilitate answering. Moreover, clear instructions were given about how the questionnaire should be completed to avoid any confusion that could lead to wrong answers; thus, students answer the questionnaire in class under the teacher's control in order to clarify and explain questions to students in addition to ensuring that all students answer all questions.

In applying the feedback from the pilot study, the final version of the questionnaire was designed. This final version was divided into two main parts. The first part was designed to collect information about the participants regarding individual variables, whereas Q1 and Q2 were devoted to collecting demographic information about the students [age & gender]. While in Q3, students were asked to provide information about their level of education.

In addition, part 2 aims to addresses the use of the computer, eBook and internet by young students who study in Libyan schools, both at school and at home. Sections A involves 13 questions (7 closed questions and 6 open questions), while section B focused on using e- book for learning proposes. The section contains seven questions. The final section (section D) focused on collecting data about using a schoolbook and defined the process used when reading schoolbooks (as seen in Table 1).

However, most of the questions were closed with predetermined answers that simply required a box to be ticked or questions with two and four points, while a ranked response was avoided because of the difficulty of selection and the ability to determine the difference between those choices.

1.2 Questionnaire Translation

The questionnaire of this study was initially drawn up and produced in English, and after all components of the questionnaire were determined, the English version of the questionnaire was prepared and then given to an independent translator to translate it into Arabic; also, the researcher has translated a copy

Table 1. Constructor of the questionnaire

Questionnaire's Parts	Section	Address of the Part	Number of Questions
Part 1		Participant's regarding individual variables	3
Part 2	Section A	the use of the computer, and internet	13
	Section B	The use of the eBook	7
	Section D	Using a schoolbook	6

of the questionnaire and compared it with the first copy. In addition, considerable attention was given to eliminating any problems and difficulties that may occur during the process of developing the Arabic draft of the questionnaire used in this study. Therefore, the Arabic version of the questionnaire was passed on to another interpreter who translated the questionnaire back into English. Comparing the two versions of the questionnaires showed some changes in the meaning of the questions, which required correcting the words and the meaning of each question.

1.3 Questionnaire Piloting

A pilot test was recommended by several researchers such as Oppenheim (2003) and Saunders et al. (2003), who argued that every aspect of the research survey should be piloted. They also argued that it can be used to help increase reliability and validity of measures and ensure that the questions' wording is clear and understood by the participants of the study.

Additionally, all aspects of the questionnaire were piloted, including question content, wording, sequence, form and layout. The first draft of the questionnaire was reviewed by the researcher's supervisor. Subsequently, an Arabic version of the questionnaire was distributed to a small sample of Libyan students studying in the UK (25 students who studied at the Libyan school in Huddersfield, UK); similar to those who were included in the actual survey, for their review and comments.

However, the feedback was very significant which resulted in reordering some sections in the questionnaire, deleting some questions from the questionnaire, dividing the questionnaire into parts to become more manageable, and rewording some of the words such as navigation حفصتلا where the majority of students cannot understand what it means.

Finally, part of the Arabic questionnaire was sent to a friend, who is a teacher at a Libyan primary school, to ensure that the questionnaire was not too long and without words that may be too difficult for students. Notes were received by e-mail which indicated that the questionnaire was clear and easy to complete. After taking all the comments, suggestions, and ideas, amendments were made, resulting in a final draft of the Arabic questionnaire which is presented in appendix (2) and the English version in appendix (1).

1.4 Population and Selection of the Sample for the Questionnaire

Research population is defined by Sekaran (2003) as "the entire group of people, events, or things of interest that the researcher wishes to investigate", while sample is described as "a subgroup of elements of the population selected for participation in the study" (Malhotra, et al. 2003).

The target population comprised of students aged 9 to 13, attending Libyan public primary schools. Because of the large size of the study population, a sample of the study population was selected that truly represents the entire research population. However, there are several ways to determine the appropriate size of a sample, all of which depends on three factors: (1) the size of the population under study; (2) the research budget; (3) the degree of error accepted; and (4) the precision required.

The total size of the participant sample was set at 504 participants where the sampling technique is a probability technique (to select the school) and non-probability sampling technique used to select participants from students in level 4, 5, and 6 for the questionnaire. This technique mainly relies on personal judgment of the researcher. The sample was distributed as follows:

- 234 males, thereby representing 46.43%; and 270 females, thereby representing 53.67%.
- The age of participants was between 9 and 13 years.
- They are distributed to the three studying stages: level 4 was 134 students, level 5 180 students, and 190 students in level 6 (as shown in Table 2).

Table 3 and Figure 1 show the distribution of the sample based on education level in each school. All students in year 4, 5 and 6 were selected in the five schools. The number of students in the year 6 was the largest in the five schools. To avoid the impact of age difference among students, a large number of students are supposed to be in the fifth grade, but were enrolled early at age 5. In addition, the sample comprising five public schools in Benghazi was selected to distribute the questionnaire more broadly. In order to ensure that the sample includes all segments of society, schools were selected from different geographical regions. In addition, schools located in the outskirts of the city have been excluded because of the difference in patterns of living which can affect the level of computer use.

Students' gender was used as a second factor to measure the usability of eBook and Internet and to report if there is a distinction in the student's skill level where some researchers have shown that there is a difference in the usability of internet and eBook according to the gender variable.

Finally, it would be useful to justify the reasons behind choosing the participants only from Libya despite the number of Arab countries (22 countries). Importantly, Libya is the home country of the researcher, which means that the researcher is able to collect the required information without any difficulties regarding time issues, obtaining permission to distribute the questionnaire, living costs, and

Table 2. Demographic characteristics of the sample

Characteristics		Frequency
Age	9	100
	10	156
	11	118
	12	110
	13	20
Gender	Male	234
	Female	270
Education level or Year of study	Year 4	134
	Year 5	180
	Year 6	190
Total		504

Table 3. The distribution of the sample based on education level in each school

	Education Level			
Schools	**Year 4**	**Year 5**	**Year 6**	**Total**
Cortba	27	42	32	101 students
Umm Habiba	28	32	39	99 students
Tariq ibn Ziyad	28	35	39	102 students
Geleana	24	36	40	100 students
Green book	27	35	40	102 students
Total	134	180	190	504

Figure 1. The distribution of the sample based on education level in each school

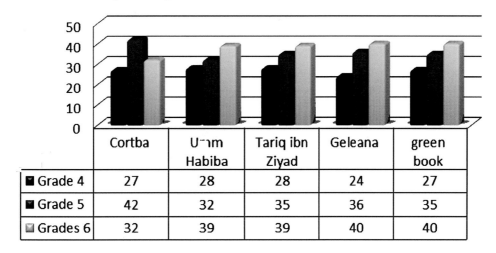

	Cortba	U⁻ɪm Habiba	Tariq ibn Ziyad	Geleana	green book
■ Grade 4	27	28	28	24	27
■ Grade 5	42	32	35	36	35
▨ Grades 6	32	39	39	40	40

so on. Notwithstanding the existence of local dialects in various Arab countries, Arabic is the language used in teaching and learning in all these countries.

2. QUESTIONNAIRE DATA ANALYSIS

2.1 Internet Access

Internet application in Libya is quite new and limited in the education field, as Libyan primary schools still could not provide Internet access for their students. Thus, there is no tangible benefit of Internet use to students in their education activities as it is simply not available. The absence of teachers' direction reduces the scientific use of the Internet. In addition, the study reported that the total average use of the Internet among participants was high, where 86.1% of responders have access to the Internet after school time without any direction from the teacher. Participants who use the Internet are mainly divided into daily users (43.84%) and weekly users (28.37%), see Table 4 and Figure 2.

Table 4. Internet use by respondents

	Number	Percentage
I do use the Internet.	445	88.29%
I use the Internet daily.	224	50..34%
I use the Internet at least once a week.	143	32.13%
I use the Internet occasionally.	78	17.53%
I do not use the Internet at all.	59	11.71%

Figure 2. Internet use by respondents

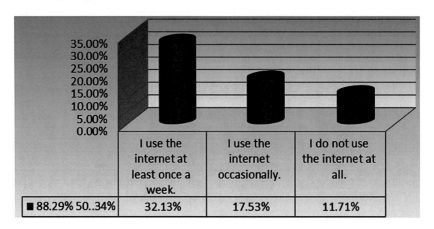

Furthermore, the hours of using the Internet daily differed among users, as seen in Table 5 which show the distribution of using the internet among participants. For example, 37.10% of respondents used the internet an hour daily and 30.76% spent just half an hour daily on the internet. The high average of using the internet for only a short time highlight the need to know the reason behind this limited use by asking questions such as: is this because respondents find the internet boring or because they do not have enough skills to use the Internet? Examining the quantitative data showed that the majority of students who use the internet for a short time did not have access to the internet at home. In addition, 35% indicated that they did not have good skills to work effectively with a computer, although students start learning computer from year five. Therefore, schools should work to develop students' and parents' skills on using the internet for learning purposes effectively. Then, the designer should take the next step by providing reliable e-material that meets students' requirements and encourage them to move from using the paper book to eBook.

In developing countries there are several barriers that reduce using the Internet widely such as a lack of access and slow internet speed, but the high price of getting ITC is the main barrier between all these (Paterson, 2007). In Libya, the case was different; getting a laptop or PC is not the main barrier that reduces the use of the Internet since the survey reported that 86.1% of participants had indicated that they have a laptop or PC at home and 49.08% have more than one PC at home as seen in Table 6). Thus, limitation in Internet use could be due to the quality of service, the limited range of available e-Arabic books for children, and the quality of eBooks, poor design of free e- Arabic books, poor Arabic children's websites, and a lack of support from the schools.

Table 5. The average daily use of the Internet

How Long Do Students Use the Internet Daily?	Number	Percentage
Half an hour	168	37.08%
One hour	152	33.55%
Two hours	102	22.51%
More than three hours	31	6.84%

Table 6. The average having computer and access to the Internet at home

	Have a Computer at Home		Connect to the Internet		Have More than One Computer at Home	
	Number	Parentage	Number	Parentage	Number	Parentage
Yes	434	86.1%	316	62.7%	213	49.08
No	70	13.9%	174	34.5%	221	50.92
Total	504	100.0	504	100.0	434	100

Table 7 demonstrates where students usually access the Internet: at home, at school or public centre. 64.05% of students do not have access to the Internet at home and thus use it at public centres where usually a private space for children's use costs 50p per hour. This explains the high rate of Internet use between one hour and half an hour. Still, 8.33% of students who have access to the Internet at home also go to public centres with friends and use the Internet for entertainment purposes.

2.2. Students' Awareness of eBook

According to previous research, there is a certain lack of awareness on eBook among students and educators especially young users, so that the field survey began by asking several benchmark questions which show whether students are familiar with eBook. The findings demonstrated that eBook is not a familiar source of information for students in primary schools in Libya. The majority of participants (71.4%) in this study pointed out that they were not familiar with the eBook, although 86.1% of participants have a computer at home and the daily average use of the internet was high. In addition, 83% of participants thought that any text on the internet was eBook, while 13.9% did not provide any answer to this question which means that they did not actually have any idea about the meaning of eBook. This finding could be summarized as follows:

Table 7. Where students usually access the Internet

Access into Internet	Number	Parentage
At school	-	-
At home	156	35.94
At public centre	278	64.05
At both (home & public centre)	291	67.05

- **Using the Internet Randomly Without Support from School:** As mentioned earlier, all students use the Internet outside of school and 64.05% have access to the Internet at commercial centres; thus, they did not get any guidance from their parents or teachers. Also, 30% of students who use the Internet at home have parents who manage their internet use but in some cases the parents do not know how to help their children use the internet safely and effectively.
- **Lack of or Poor Arabic Online Sources:** Searching for an Arabic online book for children (35 eBooks) showed only poor quality books compared to eBooks written in English, where the majority was presented in PDF file and did not include sound and animation. In addition, 53.2% of responders pointed out that they were not aware of the availability of websites that provided electronic Arabic books.

In addition, the findings revealed that 85.11% had not used an eBook before the survey (as seen in Table 8). This finding is not surprising in terms of the absence of a real understanding of the meaning of eBook and students not getting any guidance from school which could lead to misuse among students. Similar percentages were recorded in the UK and USA, although the difference is in terms of the type of respondents that were involved [e.g. students from higher education and staff]. 75 students (14.88%) had already used an eBook, 23 students (4.56%) had read or used fewer e- stories available on the internet, and 56 students (11.11%) used e- Quran. On the other hand, participants who had not used eBooks tended to state several reasons for this: 69.64% never heard of the term 'eBook', or otherwise had not seen it; 6% could not access an e-book; and 11% used it because it is as portable as the paper version.

In addition, it was expected that the level of eBook usage might be affected by the participants' age, education level and gender. Consequently, a Chi-Square test χ^2 test was implemented to define whether any connection exists. The test revealed that there is no strong association between age and using eBook, and gender has little influence on the average use of eBook (as can be seen in Table 9). Starting with the age variable where several previous research predicted an association between students' age and using eBook, the test found $X^2 = 3.495$, p > 005 (.479) which confirms that there is no association between age and usage of e- book among children.

Moreover, an association between gender and using eBook was found X^2 (1, N= 496) = 2.369, p >0.005 where p – value should be <05 or =05 to accept the association. According into this finding there is no significant association between gender and using eBook.

Table 8. Students' awareness of eBook

	Responders	%
Were You Familiar with the Term eBook before This Survey?		
Yes	67	13.29
No	351	69.64
No answer	84	16.66
Have You Read an eBook Before?		
Yes	75	14.88
No	429	85.11
No answer	-	-

Table 9. Association between age and usage of eBook among children using chi-Square test

Association	No. of Valid	Value (Pearson X²)	df	P
Is there an association between students' age and using eBook?	496	3.495	4	.479
Is there an association between gender and using eBook?	496	2.369	1	.124
Is there an association between educational level and using eBook?	496	2.615	2	.270

2.3 The Purpose of Using the Internet

As indicated earlier, students have used the computer and Internet for various purposes such as communication, entertainment, share information, or because of their interest and hobbies. Therefore, it is necessary to identify the area where using the Internet and computer would address students' attitudes to ICT. So, a key question was asked to determine their motives for using the Internet. At this point, our survey finds that students use the Internet for two purposes: academic and non- academic purposes.

2.3.1 Academic Use of Internet

Using the Internet for academic purposes has increased day after day with the improvement in learning and research tools which support students in their day-to–day learning. Consequently, participants were asked to indicate different academic purposes for using the Internet. The survey ranks five purposes for academic use to help students in their selection. The finding of the survey as shown in Table 10) indicated that the majority of participants did not use the Internet for one of the five purposes suggested based on previous research in the usage of the Internet. The survey results indicate that learning comes second with 19.82%, thus, the Internet is not used by Libyan students mostly for academic activities. In addition, students who selected the "other" option provided the following two additional reasons for using the Internet: 26.2% of participants (48 students) use it for learning English, while 71% (130 students) of participants use it for learning the Quran and stories from the Quran. Another 27.3% (50 students) use it to improve their skills, e.g. to learn how to create e-mail or design websites (those students generally use English sources, studied in the UK and can speak English). Moreover, teachers in Libyan schools

Table 10. The academic purposes of using the Internet

Purpose of Use	Number	Percentage
To look up the answer to specific questions	2	0.4
To find material for the project	2	0.4
To support research work	5	1.10
To read eBook related to school	-	-
To visit recommended websites	-	-
Other	176	39.51
Total using the Internet	453	

did not set homework to be done using the Internet because students would use it out of school rather than under the teachers' direction, and schools did not provide this service for students at school.

Furthermore, the survey reported a relationship between age and treason of using the Internet, where students in year 6 use the Internet for academic purposes more than any other groups. On the other hand, all the schools do not have a website to support home school links and to ensure that information about school Intranet is shared. Schools therefore miss out on the use of the Internet as a means of communication between staff, students and parents.

However, applying the Internet as an assisting tool in education in Arabic countries is still under investigation among several of countries such as Libya and Saudi Arabia, but more research should be done to evaluate available sources and define the types of e- sources based on education systems and learning requirements.

2.3.2 Non-Academic Use of the Internet

Students in this survey used the Internet after school time without any direction from teachers, so it is not surprising that the highest percentage of students who used the internet did it for entertainment. This finding is similar to other research that reported students' tendency to use the internet for multiple reasons such as (Chien Chon 2009). As shown in Table 11 and Figure 3, the most common reason for using the Internet was to "play games" (87.1%) and "chatting" (48.2). Emailing is less popular among participants who just create an email for subscribing to a website that asks for email.

In addition, because most students use the Internet without any guidance from school or parents, they may access sites that are not suitable for their age, while 43.56% of respondents who use the Internet for communication have an account on Facebook, 13% of participants have accounts on Twitter, and 22% have accounts on both.

Alternatively, students' attitudes towards the Internet differed according to gender and education level. According to the age variable, the survey shows that using the Internet among younger children was lower compared to older children. Playing online games was the first choice for using the Internet for participants aged 9 (24 participants), while watching video came in second (12 students). Older children used the internet for a variety of purposes but the majority used it to play online games (200 responders). also, playing online games and reading sports news were more popular for males, while females spent the majority of their time online chatting. Moreover, listening to music and downloading videos were used by girls more than boys.

Table 11. Non- academic use of the Internet

Non-Academic Use of the Internet	Number	Mean	%
Listening to music	290	.576	57.5
Watching or downloading the video	132	.262	26.2
Chatting	243	.482	48.2
Emailing	100	.198	19.8
Playing online games	439	.871	87.1

Figure 3. Non- academic use of the Internet

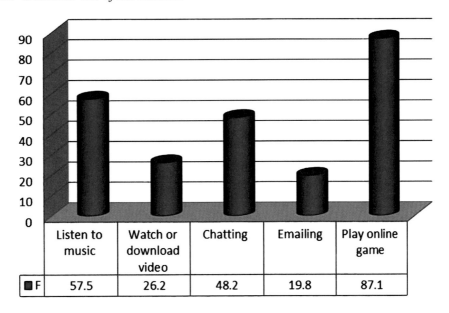

	Listen to music	Watch or download video	Chatting	Emailing	Play online game
■ F	57.5	26.2	48.2	19.8	87.1

3. CONCLUSION

This chapter indicates several important findings that can be classified into two aspects: the use of the Internet, and the use of eBook. The finding of this survey showed that students are confident with using the Internet at home or at public centres for multiple purposes that may be classified into two categories: academic and non- academic use. A deeper analysis showed that boys and girls use the Internet for the same purposes such as gaming and mailing, but the average use is different where boys tend to use the Internet for gaming more than girls, and the latter tend to listen to music and download videos. Moreover, participants state several reasons for not using eBook such as the low quality of Arabic eBooks and a lack of knowledge about their existence. Moreover, the findings show that, there is no strong association between age, gender and using eBook, and there is a certain lack of awareness on eBook among students and educators especially young users.

Therefore, eBooks should be designed in order to be able to satisfy the educational requirements of students. To achieve this aim, a thorough investigation would require defining reader requirements.

The collecting data helps in building up a picture about the usability of the Internet, selecting the sample for the observation of students who have experience in using the internet and e – text, defining impediments to the use of eBook, and outlining the purpose of using the internet and eBook.

REFERENCES

Bell, A. (2007). Designing and testing questionnaires for children. *Journal of Research in Nursing, 12*(5), 461–469. doi:10.1177/1744987107079616

Boynton, P. M., & Greenhalgh, T. (2004). Selecting, designing, and developing your questionnaire. *BMJ (Clinical Research Ed.), 328*(7451), 1312–1315. doi:10.1136/bmj.328.7451.1312 PMID:15166072

Chien, C. S., Chao, C., Hsiu, C., & Wu, H. S. (2009). Tool, Toy, Telephone, Territory, or Treasure of information: Elementary school students attitudes toward the internet. *Computers & Education*, *53*(2), 308–319. doi:10.1016/j.compedu.2009.02.003

Collis, J. & Hussey, R. (2009). *Business research: A practical guide for undergraduate & postgraduate students*. Academic Press.

Kumar, R. (2011). *Research Methodology: a step- by- step guide for beginners*. London: SAGE.

Malhotra, N. K., Birks, D. F., & Wills, P. (2003). *Marketing research: An applied approach*. Essex, UK: Prentic Hall.

Oppenheim, A. N. (2003). *Questionnaire design, interviewing and attitude measurement*. London: Continuum.

Paterson, A. (2007). Costs of information and communication technology in developing country school systems: The experience of Botswana, Namibia and Seychelles. *International Journal of Education and Development using Information and Communication Technology, 3*(4), 89-101.

Phillips, P. P., & Stawarski, C. A. (2008). *Data collection planning for and collecting all types of data*. Wiley.

Saunders, M. N. K., Thrnhill, A., & Lewis, P. (2003). *Research methods for business students*. Harlow, UK: Financial Times Prentice Hall.

Sekaran, U. (2003). *Research methods for business: a skill-building approach*. New York: Wiley.

Chapter 10
Experiment 1:
On Reading Process of Schoolbook in Two Formats (Electronic and Paper Formats)

Azza A Abubaker
Benghazi University, Libya

Joan Lu
University of Huddersfield, UK

ABSTRACT

In order to be sure that the level of e-text usability in early education can be improved, the following questions should be answered by the end of this chapter: RQ1: What are the existing prototypes (structure) of schoolbooks in primary education (PE)? RQ2: How are students interacting with schoolbooks in the electronic and printed version? RQ3: Is there a difference in the reading process between e-school textbook and p-school text-book? Quantitative and qualitative data were used in order to answer these three questions. The outcome was two flow charts which explain the interactions among students when reading e- schoolbook and paper schoolbook. In addition, it draws a clear picture of the design and structure of schoolbooks in Libya which are similar to schoolbooks used in other Arabic countries at the same educational level. The chapter comprises two main sections. The first section presents the data collection methods and research type. The second section displays the results of the observation. The chapter ends with a conclusion highlighting the main points that has discussed in the chapter.

DATA COLLECTION METHODS AND RESEARCH TYPE

Qualitative and quantitative data collection methods were applied at this stage to address aspects of reality that are difficult, or if not impossible, to measure (as previously indicated to it in section 1.4). Observation was used to record the reading stages of both e-schoolbook and paper format of the schoolbook. In this case, it is important to describe students as a group not as individuals.

Applying the observation has led the researcher to face two problems on observing students: how to observe and how to record. To solve the first difficulty, the researcher listed several possible interactions

DOI: 10.4018/978-1-5225-1884-6.ch010

based on previous findings (Juan and Ruiz-Madrid, 2009), using left space for adding new actions that could be noted (see Appendix 3). Thus, it becomes clear which aspects should be observed which can be summarised as follows:

- What does students1 emphasises when reading a school book?
- How do students browse the text of a schoolbook?
- What options do students have when using schoolbook and how do they use them?
- How do students read a textbook?

Produce

The process of observation begins by taking everything in and recording it in as much detail as possible, with as little interpretation as possible:

- Every note card is headed by the date, name of school, education level, the title of the lesson, and time of observation (as seen in Appendix 3).
- Use the code for the process to save time.
- Divide the note code as a sample size to be sure the action of all students at each stage is recorded.

The participants carried out three different observations, which required dividing the participants into 8 groups, each of which comprised 5 participants. Four groups used eBooks (available at: http:// skooollibya.com/) the website by Intel corporation which is currently unavailable, while the other four groups used paper versions. The total number of participants was 40, 26 females and 14 males with their age ranging from 11 to 12. During the first observations, participants were asked to prepare a lesson for discussion in class. They were given an open time to complete the task. The next day, teachers discussed the lesson with the students and provided explanations, which lasted 45 minutes. Finally, the students were asked to search the text, answer the questions, and take a small quiz. Figure 1 shows the steps involved in the follow-up study. The total time takes to do the experiment was two weeks.

The talk-aloud technique was used in order to identify users' cognitive and behavioural processes, and to collect quantitative data, which could not be obtained via any other method. It was also used to obtain more in-depth details from participants, such as describing their actions and reactions to the book interface, and where students were asked to describe whatever they are reacting to, acting out, thinking about without trying to interpret their actions. In addition, students in each group sit in a straight line to facilitate the observation process. The teacher stands in front of the students, while the researcher stands behind the students. On the other hand, the teacher was informed of the observation's aims. Each student uses their own laptop brought from home, using a laptop with the same standards is not essential because the observation aims to address the reading stages without consideration of speed.

The basic idea of the test is to observe readers' interaction with the book from the moment of first picking it up to the time of fishing it. The students' interaction had not been recorded, according to the desire of the teacher and student. In order to save time, a model for taking notes was built, which includes the expected reading process according to the related literacy in the area of online reading. Therefore, the description of the reading process is created based on these steps that students follow when reading the lesson. As mentioned earlier, the usage description in this study is made according to

Figure 1. The follow-up survey stages

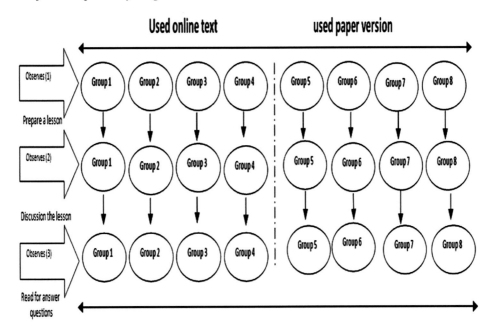

four principles: why do students use a schoolbook? What type of information is in the text? How is a schoolbook organised? And how is a schoolbook read?

The first two questions were answered using the questionnaire applied in the first phase of the research, while analysing the text was used to answer the third question. Origination of the schoolbook text differs between e- format and paper version, as seen in Table 1 and Figures 3 and 4. For example, the number of pages in the paper format was less than that of the e- format. In addition, the number of words per page in the paper version was 95 to 110 words with no images included, while in the e- format the average number of words is 20 to 33 words per window. This led to the difference in the number of pages between the two formats, e.g. the average number of pages in the paper format was 2 to 3, while in the e- format it was 9 to 17 windows.

Moreover, a schoolbook print in two sizes, A4 [210mm (8.3in) × 297mm (11.7in)] and in mathematics and science which include a large number of images it is printed in C4 [229mm (9.0in) × 324mm (12.8in)]. However, the layout of the e- format was similar in all subjects as seen in Figure 2 which presents the layout of the main page, and Figure 3 displays the layout of the lesson's content.

Table 1. Comparing the structure of textbook in the two formats

	Paper Format	**Electronic Format**
Number of words	60 to 74 with image 94-110 without image	18 to 27 with image 34 to 45 without image
Number of lines	8 to 11	2 to 4
Number of pages	3 to 4	9 to 17

Figure 2. Text presented in the e- format of schoolbook

Figure 3. Example of schoolbook for grade 5 in a page of the paper format

كَانَ الإيطَالِيُونَ قَدْ دَخَلُوا مَعْرَكَةَ الْقُرْضَابِيَّةِ بَعْدَ هَزِيمَةٍ شَدِيدَةٍ لَحِقَتْ
بِهِمْ فِي وَادِي ((مَرْسِيطِ)) سَنَةَ 1344 مِنْ مِيلَادِ الرَّسُولِ ــ صَلَّى اللهُ
عَلَيْهِ وَسَلَّمَ، مِمَّا حَمَلَ هَؤُلَاءِ الْمُسْتَعْمِرِينَ يَسْتَعِدُّونَ أَتَمَّ الاسْتِعْدَادِ،
سَعْياً وَرَاءَ اسْتِرْدَادِ مَجْدِهِمُ الْعَسْكَرِيِّ، وَكَرَامَتِهِمُ الْمَجْرُوحَةِ، وَهَيْبَتِهِمُ
الَّتِي ضَاعَتْ، فَأَعَدُّوا حَمْلَةً كَبِيرَةَ الْعَدَدِ وَالْعَتَادِ، وَسَارَتْ مَعَ تِلْكَ
الْحَمْلَةِ قُوَّةٌ لِيبِيَّةٌ، فِيهَا بَعْضُ الزُّعَمَاءِ الْبَارِزِينَ، مِمَّنْ تَظَاهَرُوا بِالْوَلَاءِ
لِلْقُوَّاتِ الإيطَالِيَّةِ. وَعِنْدَمَا وَصَلَتِ الْحَمْلَةُ إِلَى الْقُرْضَابِيَّةِ الْقَرِيبَةِ مِنْ
((سِرْت)) فِي 1344 /4/28، بَادَرَهَا[1] الْمُجَاهِدُونَ بِالْهُجُومِ، وَمَا
كَادَتِ الْمَعْرَكَةُ تَبْدَأُ حَتَّى انْضَمَّتِ الْقُوَّةُ اللِّيبِيَّةُ إِلَى قُوَّةِ الْمُجَاهِدِينَ،
وَوَحَّدُوا صُفُوفَهُمْ، وَوَجَّهُوا جَمِيعاً ضَرَبَتَهُمْ إِلَى الأَعْدَاءِ، مِمَّا أَدَّى إِلَى
ارْتِبَاكٍ[2] فِي صُفُوفِهِمْ مِنْ هَوْلِ[3] الْمُفَاجَأَةِ، وَتَلَقَّى

(1) بَادَرَهَا: عَالَجَهَا وَأَسْرَعَ إِلَيْهَا.
(2) ارْتِبَاكٌ: اضْطِرَابٌ.
(3) هَوْلٌ: فَزَعٌ وَأَمْرٌ شَدِيدٌ

119

Experiment 1

Figure 4. The layout of the main page

```
http://www.skoool.com.eg/latest_content/new/KSSPRIM5_ARAB_R_L1A_ST2/index.html - Original Source

File   Edit   Format

1  <html xmlns="http://www.w3.org/1999/xhtml" xml:lang="en" lang="en">
2  <head>
3  <meta http-equiv="Content-Type" content="text/html; charset=iso-8859-1" />
4  <title>skoool&#8482;</title>
5  </head>
6  <body bgcolor="#ffffff" style="margin:0px">
7
8  <object classid="clsid:d27cdb6e-ae6d-11cf-96b8-444553540000"
   codebase="http://fpdownload.macromedia.com/pub/shockwave/cabs/flash/swflash.cab#version=
   6,0,0,0" width="100%" height="100%" id="cm_standalone" align="middle">
9  <param name="allowScriptAccess" value="sameDomain" />
10 <param name="movie" value="cm_standalone.swf" /><param name="quality" value="high" /><param
   name="bgcolor" value="#ffffff" /><embed src="cm_standalone.swf" quality="high"
   bgcolor="#ffffff" width="100%" height="100%" name="cm_standalone" align="middle"
   allowScriptAccess="sameDomain" type="application/x-shockwave-flash"
   pluginspage="http://www.macromedia.com/go/getflashplayer" />
11 </object>
12
13 </body>
14 </html>
15
```

Figure 5. The layout of the lesson's content

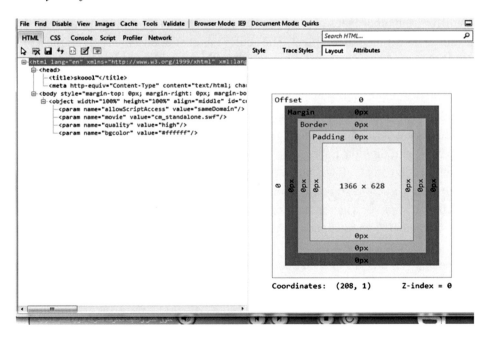

189

Population and Selection of the Sample for Observation

In order to follow-up and investigate in-depth users' cognitive behaviours with eBooks, a sample of 40 participants—all of whom were considered more confident with eBooks and who answered the questionnaire—was selected and distributed as follows:

1. 14 males representing 35%; and 26 females representing 65%;
2. The age of participants was between 11 and 13;
3. The sample was distributed across the three study stages.

DATA ANALYSIS

Using eBook and Paper Books in Primary Education

As was previously mentioned, a lot of evidence points to users preferring to use paper books rather than e- formats. There are several reasons for the low use of electronic text; one of these is the use of the same structure as the paper book. Therefore, the follow-up survey was selected to collect students' opinions and their interactions with both formats of schoolbooks, and analyse the structure of schoolbooks in order to obtain a clear understanding about the organization of such books and to identify the differences that lead to problems in the process of reading.

Analysis of Structure of School Book

Schoolbooks differ from other types of resources by way of presentation of information, the amount of information, and the structure of the content. The author has examined a random sample from the schoolbook in order to identify the main combination of schoolbooks, and has provided a document model, as shown in Figure 6, which illustrates the document in a top-down method, complete with independent descriptions of the document elements. The document is expressed in a set of parts that start with the cover of the book which includes title, authors, education level (EL), and date of publication (DOP). The document's contents are divided into several parts. The text part is divided into many sections, such as the table of contents, introduction, abbreviation, and lessons. Each lesson component comprises several sections, and each section breaks down into paragraphs, with each paragraph combining sentences which break down into words. Each lesson ends with questions that summarize the whole lesson. In addition, each document then comprises a hierarchical structure of abstraction levels, with each level representing elements in the document. The final part of the document is the back cover of the book which contains the name of the publisher.

However, the analysis of Libyan schoolbooks shows that all the schoolbooks' content, as shown in Figure 6, exhibits slight differences:

- The majority of the books' content in the first three levels comprises images, limited exercises, which mean the focus is on colour dynamics and flexibility.

Experiment 1

Figure 6. The document in a top-down method

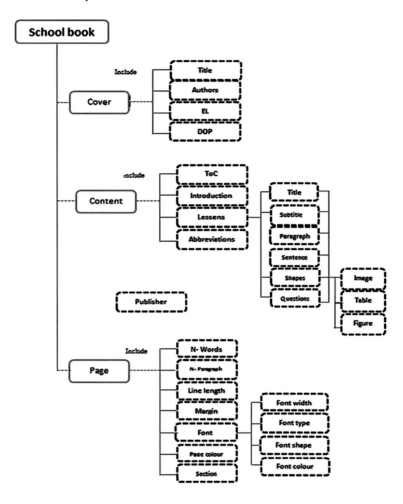

- The books of years 4, 5 and 6 are completely different to those of other levels of education in many aspects, such as the technique in which information is offered and organised, the structure, and the amount and type of information.
- The number of words increases as the level becomes higher. The average text in a schoolbook for year 6 is more comparable to a schoolbook for year 4 and 5.
- There exist fundamental differences between a schoolbook and other sources of information used for academic purposes such as articles and reference books.

According to researchers, there is confirmation of the relationship between readers' attitude, reading purpose, text presentation, and reading behaviour, all of which should be defined in order to understand the way students interact with the text.

On the other hand, searching the literature on designing texts would seem to show that there is no particular order or rules to follow when designing electronic text which is usually dependent on the subject, purpose of the text, age of the reader, the size of the text, and screen size. Alternatively, the structure of e-learning material usually depends on what the education system is aiming to achieve. In many cases, learning material is presented as a package and mainly relies on such format to transmit understanding to the learner. This special structure of educational material requires from designers the creation of a method for displaying content which can help the learner access and define the relation between contents of various learning packages.

Students' Attitudes toward the School Book

Understanding the students' attitudes towards schoolbooks and analysing their structure will lead to a good understanding of the most effective way of presenting a textbook online. Therefore, in this part of the research, students' attitudes in elementary school in Libya have been examined. Shape is one of the components of the textbook that is used as an instrument to assist in the learning process, so that the location of the shapes should enable the reader to link texts and shapes. The quantitative data show that 42% of participants from different levels of education always use the shape in a schoolbook, whilst 15.4% of them use it only sometimes. Furthermore, there are slight differences between participants when using shapes, as participants in levels 4 and 6 (49.2%, 68%) are more dependent on shapes than students of level 5 (31.1), as can be seen in Table 2 and Figure 7.

In order to define the suitability of a shape's location, participants were asked how easy it was to link the shape with a related text. 54.44% of participants in level 5 found linking shapes with text to be sometimes difficult in the paper format, while 46.3% of students in level 6 usually found it difficult to link text with shapes where the average number of words had increased in comparison with levels 4 and 5 (as seen in Table 3 and Figure 8). This difficulty appears when the graphic is located in different pages of the text. Therefore, a long line should be avoided when using graphic with texts, and pages should be divided into two parts using a short line.

Moreover, students tend to write down the main elements of the lesson, which helps them remember the lesson for the next class, and this can also save up on students' time in exams, where 42.4% of participants always write down the basic elements of the lesson and 15.4% only do so sometimes. Furthermore, the survey reports that there is a connection between the level of education and recording of the lesson's main elements, as can be seen in Table 4.

In addition, taking notes was reported to be a key element in the reading process for learning. The type and amount of notes differ according to the reader's age and reading strategy. Generally, participants tend to take notes during reading schoolbooks, e.g. all participants take notes during reading with a difference in the average of the amount of notes and when they take those notes. As seen in Table 5 and Figure 9, 25.39% of students sometimes take notes while more than 70% of participants take notes. In addition,

Table 2. The average use of shapes in schoolbooks

Year of Education	Comparing Text and Shapes						Total
	Always		Usually		Sometime		
	Number	Percentage	Number	Percentage	Number	Percentage	
Year 4	66	49.2	48	35.6	20	14.5	134
Year 5	56	31.1	92	51.1	32	17.7	180
Year 6	92	68.6	72	37.6	26	13.6	190
Total	146	28.9	212	42.6	78	15.4	504

Experiment 1

Figure 7. The average use of shapes in schoolbooks

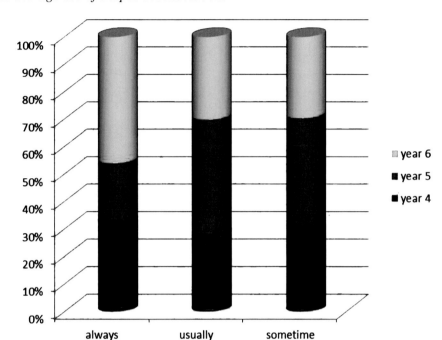

Table 3. The difficulty of making links between shapes and text

Year of Education	It Is Difficult to Link the Text with Shapes						Total
	Always		Usually		Sometime		
	Number	Percentage	Number	Percentage	Number	Percentage	
Year 4	50	37.31	40	29.85	44	32.83	134
Year 5	40	22.22	42	23.33	98	54.44	180
Year 6	56	29.47	88	46.31	44	23.15	190
Total	146	28.9	170	33.7	60	36.9	504

students in years 5 and 6 tend to take notes more than students in year 4. The survey also reported that 38.49% of participants always take notes when they are reading. The teacher has a significant impact in terms of encouraging students to record their observations during the lesson.

According to Table 6, the Table of Contents (TOC) is the only tool which is used to search the paper format of the school book, and the total number of students using the TOC was 54.7%, whilst 11.9% used it sometimes. Furthermore, students on Level 4 (13.4%) use the TOC less compared to students of years 5 and 6, where the teacher would tell students the page number of the lesson. Therefore, the survey reports that there is a relationship between using the TOC and the level of education, wherein the percentage increases as students increase their level of education.

Figure 8. Difficulty of making links between shapes and text

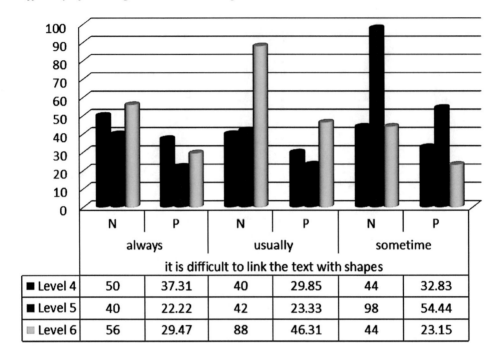

	always N	always P	usually N	usually P	sometime N	sometime P
it is difficult to link the text with shapes						
■ Level 4	50	37.31	40	29.85	44	32.83
■ Level 5	40	22.22	42	23.33	98	54.44
▨ Level 6	56	29.47	88	46.31	44	23.15

Table 4. Writing down the main elements when finishing studying

Education Years	Write the Main Element when Finish Studying						Total
	Always		Usually		Sometime		
	Number	Percentage	Number	Percentage	Number	Percentage	
Year 4	72	49.2	48	35.6	20	14.5	134
Year 5	126	31.1	92	51.1	32	17.7	180
Year 6	112	68.6	72	37.6	26	13.6	190
Total	214	42.4	212	42.6	78	15.4	504

Table 5. Taking notes when reading

Education Levels	Take Note when Studying						Total
	Always		Usually		Sometime		
	Number	Percentage	Number	Percentage	Number	Percentage	
Level 4	66	49.25	40	29.85	28	20.89	134
Level 5	44	24.44	74	41.11	62	34.44	180
Level 6	84	44.21	56	29.77	40	21.05	190
Total	194	38.49	170	33.73	128	25.39	504

Experiment 1

Figure 9. Taking notes when reading

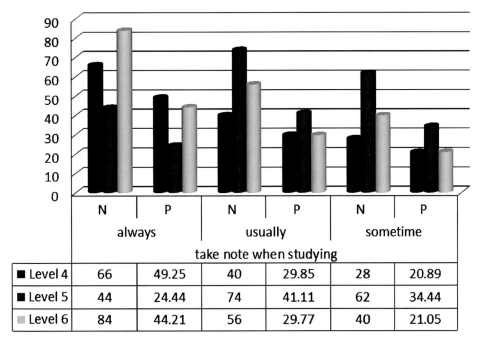

	N always	P always	N usually	P usually	N sometime	P sometime
■ Level 4	66	49.25	40	29.85	28	20.89
■ Level 5	44	24.44	74	41.11	62	34.44
▨ Level 6	84	44.21	56	29.77	40	21.05

Table 6. Using TOC

Level of Education	Using TOC						Total
	Always		Usually		Sometime		
	Number	Percentage	Number	Percentage	Number	Percentage	
Level 4	68	13.4	34	6.7	32	6.3	134
Level 5	94	18.6	78	15.4	8	1.5	180
Level 6	114	22.6	52	10.3	20	3.9	190
Total	276	54.7	164	32.5	60	11.9	504

In order to investigate the strategies of reading used by students, two questions were asked: 'Do you read the lesson first?' or 'Do you read the questions first?' Table 7 presents the reading strategy used in (PE). 65.8% of participants always read the lesson first and then answer the question, whereas 34.1% read the questions first. Usually, both strategies are used by students based on the purpose of the reading, e.g. if the student is reading for an exam, he/ she will read just the questions, whereas if he/she was reading for understanding, s/he would then read the lesson first.

Finally, students' satisfaction level is affected by several factors related to usability. Simplicity of presentation, clarity of structure, and ease of use are reported as the main factors affecting the usability of schoolbooks. In addition, students prefer viewing the text and graphics in parallel to reducing flipping between the pages which will increase their focus during the reading for this reason. Short line is the optimal line length for designing e-books for readers at this age.

Table 7. Strategies of reading through a schoolbook

Strategies	Read the Lesson First						Read the Question First					
	Always		Usually		Sometime		Always		Usually		Sometime	
	Number	Percentage	Number	Percentage	Number	Percentage	Number	Percentage	Number	Percentage	Number	Percentage
Year 4	92	18.2	22	4.3	20	3.9	16	3.1	32	6.3	44	8.7
Year 5	104	20.6	50	9.9	26	5.1	88	17.4	60	11.9	32	6.3
Year 6	136	26.9	36	7.1	18	3.5	68	13.4	48	9.5	64	12.6
Total	332	65.8	108	21.4	64	12.6	172	34.1	140	27.7	140	27.7

MODELS OF READING STRATEGIES

In order to improve reading on-screen, student behaviours need to be studied at the first stage in order to define their reading process. This requires clarification of the reading stages which the student follows, and thereby to define the reading strategy used.

In this phase of the research, the Reader Response Theory (RRT) has been used to understand the interaction of students when reading school textbook in two formats (Hirvela 1996), where this theory was applied widely to exam human interaction as mention in section 2.3. Applying the theory with schoolbooks shows certain shortcomings, in that the theory mainly concentrates on three elements (text, reader, and author) while the reading process of a schoolbook includes a new element; teacher and parent. To fill this gap, a little modification was suggested by adding a new element according to the analysis of the reader's act (as illustrate in Figure 6 in section 2.3).

Notably, it is clear that participants prefer the paper format to the e-format. For instance, 75% of participants found using the e-format very difficult, whilst 88% of participants could deal with the paper book easily. Navigation is another challenge which participants face in e-formats, with 91% of respondents finding the transition from one page to another difficulty, which in turn influenced the communication between the student and the teacher. On the other hand, 67% of participants found browsing the lesson easier in the paper version. Identifying the location of information in both versions was not easy, but was more difficult in the case of the eBook (74%) than the paper book (45%) as seen in Table 8.

Table 8. Participants' opinions about e- version of schoolbook compared to the paper version

	Electronic Format		Paper Format	
	Yes	No	Yes	No
Easy to use.	25%	75%	88%	12%
Can use without any help.	44%	66%	93%	7%
Easy to search.	9%	91%	67%	43%
Easy to find answers.	12%	88%	67%	33%
Sound help to learn	19%	81%	-	-
Easy to identify the location of information.	26%	74%	55%	45%

The survey reports that there are several scenarios used when reading a school book. These scenarios are based upon the purpose of using the school book: the schoolbook is always used at school or at home. In each case, the purpose of use is different.

- **Use at School:** At school, the teacher also directs students by telling them the page number, the lesson title, the number of questions, and so forth. These stages, in this case, were controlled by the teacher.
- **Use at Home:** At home, some students get support from their parents, whilst others do not. In both cases, students use the schoolbook for two purposes: firstly, to memorise the lessons taught at school; or preparing for the next lesson. In the case of the latter, the teacher prefers comprehensive reading.

Notably, 34.1% of students simply read the questions when they have an exam. Thus, how students use the schoolbook changes according to where the book is read (at school or at home), and why they read it (extract information or read to learn). 15 actions (AC) were recorded on observation form, as seen in Appendix 3 and as listed here below:

AC1: Read the instructions.
AC2: Identify a purpose for reading.
AC3: Read through the questions.
AC4: Skim the passage to have a general idea.
AC5: Quickly read the whole passage.
AC6: Read the whole passage quite slowly.
AC7: Underline the key words in question
AC8: Underline the key words in the passage.
AC9: Underline the main idea of each paragraph.
AC10: Scan the passage in order to find the key word.
AC11: After finding the key word in the passage, read the text around it carefully.
AC12: Connecting one part of the text to another.
AC13: Take general notes.
AC14: Re-reading.
AC15: Anything else.

Students show different attitudes when reading a schoolbook in both versions. As seen in Table 9, action 2 (AC2), action 3 (AC3), action 6 (AC6) and action 9 (AC9) were used by all students and the difference was only noted in the order of use between electronic text and paper text. For example, 95% of participants identify their aim before reading school e-textbook as searching for answers or reading for an exam. Reading through the questions is a popular action among students when reading for an exam. Students who use the e-text of a schoolbook found it is so hard to go through the text between the questions and the content of the lesson which led some of them to use a paper version to write down the questions. The left column in the Table 9 presents the actions that recorded in the observation and the second column present type of the text (electronic or paper format) while, top row of the table present the order of the step that follow when dealing with the text. For example, 16 students who read through

Table 9. Students' action when using a schoolbook in the two formats

Actions	Type	Step 1	Step 2	Step 3	Step 4	Step 5	Step 6	Step 7
AC1	Electronic	-¹	-	-	-	-	-	-
	Paper	-	-	-	-	-	-	-
AC2	Electronic	16	-	-	-	-	-	-
	Paper	9	-	-	-	-	-	-
AC3	Electronic	2	1	13	-	-	-	-
	Paper	4	4	8	-	-	-	-
AC4	Electronic	-	9	-	-	-	-	-
	Paper	5	2	-	-	-	-	-
AC5	Electronic	-	4	-	-	-	-	-
	Paper	1	3	-	-	-	-	-
AC6	Electronic	-	-	7	9	3	-	-
	Paper	-	-	4	8	7	-	-
AC7	Electronic	-	2	-	-	-	-	-
	Paper	-	4	2	-	-	-	-
AC8	Electronic	-	-	-	-	-	-	-
	Paper	-	2	5	-	-	-	-
AC9	Electronic	-	-	-	-		-	-
	Paper	-	-	-	-	5	-	-
AC10	Electronic	-	3		2	-	-	-
	Paper	-	2	-	-	-	-	-
AC11	Electronic	-	-	-	3	8	-	-
	Paper	-	-	-	5	5	-	-
AC12	Electronic	-	-	-	2	-	1	2
	Paper	-	-	3	-	-	6	5
AC13	Electronic	-	-	-	2	-	-	-
	Paper	-	-	-	7	-	-	-
AC14	Electronic	2	1	-	-	-	12	-
	Paper	1	3	-	-	-	9	-
Total								

¹ Dash mean it is not use.

electronic text firstly identify a purpose for reading (AC2) this may go back to difficulty to move from page to page in the electronic format of the text.

Moreover, it is notable that, students have more freedom when a reading paper format compared with students who read an electronic format. For instance, students cannot use their fingers or pencil when navigates electronic text as students who read through the paper where they put their fingers between page when move to a new page and return to the previous one.

In addition, the survey reported that students use three strategies when reading the schoolbook: comprehensive strategy; skimming strategy; and scanning strategy. Using these strategies differs according to two elements: the aim of reading and the book type (electronic or paper). For example, using a scanning strategy in both formats is preferred when reading to extract information in order to answer questions (47%). Whereas, 80% of participants who use the eBook and 87.5% of participants who use the paper version prefer using a comprehensive strategy when reading the lesson for the first time.

Moreover, participants who used the eBook record a higher average in terms of time compared to students who used the paper book. This may be due to using a paper structured book without applying the tools to support the reading, e.g. the average comprehensive reading for the whole lesson in an eBook was 25 min. While doing the same task with a paper book would only take 15 min.

Furthermore, it is notable that using a comprehensive strategy was difficult in the case of reading an online text where the text is divided into various segments made for browsing back and forth and thus takes a longer time than the paper format. Moreover, there are no different records between the two formats when scanning or skimming the text. Table 10 shows the percentage using each strategy among students and the average time taken to read according to their selected approach.

Finally, during the reading it is noted that students used different techniques such as taking notes, highlighting text, writing the answers on the same page, or asking questions. These techniques are affected by the reading scenario, e.g. participants using paper tended to take notes in the book when they read the lesson for the preparing the lesson or reading for discussion as seen in Table 11. In addition, highlighting words or concepts in the text is preferred by students as 89% of participants use this technique during reading. On the other hand, students who used the eBook version were not able to use this technique even though many wanted to try it. Also, the teacher tended not to let students use Microsoft Word for taking notes because this will not lead to improvement in handwriting or spelling which is necessary for students at this level of education.

Table 10. The strategies used in different reading scenarios and the medium time

Reading Strategies	E-Format Group						P-Format Group					
	Prepare Lesson		Reading for Discussion		Reading for Answering Questions		Prepare Lesson		Reading for Discussion		Reading for Answering Questions	
	Percentage	Time	Percentage	Time	Percentage	Time	Percentage	Time	Percentage	Time	Percentage	Time
Comprehensive strategy	80%	25M	25%	21M	10%	29M	87.5%	15M	7.5%	6M	-	-
Skimming strategy	7.5%	24M	32.5%	20M	42.5%	20M	2.5%	10M	37.5%	4M	32.5%	4M
Scanning strategy	12.5%	20M	42.5%	22M	47.5%	25M	10%	9M	55%	3M	67.5%	3M

Table 11. Illustrating the techniques used by students during reading

Reading Strategies	eBook Group			P-Book Group		
	Prepare Lesson	Reading for Discussion	Reading for Answering Questions	Prepare Lesson	Reading for Discussion	Reading for Answering Questions
	Percentage	Percentage	Percentage	Percentage	Percentage	Percentage
Taking notes in the book	-	-	-	73%	80%	3%
Highlight words	-	-	-	89%	89%	1%
Write the answer in the school book	-	-	-	10%	13%	93%
Taking notes in notebook	-	54%	72%	-	9%	5%

Flow Chart of Reading Process

Analysing the collecting data from the observation and that presentenced in section 5.4 two models for reading process were built; reading strategy for paper schoolbook format (RSPSBFM) and reading strategy for electronic schoolbook format (RSESBFM). These two models describe the student's attitude and action when dealing with schoolbook in different formats to provide formal and reusable models. Figure 12 summarises the schoolbook reading strategy used by students at school or at home, which starts with opening the book and skimming the table of contents (TOC). 54.7% of participants always use the TOC to access the lesson, whereas 11% of participants access the lesson via the page numbers when using the book at home.

In the case of using the book at school, usually the teacher tells students the number of the page, wherein 85% of students would not need to use the TOC. Subsequently, students usually check a lesson by identifying the subtitle, how long it would take, and the number of questions before starting to read. This technique is also used when students read the lesson for the first time. In addition, when students decide to read the lesson, there are two ways to view the text, as the survey reports: either by viewing the text or viewing the questions. In each case, students use different reading methods. Moreover, dotted lines in the right of the Figures 10 and 11 refer to return action.

On the other hand, based on qualitative feedback, the e-reading strategy for the schoolbooks was built. Figure 11 shows a generic description of the e-textbook reading strategy, which starts by viewing the homepage of the system. Subsequently, students can access the book by viewing the models and then selecting the level, or by otherwise viewing the education levels and then selecting the model. The first action will be opening the book. At this point, the student has two options: to view the text or to view the questions. In the case of viewing the questions, the students will have access to the questions which link the parts that include the answer rather than answering the questions, simply because the aim is to encourage students to read. Notably, if students select and view the text, they will then start with the introduction to the lesson before going through the lesson and learning the main bulk. Students can take notes and save those notes. This function was not available in the book used in this test where students used paper for taking notes during reading which confused them.

Experiment 1

Figure 10. Model of reading strategies for Arabic school book in paper format (RSPSBFM)
Abubaker & Lu, 2011.

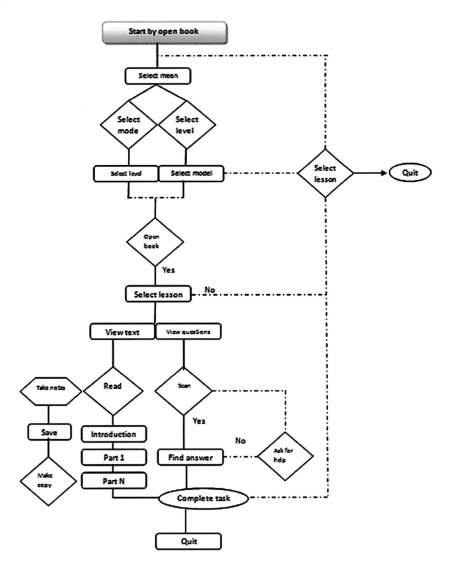

Finally, there are no changes required to user needs when students read either the paper version or e-version of the schoolbook, but the change appears in the way that students interact with the material. However, the students' reading action changes in each format; this makes a difference in the overall reading process. For example, the page number is the main tool used by students to access the book's content in the paper version, but just 54% of participants use TOC, while in the eBook the number of pages does not support the reading process. On the other hand, in the case of the e-format, students' access the lesson by concept of the lesson. Thus, defining the reading process can help define searching and reading steps. During the searching stops, students frequently search for a title or subtitle, or question and answer; this requires searching the content for concepts and titles. In the reading stage, students exploit two reading strategies: scanning and comprehension strategies.

Figure 11. Reading strategy model of Arabic e-schoolbook (RSESBAFM)
Abubaker & Lu, 2011.

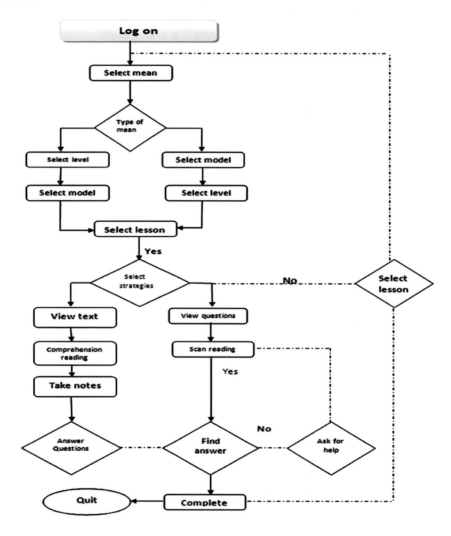

CONCLUSION

It is becoming clear from analysis of the quantitative and qualitative data that Libyan students' usability of schoolbook differs according to text format. This difference stemmed from the structure of the schoolbook and aims of use. In addition, these differences resulted in numerous requirements that should be understood by designers who ought to create functions that meet those requirements. The reading process is affected by the type of material and the aim of using the material, where the reading action and interaction changes in each version of schoolbook (electronic and paper format).

Generally, using the paper metaphor is not the correct way to represent the lesson in electronic format although a thorough investigation into user behaviour and the identification of their skills and requirements can ultimately help design an eBook interface which can cover all user needs. Students' satisfaction is affected by several factors related to usability. Simplicity of presentation, clarity of structure, and ease of use are reported to be the main factors affecting the usability of the schoolbook. In addition, students prefer viewing the text and graphics parallel to reducing flipping between pages which will increase their focus during the reading for this reason. A short line is the optimal line length for designing eBooks for readers in this day and age.

Finally, students use different actions when reading a schoolbook. These actions are affected mainly by the way the text is designed, while aim of use was reported as a second factor. Two models for reading process were built; reading strategy for paper schoolbook format (RSPSBFM) and reading strategy for electronic schoolbook format (RSESBFM). These two models describe the student's attitude and action when dealing with schoolbook in different formats to provide formal and reusable models. In the next phase of study wills examine the relationship between text layout and reading strategy in order to provide principles for designing Arabic academic text online.

REFERENCES

Abubaker, A., & Joan, L. (2011). E-reading strategy model to read E-school book in Libya. *Proceedings of the International Conference on Internet Computing ICOMP*.

Abubaker, A., & Lu, J. (2011). Model of E-Reading Process for E-School Book in Libya. *International Journal of Information Retrieval Research*, *1*(3), 35–53. Retrieved from http://www.irma-international. org/viewtitle/64170/ doi:10.4018/ijirr.2011070103

Usó, E., & Ruiz-Madrid, M.N. (2009). Reading printed versus online texts. A study of EFL learners strategic reading behavior. *International Journal of English Studies*, *9*(2), 59-79.

Chapter 11
Experiment 2:
Readable Font Size and Type for Display Academic Arabic Text on Screen

Azza A Abubaker
Benghazi University, Libya

Joan Lu
University of Huddersfield, UK

ABSTRACT

The outcomes for the previous experiment in this research indicated that students' attitudes differ according to the way of presenting the text and text layout. As the aim of the study was to investigate the three main typographic variables [font size, font type and line length] we will start by font size and font type. Much research has highlighted the character size as a factor in visual display, and reported that font size has a significant effect on readability of texts in both versions. Therefore, defining a readable font size for the Arabic language is the main focus of this experiment, taking into account the effect of one dependent variable, four controlled variables and two independent variables: content length and font type. Students were required to make different judgments of letter pairs, thus indicating which letters were distinguishable. Based on the findings of this experiment, subsequent experiments were designed. In addition, the findings of this experiment will be able to address the issues related to reading Arabic text from screen by children in relation to the following: RQ1: In which font size is the Arabic text read most effectively? RQ2: Is there any correlation between age of the reader and font size? RQ3: Which font type is more readable?

DESIGN INTERFACE

Taking into account the previous findings which show that there is a positive correlation between content's length and reading rate, the text used in the experiment was divided into four parts, each part representing a separate window. In each test, different lessons were used, although all the lessons were taken from the reading school book for primary stage in Libya and the eight lessons discussed different

DOI: 10.4018/978-1-5225-1884-6.ch011

subjects of general interest. In addition, the four windows have equal length (31 words per lines, 27 lines per text and non-margins). The sentences were printed with black letters on white background. Four font sizes (10, 14, 16, and 18) were tested with two font types as shown in Table 1. Finally, the text in both conditions was presented in a single column.

In addition, Table 2 shows an example of text layout using 10,14 16 and 18 points as font size and five font types. The total number of windows displayed in this experiment was four slides, dealing with a long text. All lessons were checked by the teacher to determine their suitability for the students' education level and all terms have been studied by students.

EXPERIMENTAL DESIGN

Conditions of Workplace

The display medium was placed in a 140 cm-high table. The distance from the screen to the surface of the table was 100 mm. The distance of eye-to- screen was 500 mm. The screen inclination was 105. Moreover, participants all used the same (PE) Pavilion dv6 [Intel i5 core processors] laptop, with the choice of using a mouse attached peripherally. The screen size of the laptop was 15.6 inches with a display setting of 1366 x 768 pixels. Internet Explorer 6.0 was used as the browser environment to present the test software and task.

Procedure

Each student was tested individually, and each test lasted approximately between 30 to 40 minutes. Before starting the test, it was emphasised that participants should work as quickly and accurately as possible, and then the experimenter told them about the aim of the experiment. They were then asked to read aloud in order to measure their ability to read. The experiment was controlled using a digital watch with a precision of one second. Each lesson was timed separately using the same procedures. The experimenter noted how participants read the text and reported the difficulty faced by each student when reading. These comments were later used to interpret the quantitative data using the form in Appendix 6. Following each lesson, and on a separate page, there was a question and answer sheet to test the ac-

Table 1. The structure of the text in each window

Test (1)	Test (2)	Test (3)	Test (4)
Black font White background **Font size**: title: 18 **Font size**: 10 **Font type:** Traditional Arabic, Arial, Times new roman, Courier New and simplified Arabic **Display:** one Colum, Single space between lines **Word number**: 279	Black font White background **Font size**: title: 18 **Font size**: 14 **Font type:** Traditional Arabic, Arial, Times new roman, Courier New and simplified Arabic **Display:** one Column, Single space between lines **Word number**: 191.	Black font White background Font size: title: 18 **Font size**: 16 **Font type:** Traditional Arabic, Arial, Times new roman, Courier New and simplified Arabic. **Display:** one Column Single space between lines **Word number**: 275.	Black font White background **Font size**: title: 18 **Font size**: 18 **Font type:** Traditional Arabic, Arial, Times new roman, Courier New and simplified Arabic **Display:** one Column, Single space between lines Word number: 254.

Table 2. Example of text layout using four different points as font size and five different font types

Font Type	Font Size (10)
Simplified Arabic	أرسل الله تعالى نبيه إبراهيم إلى قومه
Time New Roman	أرْسَلَ اللهُ تَعَالَى نَبِيَّهُ إِبْرَاهِيمَ إِلَى قَوْمِه
Arial	أرْسَلَ اللهُ تَعَالَى نَبِيَّهُ إِبْرَاهِيمَ إِلَى قَوْمِه
Traditional Arabic	أرْسَلَ اللهُ تَعَالَ نَبِيَّهُ إِبْرَاهِيمَ إِلَى قَوْمِه
Courier New	أرْسَلَ الله تَعَالَى نَبِيَّهُ إِبْرَاهِيمَ إِلَى قَوْمِه

Font Size(14)

Simplified Arabic	أرْسَلَ اللهُ تَعَالَى نَبِيَّهُ إِبْرَاهِيمَ إِلَى قَوْمِه
Time New Roman	أرْسَلَ اللهُ تَعَالَى نَبِيَّهُ إِبْرَاهِيمَ إِلَى قَوْمِه
Arial	أرْسَلَ اللهُ تَعَالَى نَبِيَّهُ إِبْرَاهِيمَ إِلَى قَوْمِه
Traditional Arabic	أرْسَلَ اللهُ تَعَالَ نَبِيَّهُ إِبْرَاهِيمَ إِلَى قَوْمِه
Courier New	أرْسَلَ الله تَعَالَى نَبِيَّهُ إِبْرَاهِيمَ إِلَى قَوْمِه

Font Size (16)

Simplified Arabic	أرْسَلَ اللهُ تَعَالَى نَبِيَّهُ إِبْرَاهِيمَ إِلَى قَوْمِه
Time New Roman	أرْسَلَ اللهُ تَعَالَى نَبِيَّهُ إِبْرَاهِيمَ إِلَى قَوْمِه
Arial	أرْسَلَ اللهُ تَعَالَى نَبِيَّهُ إِبْرَاهِيمَ إِلَى قَوْمِه
Traditional Arabic	أرْسَلَ اللهُ تَعَالَ نَبِيَّهُ إِبْرَاهِيمَ إِلَى قَوْمِه
Courier New	أرْسَلَ الله تَعَالَى نَبِيَّهُ إِبْرَاهِيمَ إِلَى قَوْمِه

Font Size (18)

Simplified Arabic	أرْسَلَ اللهُ تَعَالَى نَبِيَّهُ إِبْرَاهِيمَ إِلَى قَوْمِه
Time New Roman	أرْسَلَ اللهُ تَعَالَى نَبِيَّهُ إِبْرَاهِيمَ إِلَى قَوْمِه
Arial	أرْسَلَ اللهُ تَعَالَى نَبِيَّهُ إِبْرَاهِيمَ إِلَى قَوْمِه
Traditional Arabic	أرْسَلَ اللهُ تَعَالَ نَبِيَّهُ إِبْرَاهِيمَ إِلَى قَوْمِه
Courier New	أرْسَلَ الله تَعَالَى نَبِيَّهُ إِبْرَاهِيمَ إِلَى قَوْمِه

curacy of locating particular information. Finally, after reading and answering the task, students made their judgements about the different text layouts [different font sizes matching different font types] by answering a brief questionnaire which recorded their personal details combined with these three questions:

- Which characters are more difficult to read?
- Which font size is easier to read?
- Which font type is more legible?

Four font sizes tested; 10,14,16 and 18. The range of increase should be two and 14 was selected according to Asmaa, A. & A. O. Asma (2009) finding where she confirms that Arabic text can be read from size 14 for adult, thus, in the begging it used as the start point in test, but the researcher wanted to enrich the study by testing the difficulties that children face when reading electronic Arabic text in small size.

Participants

30 students studying in a Libyan school in the UK volunteered as participants in the experiment. Their ages ranged from 10 to 12. There were 15 females and 15 males. As seen in Table 3, and 26 were studied in an English school for more than one year, and 9 were born in the UK but Arabic is their first language. Because of the cultural factor outside the scope of the study and that the most important factor is the reading level, The sample was selected from students living in the UK. Students were also classified based on education levels and reading scores which divided them into two groups; the first group included students who scored in reading course marks above 5 of 10 mean that they have a high level of reading, whilst the second group included students whose scores were less than 5 this group include students who has a low level of reading (this is the using method to evaluate students in Libya school).

Students were asked if they have vision problem when sending questionnaires to their parents, as seen in Appendix 4. The questionnaire combines 6 questions which aim to make sure there are no problems with the vision of each participant.

Study Variables

A number of variables were recognized and outlined earlier to the implementation experiments. These variables are of three types; independent, dependent and controlled.

- **Controlled Variable:** These variables expected to affect the experimental procedure;
  - **Task and Topic:** All students read the same text in both print and electronic formats of the school book in a different font size and types. The task was selected from the school book and was checked by the teacher to be sure there is no difficulties or new words.
  - **Consistency:** The experiments were examined with the same students' age and education level. In addition, the same procedure was followed throughout the process of the experiment as well using the same computer design and measurements.
  - **Computer Familiarity:** All the students were familiar with using the computer and were able to read online text.
  - **Readers' Vision:** All students did not have problems with the vision of each participant
  - **Time:** In the experiment 1 student had a time range to complete each task in the classroom with monitoring from the teacher, while in experiments 2 and 3 students take as much time to finish the task.
- **Dependent Variable:** The dependent variable was definitely at, time taken by each participant and number of correct answers.
- **Independent Variables:** The independent variables were defined on, content length and font type.

Table 3. The sample size

Age	Number	Total	Gender	
10	10	30	Male	15
11	10			
12	10		Female	15

Statistical Technique to Analysis Data

Several of the tests were used to answer the research questions of this phase:

- **Normality Test:** In many statistical analyses, normality is frequently accepted before using the Friedman test. The normality test has been done using SPSS software to analyse the time and correctness of a data in this experiment, the final conclusion started here is that all variables are significantly non- normality distributed and non-parametric test Friedman test used to estimate and find out the differences in conditions (Abuabker & Lu, 2012).
- **Friedman's ANOVE Test:** As mentioned in the earlier point above that all variables are non- normally distributed, the Friedman Test is used for testing differences between the four conditions. The same students have been used in all appearance using in all conditions. This test has been conducted again the time and correct answers for four conditions using the SPSS statistical software.
- **The Wilcoxon Signed- Rank Test:** This test is used in this experiment to know the condition in which the student performances are significantly better in comparison with others, where this test is based on the differences between scores in reading time and errors. Once these differences have been calculated they are ranked. For this reason, in this experiment each two condition has been tested separately.
- **Median:** It is the numerical value separating the higher half of a data sample, a population. It is used in this study because the distribution of the sample is un normal.

RESULTS

Reading Performance of Arabic Traditional Font

According to Table 4, which demonstrates the results of descriptive statistics for the Arabic Traditional font in four sizes [10, 14, 16 and 18], it is obvious that the highest error is made by font size ten, and this is followed by sizes fourteen, sixteen and eighteen, respectively. Notice that since the distribution of each font group is found to be non-normal, we rely on the median as an indicator of error level. E.g., the medians for sizes ten and fourteen are .397 (about 39.7%) and .317 (about 31.7), respectively, which are high. However, the error rate drops dramatically when the size of the font is increased to sixteen and eighteen, i.e. the errors for both fonts are .048 (about 4.8%) and .054 (about 5.45%), respectively. From Figure 1, we notice how substantial the differences between the size groups are, where it seems that the fonts of sizes sixteen and eighteen are more readable than any font smaller than sixteen. Based on the maximum values given in the table, it is worth mentioning that the error percentage in reading can reach 45.9% for size ten and 3.9% for size fourteen, which is remarkably high.

However, to investigate the relationship between the four sizes of traditional Arabic fonts and the error percentages resulting from using these sizes, the Friedman test was used to test the difference in median error for the four font sizes. The Friedman test indicated a strong difference in error percentages among the four groups ($\chi2= 82$, p-value < .001) as seen in Table 5, which rejects the null hypotheses.

Next, follow-up tests will need to be conducted in order to evaluate comparisons between pairs of medians. The Wilcoxon test was applied as seen in Table 6. Using the Bonferroni adjustment for controlling adequately various types of error, the adjusted level of significance will be .05/6 = .008. Based on the

Experiment 2

Table 4. The results of descriptive statistics for the Arabic Traditional font in four sizes [10, 14, 16] and 18]

Statistic	10 Traditional Arabic	14 Traditional Arabic	16 Traditional Arabic	18 Traditional Arabic
Mean	.393	.305	.050	.054
Median	.397	.317	.048	.054
Mode	.358	.322	.058	.054
Variance	.012	.001	.001	.000
Minimum	.315	.254	.028	.031
Maximum	.459	.390	.093	.071

Figure 1. The mean error when reading the Arabic Traditional font in four sizes [10, 14, 16 and 18

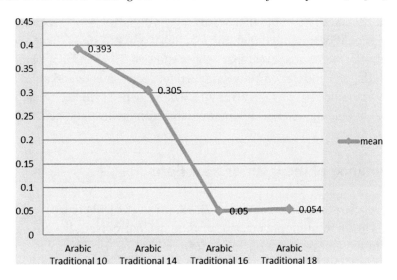

Table 5. Error percentages among the four group font sizes using Friedman test

Font Size	Mean Rank	Chi-Square	p-Value
Ten	4.00	82	.000
Fourteen	3.00		
Sixteen	1.33		
Eighteen	1.67		

Table 6. Pairs comparison using the Wilcoxon test in terms of the Traditional Arabic font groups

	10-14	10-16	10-18	14-16	14-18	16-18
Z	-4.782	-4.782	-4.782	-4.784	-4.782	-2.149
p-value	.000	.000	.000	.000	.000	.032

adjusted p-value, the median error percentage of the Traditional Arabic font for size ten is significantly higher than the median error for sizes fourteen, sixteen and eighteen, p-value < .008. Also, the median error percentage for size fourteen is found to be significantly higher than the median error for sizes sixteen and eighteen. However, the median error percentage for size sixteen does not differ significantly from the median error for size eighteen. Notice that these two sizes show the lowest error made by the students at about .048 (4.8%) and .054 (5.4%), respectively.

To measure the degree of association between age and gender with speed and error, Spearman's correlation is conducted for each font size. Based on Table 7, we observe that the age of students tends to have a negative correlation with speed; this means that as age increases, the time spent on reading decreases. The correlation becomes stronger as long as the font size becomes bigger. It is noticeable that all of the correlations are found to be significant. In terms of errors in reading, the data show that for age the correlation is negative and significant for all font sizes. It is obvious that the correlation drops when the font becomes larger. In other words, age will have a low association with error if the font is large but one should bear in mind that this relationship is still significant, and hence should not be ignored. Alternatively, the results reveal that gender shows a very weak correlation with both speed and error. For measuring the correlation between speed and error, it is remarkable that a high speed of reading is positively combined with a high error rate. This may be attributed to the following: students who have a low level of reading will take a long time to finish the text and hence time will not lead to them reducing their error rate.

Reading Performance of the Courier New Font

Courier new font was tested in 4 different sizes [10, 14, 16 and 18] wherein this font is widely used to present Arabic text. On the resulting statistics of reading in Courier New, the error in reading becomes smaller as the size of the font becomes bigger as seen in Table 8. However, the error made with size 14 is larger than that made with size 10; as mentioned earlier, this may be attributed to the relative text difficulty. The box plot given in Figure 2 indicates that fonts 10 and 14 are much closer to each other than fonts 16 and 18 which are much smaller. Also, the statistical data show that the distribution of the four sizes is somewhat asymmetric, and hence the Freedman test will be used.

Based on the results in Table 9, the Friedman test is found to be 83.84 with p-value< .000, indicating that there is a highly significant difference between the median errors of the four font sizes.

As a result, the Wilcoxon test is conducted; the results of this test are shown in Table 10. It is obvious that all pairs of font sizes result in a significant difference in reading error. We should mention that

Table 7. Spearman's correlations between the variables using the Traditional Arabic font

	Ten		Fourteen		Sixteen		Eighteen	
	Speed	**Error**	**Speed**	**Error**	**Speed**	**Error**	**Speed**	**Error**
Age	-.302*	-.661***	-.603***	-.379**	-.775***	-.781**	-.664***	-.408**
Gender	-.055	-.127	-.019	-.402*	.070	.062	.027	.012
	Speed		**Speed**		**Speed**		**Speed**	
Error	.377*		.413**		.816**		.469**	

Experiment 2

Table 8. Descriptive statistics for the reading error using four sizes of the Courier New font

Statistic	10 Courier New	14 Courier New	16 Courier New	18 Courier New
Mean	.205	.220	.0546	.0350
Median	.207	.223	.0546	.0350
Mode	.186	.202	.0482	.0370
Variance	.0005	.0008	.000	.0000
Minimum	.154	.1608	.0257	.022
Maximum	.247	.3055	.0836	.045

Figure 2. Boxplot shows the reading error using four sizes of the Courier New font

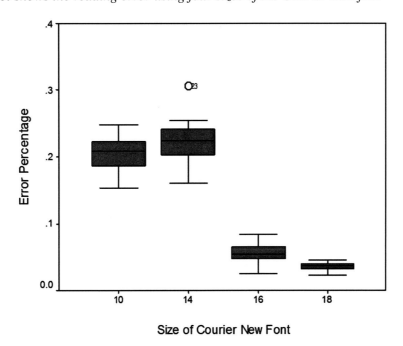

Table 9. Error percentages among the four group font sizes using the Friedman test when reading in Courier New font

Font Size	Mean Rank	Chi-Square	p-Value
Ten	3.17	83.84	.000
Fourteen	3.83		
Sixteen	1.97		
Eighteen	1.03		

Table 10. Pairs comparison using the Wilcoxon test in terms of Courier New font groups

	10-14	10-16	10-18	14-16	14-18	16-18
Z	-3.795	-4.783	-4.782	-4.787	-4.782	-4.742
p-value	.000	.000	.000	.000	.000	.000

Table 11. Spearman's correlations between the variables using Courier New font

	Ten		Fourteen		Sixteen		Eighteen	
	Speed	Error	Speed	Error	Speed	Error	Speed	Error
Age	-.781***	-.617***	-.711***	-.623**	-.692***	-.599**	-.328***	-.570**
Gender	.039	-.015	-.031	-.112	.004	-.193	.078	.167
	Speed		Speed		Speed		Speed	
Error	.674***		.688**		.618**		.651**	

the difference between sizes 16 and18 is noted to be highly significant here, while it is not so for the Traditional Arabic font.

In terms of relationship, age supplies a good degree of significant negative correlation with error for all font sizes; namely, the older the student, the less mistakes s/he makes. Also, we notice that the speed of reading will be slower when the age is older. As a result, we can say that when a student becomes older, the concentration on reading will be better; and although taking a longer time to finish the text, the mistakes made will be lower. Gender is found to have a very weak relationship with speed and error, and hence it will be ignored when interpreting errors resulting from using the four sizes of the Courier New font. To see how speed correlates with errors, we observe from Table 11 that a high speed of reading will result in a somewhat high number of errors. All sizes of the font show a very similar degree of highly significant correlation.

Reading Performance of Times New Roman Font

The Times New Roman font was the third font tested. The error percentage declined from 41.1% in size ten to 3.6% for size 18 using mean; a similar result is noted by the median. The error percentage can reach 50.5%, 28.3%, 9.7% and 5.1% for sizes 10, 14, 16 and 18, respectively, as seen in Table 12. The Figure 3 displays how the apparent difference between the four sizes is great. According to the plot, high variability can be seen between the errors of size ten. Variability in error becomes smaller as the font size increases.

To determine the significant differences in errors among the four sizes, the Freidman test using mean ranks is found to be 90.00 with p-value <.0001, indicating that there is a very highly significant difference, see Table 13. Therefore, an error in reading made by the student will be highly affected by font size, namely, a low error rate can be observed by sizes 16 and 18. From the Wilcoxon test given in Table 14, we find that the difference between sizes 16 and 18 is highly significant, indicating that more significant reductions in reading errors can be achieved by size 18 than by size 16.

Experiment 2

Table 12. The results of descriptive statistics for Times new Roman font in four sizes [10, 14, 16 and 18]

Statistic	10 Times New Roman	14 Times New Roman	16 Times New Roman	18 Times New Roman
Mean	.411	.257	.072	.036
Median	.403	.260	.069	.037
Mode	.358	.257	.064	.0400
Variance	.0028	.0004	.0001	.00007
Minimum	.323	.203	.055	.011
Maximum	.505	.283	.097	.051

Figure 3. The results of mean for Times New Roman font in four sizes [10, 14, 16 and 18]

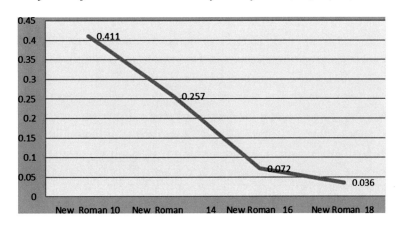

Table 13. Error percentages among the four group font sizes using Friedman test

Font Size	Mean Rank	Chi-Square	p-Value
Ten	4.00	90.00	.000
Fourteen	3.00		
Sixteen	2.00		
Eighteen	1.00		

Table 14. Pairs comparison using the Wilcoxon test in terms of Times New Roman font groups

	10-14	10-16	10-18	14-16	14-18	16-18
Z	-4.782	-4.782	-4.782	-4.788	-4.782	-4.782
p-value	.000	.000	.000	.000	.000	.000

Using Spearman's correlation in Table 15, age provides a negative association with both speed and error. The association is found to be significant for all font sizes but its degree is low for some sizes and high for others. Namely, error and speed will be low when age is older, wherein students sometimes guess the word from the order of the text. Similar to previous fonts, gender shows a very weak association and is thus not significant.

Reading Performance of Arial Font

Regarding the Arial font, it is clear from Table 16 that size 10 leads to the highest error rate (about 42.5% using mean) and longest time followed by sizes 14, 16 and 18, respectively. The resulting median leads to similar results given by the mean. The highest error percentage is 42.5% for size 10 whereas the lowest is 3.6% for size 18. Based on the maximum values, it is worth mentioning that the error percentage in reading for size 10 can reach as much as 54.1% while in size 14 it was 32.5%. Figures 4 show that the errors made by sizes 10 and 14 are very different from those made by sizes 16 and 18.

Using the Friedman test shows that all the font sizes result in very highly significant differences in the median errors, as seen in Table 17. Comparing each two pairs of font sizes using Wilcoxon confirms that the differences between all of the pairs are highly significant which means that the reduction in errors is remarkable when the font size becomes larger, as seen in Table 18.

In terms of association, Table 19, shows that speed and error for the majority of sizes are strongly and negatively linked with age. Gender does not reveal any interesting correlation with either speed or error although it shows the different directions of correlation with speed and error. For font sizes 10, 14 and 18, error is highly and positively linked with speed, resulting in a very highly significant correlation, while for size 16 the correlation is found to be very weak. The reason for this may be attributed

Table 15. Spearman's correlations between the variables using the Times New Roman font

	Ten		Fourteen		Sixteen		Eighteen	
	Speed	**Error**	**Speed**	**Error**	**Speed**	**Error**	**Speed**	**Error**
Age	-.315*	-.727***	-.665***	-.501**	-.819***	-.154**	-.570**	-.494**
Gender	.090	-.104	.112	-.158	-.039	.035	.167	.252
	Speed		**Speed**		**Speed**		**Speed**	
Error	.455*		.554**		.218		.701**	

Table 16. The results of descriptive statistics for the Arial font in four sizes [10, 14, 16 and 18]

Statistic	**10 Arial Font**	**14 Arial Font**	**16 Arial Font**	**18 Arial Font**
Mean	.425	.301	.072	.036
Median	.434	.305	.073	.037
Mode	.462	.306	.061	.0370
Variance	.0041	.0003	.0002	.000003
Minimum	.326	.254	.048	.026
Maximum	.541	.325	.106	.046

Experiment 2

Figure 4. The means of the error when reading Arial font in four sizes [10, 14, 16 and 18]

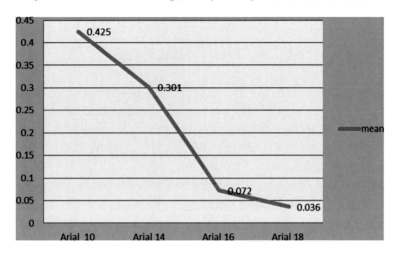

Table 17. Error percentages among the four group font sizes using Friedman test

Font Size	Mean Rank	Chi-Square	p-Value
Ten	4.00	90.00	.000
Fourteen	3.00		
Sixteen	2.00		
Eighteen	1.00		

Table 18. Pairs comparison using the Wilcoxon test in terms of Arial font groups

	10-14	10-16	10-18	14-16	14-18	16-18
Z	-4.782	-4.782	-4.782	-4.785	-4.783	-4.783
p-value	.000	.000	.000	.000	.000	.000

Table 19. Spearman's correlations between the variables using the Arial font

	Ten		Fourteen		Sixteen		Eighteen	
	Speed	Error	Speed	Error	Speed	Error	Speed	Error
Age	-.710***	-.760***	-.728	-.640	-.710***	-.133	-.625**	-.555**
Gender	.066	-.039	.008	-.046	-.116	-.182	.184	-.027

	Speed		Speed		Speed		Speed	
Error	.840***		.889***		.177		.765**	

to the difficulty of the text. Generally, a low error rate is significantly correlated with a larger font and lower speed of reading.

Reading Performance of the Simplified Arabic Font

For simplified Arabic font, error seems to dramatically drop as demonstrated by the computed mean, median and mode given in Table 20. It is observed that a considerable reduction in the error percentage results from fonts of sizes 16 and 18, with mean percentages of 7.4% and 2.6%, respectively. This result is confirmed by the boxplot given in Figures 5 and 6 which present the mean reading error using four different sizes of Simplified Arabic font.

Similar to the aforementioned fonts, the Friedman test which is 90.00, as shown by Table 21, indicates a highly significant difference between errors resulting from reading the four sizes of simplified Arabic fonts. The Wilcoxon test given in Table 22, shows a very highly significant difference is determined by each of the pairs of two font sizes. Hence, to reduce the percentage of reading error, it is better to use a larger font.

Table 20. The results of descriptive statistics for simplified Arabic font in four sizes [10, 14, 16 and 18]

Statistic	10 Simplified Arabic Font	14 Simplified Arabic Font	16 Simplified Arabic Font	18 Simplified Arabic Font
Mean	.383	.145	.074	.026
Median	.364	.143	.075	.026
Mode	.358	.127	.084	.026
Variance	.0021	.0003	.0001	.00003
Minimum	.287	.119	.054	.017
Maximum	.484	.177	.093	.037

Figure 5. Boxplot of the error when reading simplified Arabic font in four sizes [10, 14, 16 and 18]

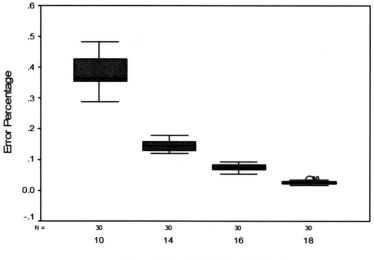

Figure 6. The mean error when reading simplified Arabic font in four sizes [10, 14, 16 and 18]

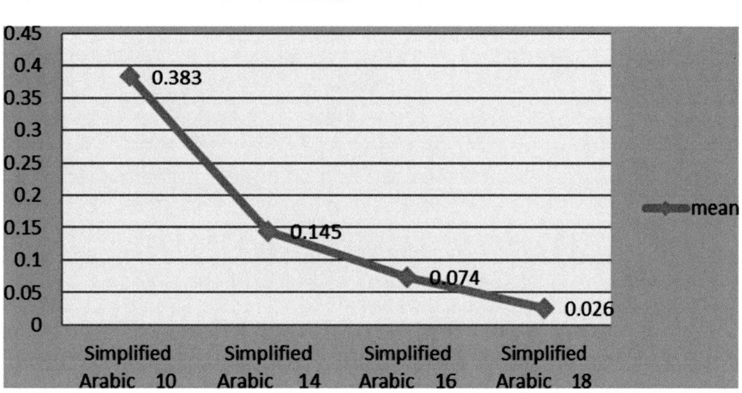

Table 21. Error percentages among the four groups of font sizes using Friedman test

Font Size	Mean Rank	Chi-Square	p-Value
Ten	4.00	90.00	.000
Fourteen	3.00		
Sixteen	2.00		
Eighteen	1.00		

Table 22. Pairs comparison using the Wilcoxon test in terms of simplified Arabic font groups

	10-14	10-16	10-18	14-16	14-18	16-18
Z	-4.782	-4.782	-4.782	-4.787	-4.783	-4.783
p-value	.000	.000	.000	.000	.000	.000

For Spearman's correlation, age tends to have a moderate correlation with speed and error of reading. But this correlation is highly significant and hence it is possible to say that when a student grows, the chances of reading errors occurring will be lower. By looking at gender, we do not observe any significant correlation with speed and error. In terms of the relationship between speed and error, the highest correlation which is .602, is obtained for size ten, then the correlation becomes somewhat weak for the rest of the sizes as seen Table 23.

Stratification of Students

At the end of the test, each student was asked to answer a short questionnaire (as seen in Appendix 6) to determine whether the text is easy through answering eight questions. Finally, answering the short questionnaire shows that all students find words in the text to be easy. All mistakes that students make when reading the text are due to a vision problem. In addition, all students do not have any problem reading from the screen or use a computer. Moreover, students aged 10 to 11 who represent 80% of the sample prefer size 18 as a readable size, while 4 students aged 12 found the text clearer to read in size

Table 23. Spearman's correlations between the variables using Simplified Arabic font

	Ten		Fourteen		Sixteen		Eighteen	
	Speed	**Error**	**Speed**	**Error**	**Speed**	**Error**	**Speed**	**Error**
Age	-.488**	-.542**	-.645**	-.206**	-.580**	-.106	-.429*	-.483*
Gender	-.056	-.075	-.076	-.033	-.053	-.070	.204	.027
	Speed		**Speed**		**Speed**		**Speed**	
Error	.602**		.351*		.249		.471*	

16 (20%). In addition, 30% of the participants recognized certain letters according to the position of the words. On the other hand, analysing the list of errors for each student in Appendix (6) shows that the errors are mainly due to the shape of the characters. Data analysis led to the classification of these errors into four types:

- Two characters are connected in the middle and have dots at the top or bottom.
- More than two characters are connected in the middle and have dots at the top or bottom.
- Characters have dots and vowels.
- Characters without dots and with similar letters have dots.

Table 24 presents the case that readers made errors according to the shapes of the letters or words. Letters that have dot or more come on the top of the average of errors especially when the size of the words is small. Vowels also led to difficult to recognize on reading the letter that has dots, thus, test two factors recorded as main factors affected the readability of Arabic text in size 10 and 14.

Reading Speed

Sequentially, age has been measured as an independent variable to define the optimal font size and type. According to Tables 25, 26, 27, 28 and Figure 7 which display the mean and standard definition of all fonts in different sizes, a readable font size is different according to the age of the reader. E.g. the reading speed of students aged 10, when reading text presented using Arabic Traditional in size 18 (M= 13.50/ SD= 2.76), is longer than students aged 12 who read the same text in size 16 (M= 8.20/ SD= 1.69) by 55.67%. In addition, it is notable that the difference in reading performance between age groups 10 and 11 is similar in all font sizes and types. For instance, comparing the reading speed of students aged 10 in size 10 (Simplified Arabic) with students aged 11 shows a slight difference (3.6%). This convergence in the performance of students in ages 10 and 11 is clearly in sizes 10, 14 and 16. .

CONCLUSION

Defining a readable font size and type for the Arabic language is the main focus of this experiment. Five types (Arabic traditional, Arial, Times New Roman, Simplified Arabic, and Courier New) were tested in four different sizes (10, 14, 16 and 18). The experiment mainly reported that sizes 10 and 14 are not the best font sizes to read present Arabic characters for children aged 9 to 13, wherein the average error

Experiment 2

Table 24. The factors that have a negative effect on reading

Font Size	Font Type	Factors Have a Negative Effect					
		Dots		Vowels and Dots		Similarity between Letters	
		N	P	N	P	N	P
	Test 1						
10	Traditional Arabic	879	96.9	879	99.4	73	89
10	Courier New	733	88	774	92.9	65	77.9
10	Times new roman	820	98.3	830	99.5	78	93.8
10	Arial	826	99.5	815	97.8	73	87.9
10	Simplified Arabic	819	98.2	829	99.4	68	82.1
	Total	1000	100	1000	100	264	100
	Test 2						
14	Traditional Arabic	618	61.8	258	25.8	56	21.2
14	Courier New	300	35.9	195	19.5	32	21.1
14	Times new roman	533	53.3	196	19.6	79	29.9
14	Arial	574	57.4	147	14.7	81	30.7
14	Simplified Arabic	605	60.5	135	13.5	39	14.8
	Total	1000		1000		264	
	Test 3						
16	Traditional Arabic	107	10.7	79	7.9	64	24.2
16	Courier New	239	23.9	29	2.9	29	11
16	Times new roman	254	25.4	91	9.1	45	17
16	Arial	377	37.7	93	9.3	35	13.3
16	Simplified Arabic	594	59.4	87	8.7	16	6.1
	Total	1000		1000		264	
	Test 4						
18	Traditional Arabic	39	3.9	23	2.3	8	3.03
18	Courier New	76	7.6	30	3	6	2.27
18	Times new roman	53	5.3	33	3.3	11	4.2
18	Arial	81	8.1	41	4.1	5	1.89
18	Simplified Arabic	97	9.7	25	2.5	3	1.14
	Total	1000		1000		264	

Table 25. Mean and standard definition of all fonts in size 10

Age	TA		CN		TNR		A		SA	
	M	SD	M	SD	M	SD	M	SD	M	SD
10	21.20	3.26	18.10	1.80	19.50	2.01	22.90	3.11	22.20	2.62
11	20.20	1.81	17	2.05	18.40	2.01	19.50	2.95	21.40	2.84
12	18.80	5.73	9.70	2.31	17.50	2.46	17.10	2.03	16.70	3.40

Table 26. Mean and standard definition of all fonts in size 14

Age	TA		CN		TNR		A		SA	
	M	SD	M	SD	M	SD	M	SD	M	SD
	18.80	1.75	18.80	1.87	18.40	2.46	18.20	1.87	17.90	2.38
11	17.40	4.01	17.50	2.64	18.30	2	17.10	2.33	17	2.11
12	12.90	2.69	12.20	2.94	11.60	3.17	12.10	2.64	10.90	1.45

Table 27. Mean and standard definition of all fonts in size 16

Age	TA		CN		TNR		A		SA	
	M	SD	M	SD	M	SD	M	SD	M	SD
10	18	2.11	17.40	1.51	17.30	1.95	17.80	1.48	16.80	2.49
11	17.60	1.51	17.90	2.13	14.80	2.97	17.80	1.96	16.90	1.91
12	8.20	1.69	8.90	1.79	8.80	2.30	8.70	1.49	8.40	2.12

Table 28. Mean and standard definition of all fonts in size 18

Age	TA		CN		TNR		A		SA	
	M	SD	M	SD	M	SD	M	SD	M	SD
10	13.50	2.76	12.80	2.49	11.30	3.02	11.80	2.44	10.60	2.07
11	13.70	1.49	10.10	2.03	9.80	2.09	10	1.89	8.80	2.15
12	6.40	2.22	8.30	1.49	7.30	2.45	8	1.70	7.80	1.62

Figure 7. Comparing the mean reading error and speed in size 10 for the five font types

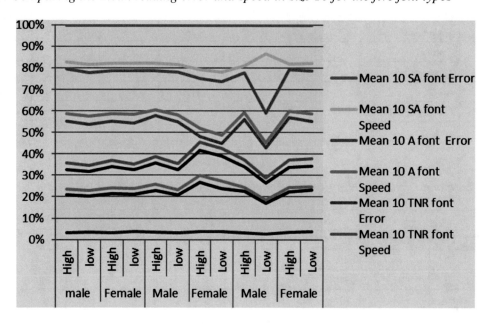

rate was higher. However, in font size 16, the average error rate decreased and the reading speed was also improved.

Moreover, age was reported as having a significant negative correlation with error for all sizes, while gender is found to have a very weak relationship with speed and error. On the other hand, examining the list of errors for each student shows that the difference in reading is caused by one of these reasons: (1) connecting two or more characters that have a dot at the top, bottom or middle; (2) characters have dots and vowels; and (3) characters have the same shape but some have dots others do not.

On the other hand, Gender is found to have a very weak relationship with speed and error, and hence it will be ignored when interpreting errors resulting from using the four sizes.

REFERENCES

Abubaker, A., & Joan, L. (2012). The optimum font size and type for students aged 9-12 reading Arabic characters on screen: A case study. Journal of Physics: Conference Series, 364. Retrieved from http://iopscience.iop.org/1742-6596/364/1/012115/

Asmaa, A., & Asma, A.-O. (2009). Arab children's reading preferences for e-learning programs. *Proceedings of the 2009 conference on Information Science, Technology and Applications*, Kuwait. ACM.

Chapter 12

Experiment 3:
Optimal Line Length for Reading Electronic Schoolbook on Screen

Azza A Abubaker
Benghazi University, Libya

Joan Lu
University of Huddersfield, UK

ABSTRACT

Although experimental studies have shown a strong impact of text layout on the legibility of e- text, many digital texts appearing in eBook or the Internet use different designs, so that there is no straightforward answer in the literature over which one to follow when designing e- material. Therefore, in this chapter we shall focus on the text layout, particularly the influence of line length. This experiment is divided into two parts. The first part focuses on the factor of line length by studying its effect on reading speed and accuracy using various columns [one column and two columns] with each page having the same amount of information. The second part tests a new approach which basically assumes that by using different colours for the first and last word of each line, it will improve students' reading level. This hypothesis was based on pervious findings over the difficulty of being able to immediately locate the following line (Chan and Lee 2005). In addition, this approach was based on explanation of the eye movement which, in the reading process, does not scan a line but stops for about ¼ of a second before jumping to new place such as at the end of the line when the eye goes back to the beginning of the new line.

DOI: 10.4018/978-1-5225-1884-6.ch012

HYPOTHESIS

The third experiment comprise seven hypotheses to be measured in order to define optimal line length for reading a school book using two reading strategies these hypothesis are;

H1: The efficiency of line length will be different in terms of time taken to search the same tasks.

H2: The efficiency of line length will be different in terms of number of correct answers made in each type of question.

H3: There will be a difference between the single line (SL) without colour, double line (DL) without colour, single line) SL (with colour and double line (DL) with colour in terms of the users' satisfaction.

H4: Line with colour is more readable than a line without colour in terms of easy to search.

H5: Line with colour will be more effective than line without colour in terms of reducing the frequency of incorrect answers.

H6: Reading strategies affect the line length in terms of shortening task accomplishment time.

H7: Reading strategies, readers' age and reading level are more effective than gender in terms of users' stratification.

DESIGN INTERFACES

Four interfaces were designed to test. These were segmented according to the number of columns and colour. The instructional module interface was designed for experimenting using Microsoft's expression web software. Each test had two different interfaces. Each web text module was designed in the light of the recommendations given in the literature and controlled by two independent variables: (1) line length; (2) type of questions. All the sentences were extracted from a lesson in the Libyan schoolbook. The lessons had no extremely rare words, such as names of people or exotic places, technical terms or unusual mechanisms. Table 1 shows the attributes of the experiment and the observed elements.

First Text Interface: Double Column without Colour (DLWOC)

A total of 19 Arabic sentences was used in the experiment. The length of the text was between 10 to 15 words (as seen in Figure 1). A total number of words approximately were 80 words using vowels.

Table 1. The experiment design

Attributes	Observed Elements	Applied to Interface
Body text	Font size, line length, colour of text.	Black font+ right alignment+ two and single column+ … Words. Words per a line.
Background	Colour	White
Margin	Larger than 2.5 inches.	
Type of question	Information recall and reading faster.	Multi choices, open questions and true and false.

Figure 1. The experiment interface for text display in a short line

Second Text Interface: Double Column with Colour (DLWC)

The way of presenting the text in this interface is similar to the previous interface in the number of words and lines. But the interface provided text by using red colour for the first and last word of each line (as seen in Figure 2).

Third Text Interface

A total of 19 Arabic sentences was used in the experiment. The length of the text was between 8 and 12 lines, the number of words per line in one column was between 23 and 26 (as seen in Figure 3).

Figure 2. The experiment interface for text display in short line using red colour for increased legibility of online text

Figure 3. The experiment interface for text display in a long line

Figure 4. The experiment interface for text display in a long line using red colour for increased legibility of online text

Fourth Text Interface

The interface was designed to present in a single column using red color for first and last word in each line (as seen in Figure 4).

EXPERIMENTAL DESIGN

Procedure

Each participant was seated in a closed room environment facing the laptop. All participants used the same PH Pavilion dv6 [Intel i5 core processors] laptop, with the choice of using a mouse attached peripherally. The screen size of the laptop was 15.6 inches with a display setting of 1366 x 768 pixels. Internet Explorer 6.0 was used as the browser environment to present the test software and task. Because of the age of the students, the observer sat behind the participants to record time and encourages them to continue with the experiment and take notes. Participants scanned the tasks in four conditions [one column with colour and without colour, two columns with colour and without colour] in looking for answers to 12 questions (Appendix 7).

Performance was assessed through two dependent variables: (1) time to complete each task; and (2) accuracy of the answers. Accuracy data were based on the number of correct answers the students provided and the total score was 12 points. In this experiment, satisfaction was measured as a dependent variable using the questionnaire. The questionnaire has 8 questions with a response as yes or no or no difference. The satisfaction questions relate to how easy it was to read the text or recall information in it. In addition, disorientation is expected to measure user perceptions towards ease of searching the lesson, becoming lost in the text, and being comfortable with the text layout.

Participants

The test sample of this experiment consisted of 48 native Arabic students (24 male and 24 female) who volunteered for this experiment. The participants' age ranged from 9 to 13. They all used the computer and the internet. Participants were divided into four groups and each group read from the same text presented in different conditions (as seen in Table 2). 29 of the participants had participated in the previous experiment (font size and type), while 19 participants taking part for the first time.

Study Variables

A number of variables were recognized and outlined earlier to implementation experiments. These variables are of three types; independent, dependent and controlled.

Controlled Variables

There is variable expected to affect the experimental procedure. These variables are summarised as followed;

- The tasks were the same for all users.
- The level of difficulty of the subject matter was the same.
- Reading scour; high level or low level [student scour according to their score in reading in Libya school while low level students who get low than 5 in reading exam].

Table 2. The size of the sample

Gender	One column	Two columns	Total
Female	12	12	24
Male	12	12	24

Dependent Variables

The dependent variable was defined in;

- Time spent searching for answers.
- Number of correct answers.
- Satisfactions.
- User reaction (use their fingers, scrolling, etc.).

Independent Variables

Three types of questions were defined as independent variables [open questions, True and false questions and multi answer]. Each type used to apply to investigating the reading strategies that were used.

Statistical Technique for the Analysis of Data

The following are the results of using three types of questions with respect to the answer speed (time) needed to finish each type and the corresponding errors in the answers. Four descriptive statistics, which are mean and standard deviation (SD) as well as minimum and maximum values, are calculated. It is expected that age, reading level and gender may lead to different speeds and errors. Therefore, Kruskal Wallis' one-way analysis of variance test is used to compare ages, while the Mann-Whitney test for assessing whether two independent samples are equal is used to compare (1) gender and (2) reading levels. In addition, the Friedman test and Wilcoxon test will be conducted to test the difference between the question models. Spearman's correlation will be used to measure the correlation between the underlying measurements. The results are organized according to questions with colours and those without colours.

DATA ANALYSIS

Comparing Reading Performance Using Single and Double Column

Reading Times

Reading times were measured for the best line length in each reading strategy, i.e. skimming or scanning. The collected data show that the computed time seems to decrease as long as students' age increases when reading through single and double columns. This finding is to be expected since age in the early stage of education affects the reading speed. Otherwise, students tend to show a different speed when answering the three types of questions. For example, the comparison between the mean reading speed to answer multi answer question [MAQ] from reading text on a single column with double line shows that the reading process is affected by the students' age, as older students were faster when reading through double lines, while students aged 9 prefer the single line in both reading processes. In addition, the mean reading time of students aged 13, 12 and 11 when reading a single line was [.905, .575, and .988] respectively, while in the double lines it was [.360, .614, and .723] in the same order. Thus, students who read the entire text searching for specific words prefer to use a double line, e.g. the mean reading speed of the entire text by older students [13 years old] was less when reading the text in a double line [MAQ/ M = .360 and true/ false question (T/FQ) M .185] and [MAQ/ M = .905 and T/FQ/ M = .905] than in double columns, as can be seen in Table 3 and Figure 5.

The reading level of students, as defined by the teacher, was considered as an independent variable. The collected data shows that the reading speed of students with a low-level of reading was less when reading a single column according to the mean reading time (m = .921,1.643, .726) as presented in Tables 4 and 5 and Figure 6. Students prefer long line because they can see a whole sentence in the same line but they face difficulty when dealing with a sentence that is broken up into two lines. Thus, displaying a complete sentence in one line is preferred by students compared to displaying it in a short or long line. In addition, short line was preferred by students with a high level of reading. This finding is in line with the findings of Dyson and Haselgrove (2001). For the multi answer model, it seems that students with

Table 3. The average reading time for three different types of questions in two different line-lengths according to the reader's age

Age		Single Column						Double Column					
		Multi Answer		Open Question		T/F Question		Multi Answer		Open Question		T/F Question	
		M	SD	M	SD	M	SD	M	SD	M	SD	M	SD
9	Speed	1.226	.153	1.857	.445	1.061	.074	1.446	.338	1.858	.445	1.061	.0742
10	Speed	1.29	.157	2.105	.469	.957	.294	1.083	.165	2.105	.469	.957	.294
11	speed	.988	.325	1.432	.343	.514	.271	.723	.314	1.461	.346	.555	.313
12	speed	.575	.230	1.317	.298	.378	.363	.614	.235	1.305	.129	.290	.075
13	speed	.905	.905	.905	0	.905	0	.360	0	1.030	0	.185	0
Kruskal-Wallis test		Chi = 10.601 p-value = .014		Chi = 5.430 p-value = .066		Chi = 9.292 p-value = .010		Chi = 11.443 p-value = .010		Chi = 7.703 p-value = .053		Chi = 13.193 p-value = .004	

Figure 5. A mean for testing three types of questions and reading through single and double columns

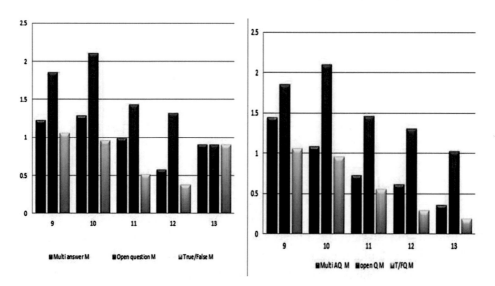

Table 4. Descriptive statistics and test for the three types of questions with respect to the reading level (single line)

Reading Level		Multi Answer (MAQ)				Open Question (OQ)				True/False (T/FQ)			
		Min	Max	M	SD	Min	Max	M	SD	Min	Max	M	SD
High	Speed	.515	1.380	1.014	.248	1.220	2.390	1.591	.416	.280	1.115	.600	.307
Low	Speed	.360	1.365	.921	.390	.795	2.380	1.643	.529	.180	1.220	.726	.437
Mann-Whitney	Speed	$Z^1 = -.231$ p-value = .817				Z = -.231 p-value = .817				Z = -.433 p-value = .665			

Table 5. Descriptive statistics and test for the three types of questions with respect to the reading level (double lines)

Reading Level		Multi Answer (MAQ)				Open Question (OQ)				True/False (T/FQ)			
		Min	Max	M	SD	Min	Max	M	SD	Min	Max	M	SD
High	Speed	.300	1.950	.785	.489	.795	2.390	1.438	.491	.180	1.115	.557	.353
Low	Speed	.555	1.310	.984	.291	1.315	2.380	1.797	.380	.280	1.220	.769	.380
Mann-Whitney	Speed	Z = -1.89 p-value = .068				Z = -2.309 p-value = .020				Z = -1.357 p-value = .178			

Figure 6. The average reading time for three different types of questions in two different line-lengths according to the reading level

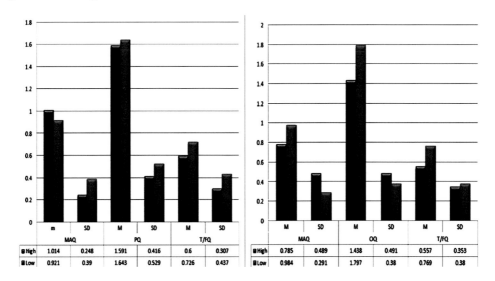

low level need more time when reading a short line than those with a high level, even though according to the median test where Z = 1.89 with p-value = .068, the preference is statistically not accepted. The same pattern is observed for the open question model, but this difference in median between both levels is statistically significant. No obvious difference in the True/false model between the two levels needs to be mentioned. This finding confirms that reading speed is influenced by the reading strategy used by the reader.

The number of studies which considered gender as a strong demographic variable that influences information behaviour (e.g. Hupfer and Detlor 2006; Liu and Huang 2007). Little difference in mean time was reported by testing differences in responses to question models due to gender. When looking at the differences in responses to the question models between genders reading short line, male and female tend to show very little difference in descriptive statistics. Based on average speed, males are somewhat better than females with regard to the multi answer and true/false questions, whereas females are better with regard to the open question. The Mann-Whitney test does not find any significant difference, and hence both males and females are expected to share more or less the same level of performance, see Table 6 and 7 and Figure 7.

Accuracy of Reading

The errors made for the question models are measured to define optimal line length for the sake of obtaining a high level of comprehensibility. Descriptive statistics and test for the three types of questions in Table 8 and Figure 8 show that the error rate decreases as age increases, where it becomes .875 for age 12 compared to 1.446 for age 9. The chi-test is 9.126 with p-value = .028, indicating a significant difference. This finding supported a line of thought considered by several of researchers such as (Cheyne 2005; Salmerón and García 2011).

In addition, the number of errors becomes higher for the second type of question (OQ), which requires reading a whole paragraph to determine the answer. According to the chi-test which is 7.266 with p-value = .064, ages do not reduce the error resulting from the open question. It is noted that the error consistency within each age is low. In terms of the true/false question, the error drops as age goes up. Despite this difference, the chi-test is reported to be not significant. The lowest is zero for ages 11 and

Table 6. The average reading time for three different types of questions in two different line-lengths according to gender (single column)

Gender		Multi answer				Open question				True/False			
		Min	Max	M	SD	Min	Max	M	SD	Min	Max	M	SD
Male	Speed	.415	1.380	.991	.354	.795	2.390	1.712	.551	.180	1.140	.619	.359
Female	Speed	.360	1.305	.944	.304	1.030	2.170	1.515	.359	.185	1.220	.707	.401
Mann-Whitney	Speed	Z = -.577 p-value = .564				Z = -.924 p-value = .356				Z = -.404 p-value = .686			

Table 7. The average reading time for three different types of questions in two different line-lengths according to gender (double column)

Gender		Multi Answer				Open Question				True/False			
		Min	Max	M	SD	Min	Max	M	SD	Min	Max	M	SD
Male	Speed	.375	1.310	.877	.356	.795	2.390	1.712	.552	.180	1.140	.619	.359
Female	Speed	.300	1.950	.895	.466	1.030	2.170	1.515	.358	.185	1.220	.708	.400
Mann-Whitney	Speed	Z = -.173 p-value = .887				Z = -.924 p-value = .378				Z = -.404 p-value = .713			

Figure 7. Boxplot for speed using the three question models in two different line-lengths according to gender

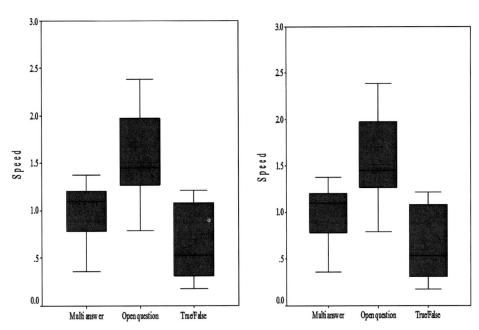

Table 8. Descriptive statistics and test for the three types of questions with respect to age reading through single and double column

Age		Single Column						Double Column					
		Multi A		Open Q		T/F Q		Multi A		Open Q		T/F Q	
		M	**SD**	**M**	**SD**	**M**	**SD**	**M**	**SD**	**M**	**SD**	**M**	**SD**
9	Error	2.000	.408	2.250	.645	1.875	.478	1.750	.289	2.125	.479	.875	.479
10	Error	1.700	.273	3.200	.836	1.600	.418	1.300	.447	3.000	.500	1.000	.354
11	Error	1.611	.486	2.278	.565	1.666	.935	1.050	.284	2.000	1.027	.850	.529
12	Error	1.100	.652	2.000	1.274	1.100	.894	.875	.478	1.500	.577	.500	.408
13	Error	1.500	1.500	1.000	0	1.500	0	1.000	0	2.000	0	.000	0
		Chi = 5.673 p-value = .129		Chi = 5.567 p-value = .135		Chi = 2.283 p-value = .516		Chi = 9.126 p-value = .028		Chi = 7.266 p-value = .064		Chi = 2.697 p-value = .441	

12. In addition, the average error for these ages is similar but varies from age 9 to 10, and hence the Chi-square = 13.193 with p-value = .004 (highly significant).

Moreover, the average error in a single column becomes .575 for aged 12 compared to 1.446 for aged 9. The chi-square is 5.673 with p-value = .129, meaning that the difference is not significant. The number of errors looks higher for the second model of questions. According to the value of chi-square which is 5.567 with p-value = .135, ages do not have any effect on the differences in errors resulting from the open question model. It is noted that the error consistency within each age group is low. For true/ false question model, the errors goes down as age goes up. The chi-square (which is 2.283) is reported

Figure 8. Mean (M) and standard deviation (SD) of average of errors in single and double column according students' age

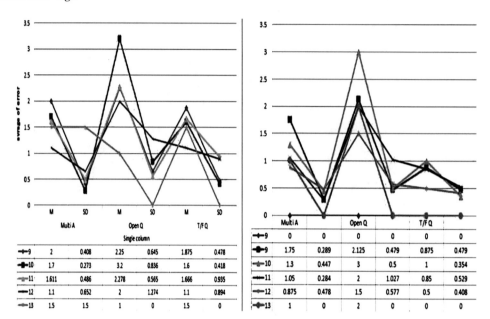

Single column

	MultiA		OpenQ		T/FQ	
	M	SD	M	SD	M	SD
9	2	0.408	2.25	0.645	1.875	0.478
10	1.7	0.273	3.2	0.836	1.6	0.418
11	1.611	0.486	2.278	0.565	1.666	0.935
12	1.1	0.652	2	1.274	1.1	0.894
13	1.5	1.5	1	0	1.5	0

	MultiA		OpenQ		T/FQ	
9	0	0	0	0	0	0
9	1.75	0.289	2.125	0.479	0.875	0.479
10	1.3	0.447	3	0.5	1	0.354
11	1.05	0.284	2	1.027	0.85	0.529
12	0.875	0.478	1.5	0.577	0.5	0.408
13	1	0	2	0	0	0

to be not significant (p-value = .516). The lowest error found is zero for aged 12 while the highest is 3 for aged 11. While comparing the mean of error in single and double column shows differences in students' preference, where the double column was preferred by students of all ages, several explanations are provided to explain this. Some students aged 9 to 10 prefer short line because they can move easily from line to line searching for a specific word or information, while older students can scan the whole page to get a general idea which helps in finding more than one answer at the same time. Additionally, when the eye is fixed on the short line, the latter is higher compared to the long line. Some of the older students find the short line easier to scan and for moving from sentence to sentence.

On the other hand, the outcomes of analysing reading level are demonstrated in Tables 9 and 10 and Figure 9 for reading long and short lines. The Mann-Whitney test does not detect any significant difference for all the question models. In addition, little improvement was reported when reading text in a short line by students with a low level of reading skill. The mean reading time to answer true and false question type [T/FQ] decreased from .600 min in single column to .557 min when reading a short line. In addition, a significant difference in the mean reading time was reported when answering multi answer choices [MAC] (M = .785) from reading short lines, whereas the mean time for answering the same type of question from reading long lines was 1.014 min which is high (Abubaker, A & Lu, J 2013).

The errors made in all the models do not differ significantly between males and females as shown by the Mann-Whitney test in Tables 11, 12 and Figure 10. In general, performance in terms of finishing the answer due to gender is regarded as very similar. Also, males and females have the same error scores in all the question models. The error rate for both male and female decreased from T/FQ [M = 1.375] in a single column to [M = 0.75] in double column. Comparing students' performance in two different line lengths shows that the double column was the best for both male and female. Although some researchers such as (Hupfer and Detlor 2006; Liu and Huang 2007) reported differences in the information behaviour for the reader according to gender, our finding has rejected it.

Table 9. The average reading error for three different types of questions for single column according to the reader's reading level

Reading Level		Multi Answer				Open Question				True/False			
		Min	Max	M	SD	Min	Max	M	SD	Min	Max	M	SD
High	Error	.500	2.500	1.625	.569	1.000	4.500	2.417	.925	.500	3.00	1.708	.722
Low	Error	.500	2.000	1.542	.498	.500	4.00	2.229	.940	.000	2.500	1.416	.793
Mann-Whitney	Error	Z = -.213 p-value = .831				Z = -.088 p-value = .930				Z = -.853 p-value = .394			

Table 10. The average reading error for three different types of questions for single column according to the reader's reading level

Reading Level		Multi Answer				Open Question				True/False			
		Min	Max	M	SD	Min	Max	M	SD	Min	Max	M	SD
High	Error	.500	1.500	1.083	.358	.500	3.500	.1956	.988	.000	1.500	.667	.443
Low	Error	.500	2.000	1.292	.498	1.000	3.500	2.333	.748	.000	1.500	.916	.515
Mann-Whitney	Error	Z = -.936 p-value = .410				Z = -1.055 p-value = .319				Z = -1.208 p-value = .266			

Figure 9. The average reading error for three different types of questions in two different line-lengths according to the reading level

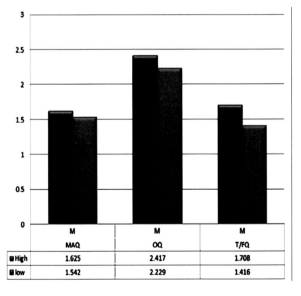

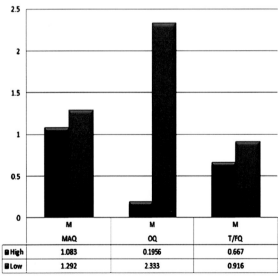

Table 11. Descriptive statistics and test for the three types of questions with respect to gender reading through single column

Gender		Multi Answer				Open Question				True/False			
		Min	Max	M	SD	Min	Max	M	SD	Min	Max	M	SD
Male	Error	1.000	2.500	1.667	.492	.500	4.500	2.375	1.068	.500	3.000	1.375	.772
Female	Error	.500	2.500	1.500	.564	1.000	4.000	2.333	.778	.000	2.500	1.750	.723
	Error	Z = -.730 p-value = .466				Z = -.117 p-value = .907				Z = -1.530 p-value = .126			

Table 12. Descriptive statistics and test for the three types of questions with respect to gender reading through double columns

Gender		Multi Answer				Open Question				True/False			
		Min	Max	M	SD	Min	Max	M	SD	Min	Max	M	SD
Male	Error	.500	2.00	1.250	.452	.500	3.50	2.167	.985	.000	1.500	.750	.452
Female	Error	.500	2.00	1.250	.433	1.000	3.500	2.125	.801	.000	1.500	.833	.536
Mann-Whitney	Error	Z = -.655 p-value = .551				Z = -.176 p-value = .887				Z = -.483 p-value = .671			

Figure 10. The average reading error for three different types of questions in two different line-lengths according to the reader's gender

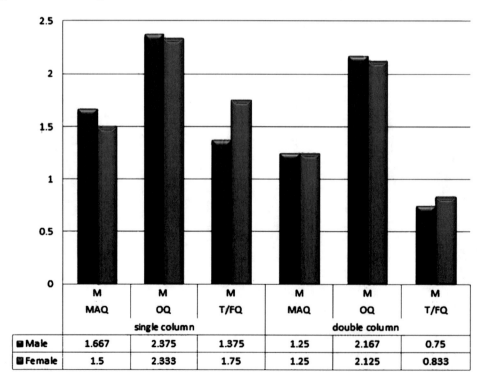

	M MAQ	M OQ	M T/FQ	M MAQ	M OQ	M T/FQ
	single column			double column		
Male	1.667	2.375	1.375	1.25	2.167	0.75
Female	1.5	2.333	1.75	1.25	2.125	0.833

With respect to the errors in single column, the open question model shows the highest error, followed by the multi answer and true/false models, while the chi-square test is 9.379 with p-value <.009, which is a confirmation of highly significant differences between the errors of the three models. The Wilcoxon test proves that the errors in true/false questions are significantly smaller than the remaining models, and errors in multi answer questions are significantly smaller than the open question models. However, it seems interesting to discover that no significant difference is found between the multi-answer and true/false model (as seen in Table 13).

Finally, Table 14 provides a summary of several recommendations from analysing collected statistical data through current experiments, which could be used as a guideline when designing academic Arabic online text for students aged 9 to 13. The reading strategy was considered as a strongly affected variable for selecting the perfect line length according to the reading speed. In addition, the readers' age and reading level have a significant influence on the human information process. For instance, the study has recommended double column for fast reading for students whose reading performance is satisfactory. However, long line is suggested for students with difficulty in reading.

USING COLOUR TO INCREASE THE ABILITY TO FOCUS VISION WHEN MOVING FROM ONE LINE TO ANOTHER

Younger students attribute the slow reading of the text displayed on screen in double column to difficulty by scrolling the text, where their experience in using computer tools especially the mouse was weak. This does not mean that students do not find it difficult to read from a long line, but students find this format similar to the print book and they deal with it by placing the finger at the beginning of each line to make it easier to move to the next line. In order to solve this problem, a new method has been proposed in this

Table 13. Pairs comparison using the Wilcoxon test in terms of speed and errors

	Speed			Error		
	Multi-Answer-Open Question	Multi-Answer-True/False	Open Question-True/False	Multi-Answer-Open Question	Multi-Answer-True/False	Open Question-True/False
Z	-4.296	-3.915	-4.286	-3.165	.000	-3.041
p-value	<.001	<.001	<.001	.002	1.000	.002

Table 14. Optimal line length to read school book on screen according to reading strategy

Age	Reading Strategy		Reading Level	Reading Strategy		Gender	Reading Strategy	
	Scan	Skim		Scan	Skim		Scan	Skim
9	Single column	No difference	High	Single column	Single column	Male	No difference	No difference
10	Single column	No difference						
11	Double column	Single column	Low	Double column	Double column	Female	No difference	No difference
12	Double column	Double column						
13	Double column	Single column						

research; the method was built based on the eye movement theory. The idea assumes that using different colours for the first and last word of each line could help the eye in fixing and moving easily through the text. Reading performances of students were compared in order to define which design [single or double column] is read most effectively by students of different ages.

Reading Speed

The student's performance when reading a text in two columns was tested. It is expected that students may have the ability to show a different degree of performance by using different models of questions. This performance is expressed by the time (speed) needed to complete answering each question. By comparing times obtained from reading a single column with colour and double column, it shows a significant difference as can be seen in Table 15. It is clear that the speed for students of all ages is faster when reading a double column in three types of questions. For example, the mean reading time of short line for students aged 13 when answering multi answer choices were .795 min, open question 1.070 min, and true/ false question .710 min, while of a long line the average reading speed for the three questions was 1.070 min, 2.020, .875 min, respectively.

In addition, we notice in general that more time is required than for the type one question. Likewise, with multi-answer questions, the time spent on answering becomes lower as age increases. According to the results, ages 9 and 10 had a similar average speed, so were ages 11 and 12. This result is enhanced by the Kruskal-Wallis test, which is 9.58 with a p-value = .022, meaning that time spent on open questions is statistically different from young students to older students. Based on dispersion measures, the speed seems to be more consistent with ages 11 and 12 than with ages 9 and 10. For the true/false model, we observe the manner of speed seen in the open question model, where students aged 9 and 10 seem much closer to each other than those aged 11 and 12. The Kruskal-Wallis test is 10.48 with a p-value = 0.00, which is statistically significant denoting that age can lead to different responses in speed. The same results are observed for errors made by this type, where the value of the Kruskal-Wallis test is 15.863 with a p-value = .001 which is highly significant.

In addition, students in age 9 show a wider range of time using minimum and maximum values (.851 and 2.110). The difference in speed is statistically not significant where chi-square = 7.013 with p-value

Table 15. Comparing reading performances of students using single column and double column with colour based on students' age

Age		Double Column						Single Column					
		Multi A		Open Q		T/F Q		Multi A		Open Q		T/F Q	
		M	SD	M	SD	M	SD	M	SD	M	SD	M	SD
9	Speed	.956	.202	1.927	.556	.665	.1696	1.310	.561	2.075	.795	.950	.278
10	Speed	.738	.299	1.875	.499	.568	.226	.919	.260	1.987	.472	.789	.352
11	speed	.624	.351	1.320	.132	..375	.57	.771	.425	1.387	.123	.469	.061
12	speed	.431	.073	1.205	.203	.352	.101	.541	.146	1.356	.077	.472	.181
13	speed	.795	-	1.495	-	.710	-	1.070	000	2.020	0	.875	000
Kruskal-Wallis test	Speed	Chi = 8.378 p-value = .039		Chi = 9.58 p-value = .022		Chi = 10.48 p-value = .015		Chi = 7.013 p-value = .071		Chi = 6.514 p-value = .089		Chi = 12.698 p-value = .005	

= .071. Also, for the open question, although the increase in the age of students seems to show some influence on reducing the time for the answers, the statistical test given by Kruskal-Wallis is found to be not significant (p-value = .089). The variation in speed using SD, min and max values is noted to be lower for older students. Unlike the multi answer and open question models, the difference in speed for true/false model between age groups is highly significant where chi-square = 12.698 with p-value = .005; this difference is in favor of older students. Based on the variation measurements, the speed seems to be more consistent than in the other models.

On the other hand, the reading performance of students with high level and low level of reading was improved when the reading text is presented in short lines. By looking at the multi answer choice model as see in Table 8, the average speed for high level is .666, which is slower than students read a single column as can be seen in Table 16. In addition, when scanning the text for students with high level of reading, the reading speed is faster when reading a short line with colour [M = .518 min, SD = .229], while in long line it was M = .710 min, SD = .358] as seen in Table 16.

By comparing differences in time spent on answering the three question modes due to the gender, the Mann-Whitney test is found to be not significant as given in Table 17 and 18. Based on the variation measurements, males and females show similar homogeneity.

Overall, the reading performance of all students at different ages was faster when reading a short line using red colour from the beginning and the end of the line. Therefore, using a red colour for the first and last word of each line showed improvement in reading speed for all students when scanning and skimming the text. In addition, students with both high and low reading levels are faster when reading a short line. To assess whether this difference in speed is caused by the type of question, the Freidman test given in Table 19 is 24.082 with a p-value = 0.00, meaning the type of question leads to a significant difference in speed. Therefore, it is better to examine the difference between each of the question

Table 16. Comparing reading performances of students using single column and double column with colour based on students' reading level

Reading Level		Double Column						Single Column					
		M A C		**O Q**		**T/F**		**M A**		**O Q**		**T/F**	
		M	**SD**	**M**	**SD**	**M**	**SD**	**M**	**SD**	**M**	**SD**	**M**	**SD**
Low level	speed	.675	.304	1.411	.215	.427	.112	.815	.420	1.522	.294	.553	.156
High level	speed	.666	.323	1.630	.571	.518	.229	.898	.521	1.779	.610	.710	.358

Table 17. Descriptive statistics and test for the three types of questions with respect to gender reading single column

Gender		Multi Answer				Open Question				True/False			
		Min	**Max**	**M**	**SD**	**Min**	**Max**	**M**	**SD**	**Min**	**Max**	**M**	**SD**
Male	Speed	.395	1.405	.887	.367	1.185	2.445	1.651	.429	.370	1.190	.589	.272
Female	speed	.286	2.110	.825	.493	1.265	3.060	1.641	.555	.330	1.220	.674	.296
Mann-Whitney	Speed	Z = -.606 p-value = .551				Z = -.577 p-value = .564				Z = -.808p-value = .443			

Table 18. Descriptive statistics and test for the three types of questions with respect to gender reading double column

Gender		Multi Answer				Open Question				True/False			
		Min	Max	M	SD	Min	Max	M	SD	Min	Max	M	SD
Male	Speed	.365	1.330	.703	.358	1.180	2.370	1.567	.400	.305	.800	.446	.171
Female	Speed	.395	1.095	.638	.258	.865	2.445	1.474	.483	.260	.830	.499	.197
Mann-Whitney	Speed	Z = .041 p-value = .840				Z = .480 p-value = .488				Z = 654 p-value = .419			

Table 19. Friedman test for the three question models in terms of speed reading double column

Question Type	Mean Rank	Chi-Square	p-Value
Multi-answer	1.96	24.082	.000
Open question	3.00		
True/false	1.04		

models. Based on Table 20, all the results using the Wilcoxon test confirm highly significant differences between each of the two models.

Accuracy

Regarding the errors made in each question model, the only significant difference is identified in the true/false model where chi-square = 8.540 with p-value = .036. It is worth mentioning that for the true/false model, the low errors are not systematically influenced by older students. Reading speed according to the reading score shows little difference. For example, the Mann-Whitney for students with a high reading score was in the multi choices answer = .815, open question = 1.522, and true/ false question = .553. This difference occurs in this type of questions (True/False), while the Mann-Whitney for students with low scores was in multi choices answer = .898, open question = 1.779, and true/ false question = .710 (as seen in Table 21). The significant difference in answering time was reported between the types of questions, where students take more time when searching for answers for the open question. In addition, the Mann-Whitney indicated a significant difference in answering time for true and false questions between students with difficulty in reading and students with high scores. The reading levels do not lead to any significant difference in errors for the three types of question models where the p-values from the Mann-Whitney test is larger than .05. Similarly, for the open model, the Mann-Whitney is -.751 with p-value = .478, while for the true/false model, the Mann-Whitney is -.520 with p-value = .603.

Table 20. Pairs comparison using the Wilcoxon test in terms of speed double column

	Multi-Answer: Open Question	Multi-Answer: True/False	Open Question: True/False
Z	-4.286	-4.172	-4.286
p-value	.000	.000	.000

Table 21. Comparing reading performances of students using single column and double column with colour

Age		Double Column						Single Column					
		Multi Answer		Open Question		T/F Question		Multi Answer		Open Question		T/F Question	
		M	SD	M	SD	M	SD	M	SD	M	SD	M	SD
9	Error	1.625	.478	2.375	1.108	1.500	.707	2.000	0	2.625	.479	1.875	.479
10	Error	1.200	.671	2.500	.353	1.500	.612	1.600	.418	2.300	.570	2.000	.612
11	Error	.9444	.634	2.055	.882	.333	.354	1.556	.463	1.833	.500	1.166	.661
12	Error	.900	.418	1.200	1.036	.200	.273	1.700	.671	1.600	.224	1.200	.447
13	Error	1.00	-	1.00	-	0.00	-	2.50	000	1.500	0	.500	000
Kruskal-Wallis test	eError	Chi = 4.249 p-value = .236		Chi = 5.027 p-value = .170		Chi = 15.863 p-value = .001		Chi = 3.378 p-value = .337		Chi = 9.098 p-value = .028		Chi = 8.540 p-value = .036	

With respect to the errors, the lowest and largest number of errors made by the high level group is lower than that made by the lower level group. Apparently, the average number of errors for the low level group, which is 1.292, is higher than for the high level group, which is .917. By relying on the test, which is 2.041 with a p-value = .153, we reject any statistical difference and confirm that both groups are equal as seen in Table 22.

By looking at the corresponding errors when reading through short line, it is observed that the number of errors resulting from using open question is highest with the biggest variation within the errors. The multi-answer model comes second and the true/false model third with a similar degree of variation. By examining these differences in error, the Freidman test, which is 31.5 with a p-value = .000, denotes a highly significant difference (see Table 23). For more details, the Wilcoxon test given in Table 24 shows that there is a highly significant difference between any two of the question models.

Table 22. The average reading error for three different types of questions for single column according to the reader's reading level

Reading Level		Double Column						Single Column					
		M A C Question		Open Question		True/False Question		M A C Question		Open Question		True/False Question	
		M	SD	M	SD	M	SD	M	SD	M	SD	M	SD
High	Error	.917	.468	1.667	.651	.625	.569	1.708	.542	1.958	.655	1.416	.596
Low	Error	1.292	.655	2.292	1.117	.8333	.913	1.708	.450	2.042	.498	1.458	.782

Table 23. The Friedman test for the three question models in terms of error reading through short line

Question Type	Mean Rank	Chi-Square	p-Value
Multi-answer	1.88	31.50	.000
Open question	2.81		
True/false	1.31		

Table 24. Pairs comparison using the Wilcoxon test in terms of error

	Multi-Answer: Open Question	**Multi-Answer: True/False**	**Open Question: True/False**
Z	-3.643	-2.513	-4.223
p-value	.000	.000	.000

According to Figure 11, it is very clear that the open questions need more time to answer than the other two models, so the multi-answer model comes second and the true/false model is third (time for writing the answer was not measured). From the figure, it is noted that a higher variation in answering speed can be observed regarding true/false questions as opposed to open questions, but more homogeneity of speed is observed within the speed for answering the true/false model.

COMPARING READING PERFORMANCE USING COLOUR AND WITHOUT COLOUR IN TWO CONDITIONS

Reading Speed

Reading performances of students were compared in order to define which design is read effectively by students and which variables have negative or positive influences using Mann-Whitney test. In Table 25, it is notable that the mean times for with and without a colour seems to be fairly close, especially for the open question and true/false morels. However, since the p-value computed from the test is more than .05, using colours will not lead to any statistical difference compared to not using colours for all types of questions. Although the difference is not statistically significant, it can be seen that there is a clear improvement especially when browsing the full text. The results of comparing two columns with and without colours using the Mann-Whitney test are summarised in Table 26. The descriptive statistics summarized in Table 66 shows that the mean rank speeds for with and without colours are apparently

Figure 11. Boxplot for error using the three question models

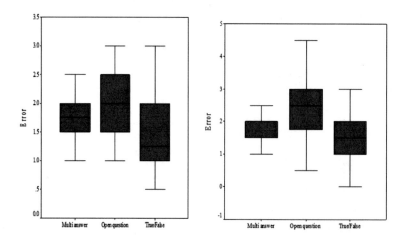

Table 25. The Mann-Whitney test for with and without colours in terms of speed (single column)

	Time	Mean	Median	Mean Rank	z-Value	p-Value
Multi answer	With colour	.856	.803	21.73	-1.160	.246
	Without colour	.957	1.055	26.37		
Open question	With colour	1.646	1.442	24.44	-.223	.823
	Without colour	1.630	1.460	23.54		
True/False	With colour	.631	.515	24.17	-.085	.932
	Without colour	.680	.550	23.83		

Table 26. The Mann-Whitney test for with and without colours in terms of speed (double column)

	Speed	Mean Rank	z-Value	p-Value
Multi answer	With colour	20.60	-1.928	.054
	Without colour	28.40		
Open question	With colour	23.06	-.711	.477
	Without colour	25.94		
True/False	With colour	21.48	-1.495	.135
	Without colour	27.52		

similar. The p-value computed from the test is more than .05, and hence colours will not lead to any statistical difference from not using colours for all types of questions.

The dataset is also analyzed by comparing the performance of with and without colors for each age. Table 27 demonstrates the results from using the Mean rank test. It is clear that the speed for students who are in age 9 and 10 is statistically different in terms of the multi answer model, but for the true/false model, the significant difference is reported for age 9 only. As the sign of z-value is negative for some models, the students seem to be faster with colors than without colors. This is noted for most ages and question models. However, since we do not detect any significant results (p-value>.05), it may not be recommended to use colors, especially for those who are older than 9 years.

The aim is to investigate the effect of using one and two columns for the time spent to answer the question models in terms of texts based on using colour or without colour. Starting with coloured text, Table 28 shows that the difference in time needed to answer the questions resulting from using one and two columns is not statistically significant. Similarly, the results are not significant for the models without colouring. Hence, using any design will lead to the same time.

Accuracy

By comparing errors obtained from with and without colours, Table 29 explains that for any question models, the errors for both groups do not differ significantly since the resulting p-value is bigger than .05. Using colour reduced the average error in the three different types of questions. This confirms that the use of colours reduces the proportion of errors.

Table 27. The Mann-Whitney test for with and without colours in terms of speed for each age

Age	Speed		Mean Rank	z-Value	p-Value
9	Multi answer	With colour	2.50	-2.309	.021
		Without colour	6.50		
	Open question	With colour	5.00	-.577	.564
		Without colour	4.00		
	True/False	With colour	2.50	-2.323	.020
		Without colour	6.50		
10	Multi answer	With colour	3.40	-2.193	.028
		Without colour	7.60		
	Open question	With colour	4.80	.465	.548
		Without colour	6.20		
	True/False	With colour	3.80	-1.776	.076
		Without colour	7.20		
11	Multi answer	With colour	8.72	-.940	.347
		Without colour	11.15		
	Open question	With colour	8.33	-1.225	.221
		Without colour	11.50		
	True/False	With colour	7.94	-1.513	.130
		Without colour	11.85		
12	Multi answer	With colour	4.00	-1.225	.221
		Without colour	6.25		
	Open question	With colour	4.20	-.980	.327
		Without colour	6.00		
	True/False	With colour	5.70	-.861	389
		Without colour	4.13		

By comparing errors obtained from with and without colours, Table 30 explains that for any question models, the errors for both groups do not differ significantly as the resulting p-value is bigger than .05. Although the negative sign of z indicates that the colours may lead to less time needed to answer the questions, the test says that both groups are statistically the same.

In conclusion, the performance of the students is not affected by incorporating colours for designing questions, whatever the question model. Therefore, using colours will not decrease the time needed to complete their answers or lead to a reduction in errors. On the other hand, the time and errors are significantly correlated whether we use colours or not.

According to Table 31, for all question models, the test does not find any statistical difference, and hence errors from designing questions with and without colors are the same for all ages although it is noted that color may lead to fewer errors as the sign z is found to be negative.

Table 28. The Mann-Whitney test for speed according to with and without colours in terms of reading score

Reading Score	Speeds		Mean Rank	z-Value	p-Value
With colour	Multi answer	One column	28.02	-1.743	.083
		Two columns	20.98		
	Open question	One column	26.75	-1.114	.265
		two columns	22.25		
	True/False	One column	29.71	-2.578	.010
		Two columns	19.29		
Without colour	Multi answer	one column	25.70	-.830	.406
		Two columns	22.38		
	Open question	One column	24.20	-.096	.924
		two columns	23.81		
	True/False	One column	24.33	-.601	.873
		two columns	23.69		

Table 29. The Mann-Whitney test for with and without colours in terms of error

Error		Mean	Median	Mean Rank	z-Value	p-Value
Multi answer	With colour	1.708	1.750	25.90	-1.016	.310
	Without colour	1.543	1.500	22.02		
Open question	With colour	2.000	2.000	21.02	-1.558	.119
	Without colour	2.369	2.500	27.11		
True/False	With colour	1.438	1.250	22.40	-.839	.402
	Without colour	1.587	1.500	25.67		

Table 30. The Mann-Whitney test for with and without colours in terms of error

Error		Mean Rank	z-Value	p-Value
Multi answer	With colour	23.44	-.548	.584
	Without colour	25.56		
Open question	With colour	23.33	-.560	.558
	Without colour	25.67		
True/False	With colour	22.79	-.873	.383
	Without colour	26.21		

Table 31. The Mann-Whitney test for with and without colours in terms of error for each age

Age	Error		Mean Rank	z-Value	p-Value
9	Multi answer	With colour	4.25	-.316	.752
		Without colour	4.75		
	Open question	With colour	4.88	-.438	.661
		Without colour	4.13		
	True/False	With colour	5.63	-1.348	.178
		Without colour	3.38		
10	Multi answer	With colour	5.30	-.216	.829
		Without colour	5.70		
	Open question	With colour	4.10	-1.571	.116
		Without colour	6.90		
	True/False	With colour	6.80	-1.469	.142
		Without colour	4.20		
11	Multi answer	With colour	9.28	-.567	.571
		Without colour	10.65		
	Open question	With colour	10.17	-.124	.901
		Without colour	9.85		
	True/False	With colour	7.22	-2.150	.032
		Without colour	12.50		
12	Multi answer	With colour	5.10	-.131	.896
		Without colour	4.88		
	Open question	With colour	4.20	-1.033	.302
		Without colour	6.00		
	True/False	With colour	4.10	-1.207	.227
		Without colour	6.13		

Unlike the results from the time analysis, the results of error analysis are considered interesting as seen in Table 32. In terms of using colours, the results reveal that for multi-answer and true/false models, the errors made by one column is significantly higher than those made by two columns (p-value = .001). On the other hand, using columns for open questions does not have any effect on the number of errors. Similarly, if no colour is used for designing the questions, one column is significantly different from two columns (p-values = .01) for multi-answer, and the difference is highly significant (p-value<.001) as observed form the true/false model where in both cases using one column leads to a reduction in the student's performance. For the open question, the number of errors is the same for using either one or two columns (p-value = .489).

Table 32. The Mann-Whitney test for error according to with and without colours in terms of reading scores

Reading Score	Error		Mean Rank	z-Value	p-Value
With colour	Multi answer	One column	31.00	-3.308	.001
		Two columns	18.00		
	Open question	One column	24.69	-.094	.925
		Two columns	24.31		
	True/False	One column	30.98	-3.273	.001
		Two columns	18.02		
Without colour	Multi answer	One column	29.02	-2.566	.010
		Two columns	19.19		
	Open question	One column	25.39	-.691	.489
		Two columns	22.67		
	True/False	One column	31.20	-3.597	<.001
		two columns	17.10		

CONCLUSION

This chapter mainly focuses on the layout of the text, particularly the influence of line length. This experiment was divided into two parts. The first part focused on the factor of line length by studying its effect on reading speed and accuracy using different types of columns [one column and two columns] with each page having the same amount of information. The second part tests a new approach which assumes that using a different colour for the first and last word in each line will improve the reading level of students. Generally, the findings from the result above indicate that the time needed to complete all question models is significantly lower for elder students. Errors from all the question models are apparently lower for older students in both the long and short line.

In addition, the high level of reading neither plays an important role in reducing the time needed to complete the answers nor leads to alleviating errors which could be made in answering the questions. The degree of association describing the relationship between speed and error for the true/false model is found to be the highest and most positive. Similar to models with colours, one interpretation of this relationship is that, usually, if students understand the question, then they do not need to spend more time on answering any question model; however, if they do not understand, then they need more time and hence their results will be inaccurate.

Overall, the conclusion from these results is that the time needed to complete all the question modules becomes significantly low when students are elder. Errors for all the question models are expected to be significantly lower for elder students.

For speed or errors, the reading scores show a positive correlation with all the question models but this correlation is generally weak and not significant. The highest correlation, which is .393, is seen in the errors from the multi answer. Therefore, no real association with reading scores has been detected by using Spearman's correlation.

For the double column, the degrees of association describing the relationship between speed and error are evaluated as moderately positive (around .550), and considered to be highly significant. In other words, more time spent on answering the questions will lead to higher errors. Similar to models with colours, one interpretation for this relationship is that, usually, if students understand the question, then they do not need to spend more time answering any question model; however, if they do not understand the question, then they need more time and hence their results will not be accurate.

In terms of gender, generally, a relationship does not exist between the question models. However, females seem to negatively correlate with speed errors resulting from answering multi-answer and open questions, whereas males seem to show a negative correlation with the true/false model, but we should bear in mind that these relationships are weak and not important. The degrees of association describing the relationship between speed and error are found to be moderate, positive and highly significant. Namely, a low speed is combined with high errors for all the question models.

REFERENCES

Chan, A., & Lee, P. (2005). Effect of display factors on Chinese reading times, comprehension scores and preferences. *Behaviour & Information Technology*, 24(2), 81–91. doi:10.1080/0144929042000267073

Cheyne, S. M. E. (2005). can electronic textbook help children to learen. *The Electronic Library*, 23(1), 103–115. doi:10.1108/02640470510582781

Salmerón, L., & García, V. (2011). Reading skills and childrens navigation strategies in hypertext. *Computers in Human Behavior*, 27(3), 1143–1151. doi:10.1016/j.chb.2010.12.008

ENDNOTE

[1]   Z is scores are measures of standard deviation.

Chapter 13
Major Findings, Contributions, and Areas for Future Research

Azza A Abubaker
Benghazi University, Libya

Joan Lu
University of Huddersfield, UK

ABSTRACT

Selecting an optimal layout of academic text for display on screen was affected by several factors such as; type of material, subject or readers` age. In this study researcher assumed that each reading strategy requires a specific layout. Thus, the study starts with an understanding of the way that students interact with the text in both formats [electronic and paper]. Findings from this phase were linked with three common typography variables to provide standards for optimal design. In this chapter, the findings of this research are interpreted in the light of the theoretical perspective of the study by linking it with the objectives of the study already set out in chapter one. The first section is devoted to debating the outcomes related to the use of the Internet and eBooks by children at school and at home. This is identified as the first layer of the children's usability of online text, suggesting a further analysis of the children's experience of the e- text with a focus on the reading processes of the schoolbook in both versions [paper and online]. The third section is devoted to discussing the results related to readable Arabic font size and type. Section four is concerned with the findings from testing the effect of line length on reading speed and comprehension of Arabic text; whereas, the fifth section is devoted to debating the outcomes related to the new method for presenting Arabic texts.

DISCUSSION OF THE FINDINGS IN VIEW OF THE RESEARCH QUESTIONS

The current research, as mentioned earlier, is concerned with the factors that affect reading online Arabic text by children aged 9 to 13. A broad analysis of the related theoretical and empirical literature was provided in chapters two and three. A few researchers seem interested in explaining the relationship between these variables. The literature on reading online has come to the conclusion that there are several factors which can be grouped into three main categories of variables (user, usability, and legibility) as

DOI: 10.4018/978-1-5225-1884-6.ch013

seen in chapter three. The questionnaire and observations among grades 4, 5 and 6 in five schools in Benghazi and Huddersfield in the UK have generated extensive data.

Using the Internet and eBook among Libyan School Children at Primary Level

Due to the lack of studies, it has highlighted the use of the Internet and eBook in Libya in particular and the Arab world in general. The study began by collecting quantitative data about the use of the Internet and eBook among school children in Libya as a starting point for investigating the factors that affect the readability of Arabic text on screen. In general, it can state that, the results of this study have supported the next stages of the research in various aspects. Firstly, it supported picking the sample for the research's experiments from students who have already used eBooks and the internet for learning purposes. The results as illustrated in chapter four points out the following:

- The majority of students aged 9- 13 from primary schools in Benghazi have access to the Internet at home or at commercial centres especially where schools did not provide access to the Internet for their students. This finding was similar to several previous studies that reported an increase in the number of children who used the Internet on a daily basis especially in developed countries (Ma, 2005; Ma, 2005; Ma, 2005; Buzzetto-More, Sweat-Guy, Elobaid, 2007; Rowlands, Nicholas et al., 2007). On the other hand, several findings confirm that they use the internet at home as much as they use it at school where they have more freedom to use it for different activities, while at school they just use it for doing research online and for a short time (Park, 2009). This finding is in line with that of this study, that 54% of participants use the internet at home by themselves without any monitoring by parents which can be very dangerous and unsafe.
- Use of the Internet was affected by several factors such as the high cost, poor quality of access, slow download, and control of use by the government. In Libya, the case is different where the main barrier is associated with a lack of internet skills, where students do not learn at school how to use the Internet. The survey reported another factor that influences using the computer and Internet effectively by children at home, namely, "parents' experience with using computer and the Internet" where a majority had no experience with using the Internet and computer, and 29.3% of children get support from their older brothers and sometimes from friends. This barrier was previously defined by Tripp (2010), which requires schools to educate parents through training courses on the use of the Internet or publish bulletins that describes the most important educational sites on the internet. Moreover, more research should be done to evaluate the Arabic websites for children in order to determine their suitability for the purposes of learning.
- The findings indicated that most of the students use the Internet for multi activities but mostly for non-academic purposes. This was possibly influenced by the use of the Internet at home while the education system just focused on the textbook at school. At the same time, Polly et al. (Polly, 2009) reported similar findings despite the fact that English schools apply technology to the education system and all schools provide Internet access for students at school, while a part of the homework requires using the Internet. However, the majority of students in the UK aged 7- 17 are more likely to socialise than doing homework online, wherein 62% of them have profiles on social networks. This case was reported for Libyan students aged 9- 13 where 78.3% have accounts on Facebook and Twitter.

- The study demonstrated that the most common reason for using the Internet was for "playing games online" and "chatting." This is in agreement with results from Tripp (2010) and Curtis, Polly et al. (Polly, 2009) where the participants tended to use the internet for playing games online

- Non- users indicated that they had not used eBooks because they were unaware of their availability, they did not know how to access eBooks, they had limited knowledge about eBook, and they disliked reading on screen. In previous studies in higher education, it was pointed out that an eBook was often used to search for information but students usually prefer a print copy for reading (Shiratuddin, Landoni et al., 2003; Bennett, 2005; Anuradha, 2006; Abdullah, 2007; Milloy, 2007; Noorhidawati and Forbes, 2008; Lam, Lam, Lam et al., 2009; Segal-Drori, Korat et al., 2009)

- It is notable that the majority of previous studies on applying the Internet to the education field had focused on university students (Bennett, 2005; Anuradha, 2006; Asmaa and Asma, 2009; Tenopir, 2009), while little scholarly attention has been directed to studying the use of the Internet in the early stage of education. Students have no idea about the types of eBooks available and they deal with all kinds of texts available on the net as eBooks. This confusion is normal in the absence of any guidance from educators over who should be responsible for educating students on the possibilities available to them on the Internet and the quality of books and resources there that could be used.

- Finally, from what the children said about the general issues on using the Internet at home or at school, it can be concluded that using the Internet and e- sources by young people for education and in their everyday life has increased. But it is notable that the influence of the Internet and e- sources on teacher teaching and student learning is not as in other areas. For example, ICT can make education possible anywhere and at any time, and although ICT offered more flexible learning, the use of ICT by teachers is still limited and very basic. However, new generations tend to use the computer and the Internet for learning purposes more than previous generations who relied basically on a hard copy e.g. (Crestani, Landoni et al., 2006; Buzzetto-More, Sweat-Guy, Elobaid, 2007). Several researchers such as (Salmerón and García, 2011) confirmed that digital learners are very excited about trying this new learning environment, taking into account the area of learning, education level, and learners' age.

E-Reading Process for Schoolbook Based on Users' Cognitive and Behaviour Processes

The literature on e- reading indicates that reading process can be significantly different depending on information sources and readers` age. From the result of this study it can surely confirm that the reading process differs according to the several variables related to the reader, the text and applying technology as shown in chapter three. In addition, theoretical perceptive into theories that related into reading online has already showed limit and gaps where the majority of the theories just focused on the psychology aspect of the readers. In this phase of the research reader response theory (RRT) was applied in order to investigate the reading process of reading a school text book in two different formats. An insignificant modification was made in the structure of the theory by putting this text in the heart of the process which helps to clarify the factors that influence the reading process and adds a new element; educator and parent as seen in Figure 8 in chapter two. These elements were considered as a main element in reading process when reading an Arabic school text book. In the presenting model, the text is presented in the middle of the reading process where all the other elements deal with the text in different levels and methods. While, the reader comes in the top of the d shape and the parent and teacher come with the same level. Through this amendment, it can be applied this model to measure the behaviour of students when reading Arabic school book.

The findings of this phase of research support the idea that the reading process is different according to the readers' characters and education level, e.g. the reading process was completely different to that presented by Dillon for using text in journal and manuals (Dillon, 2001) or to that presented by Terras for reading ancient texts (Terras, 2005). Table 1 provided a comparison to the reading process between four different information resources with the reading process of a school book. It is clear that there are substantial differences, for example, aim of reading for each source was differ and this led to a distinction in the method that readers follow when reading text where the presentation of the text was affected also. The second distinction noted, related to content layout according into material types [paper or electronic version] where reading processes differ between e-book and p-book, which seem to have resulted from the difference in the designing of the text and the tools that are used.

Moreover, there are several factors contributing to students' performance when reading paper versions of school books, some of which relate to technical aspects such as cohesion of content, linking, navigation and screen layout, segmentation of data, interface design and location of data.

However, Students show different attitudes when reading a schoolbook in both versions. AC2, AC3, AC6 and AC9 were used by all students and the difference was only noted in the order of use between e- version and paper version. For example, 95% of participants identify their aim before reading an e-school textbook as searching for answers or reading for an examination. Reading through the questions is a popular action among students when reading for an examination. Students who use the e- format of a schoolbook found it is so hard to go through the text between the questions and the content of the lesson which led some of them to use a paper version to write down the questions.

Design Recommendations for Arabic School Book

The view in chapter two had confirmed several factors that influence electronic reading. But drawing a clear conclusion from these studies is difficult for several reasons. For example, it is not possible to present the relationship between these variables and define the level of each factor's impact. Therefore, this study aims to highlight some of these aspects and fill part of this gap through investigating its influence on Arabic texts. In addition, because of the large number of factors that had been identified from previous studies, which are difficult to be covered in this study, three factors were selected: font size, font type, and line length.

First Variable: Font Size

In experiment (2), Arabic text was tested to define the optimum font size and type to read from screen for students aged 9 to 13. Accuracy of reading was measured by the average number of errors that students made when reading the text, while reading speed was determined by the time it took students to read the text. The results of this experiment showed that the highest error is made with font size ten, and this is followed by sizes fourteen, sixteen and eighteen, which confirm the relationship between font size and word vision.

In the same perspective, previous studies demonstrate that the text is readable in font size 10 to 12 for adults using English characters (Wijnholds, 1997; dos santos Lonsdale, 2006). This result is not

Table 1. Comparing reading process into different information sources

Type of Resource	Aim of Use	Ways of Reading and Searching	Organisation/Issues Related to Designing
Journal (Dillon, 1992)	• Background material for work purposes. • Personal interest. • To answer a particular question. • To keep up with developments in an area. • To read an author`s work. • To get advice on a research problem.	• A quick scan of an abstract and major headings; • Non serial scan of major sections; • Full serial read of the text.	• Introduction- method- result- discussion/ conclusion.
Manual (Dillon, 1992)	• Reference. • Introduction. • When in trouble.	• Check the contents page or index sections; • Dipping; • Scanning sections of the text; • Lengthy serial reading is rare.	• Contents- getting started- simple tasks- more complex tasks- index.
Ancient text (Terras, 2005)	• Try to restructure past actions or to discover unidentified details.	• Experts use different methods to examine the document. • They spent a long time checking the text and the words in different orders. • They deal with visual features and then build up knowledge about the document.	• Page- text- mark- image- stamp and signature
Siegethaler (Siegenthaler, Wurtz et al., 2010)	• Investigate e-reading process [iReyiLiad/SonyPRS,505/ BeBook/ ECTACO jet- book/ Bookeen Cybook].	• E-reading process is very similar to reading from paper.	• Eye movement method.
Schoolbook	• Learning. • Use at home and school. • Prepare for exam.	• Two strategies: skim & scan. • View the text and then answer the questions. • View the questions and then search for the correct answer.	• Does not take on the electronic version. • Reading process changes according to the reading purpose and type of resource. • Students usually use two strategies; each strategy requires specific tools and techniques such as highlighting the sentence, taking notes, or using a finger when reading the text. • Reading processes differ between e-book and p-book, which seem to have resulted from the difference in the designing of the text and the tools that are used. • Dividing the text into check affects the reading comprehension process where students are not trained to manage this type of text layout and affects memory which works by the fixed relationship of a point and its location on a page.

consistent with Alotaibi's (Alotaibi, 2007) survey which determines that the 14 point is the best font size for reading Arabic characters in print material by students aged 18 to 28. Also, it supports the finding that age tends to have a negative correlation with reading speed; in other words, when age increases the reading time decreases. This correlation is strong in Arabic texts because of the Arabic vowels which are key factors for defining the legible font size for children. Thus, the legible font should be able to show the difference between dots and vowels, and this cannot be achieved using font size 10, 12, 14 or even 16 in spite of the low rate of errors. Therefore, font sizes 14 and 16 are readable for readers aged 12 and over and can be used to display Arabic texts on screen. In the same way, font size 18 is recommended for reading Arabic texts online.

Sequentially, age has been measured as an independent variable to define the optimal font size and type. a readable font size is different according to the age of the reader. E.g. the reading speed of students aged 10, when reading text presented using Arabic Traditional in size 18 (M= 13.50/ SD= 2.76), is longer than students aged 12 who read the same text in size 16 (M= 8.20/ SD= 1.69) by 55.67%. In addition, it is notable that the difference in reading performance between age groups 10 and 11 is similar in all font sizes and types. For instance, comparing the reading speed of students aged 10 in size 10 (Simplified Arabic) with students aged 11 shows a slight difference (3.6%). This convergence in the performance of students in ages 10 and 11 is clearly in sizes 10, 14 and 16.

The effects of character size on participants were more significant with characters of the Arabic language; this is contrary to some research findings that font types impact the reading speed in different languages such as English (Feely, Rubin et al., 2005). Besides, Alotaibi (2007) investigated the effect of font size and type on reading speed in printed Arabic text and concluded that font type as well as font size impact the reading speed. Therefore, reading Arabic on screen for children aged 10 to 12 is not influenced by font types as in other languages.

In order to investigate the difference in reading performance among students based on gender, this is used as an independent variable to clarify its impact on this type of research. Most previous research was not concerned with finding out if there was a difference in reading performance to avoid this variable in future research. However, the findings of this experiment showed no difference in reading performance between male and female students .

Analysing the list of errors for each student shows that the errors are mainly due to the shape of the characters. Data analysis led to the classification of errors into four types:

- Two characters that are connected in the middle and have dots at the top or bottom.
- More than two characters being connected in the middle and have dots at the top or bottom.
- Characters have dots and vowels.
- Characters are without dots and have similar letters with dots

Finally, the main findings are summarized in Table 2.

Table 2. The summary of findings

Task	Measures	Findings
Font 10	Reading speed	• The mean time spent to read Times New Roman and Arial is similar (M= 19.83 and M= 18.47 respectively). • The highest mean is 20.10 m. • Courier New font records less time than the other fonts. • Reading speed is slow in all font types compared to other sizes.
	Word error	• The average word error is high in all font types. • The average error differs between font types, where the mean error in the Arial font is the highest (.424) while Courier New font records the lowest error in this size. • No statistically significant difference in error between students in different age groups.
General findings		• Arabic text in font size 10 is not readable by students aged 10 to 12. • There is no significant difference between readers in the five font types. • The average error is the highest compared to other sizes.
Font 14	Reading speed	• The average time spent in size 14 is less in all font types than size 10 with the exception of Courier New font which takes (1.84 m) more than a size 10. • There is no significant difference in the mean time taken to read Traditional Arabic (M= 16.37), Courier New (M= 16.17) and Times New Roman (M= 16.10).
	Word error	• The median error percentage for size fourteen of Arabic Traditional is found to be significantly larger than the error provided by the median error for sizes sixteen and eighteen.
General findings		• Reading speed is a little faster than font size 10 but is still slow compared to sizes 16 and 18.
Font 16	Reading speed	• The average of time is reduced in all font types. • The mean time for Times New Roman (M= 13.63) is less compared to other fonts. • The mean time spent in reading is similar to Arabic Traditions (M= 14.60), Courier New (M= 14.73), Simplified Arabic (M= 14.67) and Arial (M= 14.03).
	Word error	• The average reading error is decreased notably in all font types. • The percentage of error in Arabic Traditional font in size 16 is less than size 14 by 61%. • Simplified Arabic font has the highest mean of the error (M= .074).
General findings		• It is more readable for readers aged 12 than 10 and 11. • There is no significant difference in reading speed between students aged 10 and 11 in this size.
Font 18	Reading speed	• Reading speed is improved in all font types. • Traditional Arabic has the longest time in reading (M= 11.20m) while Simplified Arabic has the shortest time (M= 9.07).
	Word error	• The averages of error in this size improve in all font types. • The percentage of error in Simplified Arabic font is less than Arabic Traditional font by 51.85%; the percentage of error in the Simplified Arabic font is less than the Courier New font, Arial and Times New Roman by 38.46%. • There is no significant difference in error mean between Courier New, Arial and Times New Roman (0.035, 0.36, 0.035) respectively.
General findings		• All students aged 10 and 11 prefer font size 18 for reading from the screen. • Age has a significant effect on reading speed. • Gender has no significant effect on reading speed. • There is a correlation between reading level and reading speed. • Fonts of sizes sixteen and eighteen are more readable than any font smaller than sixteen. • There is a strong difference in error percentages among the four Arabic Traditional groups ($\chi 2$= 82, p-value < .001). • The median error percentage for size sixteen in Arabic Traditional does not differ significantly from the median error for size eighteen. • A high reading speed is positively combined with a high error rate.

Second Factor: Font Type

Font type was reported by several researchers as one of the factors that has significant influence on the legibility level of online reading (Alotaibi, 2007; Asmaa and Asma, 2009; Banerjee, Majumdar et al., 2011). The width of the characters is not the same in all the font types which leads to a different level of vision. The average error rate was different between the five fonts, e.g. the average error in sizes 16 and 18 in font Courier New is noted to be highly significant, more than in the Arabic Traditional font. In addition, the average error in font 10 and 14 of the same font type is much closer to each other than in sizes 16 and 18.

Courier New was reported as a more legible font for children because the space between the words is wider than in other fonts; in the same perspective, no significant difference was noted between three font types: simplified Arabic, Times New Roman, and Arial. This finding goes in the same line as Asmaa and Asma (2009) who recommend using Simplified Arabic font for children's reading, while Alotaibi (2007) claimed that Times New Rowan was read faster in Arabic print texts.

Arabic traditional font should be avoided when designing Arabic texts for children even if the Arabic traditional font in size 16 was more readable than the Simplified Arabic font of the same size. Table 3 provides a summary for the main findings that help the designer and educator when selecting optimal font types for presenting text in a school book.

Third Factor: Line Length

In chapter three, several questions related to defining the optimal length line for reading from screen was asked, and the literature on the reading area did not provide any clear consensus in this case, with some emphasising the influence of line length on reading speed and accuracy (Creed, 1987, Dyson and Kipping, 1997, Chaparro et al., 2005, dos Santos Lonsdale, 2006)(Asmaa and Asma 2009), while others deny or at least reduce the influence of this factor on the legibility of the online text (Dyson and Kipping, 1997). Examining the procedure followed by a majority of these studies showed a weak relationship between factors in the one side, and reorientation of the age-group of readers being the cause of these differences

Table 3. Summary for the main findings

Task	Measures	Findings
Arabic traditional	Word error	• The average of error is the high between all the testing fonts. • There is no significant different in readability between size 16 and 18. • It is more readable than courier new in size 16.
Courier new	Word error	• The average of error between students is the best in size 10 and 14 comparing the other font types. • There is a significant different in reading speed and word error between 16 and 18 in the same font.
Times New Roman	Word error	• There is a significant different in mean of number of error between sizes 10 and 14. • There is no significant different in mean of error in size 16 between times new roman and Arial font (M=.072).
Arial	Word error	• Average of error in size 10 is the high comparing with other fonts.
Simplified Arabic	Word error	• It is the best in size 16 and 18. • it is the best to present Arabic text in size 18 for young children.

on the other. Therefore, in this research more attention was given to factors that impact the legibility of online texts in chapter 3 in order to understand the interaction between these variables and their effect. Based on previous studies that focused on children who viewed e- books (written in English language), two formats were used in this research, a single column and a double column using the Arabic script.

A further comparison of times is taken to answering three different types of questions shows different reading speeds. This difference is influenced by multiple factors such as the reading process [scan or skim]. The comparison between the mean reading speed for answering multiple choices through reading texts on a single column and double columns shows that the reading process is affected by students' age, wherein older students were faster when reading through double columns, while students aged 9 preferred a single column in both reading processes.

In the same perspective, Dyson and Kipping (1997) came up with the same finding that people over 24 years old show no differences in reading rate across three columns, while people aged 18-24 are faster when reading a single page column. Simmonds (Simmonds, 1994) has looked into the effect of information source types as factors influencing the optimal line length. The study suggested using a single column with wide margins for scientific journals.

In addition, the current research discovered that students who read the entire text searching for answers prefer using a single column. This finding was supported by the findings of Maria dos Santos Lonsdale (dos santos Lonsdale, 2006). On the other hand, Asmmaa and Asma (2009) reported different findings which suggest using 2/3 screen line length to improve reading speed for Arab children without any explanation of the factors that lead to this finding.

Moreover, the reading level was used as a second independent variable to investigate the optimised line length using different reading processes, wherein this variable was reported as significant. Students with a high reading level found a single column quicker to read when searching for answers to three different types of questions. In addition, little improvement was reported when reading texts presented in short lines by students with a low level of reading.

In general, it can be concluded that selection of the appropriate line length depends on two main factors: reader's age and reading level. The study has shown that readers who are 10 years old or less prefer to read from the long line, while older students prefer the long line in comprehensive reading and short line when searching for specific information.

Using Colour to Increase the Ability to Focus Vision when Moving from One Line to Another

Younger students' slowness in reading text displayed on screen in double column is due to difficulty scrolling the text as their experience in using computer tools especially the mouse was weak. This does not mean that students do not find it difficult when they read from a long line, but students find this format similar to print book and they deal with it by placing a finger at the beginning of each line to make it easier to move to the next one.

In order to solve this problem, new methods have been proposed in this research; the method was built based on visual theory (Bundesen, 1990). The idea assumes that using different colours for the first and last word of each line would help:

1. Eyes are fixed and move easily through the text which will enhance reading performance of students when reading through the school textbook.
2. Increased retention of text read.
3. Improved comprehension.
4. Increased accuracy in reading compared with reading text using black text.

The colouring text format (CTF) group shows significant improvement in reading performance compared to the control group who read from black text. The improvement included quiz scores, comprehension and retention. For example, students in control group were scoring less compared with those who read the (CTF) text. Students with both higher and lower were reading levels had significant improvements in reading performance with (CTF) compared to the control group.

Although differences statistically are not significant, it can be seen that there is a clear improvement especially when browsing the full text presented in a single column.

In addition, the mean reading speed improved for a single column with colour to .101 min. In the case of a double column, a significant improvement was noted in reading speed by using colours in double column which also shows improvement in reading speed for younger students (p- value= .021).

Finally, it is difficult to compare this finding with previous results because of the difference in the research conditions such as language, age, type of text, and reading process. For example, a majority of studies (Dyson and Kipping, 1997; Youngman and Scharff, 1998; Dyson and Haselgrove, 2001; dos santos Lonsdale, 2006) has determined the length of the line number of characters, making it difficult to compare. On the other hand, in the Arabic language letters are related to each other and the word count is based on the number of the word.

Guideline for Displaying Academic Arabic Text on Screen

Analysis of the quantitative and qualitative data show several rules to recommend of designers and educators to follow when designing Arabic academic text on screen. As the summary of the result in chapters 6 and 7 points out, there was an effect of reading strategy of selecting a right font size, font type and line length. These results have practical implications for readers involved with Arabic academic text on screen for young readers.

Font size:

R1: Font size 10 should be avoided for all students especially for younger students where they cannot distinction between the dots and vowel.
R2: Font size 16 and 18 should be used, 18 is recommended for reader age 9 to 10.

Font type:

R3: Arabic Traditional font should be used with size 16 where it is more readable than other font type. In addition, it is a suitable with size 18 for students with difficulty in reading.
R4: In size 18, Simplified Arabic font should be used for to present Arabic text on screen especially for young readers.

Line length:

R5: Single column should be used for young students aged 9 to 10 when text presented needs to be scanned carefully, while, there is no difference in line length when skim academic text quickly.

R6: There is no difference in reading performance between the two conditions according to gender.

R7: Short line should be used when designing for students with difficulty in reading in both types of reading quickly or slowly.

R8: Using a different colour for the first and last word of each line was strongly recommended.

R9: Double column with using colour for the first and last word of each line should be used when presenting Arabic academic text online.

Framework of Reading Factors Considered by This Research

The literature review has already shown that there are several factors affecting the legibility of online texts. A schematic representation of the framework is presented in Figure 9 in chapter two where the factors were classified into three groups: human factors, usability factors, and legibility factors. But the conceptual framework merely gathered these factors based on their effect, making it difficult to draw a clear conclusion that shows the relationship between these variables and the level of their effect. The variables basically were divided into three levels;

Level One: Factors at this level have a significant effect on readability of the screen. According to previous research on reading and usability field, font size and colour have a significant impact on the readability level of e-text. The font size was reported as the main factor that affects online reading according to the majority of research (Sanocki, 1991; Feely et al., 2005; Bernard et al., 2003; Bouma, 1971; Rudnicky and Kolers, 1984; Mills and Weldon, 1987; Boyarski, Neuwirth et al., 1998).

Level Two: Consists of three factors: interlinear spacing (which refers to the space between two lines) and the words [single or double spacing], background colour, and finally the line length (which refer to the number of characters in a line). This latter factor is also associated with a font size. In addition, factors in this level mainly related to page design.

Level Three: Factors at this level are less influential than previous factors. These factors are: margins, image, and text location. This is generally related to the structure of the text. A small number of researchers considered the effect of these factors when designing eBook but they have to be considered when designing web pages.

In this project, three topographical variables were measured for their effect on reading performance according to reading processes, taking into account for human variables: age, education level, gender, and reading level. Figure 1 presents a framework explaining the relationships between these three variables where the quantitative data collected in experiments (2) and (3) show that there is a significant correlation between font size and line length, especially when using a number of words or characters to define the line length. At the end of the research, it has become clear to the researcher that there is a group of elements related to each other and should be considered by designers and researchers. In addition, when a designer plans to design e- material, s/he must understand the relationship between several of these elements and consider the impact level to each other and on each variable. For example, the designer should start designing by identifying the age of the reader as the first stage which is directly related to the size of the font, which in turn determines the size of the text on the screen. The framework aims to explore the relationship and type of interaction between elements in order to give assistance to designers; in addition, it is still able to add additional elements.

According to the framework (as seen in Figure 1), there are two types of interaction between elements: direct and indirect interaction. This will now be described in detail.

- **Direct Interaction (DI):** There are two levels of direct interaction between the variables, one between elements in the same level e.g. there is direct interaction between font size and line length where increasing the font size will decrease the number of characters per line. In addition, other direct interaction was recorded according to the analysis of qualitative data in chapter (2) between the reading strategy and purpose of reading the text. The second type of direct interaction occurs between elements from a different group, e.g. findings of experiments (3) that investigate the

Figure 1. Framework for interaction between three typographical variables and other factors

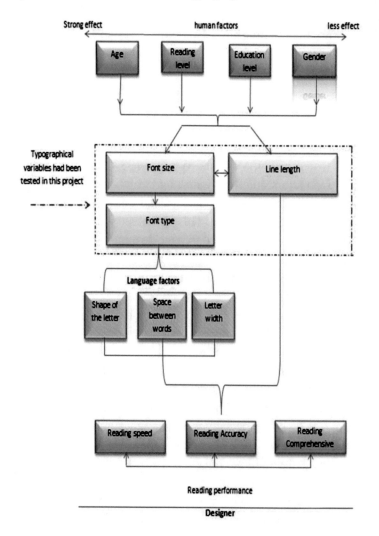

optimal line length for reading based on type of questions, and reported a significant relationship between the strategy of reading and line length.

- **Indirect Interaction (II):** This type of interaction occurs during the interaction between different variables. For example, font size differs from font to font. This difference affects the size of the text and the number of characters in each line in an indirect way. In addition, the reading speed is affected by font size indirectly, making it easier to distinguish between characters and dots. In addition, factors related to reading performance are influenced by human factors such as age and reading level. These will also be affected by typographical factors.

CONCLUSION

This chapter mainly addressed the findings of this research which may be summarised into four aspects:

- Investigating the use of the internet among students in years 4, 5 and 6 in a Libyan school. The collected data was used as a starting point for next phases of research.
- Defining the reading process in terms of the schoolbook by building two reading models each model present action of students when reading Arabic schoolbook in electronic and paper format.
- Defining the factors that influence the reading of e-texts by children with focus on the effect of three factors in the Arabic text: font size, font type, and line length. Through exam the previous researches, a model show the factors affect using electronic text was built. This model has the ability to present affected factors as a group.
- Using colours to enhance the ability to focus vision when moving from one line to another.

In addition, several explanations and interpretations were made regarding the various associated factors that influence the reading of Arabic texts.

REFERENCES

Abdullah, N. (2007). A Study into Usability of Tools for Searching and Browsing E-books with Particular Reference to Back-of-the-Book Index.

Alotaibi, A. Z. (2007). The effect of font size and type on reading performance with Arabic words in normally sighted and simulated cataract subjects. *Clinical & Experimental Optometry*, *90*(3), 203–203. doi:10.1111/j.1444-0938.2007.00123.x PMID:17425766

Anuradha, K., & Usha, H. S. (2006). Use of e-books in an academic and research environment: A case study from the Indian Institute of Science. *Program*, *40*(1), 48–62. doi:10.1108/00330330610646807

Asmaa, A., & Asma, A.-O. (2009). Arab children's reading preferences for e-learning programs.*Proceedings of the 2009 conference on Information Science, Technology and Applications*, Kuwait. ACM.

Banerjee, J., & Majumdar, D., & Dhurjati, M. (2011). Readability, Subjective Preference and Mental Workload Studies on Young Indian Adults for Selection of Optimum Font Type and Size during Onscreen Reading. *Al Ame. en J. Medical Science*, *4*(2), 131–143.

Bennett, L., & Landoni, M. (2005). E-books in academic libraries. *The Electronic Library*, *23*(1), 9–16. doi:10.1108/02640470510582709

Bernard, M. L., Chaparro, B. S., Mills, M. M., & Halcomb, C. G. (2003). Comparing the effects of text size and format on the readibility of computer-displayed Times New Roman and Arial text. *International Journal of Human-Computer Studies*, *59*(6), 823–835. doi:10.1016/S1071-5819(03)00121-6

Bouma, H. (1971). *Visual recognition of isolated lower case letters*. Vision Research DOI.

Boyarski, D., Neuwirth, C., Forlizzi, J., & Regli, S.H. (1998). A study of fonts designed for screen display. *Proceedings of CHI'98*. doi:10.1145/274644.274658

Bundesen, C. (1990). A Theory of Visual Attention. *Psychological Review*, *97*(4), 523–547. doi:10.1037/0033-295X.97.4.523 PMID:2247540

Buzzetto-More, N., & Sweat-Guy, R. et al.. (2007). Reading in A Digital Age: e-Books Are Students Ready For This Learning Object? *Interdisciplinary Journal of Knowledge and Learning Objects*, *3*, 239–250.

Creed, A., Dennis, I., & Newstead, S. (1987). Proof-reading on VDUs. *Behaviour & Information Technology*, *6*(1), 3–13. doi:10.1080/01449298708901814

Crestani, F., Landoni, M., & Melucci, M. (2006). Appearance and functionality of electronic books. *International Journal on Digital Libraries*, *6*(2), 192–209. doi:10.1007/s00799-004-0113-9

Dillon, A. (1992). Designing usable electronic text. New York: CRC Press.

Dillon, A. (2001). Designing usable electronic text: ergonomic aspects of human information usage. London: Taylor & Francis Inc.

dos Santos Lonsdale, M., Dyson, M.C., & Reynolds, L. (2006). Reading in examination- type situations: the effects of text layout on performance. *Research in reading*, *29*(4), 433- 453.

Dyson, M. C., & Haselgrove, M. (2001). The influence of reading speed and line length on the effectiveness of reading from screen. *International Journal of Human-Computer Studies*, *54*(4), 585–612. doi:10.1006/ijhc.2001.0458

Dyson, M. C., & Kipping, G. J. (1997). The legibility of screen formats: Are three columns better than one? *Computers & Graphics*, *21*(6), 703–712. doi:10.1016/S0097-8493(97)00048-4

Feely, M., Rubin, G. S., Ekstrom, K., & Perera, S. (2005). Investigation into font characteristics for optimum reading fluency in readers with sight problems. *International Congress Series*, *1282*, 530–533. doi:10.1016/j.ics.2005.05.121

Siegenthaler, E., Wurtz, P., & Groner, R. (2010). Improving the Usability of E-Book Readers. *JUS*, *6*(1), 25–38.

Lam, P., Lam, S.L., Lam, J., & McNaught, C. (2009). Usability and usefulness of ebooks on PPCs. *Australasian Journal of Educational Technology*, *25*(1), 30-44.

Ma, H. (2005). Interpreting middle school students` online experiences a phenological approach. Ohio university.

Mills, C. B., & Weldon, L. J. (1987). Reading text from computer screens. *ACM Computing Surveys, 19*(4), 329–358. doi:10.1145/45075.46162

Noorhidawati, A., & Forbes, G. (2008). Students attitudes towards e-books in a Scottish higher education institute: Part 1. *Library Review, 57*(8), 593–605. doi:10.1108/00242530810899577

Park, H.W. (2009). Academic internet use in Korea: Issues and lessons in e-research. Proceedings of WebSci"09: Society online, Athens, Greece.

Polly, C. (2009). National: Internet generation leave parents behind: Change in communication creating divide, says study: Children spend six hours a day in front of screens. *The Guardian.*

Rowlands, I., Nicholas, D., Jamali, H. R., & Huntington, P. (2007). What do faculty and students really think about e-books? *Aslib Proceedings: New Information Perspectives, 59*(6), 489–511. doi:10.1108/00012530710839588

Rudnicky, A. I., & Kolers, P. A. (1984). Size and case of type as stimuli in reading. *Journal of Experimental Psychology. Human Perception and Performance, 10*(2), 231–247. doi:10.1037/0096-1523.10.2.231 PMID:6232342

Segal-Drori, O., O. Korat, et al. (2009). Reading electronic and printed books with and without adult instruction: effects on emergent reading. Springer Science+Business Media B.V.

Shiratuddin, N., & Landoni, M., Gibb, F., & Hassan, S. (2003). E-book technology and its potential applications in distance education. *Journal of Digital Information, 3*(4).

Simmonds, D. R. L. (1994). *Data presentation and visual literacy in medicine and science.* Oxford: Butterworth-Heinemann.

Tenopir, C., King, D. W., Edwards, S., & Wu, L. (2009). Electronic journals and changes in scholarly article seeking and reading patterns. *Aslib Proceedings, 61*(1), 5-32.

Terras, M. (2005). Reading the Readers: Modelling Complex Humanities Processes to Build cognitive System. *Literary and Linguistic Computing, 20*(1), 41–59. doi:10.1093/llc/fqh042

Tripp, L.M. (2010). The computer is not for you to be looking around, it is for schoolwork: Challenges for digital inclusion as Latino immigrant families negotiate children access to the internet. *New media & society, 13*(4), 552-567.

Wijnholds, A.D.B. (1997). *Using type: The typographer's craftsmanship and the ergonomist's research.* The Netherlands: Utrecht University.

Youngman, M., & Scharff, L. (1998). *Text width and margin width influences.* South Western Psychological Association.

Chapter 14
Conclusion and Future Work in E-Reading Context

Azza A Abubaker
Benghazi University, Libya

Joan Lu
University of Huddersfield, UK

ABSTRACT

This research is an attempt to examine the effect of reading processes on designing e-texts for children using Arabic script. In addition, it aims to develop a model for designing acceptance that will have the power to demonstrate acceptance and usage behaviour of the e-school text using a schoolbook for primary schools in Libya. Alternatively, dealing with the research problem led to the specification of the following research objectives, which were achieved through four inter- related surveys: to build an e-reading strategy for a schoolbook based on users' cognitive and behaviour processes, to define the typographical variables that affect reading Arabic texts from the screen such as font size, font type, background color, line length and text format from a literature survey, to provide a standard that can help keep children's concentration on the text, to create a guideline that could help designers when designing e-Arabic texts for children, to examine in-depth the challenges of reading Arabic e-texts, to study the efficiency of Arabic text reading and the factors impacting the efficiency of reading and comprehension, to understand children's behaviour when reading from a screen. The aim of this chapter is to discuss the study's contribution to knowledge and provide recommendations for future research.

SIGNIFICANCE OF THE STUDY

Several studies have reported that reading electronic text leads to changes in the reading and learning processes. This calls for research aimed at understanding the reading processes, cause of these changes, defining the requirements for meeting these changes, and then to connect it with the reading purpose. This in turn will lead to designing e-learning material that is able to meet readers' requirements and educators. This study seeks to examine the general significance of the reading process of electronic text and the factors that affect reading Arabic electronic texts for children so as to provide a standard to help

DOI: 10.4018/978-1-5225-1884-6.ch014

the interface designer to design an interface that makes the user feel comfortable and work efficiently as well as developing a theory of presenting e-texts for children's learning.

Thus, this study will be useful for at least three aspects; designing the electronic resources, e-reading, and educational aspect. In addition, understanding the proposed model may help analyse the reasons for the resistance toward the e- text and would also help to bring about efficient measures to improve reading on screen. In the same context, highlighting the reading stage in terms of the schoolbook will help consolidate factors such as the social and learning processes.

Moreover, e-text will enable changes in the reading and learning processes. Also, reading an e-text can have several advantages over traditional reading as the reader or learner is able to apply animation in learning, and increase control and interaction with the learning material. All these will lead to improvement in the quality of learning. Thus, analysis of the text and connecting it with the reading purpose and reader's skill will help meet those requirements that should be available when displaying texts on screen. In addition, the findings of this research can help build e- curricula that are easy and effective to be read and used by all Arabic learners.

On the other hand, most of the research on reading e-texts among children have been done in the context of Western languages e.g. (Reimer, Brimhall, Cao et al., 2009) and a few in Chinese e.g. (Tsai et al., 2008). This study extends the work already started by Asmaa Alsumait and Asma Al-Osaimi (NISO, 2005; Asmaa and Asma, 2009) using Arabic language. Both works have addressed a small part of the whole field without providing explanations to show how and when these factors can influence e- reading.

Moreover, the quality of screen display is usually discussed in terms of the resolution, that is, the maximum number of dots or pixels. In this study, we try to examine all the factors that affect reading on screen such as presentation factors, reader factors and physical factors, but the main focus will be on factors related to displaying the text.

Contribution to Knowledge

The contribution of this research is mainly in the area of reading. This contribution is related to the gap reported in this area as reviewed in chapters (2) and (3). Furthermore, many studies have demonstrated the extent of interest in measuring the effectiveness of the use of electronic text in higher education and how to employ e-material by academic libraries without giving the same attention to the use of information technology (IT) in early learning. This means that most children's e- books are not satisfactory as tools for supporting learning (Wilson, Landoni et al., 2003; Korat and Shamir, 2004).

In general, the objectives of research are to bring more qualitative results into a quantitative area, drawing a balance between quantity and quality of results and developing more effective information in the legibility area. The experimental findings demonstrated that;

- The questionnaire survey has evaluated the present situation of eBook and internet usage in primary schools based on the five schools in Libya as a sample population. This is supportive in terms of achieving a good awareness of how eBooks and the Internet are being managed by students and the reasons why students do, and do not, use eBooks and the Internet. The findings are of value to educators and designers who wish to increase eBook awareness and usage amongst students.
- The follow-up study findings are useful in considering students' reactions and attitudes towards the schoolbook in two formats paper and eBooks, particularly on how students consult e-books for the learning purpose. The study is important, for designers in terms of improving eBook layout,

for educators in terms of using the eBook effectively, and to school and children libraries in terms of improving e-book collection management.

- The research contributed to producing guideline rules that could, potentially benefit the designers of academic Arabic text for readers age 9 to 13. This need has come from the specialization of Arabic characters. However, the guideline provides to designers a package of rules such as; defining readable font size and determining the optimal font type.
- The experimental findings demonstrated that the reading process has a significant influence in designing online text. In the literature there are attending that the designing requirements are affected by several elements such as type of material (web page (Scane, 2003; Hartley, 2004), e- news or eBook (Dillon, 2001; Dyson, 2004)), readers' age (Cheyne, 2005), prior knowledge (Panayiota and van den, 2007) or subject (history, math or story (Wolf, 2007)).
- The findings of experiment 3 consistently suggest that the reading strategy used by readers has a significant effect on selecting the optimal line length for reading online Arabic academic text. Thus, double column was suggested for presenting text for slow reading between students age 11,12, and 13 and a single column for quick reading, while, students' age 9 and 10 prefer the single column in both strategies.

The contributions of this project are summarised in Table 1 and may be divided into four aspects: reading process, designing e- text for children, using the internet and eBook in education, and method to increase the ability of reading.

LIMITATION

There is no doubt that in all academic research, it is impossible to be free from borders which prevent the generalization of results to other populations; consequently, this study, like all studies, has limitations. These can be summarised as follows:

1. The study is restricted to Arabic script. Because the studies are concerned with the structure of the Arabic language and to compare it with other languages, several differences become apparent such as the writing direction and use of vowels, which may lead to differences in the way of dealing with it.
2. Reading performance is affected by the reader's age as several researchers have reported; thus, this study is confined to children aged 9 to 13. Also, this study is focused on the development of e-Arabic literacy from the perspective of improving the way of presenting e-texts to children. However, in the current study, there was no opportunity to involve other participants from other Arab countries, even though all the participants are studying in a school in Libya and in a Libyan school in the UK.
3. The e-text legibility evaluation only focused on factors related to displaying text, with a particular focus on font size, font type, using colour and line length which have been highlighted in some studies as influential factors (Huang, Rau et al., 2009; Shu and Zhou, 2010). But in this study, tested using different methods, language, information resources and age range.

Table 1. The gap in the field and the contributions of this research

Related Area	Major Trends and Issues	Identified Gaps	This Study's Contribution
Reading process	• Empirical literature present two implicit views; scanner of short texts searching out spelling mistakes, and searching for target information. • Most of the research on reading process is from cognitive psychology. • Theoretical input in reading domain commonly concerned with issues such as memory organisation or learning. • The majority of research focused on how humans extract information from the text	• Absence of a suitable descriptive framework of the reading process that would enable designers concerned with electronic texts to find guidance for specific design applications. • Psychological models of reading that consider text manipulation are limited.	• Developing more reading approaches in this area. • Bring more qualitative findings in the online reading area to enrich it. • Two models of reading process were built according to users' interaction with the school textbook. These models will not only help define the interaction amongst users and e-books, but will also help designers to understand user behaviour re e-books and thereby to establish the most appropriate functions/features when building an e-book interface.
Designing e- text for children/ Factors influencing reading from screen	• Empirical literature shows quite a number of factors that influence reading through the screen but a limited number of these research focus on explaining the relationship between these variables and provide a framework to help understand this effect when designing e- text. • Studying of typographical factors shows a significant influence of these factors on reading performance.	• The studies in general focus on reading a web page while few researchers focused on reading e- book. • Three studies were focused on Arabic script. • A limited number of studies concentrated on children. • Paying less attention to factors that affect the legibility of Arabic texts. • Shortage of in-depth understanding of end users' feeling, action and attitude.	• The framework can be the basis for digital document usage. It is used as a starting point and is intended to offer a conceptual aid in electronic text design. • Identify the optimal font size for reading an Arabic script from screen by children aged 9 to 13. • Producing more in-depth results to develop more effective designing principles for online texts. • Based on collecting data from experiments (2) and (3), the model explains the interaction between three topographical variables [font size, font type and line length] and their relationships with independent variables were also provided. • Framework shows the factors that influence reading, and using e- content was suggested according to previous studies.
Using the internet and e- book in education.	Theoretical perspective on this subject shows an increase in the number of people who use the internet and e- book for different reasons.	The majority of the research merely focused on defining the average use and paid little attention to issues related to the theory aspect.	• Students use the internet for multiple purposes that may be classified into two categories: non-academic and academic use. • Boys and girls use the internet for the same purposes such as gaming and mailing but the average use is different where boys tend to use the internet for gaming more than girls, while girls tend to listen to music and download videos more than boys. • Participants state several reasons for not using the e- book such as quality of Arabic e- book and lack of knowledge of their existence. • E- book is not a familiar source of information for students in Libya's primary schools.
Increase the ability of reading from screen.	Focus on improving the technology such as speed and storage capacity, more than improving the way of presenting the context.	Absence of methods that take into account the needs of each reader and information source.	• Using colour to increase the ability to focus vision when moving from one line to another so as to improve the screen display. • Create a new display technique to improve the legibility of reading Arabic online texts.

4. In this study, all materials used were taken from the Libyan schoolbook. This type of material was chosen because it has been evaluated by educators in terms of relevance to students' age and their level of education.

5. Finally, this study focused on viewing e-texts on a computer screen; it is hard to generalize the findings to other type of viewing text such as PDF files.

RECOMMENDATIONS FOR FURTHER RESEARCH

The new perspectives emerging from the investigations of this research open up the field for further studies including:

- Investigating the effect of the colour factor on improving the legibility of Arabic texts on screen for children, e.g. use different colours to distinguish between dots and vowels.
- Exploring and developing an e-reading model based on all the factors discussed in the empirical studies on the reading field which will lead to building more theories on e- reading.
- Investigating the influence of the subject as a variable affecting the reading process and the variables that have a positive or negative impact on it.
- Applying a model that uses colour to increase the ability to focus vision using different ages and types of information such as journals or books.

REFERENCES

Asmaa, A., & Asma, A.-O. (2009). Arab children's reading preferences for e-learning programs.*Proceedings of the 2009 conference on Information Science, Technology and Applications*, Kuwait. ACM.

Cheyne, S. M. E. (2005). can electronic textbook help children to learn. *The Electronic Library, 23*(1), 103–115. doi:10.1108/02640470510582781

Dillon, A. (2001). designing usable electronic text: ergonomic aspects of human information usage. London: Taylor & Francis Inc.

Dyson, M. C. (2004). How physical text layout affects reading from screen. *Behaviour & Information Technology, 23*(6), 377–393. doi:10.1080/01449290410001715714

Shu, H., Zhou, W., Yan, M., & Kliegl, R. (2010). Font size modulates saccade- target selection in Chinese reading. *Attention, Perception & Psychophysics, 73*(2), 482–490. doi:10.3758/s13414-010-0029-y PMID:21264735

Korat, O., & Shamir, A. (2004). Are electronic books for young children appropriate to support literacy development? A comparison across languages. *Journal of Computer Assisted Learning, 20*, 257–268. doi:10.1111/j.1365-2729.2004.00078.x

Huang, D.-L., Patrick Rau, P.-L., & Liu, Y. (2009). Effects of font size, display resolution and task type on reading Chinese fonts from mobile devices. *International Journal of Industrial Ergonomics, 39*(1), 81–89. doi:10.1016/j.ergon.2008.09.004

National Information Standards Organisation (NISO). (2005). Information services & use: metrics & statistics for libraries and information providers: data dictionary.

Panayiota, K., & van den Broek, P. (2007). The effects of prior knowledge and text structure on comprehension processes during reading of scientific texts. *Memory & Cognition, 35*(7), 1567.

Tzeng, O. J.-L., & Tsai, J.-L., Tzeng, O.J.L., & Hung, D.L. (2008). Eye movements and parafoveal word processing in reading Chinese. *Memory & Cognition, 36*(5), 1033–1045. doi:10.3758/MC.36.5.1033 PMID:18630209

Wilson, R., Landoni, M., & Gibb, F. (2003). The WEB Book experiments in electronic textbook design. *The Journal of Documentation, 59*(4), 454–476. doi:10.1108/00220410310485721

Wolf, M. (2007). Proust and squid: the story and science of the reading brain. New York: Harper Collins.

Reimer, Y.J., Brimhall, E., Cao, C., & O'Reilly, K. (2009). Empirical user studies inform the design of an e- note taking and information assimilation system for students in higher education. *Computers & Education, 52*(4), 893–913. doi:10.1016/j.compedu.2008.12.013

Section 3

Neural Trust Model for Multi-Agent Systems

Chapter 15
Introduction to the Investigating in Neural Trust and Multi Agent Systems

Gehao Lu
Yunnan University, China

Joan Lu
University of Huddersfield, UK

ABSTRACT

Introducing trust and reputation into multi-agent systems can significantly improve the quality and efficiency of the systems. The computational trust and reputation also creates an environment of survival of the fittest to help agents recognize and eliminate malevolent agents in the virtual society. The research redefines the computational trust and analyzes its features from different aspects. A systematic model called Neural Trust Model for Multi-agent Systems is proposed to support trust learning, trust estimating, reputation generation, and reputation propagation. In this model, the research innovates the traditional Self Organizing Map (SOM) and creates a SOM based Trust Learning (STL) algorithm and SOM based Trust Estimation (STE) algorithm. The STL algorithm solves the problem of learning trust from agents' past interactions and the STE solve the problem of estimating the trustworthiness with the help of the previous patterns. The research also proposes a multi-agent reputation mechanism for generating and propagating the reputations. The mechanism exploits the patterns learned from STL algorithm and generates the reputation of the specific agent. Three propagation methods are also designed as part of the mechanism to guide path selection of the reputation. For evaluation, the research designs and implements a test bed to evaluate the model in a simulated electronic commerce scenario. The proposed model is compared with a traditional arithmetic based trust model and it is also compared to itself in situations where there is no reputation mechanism. The results state that the model can significantly improve the quality and efficacy of the test bed based scenario. Some design considerations and rationale behind the algorithms are also discussed based on the results.

DOI: 10.4018/978-1-5225-1884-6.ch015

INTRODUCTION

The characteristic of "intelligence" is usually attributed to humans. Grant more intelligence to machines has always been a fascinating dream in fictional movies, however, it is an important research direction for computer scientists as well. The traditional symbol based artificial intelligence is confined to an individual program or an application in the form of strict logic representation. The distributed artificial intelligence focuses on sociality of the systems and the computing intelligence emphasizes the emergent properties of the intelligence. A multi-agent system is an attempt to create intelligent applications that exploit the advantages from these different types of intelligences. It is an aggregate or even a society of intelligent agents, at the same time, those agents posesses the abilities that different intelligent theories bestow. The coordination and cooperation is the main research subject in multi-agent systems. Inside these two relationships, the idea of intelligent agents capable of trusting each other and be able to build a reputation network analogous to human society is an interesting and important question which is deserved to research. Such trust and reputation is especially designed for computer programs. It can be named as computational trust and computational reputation, or more specifically, it can be called as agent trust and agent reputation in multi-agent systems. Adding computational trust into the multi-agent system can bring many benefits. The efficiency of the interactions is greatly enhanced because the agents no longer need to waste time on negotiation with other agents due to lack of trust, and the agents no longer need to interact with agents with bad reputations. The existence of trust and reputation forms an environment that pursues the rule of survival of the fittest. If an agent loses trusts or even reputation, the chance of further interactions are reduced or removed. Thus, the quality of the interaction is also greatly improved because of the elimination of the bad agents.

IMPORTANCE AND SIGNIFICANCE

There many mechanisms and algorithms that have been proposed for determining the computational trust and the computational reputation. Some of them have already been put into practice in industries such as eBay's reputation system (Resnick et al.,2006), while some are still research topics or research results such as (Zacharia et al.,1999), Marsh's Model (Marsh, 1994b), RegreT (Sabater and Sierra, 2002), Referral Reputation (Yu and Singh, 2000), FIRE (Huynh et al., 2004) and TRAVOS (Teacyet al., 2006). Most models are mathematical models that are based on summation or product of different dimensions with selected weights representing their influences. Some models (Teacy et al., 2006) are based on probability theory or statistical methods while most models presume the semantics behind trust is consistent to all the agents.

Although the research on trust and reputation has achieved great process, there are some still some problems that need to be solved:

- **Lack of Adaptability:** Most models (Marsh, 1994b; Resnick et al., 2006; Sabater and Sierra, 2002; Zacharia et al., 1999) are based on delicate arithmetic equations or probabilistic statistical methodologies such as the Bayesian system. These models may work fine in specific domains and specific scenarios but once the domains are changed or scenarios are changed, there is no way to adjust the equation of calculating trust. The rigidity of the mathematical models prevents them from adapting to the ever-changing environments. Unluckily, the environments for most multi-agent system are complex and dynamic. Autonomous agents are not simple task assigned programs. They have to be proactive and reactive in a complex environment. Thus they need the ability to learn from outside environments, learn from their interactions, and learn from the other agents.

- **Lack of Systematic Approach:** Some models (Marsh, 1994b) separate the trust and reputation as two different areas. They either carry out study simply on trust or simply on reputation. But trust and reputation are two facets of a systematic whole. Trust is a facet viewed from the individual level and reputation is the other facet viewed from the social level. Reputation is the generated product of trust and trust spreads itself through reputation. Any solution which simply focuses on trust or reputation is not a systematic or complete solution.

- **Lack of Object Semantics:** Some models (Marsh, 1994b; Resnick et al., 2006; Zacharia et al., 1999) assume that the trust is put in a single background, thus they do not care what the difference of the backgrounds might lead to. In fact, most of the time, the backgrounds are different. In different backgrounds, or say "domains", the object of trust is various so that semantics of trust relationship is also variable. The scarcity of the research into concepts like domain, object, and semantics may impede the multi-agent from forming federated societies which cross many domains.

- **Lack of Difference between Trust and Trustworthiness:** Some models (Huynh et al., 2004; Marsh, 1994b; Resnick et al., 2006; Teacy et al., 2006; Yu and Singh, 2000) do not differentiate trust and trustworthiness, they usually use a numeric value to represent both of them. Such simplification works in simple arithmetic model and covers the nature of learning of autonomous agents. Take human trust model as a comparison, trust is a recognition process and trustworthiness is a decision making process. An autonomous agent should also have such two level models.

Through the analysis against these problems, the research builds a systematical model for trust and reputation. This model is named as neural trust model for multi-agent system which combines the techniques from both distributed artificial intelligence and computing intelligence. The significances of the model are described as follows:

- The neural trust model proposes that the recognition of trust is actually a problem of machine learning and the model is designed and implemented based on this viewpoint. This gives the multi-agent trust system the ability to adapt to the environment. This also makes the detailed information of interactions become the foundation of trust learning.

- The neural trust model is a systematic and complete model which contains learning of trust, estimation of trust, reputation generation and reputation propagation. In this model, reputation is not separated from trust; it is the calculated result of trust. The reputation is based on the estimation against specific agent. The computational trust is transformed to reputation to propagate on the network.

- The neural trust model can be applied in different domains instead of single domain. Single domain can only represent one set of related concepts. In order to represent various sets of concepts in the real world, it is necessary to use multi-dimensional trust to cope with the varieties of domains. In each domain, the trust learning is against a few specific dimensions so that the change of domain only changes the dimensions of learning algorithm.

- The neural trust model presents a two level trust mechanism: one level for learning trust from interactions and reputations, the other level for estimation and decision making. The model explicitly separates these two processes so that each process can be independently executed. This means an agent can also do these two jobs concurrently instead of sequentially execution.

Aims and Tasks

The aim of the research is to propose a computational trust model for multi-agent systems. The model should be capable of learning trust, estimating trust, generating reputation, and propagating reputation. In order to realize this aim, several tasks must be done.

1. Define the concept of trust and reputation and analyze the influential factors of the concept.
2. Design a model framework that specifies the components and the relationship among components. Design the process how the model should work.
3. Propose the algorithm for learning trust and estimating trust, also find out the solution of using trust learned as trustworthiness decision making criteria.
4. Design the mechanism of reputation generation and reputation propagation. The generation should be based on results of trust learning. The propagation should specify the process and path.
5. A test bed should be designed to evaluate the proposed model, algorithms and mechanisms in the above tasks.

Contributions

The research analyzes the idea of learning trust, proposes a systematical model for trust and reputation, proposes the STL algorithm and STE algorithm, designs the reputation generation and propagation mechanism, and implement a test bed. The research believes that the computational trust is a combinatory problem of machine learning and decision making. The form of representation is patterns that are emerged from information collected during agent interactions. The research also points out that the trustworthiness and untrustworthiness are actually decision making problems. Most of the traditional computational trust models are arithmetical or statistical models which deem the trust and reputation as a numeric value generated from delicate equations. The research proposes a trust and reputation model named "Neural trust learning and estimation model". This model establishes a complete framework to accomplish trust related activities. It depicts the relationship among algorithms and mechanisms. It defines the processes of trust learning, estimating and reputation generating, propagation. Two algorithms are proposed. One is SOM based Trust Learning algorithm and the other is SOM based Trust Estimation algorithm. Both algorithms modify the original Self Organized Map to produce patterns suitable for representing trust. The estimation algorithm helps agents make trustworthiness decision according to its memorized patterns. The research proposed a reputation propagation mechanism to support the generation and propagation of reputations. The mechanism designs three types of reputation propagation paths: Point-to-point based inquiry, broadcasting based propagation and observer. The reputation is produced as the difference between macro pattern and agent pattern. An equation for calculating the reputations is proposed and issues such as decaying along the propagation are also modeled in it. In order to evaluate the model, a computational trust test bed is designed and implemented. The test bed is built upon Java Agent Development Environment platform and it constructs a simulated electronic market which contains many autonomous agents divided into different roles. The test bed not only can be used in this research related experiment, but it also can be used to test the other types of agent trust models.

Application Domains

The neural trust model is initially designed for multi-agent systems. In many scenarios of using autonomous agents, the model can be applied to improve qualities and efficiencies. In automated electronic commerce, the model can be used as a commercial reputation system. Agents receives transactional task and automatically execute the transaction in a virtual market. They evaluate the trust toward each other and finally form a reputational network. In computer games, the NPC (Non Player Character) can make use of the proposed model to learn trust from the interaction between NPCs or between NPC and human players. In agent based planning, the agents can find trustworthy partner agents to form an optimized plan based on the proposed model. In case there are interactions, the model can be exploited to some extent to help lubricate the virtual groups or virtual societies.

The application of the model is not limited to the field of multi-agent systems. It can also be used in regular computing tasks. In network security, trust is deemed as soft security (Barber and Kim, 2003) which restricts the relationship between programs or components. The proposed model can be transformed against trust of programs or trust of components instead of agents. The model can also be applied to the program that needs trust or reputation mechanisms.

REFERENCES

Barber, K.S. & Kim, J. (2003). Soft security: Isolating unreliable agents from society. In *Trust, Reputation, and Security: Theories and Practice, LNCS* (Vol. 2631, pp. 224-234).

Dong-Huynha, T., Jennings, N.R., & Shadbolt, N.R. (2004). Fire: An integrated trust and reputation model for open multi-agent systems. Proceedings of 16th ECAI conference (pp. 18-22).

Marsh, S. (1994b). Trust in distributed artificial intelligence. In *Artificial Social Systems, LNCS* (Vol. 830, pp. 94-112).

Resnick, P., Zeckhauser, R., Swanson, J. and Lockwood, K. (2006). The value of reputation on ebay: A controlled experiment. *Experimental Economics*, 9(2), 79-101.

Sabater, J., & Sierra, C. (2002). Social regret, a reputation model based on social relations. *ACM SIGecom Exchanges*, 3(1), 44-56.

Teacy, W.T., Patel, J., Jennings, N.R. & Luck, M. (2006). Travos: Trust and reputation in the context of inaccurate information sources. *Autonomous Agents and Multi Agent Systems*, 12(2), 183-198.

Yu, B., & Singh, M. P. (2000). *A social mechanism of reputation management in electronic communities*. Cooperative Information Agents IV - The Future of Information. doi:10.1007/978-3-540-45012-2_15

Zacharia, G., & Maes, P. (1999). Collaborative Reputation Mechanisms in Electronic Marketplaces. *Proc. 32nd Hawaii International Conf. on System Sciences*.

Chapter 16
Background Review for Neural Trust and Multi-Agent System

Gehao Lu
University of Huddersfield, UK & Yunnan University, China

Joan Lu
University of Huddersfield, UK

ABSTRACT

This chapter provides a systematic background study in the neural trust and multi-agent system. Theoretic models are discussed in details. The concepts are explained. The existing systems are analyzed. The limitations and strength of previous research are discussed. About 59 references are cited to support the study for the investigation. The study did address the research importance and significance and finally, proposed the future directions for the research undertaken.

1. INTRODUCTION

Multi-agent systems are initially introduced as a branch of distributed artificial intelligence. In 1986, Minsky and Murata proposed the concept of agents and he thought some problems could be solved through the negotiation among the social individuals (Minsky & Murata, 2004). These social individuals are agents. Agents should be highly interactive and intelligent. Hewitt thought that it is difficult to define agent as it is to define intelligence (Hewitt, 1985). Wooldridge and Jennings thought that agents should be autonomous, social interactive, proactive, and reactive (Wooldridge & Jennings, 2002). Eberhart & Shi thought that agents can react through sensing the outside environments (Eberhart & Shi, 2007).

With the increased size and complexity of the computer systems, it is nearly impossible to design a system from scratch and control every details of the system purely by human brain (Simon, 1996). It is difficult to control millions of transactions occurring in a large-scale E-market. It is also difficult to monitor an enterprise information system which encompasses huge amounts of heterogeneous devices which covers thousands of different geographical locations (Rothkopf, 2003; Coulouris, Dollimore & Kindberg, 2000a). Grid Computing, Autonomous Computing, Pervasive computing and Multi-agent systems, are all committing themselves to challenging the design of large-scale distributed system (Coulouris et al.,

DOI: 10.4018/978-1-5225-1884-6.ch016

2000b). Computational trust is to make an intelligent agent trust another agent and delegate part of their tasks to the target agent in a heterogeneous distributed multi-agent environment. Delegation of action is the result of trust and it also forms the foundation of future large-scale cooperative computer systems. Generally, trust toward specific agent is generated through recognition and experience under repeated transactions with that agent. Reputation is the socialized trust which can be propagated through a social network of agents. It helps agents trust the target agent without any direct interaction with the target agent. The benefits of introducing trust and reputation into multi-agent system include:

- As a lubricant, trust can eliminate much of unnecessary communications which are currently necessitates many interaction protocols thus greatly improve the performance of the multi-agent systems.
- An agent can make decision easier based upon the evaluation of the trustworthiness of another agent. Computational trust is also a very beneficial addition to the traditional decision theory.

Trust is a kind of soft security which complements the traditional hard security like encryption, authorization, and authentication. An agent that exists in complex heterogeneous environment must possess both securities in order to be safe and effective.

The mechanisms for coordinating interactions among agents are always pre-defined, that is, the designer specifies how one agent responses to another agent in a fixed protocol (Huynh, 2006). Such mechanisms are not flexible enough because of the intrinsic high openness and variability of the distributed systems (Ferber, 1999). For example, in open MAS (Multi-agent Systems), an agent cannot expect to always interact with the agents in the predefined application domain in a predetermined way (Subrahmanian, Bonatti, Dix, Eiter, Kraus, Ozcan & Ross, 2000). Agents will interact with different agents coming from heterogeneous applications and they may face challenges from lying, deceiving and accidental incidents (Ferber, 1999). Such complexity creates the following questions: can agents accept services from other unfamiliar agents? Can agents make use of the interaction history and transform them into experiences? Can agents avoid excessive negotiation with a familiar agent in an efficient way? Computational trust seems to be the answer and the next step of research for the multi-agent systems. Thus, a systematic review on the existing trust models is necessary.

Trust actually is a belief that someone or agents can delegate the host to finish some actions. There are two layers of meaning in the expression: first, agents should generate the belief of trustworthiness toward some other agents in some specific form; second, agents should make decision whether to delegate actions to the trusted agent. The first layer is actually to study how agents generate and update their belief which is part of research from computational intelligence. The second layer is an extension of the traditional decision theory which adds agent's belief and trustworthiness as one of the concerns during decision making.

There are a few computational trust models and reputation models that have been proposed from (Subrahmanian et al., 2000) to (Huynh, 2006). From a point of dimensional view, there are two types of models involved, i.e. local trust based and reputation based models. For local trust based model, the early model developed by Marsh, University of Stirling, 1994, only considers the local trust dimension which only derives trust from the agent's direct interaction without referencing to the recommendations from other witness agents (Marsh, 1994a). For reputation based models, like SPORA (Zacharia, 1999), they only consider the reputation (witness trust) dimension without looking at the local experience of the agent itself. Recently RegreT, Referral Network and TRAVOS take both local trust and witness trust into account (Teacy et al., 2005; Sabater, 2003). They combine the value of the two dimensions with relative weights and finally get a sum. Some models, such as FIRE, even introduce additional dimension called as role-based trust and certified reputation (Huynh, 2006; Huynh et al., 2006).

From a point of algorithmic view, different ways of calculating trust and reputation are proposed. For example, Bayesian systems take binary ratings as input and are based on calculating reputation scores by statistical updating of beta probability density functions. Such models include TRAVOS (Teacy, 2006; Teacy et al., 2005). Models such as RegreT (Sabater & Sierra, 2001) are based on discrete trust model to represent trustworthiness and untrustworthiness as a discrete value. A detailed analysis about the composing elements of trust and reputation model will be given.

The objective of the study is finding out the current situation and future trends of computational trust for multi-agent systems. It also aims at looking for common necessary compositional elements that compose the models through extracting the essence of those representative models and summarizing their common weaknesses through comparison, discussion and analysis. Finally, a clear research path is proposed to help the community to promote the research of computational trust.

2. BACKGROUND STRUCTURE

2.1 Distributed Artificial Intelligence

Intelligence and distribution are the future direction of software design. The subject of Distributed Artificial Intelligence (DAI) is a combination of Artificial intelligence and distributed computing. The Distributed Artificial Intelligence attracts the interests from researchers. The other requirement is interoperability, that is, the capabilities to exchange information and cooperate in fast changing heterogeneous environment.

In DAI, the intelligence is not an independently existing concept as it only exists in a group of agents. The interaction and cooperation among agents are the major research areas in DAI. DAI can be divided into two parts: Distributed Problem Solving (DPS) and Multi-agent System (MAS). DPS mainly considers how to decompose a problem into tasks that can be allocated to cooperating and knowledge sharing modules or nodes. The multi-agent system mainly focuses on the coordination of behaviors among autonomous agents.

Both fields need to investigate the division of knowledge, resource and control. However there is big difference between DPS and MAS. In DPS, there is only one conceptual model, one global problem, and success criteria; while in MAS, there are multiple local conceptual models, problems and success criteria. The purpose of DPS research is to create a coarse grained cooperating module. The modules in DPS cooperate to solve a problem. The problem is usually decomposed into several tasks. Each task is executed by a specialized module. All the policies of interactions are integrated as a whole. DPS is a top down approach of designing systems. On the contrary, MAS is a bottom up approach of designing systems. There are no global controls or global criteria for agents. The dispersed agents are defined first and then the problem is decomposed into several tasks which can be assigned to different agents. The relationship among agents may be cooperative, competitive or even hostile.

2.2 Intelligent Agent

2.2.1 Concepts

Although the word "agent" is widely used in different areas, "agent" is still an ambiguous concept. It is difficult to find a definition accepted by all researchers. The most common viewpoint is that an agent is a computer system designed for some purpose and the system is autonomous and flexible. Wooldridge and Jennings summarize the work done in this field by pointing out that it is better to understand agent from the broad sense and the narrow sense (Wooldridge, 2002).

From the broad sense, nearly all agent based software or hardware have the following characteristics:

- **Autonomy:** Agents are not controlled by humans or other programs. They have control over the behaviors and the internal states.
- **Social Ability:** Agents can exchange information through agent communication languages. This is also called communicability.
- **Reactivity:** Agents can sense from the environment and also influence the environment. Whether the agents in real world or the agent in virtual society, they need to sense their environments and change their environments. A program which cannot influence the environment cannot be called as an agent.
- **Pro-Activeness:** The traditional application is passively run by the users and strictly follows the instructions from the users. Agents behave actively or spontaneously. Through sensing the changes in the environments, agents can perform some goal directed behaviors.

Some researchers believe that agents should have some human like characteristics such as knowledge, belief, intention, and desire. Some researchers even propose emotional agents (Bates, 1994; Bates et al., 1992). According to (Shoham, 1992, 1993), an agent is an entity with states composed of belief, capability, choice, commitment and mental component.

1.2.2 Theoretical Models

Mind elements in order to adapt to the environment and cooperate to solve problems, intelligent agents must use knowledge to change its internal status, that is, the mental state. The mental state drives the actions of the agents. It is possible to build an agent mental state from three aspects: emotion, feeling, and intention. The most famous model based on formal method is the BDI (Belief, Desire, and Intention) model. Belief represents the basic opinions owned by agents toward the environment; an agent also can use it to represent the future possible states. Desire is derived from belief. Desire includes the estimation of the future for agents. Intention confines the activities of agents; it is the subset of goals.

Logic is the most important tool to depict the mental state. Moore is one of the first researchers who used formal logic to model agents (Moore, 1990). His research focuses on the relationship between knowledge owned by agents and the realized activities. He introduces modal operator of knowledge into logic and use dynamic logic to represent actions. Such formalization allows agents to own beliefs about how to achieve goals. And agents can acquire information through executing actions. The disadvantage is his modeling is too simple and incomplete. Cohen and Levesque designed a formal model which is based on linear sequential logic (1990). The model introduces concepts like time, event, behavior, goal, belief, and intention. The model also depicts the relationship among these concepts. However, the model does not reveal the relationship between intention and goal, and the model is also very abstract and difficult to implement. Kinny proposes the BDI model of rational agent based on nonlinear branch temporal logic (Kinny, George & Rao, (1996)). They use three modal operators, belief, desire and intention, to build a BDI model. Singh uses agent logic to describe intention, belief, knowledge and communication. Its logic is also based on branch temporal logic (Singh, 1994).

The behavior of rational agent cannot be driven directly from belief, desire or their combination. There should be an intention between the desire and the plan. The reason is that the behavior of agents is confined by limited resources. Once an agent decides to do some task, it needs to build a commitment with limited form. In a multi-agent environment, there must be a commitment to coordinate the behaviors of agents. Without commitment, there are no actions. Intention is just one type of commitments. In an open environment, a rational agent's behavior must be restricted by intention. If an agent changes its own intention, the changes must have some reasons. An agent cannot ignore the changes in environment and keep unimportant or not realistic activities.

1.2.3 Structures

An agent can be looked as a black box with sensors and effecters. Agents use sensors to sense the environment and use effecters to change environment. Except when interacting with environment, agents need process and explain information received from outside. The information is merged and processed into understandable data. There are three types of agent structures: deliberative agent, reactive agent, and mixed structure.

Deliberative agent is also called cognitive agent. It is an explicit symbol based model which has abilities of logical deductions (Wooldridge, 2002). It is a knowledge based system that keeps the essence of the traditional artificial intelligence. There is an environment model implemented as the major component of the knowledge library. Agents using this structure will face two basic problems (Castelfranchi, 1999): (1) transformation problem: how to translate the real world into an accurate, appropriate symbol description; (2) Representation/deduction problem: how to use the symbols to represent the entities and processes in the real world, and how to let agents make decision through deducing the information. The BDI model (Kinny et al., 1996) is a typical deliberative agent structure. The biggest disadvantage for deliberative agent is its fixed structure. In a complex, fast changing environment, it is too stationery to be reactive. The reactive agent is an agent without complex symbol deduction and symbol based world model (Cruces, 2000). It uses the condition-action rule to connect perception and action.

Neither the symbol base deliberative agent nor condition-action based reactive agent can be built into a perfect agent. Some researchers propose the mixed structure in order to combine the advantages of both types. The most direct method is to build two sub systems in an agent: one for deliberative structure, the other for reactive structure. Usually the reactive sub system has higher priority than the deliberative sub system because the agent needs to react to important event in real-time. Each agent contains a series of modules including sensory, action, reaction, modeling, planning, communication and decision making. The agent has an agent kernel which allows additional modules be attached to the kernel dynamically. The kernel is made up of internal database, mail box, and blackboard and execution engine.

1.2.4 Communications

The commonly used communication methods include the black board system and the message/dialog system. The black board system provides a public working area; agents can exchange information, data, and knowledge there. The black board is the medium between agents. Agents do not communicate with each other directly. Message based communication is the foundation of realizing complex coordination policies. Through the specified protocol, agents can exchange messages to build communication and coordination. It is different from the black board system in that the messages are directly exchanged between two agents without any caches. Message is sent to one specific agent or specific group. Only the agent or group with that address can read the message. The protocol must specify the process of communication, format of messages, and languages of communication. Of course, agents must understand the semantics of the language.

Knowledge Query Manipulation Language (KQML) is a uniform agent communication language (Labrou & Finin, 1997). KQML specifies the format of messages and the message transmitting system. It also provides a group of protocols for recognizing, establishing connection and exchanging messages. But the semantics of message content is not specified clearly in KQML. KQML can be analyzed from three layers: communication, message and content. The communication layer specifies the techniques, and the parameters of communications. The message layer specifies message related types of speech acts. The content layer specifies the content.

FIPA (Foundation for Intelligent Physical Agents) defines a language and designs supporting tools. The language is called Agent Communication Language (ACL) (Labrou et al., 1999). The thoughts of ACL are originated from interaction of human society. It does not specify any low level service like network protocol or transmitting services. It assumes the physical infrastructure exists. The characteristics of ACL including: defining goal driven behavior, defining autonomous decision making processes for agent actions, building interaction protocol through negotiation and delegation, creating models of mind states, and enhancing the adaptability to environments and requirements. In this research, ACL is followed as the communication language among agents.

2.3 Multi-Agent System

2.3.1 Coordination and Cooperation

Coordination and cooperation is the core research topics for multi-agent systems. It is also the major difference between multi-agent systems and the other types of computer systems. The purpose of build system in a multi-agent way is to coordinate the knowledge, desire, intention, planning, and actions so that the agents can cooperate to complete the tasks.

Coordination is to change the intention of the agents. Cooperation is a special case of coordination. In an open dynamic environment, agents with different goals need to coordinate its goals and resources. If there is a conflict in using resources, without a good coordination, there will be a dead lock. In another scenario, if a single agent cannot finish its goal, it may need helps form other agents, this requires coordination.

Cooperation can improve the performance of the multi-agent system and enhance its capability to solve problems. It also improves the flexibility of the system. While individual agents are independent from other agents and only care about its own needs and goals, when in a multi-agent system, agents must follow the predefined social rules and its behaviors must meet the preset social norms. The interdependency among agents strictly restricts the interaction and cooperation of agents. Based on different mechanisms of interaction and cooperation, the implementation of agents in a multi-agent system is different.

Nowadays, the researches on agent cooperation mainly fall into two types. The first type is to migrate the theories into other domains (Game theory, classical dynamics) for agents (Kraus, 1997). The second type is to research the cooperation from the idea of mind attitude as goals, intension, planning like model named as FA/C (Kraus, 1997), joint intention framework (Levesque, 1990; Wooldridge & Jennings., 1994), and shared planning (Grosz & Kraus, 1996). The first type of mechanisms is not as widely used as the second because once the environment changes, the number of agents, types, and interaction relationships might be different from the situations that are suitable for the theories. The theory based interaction thus loses its advantages. The second type focuses on problem planning and solving.

2.3.2 Contract Net

Contract net (Smith, 1980) is widely used in coordination of multi-agent systems. The communications among agents are usually built on agreed message formats. Contract net is actually a contract or a protocol that is based on formats of contract net. The contract net specifies task assignments and roles of agents. It is made up by task processor, contract processor, communication processor and local database.

The local database contains the nodes related knowledge base, information about the current states, and problem solving processes. The other three components use the local database to execute their tasks. The communication processor is responsible for communicating with other nodes. All nodes connect to the network through this processor. The contract processor receives the tasks from bidding. It sends application and finish jobs. It also explains and analyzes the received information. The contract processor executes the coordination among nodes. The task processor is responsible for processing and solving the assigned tasks.

The working process of the contract net is as follows: the problem is decomposed into several sub problems. A node is chosen as the manager to manage the bidding processes. The manager encapsulates the sub problems as bids and publishes them to the nodes. The bids are open to all agents and can be processed through contract processor. The contract processor decides whether to accept the bid. If it accepts, it will inform the manager. The manager chooses the appropriate sub problem for the agent. The agent sends an acknowledge confirming it has accepted the contract. When the processing or solving is completed, the result is sent back to the manager. The essence of the contact net is task distribution. Figure 1 illustrates the process of the contract net with a sequence diagram.

2.3.3 Cooperation Planning

When an agent believes that cooperation bring benefits like improving efficiency or finishing unavailable tasks for single agent, it will have the desire of cooperating and looking for partner to do it. Or when multiple agents find that they can achieve bigger goals, they will form federations and take cooperative actions. The principle of cooperation is setting roles on demand and acquiring roles through competition. The roles are preset according to the goals and the needs of cooperation. The agents play specific roles only when they win in the competition attended by multiple agents.

The process of cooperation can be divided into six steps:

Figure 1. How a contract networks

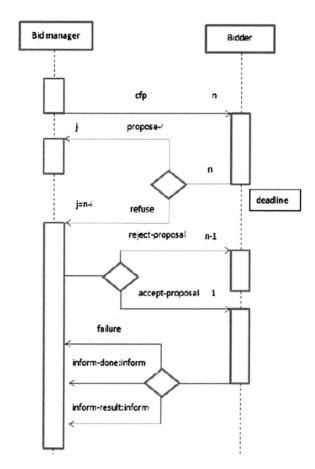

- Set goals and produce requirements;
- Cooperation planning and decide cooperation structure;
- Search for cooperating partners;
- Choose a cooperation solution;
- Realize goals;
- Evaluate results.

There are many formal methods to describe the cooperation process. Fox example, d'Inverno uses Z notation (Luck & d'Inverno, 1995), Fisher use sequential logic (Fisher & Wooldride, 1997), Kinny uses modal logic base on derived channel (Kinny et al, 1996). Although the logic based formal method can accurately describe the mind attitude and time series for agents, the action norms depicted by logics is still far away from implementation. The logic method is good at depicting the static properties and social norms, but it is not good at depicting communication and interaction structure among agents. Some researchers use process calculus in process algebra such as calculus to describe the dynamic behavior processes, concurrent interactions and cooperating structures. Some researcher combines the formal methods and process calculus into a uniform formal structure (Werger, 1999). Using sequential logic depicts goals of cooperation while using calculus depicts interaction processes and cooperation structures.

2.3.4 Ecology Based Coordination

The distributed computing system has similar social, organic characteristics as living beings. Such open system is different from the current computing system. It can do asynchronous computing against complex tasks; it can generate nodes in different types of machines. Each node may make local decision according incomplete knowledge and delayed information. There is no central control; instead, it uses interaction among nodes to cooperate to solve problems. These characteristics form a concurrent composition. Their interactions, policies and competitions for resources are similar to pure ecology.

Ecology computing looks the computing systems as an ecosystem. It introduces many biological mechanisms such as mutation and evolution. The mutation leads to genetic variation and create diversities of species with stronger adaptation. The policies of mutation can be a method to improve the ability of agents in artificial intelligence.

Lenat and Brown (Lenat & Brown, 1984) introduce mutation mechanism into their AM and Eurisoko system through grammar mutating in Lisp programs to discover mathematical concepts. They believe the future successful systems should be a series of social systems with abilities of evolution and self-organization. Miller and Drexler (Drexler, 1988) discuss models of evolution such as biological ecosystem, commodity market and points out the difference between ecosystems and computing systems. They also think that a direct computing market is the most ideal system model. Huberman and Hog propose and analyze the process of the dynamic game (Huberman & Hogg, 1995). When different processes interact to finish the computing tasks, if there are multiple optional strategies, the dynamic gradual process may turn into nonlinear oscillation and chaos. This means that there are no stable strategies of evolution for computing ecology systems. Rosenschein and Zlotkin (1994) propose to use static game theory to solve conflicts in multiple computing nodes with different goals (Parsons, 2002).

The most famous ecosystem model includes biological ecosystem model, species evolution model, economic model, and social model of scientific group. The intelligence for the ecosystem usually supersedes the individual intelligence.

2.4 Learning

The basic learning mechanism tries to transfer a successful behavior in one circumstance to another similar circumstance. Learning is a process to gain knowledge, accumulate knowledge, improve performance, discover order, and adapt to environments. There are four basic nodes in a learning system: learning node, execution node, knowledge base and environment. The environment provides outside information. The learning node (or learning algorithm) process the information provided by the environment (Panait, 2005). The knowledge base stores the information in some knowledge representation form. The execution node uses the knowledge from the knowledge base to accomplish some tasks and provides the feedback regarding the execution to the learning node. Learning improves the performance of the system.

The quality and level of information that is provided by the environment directly influences the ways and effects of learning. The level of information refers to the degree of abstracting information. The low level information refers to detailed, concrete and raw information while high level information refers to processed abstract information. The quality of information decides the difficulty of learning. If the information is incorrect, incomplete or imprecise, it is impossible to gain the right knowledge.

The learning node is actually learning methods and algorithms; it is also called the learner. There are many methods and algorithms for machine learning such as inductive learning, learning by analogy, analytic learning, genetic learning and connectionist learning. The knowledge base is place for storing knowledge. It should select the appropriate ways of representing knowledge and it should allow modification and extension. The execution node use knowledge to guide actions and to change environments. The results of the execution are provided to the learning node so that the learning node can be improved. Only through the effect of the environments can the learning algorithm be evaluated.

In agent learning, there are two streams: one is to improve performance of the system through agent learning; the other one is to improve learning efficacy and quality of knowledge through agent learning (Alonso & Noble, 2001).

2.4.1 Active Learning

When an agent works in an environment, the method of gaining experiences of the autonomous agent is active learning. It is different from passive learning. In passive learning, the teachers or domain experts need to choose groups of training data. In active learning, agents learn the effects of actions or plans and amend their domain knowledge. There two types of learning methods for domain knowledge. The first type is theory amendment system such as EITHER (Ourston & Mooney, 1994), OCCAM (Pazzani & Kibler, 1991), CLIPS-R (Pazzani et al., 1994). These systems are representatives of the passive learning. They have preselected one group of training data which is unrelated to the status in training. The second type is reinforcement learning such as Q-learning, classifiers, back propagation. These types of systems do not explicitly focus on the correctness of the learned domain knowledge. They care about the results of executions. The reinforcement learning is widely used. Agents make a plan based on their current knowledge. The execution of the plan produces results which become a feedback to the learning algorithm.

2.4.2 Case Based Reasoning

In case based reasoning, the situations or problems that the agent face are called target case. The memorized situations or problems are called source case. CBR is a strategy that let agent search source cases according to target cases and uses the source cases to help solve the target cases.

Cases are the fundamentals of knowledge representations in CBR (de Mantaras, 2001). Acquiring cases is easier than acquiring rules. This can greatly simplify the process of knowledge acquisition and reuse the experiences of past processes. Agents do not need to start everything from scratch so that the efficiency of processing new problems is improved. Past successful or failure experiences can provide hints to solving current problems and to avoid future failures.

There are two types of CBR in multi-agent systems: process oriented multi-agent CBR and task oriented multi-agent CBR. The process oriented CBR focuses on the processes. Each process can be implemented as an agent. The process oriented CBR is made up of five agents. The case maintenance agent is responsible for maintaining the case library; The case searching agent is responsible for searching and matching the new case; The case modification agent is responsible for the transformation of the case solutions; The case reuse agent is responsible for dealing with the target case according to the transformed solution; The case storing agent is responsible for putting the new case into the case library.

Task oriented CBR focuses on the tasks instead of processes. It provides a CBR agent with multiple strategies to deal with complex tasks. According to the requirements of the specific tasks, it constructs and organizes agents with different functionalities. Every agent is a small CBR system doing specified tasks. Such agent is called a CBR agent. The functionalities of the agents are relatively independent to each other and these agents have their own unique capabilities. Multiple CBR agents can cooperate to finish complex tasks through the form of contract net.

2.5 Research Areas

Design new theoretical model for intelligent agents is one of the interesting research areas. Nowadays, researchers are trying to build better theoretical agent models. The models should be based on the autonomous agents and should find the balance between social interactivity and individual intelligence. Some researchers propose to build rational agents and multi-agent system made up of the rational agents. For example, the logic rationality based BDI model (Kinny et al., 1996); the behavior rationality based Rational Agent (Wooldridge, 2000); The MAS sociality based semantics of open information systems and economic methodologies using game theory and decision making theory.

Negotiation mechanisms and organizations are also important topics that attract many researchers. Another important stream is to research the MAS frameworks and MAS related methodologies for the opening dynamic environments. Such research covers negotiations, cooperation, and task allocation mechanisms, social rules, filtering strategies, behavior normalization and federations. An agent organization is a structured agent group with clear goals. In agent organization researches, the hotspots include the models for agent organization, the formation and evolution of the organization, rules of organizations and patterns of organizations. Sociality is an important aspect to indicate the social abilities of agents in MAS. The modern organization theory based agent sociality can become the foundation of the agent theories. It also stands for the research direction of agent theories and technologies.

Implementation tools and applications are the research areas that focus on how the theoretical models can be applied into the real world. The implementing technologies for Agent and MAS are also hot research topics. The current technologies are based upon the existing social organization theory and modeling theories. Many tools have been developed to support MAS including experimental test beds, integrated systems, blackboard framework and object oriented concurrent programming OBCP (Briot & Gasser, 1998). The most representative work in this area is the Agent Oriented Program (AOP) program designing (Bresciani et al., 2004). There are lots of applications with logically distributed problems or physically distributed problems. Nowadays, the major application domains include: language processing, industry manufacturing, organizational information systems, air traffic controls, concurrent engineering design, distributed sensor systems, transportation planning, monitoring and robots. With the high speed development of the Internet, the integration technology based on mobile agents and multi-agent also become new hot research spots.

Intelligent agent should have the ability of learning from their environment. Trust and reputation are important mechanisms that support coordination and cooperation. 22 If agents can evaluate the trust or reputation of another agent, the performance and reliabilities of the coordination and cooperation can be greatly enhanced. If the agent can learn the trust and reputation through its past interaction experiences, the agent can then dynamically adjust its belief about other agents in the fast changing environments. Thus the framework, mechanisms and algorithms that the research proposes contributes both to the agent coordination and agent learning. The trust learning algorithms give agents learning ability while the reputation mechanisms improve the quality of coordination and cooperation.

3. EXISTING SYSTEMS

3.1 Method Employed

The investigation is carried out through viewing and analyzing conference papers, journal papers and technical reports on computational trust from varieties of sources. The criteria of choosing analyzing target are based on whether the model is representative and whether the model reflects the latest trend of the research. To achieve a comparative result, the first thing is to figure out the common basic compositional elements of different models. Taking the elements as parameters then compares the above models in the form of table; it will also try to find out the significance of the result table.

The results will be organized in the form of spider graph to show the reader a clear relationship between the evaluation criteria. The study will also differentiate research paths of different models through quantitative analysis and statistics.

3.2 Investigation Results

Results are shown from two approaches, i.e. centralized approach and distributed approach. The centralized approach saves all the rating procedure, storage of reputation, query of reputation, searching of comments to the computer server, while the distributed approach finishes all these jobs by agents themselves.

3.2.1 Centralized Approach

There are two existing models that take the centralized approach. They are eBay (Ebay, 2012) and SPORAS (Zacharia, 1999). eBay has built a feedback reputation system for its customer-to-Customer web-sites. The goal of designing such a system is to transfer the trust and reputation mechanism in the real life human market to the internet-based e-Market. SPORAS is a reputation model was developed by Zacharia in MIT, 1999. It is an evolved version of the eBay's online reputation models. In this model, only the most recent rating between two users is considered. Another important characteristic is that users with very high reputation values experience much smaller rating changes after each update than users with a low reputation. SPORAS incorporates a measure of the reliability of the users' reputation based on the standard deviation of reputation values.

3.2.2 Distributed Approaches

The research lists five existing models that take the distributed approaches and analyze their characteristics respectively. They are Marsh's Model (Marsh, 1994a), RegreT (Sabater & Sierra, 2001), Referral Reputation (Yu & Singh, 2002, 2003), FIRE (Huynh, 2006; Huynh et al., 2006), and TRAVOS (Teacy, 2006; Teacy et al., 2005).

The pioneer work on computational trust model was done by Marsh (Marsh, 1994a) in 1994. Marsh thought that knowledge, utility, importance, risk, and perceived competence are important aspects related to trust. He defined three types of trust: dispositional trust, general trust and situational trust. The trust management provided by Marsh does not treat the collection of recommendations provided by other agents; he only models direct trust between two agents. The aspect of risk is dealt with explicitly based on costs and benefits of the considered engagement. The decision making is threshold based. Among other parameters, the cooperation threshold depends on the perceived risk and competence of the possible interaction partner. If the situational trust is above the value calculated for the cooperation threshold, cooperation will take place otherwise it will not. Furthermore, the decision making can be extended by the concept of reciprocity, i.e. it is expected to be compensated at some time, if one does another one a favor.

RegreT takes trust as a multi-facet concept and a combination of pieces of information (Sabater & Sierra, 2001). In RegreT, reputation is a combinatorial product of individual dimension, social dimension, and ontological dimension. The calculation of reputation is same as the calculation in individual dimension. The only difference is that all the reputation under each sub-ontological dimension should be summarized. The model deals with three dimensions of trust or reputation. The individual dimension is based on self-made experiences of an agent. The trust values are called direct trust or outcome reputation. The social dimension is based on third party information (witness reputation), the social relationships between agents (neighbor-hood reputation), and the social role of the agents (system reputation). The ontological dimension helps to transfer trust information between related contexts. For all trust values, a measurement of reliability is introduced, which depends on the number of past experience and expected experience (intimate level of interaction), and the variability of the ratings.

The underlying computational framework for Referral Reputation (Yu & Singh, 2002, 2003) is based on Dempster-Shafer theory (Dempster & Arthur, 1968). The model has a well-defined trust network to propagate the trust value from the witnesses, the proposed approach does not concern the uncertainty which surely occurs in the interaction and there is no risk management in this model.

The FIRE model (Huynh, 2006; Huynh et al., 2006) believes that most of the trust information source can be categorized into the four main sources: direct experience, witness information, role based rules and third party references. FIRE integrates all four sources of information and is able to provide trust metrics in a wide variety of situations. The reliability value bases on the rating reliability and deviation reliability to counteract the uncertainty due to instability of agents.

TRAVOS (Trust and Reputation model for Agent-based Virtual OrganizationS) is based on probability theory (Teacy, 2006; Teacy L, W. T., Patel, J., Jennings, N. R. & Luck, M, 2005) and Bayesian system (DeGroot & Schervish, 2002). The prominent feature of TRAVOS is that it takes confidence into account and the trustor makes decisions based upon the confidence level instead of the trust value. The reputation is not simply added to the direct trust value or confidence value, the introduction of reputation depends on the value of confidence level. If the agent can achieve the minimum confidence level through checking belief of its direct interaction, then it does not have to query other agents. But if the agent cannot find enough confidence, then the agent needs to seek more evidence from the witness.

The researcher needs to build a test-bed for implementing TROVOS model. Such test-bed is also useful for future evaluation of the researchers own model and other models. The test-bed can mimic a general market where agents carry on business by automatically standing in for humans. Each agent seizes some resources and cost specific amount of resources with time elapsing (charging energy). The lifetime of the agent ends when the agent owns nothing (starving to death). The goal of each agent is to maximize their assets (resources) and keep itself alive as long as possible. Transaction is the only way to accumulate resources and avoid dying because the system is designed to make agents achieve more resources in transaction than the resources elapsing with time. There are two attitudes held by the agents:

benevolence and malevolence. Under the attitude of benevolence, the agent tends to give full value to the other agent in a transaction; under the attitude of malevolence, the agent tends to give partial value to the other agent in a transaction.

Before any transaction, an agent should find out a target agent and evaluate the trustworthiness of that agent. To find out a target agent, the usual way is to use Contract Net Protocol, the agent broadcast its needs and the other capable agents who are willing to sell goods will response to the request listing their preferred price and quantities. However, in our design, to simplify the scenario and focus on the effect of trust model, the target agent is selected randomly by the simulation engine. The trustworthiness is calculated by the agent through combining the reputation from other agents and the experience accumulated in past transactions with the target agents. The evaluation engine is based on TRAVOS model. Agents must consult other agents through broadcasting request for reputation. If the agent has knowledge (experience) about the target agent then the agent should respond to the request and send their experience to originated agent. The originated agent then combine these experience with its own experience according to the TRAVOS model to decide whether to make transaction with the target agent.

- Dimension is to study what the sources of the trust values are.
- The semantics focus on the meaning behind the trust in case that the outcome from the trust is a composite product.
- The mathematical model employed in calculating trust or reputation is sometime called trust computation engine (Josang, Ismail & Boyd, 2007).Trust network is the study on the topology of organizing witness agents and the host agent.
- Uncertainty refers to the management of risk which monitors the accidental incident and environmental changing, and reliability which ensures that the trusted agent is reliable enough even though it is trustworthy that is based upon the result of mathematical calculation.

3.2.3 Observations

Different models are compared in Table 1. Significant observations from the table can be listed as follows.

Table 1. Comparison: the difference among different computational trust models

Model Name	Dimension	Semantics	Architecture	Trust Network	Uncertainty	
					Reliability	Risk
eBay	Reputation	Single	Centralized	N/A	N/A	N/A
Marsh	Local trust	Single	Distributed	N/A	N/A	N/A
SPORAS	Reputation	Single	Centralized	N/A	Exogenous	N/A
Referal System	Local trust reputation	Single	Distributed	Directed graph With depth limit	N/A	N/A
Regret	Local trust Reputation	Ontology-based	Distributed	N/A	Endogenous	N/A
FIRE	Local trust Reputation Role-based trust Certified trust	Single	Distributed	Directed graph with depth limit	Exogenous	N/A
TRAVOS	Local trust reputation	Single	Distributed	N/A	Exogenous	N/A

1. There are multiple facts (cardinality of dimensions) to forge the trust or reputation. 3 models are single dimension and 4 models are multiple dimensions.
2. 6 models presume the semantics behind trust is consistent to all agents except that RegreT adds an ontological dimension to deal with the semantic difference.
3. 5 models choose distributed architecture rather than centralized architecture.
4. 6 mathematical models are based on summation or product of different dimensions with selected weights representing their influences. TRAVOS is an exception which is based on Bayesian probability theory. (The evaluation criterion is the confidence level instead of the trust or reputation value).
5. 5 models, except Referal System and FIRE, don't take trust network and trust transitivity into account.

Their hypothesis is that trust propagates from the target witness to the host agent without any distortion or loss. The findings are: semantics, risks, trust network pose weak points for most models, whereas the dimension, architecture and mathematical models are intensively studied by researchers.

4. DISCUSSIONS

Most models have two basic dimensions: local trust and reputation. But they aren't the only dimensions that can be used to deduce trust. FIRE (Huynh, 2006; Huynh et al., 2006) introduces role-based reputation, which models the trust to the specific role in the society. This is similar to the situation that people always tend to trust some group of people with occupations like professor, doctor or police in real world society. FIRE (Huynh, 2006; Huynh et al., 2006) also has a design called "certified reputation" which is reputation collected by the trustee from its previous interactions. The truster then does not need to contact its acquaintances to know about the trustee thus the design improves the efficiency of communication. Some idea can be borrowed from social science study on trust; cultural trust and mechanism trust (Sztompka, 2000) are trust that may find their places in computational trust. Their potential hypothesis is that their trust is restricted to a predefined topic. For example, in eBay, trust (reputation) to the seller implicitly means the belief held by the buyer that the seller will send the correct product to the correct location within the right time frame (Ebay, 2012). However, this is an ambiguous semantic. Some sellers may believe that the correct product to the correct location with a little delay deserves the buyer's trust. Such gaps of semantics lead to disruption between buyers and sellers. In multi-agent systems, if two agents with different trust semantics meet, do they simply refuse to trust the other because of incompatible semantics or they need to build up a consensus through negotiation? If the semantics of trust can be adjusted, how often should such adjustment happen and to what extent? It is necessary to create an ontology built upon XML and RDF that allows systems to provide machine-readable semantic annotations for the trust of specific domain. Most models do not explain how the trust network work and what mechanism the trust transitivity is based. How the trust or reputation value is transferred? Does it simply keep the original value from the witnesses? Or does its value attenuate a long distance as same as what happens in the transitivity of human reputation? The solutions to these questions are keys to implement a practical system. Theories about social network analysis in social science make sense to build algorithms for searching witnesses in the network of intelligent agents. The transitivity or propagation algorithm can also benefit from studying the social network analysis. Some researchers have already noticed the transitive trust and proposed their ideas (Josang & Pope, 2005).

None of the reviewed models introduce risk management to control the uncertainty due to the environmental influence or accidental incidents, although they do define reliability to counteract the uncertainty due to instability of individual agent. It is necessary to use risk evaluation to evaluate the risk associated with the prospective transaction under specific environmental facts. The risk here mainly means the risk derivate from the environmental influence or accidental incidents. For example, agent A trust a reliable agent B, but B's environment is instable (B's system often breaks down due to an accidental power off). Such type of risk can be called as environmental reliability. If agent A has assessed the risk of B's unstable environment additional to its reliability and trust, it will be more careful when making decision about whether to trust B or not.

An important part is not listed in the comparison table but deserves discussions. Most models stay as a theoretical model without performing a strict experiment in the real system. A few of them do have simple test but are not complete. A complete experiment to assess the trust model for MAS should at least pass the functionality test, the performance test and the security test. The functionality test focuses on whether the model supports heterogeneous agents to effectively cooperate with each other in different scenarios. The performance test focuses on measuring the efficiency of the model in the form of comparison with other models. The security test needs to measure whether the trust model enhances or does harm to the traditional security like authorization and authentication. The test environment should firstly be a simple but complete multi-agent system. Some tools of building multi-agent system can be applied to the experiment like JADE (Java Agent Development Environment), FIPA-OS, zeous, etc. The details about different tools can be seen in technical report from Gerstner Laboratory (Laboratory, 2005).

JADE (Bellifemine, Caire & Greenwood, 2007), FIPA-OS (coordinating team, 2012), and ZEUS (Nwana, Ndumu, Lee & Collis., 1999) are the most prominent and prevalent platforms that support MAS development. The similarities among the three platforms are: all of them are based on Java programming language, all of them are open-source project, and all of them claim to strictly follow the FIPA (Foundation for Intelligent Physical Agents) specification. Through comparing these tools, the following observations and conclusions can be made:

- JADE platform is a better choice for MAS development than FIPA-OS and ZEUS in FIPA compliancy, platform maturity, and non-technical concerns.
- Adopting XML as the specification message encoding, representation, and content language can be a good choice to alleviate interaction problems.
- It is necessary to extend the range of applicability of the agent mobility to low-end devices.
- Web Service enhanced agent can freely integrate with any system that supports Web Services; The combination of agent paradigm and the Web Service paradigm may form an intelligent service provision network to complement the traditional static service oriented architectures (SOA).
- It is necessary to introduce agent oriented software engineering process and agent based modeling tools such as AUML (Luke, 2006) into MAS platforms.

The continuity of development efforts is important for the maturity of a successful agent platform. For the MAS research community, it is possible to develop better tools and platforms to support the agent development through three routes. The first route is to update the FIPA specification with continuously absorbing new findings and new mechanisms, to incorporate with the existing widely adopted specifications such as XML and UML; the second route is to build more powerful application platform through strengthening the administration, monitoring, debugging and logging functionality, to exploit the successful development tools like eclipse, to incorporate Web Service and agent oriented software engineering; the third route is to maintain and enlarge the open source communities and let more researchers take part in and contribute to the development of platforms. A framework is designed for the computational trust and reputation. In the mental space, agents carry out trust learning through observing the results of actions. Such learning leads to the generation, increasing or decreasing of trustworthiness. The learning process is discussed later in details. Next to the mental space is the decision space where agents use trustworthiness derived in the learning process to make delegation decisions. It is combinatory decision making process in that the risk and utility evaluation are also included. The outcomes of specific transaction are constantly observed by the other agents. The observation will become the input of next round trustworthiness learning. Apart from the agents own experience, the trust from the other agents, reputation, is also part of the input of trust learning. The reputation from an organized social network and its propagation mechanism is also a research topic in future work. Most aforementioned trust and reputation models are mathematically based upon simplistic algebraic summation or explicit statistical deduction through counting the success or failure of historical transactions toward the target agents. Surely these methods can produce reasonable numerical results and then translate them into thresholds which help agents make decisions. However, the assumption that the agents always repeat the same transactions with the same target opponents is impossible in an ever changing complex multi-agent environment.

- First, the semantics are various among objects and it does not make sense to hold some invariable elements as formula to calculate the trustworthy or not trustworthy.
- Second, the count of success or failure of transaction is non-sense when the target of discussion is different. It is impossible to draw an equivalence between a successful coke transaction and a successful airplane transaction.
- Third, there is no sure clear border between trustworthiness and distrust-worthiness, that is, trustworthiness or its opposite should be a pattern generated from the repeated transactions instead of a simplistic value.

The above analysis leads the modeling of trust and reputation to the area of computational intelligence. Actually, trustworthiness is one kind of belief. The research on generation of trustworthiness is to model a specialized kind of belief for the computer agent. In the study of computational intelligence, several streams are popular and focused in recent years: neural networks, evolutionary computation, swarm intelligence and fuzzy systems. Since 1970s, neural network becomes one of the main research streams of computational intelligence. It is widely applied in machine learning, pattern recognition, and biological science. The reasons of choosing neural network as the basic calculating mechanism are listed as below:

- Instances are represented by many attribute-value pairs. The target function to be learned is defined over instances that can be described by a vector of predefined features.
- The target function output of the computational trust can be discrete-valued, real-valued or a vector of several real or discrete-valued attributes.
- Neural network learning is good choice for fast evaluation of the learned target function. Usually, the recognition of trustworthiness should be finished several times per second by the agents.

- The ability of humans to understand the learned target function is not important. The weighted learned by neural networks are often difficult for humans to interpret.

The input layer is composed by dynamically organized element. The elements are extracted from the semantic library according to the target object. For example, if the target object is digital camera, then the elements extracted maybe price, quality, guarantee and delivery. The neural network will gradually adjust its weights in a way of unsupervised learning.

5. SUMMARY

Here the background knowledge of intelligent agent and multi-agent systems has been reviewed. The difference between DPS and DAI has been explained with a detailed description. Then the intelligent agent is reviewed from its concept, structure and communication. The explanations cover the concepts and meanings of agent in both broad and narrow sense. The popular theoretical models are listed. The differences of these models are compared. The discussions are focused on rational agent and Belief, Desire, Intention model. The intelligent agents are the fundamentals of multi agents. The investigation also includes the coordination and cooperation mechanisms. The advantages and disadvantages of different mechanisms are analyzed. The agent learning topics is also covered. The rational of learning is explained and the common algorithms such as active learning and CBR are mentioned. Finally, some interest topics in the field are listed and stated how the related results are located in the background.

Plenty of interests have been attracted to the construction of computational trust from various research communities. Through analyzing and comprising these models, the research proposes that a complete computational trust model should at least have seven fundamental elements. Some conclusions are drawn as follows:

- The current trust dimensions are not enough to represent trust in multi-agent systems and new dimension can be modeled through introducing concepts in sociology.
- Agents from different domains must fill their semantic gaps through constructing ontology with XML and RDF.
- The searching algorithm for trust network and the propagation mechanism for trust network can be progressed through introducing techniques in social network analysis.
- Except for the reliability of target agents, agents also need to manage the risk (or environmental reliability) due to environmental changes or accidental incidents.
- A complete experimental platform which used to test the functionality, performance and security of computational trust model is a necessity.
- The future work of the research domain can also be naturally derived from the above conclusions.
- The dimension of trust can be extended based on the study of trust in sociology and psychology. It is necessary to categorize the scenarios where the dimension is appropriately used.
- The results in the research of semantic web can be used in the computational trust model. It is necessary to create an ontology built upon XML and RDF that allows systems to provide machine-readable semantic annotations for trust of specific domains.

- Theories about social analysis in social science can be used to build algorithms for searching witnesses in the network of intelligent agents. It is necessary to develop a trust transitivity or propagation mechanism which fulfills the requirement of different situations.
- There is still a need for a simplified, effective mathematical model which can be evaluated through appropriately constructing experiments.

REFERENCES

Cruces, A., & Arriaga, F. D. (2000). Reactive agent design for intelligent tutoring systems. *Cybernetics and Systems: An International Journal, 31*(1), 1–47. doi:10.1080/019697200124900

Alonso, E., Dinverno, M., Kudenko, D., Luck, M., & Noble, J. (2001). Learning in multi-agent systems. *The Knowledge Engineering Review, 16*(03), 277–284. doi:10.1017/S0269888901000170

Bates, J. (1994). The role of emotion in believable agents. *Communications of the ACM, 37*(7), 122–125. doi:10.1145/176789.176803

Bates, J., Loyall, A. B., & Reilly, W. S. (1992). *An architecture for action, emotion, and social behavior.* Technical Report CMU-CS-92-144. School of Computer Science, CMU.

Bellifemine, F., Caire, G., & Greenwood, D. (2007). *Developming multi-agent systems with JADE.* John Wiley and Sons. doi:10.1002/9780470058411

Bresciani, P., Perini, A., Giorgini, P., Giunchiglia, F., & Mylopoulos, J. (2004). Tropos an agent-oriented software de- velopment methodology. *Autonomous Agents and Multi-Agent Systems, 8*(3), 203–236. doi:10.1023/B:AGNT.0000018806.20944.ef

Briot, J. P., & Gasser, L. (1998). Agents and concurrent objects. *IEEE Concurrency, 6*(4), 74–77. doi:10.1109/4434.736431

Castelfranchi, C., Dignum, F., Jonker, C. M., & Treur, J. (1999). Deliberate normative agents: Principles and architecture. *Lecture Notes in Computer Science, 1757,* 364–378. doi:10.1007/10719619_27

Cohen, P. R. & Levesque, H. J. (1990). Intention is choice with commitment. *Artificial Intelligence, 42*(3).

Coordinating Team. F.-O. (2012). *Fipa-os developers guide.* Retrieved from http://citeseer.ist.psu.edu/477218.html

Coulouris, G., Dollimore, J., & Kindberg, T. (2000). *Distributed systems: Concepts and design.* Addison-Wesley Longman Publishing Co., Inc.

Dempster, A. P. (1968). A generalization of bayesian inference. *Journal of the Royal Statistical Society. Series A (General), 30,* 205–247.

DeGroot, M., & Schervish, M. (2002). *Probability and statistics* (3rd ed.). Addison Wesley.

Eberhart, R. C., & Shi, Y. (2007). *Computational intelligence: concepts to implementations.* Morgan Kaufmann. doi:10.1016/B978-155860759-0/50002-0

Ebay. (2012). Retrieved from http://www.ebay.com

Hewitt, C. (1985). The challenge of open systems. *Byte, 10*(4), 223–242.

Huberman, B. A., & Hogg, T. (1995). Communities of practice: Performance and evolution. *Computational & Mathematical Organization Theory, 1*(1), 73–92. doi:10.1007/BF01307829

Huynh, T. D. (2006). *Trust and Reputation in Open Multi-agent Systems* (PhD thesis). Schools of Electronics and Computer Science, University of Southampton.

Huynh, T. D., Jennings, N. R., & Shadbolt, N. R. (2006). An integrated trust and reputation model for open multi-agent systems. *Autonomous Agents and Multi-Agent Systems, 13*(2), 119–154. doi:10.1007/s10458-005-6825-4

Ferber, J. (1999). *Multi-Agent Systems: An Introduction to Distributed Artificial Intelligence*. Addison-Wesley.

Josang, A., Ismail, R., & Boyd, C. (2007). A survey of trust and reputation systems for online service provision. *Decision Support Systems, 43*(2), 618–644. doi:10.1016/j.dss.2005.05.019

Rosenschein, J. S., & Zlotkin, G. (1994). *Rules of Encounter: Designing Conventions for Automated Negotiation among Computers*. The MIT Press.

Josang, A., & Pope, R. S. (2005). *Semantic constraints for trust transitivity. APCCM 2005*. University of Newcastle.

Grosz, B., & Kraus, S. (1996). Collaborative plans for complex group actions. *Artificial Intelligence, 86*(2), 269–357. doi:10.1016/0004-3702(95)00103-4

Drexler, K.E. (1988). Incentive engineering for computational resource management. In *The Ecology of Computation* (pp. 231-266). Academic Press.

Kinny, D., George, M., & Rao, A. (1996). A methodology and modelling technique for systems of bdi agents. *Lecture Notes in Computer Science, 1038*, 56–71. doi:10.1007/BFb0031846

Kraus, S. (1997). Negotiation and cooperation in multi-agent environments. *Artificial Intelligence Journal*.

Labrou, Y., & Finin, T. (1997). *A proposal for a new kqml specification. TR-CS-9703*. UMBC.

Labrou, Y., Finin, T., & Peng, Y. (1999). IEEE intelligent systems and their applications. *IEEE Intelligent Systems & their Applications, 14*(2), 45–52. doi:10.1109/5254.757631

Laboratory, G. (2005). Agent system development hands-on exercise, easss-05 (7th European agent systems summer school). Technical report, Utrecht.

Lenat, D. B., & Brown, J. S. (1984). Why am and eurisko appear to work. *Artificial Intelligence, 23*(3), 269–294. doi:10.1016/0004-3702(84)90016-X

Levesque, H. J. (1990). All i know: A study in autoepistemic logic. *Artificial Intelligence, 42*, 263–309.

Luke, T. W. (2006). *Agent-based trust and reputation in the context of inaccurate information sources* (PhD thesis). Schools of Electronics and Computer Science, University of Southampton.

Teacy L, W. T., Patel, J., Jennings, N. R. & Luck, M. (2005). Coping with inaccurate reputation sources: Experimental analysis of a probabilistic trust model. *AAMAS05*.

Panait, L., & Luke, S. (2005). Cooperative multi-agent learning: The state of the art. *Autonomous Agents and Multi-Agent Systems*, *11*(3), 387–434. doi:10.1007/s10458-005-2631-2

Nwana, H., Ndumu, D., Lee, L., & Collis, J. (1999). Zeus: a toolkit and approach for building distributed multi-agent systems. *Proceedings of the Third International Conference on Autonomous Agents*, 360-361 doi:10.1145/301136.301234

Marsh, S. (1994a). *Formalising Trust as a Computational Concept* (PhD thesis). Department of Mathematics and Computer Science, University of Stirling.

Marsh, S. (1994b). Trust in distributed artificial intelligence. *Lecture Notes in Computer Science*, *830*, 94–112. doi:10.1007/3-540-58266-5_6

Minsky, N. H., & Murata, T. (2004). On manageability and robustness of open multi-agent systems. *Lecture Notes in Computer Science*, *2940*, 189–206. doi:10.1007/978-3-540-24625-1_11

Moore, R. (1990). *A formal theory of knowledge and action', In formalizing common sense*. Ablex Publishing Corporation.

Ourston, D. & Mooney, R. J. (1994). Theory refinement combining analytical and empirical methods. *Artificial Intelligence, 66*(2), 273-309.

Pazzani, M., & Kibler, D. (1991). The utility of knowledge in inductive learning. *Machine Learning*, *9*(1), 57–94. doi:10.1007/BF00993254

Pazzani, M., Merz, C., Murphy, P., Ali, K., Hume, T., & Brunk, C. (1994). Reducing misclassication costs. *Proceedings of the Eleventh International Conference on Machine Learning*, 217-225.

Rothkopf, M. H. (2003). The future of e-markets. *Journal of Economic Literature*, *41*(1), 214.

Sabater, J., & Sierra, C. (2001). Regret: areputation model for gregarious societies. *Fourth workshop on deception fraud and trust in agent societies*, 61-70.

Singh, M. P. (1994). Multiagent systems: A theoretical framework for intention as, know how, and communications. *Lecture Notes in Artificial Intelligence, 799*.

Shoham, Y. (1992). Agent-oriented programming: An overview and summary of recent research. *Proc. of Artificial Intelligence*.

Shoham, Y. (1993). Agent-oriented programming. *Artificial Intelligence*, *60*, 51–92.

Simon, H. A. (1996). *The Science of Artificial* (3rd ed.). The MIT Press.

Smith, R. G. (1980). The contract net protocol: High-level communication and control in a distributed problem solver. *IEEE Transactions on Computers*, *C-29*(12), 1104–1113. doi:10.1109/TC.1980.1675516

Simon, H. A. (1996). *The Science of Artificial* (3rd ed.). The MIT Press.

Simon Parsons, M. W. (2002). Game theory and decision theory in multi-agent systems. *Autonomous Agents and Multi-Agent Systems, 5*(3), 243–254. doi:10.1023/A:1015575522401

Subrahmanian, V. S., Bonatti, P., Dix, J., Eiter, T., Kraus, S., Ozcan, F., & Ross, R. (2000). *Heterogeneous Agent Systems*. The MIT Press.

Werger, B. B. (1999). Cooperation without deliberation: A minimal behavior-based approach to multi-robot teams. *Artificial Intelligence, 110*(2), 293–320. doi:10.1016/S0004-3702(99)00023-5

Wooldridge, M. J. (2002). *An introduction to multiagent systems*. John Wiley and Sons.

Wooldridge, M. J. (2000). *Reasoning about rational agents*. The MIT Press.

Wooldridge, M., & Jennings., N. R. (1994). Towards a theory of cooperative problem solving. *Proc. of Modelling Autonomous Agent in a Multi-Agent World*.

Zacharia, G., & Maes, P. (1999). Collaborative Reputation Mechanisms in Electronic Marketplaces. *Proc. 32nd Hawaii International Conf on System Sciences*.

Yu, B., & Singh, M. P. (2000). *A social mechanism of reputation management in electronic communities*. Cooperative Information Agents IV - The Future of Information. doi:10.1007/978-3-540-45012-2_15

Chapter 17
Neural Trust Model

Gehao Lu
University of Huddersfield, UK & Yunnan University, China

Joan Lu
University of Huddersfield, UK

ABSTRACT

The problems found in the existing models push the researcher to look for a better solution for computational trust and computational reputation. According the problem exposed earlier, the newly proposed model should be a systematic model which supports both trust and reputation. The model should also take the learning capability for agents into consideration because agents cannot quickly adapt to the changes without learning. The model also needs to have the ability to make decisions according to its recognition of trust. Before actually building the model, it is necessary to analyze the concept of trust. Usually when people say trust they mean human trust, however, in this research trust refers to computational trust. How human trust is different from computational trust is a very interesting question. The answers to the question helped the researcher recover many features of computational trust and built a solid theoretical foundation for the proposed model. The definitions of trust in different disciplines such as economy, sociology and psychology will be compared. A possible definition of computational trust will be made and such trust from several different perspectives will be analyzed. The description of the model is important. As a whole, it is represented as a framework that defines components and component relationships. As the concrete components, the purposes and responsibilities of the specific component are explained. This is to illustrate the static structure of the model. The dynamic structure of the model is described as the process of executing the model.

1. CONCEPT ANALYSIS

1.1 Trust in Human Society

In any dictionary, trust is defined both as a noun and as a verb. There are three major dictionaries are chosen to gain insight into the meaning. In Oxford online dictionary (Oxford, 2011), the word trust is defined as: \1) (noun) firm belief in the reliability, truth, or ability of someone or something; 2) (noun)

DOI: 10.4018/978-1-5225-1884-6.ch017

an arrangement whereby a person (a trustee) holds property as its nominal owner for the good of one or more beneficiaries; 3) (verb) believe in the reliability, truth, or ability of "; In the Merriam-Webster online dictionary (Merriam-Webster, 2011), the word trust is defined as: \1) assured reliance on the character, ability, strength, or truth of someone or something; 2) dependence on something future or contingent; 3) a property interest held by one person for the benefit of another; 4) a charge or duty imposed in faith or confidence or as a condition of some relationship. 5) (verb) to place confidence ". In the Longman online dictionary (Longman, 2011), the word trust is defined as:

1.   A strong belief in the honesty, goodness etc. of someone or something;
2.   (Verb) to believe that someone is honest or will not do anything bad or wrong;
3.   Facts/judgment to be sure that something is correct or right ".

All these definitions have something in common: First, in essence, trust is a human belief which is held by the host. Second, the object or the target of the trust is the trustee. The contents of the trust are the ability of trustee, and the truth told by the trustee or the reliability of the trustee. Third, the relationship between the host and the trustee is reliance or dependence. The host delegates its benefit related activities to the trustee and relies on or depends on the trustee.

The typical definition of trust in sociology (Mayer et al., 1995) follows the general intuition about trust and contains such elements as: the willingness of one party (trustor) to rely on the actions of another party (trustee); reasonable expectation (confidence) of the trustor that the trustee will behave in a way beneficial to the trustor; risk of harm to the trustor if the trustee will not behave accordingly; and the absence of trustor's enforcement or control over actions performed by the trustee (?).

In psychology, according to the psychoanalyst Erik Erikson, trust believes that the person whom is trusted will do what is expected (Cofta, 2007). Trust is integral to the idea of social influence: it is easier to influence or persuade someone who is trusting. The notion of trust is increasingly adopted to predict acceptance of behaviors by others, institutions (e.g. government agencies) and objects such as machines. However, once again, the perception of honesty, competence and value similarity (slightly similar to benevolence) are essential.

In Economics, trust is also seen as an economic lubricant, reducing the cost of transactions, enabling new forms of cooperation and generally furthering business activities, employment and prosperity. This observation created a significant interest in considering trust as a form of social capital and has led research into closer understanding of the process of creation and distribution of such capital (Fukuyama, 1996).

All the above discussion about trust refers to human trust or trust in human society. For a multi-agent system, thousands of autonomous agents interact with each other without a moment's pause and also create or emerge as a virtual society. These agents are proactive agents with clear goal to pursue. As an important social mechanism, trust can also play a critical role in the agent society to promote the effectiveness of the interactions. Such trust for an agent or for a computer program can be called "computational trust". Computational trust is a simulation of human trust but with its own unique characteristics. Next, the concept of the computational trust will be explained in details.

2. COMPUTATIONAL TRUST

2.1 Definition

After analyzing the concept of trust from different aspects and disciplines, the research needs to make its own definition so that this definition can be the foundation of further discussions. The definition of the computational trust in this research is defined as:

Computational trust is a belief that an agent (trustor) perceived for another agent (trustee) in a specific domain and in a specific duration, the belief is that the trustee is honest, reliable and capable of delegating the trustor's benefit. Namely, the information provided by the trustee is true; the trustee has the ability to successfully finish the trustor's delegated jobs; the trustee is a reliable partner to cooperate in specific tasks.

There are some important composing words for this definition: belief, trustor, trustee, object, duration. These words also reflect some features of the computational trust. Figure 1 illustrates the features of the computational trust.

- **Belief:** Belief is introduced into many agent design models. It is also the core part of Belief, Desire and Intention (BDI) model (Kinny et al., 1996). The computational trust is a special type of belief which only focuses on social agents in a virtual society.
- **Trustor and Trustee:** Every trust relationship must have a pair of trustor and trustee. Trustor and trustee are just role name in a trust relationship. In a virtual society, an agent could be a trustor in one scenario and be a trustee in another scenario. Such role allocation also implies a direction in the trust relationship. If a line with arrow is drawn to represent the relationship, then the arrow

Figure 1. Features: the features of the computational trust

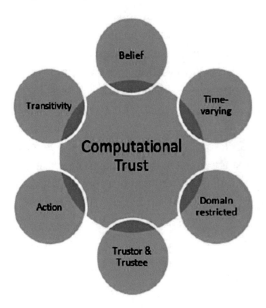

should point to the trustee form the trustor. Take an electronic transaction as an example. The buyer agent is the trustor who will trust the seller agent. The seller agent is the trustee who will be trusted by the buyer agent.

- **Domain Restricted:** The computational trust is domain restricted because the trust without domain is nonsense and impossible to operate. An agent trusts another agent only on some specific domain. A domain is just a concept of set or collection. It reveals a fact that an agent is trusted only in its familiar scope. A domain can be an industry, a type of product, a geographical area, etc. It is possible to generalize the model in the future through introducing an ontology layer which supports the semantics from multiple domains so that the agent can carry out trust recognition tasks in different standard domains. Take figure 3 as an example. In an electronic market, Agent A trust Agent B in the domain of publishing and book sales, while Agent A does not trust Agent B in the domain of food and restaurant because B is only a dealer agent for publishing industry.

- **Time Sensitivity:** The computational trust is dynamical, that is, it will not stay in an unchangeable state, and it is always changing with the outside environment. Time is a dimension that measures the sequence of state changing. Thus the computational trust can be said as Time sensitivity. The state of the trust is changing as time elapses.

- **Transitivity:** In a multi-agent context, computational trust is not just a belief in the individual agent. It is a social mechanism. It is generated from the individual agent and propagated to the other agent in the society and so the computational trust is transitive. Most of the time, the transitive message is also called reputation. Of course, it cannot be propagated without any boundary and any loss. The mechanism of reputation is discussed later.

- **Action:** As a belief, the computational trust will not directly lead to actions between agents. The belief is only knowledge about some specific agent. Such knowledge is only used to support the decision making on whether to start an action. The computational trust helps an agent decide whether to take actions or give up actions based on the result of trustworthiness or untrustworthiness. Trustworthiness is also an important topic that will be discussed later.

Figure 2. Domain difference: computational trust should be designed to use in a specific domain because the trustworthiness is estimated from different perspective in different domain.

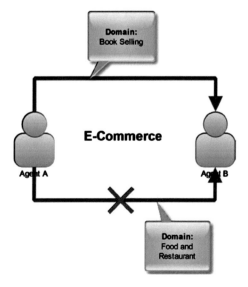

Computational trust can be used in the transactions of Electronic Commerce which are participated by autonomous agents. Agents can choose to trust or not trust its potential trading partner. Such trust may lead to subsequent transactions or denial of transactions depending on the belief of trust. Computational trust can also be used in a cooperation scenario which requires the participating agents to interact with each other. For example, in robot soccer game, whether two agents cooperate with each other to make a shoot or pass depends on whether they have belief of trust in the other one. If they do not have the trust then such cooperation is not considered and they will look for another agent that they trust to cooperate. In fact, like human societies, computational trust is also an important lubricant that makes the virtual society operate in a more efficient and effective way. Once multiple agents are assembling, there must be a space for the computational agent. Just like a machine, it needs to be lubricated by the machine oil in order to keep its different components running without wearing and tearing.

2.2 Computational Trust vs. Human Trust

The idea of computational trust is borrowed from human societies. Just like the autonomous agents are simulations of human individuals. The computational trust is also a type of simulation based upon human trust. However, the physical foundation of the computational trust is the electronic computer. The living context of agents is an Internet based virtual society which is different from the real world of human being. Such facts decide that computational trust must have some characteristics that human trust does not have. The difference between the two types of trust is deserved to be investigated. Through studying their differences, the researcher can learn the advantages and disadvantages of human trust and what mechanisms those advantages are based upon. The researcher can also see how computational trust avoids the disadvantages of human trust due to its physical limitations. The researcher can obtain the ideas of how to design good mechanisms appropriate for multi-agent systems.

Table 1 tries to analyze the differences between the computational trust and the human trust from seven facets. These facets cover the actor involved, the physical and social foundation, the belief model, the capability of storage and transitivity, the range of domains and the applicability.

The involved actors in computational trust are the autonomous agents in multi-agent systems while the involved actors in human trust are the human individuals in the human society. Both forms of trust can use the same roles to represent the functions played by the actors, that is, the trustor who generates the trust and the trustee who is endowed with the trust.

All autonomous agents are actually computer programs in the form of agents. The physical representation of computational trust is electronic computers. These agents are theoretically imperishable although they might have their usage life cycle. Human trust is the emergent product of the human brain, and the human brain is materially supported by the human body. Such brain and body are mortal and suffer from aging and death.

The Internet is the basis of multi-agent systems. It connects agents from different applications, autonomous domains or virtual societies. It is the communication foundation and the protocol foundation of the heterogeneous agents. For human trust, the real society connects every person. Human individuals use languages to communicate with each other. The trust emerged from the brain is also expressed and propagated through messages in the form of languages.

Whether in dictionary explanations for human trust or in the above explanations for the computational trust, they both define the trust as a belief. The only difference is one is a belief emerged from the biological brain, the other is a belief represented by electronic circuits. This now also brings the researcher

Table 1. Computational trust vs. human trust: the difference between computational trust and human trust

	Computational Trust	Human Trust
Involved actors	Autonomous agents (as role of trustors and trustees)	Human individuals (as role of trustors and trustees)
Physical foundation	Programs designed for agents running on electronic computer	Human brain and human body
Social foundation	Internet based virtual society which is highly specialized and motivated.	Individual human and their society
Belief models	Usually based on the simple arithmetic models, the statistic models, or the machine learning models	Human nervous system
Storage capability	Based on the computer memories which can be extended, thus the capability is theoretically unlimited.	The human brain has its biological lifecycle. The memory can be forgotten due to aging. Thus the capability is limited and volatile.
Transitive capability	The transitive speed is high enough to ignore the geographical difference. The information can be intact.	The transitive speed is slow and the information tends to be distorted to form "rumors".
Range of domains	Highly specialized to a specific object, a set of tasks, an industry or a designed virtual society.	Highly general, cover all the areas of the human cognition. The trust in human tends to be more generalized and can be applied across different domains.

to the most difficult question: what is a belief and how to represent it? Until now, the mystery of human brain has not been fully explored by the neurological science (Ralph, 1999). For computational trust, the simplest way to represent the belief is to use an arithmetic equation to reflect it. The statistic method is also widely used to express the belief in a statistical way. Machine learning is another way which emphasizes the computational trust as a belief that can be learned. The human trust is emerged from the human nervous system. As the other type of beliefs, the trust belief is the product of connection of millions of neurons (Adolphs, 2002).

There is a big difference between the computational trust and the human trust in the facet of the storage capabilities. The computational trust can be stored in the computer's secondary storage as binary data while the human trust can only be stored in some part of the brain. The computer is theoretically everlasting and the memory is theoretically infinite. This means computer based agents can memorize every single detail that is related to the computational trust. Human memory is much less powerful and often suffers from the forgotten due to aging and death.

The transitivity capability is also the strength of the computational trust. The message about trust (reputation) propagated along the network. The speed of transmission equals to the speed of electrons without considering the time spent for the congestion and routing. The accuracy of the message is also pretty good because there is no loss or intended distortion even after it passes through thousands of nodes. The human trust is unavoidably limited by its physical foundation. The speed of human to human transmission is slow even after using the modern communication technologies. The more serious problem is inaccuracy: the message (reputation) sent out is always magnified, dwindled, or distorted because of intended or unintended reasons. The spreading of rumors is a typical example of the problematic human reputation propagation.

There is also big gap between these two types of trust in the range of domain. For computational trust, it is highly specialized and motivated for some specific domain. For example, an agent designed to be used in a game will not have the same domain of trust as an agent designed for an e-business scenario. However, the human trust is different, it is much more general. Sometimes such generality may lead to some interesting trust transferring phenomenon. For example, if a person trusts a movie actor or actress because of his or her performance, they will transfer such trust to the product that the actor or actress is endorsing. In this example, the domain of trust has been shifted from the movie into the commercial product. The reason of the gap is that the computational trust is a designed trust whereas the human trust is a natural product which is emerged from the human society. Trust transferring phenomenon is useful for agents in some scenario. For example, when agents learn trust from a domain of the desktop computer transaction, such trust is valuable referential experience for a domain of the computer peripherals in case two domains belong to semantically related ontologies.

In a word, there is the necessity to simulate the human trust in the multi-agent system and virtual society in order to lubricate the interaction of agents. The computational trust can apply many ideas and mechanisms which appear in human society but that does not mean computational trust must strictly follow the ways of human trust. Strictly following human's way only leads to simulated human trust instead of computational trust. In fact, the transitivity and storage capability can be designed as even more powerful than the human trust. The best solution is to select the appropriate idea from human trust while rejecting inappropriate. Thus the researcher makes a list which states the points that the computational trust can learn from the human trust and another list which states the points that the computational trust can improve based on the human trust:

- Points can be borrowed:
  - Belief including trust belief is generated from human nervous system. The mechanism can be explained from theory of neuroscience. This reminds the researcher that the computational trust can also be designed in technology of artificial neural network.
- Points need improvement:
  - The ability of speedy transitivity for the computational trust should be promoted. The reputation network can be extended to a reasonably far distance. The computational trust should be propagated without any loss and distortion. There should not be things like "rumors" in the virtual society.
  - The autonomous agent should remember all the information that is related to its trust belief because it does have such storage space and extending potentials. There is no such thing as "forgetting" for agents. The computational trust is based upon all the interaction experiences that the agent might have in its life cycle.
  - For each domain, an agent needs one type of trust to support. Agents can freely extend its domains in case they need to take part in additional domains. The human trust can be transitive between domains. Trust to a good performance of a movie star can be transferred to trust to the product represented by the movie star. However it is not necessary for agent to behave like human in this transitivity issue. Agent can have ontology designed for standardizing the trust domain and the related semantics.

2.3 Trustworthiness and Untrustworthiness

In Oxford online dictionary (Oxford, 2011), the word "trustworthy" means: "able to be relied on as honest or truthful". In this research, the trustworthiness and the untrust-worthiness are defined as: they are decisions that are made by the autonomous agent based on the belief of computational trust. The positive decision, i.e., trustworthiness, will lead to actions of agent cooperation, delegation or transaction, while the negative decision, i.e., untrustworthiness will stop any further actions.

Figure 3 illustrates the relationship between the computational trust and the trustworthiness/untrustworthiness. The computational trust provides a belief basis for decision making. When an agent needs to start a task that involves another agent, the host agent first initiates a trustworthy judgment. It checks its belief to see whether the specific target agent can be trusted. The result is either trustworthiness that allows the agent to carry out its action or untrustworthiness that forbids the agent to go ahead.

2.4 Reputation

In Oxford online dictionary (Oxford, 2011), the word "reputation" means: "the beliefs or opinions that are generally held about someone or something, or a widespread belief that someone or something has a particular characteristic". In this research, the computational reputation is defined as: a message that is transmitted between agents. The content of the message is information about the trustworthiness or untrustworthiness of another specific target agent. Such information is generated according to the belief of trust hold by the initiator agent toward the target agent. The purpose of the reputation is to give recommendation to the other agents who lack the direct interaction experience with the target agent so that the target agent can make better decision with ease. Thus the reputation can increase the efficiency of the whole system.

The computational reputation is the byproduct of the computational trust. But it does not equal to the computational trust. Because the trust is an individual belief that needs to be generated from many times of direct interactions, the reputation is only a recommendation which cannot substitute the agents' own experiences and cognitions in their special environments. The reputation can influence the formation of the belief of trust and vice versa. It can be looked as an influential element of the trust belief, though such element is introduced as indirect experiences from other agents.

Figure 3. Relationship: the relationship between computational trust and trustworthiness

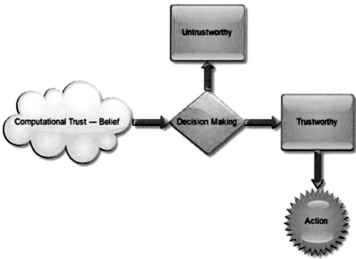

The transitivity (propagation) is the basic characteristic of the computational reputation. The propagation can take many forms. The initiator agent can only send the reputation to its close neighbor or it can send the reputation to all the agents in the system or in the virtual society. The distance of transmission is a design variable for the propagation mechanism. Additionally, whether the reputation can be propagated intact is another consideration. It is reasonable to introduce the concept of decaying to make the reputation transmit more naturally. When the reputation is propagated relatively long, it can decay according with the distance so that the reputation will not be transmitted unrestrictedly. The distance of propagation is controlled by the rate of decaying and its initial strength.

Figure 4 is an example of the reputation propagation. Agent A has experiences of transactions, cooperation or delegations with Agent B. In the virtual society, Agent C is preparing to have some type of interactions with Agent B. It needs indirect experience with Agent B to help it enhance successful possibility of the potential interactions. It turns to Agent A for recommendations. According to the belief of trust toward Agent B, Agent A sends out a reputation to Agent C. Agent C receives the reputation and takes it as an influential element to update its own belief of trust. Then according to its updated belief of trust, Agent C decides whether to take further action with Agent B. Furthermore, Agent C also sends the reputation to Agent D when it learns that Agent D might also have the needs to interact with Agent B. But the reputation sent by Agent D is possibly decayed because it is already second layer node relative from Agent A.

2.5 Design Consideration

2.5.1 Learning Trust Patterns

In multi-agent systems, "Beliefs represent the informational state of the agent, in other words its beliefs about the world (including itself and other agents). Beliefs can also include inference rules, allowing

Figure 4. Example: the example of reputation propagation

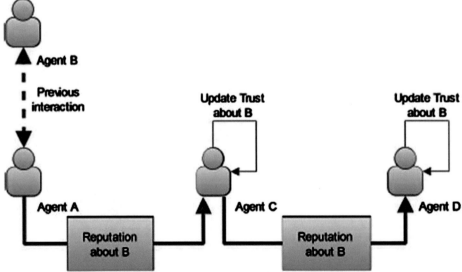

forward chaining to lead to new beliefs. Using the term belief rather than knowledge recognizes that what an agent believes may not necessarily be true (and in fact may change in the future)" (Wikipedia, 2012). From this dentition, it is clear that the belief is also information. Representing beliefs is actually a task of representing the information state of the agent. There are a variety of methods to represent information. In the hardware level, the computers use the binary or octal number system to record information. In the application level, the programs make use of the relational algebra based relational database or make use of the Unicode text file to record information. For information in the belief, these above methods are all applicable. But a more abstract higher level of description is still needed.

In traditional methods like Marsh model (Marsh, 1994b), basically, they deem the computational trust as a numerical value. So that they can use mathematical equations or statistical equations to produce a numerical trust value. Such value is also a good indicator for trustworthy level. The decision making is simply to set a threshold for the value: over the threshold, trustworthy; and under the threshold, untrustworthy. For example, in Marsh model (Marsh, 1994b), the trust value is calculated using his equations (Marsh, 1994b):

$$T_x(y,\alpha) = U_x(\alpha) \times I_x(\alpha) \times \widehat{T_x(y)}$$

$$CT_x(y,\alpha) = \frac{PerceivedRisk_x(\alpha)}{PerceivedCompetence_x(\alpha,y)} \times I_x(\alpha)$$

In the above equations, the conceived trust value (CTx(y,)) is the threshold. If the value of Tx(y,) is greater than or equals to the conceived trust value (CTx(y,)), an agent x will cooperate with another agent y. The problem of such traditional methods is: the numerical value is not adaptive enough to reflect the changes of the trust relationship. They are single dimensional instead of multi-dimensional.

To perceive the beliefs of computational trust, agents need to learn from their historical interactions and extract beliefs from the experiences. For computational agents, learning refers to machine learning and the intuitive results of learning are patterns that reflect the emerged characteristic of the interactions. Such characteristics are the informational states that the computational trust requires. And so the research proposes to use matrix like pattern learned from agents' interactions to realize the belief of the computational trust. The topological structure of the matrix like pattern can represent the changes of the trust relationship quickly and efficiently. The following matrix is an example which can represent a trust belief.

$$\begin{pmatrix} 0 & -3 & 0 \\ -1 & 8 & 6 \\ -2 & 0 & 1 \end{pmatrix}$$

The next question is which type of machine learning mechanism is appropriate for learning the computational trust and what kind of patterns is suitable for representing the computational trust. The mechanisms used should meet the following requirements of the belief information, especially the trust belief information:

- The patterns of agents' beliefs should be a form that meets the need of frequently mutable and updatable informational state. Agents keep on interacting with each other and every interaction will lead to changes to the informational state of the beliefs. Thus the representing form should record the changes and update the original belief as soon as possible. The best way is to enforce the real-time updating of the agents' beliefs.
- The patterns of agents' beliefs should be a form that meets the need of continuous accumulation of the informational state. Beliefs are deposits of experiences based on thousands of interactions. Every piece of results needs to be reflected on the patterns. The pattern should be compact enough in order to save storage space while it should be complete without losing any details of interactions as well.
- To record the information for each interaction only finishes the first stage of the patterns. The ultimate goal of choosing an appropriate pattern is to find out the characteristics which exhibit from the form. Because only through finding the characteristics in the belief can agents carry out trust related decision making and actions. Thus the form needs the ability to show the characteristics from the seemingly unrelated data in an organized or emerged way.
- The mechanism that generates the pattern should allow multiple input dimensions because most agents' interactions generate multi-dimensional raw information. The mechanism should transform that raw information to some sensible characteristics.

There are many types of machine learning algorithms. The requirements discussed above support the choice of a neural network as the basic trust learning architecture. The neural network is highly adaptable to the changes in the environments. It can adjust the weight to reflect the changes. This makes the neural network a robust solution for learning computational trust. The pattern generated from neural network can represent the belief precisely. Figure 5 illustrates the relationship among trust belief, trust pattern and learning methods.

Figure 5. Relationship: trust belief, trust pattern and learning methods

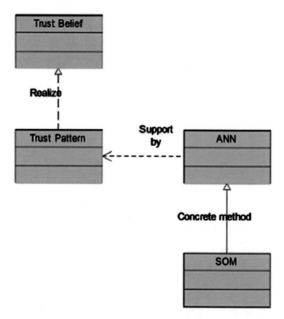

1. **Supervised or Unsupervised:** Most of the time, neural network is used as a supervised learning mechanism. The network is fed with prepared training data and learns typical patterns from these typical data. This is good solution for problems like handwriting recognition and natural language recognition because the typical training data is easy to be organized. However, in the virtual society of autonomous agents, to prepare the typical training data is a much more difficult job to do. The behaviors of agents are versatile. It is difficult to define a standard behavior that is "good" for agents. There are too many types of domains with too many types of agents. There are no consensuses on the definition of "good".

    Furthermore, the dimensions of the input data for the network changes with different domains. This means that if a set of data in one domain is selected as the training data. Such training data is not representative enough to cover varieties of domains. Thus, the learning of computational trust should be unsupervised learning, that is, there is no prepared training data. The process of learning is totally based on the input data generated from the real time interactions. Each round of the interaction is accompanied with a round of the trust learning. The learning process is all throughout an agent's life cycle.

2. **Organized or Emerged:** The representations of the beliefs can be as simple as expressions like "x=x+1" or "x=x-1". The variable x represents the belief of the computational trust for a specific agent. And after each round of the interaction, the host agent accumulates or decreases the variable according to the result of the interaction. A positive result leads to "+1" while the negative result leads to "-1". Such kinds of equations are simple but effective. They become the basic foundations of the trust model for many current successful commercial web sites. Some models also use the statistical theories to construct their computational trusts. In this case, the computational trust is deemed as a mathematical probability. These models in details have been discussed earlier, whether the variables or the probabilities are an organized way of representing the computational trust. The mathematical models are applied to abstract the process of the belief generation. In a specific case like Electronic commerce, it works perfectly. However, the mathematical models are not general enough. The researcher has to build a specialized one for each domain or each application. Take the human brain as a comparison, the belief of the trust is more or less a feeling instead of a real number of rank or a probability. It is an emerged product of the millions of connected neurons in the brain. The autonomous agents need the generality and adaptability like the human brain and the autonomous agents needs to learn trust in their life cycle gradually. The problem of acquiring computational trust should be looked as a problem of machine learning. The computational trust is a pattern that emerged from the experiences of the interactions. There is no fixed formulation to produce trust as in the mathematical models. In this research, computational trust tends to be created as a "feeling" of the autonomous agent.

2.6 Decision Making for Trustworthiness

The computational beliefs are only patterns that reflect some characteristics of the interactions. Actions are not the direct result of the belief. The beliefs are mind level foundations for the action. It is not compulsory that the belief of trust must leads to actions. Only when the autonomous agents have an intention to start an interaction with another specific agent, then the belief is used to support the decision on whether to perform the action or not. The results of the decision as mentioned previously are either trustworthiness or untrustworthiness. The way of using the beliefs of the computational trusts is the interest of the research.

In fact, the judgments on trustworthiness or untrustworthiness can be deemed as a problem of decision making. Decision making can be regarded as the mental processes (cognitive process) resulting in the selection of a course of action among several alternative scenarios. Every decision making process produces a final choice (McK-night and Chervany, 1996). The computational trust provides the information that the decision making needs. The result of decision making is the trustworthiness and untrustworthiness that leads to action or rejection.

As mentioned previously, all beliefs of the computational trust are patterns that emerged from the historical interactions between agents. In the human brain, a recent neuro-imaging study (Castelfranchi and Falcone, 2000) found distinctive patterns of neural activation in these regions depending on whether decisions were made on the basis of personal volition or following directions from someone else. Patients with damage to the ventromedial prefrontal cortex have difficulty making advantageous decisions (Mollering, 2005). This research has given the researcher some inspirations that the decision making for trustworthiness or not can also be based on the distinctive patterns that resides in the memory of the agents. Every interaction occurs will generate a pattern and each of the patterns shows some characteristics of the interactions. If a hypothesis, namely, all the agents are played in the domain, exists, the pattern generated from a successful interaction must be different from the pattern generated from a failed interaction. This difference can exhibit the good features and bad features of the patterns in the interactions. So to make a decision on trustworthiness, an agent can turn to its own beliefs and compare its patterns from positive interactions and from negative interactions. The result of comparison not only tell us whether the target agent is trustworthy or not, but also tell us how much the host agent can trust the target agent because the magnitude of the difference is an indicator how the bad pattern deviates from the good pattern. Figure 6 illustrates idea of comparing patterns from successful and failed interactions.

Figure 6. Decision making: how comparing patterns help make decision for trust-worthy or untrustworthy

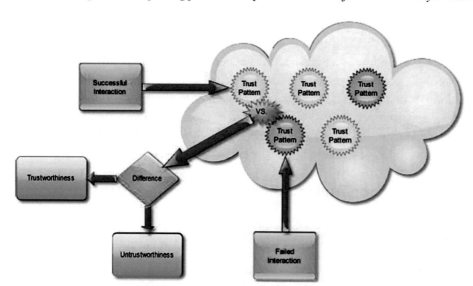

2.7 Trust with Reputation

The computational reputation is a not synonym of the computational trust. The reputation is a by-product of the society while the trust is an individual belief which is only suitable for an individual agent. The computational trusts are patterns learned from their interactions. The computational reputations are messages that are transmitted from one agent to another. It is the lubricating oil for the multi-agent based virtual society. The computational reputation is originated from the computational trust. An agent learns trust first and then produces reputation for its partner agents.

The reputation should reflect the host agent's impression toward the target agent. When an agent is asked to give reputation for a specific agent, it needs to check whether it has interacting experiences with the target agent before. If it does not, it stays neutral and rejects sending the reputations. If it has, it might have some patterns that are generated during the interactions with the target agent. To only send out these patterns as the reputation is not complete, because every pattern is a product of a concrete environment with many specific factors and every pattern is also a unique result of an agent learning. One agent's pattern should not be used by another agent directly. The other agent does not have the same pattern generating context as the initiate agent and the networks of recognizing trust for both agents are also formed in very different ways. The reputation can be simple messages that reflect recommendations of the host agent toward the target agent. When the agent requiring reputations receives the messages, the messages also become part of the input data of the trust learning algorithm. Such design is good because even the initiate agent send biased reputation; the receiver agent has the ability to learn it and adapt to the "lying" reputation. Figure 7 illustrates the process of generating, transmitting and receiving reputations.

Propagation is the major feature of the computational reputation. It lets the reputation transmit to two or more agents and it also makes the computational trust become a social influential factor for the virtual society. The agents in the propagating path create a chain of reputation propagation. The length of the chain equals the number of agents in that chain. The chain cannot be infinite due to the physical limitations and it is also bounded by the size of the virtual society. The maximum propagating distance is the length of the reputation chain. The distance can be set as a fixed length so that all the agents in the radius of the length are included and propagated. The distance can also be set to be dynamic. The concept of decay will help determine the dynamic distance.

There are three types of propagations: amplifying propagation, unaltered propagation and decaying propagation. In the amplifying propagation, the reputation is amplified a bit through every agent in

Figure 7. Reputation generation: the process of generating, transmitting and receiving reputations

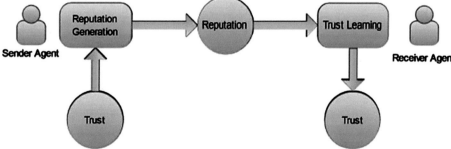

the propagating chain. It is not an ideal way of propagation. In human society, rumor spreading is an example of such type of propagation (Moreno et al., 2004). Such amplification is not controlled and sometimes it is negative and unpredictable. In a virtual society, amplifying propagation is superfluous or even harmful. So it should be avoided instead of being taken into consideration. In the unaltered propagation, the reputation remains unchanged regardless how many agents it has been passed through. The computer based agents are capable of memorizing all the related information. They do not suffer from aging and forgetfulness like human being, the reputation can reach the receiver agent intact. This is a good feature for keeping the accuracy and reliability of the reputations. In the decaying propagation, the reputation simulates the decaying phenomenon that happens in human society, the magnitude of the reputation decay along the transmitting chain. Each agent receives a shrunken reputation from its upper node. Decaying can keep the length of the propagation chain down dynamically. When the magnitude of reputation shrinks to zero at some agent, the chain is ended and the propagating is over.

From the initiative of the propagating reputations, there are two types of propagation: active propagation and passive propagation. In active propagation, an agent initiates the reputation propagation to its neighboring agents after it finishes an interaction with another agent. The reputation network is updated once an interaction happens between any two agents. For multi-agent system, the advantage of such mechanism is the timely updating of reputations. The disadvantage is that it may lead to big burden on performance. In the passive propagation, the agent does not initiate any active propagation unless it is inquired to do so. The advantages of passive propagation are that the system can avoid redundant propagation and improve performance. The disadvantage is that the update of reputations lags behind the interactions.

3. MODEL FRAMEWORK

After the analysis and discussions about the trust and the reputation, it is time to have a global framework designed for the computational trust and reputation. The frameworks design needs to reflect the design considerations earlier. Each facet of the considerations can be transformed into a mechanism design in the framework. The framework then becomes a systematic composition that is composed by several components.

3.1 Model Structure

Figure 8 illustrates structure of the computational trust and reputation framework. The outside rectangle delimits the bounds between the internal mechanisms of an autonomous host agent and the external environment that the other agents participate. The inside rectangles represent the processes for specific calculations or algorithms. The cycles represent data, information or results fed into the agent or sent out from the agent. The rounded rectangles represent the processed information, knowledge or patterns that are generated by the host agent. The actors represent the host agent and the receiver agent who receives reputations from the host agent. The arrows show the direction in which the information flows.

The framework is constructed with five major mechanisms (components). Inside the host agent: Trust learning mechanism, Trust estimation mechanism, decision making mechanism and reputation generation mechanism. Outside the host agent: the reputation propagation mechanism. There are no priorities for

Figure 8. Framework: framework of computational trust and reputation

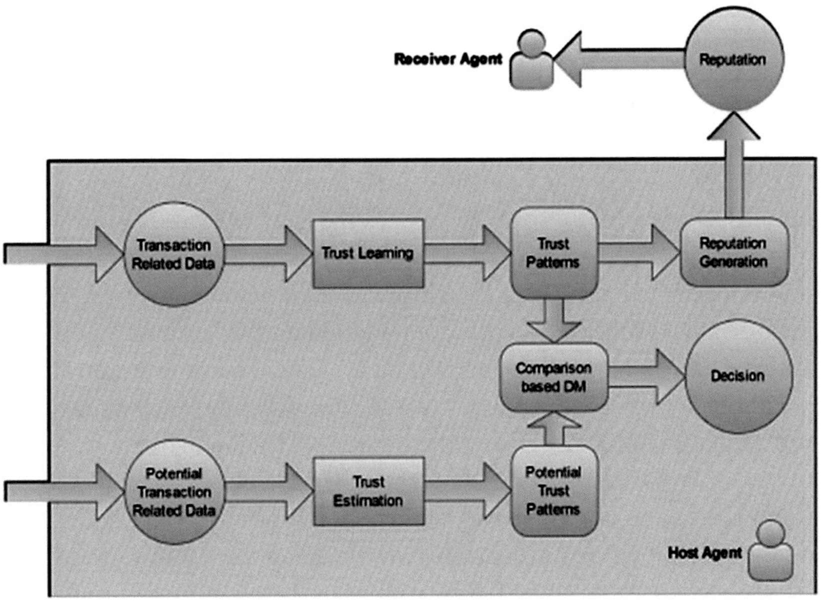

these mechanisms. Each mechanism can work independently, that is, each one can work parallel to one another. The direction of the arrows indicates where the information about transactions flow to which component in the framework. They also indicate the order that the transactional information is processed. Thus the framework works in three ways simultaneously.

- **Continuous Trust Learning:** The first way is continuous trust learning. An agent perceives and extracts the transaction or interaction related data as input to its learning algorithm. The algorithm processes the input data and generates the computational trust patterns. Those patterns are stored for future queries and comparisons. The continuous trust learning is the regular learning accompanied with any agent interactions. Each interaction leads to a repeated learning process. This learning is also the most frequent operation among the mechanisms of the framework.
- **Trust Estimation and Trustworthiness Decision Making:** The second way is trust estimation and trustworthy decision making. An agent prepares to have an interaction with another agent. Before the interaction actually occurs, the agent collects domain related information about the target agent. According to the potential interaction related data, the algorithm makes estimation and produces an estimated trust pattern. This estimated pattern is compared with the existing patterns that generated in the previous interactions. The result of the comparison is then an indicator of the trustworthiness or untrustworthiness toward the target. It helps the agent make a decision whether to trust a specific target agent to start an interaction or transaction.
- **Reputation Generation and Propagation:** The third way is reputation generation. When an agent initiates reputation propagation or it is required to do so, the historical patterns of the target agent are found out and compared with the memorized patterns. The result of comparison is also indicator of the trustworthiness of the target agent. This result is transformed into a form of

message that is fit for propagation and then is sent out to the receiver agents. The propagation mechanism controls the active/passive transmission of the reputation, the path of reputation transmission, the distance of the transmitting, and the decaying rate of the transmission.

3.2 Trust Learning Mechanism

In this research, the computational trust is deemed as patterns learned from agent interactions. The use of neural networks as the basic algorithm that generates the trust patterns is proposed earlier to address that the learning of trust patterns is emerged and unsupervised. This creates some preconditions for choosing appropriate specific algorithm in the alternatives of neural networks. The research chooses Self Organizing Map (SOM) as the basis of the computational trust learning algorithm. The researcher improves the traditional SOM and proposes a SOM based Trust Learning Algorithm (STL).

The STL algorithm can be executed in 9 steps: weight initialization, fetching input data, feed forward input, feed forward output, marking patterns, storing patterns, finding neighbors, updating weights and continuation. The task of initialization is to decide the initial weight of the neurons in the network. For each transaction that occurs, an agent receives various dimensions of transaction related results. The information about those results is organized into a vector. Then the feed forward input feeds the input vector to the STL network. After fetching the input vector, the input data is sent to the STL neurons. The major task of Feed forward output is to find out the winning neuron. As the author introduces in the SOM theory background, finding the largest value of product of weight and input vector is equivalent to find out the smallest distance between the weight vector and the input vector. To make the patterns useful, it is necessary to do a qualitative analysis against it as well. If the interaction is successful, then the pattern generated can be marked as good pattern; if it fails, then the pattern generated can be marked as bad. The drop points that compose the pattern can also be marked as good points or bad points. The perceived patterns can be stored as a two dimensional array. After storing the patterns, the network tends to adjust weights of the neighboring neurons around the center winning neuron. If the neighboring neurons are in the area of the radius, they are excited neighbors. All the neurons in the range of excited neighbors will get positive updating. If there exists multiple transactions that happened successively, the algorithm is executed in a loop.

The STL algorithm produces three types of patterns: transactional trust general, agent trust pattern and macro trust pattern. The transactional trust pattern is the direct product of the STL algorithm. The pattern records the recognized features of a specific transaction that happens between the host agent and its opponent agent. The agent trust pattern is the indirect product of the STL algorithm. It is an aggregation of transactional patterns for one specific agent over a specific duration. It is the agent's memory toward another agent that forms the basis of their interaction experiences. The macro trust pattern is also the indirect product of the STL algorithm. It is an aggregation of the agent patterns for all transactions. The reason of setting a macro trust pattern is that an agent needs a balanced view of trust over different agents and different transactions.

3.3 Trustworthiness Based Decision Making

Once the computational trust is recognized, another problem to be solved is how an agent makes a trustworthy decision which will lead to a future transaction or a future cooperation based upon the recognized trust patterns. The research proposes a "Trust-worthiness Estimation Algorithm" to solve the problem. The algorithm absorbs neural network component of the STL algorithm to do pre-recognition jobs and adds a search and comparison components to do estimation and recommendation jobs.

The algorithms can be expressed as having 6 steps: fetch input data, feed forward input, feed forward output, searching patterns, comparing patterns and giving recommendations. The process of fetching input data is as same as the first step in the STL algorithm. The input data are fed to the network in the form of input vector with various dimensions. The feed forward input in the estimation algorithm is as same as the feed forward input in the STL algorithm. The process of feed forward output in the estimation algorithm is as same as the process of feed forward output in the STL algorithm. But the result is processed in a different way. Once the predicted pattern is generated, a corresponding pattern should be retrieved from the agent pattern library. The identity of the target agent becomes the key to searching. Comparing patterns is the most critical step in the estimation algorithm. The basic principle of comparison is to put two patterns together and measure how big the differences are. There are mainly two types of difference: different drop points and different size of drop points. After calculating the result of the comparison between the macro trust pattern and the predicted trust pattern, the result can be an indicator of the degree of trustworthiness.

Here is a simple example of pattern comparison. The following matrices are used to represent different patterns. Matrix 1 represents the macro pattern:

$$\begin{pmatrix} 0 & -3 & 1 \\ 3 & 10 & 0 \\ 6 & -5 & 0 \end{pmatrix}$$

matrix 2 represent the estimated trust pattern 1:

$$\begin{pmatrix} 0 & 0 & 0 \\ 0 & 1 & 0 \\ 0 & 0 & 0 \end{pmatrix}$$

and matrix 3 represent the estimated trust pattern 2:

$$\begin{pmatrix} 0 & 0 & 0 \\ 0 & 0 & 0 \\ 0 & 1 & 0 \end{pmatrix}$$

In the macro pattern, the value as the element of the matrix represents the sum of the drop points which is the result of trust recognition after each round of transactions. In the estimated trust pattern, the value as the element of the matrices represent the exact drop point from the trust estimation before the transaction actually happening. Compare matrix 1 and matrix 2, the drop point of matrix 2 matches the point in matrix 1 with larger positive value which means better chance to be trustworthy. Instead, compare matrix 1 and matrix 3, the drop point of matrix 3 matches the point with negative value that represents less trustworthy.

3.4 Reputation Generation and Propagation

The basic trust pattern for an agent is a matrix with two types of drop points. The size of the success point or failure point is proportional to the times of successful interactions or failure interactions. The size difference provides a foundation about how the agent believes the trustworthiness is. The history of past interaction can also be recorded using the same style of pattern like the general trust pattern. The only difference is that the general pattern is design to contain all the drop points in all previous interactions. The drop points appeared in the specified pattern must be accumulated to the points on the general pattern. A reasonable reputation should consider both the general pattern and the specified pattern so that the individual performance can be compared with the general performance. The calculation of the difference should be put into a mathematical framework so that the result of the calculation is a numerical value which can be propagated along the network, accepted and absorbed by the inquiry agent.

The initiative agent sends the reputation value to the inquiry agent. The reputation receiving agent should also take the sender's reputation into account. Propagating the reputation through inquiry method may form a chain that connects multiple agents which forward or respond to the inquiry request. The research introduces a variable called "decaying coefficient", which can help adjust the degree of decaying speed. The coefficient could be moderate so that the distance of propagation is confined to reasonable clusters. When an agent accepts the reputation, it needs to update its trust pattern against specific agent using this reputation. The updating method is to simply put the reputation as the input data for the STL learning algorithm.

The research designs three forms of reputation propagation mechanisms: point-to-point based inquiry, broadcasting based propagation and observer based propagation. The point-to-point based Inquiry is the simplest and most effective way of the reputation propagation. In order to have some knowledge of the target agent, an agent can send a request to its own acquaint agents. The broadcasting propagation can cover wider propagation scope in a short time. Once the initiative agent has interacted with some specific target agent, it will generate a reputation reference and send this reference to all the agents in its domain or society. In the observer propagation, agents can be categorized into four roles: subject, target, subscriber and un-subscriber. The subject is an agent being watched by the other agent. Its behavior and its interaction with the other agents are interested by other agents. The key to design a subject agent is that it holds a subscriber list that contains all the agents' identities who are interested in the subject. A target agent is the agent that interacts with the subject agent. The result of their interaction will be propagated as a reputation reference.

Point-to-point based inquiry is appropriate for scenario that agents have clear list of the other agents in the virtual society. The efficiency of propagation is high because there is no redundant communication channel between agents who do not involve in the interaction. Broadcasting propagation is good for a simple scenario with limited number of agents and there is a necessity to let every agent in the society to know what happens. The efficiency of propagation is low because large bandwidth is wasted to build communications with every agent. Observer propagation is good for large scale virtual society like electronic commerce market. An agent only propagates reputation to those who have registered in its subscriber list. The efficiency of propagation is between the broadcasting propagation and point-to-point based inquiry.

4. SUMMARY

First, the concept of the computational trust and computational reputation is analyzed. The six core features of the computational trust have been figured out. The influences of each feature are explained. The comparison between the computational trust and the human trust is conducted, thus the reader can understand the origin of the computational trust and have insight about how computational trust is superior to the human trust. Then a systematic framework has been designed for the neural trust model which includes mechanisms and algorithms such as trust learning, trust estimation and reputation generation, and reputation propagation. The relationships among components are introduced and each component is also described briefly.

REFERENCES

Adolphs, R. (2002). Trust in the brain. *Nature Neuroscience, 5*(3), 192-194.

Castelfranchi, C., & Falcone, R. (2000). Trust is much more than subjective probability: Mental components and sources of trust.*Proc. of the 33rd Hawaii International Conference on System Sciences.* 52 doi:10.1109/HICSS.2000.926815

Cofta, P. (2007). Trust, Complexity and Control: Confidence in a Convergent World. John Wiley and Sons.

Fukuyama, F. (1996). *Trust: The Social Virtues and the Creation of Prosperity.* Touchstone Books.

Kinny, D., Georgeff, M., & Rao, A. (1996). A methodology and modelling technique for systems of bdi agents. *Lecture Notes in Computer Science, 1038*, 56-71.

Longman. (2011). *Longman online dictionary.* Retrieved from http://www.ldoceonline.com/dictionary/trust2:36

Marsh, S. (1994). Trust in distributed artificial intelligence. *Lecture Notes in Computer Science, 830*, 94.

Mayer, R., Davis, J. H., & Schoorman, F. (1995). An integrative model of organizational trust. *Academy of Management Review, 20*(3), 709-734.

McKnight, D. H., & Chervany, N. L. (1996). The meanings of trust. Technical report. University of Minnesota.

Merriam-Webster. (2011). *Merriam-Webster online dictionary.* Retrieved from http://www.merriam-webster.com/dictionary/trust

Mollering, G. (2005). The trust/control duality: An integrative perspective on positive expectations of others. *Int. Sociology, 20*(3), 283-305.

Moreno, Y., Nekovee, M., & Pacheco, A. F. (2004). Dynamics of rumor spreading in complex networks. *Physical Review Series E, 69.*

Oxford. (2011). *Oxford online dictionary.* Retrieved from http://oxforddictionaries.com/de_nition/trust

Ralph, A. (1999). Social cognition and the human brain. *Trends in Cognitive Sciences, 3*(12), 469-479.

Wikipedia. (2012). *Belief in Wikipedia.* Retrieved from http://en.wikipedia.org/wiki/Belief

Chapter 18
Trust Learning and Estimation

Gehao Lu
Yunnan University, China

Joan Lu
University of Huddersfield, UK

ABSTRACT

Predict uncertainty is critic in decision making process, especially for the complex systems. This chapter aims to discuss the theory involved in Self-Organizing Map (SOM) and its learning process, SOM based Trust Learning Algorithm (STL), SOM based Trust Estimation Algorithm (STL) as well as features of generated trust patterns. Several patterns are discussed within context. Both algorithms and how they are processed have been described in detail. It is found that SOM based Trust Estimation algorithm is the core algorithm that help agent make trustworthy or untrustworthy decisions.

1. INTRODUCTION

In the neural trust model constructed in the previous section, it is obvious that the component used for learning and making decisions is the most important component. So the algorithms inside the component are major topics of this section. The requirement of the model is to make the agents learn the experiences of their past interaction. This determines that the algorithm must be a learning algorithm. Additionally, the pattern produced by the algorithm should be easy to memorize, store and reuse.

As an unsupervised learning scheme, Self-Organizing Map (SOM), is the best choice for recognizing interaction data and find out features of the interaction. This section discusses the rationale of choosing SOM, and introduces the SOM theory in detail and describes the standard algorithm.

Based on SOM, two new algorithms are proposed: SOM based trust learning (STL) algorithm, and SOM based trust estimation (STE) algorithm. STL is designed as learning the trust from the interactions while STE is design to learn the potential interaction data and compare the related pattern with the STL generated pattern so that it can decide whether the specific agent is trustworthy. The key results of both algorithms and the patterns are categorized as three types and each type get explained thoroughly.

The section contains six sections. The organization of the content is from general to specific, from basic to advance. Section 2 describes the theory about Self Organizing Map, introduces its features and

DOI: 10.4018/978-1-5225-1884-6.ch018

depicts the process and algorithm. Section 3 proposes SOM based trust learning (STL) algorithm and describes this algorithm step by step. Section 4 differentiates the different patterns generated from the STL algorithm and discusses their characteristics and possible usages. Section 5 proposes SOM based trust estimation (STE) algorithm and describes this algorithm step by step. The section also presents the mechanism of decision making based on the results of STE algorithm. Section 6 summarized the section.

2. THEORY OF SELF ORGANIZING MAP

2.1 Self Organizing Map

Self-organizing map (SOM) is one type of neural networks based on competitive learning (Kohonen, 1998). The features of SOM include: approximation of input spaces, topologically ordering, density matching and feature selection (Haykin, 1999). The belief of trust is frequently mutating and updating, the chosen algorithm should be highly adaptive. This is what SOM is capable of. The belief of trust is a continuous accumulation of information. The output of SOM is compact and completes enough to reflect every piece of changes. Also, the output of SOM can reveal obvious characteristics of the trust belief. It is easy for a computer program to discover the belief of trust which comes from multiple sources.

The SOM can approximate the input space. The statistical characteristics can be extracted from the input data. The result map reveals an approximation of the input space through the synaptic weight of the output space. The SOM can discover the topological ordering of the input data. The location of the excited neurons constructs a spatial pattern that represents the geometric characteristics of the input space. Because the neighboring neurons are also excited, the zone that reflects the input space has better chances to be selected. This results in a good density matching. Thus, the features hided in the input space can be found through discovering the special distribution of the neuron groups.

The basic process of SOM is made up by three processes: competitive process, cooperative process and adaptation process. After initializing the synaptic weights of the network, in the competitive process, the data of the input pattern are provided to the discrimination function of the network, for each input pattern at each neuron, there will be a value of the discrimination function. The highest value gained neuron will be the winner of the competition. In the cooperative process, the neighbor function decides which neighbor neurons around the winning neuron are excited as well. In the adaptation process, the synaptic weights are adjusted so that the similar pattern leading to the winning neuron will be enhanced.

2.2 Learning Process

Based upon the traditional SOM algorithm, the trust learning process is composed by three processes: competitive process, cooperative process and adaptive process. In the competitive process, the discriminative function will help the network identify the winning neuron which produces the largest value of the discriminative function; in the cooperative process, according to the winning neuron's topological location, the neighboring neurons are calculated to be excited; in the adaptive process, the excited neurons and the winning neuron can adjusted their weight so that the ability of recognizing the next similar patterns are gradually enhanced.

Mathematical or formal description:

- **Competitive Process:** Let n denotes the dimensions of the input data to the network. Then the input data can be described using a vector in the form of a transpose matrix.

$$x = \left[x_1, x_2, \ldots, x_n \right]^T n \geq 1$$

The dimension of the trust is already discussed in Section 3. Theoretically speaking, the dimension should not be limited in its size. But the reality is different. The size is confined by the physical capability of the computer which holds the agents. It is impossible to increase the dimension indefinitely and it is also not necessary to increase the dimension indefinitely. In this section, the dimension is mainly focused in a simulated way, that is, only up to 7 dimensions are used to illustrate how the agent trust is recognized.

For each neuron in the network, there is a corresponding synaptic weight. The weight of each neuron is represented as w. The number of weights is equals to the number of dimensions (n). So the weights can be depicted as:

$$\omega = \omega_{j1}, \omega_{j2}, \ldots, \omega_{jn} j = 1, 2, \ldots, l$$

l is the total number of the neurons in the SOM network. In order to find out the winning neuron from the network, it is necessary to look for the biggest value of the inner product of ω and x. Because the same threshold is negative bias and is applied to all the neurons. When the largest inner product ω_j^T is selected, the corresponding neuron can be determined as the center of excited neurons. This is equal to find out the smallest Euclidean distance between vectors ω_j and x.

If i(x) is used to represent the distance, then in order to get the biggest inner product ω_j^T x, the i(x) should be:

$$i(x) = \arg \min \left\| x - \omega_j \right\| j \in A$$

A represents all the neurons appeared in the network. i(x) is the neuron that hold the biggest inner product value. The index of this i(x) can determine the topological position of the excited neuron. The neuron is called winning neuron or best matching neuron in SOM algorithm.

- **Cooperative Process:** The key operation of the cooperative process is to find out the neighboring neurons which should be excited with the winning neuron. The method is to use the function to calculate whether the neighboring neurons are in the excited range of the winning neuron. There are three main types of neighboring functions: Mexican hat function, Stovepipe hat function and Chef hat function (E. and Yuhui, 2007). The most often used function is the Mexican hat function (it is formally called Gaussian function (E. and Yuhui, 2007)). Let h(j, i(x)) represents the set of neighboring neurons that will be excited. Let d(j, i) represents the distance between the winning neuron and the neighboring neuron. The rule is simple, the distance decides whether the neurons get excited or not. It is obvious that d(j, i) is inverse proportion to h(j, i(x)). When the distance d(j,

i) = 0, the h(j, i(x)) will get the maximum value at the winning neuron. The distance d(j, i) can be infinitely large, that is, there can be infinite number of neighboring neuron, but the h(j, i(x)) tends to be zero.

- **Adaptive Process:** After finding out the excited neighboring neurons around the centered winning neuron, it is time to update the weights of those excited neurons. This is the most critical part of self-organizing. The weight change can be calculated as follows:

$$\Delta\omega_{ji} = \eta(t)(\alpha_{ki-}\omega_{ji})$$

$\eta(t)$ is a decreasing function of time which represents the decaying of the weight changes. ($\alpha ki - \omega j$ i) is the smallest Euclidean distance of the input vector and weight vector. $\Delta\omega j$ i should be added to the weight so that the winning neuron can be rewarded with more weight to reflect the classification of the input vectors. So the weight can be calculated as follow:

$$\omega_{ji}(t+1) = \omega_{ji}(t) + h_{(j,i(x))}(t)$$

In this formula, h(j, i(x))(t) is the neighboring function as mentioned above. ωj i(t) is the old weight for the particular neuron. ωj i(t + 1) is the new weight after combining the positive feedback. All the neurons in the range of excited neighbors will get positive updating.

3. SOM BASED TRUST LEARNING ALGORITHM (STL)

In order to let agents fully exploit their previous experiences of interaction, it is necessary to make agents learn trust from their old experiences. The research proposes an algorithm called "SOM based Trust Learning Algorithm (STL)" to help agents recognize the features related to trust through their repeated transactions. The algorithm is also the prelude of decision making toward trustworthiness in the next stage. The algorithm can be executed in 9 steps: weight initialization, fetching input data, feed forward input, feed forward output, marking patterns, storing patterns, finding neighbors, updating weights and continuation. The following pseudo code describes the STL algorithm:

1. Weight initialization;
2. While(transaction occurs;){
3. Fetching input data;
4. Feed forward input;
5. Feed forward output;
6. Marking pattern;
7. If (review result is good)
8. { Marking patterns as good;}
9. else
10. { Marking pattern as bad;}

11. Storing patterns;
12. Finding neighbors;
13. Updating weights;
14. Next round;

Figure 1 uses a process graph to depict these steps.

1. **Weight Initialization:** The task of initialization is to decide the initial weight of the neurons in the network. In the STR algorithm, each weight is assigned a random weight as its initial weight. The random value is in the range of 0.4 to 0.6. The bias of initial weight does influence the performance of the recognition. However, in an unsupervised trust learning, trust dimensions are provided to the STR algorithm one at a time when an agent transact with another agent. The STR algorithm tends to form a stable weight value through many transactions in a relatively long duration. So the initial bias on weight value only has minor influence on this prolonged process.

2. **Fetching Input Data:** For each transaction that happens, an agent receives various dimensions of transaction related results. The information about those results is organized into a vector which has been mentioned in section4. For example, an input vector with five dimensions: reputation, price, appearance, quality, delivery will look like 1, 1, 0, 1, 0. Thus the input data to the STL algorithm is actually a matrix which contains many rows of transaction related information. Such matrix is not prepared beforehand. It is collected by the agent after every transaction. Each transaction adds one row of information into the matrix and the agent fetch this row to learn and then generate the trust patterns. An agent is not trained to understand the pattern, it learned during its lifecycle in continuous business activities. The STL algorithm thus is an unsupervised learning algorithm.

Figure 1. Map structure: the structure of the SOM network

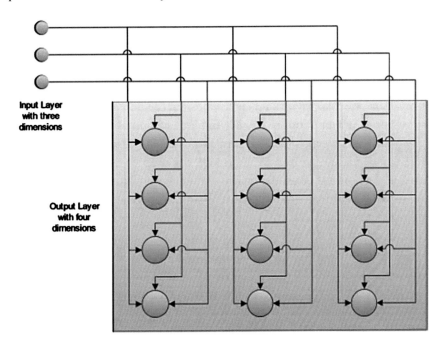

3. **Feed Forward Input:** Feed forward input feeds the input vector to the STL network. There are only two layers in the STL algorithm: the input layer and the output layer. Or they can be called the sensor layer and the recognition layer. The input layer is responsible for receiving the data from the input vector. The number of nodes in this layer depends on the number of dimensions in the input vector. One input node corresponds to one dimension in the input vector. The number of nodes is dynamic. The more sophisticated the transaction is, the more nodes might be needed to help sense more information. Section 4 has discussed how the dimension is defined and how two different agents achieve agreement on the meaning of the transaction. After fetching the input vector, the input data are sent to the STL neurons.

4. **Feed Forward Output:** The major task of Feed forward output is to find out the winning neuron. As the author introduces in the SOM theory background, finding the largest value of product of weight and input vector is equivalent to find out the smallest distance between the weight vector and the input vector. The output neuron with the minimum Euclidean distance is the winning neuron which stands for the classification that the input vector belongs to. Thus the activation function for the Feedfoward output is:

$$d = \sqrt{\sum_{i=1}^{n} \left(\alpha_{ki} - \omega_{ji} \right)^2}$$

d represents Euclidean distance, n represents the number of neurons in the output layer, α_{ki} represents the input vector and ω_{ji} represents the synaptic weight of the neuron. The distance is calculated for each neuron and all the distances are compared to find out the smallest one. Then the neuron which has the smallest distance is set to the winning neuron.

5. **Marking Patterns:** It is nonsense to talk about the goodness or badness of the pattern recognized. A pattern is just a neutral concept. Only when agents or people endow their interests to the pattern, the pattern then become valuable and useful. Like the natural concept "water", people think water is good because water help them survive, irrigate their farm, and present them with beautiful scenery. To make pattern useful, it is necessary to do a qualitative analysis against it as well. The pattern itself is not analyzable. The analyzable target is the transaction which provides the input information and generates the pattern. It is not important to know the details about the transaction. The most straightforward question is whether this transaction is successful or has failed. If it is successful, then the pattern generated can be marked as good pattern; if it has failed, then the pattern generated can be marked as bad. Furthermore, the drop points that compose the pattern can also be marked as good points or bad points. Now the pattern is useful when an agent enters a new transaction and needs to estimate the trustworthiness of the new opponent agent. They only need to compare the difference between the pattern from the new transaction and the memorized good patterns. In the next section, the research will discuss the trustworthiness estimation algorithm in details.

6. **Storing Patterns:** The research aims to find a way to estimate the trustworthiness of agents and transactions. Historical patterns are thus the source of estimation and they should be stored in a proper way so that the patterns can be retrieved conveniently in the next time. The pattern is a

matrix which is composed by blank point and drop points. It can be stored as a two dimensional array. The following matrix is an example of the array: b represents blank point and d represents drop points.

$$\begin{pmatrix} b & d & b \\ d & b & b \\ b & d & b \end{pmatrix}$$

For every new transaction with a specific agent, there will be a new pattern generated accordingly. For an agent in a transaction, there is a pattern stored in the following relational form: For a specific agent who has more than one time interaction with the host agent, there is an accumulated general pattern stored in the following relational form: For the host agent there is a meta-level pattern which can help agent deal with new transaction with new agent who has never met before. Such meta-level pattern can be called macro pattern and can be stored in the following relational form:

7. **Finding Neighbors:** The most obvious difference between SOM network (Figure 4) and the other type of neural networks is that the SOM network tends to adjust weights of the neighboring neurons around the center winning neuron. This is a lesson learned from the mechanism of the human brain. In the human brain, there is evidence that ring a biological neuron can also make the adjacent neurons to be excited (Ritter, 1999). The neighboring function is the key to control how many neighbors can be excited. The theory background has introduced three types of neighboring functions: Gaussian function, Stovepipe hat function and Chef hat function (E. and Yuhui, 2007). In the STL algorithm, the simplest method is used, that is, the Chef hat function is used as the neighboring function. The Chef hat function only sets the radius around the winning neuron. If the neighboring neurons are in the area of the radius, they are excited neighbors. Otherwise, the outside neurons are never influenced by the weight updating.

Figure 2. Example for storing transactional patterns: example of the pattern storage for each transaction

Agent id	Transaction id	Pattern generated	Marking
Agent-xxx	10645571	$\begin{bmatrix} b & d & b \\ d & b & b \\ b & d & b \end{bmatrix}$	Bad

Figure 3. Example for storing general patterns: example of the pattern storage for general patterns

Agent id	General Pattern	Marking
Agent-xxx	$\begin{bmatrix} b & d & b \\ d & b & b \\ b & d & b \end{bmatrix}$	Good

Figure 4. Example for storing macro patterns: example of the pattern storage for macro patterns

Marking	Macro Pattern
Good	$\begin{bmatrix} b & d & b \\ d & b & b \\ b & d & b \end{bmatrix}$

8. **Updating Weights:** Updating the synaptic weights of the winning neuron and its neighbors is how the network adapts to the ever changing environment. The equation of updating the weights has been mentioned in the theoretical background.

$$\omega_{ji}(t+1) = \omega_{ji}(t) + h_{j,i(x)}(t)\eta(t)(\alpha_{ki} - \omega_{ji})$$

hj, i(x)(t) is the neighboring function as mentioned above. ωj i(t) is the old weight for the particular neuron. ωj i(t+1) is the new weight after combining the positive feedback. All the neurons in the range of excited neighbors will get positive updating.

9. **Continuation:** If there is only one transaction that happens, the algorithm can be stopped. The agent can wait for another round of transaction and wait for another vector of information to be fed. If there exists multiple transactions that happens successively, the algorithm is executed in a loop. Continue with step 2 until there is no more input vector to be fed.

4. FEATURES OF THE GENERATED TRUST PATTERNS

4.1 Three Types of Trust Patterns

The STL algorithm produces three types of patterns: transactional trust general, agent trust pattern and macro trust pattern. Their abstraction level is meta-level for all the agents in all transactions, general level for a specific agent in all previous transactions and concrete level for a specific agent in a specific transaction. The hierarchy of the three levels is depicted in Figure 6. A macro pattern is an aggregation of many agent patterns; an agent pattern is an aggregation of many transactional patterns. The network of STL algorithm only directly generates the lowest level pattern, the transactional pattern. The other two types of patterns are created according to the transactional patterns indirectly. All three types of patterns are results of learning activities while only the higher two types, macro pattern and agent pattern, are used in the trustworthiness estimation activities.

4.2 Transactional Trust Pattern

The transactional trust pattern is the direct product of the STL algorithm. The pattern recorded the recognized features of a specific transaction that happens between the host agent and its opponent agent. Once

Figure 5. STR algorithm: the algorithm of SOM based trust learning

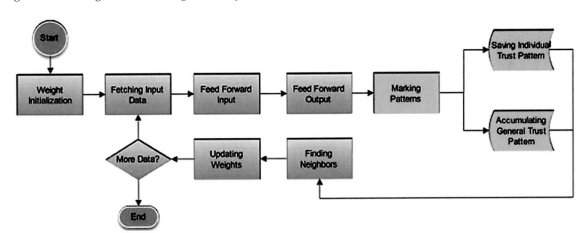

the pattern generated is marked as good or bad, the pattern becomes the source material of the above two level of patterns. The transactional pattern is stored in a matrix (two-dimensional array). Every point in the matrix represents a potential feature of the target agent. For each transaction, after the input data fed into the network, a pattern with a drop point is created. The drop point is actually the winning neuron of the algorithm. Its location is kept intact and recorded with the pattern. Figure 6 shows an example of the transactional pattern. The example presents an output layer with 3 dimensions and 9 neurons. The red point in the graph represents the drop point or the winning neuron.

4.3 Agent Trust Pattern

The agent trust pattern is the indirect product of the STL algorithm. It is an aggregation of transactional patterns for one specific agent over a specific duration. It is the agent's memory toward another agent based on their interaction experiences. The agent trust pattern is useful when the host agent is inquired by other agents about some specific agent's reputation. The agent compares the agent trust pattern with its macro trust pattern and then decides to send a reputation to the inquiring agent. The details of repu-

Figure 6. Pattern types: hierarchy among three types of patterns

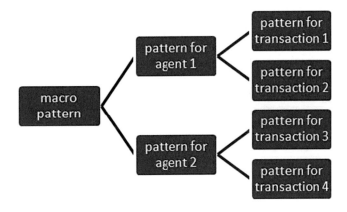

tation generation and propagation are discussed in Section 6. Because the transactional patterns have good or bad marking, the agent trust patterns have good or bad marking as well. Figure 7 illustrates an agent trust pattern marking as good as well. In this figure, the red point represents the drop points of previous transactions. The size of the point states that the same drop points has appeared in the same location for several times. Actually, the agent trust pattern can be viewed as an overlapping of many transactional patterns.

4.4 Macro Trust Pattern

The macro trust pattern is also the indirect product of the STL algorithm. It is an aggregation of the agent patterns for all transactions. The reason of setting a macro trust pattern is that an agent needs a balanced view of trust over different agents and different transactions. If there are no macro trust patterns, then the agent lacks a benchmark to measure how big the differences are among agents and among transactions. This is important especially when the host agent needs to send reputation to its partner agent. Different from the transactional trust patterns and the agent trust patterns, the macro pattern is only one integral pattern instead of division based on good or bad marking. It is an aggregation of both good agent trust patterns and bad trust patterns. It reveals the whole trust map of the host agent and builds a foundation of the reputation network. Figure 8 illustrates an example of the macro trust pattern.

In this figure, the red points represent the good drop points that are led by successful transactions and the black points represent the bad points that are led by the failed transactions. The size of the points is the result of aggregation of many agents' trust patterns. If unfortunately, the good drop point coincides with the bad drop point, they counteract each other and carry out a subtraction in effect.

5. SOM BASED TRUST ESTIMATION ALGORITHM (STE)

The STL algorithm help agents find trust patterns through process the previous transaction experiences. It also helps agents store those patterns into its memory as three abstraction levels. However, this only

Figure 7. Transactional pattern: an example of the transactional pattern

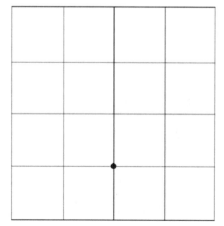

Figure 8. Agent trust pattern: an example of the agent trust pattern

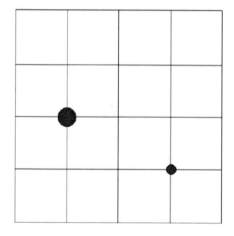

solves the first fold of the problem: seek the trust patterns for the agents. The second fold of the problem is how an agent makes a trustworthy decision which will lead to a future transaction or a future cooperation based upon the recognized trust patterns. The research proposes a "Trustworthiness Estimation Algorithm" to solve the latter problem. The algorithm absorbs neural network component of the STL algorithm to do pre-recognition jobs, and adds a search and comparison components to do estimation and recommendation jobs. The algorithms can be expressed as 6 steps: fetch input data, feed forward input, feed forward output, searching patterns, comparing patterns and giving recommendations (Figure 9). The following pseudo code depicts the STE algorithm:

1. While (meet new potential transaction;){
2. Fetch input data;
3. Feed forward input;
4. Feed forward output (transaction pattern);
5. Searching macro patterns;
6. Comparing patterns (macro pattern vs. transaction pattern);
7. Generating recommendations;
8. Next round;
9. }

Figure 10 illustrates the steps of the estimation algorithm.

1. **Fetch Input Data:** The process of fetching input data is as same as the first step in the STL algorithm. The input data are fed to the network in the form of input vector with various dimensions. But the type of input data being used is different. In the STL algorithm, the input data are mainly information related to a previous transaction. A host agent gains experiences from analyzing its historical data. The pattern referring to the transaction and the target agent is also generated and stored. However in the estimation algorithm, the purpose of the estimation is to predict whether a target agent can be trusted to carry out a transaction with the host agent. The data used as the input vector is not historical information from old transaction. The data used in the estimation

Figure 9. Macro trust pattern: an example of the macro trust pattern

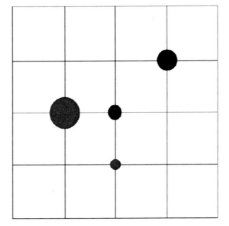

Figure 10. STE algorithm: the process of the trust estimation algorithm

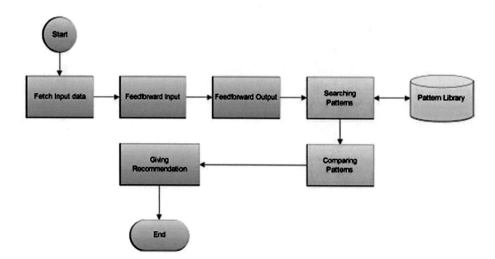

algorithm is observed data before any the transaction actually happens. The observed data also follows the format of the input vector, that is, it should have the same format and dimensions as the real transactional input vector. Otherwise it would be impossible to compare the transaction generated patterns and the estimation generated patterns. For example, if there is a book to be sold through automatic agent transaction, the information to describe the book could be organized from 5 dimensions: reputation, price, quality, appearance, delivery. The reputation can be gained from the other agent (see next section about reputation propagation). The price is clearly stated. The quality needs the book to be ranked by some expert's book review or customer's book review like what Amazon has already done. Appearance and delivery also needs a third party to give them a rank so that the agents can retrieve it directly. The mechanism of ranking is not in the scope of the research; the reader can find more information about ranking through (Koehn, 2003).

2. **Feed Forward Input:** The feed forward input in the estimation algorithm is as same as the feed forward input in the STL algorithm. They are both based on the SOM algorithm. Their structure is also two layers: one layer as input layer and the other layer as output layer.

3. **Feed Forward Output:** The process of feed forward output in the estimation algorithm is the same as the process of feed forward output in the STL algorithm. But the result is processed in a different way. In the STL algorithm, the pattern recognized are transformed into three forms: transactional trust pattern, agent trust pattern and macro trust pattern. These three forms become the foundation of the trust estimation. In estimation algorithm, the output pattern is only a predicted transactional trust pattern which aims to be compared with the macro pattern. It is only a temporary intermediary pattern which will be discarded after the estimation. Such discarded pattern will not enter the pattern library and will not form parts of the knowledge about trust.

4. **Searching Patterns:** Once the predicted pattern is generated, a corresponding pattern should be retrieved from the agent pattern library. The identity of the target agent becomes the key to the searching. If there is an id of the target agent in the library, it means that the host agent has already interacted with the target agent before. The agent trust pattern for the target agent and the macro

pattern are provided for the next comparison. If the id of the target agent is not in the library, it means that the host agent has never interacted with the target agent before. In this case, only the macro trust pattern is returned.

5. **Comparing Patterns:** Comparing patterns is the most critical step in the estimation algorithm. The basic principle of comparison is to put two patterns together and measure how big the differences are. There are mainly two types of difference: different drop points and different size of drop point. So the comparison must consider both situations. The pattern is stored as a matrix so that the difference between patterns is the difference between matrixes. Let Pm represents the predicted pattern and let Pm represents the macro trust pattern. The difference between these two patterns is: $P_d = P_m - P_e$

Now the job is transformed to measure Pd. Based on Pd, let gkl represents the successful drop points in the predicted trust pattern. Let fkl represents the failed drop points in the specified trust pattern. Let rg represent the rate of good drop points in all points in the pattern. Let rb represents the rate of bad points in all points in the pattern. Let rd represents the rate of displaced points in the pattern.

$$r_g = \frac{\Delta g_{kl}}{\Sigma g_{kl}}$$

$$r_b = \frac{\Delta b_{kl}}{\Sigma b_{kl}}$$

$$r_d = \frac{\Delta d_{kl}}{\Sigma d_{kl}}$$

Because the agent has no prior knowledge about what the displaced points are, these points can be good points or bad. In order to state the risk tendency of the agent, a risk factor γ is introduced to adjust the attitude of the agent toward the unknown facts. The value of γ is between -1 and 1. It could also be zero if the agent chooses to omit the displaced point. Let r represents the result of the comparison. So the r is generated according to the following formula:

$$r = r_g - r_b - \Upsilon r_d \ (-1 \leq \Upsilon \leq 1)$$

$$r = \frac{\Delta g_{kl}}{\Sigma g_{kl}} - \frac{\Delta b_{kl}}{\Sigma b_{kl}} - \Upsilon \frac{\Delta d_{kl}}{\Sigma d_{kl}} \ (k=1...i, \ l=1...j, \ -1 \leq \Upsilon \leq 1)$$

6. **Giving Recommendation:** After calculating the result r of the comparison between the macro trust pattern and the predicted trust pattern, r can be an indicator of the degree of trustworthiness. There are three situations that r may be:

$$\begin{cases} r < 0 \\ r = 0 \\ r > 0 \end{cases}$$

- In the first situation r < 0, there are big gap between the predicted trust pattern and the macro trust pattern for the specific agent. The bigger the absolute value of the r, the smaller the trustworthiness is.
- In the second situation r = 0, this means there is no trustworthiness evaluation. The reason might be lack of the fact supporting trustworthiness evaluation. The agent will not take any action to do further jobs.
- In the third situation r > 0, most of the drop points coincide with the good drop points of the macro pattern. In such case, the algorithm encourages the agent to take further action to cooperate, delegate or do some transaction with the target agent.

6. SUMMARY

In this section, the research analyzes the necessity of learning trust in a way of neural network. It also proposes to use self-organizing map as the basic algorithm for learning computational trust. The section describes the processes of the standard self -organizing map and illustrates its core features. Then the section proposes the SOM based Trust Learning algorithm and describes the processes of the algorithm in detail. The algorithm improves the traditional SOM algorithm according to the special requirement of trust learning. This section also proposes the SOM based Trust Estimation algorithm and depicts its detailed processes. This algorithm is used to estimate the trustworthiness of the target agent before any transactions. It is the core algorithm that help agent make trustworthy or untrustworthy decisions.

REFERENCES

Eberhart, R.C., & Shi, Y. (2007). Computational intelligence: concepts to implementations. Morgan Kaufmann.

Haykin, S. (1999). Neural Networks: A Comprehensive Foundation. Prentice-Hall.

Koehn, D. (2003). The nature of and conditions for online trust. *Journal of Business Ethics*, 43, 3-19.

Kohonen, T. (1998). The self-organizing map. *Neurocomputing*, *21*, 1-6.

Ritter, H. (1999). *Self-organizing maps on noneuclidean spaces*. Kohonen Maps.

Chapter 19
Reputation Generation and Propagation

Gehao Lu
Yunnan University, China

Joan Lu
University of Huddersfield, UK

ABSTRACT

Reputation plays an important role in multi-agent system. It is a socialized form of trust which makes agent cooperate with each other and reduces the cost of agents' interaction. In a world with only computational trust, the agent can only perceive its own interactions. Its learned trust pattern can only be used by itself. There is no socialized mechanism to magnify the trustworthiness that has been learned. To introduce reputation is the solution to efficiently exploit the trust patterns. If the NTR algorithm is designed for intelligent agents, then the reputation propagation models and reputation generation mechanism are designed for multi-agent systems. Introducing reputation into multi-agent systems brings many benefits: the agent can greatly extend its range of influence to cover other agents. The agent also can share the interaction experience with others. Such sharing will accelerate the washing out of malevolent agents and increase the possibility of transactions for benevolent agents. The reputation will improve the executive efficiency of agents by avoiding unnecessary communication and transactions. In general, reputation is the key to form a tight coupling agent society. There is no acknowledged or standard definition for computational reputation. But it is possible to describe it from five facets: interaction experience, intention of propagation, range of propagation, path of propagation, content of reputation. Interaction experience explains the reputation from the view of information source; intention of propagation explains from the view of agents' motivation; range of propagation explains from the view of spatial consideration; path of propagation explains from the view of network; content of reputation explains from the expression of the reputation. The author builds three models of reputation propagation. Point-to-point based inquiry allows an initiative agent start an inquiry request to its acquaintance. If the middle agent has intention to transfer the inquiry, then the request can be propagated far from the initiative agent and thus form a reputation network. Broadcasting based propagation is to let agent broadcast its experience about every interaction or transaction so that every other agents in the society can learn what happened.

DOI: 10.4018/978-1-5225-1884-6.ch019

DEFINITION

The meaning of reputation in dictionary implicitly refers to the reputation in the human society. There is a big difference between the human reputation and computer based reputation. In addition to the common meaning of the word "reputation" appeared in the dictionary, the author tries to depict the computational reputation, that is, agent reputation from five aspects: interaction experience, intention of propagation, range of propagation, path of propagation, content of propagation. Figure 1 illustrates these five aspects.

Interaction experience toward target agent is the source of reputation. An agent first needs to have some interaction experience with the specific target agent. And such reputation interaction needs to have some results either positive or negative. As the research describes in the previous section, the agent perceives the result and melts it with its existing pattern toward the target agent. In case of inquiry on the target reputation or in case of broadcasting, the agent will generate a reputation according to the trust pattern and propagate the reputation to some agents or some networks. Trust recognition is the very first step of reputation propagation, only when agents have interacted with some other agents, then they are qualified with the "experience", pattern of trustworthiness, to tell the other agents that agent x is good and agent y is bad.

Intention of propagation is the intent that an agent is willing to propagate its perceived reputation to the other agents. It is like a switch that controls whether the agent is willing to share its interaction experience with its fellow agents over some form of reputation networks. The set of the switch can be used with the goal of an agent to emphasize that an agent is proactive and on its own initiative to participate a network. In this research, the author assumes every agent has the initiative to share their interaction experience because the purpose of the research is to investigate the mechanism of trust and reputation in a dense network full of active sharing agents.

Figure 1. Definition of reputation: the dimension of defining a computational

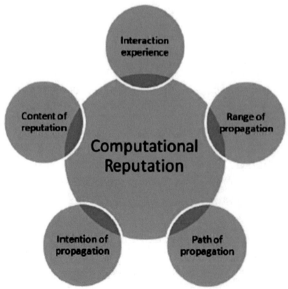

Range of propagation is the distance that an agent can affect another agent by sending its perceived reputation to. The range here refers to the number of agents that lies between the sending agent and the receiving agent. In a virtual world of computer program, the simplest scenario is to remove the limitation of propagation range, let reputation propagated without any blocking or decaying. Any agent can get undistorted reputation from the remote agent. Agents in such scenario are actually stay in a flat and homogeneous network without layers or clusters which is too nave from the real world networks. In the real world networks, the network is layered or clustered into LAN, MAN or WAN, accordingly, the agents are belong to different owner in different application domain with different goals and usages. In the complex scenario, it is not reasonable and not appropriate to propagate the reputation unchangeable. The reputation could be enhanced or decayed according to the trustworthiness between transmitting agents or the agent network structures.

Propagation Mechanism Design

Through the description in section 3, it is clear that designing ways of propagation is a critical task for spreading recognized reputation. The effectiveness of a propagation method can be analyzed from three perspectives: coverage, performance and structure. Wide coverage means that the reputation message should be propagated to as many agents as possible and as far distance as possible. High performance means that the propagation should efficiently make use of the network; the reputation message should reach the agents quickly without any distortion. Simple structure means the propagation mechanism should easy to implement and have a clear layered structure. According to those three principles, the research designs three forms of reputation propagation mechanisms: point-to-point based inquiry, broadcasting based propagation and observer based propagation. The next three subsections describe how those three mechanisms are designed, their detailed propagating processes, and their advantages and disadvantages.

Point-to-Point Based Inquiry

The initial of idea of point-to-point based inquiry comes from the p2p system (Zhou Wen-li, 2006) which shares files among various nodes. Point-to-point based Inquiry is the simplest and most effective way of the reputation propagation. In order to have some knowledge of the target agent, an agent can send a request to its own acquaint agents. In case one of these agents also has interacting experience with the target agent, this acquaint agent may respond the request and send a reputation message back.

Figure 2 depicts the point-to-point based inquiry. The process of such inquiry can be summarized as the follow:

1. The initiative agent intends to start an interaction with the target agent.
2. The initiative agent sends reputation recommending requests to its neighbor agents according to its acquaintance list.
3. Upon receiving the request, the acquainted agent checks its interacting history list to see whether it has the past experience with the target agent. If it has, it will generate a reputation recommending message to the initiative agent. On the contrary, it will send a not-found message back to the initiative agent.

4.   The initiative agent receives responses from the acquainted agents. It filters the not-found message and combines the reputation recommending message based on reputation recognition algorithm which will be discussed in the later sections. Then the initiative agent can generate its own trust pattern against the target agent.

5.   Depending on the judgment of trustworthiness toward the target agent, the initiative agent decides to or not to interact with the target agent.

The obvious advantage of the point-to-point based inquiry is its simplicity. Agents only need an acquaintance list to store their acquainted agents. The process of propagation is also a simple send and receives return. Such inquiry is actually the very basic form of reputation propagation. Other more complex forms like broadcasting and observer are derived from this basic form with a few add-ons to the way of propagation. The other advantage of the point-to-point based inquiry is its good performance. The initiative agent will not arbitrarily send too many requests out, they only send according to their acquaintance list. Such list can be limited to a relatively small size to avoid heavy network traffic. The disadvantage of the point-to-point based inquiry is that it is highly possible that all the acquainted agents in the list may not have the direct interacting experience with the target agent due to the size limitation of the list. Especially in a large computational agent society with a small acquaintance list, this situation would happen frequently. Such defect will counteract the above two advantages.

A slightly more sophisticated version of the point-to-point based inquiry is designed to allow the acquainted agents to exploit their acquainted agents again and again, i.e., constructing a chain of 2-layer or even n-layer propagation. Figure 3 illustrate such a reputation reference chain. Each agent first checks its own interaction history to see whether it has the previous interacting pattern with the target agent. If it has not, it will not stop at this point. It will try to forward this request to its own acquainted agents. Such process will go on until a reputation recommending message is returned from some nodes along the reference chain. This chained propagation solves the problem of limited acquaintance list for single agent. It composes a reputation network that allows agents search and propagate reputation. It enlarges the range of reputation inquiry for a single agent whereas keeps the acquaintance list reasonably small. But it is not to say that the depth of chain is deeper and better. Too long chain usually means heavy network transportation and worse performance. There must be some trade-off when choosing the depth of the reputation chain. Sacrificing some reputation propagation ability is to achieve better performance.

Figure 2. Point-to-point inquiry: the process of the point-to-point based inquiry

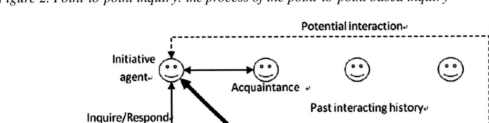

Figure 3. Chained point-to-point inquiry: the process of the chained point-to-point reputation inquiry

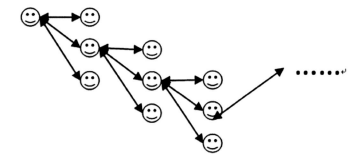

Broadcasting Based Propagation

The initial of idea of broadcasting based propagation comes from (Hedet-niemi, 2006). They studied how the gossips propagated in the society in the form88 of broadcasting. Compare to the point-to-point reputation inquiry, broadcasting can cover wider propagation scope in a short time. Once the initiative agent has interacted with some specific target agent, it will generate a reputation reference and send this reference to all the agents in its domain or society. Such broadcast is indiscrimination whereas the precondition is the initiative agent knows the identity and address of its neighbors.

Figure 4 illustrates how an agent broadcasts its experience to the other agents. The process can be summarized as the follows:

1. The initiative agent interacts with the target agent and the initiative agent updates its trust pattern through NTR algorithm mentioned in the previous section.
2. The initiative agent acquires the full agent list from the domain manager program and sends the perceived reputation reference out to all of the agents.
3. The receiving agent can choose to accept the broadcasting reference or simply just ignore the reference according to the strength of the relationship between the initiative agent and the receiving agent.

Figure 4. Broadcasting reputation: the process of broadcasting the reputation

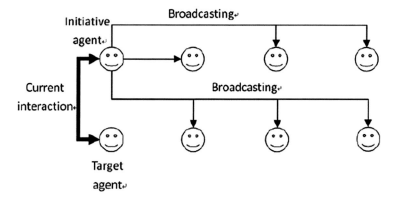

The biggest advantage of broadcasting is its wide coverage. Each agent tries to propagate its perceived reputation reference to the other agents. The reputation network is 89 updated frequently after each time of agents' interaction. This is very good for situation which needs closely watch the status of agent transaction or interaction. However, the biggest advantage can become the biggest disadvantage when used inappropriately. Broadcasting leads to performance problem because each time the initiative agent sends reputation reference to all the agents in its network. Such reference message will occupy too much of the bandwidth and sometimes it may heavily interfere the normal communication of the network and even block the whole network. Worse still, the broadcasting agent simply ignores whether the receiving agent has the requirement of the reputation reference or not. It sends the reference blindly and forces the receiving agent to accept it. In fact, there are only a few of the receiving agents who are interested in the reputation derived from the interaction between the initiative agent and target agent. This means the efficiency of broadcasting is less than the point-to-point based inquiry.

Size of the agent organization or society is the key factor that decides whether broadcasting is good or bad. The author's experiment shows, when agents built by JADE are deployed in a lab with 10 personal computers (2.4GHz, dual-core, 1Gb memory), 100M Ethernet connection, the turn point of using broadcasting based reputation propagation is 54 agents, that is, when the number of agents exceed 54, the broadcasting will severely impact the performance of the network. According to this discovery, the broadcasting propagation is not appropriate for system with vast number of agents. It is best suit for close agent society with very a few agents and with needs to closely watch the status of the agents' interaction.

Observer/Subscriber

In some cases, a better solution is to keep the wide coverage of the broadcasting while to avoid the uninterested agents being bothered to receive the reputation propagation from the initiative agents. In the objected-oriented software design, there is a design pattern called "Observer" (Hannemann, 2002), it is a pattern used to decouple the subject object and the observer object. In the paradigm of multi-agent system, agent is one kind of "intelligent object" so that it is wise to introduce this pattern into the world of multi-agent to build a solution that meets the aforementioned needs. The name can still follow the object-oriented way as the Observer, or more specifically, as the Observer based reputation propagation. In this propagation method, agents can be categorized into four roles: subject, target, subscriber and unsubscriber.

The subject is an agent being watched by the other agent. Its behavior and its interaction with the other agents are interested by some other agents. The key to design a subject agent is that it holds a subscriber list that contains all the agents' identities who are interested in the subject. A target agent is the agent that interacts with the subject agent. The result of their interaction will be propagated as reputation reference. A register agent is the agent who needs reputation reference form the subject agent. It will register itself into the subscriber list of the subject agent hence it can receive reputation propagation message from the subject when the subject interacts with the target agent. A unsubscriber is an agent who totally has no interest in this subject. So it will never receive any piece of information from the subject agent.

Figure 5 illustrate how the subject agent notifies the subscriber agent its updated reputation. The process is summarized as the follows:

Figure 5. Observer: the process of observer based reputation propagation

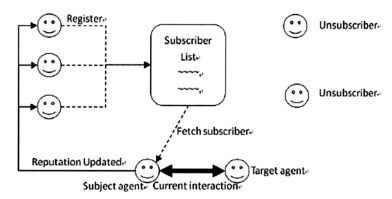

1. An agent is interested in a subject agent's behavior and it sends a registering request to the subject agent.
2. The subject agent receives this registering request and adds this identity of the request agent into its subscriber list.
3. The subject agent carries out an interaction with the target agent. The result of the interaction is transformed to update the trust pattern against the target agent through the NTR algorithm mentioned in the previous section.
4. The subject agent checks its subscriber list and sends the perceived reputation recommending message to all the agents appeared in the list. The unsubscriber will not receive any message from the subject agent because they are not in the sending list.
5. The subscriber agent receives the reputation recommending message and updates its own trust pattern against target agent accordingly.
6. The subscriber is no longer interested in the subject agent. It sends an unsubscribe request to the subject agent.
7. The subject receives the unsubscribe request. It finds out the identity of the unsubscriber from its subscriber list and then it removes this identity. Next time when it carries out another interaction, it will not notify the removed unsubscriber.

The observer based reputation propagation combines the advantages from both the point-to-point inquiry based propagation and broadcasting based propagation. On the one hand, like point-to-point inquiry based propagation, the subject agent only serves those subscriber agents who register in advance. Other unrelated agents keep silent and the network traffic will not congest due to redundant communication. On the other hand, like the broadcast based propagation, the coverage of the observer based propagation is reasonably big. The subscriber list maintained by the subject agent is a controlled, ordered broadcasting list. Such a controlled broadcasting impact big enough zone of interested agents while save much time used to inquire or respond a single agent before every interaction. Thus the observer based reputation propagation is especially good for reputation propagation in Electronic commerce. In E-commerce, the users come from all over the world; it is infeasible to realize a global reputation network which allows individuals to freely exchange reputation. A better way to design the network is to use observer based propagation. Let some highly active users/agents become subject and the other user could choose to observe those subject user and gain reputation about specific dealer or product through the active users.

REPUTATION RECOGNITION

Reputation Generation

In Section 6, computational agent can use the various transaction criteria as the input data to the STL algorithm. The algorithm then creates a matrix based trust pattern after repeated learning on these data. This matrix stores the experience gained through thousands of interaction, it is a "brain" designed for the computational agent to memorize the good behavior and the bad behavior. Section 6 points out that the value of the matrix based trust pattern is to learn the past interaction and to predict the possibility of success for the potential transactions. However, the matrix is only used in the sense of individual agent. For a multi-agent system, a learned trust do help agent improve its successful rate of transaction. But the complete advantages of multi-agent is not fully inspired unless the learned trust is put into the context of agent society, that is, generating reputation from the learned trust pattern and propagate those reputation to some interested agents. The algorithm for generating reputation is listed in the following pseudo code:

1. Send reputation request to reference agent;
2. Reference agent search patterns about target agent;
3. If (found)
4. { target pattern vs. macro pattern;
5. Got recommendation;}
6. Else { end generation;}
7. Return recommendation to host agent;

Drop Point Comparison

Initially, the basic trust pattern for an agent is a matrix with two types of drop points. The first type is success point, depicted as point in red, which represents successful transactions or interactions between the agent and its opponents. The size of the success point is proportional to the times of successful transactions or interactions. The second type is failure point, depicted as point in gray, which represents failed transactions or interactions between the agent and its opponents. The size of the failed point is proportional to the times of failed transactions or interactions. Figure 6 illustrates such a general pattern. This pattern is general matrix which is an assembled graph that accumulates the drop points of many interactions with many agents. It does not aim to reveal the trustworthiness of a specific single agent. But it does show a macro pattern about what is a good transaction and what is a bad transaction for an agent if the agent is provided with transaction related data to learn or analyze. It provides a foundation about how the agent believes the trustworthiness is. To gain the reputation against one specific agent, the interaction history with this agent is still needed.

The history of past interaction can also be recorded using the same style of pattern like the general trust pattern. The only difference is that the general pattern is design to contain all the drop points in all previous interactions. While the specific trust pattern is design to record the interaction between the initiative agent and the specified agent in the form of matrix and drop points. Figure 7 illustrates such a pattern. In this example, two features should be noticed. First, the drop points, both the success points and the failure points, are located in the same location as the general pattern. This is because the specified pattern is just a subset of the general pattern. The drop points appeared in the specified pattern must be

Figure 6. Macro pattern: the example of the macro trust pattern

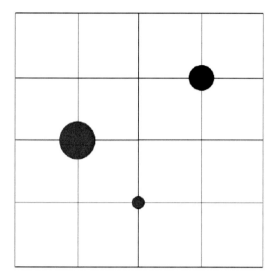

Figure 7. Agent pattern: the example of trust pattern for specified agent

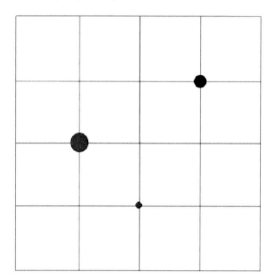

accumulated to the points on the general pattern. Whereas the drop points appeared in the general pattern might not appear in the specified pattern because some points may be plotted by some other interaction with some other agents. Reputation cannot be retrieved directly from the specified trust pattern as well because the specified pattern only shows the performance of one agent in limited interactions and there is no reference whether such performance deserves trust or not. A reasonable reputation should consider both the general pattern and the specified pattern so that the individual performance can be compared with the general performance.

The comparison between general pattern and specified pattern can be organized into a comparison on two folds. First, compare whether these two patterns have the same drop points. Usually, they will have. But in some cases, the specified pattern will miss some points that appear in the general pattern. Second, if some points lap over each other, it is necessary to compare the size of the points because the size indicates the strength of more trustworthy or less trustworthy. The size of drop points in the general pattern is definitely great than the size of drop points in the specified pattern. But how big the difference is can be an important indicator that how far the trustworthiness for specified agent biases the general pattern. This difference is also the source of the reputation. An agent receives a request to inquire a specified agent about its reputation; it will check whether it has interaction history with the specified agent. If it does, it extracts the pattern for the specified agent and compares it with the general trust pattern. It will find some difference. If the difference is small (the drop points represent trustworthiness nearly overlap each other, the size is close), then the agent can send good reputation out to the inquiry agent. If the difference is big (the drop points represent untrustworthiness are overlapped or the drop points represent trustworthiness are missed, the size difference of the overlapped trustworthy points is big), then the agent can send bad reputation out to the inquiry agent (Figure 8).

Figure 8. Result of comparison: the comparing result of the macro pattern and the agent pattern

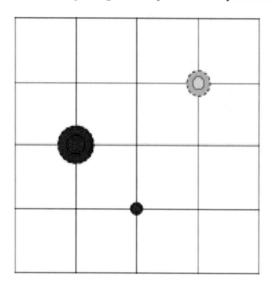

Calculation of Similarity

The calculation of the difference should be put into a mathematical framework so that the result of the calculation is a numerical value which can be propagated along the network, accepted and absorbed by the inquiry agent. Let Pg represents the matrix based trust pattern. Let dij represents the size of drop points on row i and column j; Let Ps represents the matrix based trust pattern. Let sij represents the size of drop points on row i and column j. So the pattern is mathematically described as:

$$P_g = \begin{pmatrix} d_{11} & \cdots & d_{1j} \\ \cdots & \cdots & \cdots \\ d_{i1} & \cdots & d_{ij} \end{pmatrix}$$

$$P_s = \begin{pmatrix} s_{11} & \cdots & s_{1j} \\ \cdots & \cdots & \cdots \\ s_{i1} & \cdots & s_{ij} \end{pmatrix}$$

Let k, l represent the coordinate of the drop points in the matrix. Let T represents the total number of drop points in the general trust pattern. Let rt represents the generated reputation value of the target agent. Let skl represents the successful drop points in the specified trust pattern. Let fkl represents the failed drop points in the specified trust pattern. So the rt is generated according to the following formula:

$$r_t = \frac{\Sigma s_{kl} - \Sigma f_{kl}}{T} \ (k=1\ldots i,\ l\ldots j,\ r\leq 1)$$

The first part of the formula calculates the rate of the successful drop points in the total number of interactions. The second part of the formula calculates the rate of the failed drop points in the total number of interactions. The value of r is actually reflects the difference between successful rate and failed rate, that is, a reputation value against specific agent which can be propagated to the other agents.

Received Reputation

The initiative agent sends the reputation value to the inquiry agent. As section 5.1 shows, the value expresses the opinion about the target agent from the view point of the initiative (sender) agent. To simply accept this value as the reputation of the target agent is too rough. It is necessary to consider the sender's reputation as well. If a sender agent responds a reputation message about the target agent, while this sender's own reputation is awful. To believe such sender's recommending without any deliberation is dangerous. So the reputation receiving agent should also take the sender's reputation into account. This time, the generation of reputation is not by aid of the other agents.

The process of generating reputation is controlled by the agent itself. The agent can guarantee that it will not be impacted by the biased influence at least.

Let ra represents the accepted reputation, rt represents the target reputation as stated in last section, and rs represents the sender's reputation. So the ra can be produced as the follow: $r_a = r_t(1 + r_s)$

Depends on the value of rs is positive or negative, rt is enlarged or reduced. There are three situations:

1. rs > 0, the reputation for the sender is positive, so the reputation of the target agent is also enlarged.
2. rs = 0, an agent does not have the interaction experience with the sender agent. This absence of experience leads to set the sender's reputation as 0. This means if the agent does not have interaction experience with the sender agent, it will simply accept any reputation reference from the anonymous senders.
3. rs < 0, the reputation of the sender agent is negative. The agent might have some unhappy experience with the sender. The reputation forwarded from the sender is discounted, the more negative the sender's reputation, and the more weakened the target agent's reputation.

Multi-Source and Decaying Reputation

According to section 4.1, propagating the reputation through inquiry method may form a chain that connects multiple agents which forward or respond to the inquiry request. Whether the reputation propagated along the chain is decaying or lossless is an interesting problem. If it is lossless, the remote agents can send the intact reputation to the inquiry agent across many middle agents. Such situation is not good for huge agent society which is made up of many clusters of agents. An agent might be significantly influenced by a totally unrelated stranger from a remote cluster. On the contrary, if the reputation is decaying with a long distance between sender agent and receiving agent, the reputation might reach 0 before it can arrive at the receiving agent. Both the above two situations are not perfect choice. A good solution is to introduce a variable called "decaying coefficient", which can help adjust the degree of decaying speed. Then the designer or programmer of agents can control how far the reputation should propagate. For large agent society, the coefficient could be moderate so that

98 the distance of propagation is confined to reasonable clusters; for small agent society, the coefficient could be adjusted so that the reputation can be ensured to reach the farthest agent at the border of the society.

The variable is defined as, then the variable is added to the formula mentioned in the above section:

$$r_a = \Upsilon r_t(1+r_s)$$

Without considering the situation of magnifying reputation (gossip), it is convenient to define the γ as $0 \leq \gamma \leq 1$. Let n represents the number between the sender agent and the receiving agent, N represents the total number of agents in an agent society.

Then n can be used to decide the value of γ by using a sigmoid function:

$$r_a = \frac{1}{1 - e^{-n}}$$

By substituting, the formula becomes:

$$r_a = \frac{1}{1 - e^{-n}} r_t(1 + r_s) \ (0 \leq n < N)$$

When an agent accepts the reputation, it needs to update its trust pattern against specific agent using this reputation. The updating method is to simply put the reputation as the input data for the NTR pattern. Just like the other input data, the reputation is another dimension which will contribute to the formation of the trust pattern. The process of how to emerge a trust pattern based on the input data is covered in Section 5.

SUMMARY

This section mainly discusses the reputation related topics in the neural trust learning model. The definition of the reputation is first analyzed from five aspects. The reputation mechanism is then designed from three levels: reputation generation, reputation propagation and reputation receiving. Three propagation mechanisms are proposed to construct a reputation network. They are point-to-point inquiry, broadcasting and observer. The processes of each type are described in details. Then an approach of generating reputation based on the STL algorithm is designed so that the agent can produce reputation for other agents through investigating its own experience with the target agent. A decaying covariance is also introduced to deal with the problem of reputation decaying in case the reputation is variable along the propagation chain. In the last section, the section proposes the approach of absorbing the reputation received from other agents, which is also based on the STL algorithm.

REFERENCES

Hannemann, J. Kiczales, G. (2002), Design pattern implementation in java and aspect. ACM Sigplan Notices, 37(11), 161-173.

Hedetniemi, S., M., & Hedetniemi, S.T., Liestman, A.L. (1988). A survey of gossiping and broadcasting in communication networks. *Networks*, *18*(4), 319-349.

Zhou, W.L., & Wu, X. F. (2006). Survey of P2P technologies. Retrieved from en.cnki.com.cn

Chapter 20
Findings and Discussions on the Neural Trust and Multi–Agent System

Gehao Lu
University of Huddersfield, UK & Yunnan University, China

Joan Lu
University of Huddersfield, UK

ABSTRACT

This chapter focuses on the testing for a complete systematic neural trust model developed previously based on the trust learning algorithms, trust estimation algorithm and reputation mechanisms. The focus is to describe the detailed design of the model and explain the rationales behind the model design. The purpose is to evaluate the proposed neural trust model from different aspects and analyze the results of the evaluations. Experiments have been conducted. Results are presented and discussed. Finally, based on the analysis and comparison of acquired results, conclusions are drawn.

1. INTRODUCTION

Before actually starting testing, an agent test bed is the necessity of the evaluation and should be carefully designed and implemented. It should follow some guidelines and choose an appropriate mature platform. Currently, JADE is the researcher's choice. The architecture of the test bed is presented and some of the implementation details are also presented. The experiment environment, the experiment data preparation and the simulated testing data are demonstrated as well.

In order to evaluate the model, it is necessary to compare the model with other existing models. As analyzed in background, most models are based on numeric or statistical foundation. The compared model should be built upon such mechanism, also, it should be easy to implement. The research takes a simple numeric model to be compared with the proposed model. The comparison is carried out from two perspectives. The first perspective is to compare the quality of interaction through checking the successful rate of transactions; the second perspective is to compare the efficiency of discovering

DOI: 10.4018/978-1-5225-1884-6.ch020

malevolent agents from all agents. The comparison is prepared as two stages. In stage 1, the simple numeric model is taken as the baseline to be compared with the proposed model without the reputation propagation mechanism. The result of this stage is to exhibit the evidence that the learning capability of the proposed model is better than the simple numeric model. In stage 2, the proposed model without the reputation propagation mechanism is taken as the baseline to be compared with the proposed model with the reputation propagation mechanism. The result of this stage is to exhibit the positive influence of propagating reputation among agents. It also can reveal the fact that the socialized agents are better than individual agent on recognizing trustworthiness.

2. TEST-BED DESIGN AND IMPLEMENTATION

For evaluating the effectiveness of the proposed computational trust and reputation models, a test bed is designed and implemented to provide an experimental platform. The test bed is built in Java programming language and it makes use of the agent framework JADE (Bellifemine, Caire & Greenwood, 2007) to provide agent management, agent communication and multi-agent environment. The test bed is based on the JADE API and JADE Agent Containers. The research chooses the experimental scenario as the electronic commerce activities that are finished by autonomous agents.

2.1 Objective and Requirements

The objective of the test-bed is to build an automated experimental platform to test the feasibility and effectiveness of the proposed computational trust and reputation models. In order to realize the objective, the test bed needs to meet four basic requirements during its design and implementation.

- **Agent Oriented:** The test bed should be designed and implemented as an autonomous agent based multi-agent system. The research aims to build a computational trust and reputation models for multi-agent systems. Thus the test bed should be a multi-agent system. The architecture of the test bed should also be established from units of autonomous agent. This means the basic elements of the design are autonomous agents. The system is designed and functioned through modeling the interaction among different roles of agents. The techniques of object oriented programming are also used in the implementation level instead of the system design level (The programs create agents are also object oriented programs).
- **Supporting Multiple Mechanisms:** The focus of the research is the computational trust model and reputation mechanism. In order to state the superiority of the proposed models and mechanism, the test bed should not only support the research proposing mechanisms but also support the other popular trust and reputation related mechanisms. Furthermore, agents in the test bed should have the capability of choosing the different trust and reputation mechanisms as needed. Only with such capabilities, is it possible to let the agents in the test bed to be able to run in different trust/reputation mechanisms. So the researcher can compare the performance of different trust/reputation mechanisms and figure out the advantages and disadvantages of the proposed mechanisms.
- **Simulating the Real World E-Commerce Transactions:** The autonomous agents in the test bed have to be assigned with some tasks so that they can interact for achieving the tasks. With the tasks, the test bed can reveal the results of the trust/reputation mechanisms. The tasks are orga-

nized in the form of a scenario. In this research, the researcher chooses the most ordinary electronic commerce as the scenario of the test bed. And the transactions take place in the e-commerce environments become the task of the autonomous agents. The test bed needs to simulate a virtual market with hundreds of autonomous agents which represent the authorizations and goals of the human users. The agents in the market will transact with each other to fulfill their bestowed goals. They will turn to exploit the trust/reputation mechanism before and after they start e-commerce transactions.

- **Following Standards:** The test bed should follow the standard or popular techniques of multi-agent systems, that is, the test bed should be built upon the existing agent framework. In such open source framework, many agent related functionalities are already in the state of maturity. It is convenient to directly use the application interface from the open framework instead of creating everything from scratch. The second level meaning of following standards is to let the design follow the standards in the field of agent programming. The current agreed industry standards for computer agents are Foundation International Physical Agent (FIPA) (FIPA, n.d.). The test bed should also follow this industry standard and avoid violation.

FIPA (Foundation for Intelligent, Physical Agents) specification was initially set up as a five-year mandate to specify selected aspects of MAS. It mainly focuses on the communication and interoperation specifications instead of the internal implementations of agents. The specification specifies the agent communication language (ACL) which includes content language, communicative acts and interaction protocols; it specifies the core communication support which includes naming, transport and directory service (it is also called Abstract Architecture); it also specifies additional communication support like agent management (mobility support, ontology service, and configuration management etc is still under drafting).

2.2 Development Tools

To implement the test bed, the selection of the programming language is important. Theoretically, there is no compulsion in choosing the languages. Every language can be programmed to support a multi-agent system. But in the real world, an agent is a mobile program (mobile agent) that can cross hardware boundaries. The range of the information transmission and agent migration can be as large as the range of the Internet. The actual solution has to consider the heterogeneity of the computers, networks and software implementations. Java is the best language to tackle the difference because it is a programming language that is "write once, run anywhere". Its platform independence makes it the best choice for implementing a multi-agent system which allows a fully distributed agent deployment. The low level difference is hidden so that the researcher can focus on the design of interaction schemes and agent roles.

The widespread of MAS paradigm leads to the requirement of building good MAS based development tools and platforms. Both the academic communities and industrial groups develop their platforms in the process of building the MAS projects (Lu, Lu, Yao & Yip, 2009). In these projects, JADE (Bellifemine et al, 2007), FIPA-OS (Team, 2011), and ZEUS (Nwana et al, 1999) are the most prominent and prevalent platforms that support MAS development. The similarities among the three platforms are: all of them are based on Java programming language, all of them are open-source project, and all of them claim to strictly follow the FIPA (Foundation for Intelligent Physical Agents) specification.

In order to choose the best platform from the candidate platform, the researcher uses three tables to compare them from different facets. Table 3 compares the compliancy of the three platforms taking seven layers of the FIPA 2000 specification as criteria. Y, N, P is inserted before the table: In this table, Y represents Yes, N represents No and P represents possible which means that the specific platform currently does not have the characteristic but leave interface to add such characteristic. Table 1 (Gehao et al, 2009) focuses on the maturity of the agent development platform through compare different platforms on monitoring and management, debugging, mobility, integration, and programming paradigm. Table 2 (Gehao et al, 2009) compares three platforms through their activity, popularity, accessibility and intellectual property form.

Through observing the above three tables, the compliancy percentages for JADE, FIPA-OS and ZEUS are 100.

Thus, JADE platform is a better choice for MAS development than FIPA-OS and ZEUS in FIPA compliancy, platform maturity and non-technical concerns. The test bed will be designed and implemented based on the JADE platform.

Java Agent DEvelopment Framework (JADE) (Bellifemine et al, 2007) is Java based agent platform developed by Telecom Italia Lab. It is an open source project and installation can be obtained free of charge from http://jade.tilab.com/ under GNU lesser GPL. It is fully FIPA compliant and on top of that it supports all FIPA message encodings (XML, Lisp, and binary). There is a direct support for SL, RDF, and XML content languages. It supports multiple containers that can be running on different machines forming one agent platform. FIPA compliant White and Yellow pages services are available. There is a

Table 1. FIPA compliancy: FIPA compliancy for three platforms

	Transport	Encoding	Messaging	Ontology	Content Expressing	Commutative Act	Interaction Protocol
JADE (Bellifemineet al, 2007)	Y	Y	Y	Y	Y	Y	Y
FIPA-OS (Team, 2011)	Y	P	P	Y	Y	Y	Y
ZEUS (Nwanaet al, 1999)	P	P	Y	Y	N	Y	Y

Gehao et al., 2009.

Table 2. Platform maturity: platform maturity for three platforms

	Monitoring and Management	Debugging	Mobility	Integration	Programming Paradigm
JADE (Bellifemine et al., 2007)	Administration GUI	Event monitor and logger	LEAP	Web Service	API-based Programming
FIPA-OS (Team, 2011)	Wizard based configuration	DIAGNOSITCS class used to store debug message into file	Micro-fipaos	N/A	API-based Programming
ZEUS (Nwana et al, 1999)	Utility Agents and Visualizer	Visualizer check event happening	N/A	Wrapper	Visual Programming

Gehao et al., 2009.

support for an interconnected set of these services defined by the user. A subscription for these services is available too. Agent programming is based on Java language with additional support for behaviors and events. Both ontology and mobility are supported. There is no additional support for development of agents, but there is support for debugging which includes built-in message viewer and agent introspector.

Multiple network communication protocols are supported and additional ones can be developed via Message Transfer Protocol plug-ins. There is a very good support for different virtual machines like J2ME, J2EE, and also for .NET framework. The platform offers a scalability and communication speed. Security and web services are also supported. There is a collection of add-ons and 3rd party software available since there is a community of developers that are using JADE.

2.3 Test Bed Architecture

The test bed is made up of two major parts: The JADE platform and the agent activity zone. The JADE platform provides the regular management functionalities such as agent management, container management, and communication management. It creates an environment for agents communicating and interacting. It enforces the communicating protocol and the ways of agent behaviors. The agent activity zone is the workplace for agent transactions. Agents reside in their respective container and carry out transactions with other agents. According to the functions, the zone can be subdivided into three parts: autonomous agents, trust services and pattern libraries. The trust services and pattern libraries are called just like that they are the internal components of the autonomous agents. In order to explain their design mechanisms clearly, they are separated into independent parts. Figure 1 illustrates the architecture and components of the test bed.

The JADE platform is deployed as a typical distributed system. Every computer joins the platform becomes a "Container". Agents reside in these containers and the containers have the responsibilities to manage the agents. Among the containers, one of the computers plays a role called "Main Container". The main container might be a server with more powerful computing capabilities. It is the control center of the JADE platform. The main container manages a table called the container table which registers the object references and transport addresses of all the ordinary containers. Every container also manages a LADT table and a GADT table. The LADT represents the Local Agent Descriptor table and the GADT represents Global Agent Descriptor Table. The LADT manages a list for local agents. The container uses

Table 3. Non-technical concerns: non-technical concerns for three platforms

	Activity	**Popularity**	**Accessibility**	**Intellectual Property Form**
JADE (Bellifemine et al, 2007)	Available and maintained	About 40000 downloads	From JADE homepage	Open source, general public license
FIPA-OS (Team, 2011)	The latest accounted activity is dated on 2003	About 50000 downloads	From Source-forge.net	Open source, public domain, free of charge for noncommercial use
ZEUS (Nwana et al, 1999)	The last version is dated to 2001 and the ZEUS homepage was last updated in Jan 2001	No information provided	From ZEUS homepage	Open source, Mozilla Public License

Gehao et al, 2009.

the LADT to find whether the message recipient lives in the container. The GADT caches the global agent information that the container receives, this help the system to avoid bottleneck of the main container. The AMS represent the Agent Management System. The AMS

is an agent that monitors all the agents on the platform. It controls the life cycle of each agent and the agent that needs to start an interaction also first inquires the AMS for the contact information. Agents need to register to the AMS when they start up their lifecycles. DF represents Directory Facilitator and it is also an agent that is responsible for implementing the yellow page service. Agents can publish their service onto the yellow page so that the other agents can search for their preferred services. An agent can subscribe to the yellow page service. Once the service is updated or new services added, the agent will get notification for the changes.

Each agent has an agent identifier which helps the other agents search and interact with it. The identifier is a unique name globally. The name takes the form:< local - name > @ < platform -name >. The local name is the agent's name in the container and the platform name is the name of the container. Before starting an agent, it is necessary to start the JADE platform first (The platform behaves like an application server in client/server architectures). Once an agent is started, it sends registration request to the DF agent and it stays being alive until it is terminated by the AMS. Autonomous agents have goals and tasks. The task is represented as a behavior. There can be multiple behaviors assigned to one agent. JADE provides three types of behavior: one shot behavior, cyclic behavior and generic behavior. An agent can select one type of behavior or it can embed different types of behaviors to compose more complex compound behaviors. The communication methods among agents follow the FIPA specification and Agent Communication Language (FIPA, n.d.). There are a series of ACL primitives that covers the common terms required in communication. Fox example, INFORM represents sending a piece of

Figure 1. Test bed architecture: the test bed architecture for computational trust and reputation

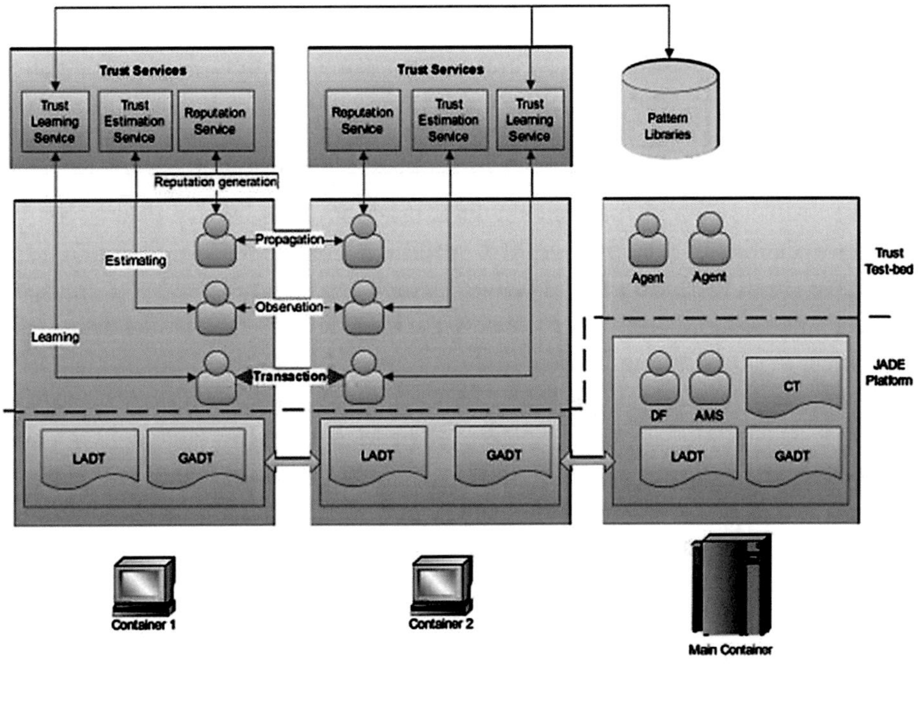

information about some facts. CFP represents call for proposal from another agent. The messages sent between agents are asynchronous. Each agent maintains a queue to manage its receiving messages. The DF agent is started with the JADE platform and it manages the yellow page service for all agents. Agents publish their services to the yellow page and some other agents may try to search the services they have interests from this page. In the scenario of electronic commerce, the seller agent post their product selling services to the page when they come created and the buyer agents tend to search products from this page.

The trust services are the core components of the test bed design. The services include the trust learning service, the trust estimation service and the reputation service. These three services are independent with each other and each of them can be executed concurrently. Autonomous agents use one of the services according to the stage that they step into. The trust learning service encapsulates the STL algorithm for learning trust patterns. The estimation service encapsulates the trustworthiness estimation algorithm. The reputation service encapsulates the reputation generation algorithm and reputation propagation mechanism. Every service is designed as one kind of behavior of the agents. Because behavior is one critical part of an agent, the behavior wrapped services are depended on the agent. When an agent starts its life cycle in the system, the trust services component generate an instance of the services as the form of a behavior and assign this behavior to the specific agent. Thus an agent owns the trust related behaviors after it comes into being. The ultimate goal of the services is to help agents achieve transactions with better quality. The behavior wrapped services should be plugged before and after the transaction behaviors so that they can take effect and protect the enclosed transactions. Before the transactions, the estimation service based behavior is executed so that the agent can predict the potential trustworthiness of its opponents. After the transactions, the trust learning service based behavior is executed so that the agent can learn from the finished transactions and improve its cognition toward the specific agents.

Pattern libraries store and manage the patterns learned from previous transactions for agents. The pattern libraries are not central to all the containers and agents. In the deployment, the solution is to assign one pattern library only for one agent. The life cycle of an agent may be temporally terminated but the pattern library is kept in the database forever. Such design is to ensure the experiences learned from the history won't be lost due to the interrupt of agents' life cycle. When an agent is revived by the AMS, it retrieves its patterns from its own pattern library to recreate its belief of trust. The pattern library is simply made up of three tables: TransactionPatterns table, AgentPatterns table and MacroPatterns table. They are corresponding to the three types of patterns. The relationships among them are an accumulating relationship. The TransactionPatterns table is the basic one that collects all the previous data about transactions. It records the pattern for each single transaction done by the agent. The AgentPatterns table is a view by accumulating the patterns of a specific agent in the TransactionPatterns table. The MacroPatterns table stores the most general patterns which are accumulated by all transactions and all agents. Patterns are the most important data stored in the library. It is a matrix like data so the researcher uses a generic object to store the pattern data in the program. It appears as binary data in the database tables. The marking attribute illustrate the results of the transactions. It is a Boolean value because the transaction is either successful (true) or failed (false). The MacroPatterns table does not need the marking attribute because the patterns recorded in the table combines all the successful patterns and failed patterns to create a macro pattern which contains the emerged feature for both successful transaction or failed transaction. The library is implemented as a cluster of databases. The physical implementation is based on MySQL relational database. Figure 2 illustrates the conceptual model of the pattern library.

Figure 2. Pattern library: conceptual model of the pattern libraries

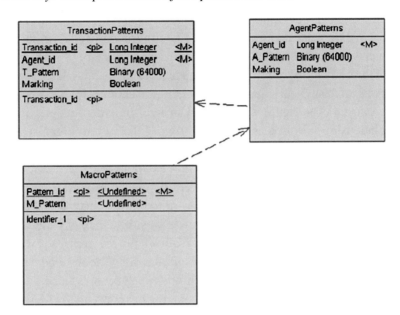

2.4 Test Bed Implementation

Figure 3 illustrates the package diagram of the test bed. The Sellers and Buyers package contains the seller agents and buyer agents. The behavior package contains the regular behavior classes for carrying out transactions. The additional trust related behaviors are accomplished through the Learning-Services package, Estimating-Service package and Reputation-Service package. The seller and buyer agents install the behaviors from the Behaviors package and finish the tasks in the way of the behaviors. The

Figure 3. Test bed implementation: test bed package diagram

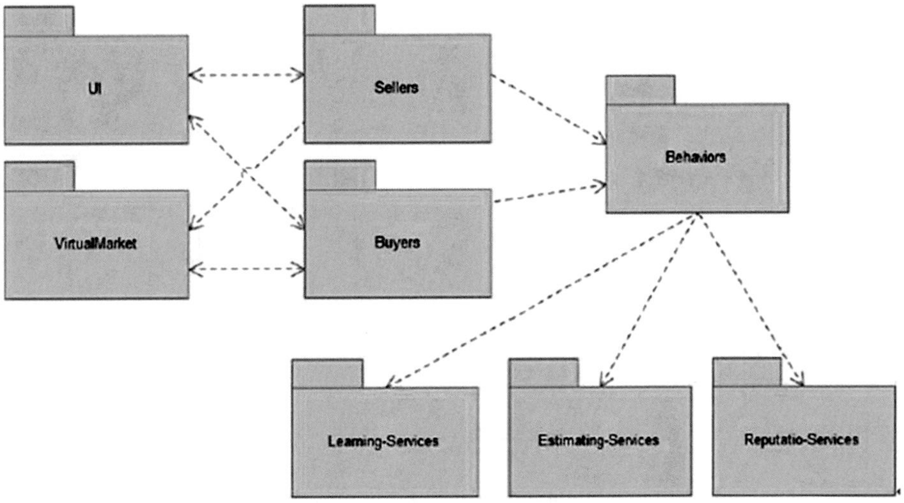

UI package contains the classes related to the graphical user interface. The process of transactions, the display of the learned patterns is all realized through this package. The VirutalMarket package contains the utility class and constant class that represents the configuration of the virtual market and it also contains the product classes that are to be sold in the multi-agent system.

The key classes of the implementation are the buyer agent class and the seller agent class. The research takes the buyer agent as an example to illustrate the internal structures. Figure 4 is the implementation diagram for the buyer agent. The figure is drawn in Unified Modeling Language and the connection is the association relationship among classes. In this figure, the system organizes the functionalities around the BuyerAgent. The behaviors of the buyer agent can be divided into two categories. The first category is the common transaction related behaviors. For example, the TransacTicker class plays a role of controlling the time. If the waiting time is up, the agent stops sending CFP request to the other agents. The purchase behavior finishes the regular transactions through messages based communication. The other category is the trust related behavior. The research uses the Strategy pattern to create a flexible selection scheme of trust behaviors. The design pattern allows the researcher to switch the trust related behaviors quickly and adds new algorithm based behaviors easily. The test bed can compare different trust mechanisms and help the researcher evaluate the proposed algorithms and mechanisms. The market model defines the configuration details of the context. For the buyer agent, the MarketModel class gives information that facilitates the potential transactions.

3. PREPARATION

3.1 Experimental Scenario

The experimental scenario for testing the computational model and reputation should be simple enough so that it can reveal the advantages and disadvantages of the specific algorithms and mechanisms. At

Figure 4. Implementation of the buyer agent: class diagram for implementing the buyer agent

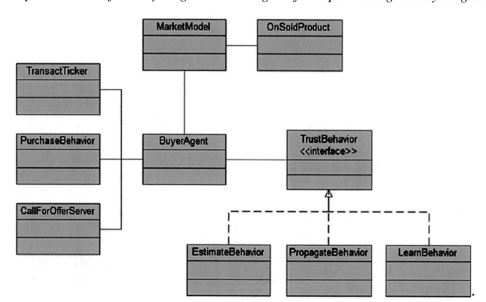

the same time, the scenario should have realistic significance so that the researcher can have intuitive experiences about the pragmatic value of the study. The common applications for multi-agent systems include games, web assistants; computer aided planning, industry process controls, and automated electronic commerce, etc. The research chooses the automated electronic commerce as the experimental scenario because its simplicity and understandability. It might be the most familiar type of interaction for the readers. The major interactions in the electronic commerce are transactions and the objects or domains for the transactions are simply the product being transacted. This scenario gives the researcher a clear structure to design the test bed and to test the algorithms.

The scenario is automated e-commerce. The word "automated" means that the transaction, including searching products, enquiry, negotiation, placing orders, payments, deliveries, are all done by the autonomous agents. At this stage, the technical development cannot avoid human intervention. Some critical authorizations and decisions have to be made by human users. The agents here behave like a representative of the transactions. The evaluations of the transactions have to be done by the users who authorize the agents to transact unless someday the agents' capability of cognition reaches the highness of understanding the goodness and badness of the transactions.

There are two roles of agents in the scenario: buyer agents and seller agents. The buyer agent is trying to search their preferred products from the service list published by the seller agents. The seller agents and buyer agents will communicate and transact with each other under the interaction protocol as mentions previously. The seller agents are more complicated. They can hold two types of attitudes during the transactions: benevolent attitude and malevolent attitude. The probabilities of providing good products from the benevolent seller agents are high, while the probabilities of providing good products from the malevolent seller agents are low. The judgments about good products are achieved through reviewing the dimensional data of the product domain. The major task of seller agent is to investigate how the computational trust and reputation can help buyer agents avoid inferior transactions with malevolent seller agents.

Books are the default product selling through the autonomous agents in the experimental scenario. Thus the domain of the product is the book. The dimensions for describing a book transaction are set as reputation, price, quality, delivery, and after-sale. Reputation refers to the transferred reputation from the other agents, price refers the soundness of the price level, quality refers to the cognition of the product quality, delivery refers to the satisfaction of the delivery speed and quality, and after-sale refers to the cognition of the after-sale service quality. For simplifying the evaluation of the dimension, every dimension is marked as 1 for good and 0 for bad. Such simplified setting is also convenient for the learning algorithm to read the product dimensional data as input vectors. The simplification is only for easier understanding. In the real case, the dimensional input is provided by the human users and the value is between 0 and 1 according to their subjective judgment. When the user feel a dimension is not good enough, he or she will give a value close to 0. In the experiments, the input data is actually generated as decimal value between 0 and 1.

3.2 Data Preparation

The experimental data are mainly the simulated transaction data that appears in the form of production dimensions. After every round of the transaction between two agents, one line (vector) of the data is provided to the buyer agent. There are two groups of transactional data. The first group is training transactional data. Data in this group are generated according the proportion of benevolent agents and malevolent agents. For each seller agent, there is a file assigned for it to be its simulated transactional data. The second group contains the test data (observation data). This group is design for testing the ability of differentiating bad transactions of the buyer agents after learning the computational trust through the first training group. The data of these two groups are generated through transactional data generating program. In the real world, all transactional data should be provided by human user who owns the agent and authorize the agent to represent him/her.

To simulate the transactional data of thousands of agents, it is not realistic to manually design the data from scratch. The better way is to set the rule of data generation and let the computer program to produce the data for testing. The researcher designs a simple program to do this job. The algorithm of data generation is described as follows:

```
1. While(!end of file){
2. if(benevolent){
Marking = 1;
At least 3 random slots = 1;
}
3. else if(malevolent){
Marking = 0;
At least 3 random slots = 0;
4. next line;
}
```

In this data generation algorithm: A new file is created for one agent. The slots and marks in this file are all initialized to 0. The algorithm will change the value of the slot and the value of the mark according to the rule in the algorithm. The size of file is 100 lines. Each line is the data of five dimensions plus the marking. The marking represent the subjective evaluation of the transaction as a whole. All the value in the table is restricted to either 1 or 0. "1" is positive result and vice versa. The transactional data is either for benevolent seller agents or for malevolent seller agents. The research set that one half of the seller agents are benevolent and the others are malevolent. For the benevolent agent, the probability of being benevolent is 80%, it still have 20% chances to be malevolent. The method of generating benevolent data is: Marking = 1, for the other 5 slots, assigns 1 to more than 3 slots. The slot being assigned is randomly specified. For the malevolent agent, the probability of being malevolent is 80%, where there is a 20% chance of being benevolent. The method of generating malevolent data is: Marking = 0, for the other 5 slots, assign 0 to more than 3 slots. The slot being assigned is randomly specified. Then generate the next line. If the line number reaches 100, then quit and start again for another new agent file.[1]

Table 4 is an example of simulated transactional data. Each line evaluates a transaction from 5 dimensions. The marking is a subjective evaluation to the transaction as a whole. The example is a fragment extracted from a benevolent agent's transactional data file.

Table 5 gives a summary of the experimental data. The number of agents attended to the scenario is 100; and 50% of them are buyer agents and the other 50% are seller agents. The attitudes of the seller agents are also split evenly: 50% benevolent and 50% malevolent. That means there will 25 benevolent seller agents and 25 malevolent seller agents. The number of simulated data files is equal to the number of agents. The size of the data files actually equals the number of transactions that one agent will do during its life cycle. Thus the number of transactions is 150,000.

Table 4. Examples of simulated data: examples of simulated transactional data

Reputation	Price	Quality	Delivery	After-Sale	Marking
1	0	1	0	1	1
1	1	1	1	1	1
0	0	0	0	1	0
0	1	1	1	0	1

Table 5. Summary of data preparation: summary of data preparations is listed in this table

The Total Number of Agents	100
Number of Buyer Agents (50%)	50
Number of Seller Agents (50%)	50
Benevolent Seller Agents	25
Malevolent Seller Agents	25
Number of Transactions	150.000
Number of Simulated data _les	50
Size of the data _le (lines)	60

¹The research provides installation guidance and testing report as the attachments. The source code of the test bed can also be downloaded fromhttp://www.ynsoft.org.

Table 6 shows the conjuration of the experiment environment. The test bed is deployed in a distributed manner. The main container is a Server with 2.13 GHz Xeon CPU and 4GB memory. The ordinary containers are three PCs with Intel Conroe i3 2100 CPU and 2GB memory. The operating system for the main container is Window 2003 Server and the operating system for the containers is Windows 7. All the computers are connected with 100M LAN.

The simulated data is generated through program and the initial marking of the transactional data is also allocated by the program according to the predefined benevolent/malevolent probability. This might be different from the real data which is generated from the real transaction and marked by the real human user. However, this won't negatively influence the validity of the test bed because the recognition of trust will reflect patterns according to the simulated data in case the data do have some regularity. In the real world, human input tends to be even less regular than the input generated from computer programs, so once the model works fine in the simulated data. It will reveal the pattern or regularity from the transactional data marked by the real human users.

Table 6. Summary of experiment environment: summary of experiment environment and configuration

Hardware	1 Server (IBM X3400 M3, Xeon 2.13GHz, 4GB memory) as the main container, 3 PCs (Lenovo i4160, Intel Conroe i3 2100) as the container. Each container uns 250 agents.
Software	JADE platform and Trust Test bed, Window Server 2003 for Server and Window 7 for PCs.
Network	100Mb LAN

4. RESULTS

After building the experiment environment, it is time to use the test bed to evaluate the proposed framework and its internal algorithms and mechanisms. The most direct choice is to compare the proposed framework with some other trust mechanisms. The precondition of the comparison is that both trust frameworks should be working in the same platform and process the same data in the same duration. The results of the comparison mainly focus on two aspects: operational effectiveness and operational performance. The operational effectiveness means that the specified algorithm or mechanism can effectively finish the designed jobs and achieve satisfied qualities. The operational performance means that the specified algorithm or mechanism can finish the designated jobs as timely as possible. These two aspects are also criteria for successfully evaluating the proposed model.

4.1 The Compared Algorithm: A Simple Number Based Model

There are many computational trust related mechanisms and algorithms developed in the past few years. Some typical algorithms have been introduced in details. Majority of these trust/reputation models are based on number or statistical methods. Here, the research chooses a simple but popular model to be compared with the proposed framework. This model is based on a simple number based method: addition and subtraction. The trust is represented as a numeric value. The initial trust value is 0. After each successful transaction, the agent simply adds 1 to its trust value. On the contrary, after each failed transaction, the agent simply minus 1 from its trust value. The sum of the addition indicates the trustworthiness of the agent toward another agent. The agent sets a threshold to be the judgment rule on decision making. For example, if the threshold is set as 30, an agent trust value less than 30 will not enter any transactions with the host agent. The trust value can also be negative number which means degree of trustworthiness is none and the untrustworthiness is big. Although such model is relatively simple, it is widely accepted as the basis of many successful e-commerce web sites. For example, the customer rating system of Taobao (Taobao, 2011), EBay (Ebay, 2012) are all advanced variations from the basic number based model. To use the number based model, the comparison can be close to the real world application. Additionally, the simple model is easy to implement on the test bed. This saves great effort in designing and programming.

4.2 Simple Number Based Model vs. Neural Trust Model

The first experiment is to compare the successful rate of buyer agents between the proposed framework and the number based model. This is a test especially designed for evaluating the operational effectiveness of the algorithms. The successful rate refers to the rate of successful transactions among all the transactions. Such rate can reflect two things about the trust models. The first thing revealed is that the high-low of the ability of avoiding malevolent agents. The second thing revealed is the accuracy of finding benevolent agents. When facing thousands of seller agents, the inferior model tends to make many wrong decisions and transact with malevolent agent thus decrease the rate of successful transactions.

There are 100 agents participate into the experiment. One half of them play the role of buyer agent and the other half plays the role of seller agent. Among the 50 seller agents, 25 of them are malevolent. The experiment is designed to see which model can achieve better and higher successful rate. The simulated transaction data contains 150,000 lines of transactional data. The testing time is about 4 hours (15000 seconds). The sniffer programs are set in the test bed to record the number of successful transactions at the sampling time. The sampling interval is 1500 seconds. Both models are first trained with a set of prepared data listed previously.

Figure 5 illustrates the result of comparing the specified two models on the successful rate of transactions. The successful rate refers to the rate of transactions that the result is marked as positive 1 by the end user. This rate is a measurement to reflect the degree how the trust model helps the agents improve their transactional quality. The horizontal axis is the time used in the transactions. The range of the time is from 1500 seconds to 15000 seconds. The vertical axis is the rate in percentage. The range is from 0% to 100%. The two lines in the figure represent the two types of models to be compared. Trust1 line represents the number based model. Trust2 represents the proposed model. Both lines start from 1500 seconds. It is clear that Trust2 line is superior to Trust1 line from the start point. The initial rate of success reaches 13% for Trust2; the Trust1 is only 1%. The difference is kept until the end of all transactions. The final rate of success for Trust2 reaches 98% while the final rate of success for Trust1 is only 36%.

The second experiment is to compare the elimination speed of malevolent agents between the proposed framework and the number based model. This is a test especially designed for evaluating the operational performance of the algorithms. Elimination refers to finding out the malevolent agents and let agents stop any further transactions with the malevolent ones. Just like the malevolent agents are eliminate from the electronic market. A better algorithm or a better model needs eliminate the malevolent agent as quick as possible so that the agents can avoid unnecessary loss in the future transactions.

There are 100 agents participate into the experiment. One half of them play the role of buyer agent and the other half plays the role of seller agent. Among the 50 seller agents, 25 of them are malevolent. The

Figure 5. Simple number based model vs. neural trust model: successful rate for the compared models

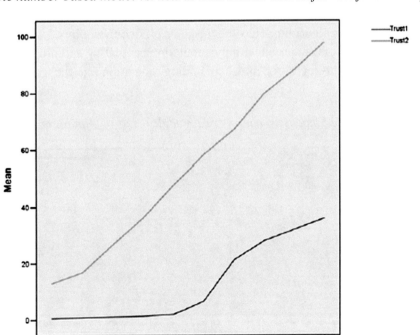

experiment is designed to see which algorithm can find all these malevolent agents as quick as possible. The simulated transaction data contains 150,000 lines of transactional data. The testing time is about 4 hours (15000 seconds). The sniffer programs are set in the test bed to record the number of eliminated agents at the sampling time. The sampling interval is 500 seconds. Both models are first trained with a set of prepared data listed earlier.

Figure 6 illustrates the result of eliminating malevolent agents in a line diagram. In this figure, the horizontal axis indicate the time that the test bed executing. The range of time is from 500 seconds to 15000 seconds. The vertical axis is the mean number of eliminated agents for both models. The range of the number is from 0 to 25. There are two lines in the figure. The line named Trust1 represents the number based model and the line named Trust2 represents the proposed model. In the first 1000 seconds, both models are uneventful and do not find any malevolent agents. Within 1500 seconds, the proposed model starts to find the first malevolent agent and the

Trust2 line exceeds the Trust1 line. The difference of two lines keeps magnifying. The Trust2 reaches the top value of 25 at the time of 12500 seconds. It keeps this number until the end of the experiment. The Trust1 only reaches 11 at the time of 14000 seconds. This indicates that the number based model does not find all the malevolent agents.

4.3 Reputation vs. Non-Reputation

The above experiments compare two different models to evaluate the operational effectiveness and performance effectiveness of the proposed framework. Next, the research turns to the test the reputation related behaviors. The goal of the next comparison is also changed to check the influence of the reputation. Thus the target of comparison is no longer the number based trust model. Now the comparison will be carried out

between two instances of the proposed framework. One instance is only equipped with trust learning algorithm and trust estimation algorithm. The other instance is not only equipped with all the algorithms of the first instance but also it is enhanced with the reputation generating and propagating mechanism. The key to the comparison is to reveal the impact of adding reputation into the transactions.

Figure 6. Simple number based model vs. neural trust model: result of eliminating malevolent agents

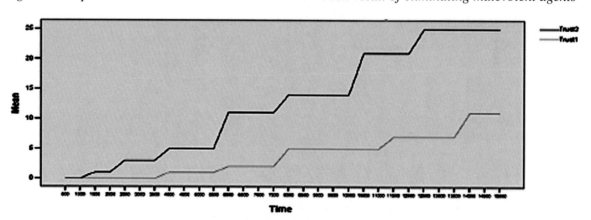

The first experiment is designed to compare the successful rate of buyer agents between the complete framework and the framework without reputations. The results can also help evaluate the operational effectiveness of two configurations. The comparison needs to prove that the existence of the reputation mechanism can improve the effectiveness of the whole framework. The speed of finding malevolent agents should also be improved. Furthermore, this experiment is a chance to explain why multi-agent systems work better than single intelligent agent.

There are 100 agents participating into the experiment. One half of them play the role of buyer agent and the other half plays the role of seller agent. Among the 50 seller agents, 25 of them are malevolent. The experiment is designed to see which configuration can achieve better and higher successful rate. The simulated transaction data contains 150,000 lines of transactional data. The testing time is about 4 hours (15000 seconds). The sniffer programs are set in the test bed to record the number of successful transactions at the sampling time. The sampling interval is 1500 seconds. Both models are first trained with a set of prepared data listed earlier.

Figure 7 illustrates the result of comparing the specified two configurations on the successful rate of transactions. The horizontal axis is the time used in the transactions. The range of the time is from 1500 seconds to 15000 seconds. The vertical axis is the rate in percentage. The range is from 0% to 100%. The two lines in the figure represent the framework and the framework without reputation respectively. They are called WithRepu line and TrustOnly line. Both lines start from 1500 seconds. The WithRepu line is superior to TrustOnly line at the starting point. The initial rate of success reaches 25% for WithRepu line; the TrustOnly is only 13%. The difference is kept until the end of all transactions. The final rate of success for WithRepu reaches 98% while the final rate of success for Trust1 reaches 94%. Although the final rate is close enough, the WithRepu quickly approach the maximum success rate while the TrustOnly approaches relatively slowly.

Figure 7. Reputation vs. non-reputation: result of comparing frameworks with and without reputation support

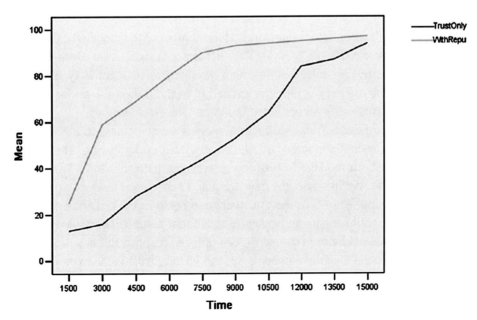

The next experiment is to compare the elimination speed under the condition with reputations and without reputations. The existence of reputations may influence the operational performance of the framework. The common sense about reputations is that an agent can avoid many unnecessary transactions if it is informed by the other agents in the form of reputations. Thus, the malevolent agents should be eliminated much more quick in an environment with reputations than in an environment without reputations. Additionally, the experiment can discover the degree of influences produced by the reputations.

There are 100 agents participating in the experiment. One half of them play the role of buyer agent and the other half plays the role of seller agent. Among the 50 seller agents, 25 of them are malevolent. The experiment is designed to see which configuration can find all these malevolent agents as quick as possible. The simulated transaction data contains 150,000 lines of transactional data. The testing time is about 4 hours (15000 seconds). The sniffer programs are set in the test bed to record the number of eliminated agents at the sampling time. The sampling interval is 500 seconds. Both configurations are first trained with a set of prepared data listed earlier.

Figure 7 illustrates the result of eliminating malevolent agents in a line diagram. In this figure, the horizontal axis indicate the time that the test bed executing. The range of time is from 500 seconds to 15000 seconds. The vertical axis is the mean number of eliminated agents for both configurations. The range of the number is from 0 to 25. There are two lines in the figure. The line named TrustOnly represents the configuration without reputations and the line named WithRepu represents the configuration with reputations. Two lines separate from the start point at 500 seconds. The WithRepu line lead the number of more eliminated malevolent agents from the beginning. Its advantages are magnified with the elapsing time. It first finishes eliminating jobs at 7500 seconds. Comparing to the TrustOnly line which reaches the top at 14000, it precedes for 6500 seconds. This saves one half of the transactional time.

5. DISCUSSION AND ANALYSIS

5.1 Analysis of Testing Scenarios

In the comparison between the proposed framework and the number based model, the final successful rate of the former precedes the later 62% (98%-36%). This difference is significant. Both models are trained before they are fed with the testing data. Both of them have generated specific type of memories. For the proposed framework, the memory is patterns learned from the training data; for the number based model, the memory is the trust value accumulated in the previous transactions.

During the testing phase, the data files used for both models are new transactional data. In these files, agents are new agents that haven't interacted with the buyer agents under testing. The transactional data are also fresh to agents for both models. In this case, the macro patterns stored in the pattern library become a solid foundation for dealing with the new agent and new data. The macro patterns are general patterns that reveal the general features of the so called good behaviors. The trust estimation algorithm can recognize the new transactional data and generate a potential pattern. Then the pattern is compared with the macro pattern. That's why the framework can quickly adapt to the new testing environment. On the contrary, though the agents in the number based model have trust value to memorize the specific agent's behavior, the trust value only takes effect when the agent meets the same agent in another round of transaction. In the testing, nothing is familiar to the agents in the model. This leads to a very slow adaptation to the environment. The agent has to interact with unfamiliar agents first and learn from

Figure 8. Reputation vs. non-reputation: result of eliminating agents between the proposed framework with and without reputations

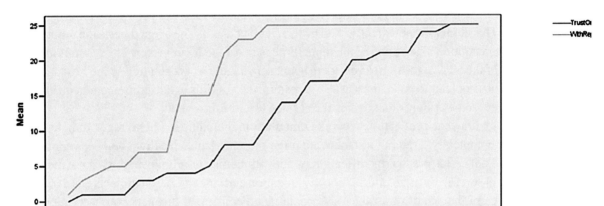

successes and failures from scratch. Figure 7 shows that during the first 9000 seconds, the successful rate is really low. After 9000 seconds, the successful rate has significant increasing. The number based model has to use lots of time and lots of negative transactions to be adapted. This is an unacceptable cost that should be avoided.

The speed of eliminating malevolent agents for the proposed framework is also higher than the number based model. The rationale of the superiority is similar to the discussion above. When facing new agents and new transactional data, there is no way for the agents in the number based model to know which agent is malevolent and which one is benevolent. They have to interact with the new agents first even these agents are all malevolent agents. They need to use failures to build the knowledge about the agents. The agents of the proposed framework are much better for adapting the new environment. The estimation algorithm provides a protection in advance. However, the number based model does have its advantage. Especially in a familiar environment, the performance of the number based model is better than the proposed framework. This is due to the complexity of the STL algorithm and the trust estimation algorithm. Both algorithms take much time to learn and to process the transactional data. The number based model does not have such complexity; all the operations are simply adding 1 or subtracting 1 from the numeric trust value. The maintenance of the trust value is also simple and direct. Thus, in a simple and restricted virtual society, the population of the agents is limited. The number based model or its improved variations are good choice. In an internet based virtual society, the heterogeneity of agents is high or the requirements of adaptation for agents are high. The framework in this research is better choice.

From the results, the reputation is proving to be an important complementary and improvement for the computational trust. In the result of Figure 35, the reputation enhanced framework greatly increases the rate of successful transaction. The biggest difference appears at the time of 9000 seconds, the difference reaches 40. The rationale behind is simple. When agents depend only on themselves to judge the malevolence and benevolence, they might be stuck into two dilemmas: either they lack the interaction experiences due to their short life cycle, or the environment changes are so significant that agents cannot adapt in a short time. In these situations, reputation become critical factor that help make up for the deficiencies.

There is another advantage of the reputation mechanism in the proposed framework. The process of receiving reputation is unique and creative. The reputation is transmitted in the form of messages which follows the format of the Agent communication language standards. The core part of the message is the reputation value. This number is not directly used by the receiver agent. The agent digests the reputations by accepting the reputation value as one of the input dimension of the input vector. The reputations then become one part of the STL algorithm. Even some agent sends incorrect reputation to the host agent. If such reputation does not lead to positive transaction results, the patterns against this agent is influenced and tend to generate some features that denies the service level of the agent.

One of the major drawbacks of neural network computation, including the SOM algorithm, has been its computational complexity. Training instances are often presented multiple times and network performance is achieved only after gradual modification of network connection/link weights. Our experience in adopting SOM in several mid-size information visualization and categorization projects (10-100 MBs, several to hundreds of thousands of abstract-size documents) confirmed this general observation. The computational complexity of the SOM algorithm has rendered it infeasible for large-scale applications (1-10 GBs, millions of documents, e.g., the entire searchable Internet WWW homepages). In order to improve the scalability of the SOM approach to textual classification, a more efficient algorithm is needed.

The computational complexity of neural networks including the SOM based algorithms is their major drawbacks because the networks need to process thousands of training instances by multiple times. The network performance is delayed by gradual modification of the synaptic weights. The above experiments also show that the STL and STE (SOM based algorithm) obey this general observation. In large scale real-time application, the STL and STE are infeasible under the current effectiveness. However, the usage of the STL and STE now is not used continuously or real-time. Basically, they are applied once after each round of agent transactions. The agent has sufficient resource and time to learn trust and estimate trustworthiness of the target agent in such circumstance.

The way of propagating reputation can also influence the performances of the agents. In this scenario, the point-to-point based inquiry is used as the default propagating method. The agent sends reputation only when it is inquired by some other agents. Such methods are appropriate for communities with middle size of agents. For bigger virtual societies, the observer propagation is the better choice because this method can greatly decrease the communications among agents. It is activated only when the registered topic or registered agent have some state changes. The message is only transmitted between the subscribers and the subject owners. For extremely small society, the broadcasting propagation is the best choice. In the small society, there are only a few agents. The host agent knows all the other agents. When the host agent has any interactions, it can report the reputation generated to all the agents it knows. This is good for small society with high real-time or high responsiveness requirement.

5.2 A Comparison between the Neural Trust Model and the Traditional Trust Models

The proposed neural trust model is going to be compared with the existing traditional trust models. The results of the comparison are listed in Table 7. There are 7 existing models which are listed to be compared with the neural trust model. They are TRAVOS (Teacy et al., 2006), FIRE (Huynh et al., 2004), ReGreT (Sabater and Sierra, 2002), Referal (Yu & Singh, 2000), Sporas (Zacharia et al., 1999), Marsh

Table 7. Neural model vs. existing models: comparison between the neural trust model and the traditional trust models

Model Name	Architecture	Trust Domain and Semantics	Belief Representation	Trust Learning	Decision Support	Reputation Generation	Propagation Mechanism
Neural Trust Model	Distributed	Ontological dimension	Patterns	Improved SOM based Neural Networks	Patterns differences reflect confidence	Pattern differences merged	Point-to-point, Broadcast, Observer
TRAVOS (Teacy et al., 2006)	Distributed	Applied to single domain	Probability (Bayesian framework)	N/A	Measure confidence in its value of trust	Weighted average of individual opinion	N/A
FIRE (Huynh et al., 2004)	Distributed	Ontology dimension	Number	N/A	reliability rating that reflects the confidence	Weighted accumulation of acquaintances	N/A
ReGreT (Sabater and Sierra, 2002)	Distributed	Applied to single domain	Number	N/A	Set threshold for the reliability	A weighted mean of the impressions' rating factors	N/A
Referal (Yu and Singh, 2000)	Distributed	Applied to single domain	Number	N/A	an upper and a lower threshold for trust	a total belief obtained from the original witnesses	Testimony propagation algorithm
Sporas (Zacharia et al., 1999)	Centralize	Applied to single domain	Number	N/A	A threshold is set for the reputation value	the weighted average of non-negative values	Directed graph representing the rating path
Marsh (Marsh, 1994a)	Distributed	Applied to single domain	Number	N/A	A threshold is set for the trust value	A weighted accumulation from agents	N/A
eBay (Ebay, 2012)	Centralized	Applied to single domain	Number	N/A	No threshold, judged by human users	Rated by human user	N/A

(Marsh, 1994a), and eBay (Ebay, 2012). The comparison is carried out from 7 selected aspects: Architecture, Trust domain semantics, and Belief representation, Trust learning, Decision support, Reputation generation, and Propagation mechanism. Each aspect reflects one facet of strength or weakness of the model. So the synthesis from different aspects can show obvious advantages of the proposed model.

- **Architecture:** 6 of 8 models are distributed models. Only eBay (Ebay, 2012) and Sporas (Zacharia et al., 1999) are centralized models. Distribution is a natural feature that a multi-agent system should possess. Agents distributed over different nodes of network across various geographical zones. Trust models should also follow the distributed deployment of agents. The neural trust model is purely distributed in that every agent has its own STL and STE algorithm embedded so that they can do trust related activities independently. There is no central repository for trusts or reputations. The trust is generated individually and the reputation is aggregated from acquaintances.

- **Trust Domain and Semantics:** Majority of the models are designed for single domain (6 of 8). Only the neural trust model and FIRE (Huynh et al.,) 2004 model considers the domain difference toward the involving objects. The neural trust model divides transaction data into dimensions according to their belonging domain. The dimensional data then is feed to the STL algorithm as multi-dimensional input. The precondition of two agents starting trust learning is that they both have consensus on ontology about their transactions.

- **Belief Representation:** 6 models use number to represent the belief of trust, the TRAVOS (Teacy et al., 2006) model use probability to represent trust and its related confidence value, the neural trust model use pattern to represent trust. The number based models are inflexible and unable to reflect sophisticated changes on belief. It is also unable to differentiate trust from different domains. The probability based is better to reflect the fuzzy characteristic of belief. However, it is still difficult to show the domain difference using probabilities. The neural trust model uses patterns to represent trust. A pattern has abundant detail to map the sophistication of the belief. Furthermore, patterns are a simulation that mimics the mechanism of belief in human brain. It can successfully deal with the problem of different domains.

- **Trust Learning:** All of the existing models do not support learning trust from previous interactions or transactions except eBay model (Ebay, 2012) which is human user based. They only evaluate and record the outcome of the interaction in a numbered or probabilistic way. They are poor to deal with the uncertainty in interactions or transactions; they cannot quickly response to a fast changing environment. The neural trust model takes the trust recognition problem as a learning problem and learns trust using improved SOM based neural networks. This makes agents flexible enough to different domains and robust enough to sudden outside changes.

- **Decision Support:** Threshold of trustworthiness decision making is common way of helping agents to decide actions. All models use threshold to control the decision making. The existing models set number as threshold, if the trust or reputation value supersedes the threshold. A trustworthy decision will be made. The neural trust model also uses threshold. However, the threshold is generated from the difference of estimated pattern and macro pattern. The value is between -1 to 1. The value is guidance to trustworthy decision or untrustworthy decision.

- **Reputation Generation:** Majority of the models (7 of 8) use weighted average or weighted accumulation to calculate the reputation value. The neural trust model takes a way to compare the target agent pattern with the global macro pattern. Then the result is accumulated to form the reputation. The advantage of adding the additional step is that the added pattern considers the difference between macro issues and a specific issue; it reflects difference between the general belief and the occasional idea. The weighted average or accumulation cannot reveal such delicate details.

- **Propagation Mechanism:** 3 0f 8 models never consider the problem of reputation propagation. The Referal model (Yu & Singh, 2000) designs a testimony propagation algorithm and the Sporas model (Zacharia et al., 1999) designs a directed graph representing the rating path. The proposed neural trust model designs three forms of propagation: point-to-point, broadcast, and observer. The idea of the design is coming from network protocols and design patterns. The advantage of three forms' propagation is that they can fit for different situations and is easy to implement. In addition, the decaying rate along the chain of reputation is also contribution of the new model.

6. CONCLUSION

The model proposes a new way to learn and estimate trust from the agent transactions. The intelligent agents can adapt to the constantly changing environments. However, the model does have some limitations due to its way of designing and implementation. The first limitation is its relatively inferior performance comparing to some statistical or numeric models. The limitation is due to the drawback of neural network based algorithms. Much time is cost to exciting neighboring neurons and update synaptic weight repeatedly. A good thing is that the usage of the model now is not real-time so that the agent has plenty of resources and time to deal with transactional data at each time. The other limitation is the way of input data. The data needs to be transformed into normalized dimensional data. The dimensions are so diversified in complex e-commerce environments. Even with different user, he or she may have different dimensions to evaluate the outcome of the transaction. There still future research to be done on the areas of semantic trust learning and e-commerce evaluation ontologies.

Generally speaking, the neural trust model proposes a new systematical model to represent, generate, and exploit computational trust. The most significant advantage of the model is the idea of trust learning and the algorithm of trust learning. Looking trust as a machine learning problem also decides that the belief should be represented as patterns. Such representation endows more ability to record delicate details of the interactions and simulates the trust in human brain. The model also proposes a new pattern based trustworthiness decision making algorithm (trust estimation algorithm). The model designs a reputation propagation mechanism to support the generation and propagation of reputations. The mechanism designs three types of reputation propagation paths: Point-to-point based inquiry, broadcasting based propagation and observer. The reputation is produced as the difference between macro pattern and agent pattern.

Finally, the experimental environment, test bed design and implementation, evaluation data preparation, evaluation configuration, and evaluation results are described and explained. The description includes the test bed design and implementation, the requirements, architecture and components. The rationale behind the design is also discussed in details. Then, the experimental preparation is introduced including environment configuration and data preparation. The results through two types of comparisons are presented. One is to compare the proposed neural trust model with a simple number based trust model; the other is compare the reputation based neural trust model with a non-reputation based neural trust model. The experimental result can support the argument that the neural trust model can have better quality and performance than the simple number based trust model. The results also state the importance of the reputation propagation in a multi-agent system. The results are also discussed from the comparison and analysis of some core design considerations and limitations.

REFERENCES

Bellifemine, F., Caire, G., & Greenwood, D. (2007). *Developming multi-agent systems with JADE*. John Wiley and Sons. doi:10.1002/9780470058411

Ebay. (2012). Retrieved from http://www.ebay.com

Lu, G., Lu, J., Yao, S., & Yip, J. (2009). *A comparison of java-based multi-agent system development platforms*. The Open Information Science Journal.

Huynh, T. D., Jennings, N. R., & Shadbolt, N. R. (2004). *Fire: An integrated trust and reputation model for open multi-agent systems*. ECAI.

Marsh, S. (1994). *Formalising Trust as a Computational Concept* (PhD thesis). Department of Mathematics and Computer Science, University of Stirling.

Nwana, H., Ndumu, D., Lee, L., & Collis, J. (1999). Zeus: a toolkit and approach for building distributed multi-agent systems. *Proceedings of the Third International Conference on Autonomous Agents*, 360-361. doi:10.1145/301136.301234

Sabater, J., & Sierra, C. (2002). Social regret, a reputation model based on social relations. *ACM SIGecom Exchanges - Chains of Commitment, 3*(1).

Taobao. (2011). *Chinese taobao web site*. Retrieved from http://www.taobao.com

Teacy, W. T., Patel, J., Jennings, N. R., & Luck, M. (2006). Travos: Trust and reputation in the context of inaccurate information sources. *Autonomous Agents and Multi-Agent Systems, 12*(2), 183–198. doi:10.1007/s10458-006-5952-x

Team, F.-O. D. (2011). *Fipa-os developers guide*. Retrieved from http://citeseer.ist.psu.edu/477218.html

Yu, B., & Singh, M. P. (2000). *A social mechanism of reputation management in electronic communities*. Cooperative Information Agents IV - The Future of Information. doi:10.1007/978-3-540-45012-2_15

Zacharia, G., & Maes, P. (1999). Collaborative Reputation Mechanisms in Electroni Marketplaces.*Proc. 32nd Hawaii International Conf on System Sciences.*

Chapter 21
Final Remarks on The Investigation in Neural Trust in Multi-Agent Systems and Possible Future Directions

Gehao Lu
Yunnan University, China

Joan Lu
University of Huddersfield, UK

ABSTRACT

This chapter provides the book's summary and conclusion on the neural trust in multi-agent systems. It also discusses possible future research directions in the field. The other chapters that make up this book collectively discuss ontology and big data.

GENERAL SUMMARY

The research carries out research on the computational trust and reputation for the multi-agent systems. It reviews the background theories for intelligent agents and multi-agent systems. It investigates the state of art on the mechanisms, algorithms and models of trust and reputation in computer science. The features of these models are compared from several typical aspects and the advantages and disadvantages of these models are also analyzed and discussed in detail. Then the research analyzes the definition of the computational trust, defines the concept from a unique viewpoint, compares the computational trusts with human trusts, and discovers the key factors hidden behind the definition. Through the insight to the computational trust gained in the profound analysis, the research proposes a complete model named "Neural Trust Learning and Estimation Model" that systematically supports all trust and reputation related activities include learning trust, estimating trust, making trustworthiness decision, generating reputation, and propagating reputation. In this model, the research innovates the traditional Self Organizing Map (SOM) and creates a SOM based Trust Learning (STL) algorithm and SOM based Trust Estimation

DOI: 10.4018/978-1-5225-1884-6.ch021

(STE) algorithm. The STL algorithm solve the problem of learning trust from agents' past interactions and the STE solve the problem of estimating the trustworthiness with the help of the previous patterns. For transforming the computational trust into a social influential mechanism, the research also proposes a multi-agent reputation mechanism for generating and propagating the reputations. The mechanism exploits the patterns learned from STL algorithm and generates the reputation of the specific agent. Three propagation methods are also designed as part of the mechanism to guide path selection of the reputation. In order to evaluate the viability and effectiveness of the model and the algorithms/mechanism in the model, the research designs and implements a test bed that is based upon the Java Agent Development Environment platform. A simulated electronic commerce scenario is used with lots of transactional data to test whether the proposed framework works well. The traditional arithmetic based trust model is compared with the proposed Neural Trust Learning and Estimation Model. The experimental results prove the superiority of the proposed model. The quality and performance of the transactions have been improved in experiments implemented with the proposed model. The experimental results also state the important influence of applying reputation mechanism. Some design considerations and rationale behind the algorithms are also discussed based on the experimental results.

CONTRIBUTIONS

The research analyzes the idea of learning trust, proposes a systematical model for trust and reputation, proposes the STL algorithm and STE algorithm, designs the reputation generation and propagation mechanism, and implement a test bed. These significant contributions are listed and explained in brief as follow:

- **New Ideas Proposed and Analyzed:** The research believes that the computational trust is a combinatory problem of machine learning and decision making. The form of representation is patterns that are emerged from information collected during agent interactions. The research also points out that the trustworthiness and untrustworthiness are actually decision making problems. Most of the traditional computational trust models are arithmetical or statistical models which deem the trust and reputation as a numeric value generated from delicate equations.
- **A Systematic Model:** the research proposes a trust and reputation model named "Neural trust learning and estimation model". This model establishes a complete framework to accomplish trust related activities. It depicts the relationship among algorithms and mechanisms. It defines the processes of trust learning, estimating and reputation generating, propagation.
- **Algorithms for Learning and Estimating Trust:** Two algorithms are proposed. One is SOM based Trust Learning algorithm and the other is SOM based Trust Estimation algorithm. Both algorithms modify the original Self Organized Map to produce patterns suitable for representing trust. The estimation algorithm helps agents make trustworthiness decision according to its memorized patterns.
- **Reputation Propagation Mechanism:** The research proposed a reputation propagation mechanism to support the generation and propagation of reputations. The mechanism designs three types of reputation propagation paths: Point-to-point based inquiry, broadcasting based propagation and observer. The reputation is produced as the difference between macro pattern and agent pattern.

An equation for calculating the reputations is proposed and issues such as decaying along the propagation are also modeled in it.

- **Application:** In order to evaluate the model, a computational trust test bed is designed and implemented. The test bed is built upon Java Agent Development Environment platform and it constructs a simulated electronic market which contains many autonomous agents divided into different roles. The test bed not only can be used in this research related experiment, but it also can be used to test the other types of agent trust models.

FUTURE WORK

The research involves the research on computational intelligence and machine recognition, the development in these areas is only a start comparing to other disciplines with hundreds of years of history. There are still more truths to be discovered and more problems to be solved. Although a lot of efforts have been put into the research for this research, there are still plenty of areas that need to be explored in future studies.

Due to the scarcity of commercial transaction data from large scale e-commerce web sites (Electronic commerce sites like eBay already has its reputation systems supporting their transactions. To test the proposed model in such a site, it is necessary to substitute their original reputation system and training their millions of users to use it. This is difficult and could lead to considerable cost. A better way to make use of the open API of the site (presume they have), take the proposed model as a site plugin and let part of the users uses and evaluates the model based trust system. Both ways need the authorization and strong support from the site owner), the experiment in the research is only based on simulated scenario of automated electronic commerce. The experimental data is also generated from the rule based computer programs. In future developments, if it is possible, it is better to find commercial web sites as the research partner and test the model in a real environment. The autonomous agents can represent the human user to do transactions, and the human user can set their evaluations as the input to the computational trust models.

In Section 4, the domains and dimension of the computational trust has been analyzed and discussed. The model also takes domain based dimensional data as input to the learning algorithm. However, even the agent knows the domain and dimension; the semantics behind the name is not unified. This could lead to problem of duplicating or misunderstanding the name of domain or dimension. Fox example, the product name or domain name in different languages may refer to the same object. Additionally, the scarce of a unified domain hierarchy is an obstacle of building large scale multi-agent societies because there might be domain name conflicts and domain structure conflicts that block extended interactions cross systems. Thus, a unified ontology structure defining domains and dimensions, and a semantic web based implementation of the structure are the prerequisites for constructing large multi-agent societies.

Multi-agent organization is a research topic in multi-agent system. It refers to the organization methods of the roles, relationships and authority structures in a multi-agent system. The research discusses the reputation generation and propagation mechanisms. Trust and reputation can actually be the adhesion of the organization or society. In future research, it is possible to implant the computational trust and related models into the organization to see the how trust influence the formation and structure of the organization. Meanwhile, the organization theory, the organization structure can change the way that reputation propagates or create new forms of propagation mechanisms.

Appendix

APPENDIX 1: QUESTIONNAIRE SURVEY FOR E-BOOKS AWARENESS AND USING THE INTERNET

Thank you for participating in this survey. This survey is being conducted to assess user awareness of e- books and to measure the level of e- book usage. Your privacy is considered to be paramount and the information you provide will be hold securely and used only for the purpose of this research. All data will be anonymous and will be destroyed at the completion of the research.

Part 1: Participant's Details

1. What is your gender?
    a. Male
    b. Female
2. Age:
    a. 9
    b. 10
    c. 11
    d. 12
    e. 13
3. What is the level of your studies?
    a. Level 4
    b. Level 5
    c. Level 6

Part 2

Section A: "Use Internet"

4. Do you have computer at home?
    a. Yes
    b. No

5. If yes, do you connect to internet?
   a. Yes
   b. No
6. I do use internet?
   a. Yes
   b. No
7. I use the internet daily?
   a. Yes
   b. No
8. I use the internet at least once a week?
   a. Yes
   b. No
9. I use the internet occasionally?
   a. Yes
   b. No
10. I do not use the internet at all?
    a. Yes
    b. No
11. Where do you use the internet?
    a. At home
    b. At school
    c. At net café
12. How long do you use the internet daily?
    a. Half an hour
    b. One hours
    c. Two hours
    d. Three hours
    e. More
13. How many computers do you have at home?
    a. One
    b. More than one
14. Do you have account in social network?
    a. Yes
    b. No
15. If yes which one?
    a. Facebook
    b. Twitter
    c. Both
16. Reason of using internet:
    a. Improve skill
    b. Share information
    c. Play computer game
    d. listening to music

e.   Doing homework

f.   E- Mailing.

g.   Chatting.

h.   All.

Section B: Use an E-Book

17.   Were you aware that e- book is available online?

    a.   Yes

    b.   No

18.   Have you used an e- book before?

    a.   Yes

    b.   No

19.   Were you familiar with the term e- book before this survey?

    a.   Yes

    b.   No

    c.   No answer

20.   If yes, for what purpose did you use these e- books?

    a.   To find material for project

    b.   To look up the answer to a specific question

    c.   To support research work

    d.   To read as a recommended course book

    e.   To entertainment

    f.   Other (please specify)

21.   What of the following types of e- book for children do you use? (please tick all which apply)

    a.   Story books

    b.   Reference books

    c.   Text books

    d.   Special internet books

    e.   Other (please specify)

22.   What types of e- book format have you used? (please select all that apply)

    a.   Computer based

    b.   Device based

    c.   Other

    d.   (Please specify) _____

23.   How have you read these e- books?

    a.   On screen

    b.   Downloaded file

    c.   Printed out

Section C: Using Schoolbook

24. Do you use the figure and image when reading schoolbook?
    a. Yes
    b. No
25. It is easy to link the shapes in the book with the text?
    a. Yes
    b. No
26. Do you take note when reading?
    a. Yes
    b. No
27. Do you use the table of content when searching for the lesson?
    a. Yes
    b. No
28. Do you read the question first?
    a. Yes
    b. No
29. Do you read the lesson first?
    a. Yes
    b. No

APPENDIX 2: QUESTIONNAIRE SURVEY FOR E- BOOKS AWARENESS AND USING THE INTERNET (ARABIC VERSION)

اعزاء الطالب:

اتقدم لكم بجزيل الشكر والتقدير الى كل من شارك في هذه الدراسة التي تهدف الى تقييم الوعي باستخدام الكتاب الالكتروني والانترنت . المعلومات التي تقدمها سوف تعامل بشكل آمن وتستخدم فقط لغرض هذا البحث. وسوف تكون جميع بيانات مجهولة المصدر وسيتم التخلص منها عند الانتهاء من البحث.

الجزء الاول: بيانات شخصية

1. الجنس - ذكر أنثى
2. العمر:
3. السنة الدراسية: الثالثة الرابعة الخامسة السادسة

الجزء الثاني:

القسم الاول: استخدام الحاسوب:

4. هل تمتلك حاسوب في البيت. نعم لا
5. اذا كانت الاجابة بنعم:هل جهاز كمبيوتر متصل بالنت في البيت. نعم لا
6. هل انت من مستخدمين الانترنت نعم لا
7. هل تستخدمه يوميا نعم لا
8. هل تستخدمه اسبوعيا نعم لا
9. هل تستخدمه شهريا نعم لا
10. انا لا استخدام الانترنت نعم لا
11. اين تستخدم الانترنت . المنزل المدرسة مركز النت
12. اذا كانت الاجابة بنعم, كم حاسوب تمتلك في البيت اكثر من 3
13. هل تستخدم الانترنت في المدرسة. نعم لا
14. اذا كانت الاجابة ب (لا). ارجو ذكر الاسباب.
15. اذا كنت تستخدم بالمدرسة فما هو الغرض من الاستخدام
16. فهم الدروس كتابة حوث ادا واجبات المدرسية
17. ما الغرض من استخدام النت
18. السماع الي الموسيقية مشاهدة الدردشة مشاهدة الافلام
19. تصفح مواقع مرتبطة بالمنهج الدراسي عن البحث مع المعلومات ترتبط بالدرس
20. قراءة الكتب الالكترونية الدردشة العابة مراسلة
21. اذا كنت تستخدمه يوميا بمعدل كم ساعة.
22. اقل من ساعة ساعة اكثر من ساعتين ساعتين من اكثر
23. هل هناك من يساعدك في اختيار المواقع. نعم لا
24. اذا كانت الاجابة بنعم من يقوم بمساعدتك. احد الوالدين احد الاصدقاء

APPENDIX 3: FORM FOR RECORDING THE READING PROCESS

Date: _____

Time: _____

Name of School: _____

Education of Level: _____

Lesson Title: _____

APPENDIX 4: SCREENER QUESTIONNAIRE

1.   Do you wear contacts or eyeglasses in order to read the computer screen?
    a.   Yes
    b.   No
2.   Are your glasses for:
    a.   Reading only
    b.   Seeing distant objects only
    c.   Both
3.   Can you read a computer screen and the web without difficulty with your contacts or eyeglasses on?
    a.   Yes
    b.   No
4.   Do you have cataracts?
    a.   Yes
    b.   No
5.   Do you have any eye implants?
    a.   Yes
    b.   No
6.   Do you have glaucoma?
    a.   Yes
    b.   No

Table 1.

The Main Active	Students									
	1	Note	2	Note	3	Note	4	Note	5	Note
Read the instructions(AC1)										
Identify a purpose of reading. (AC2)										
Read through the questions. (AC3)										
Skim the passage to have general idea. (AC4)										
Quickly read the whole passage. (AC5)										
Read the whole passage quite slowly. (AC6)										
Underline the key words in question. (AC7)										
Underline the key words in the passage. (AC8)										
Underline the main idea of each paragraph. (AC9)										
Scan the passage in order to find the key word. (AC10)										
After finding the key word in the passage read the text around it carefully. (AC11)										
Connecting one part of the text to another. (AC12)										
General notes. (AC13)										
Rereading. (AC14)										
Anything else										

APPENDIX 5: EXAMPLES OF STUDENT'S ERRORS

Table 2.

Personal details (270)		
Name:	Age:12	L of ED: 7
Reading score: over 5	Eye visual : 6	
Test : (1) font size		
time	Start time05:40: 03	End time: 05:45:54
Lesson 1: 10 point. 270	رَسَلَ اللهُ تَعَالَى نَبِيَّهُ إِبْرَاهِيمَ إِلَى قَوْمِهِ، وَكَانُوا بِالعِرَاقِ، يَعْبُدُونَ الأَصْنَامَ، فَدَعَاهُمْ إِلَى عِبَادَةِ اللهِ تَعَالَى وَحْدَهُ، وَتَرْكِ عِبَادَةِ الأَصْنَامِ الَّتِي لاَ تَسْمَعُ وَلاَ تُبْصِرُ، وَلاَ تُغْنِي عَنْ أَحَدٍ شَيْئًا. فَلَمَّا لَمْ يَسْمَعُوا لَهُ، كَثُرَ أَصْنَامَهُمْ، فَحَكَمُوا بِإِحْرَاقِهِ فِي النَّارِ، وَأَلْقَوْهُ فِيهَا، فَنَجَّاهُ اللهُ تَعَالَى مِنْهَا، فَصَارَتْ بَرْدًا وَسَلَامًا، ثُمَّ بَعْدَ ذَلِكَ خَرَجَ إِبْرَاهِيمُ عَلَيْهِ السَّلَامُ مِنْ بِلَادِ العِرَاقِ، وَذَهَبَ إِلَى الشَّامِ؛ لِيَتَمَكَّنَ مِنْ عِبَادَةِ اللهِ وَحْدَهُ، وَسَأَلَ اللهَ سُبْحَانَهُ وَتَعَالَى أَنْ يَهَبَ لَهُ بَعْضَ الأَوْلَادِ الصَّالِحِينَ فَبَشَّرَهُ اللهُ تَعَالَى بِوِلَادَةِ ابْنِهِ إِسْمَاعِيلَ، وَقَالَ: إِنَّهُ سَيَكُونُ حَلِيمًا عَاقِلاً . وَلَمَّا كَبِرَ إِسْمَاعِيلُ، وَاسْتَطَاعَ أَنَهُ يُسَاعِدَ أَبَاهُ عَلَى عَمَلِهِ، رَأَى أَبُوهُ إِبْرَاهِيمُ أَنَّهُ يَذْبَحُهُ، فَعَلِمَ أَنَّ هَذَا أَمْرٌ مِنَ اللهِ عَزَّ وَجَلَّ بِذَبْحِهِ، فَقَصَّ عَلَى وَلَدِهِ مَا رَأَى، فَامْتَثَلَ إِسْمَاعِيلُ أَمْرَ اللهِ تَعَالَى، وَقَالَ لِأَبِيهِ: افْعَلْ مَا تُؤْمَرُ، سَتَجِدُنِي إِنْ شَاءَ اللهُ صَابِرًا، فَأَخَذَ أَبُوهُ السِّكِّينَ، وَأَضْجَعَهُ عَلَى جَنْبِهِ، حَتَّى كَانَ جَبِينُهُ وَخَدُّهُ عَلَى الأَرْضِ، وَوَضَعَ السِّكِّينَ عَلَى رَقَبَتِهِ امْتِثَالاً لِأَمْرِ اللهِ تَعَالَى، وَإِسْمَاعِيلُ صَابِرٌ، لاَ يُبْدِي جَزَاكًا، وَعِنْدَئِذٍ نَادَى اللهُ تَعَالَى إِبْرَاهِيمَ: لَقَدْ نَفَّذْتَ الأَمْرَ، فَلَا تَذْبَح الغُلَامَ، وَإِنَّكَ وَابْنَكَ لَمِنَ المُؤْمِنِينَ الصَّادِقِي الإِيمَانِ بِاللهِ، وَسَيَجْزِيكُمَا اللهُ الخَلَاصَ مِنْ هَذِهِ الشِّدَّةِ؛ لِإِحْسَانِكُمَا، فَأَرْسَلَ اللهُ تَعَالَى إِلَى إِبْرَاهِيمَ كَبْشًا عَظِيمًا. وَأَمَرَهُ أَنْ يَذْبَحَهُ، وَخَلَصَ مِنْ تِلْكَ المِحْنَةِ الَّتِي صَبَرَ عَلَيْهَا هُوَ وَابْنُهُ أَحْسَنَ الصَّبْرِ. وَقَالَ إِنِّي ذَاهِبٌ إِلَى رَبِّي سَيَهْدِينِ رَبِّ هَبْ لِي مِنَ الصَّالِحِينَ* فَبَشَّرْنَاهُ بِغُلَامٍ حَلِيمٍ فَلَمَّا بَلَغَ مَعَهُ السَّعْيَ قَالَ يَا بُنَيَّ إِنِّي أَرَى فِي المَنَامِ أَنِّي أَذْبَحُكَ فَانْظُرْ مَاذَا تَرَى قَالَ يَا أَبَتِ افْعَلْ مَا تُؤْمَرُ سَتَجِدُنِي إِنْ شَاءَ اللَّهُ مِنَ الصَّابِرِينَ فَلَمَّا أَسْلَمَا وَتَلَّهُ لِلْجَبِينِ وَنَادَيْنَاهُ أَنْ يَا إِبْرَاهِيمُ قَدْ صَدَّقْتَ الرُّؤْيَا إِنَّا كَذَلِكَ نَجْزِي المُحْسِنِينَ إِنَّ هَذَا لَهُوَ البَلَاءُ المُبِينُ وَفَدَيْنَاهُ بِذِبْحٍ عَظِي .
Lesson 2: 14 point Start time 05:47:23 end time:05:49:33 3	/لِيَتَمَكَّنَ /الشَّامِ /ثُمَّ /تَعَالَى /بِإِحْرَاقِهِ /الَّتِي /تُغْنِي /تَعَالَى /إِبْرَاهِيمَ /نَبِيَّهُ /الرُّؤْيَا /نَادَيْنَاهُ /لِلْجَبِينِ /تَلَّهُ /أَبَتِ /فَانْظُرْ /فَبَشَّرْنَاهُ /شَاءَ /تُؤْمَرُ /فَامْتَثَلَ /يَذْبَحُهُ /فَبَشَّرَهُ /تَعَالَى /عَاقِلاً /إِنَّهُ /بِذِبْحٍ /فَدَيْنَاهُ /نَجْزِي
Lesson 3: 16 point Start time: 05:49:55 End time:05:53:42 2	تُؤْمَرُ /فَبَشَّرْنَاهُ /المُؤْمِنِينَ /عِنْدَئِذٍ /يُبْدِي /امْتِثَالاً /تُؤْمَرُ /فَامْتَثَلَ /بِإِحْرَاقِهِ /شَيْئًا /تُغْنِي
Lesson4:18 point Start time: 05:55:49 End time: 05:58:49 1	فَامْتَثَلَ /فَبَشَّرْنَاهُ /يُبْدِي /تُغْنِي

Table 3.

Personal details (270)		
Name:	Age:12	L of ED: 7
Reading score: over 5	Eye visual : 6	
Test : (1) font size		
time	Start time05:40: 03	End time: 05:45:54
Lesson 1: 14 point.	أزْوِع /الأشْياء /تُدْخِلِ /يَرى /شَجَرَةٌ /تَنْبُتُ /أَجْمَل /الْبَهْجَةَ /يَرى /ثَرابًا /يَتَحَوَّلُ /أَخْضَرَ /يُحِسُّ /	
Lesson 2: 14 point Start time 05:47:23 end time:05:49:33 3		
Lesson 3: 16 point Start time: 05:49:55 End time:05:53:42 2		
Lesson4:18 point Start time: 05:55:49 End time: 05:58:49 1		

Table 4.

Personal details		
Name: اصيل	Age: 10	L of ED: 5
Reading score: over 5	Eye visual : 6	
Test : (1) font size		
time	Start time: 11:48: 03	End time: 12:06:
Lesson 1: 10 point.	فَدَعاهُمْ/ تَسْمَعُ/فَلَمَّا / يَسْمَعُو/ وَأَلْقُوهُ / فَصارَتْ/ ثُمَّ / يَهَبَ/ حَليمًا عاقِلاً/ وَاسْتَطاعَ/ الْمَنامِ/ يَذْبَحُهُ/ فَقَصَّ/ فَامْتَثَل / إسْماعيلُ / لأَبيهِ/ وَأَضْجَعَهُ/ جَنْبِهِ،/ امْتِثالاً/ يُبْدِي / تَذْبَح/ نَفَّذْتَ/ وَسَيَجْزيكُمْ/ الْخَلاصِ/ الشَّدَّةِ / كَبْشًا/ يَذْبَحُهُ/ فَبَشَّرْناهُ / حَليمٍ / بَلَغَ/ إنّي / أَذْبَحُكَ/ وَتَلَّهُ/ لِلْجَبينِ/ نَجْزِي/ بِذِبْحٍ/ الْمُبينُ.
Lesson 2: 12 point	
Lesson 3: 14 point	
Lesson4:18 point	

Table 5.

Personal details		
Name: عائشة ا	Age: 10	L of ED: 5
Reading score: over 5	Eye visual : 6	
Test : (1) font size		
time	Start time: 11:18: 03	End time: 11:30:03
Lesson 1: 10 point.	تُغْني / لَمَّ / ثُمَّ / لإِحْسانِكُما/ يَهَبَ/ حَليمًا عاقِلاً/ واسْتَطاعَ/ الْمَنام / يَذْبَحُهُ/ فَقَصَّ/ فَامْتَثَلَ/ لأبيهِ/ وأَضْجَعَهُ/ جَنْبِهِ، امْتِثالاً/ يُبْدي / تَذْبَح / وسَيَجْزِيكُمُ/ الْخَلاصَ/ الشِّدَّةِ / كَبْشًا/ يَذْبَحُهُ/ فَبَشَّرْناهُ / حَليمٍ / بَلَغَ/ إِنِّي / أَذْبَحُكَ/ وَتَلَّهُ/ لِلْجَبينِ / نَجْزِي/ بِذِبْحٍ/الْمُبينِ.
Lesson 2: 12 point Start time :11:24:04 end time:11:31:34	لِيَهْتَدِيَ / والْبِناءُ/ قارِئًا/ بِما/ أَتاهُ/ اقْرَأْ / /مُجْتَمَعِهِ /وَكُلٌّ/ مُجْتَمَعِهِ / لِيَهْتَدِيَ /
Lesson 3: 14 point Start time: 11:32:55 End time:11:49:45	تُقيمُ/ تَرْفيهِيَّةٌ/ اشْتِراكِهِمِ/ سَنَنْقُلُهُمْ/ مُبْتَهِجينَ/ الْحَبيبَةُ/ الطَّبيعَةُ/ الطَّبيعَةِ/ يَتَبادَلانِ/ وَلَيْسَتْ تَخْتَلِفُ/ يَجْعَلُها/ ثَرْوَةُ//يَقْتَصِرُ/ وأَهَمِّيَّتِهِ
Lesson4:18 point Start time: 11:40:35 End time: 11:46:12	اتَّفَقْنا/ الْهَيِّنِ/ يَبْعَثُ/ وَضَيَّعْتَ/ أَسْتَفيدَ/ إِيّاكَ/ فَإِنَّني/ ثَمينٌ/ يَحْتَرَمُ/ يَتَسَبَّبُ/ الثَّمينَةِ/ الْمُسْتَقْبَلِ مُحَدَّدِ

Table 6.

Personal details		
Name:	Age: 10	L of ED: 5
Reading score: over 5	Eye visual : 6	
Test : (1) font size		
time	Start time: 10:18: 03	End time:10:30:03
Lesson 1: 10 point.	نَبِيَّهُ/ وَتَرْكِ / سَنَجِدُنِي/ رَقَبَتِهِ/ وَعِنْدَئِذٍ/ وَابْنَكَ/ تُغْنِي / أَمْ / ثُمَّ / لِإِحْسانِكُما/ يَهَبُ/ حَلِيمًا عَاقِلاً/ وَاسْتَطَاعَ/ الْمَنَام / يَذْبَحُهُ/ فَقَصَّ/ فَامْتَثَل / لِأَبِيهِ/ وَأَضْجَعَهُ/ جَنْبِهِ، امْتِثَالاً/ يُبْدِي / نَفَّذَتُ/ وَسَيَحْزِيكُمُ/ الْخَلاصُ/ الشُّدَّةِ / كَبْشًا/ يَذْبَحُهُ/ فَبَشَّرْناهُ / حَلِيم / بَلَغَ/ إِنِّي / أَذْبَحُكَ/ وَتَلَّهُ/ لِلْجَبِينِ / يَجْزِي/ بِذِبْحٍ/الْعُبِينُ.
Lesson 2: 12 point Start time :10:48:04 end time:10:52:34	لِيَهْتَدِيَ / تَسِيرُ/ سَعَادَتِهِم وَالْبِنَاءُ/ قَارِئًا/ بِهَا/ أَتَاهُ/ اقْرَأْ / /مُجْتَمَعِهِ /وَكُلٍّ/ مُجْتَمَعِهِ / لِيَهْتَدِيَ // تَنْتَظِرُ /كَثِيرًا؛ / شَرِيكَ /
Lesson 3: 14 point Start time: 11:32:55 End time:11:49:45	نُقِيمُ/ تَرْفِيهِيَّةً/ اشْتِرَاكِهِمْ سَتَنْقُلُهُمْ/ مُنْتَهِجِينَ/ الْخَبِيئَةُ/ الطَّبِيعَةِ/ الطَّبِيعَةِ/ يَتَبَادَلاَنِ/ وَبَيْسَتْ تَخْتَلِفُ/ يَجْعَلُها/ ثَرْوَةٌ// يَقْتَصِرُ/ وَأَهَمِّيَّتِهِ اشْتِرَاكِهِمْ/ مُنْتَهِجِينَ/ تَخْتَلِفُ تَأْثِيرٍ/ أَهَمِّيَّتِهِ/ تَنْفِيذِ/
Lesson4:18 point Start time: 11:40:35 End time: 11:46:12	اتَّفَقْنَا/ الْهَيِّنِ/ يَبْعَثُ/ وَضَيَّعْتَ/ أَسْتَفِيدَ/ إِيَّاكَ/ فَإِنَّنِي/ ثَمِينٌ/ يَحْتَرِمُ/ يَتَسَبَّبُ/ الثَّمِينَةِ/ الْمُسْتَقْبَلِ مُحَدَّدٍ/ يَنْتَظِرُهُ / فَاسْتَقْبَلَهُ/ انْتَظَرْتُكَ/ ثَمِينًا/

Table 7.

Personal details		
Name: روان	Age: 10	L of ED: 5
Reading score: over 5	Eye visual : 6	
Test : (1) font size		
time	Start time: 10:18: 03	End time:10:30:03
Lesson 1: 10 point.	نَبِيُّهُ/ وَتَرْكِ / سَتَجِدُنِي/ رَقِبَتِهِ/ وَعِنْدَئِذٍ/ وَابْنَكَ/ تُغْنِي / لَمْ / ثُمَّ / لِإحْسَانِكُمَا/ يَهَبَ/ حَلِيمًا عَاقِلاً/ وَاسْتَطَاعَ/ الْمَنَامِ / يَذْبَحُهُ/ فَقَصَّ/ فَامْتَثَلَ / لأَبِيهِ/ وَأَضْجَعَهُ/ جَنْبِهِ، امْتِثَالاً/ يُبْدِي / تَذْبَحْ/ نَفَّذْتَ/ وَسَيَجْزِيكُمْ/ الْخَلاَصُ/ الشِّدَّةِ / كَبْشًا/ يَذْبَحُهُ/ فَبَشَّرْنَاهُ / حَلِيم / بَلَغَ/ إِنِّي / أَذْبَحُكَ/ وَتَلَّهُ/ لِلْجَبِينِ / نَجْزِي/ بِذِبْحٍ/الْمُبِينُ.
Lesson 2: 12 point Start time :10:54:04 end time:10:58:34	جِبْرِيلُ/اقْرَأْ/ / وَالْبِنَاءُ/ قَارِئًا/ بِهَا/ أَتَاهُ/ اقْرَأْ يَكُونَ/
Lesson 3: 14 point Start time: 11:07:55 End time:11:02:45	تُقِيمَ/ تَرْفِيهِيَّةٌ/ اشْتِرَاكِهِمْ سَتَنْفَّلُهُمْ/ مُنْتَهِجِينَ/ الْخَبِيئَةُ/ الطَّبِيعَةِ/ الطَّبِيعَةُ/ يَتَبَادَلاَنِ/ وَيَسَتْ تَخْتَلِفُ/ يَجْعَلُهَا/ ثَرْوَةٌ// يَقْتَصِرُ/ وَأَهَمِّيَّتِهِ اشْتِرَاكِهِمْ/ مُنْتَهِجِينَ/ تَخْتَلِفُ تَأْثِيرِ/ أَهَمِّيَّتِهِ/ تَنْفِيذِ/
Lesson4:18 point Start time: 11:40:35 End time: 11:46:12	اتَّفَقْنَا/ الْهَيِّنِ/ يَبْعَثُ/ وَضَيَّعْتَ/ أَسْتَفِيدَ/ إِيَّاكَ/ فَإِنَّنِي/ ثَمِينٌ/ يَحْتَرِمُ/ يَتَسَبَّبُ/ الثَّمِينَةِ/ مُحَدَّدٍ/ يَنْتَظِرَهُ / فَاسْتَقْبَلَهُ/ انْتَظَرْتُكَ/ ثَمِينًا/

Table 8.

Personal details		
Name: محمد	Age:12	L of ED7
Reading score: over 5	Eye visual : 6	
Test : (1) font size		
time	Start time: 02:44: 03	End time:02:52:03
Lesson 1: 10 point.	تَعَالَى / بِالْعِرَاقِ / نَبِيَّهُ / وَتَرْكِ / رَفِيقِهِ / وَابْنَكَ / تُغْنِي / مَا تُؤْمَرُ ، / لِإِحْسَانِكُمَا / يَهَبُ / حَلِيمًا عَاقِلاً/ بِإِحْرَاقِهِ / خَرَجَ / يَهَبُ / صَابِرًا، / وَاسْتَطَاعَ / الْمَنَامَ / يَذْبَحُهُ / فَفَصَّ / فَامْتَثَلَ / لِأَبِيهِ / وَأَضْجَعَهُ / جَنْبِهِ، / امْتِثَالًا/ يُبْدِي / تَذْبَح/ نَفَّذْتَ/ وَسَيَجْزِيكُمْ/ الْخَلاَصَ/ الشِّدَّةِ / كَبْشًا/ يَذْبَحُهُ/ فَبَشَّرْنَاهُ / حَلِيمٍ / بَلَغَ/ إِنِّي / أَذْبَحُكَ/ وَتَلَّهُ/ لِلْجَبِينِ / نَجْزِي/ بِذِبْحٍ/ الْمُبِينُ.
Lesson 2: 12 point Start time :10:54:04 end time:10:58:34	/ جِبْرِيلُ/اقْرَأْ/ وَالْبِنَاءُ/ قَارِئًا/ بِهَا/ أَتَاهُ/ اقْرَأْ يَكُونَ/
Lesson 3: 14 point Start time: 11:07:55 End time:11:02:45	تُقِيمُ/ تَرْفِيهِيَّةٌ/ اشْتِرَاكِهِمْ سَتَنْفَقُلُهُمْ/ مُنْتَهِجِينَ/ الْخَبِيبَةُ / يَتَبَادَلاَنِ/ وَيَبِسَتْ تَخْتَلِفُ/ يَجْعَلُهَا/ ثَرْوَةٌ// يَقْتَصِرُ/ وَأَهَمِّيَّتِهِ/ اشْتِرَاكِهِمْ/ مُنْتَهِجِينَ/ تَخْتَلِفُ تَأْثِيرٍ/ أَهَمِّيَّتِهِ/ تَنْفِيذِ/
Lesson4:18 point Start time: 11:40:35 End time: 11:46:12	اتَّفَقْنَا/ الْهَيِّنِ/ يَبْعَثُ/ وَضَيَّعْتَ/ أَسْتَفِيدَ/ إِيَّاكَ/ فَإِنَّنِي/ ثَمِينٌ/ يَحْتَرِمُ/ يَتَسَبَّبُ/ الثَّمِينَةِ/ مُحَدَّدٍ/ يَنْتَظِرَهُ / فَاسْتَقْبَلَهُ/ انْتَظَرْتُكَ/ ثَمِينًا/

Table 9.

Personal details		
Name: اروي	Age:12	L of ED: 7
Reading score: over 5	Eye visual : 6	
Test : (1) font size		
time	Start time13:47: 03	End time: no
Lesson 1: 10 point.	يَعْبُدُونَ / بِإِحْرَاقِهِ / لِيَتَمَكَّنَ / نَبِّئْهُ / وَتَرْكِ / رَقَبَتِهِ/ وَابْنَكَ/ تُغْنِي / مَا تُؤْمَرُ، / لِإِحْسَانِكُمَا/ يَهَبْ/ حَلِيمًا عَاقِلًا/ وَاسْتَطَاعَ/ الْمَنَامِ / يَذْبَحُهُ/ فَقَصَّ/ فَامْتَثَلَ / لِأَبِيهِ/ وَأَضْجَعَهُ/ جَنْبِهِ، امْتِثَالًا/ يُبْدِي / تَذْبَحُ/ نَفَّذْتَ/ وَسَيَحْزِبُكُمْ/ الْخَلَاصَ/ الشِّدَّةِ/ سَيَهْدِينِ.
Lesson 2: 12 point Start time :10:54:04 end time:10:58:34	/ جِبْرِيلُ/اقْرَأْ/ وَالْبِنَاءُ/ قَارِئًا/ بِهَا/ أَتَاهُ/ اقْرَأْ يَكُونَ/
Lesson 3: 14 point Start time: 11:07:55 End time:11:02:45	نُقِيمَ/ تَرْفِيهِيَّةً/ اشْتِرَاكِهِمْ سَتَنْقُلُهُمْ/ مُنْتَهِجِينَ/ الْخَبِيئَةُ / يَتَبَادَلَانِ/ وَيَسَتْ تَخْتَلِفُ/ يَجْعَلُهَا/ ثَرْوَةٌ// يَقْتَصِرُ/ وَأَهَمِّيَّتِهِ/ اشْتِرَاكِهِمْ/ مُنْتَهِجِينَ/ تَخْتَلِفُ تَأْثِيرُ/ أَهَمِّيَّتِهِ/ تَنْفِيذِ/
Lesson4:18 point Start time: 02:05:35 End time: 02:07:12	no

Table 10.

Personal details		
Name:حارث	Age:12	L of ED: 7
Reading score: over 5	Eye visual : 6	
Test : (1) font size		
time	Start time14:17: 03	End time: 14:25:54
Lesson 1: 10 point.	/ يَعْبُدُونَ / بِإِحْرَاقِهِ / لِيَتَمَكَّنَ / نَبِيَّهُ/ وَتَرْكِ / رَقَبَتِهِ/ وَابْنَكَ/ تُغْنِي / مَا تُؤْمَرُ، / يَهَبَ/ حَلِيمًا بِوِلَادَةٍ / يُسَاعِدَ / فَدَيْنَاهُ /عَاقِلًا/ وَاسْتَطَاعَ/ الْمَنَامِ / يَذْبَحُهُ/ فَقَصَّ/ فَامْتَثَلَ / لِأَبِيهِ/ وَأَضْجَعَهُ/ جَنْبِهِ،/ امْتِثَالًا/ يُبْدِي / تَذْبَحَ/ نَفَّذْتَ/ وَسَيَحْزِيكُمُ/ الْخَلَاصِ/ الشِّدَّةِ / سَيَهْدِينِ.	
Lesson 2: 12 point Start time :02:45:04 end time:02:59:34	/ جِبْرِيلُ/اقْرَأْ/ لَهُ يَكُونَ/ وَالْبِنَاءُ/ قَارِئًا/ بِمَا/ أَتَاهُ/ اقْرَأْ/ وَازْدِهَارٍ /	
Lesson 3: 14 point Start time: 02:69:55 End time:03::09:06	تُقِيمَ/ تَرْفِيهِيَّةٌ/ اشْتِرَاكِهِمْ سَتَنْفُلُهُمْ/ مُنْتَهِجِينَ/ الْحَبِيبَةُ / يَتَبَادَلَانِ/ وَيَبِسَتْ تَخْتَلِفُ يَجْعَلُهَا/ ثَرْوَةٌ// يَقْتَصِرُ/ وَأَهَمِّيَتِهِ/ اشْتِرَاكِهِمْ/ مُنْتَهِجِينَ/ تَخْتَلِفُ تَأْثِيرُ/ أَهَمِّيَتِهِ/ تَنْفِيذِ/ بِمَا /اوَلِكَي	
Lesson4:18 point Start time: 03:15:35 End time: 03:23:12	all the words guse by the وَضَيَّعْتَ/ ثَمِينًا .sentences	

Table 11.

Personal details		
Name: محمد	Age:12	L of ED: 7
Reading score: over 5	Eye visual : 6	
Test : (1) font size		
time	Start time05:40: 03	End time: 05:45:54
Lesson 1: 10 point.	يَعْبُدُونَ / بِإِحْرَاقِهِ / لِيَتَمَكَّنَ / نَبِيُّهُ/ وَتَرْكِ / رَقَبَتِهِ/ وَابْنَكَ/ تُغْنِي / مَا تُؤْمَرُ، / يَهَبَ/ حَلِيمًا بِوِلَادَةٍ / يُسَاعِدَ / فَدَيْنَاهُ /عَاقِلاً/ وَاسْتَطَاعَ / الْمَنَامِ / يَذْبَحُهُ/ فَقَصَّ/ فَامْتَثَلَ / لِأَبِيهِ/ وَأَضْجَعَهُ/ جَنْبِهِ،/ امْتِثَالاً/ يُبْدِي / تَذْبَحْ/ نَقَذْتَ/ وَسَيَجْزِيكُمْ/ الْخَلَاصَ/ الشِّدَّةِ / سَيَهْدِينِ.
Lesson 2: 12 point Start time 05:47:23 end time:05:49:33	تَطْمَحُ وَالْبِنَاءُ/ قَارِئًا/ بِمَا/ أَتَاهُ/ اقْرَأْ/ كِبَ/ / إِنَّنَا/ الْمُتَفَضِّلُ/ فَتَسْعَدَ/ / جِبْرِيلُ/اقْرَأْ/ لَهُ يَكُونَ/ وَازْدِهَارٍ/
Lesson 3: 14 point Start time: 05:49:55 End time:05:53:42	تُقِيمُ/ تَرْفِيهِيَّةٌ/ اشْتِرَاكِهِمْ سَتَنْفُلُهُمْ/ مُبْتَهِجِينَ/ الْخَبِيئَةُ / يَتَبَادَلَانِ/ وَيَيْسَتْ تَخْتَلِفُ/ يَجْعَلُهَا/ ثَرْوَةٌ/ / يَقْتَصِرُ/ وَأَهَمِّيَّتِهِ/ اشْتِرَاكِهِمْ/ مُبْتَهِجِينَ/ اشْتِرَاكِهِمْ/ تَخْتَلِفُ تَأْثِيرِ/ أَهَمِّيَّتِهِ/ تَنْفِيذِ/ بِمَا /اوَلِكَي وَقُرَّانَا/ الْخَبِيئَةُ
Lesson4:18 point Start time: 05:55:49 End time: 05:58:49	no

Table 12.

Personal details		
Name: محمد	Age:12	L of ED: 7
Reading score: over 5	Eye visual : 6	
Test : (1) font size		
time	Start time05:40: 03	End time: 05:45:54
Lesson 1: 10 point.	يَعْبُدُونَ / بِإِحْرَاقِهِ / لِيَتَمَكَّنَ / نَبِيُّهُ/ وَتَرَكَ / رَقَبَتِهِ/ وَابْنَكَ/ تُغْنِي / مَا تُؤْمَرُ، / يَهَبْ / حَلِيمًا بِوِلَادَةٍ / يُسَاعِدَ / فَدَيْنَاهُ /عَاقِلاً/ وَاسْتَطَاعَ / الْمَنَامَ / يَذْبَحُهُ/ فَقَصَّ/ فَامْتَثَلَ / لِأَبِيهِ/ وَأَضْجَعَهُ/ جَنْبِهِ،/ امْتِثَالاً/ يُبْدِي / تَذْبَحُ/ نَفَّذْتَ/ وَسَيَجْزِيكُمُ/ الْخَلَاصَ/ الشِّدَّةِ / سَيَهْدِينِ.
Lesson 2: 12 point Start time 05:47:23 end time:05:49:33	تَطْمَحُ وَالْبِنَاءُ/ قَارِئًا/ بِهَا/ أَتَاهُ/ اقْرَأْ/ كِبْ/ إِنَّنَا/ الْمُتَفَضِّلُ/ فَتَسْعَدَ/ / جِبْرِيلُ/اقْرَأْ/ لَهُ يَكُونَ/ وَازْدِهَارٍ /
Lesson 3: 14 point Start time: 05:49:55 End time:05:53:42	نُقِيمَ/ تَرْفِيهِيَّةً/ اشْتِرَاكِهِمْ سَتَنْقُلُهُمْ/ الْحَبِيبَةِ / يَتَبَادَلَانِ/ وَيَبِسَتْ تَخْتَلِفُ/ يَجْعَلُهَا/ ثَرْوَةٌ// يَقْتَصِرُ/ وَأَهَمِّيَّتِهِ/ اشْتِرَاكِهِمْ/ مُنْتَهِجِينَ/ تَخْتَلِفُ تَأْثِيرُ/ أَهَمِّيَّتِهِ/ تَنْفِيذٍ/ بِمَا اوَلِكَي وَقُرَّائِنَا/ الْحَبِيبَةُ
Lesson4:18 point Start time: 05:55:49 End time: 05:58:49	no

Appendix

Table 13.

Personal details		
Name: محمد	Age:12	L of ED: 7
Reading score: over 5	Eye visual : 6	
Test : (1) font size		
time	Start time05:40: 03	End time: 05:45:54
Lesson 1: 10 point.	يَعْبُدُونَ / بِإِخْرَاجِهِ / لِيَتَمَكَّنَ / نَبِيُّهُ/ وَتَرْكِ / رَفِيقِهِ/ وَابْنَكَ/ تُغْنِي / مَا تُؤْمَرُ/ ، بَهَبْ/ حَلِيمًا بِوِلَادَةِ / يُسَاعِدَ / فَدَيْنَاهُ /عَاقِلاً/ وَاسْتَطَاعَ/ الْمَنَامِ / يَذْبَحُهُ/ فَقُصِّ/ فَانْتَقَلَ / لِأَبِيهِ/ وَأَضْجَعَهُ/ جَنْبِهِ، امْتِثَالاً/ بُيْدِي / نَذْبَح/ نَفَّذْتَ/ وَسَيَجْزِيكُمُ/ الخَلاصُ/ الشِّدَّةِ / سَيَهْدِينِ.	
Lesson 2: 12 point Start time 05:47:23 end time:05:49:33	تَطْمَحُ وَالْبِنَاءُ/ قَارِئًا/ بِمَا/ أَتَاهُ/ اقْرَأْ/ كِبْ/ إِنَّا/ الْمُتَفَضِّلُ/ فَتَسْعَدَ/ / جِبْرِيلُ/اقْرَأْ/ لَهُ يَكُونَ/ وَازْدِهَارِ /	
Lesson 3: 14 point Start time: 05:49:55 End time:05:53:42	نُقِيمُ/ تَرْفِيهِيَّةً/ اشْتِرَاكِهِمْ سَنَنْقُلُهُمْ/ مُنْتَهِجِينَ/ الخِبِيئَةُ / يَتَبَادَلَانِ/ وَيَبِسَتْ تَخْتَلِفُ/ يَجْعَلُهَا/ ثَرْوَةً// يَقْتَصِرُ/ وَأَهَمِّيَّتِهِ/ اشْتِرَاكِهِمْ/ مُنْتَهِجِينَ/ تَخْتَلِفُ تَأْثِيرِ/ أَهَمِّيَّتِهِ/ تَنْفِيذِ/ بِمَا /أَوْلَكِي وَقُرَّانَا/ الخِبِيئَةُ	
Lesson4:18 point Start time: 05:55:49 End time: 05:58:49	no	
Personal details		
Name: محمد	Age:12	L of ED: 7
Reading score: over 5	Eye visual : 6	
Test : (1) font size		
time	Start time05:40: 03	End time: 05:45:54
Lesson 1: 10 point.	يَعْبُدُونَ / بِإِخْرَاجِهِ / لِيَتَمَكَّنَ / نَبِيُّهُ/ وَتَرْكِ / رَفِيقِهِ/ وَابْنَكَ/ تُغْنِي / مَا تُؤْمَرُ/ ، بَهَبْ/ حَلِيمًا بِوِلَادَةِ / يُسَاعِدَ / فَدَيْنَاهُ /عَاقِلاً/ وَاسْتَطَاعَ/ الْمَنَامِ / يَذْبَحُهُ/ فَقُصِّ/ فَانْتَقَلَ / لِأَبِيهِ/ وَأَضْجَعَهُ/ جَنْبِهِ، امْتِثَالاً/ بُيْدِي / نَذْبَح/ نَفَّذْتَ/ وَسَيَجْزِيكُمُ/ الخَلاصُ/ الشِّدَّةِ / سَيَهْدِينِ.	
Lesson 2: 12 point Start time 05:47:23 end time:05:49:33	تَطْمَحُ وَالْبِنَاءُ/ قَارِئًا/ بِمَا/ أَتَاهُ/ اقْرَأْ/ كِبْ/ إِنَّا/ الْمُتَفَضِّلُ/ فَتَسْعَدَ/ / جِبْرِيلُ/اقْرَأْ/ لَهُ يَكُونَ/ وَازْدِهَارِ /	
Lesson 3: 14 point Start time: 05:49:55 End time:05:53:42	نُقِيمُ/ تَرْفِيهِيَّةً/ اشْتِرَاكِهِمْ سَنَنْقُلُهُمْ/ مُنْتَهِجِينَ/ الخِبِيئَةُ / يَتَبَادَلَانِ/ وَيَبِسَتْ تَخْتَلِفُ/ يَجْعَلُهَا/ ثَرْوَةً// يَقْتَصِرُ/ وَأَهَمِّيَّتِهِ/ اشْتِرَاكِهِمْ/ مُنْتَهِجِينَ/ تَخْتَلِفُ تَأْثِيرِ/ أَهَمِّيَّتِهِ/ تَنْفِيذِ/ بِمَا /أَوْلَكِي وَقُرَّانَا/ الخِبِيئَةُ	
Lesson4:18 point Start time: 05:55:49 End time: 05:58:49	no	

Table 14.

Personal details		
Name:	Age: 10	L of ED: 5
Reading score: over 5	Eye visual : 6	
Test : (1) font size		
time	Start time: 10:18: 03	End time:10:30:03
Lesson 1: 10 point.	نَبِيُّهُ/ وَتَرْكِ / سَنَجْحَدُنِي/ رَقْبَتِهِ/ وَعِنْدَئِذٍ/ وَالْبَنَكَ/ وَابْنَكَ/ تُغْنِي / ﻷَمْ / ثُمَّ / لِإِحْسَانِكُمَا/ يَهَبُ / حَلِيمًا عَاقِلاً/ وَاسْتَطَاعَ/ الْمَنَامِ / يَذْبَحُهُ/ فَقَصَّ/ فَامْتَثَلَ / لِأَبِيهِ/ وَأَضْجَعَهُ/ جَنْبِهِ،/ امْتِثَالاً/ يُبْدِي / تَذْبَحُ/ نَقَذْتَ/ وَسَيَجْزِيكُمُ/ الْخَلاَصِ/ الشَّدَّةِ / كَبْشًا/ يَذْبَحُهُ/ فَبَشَّرْنَاهُ / حَلِيمٍ / بَلَغَ/ إِنِّي / أَذْبَحُكَ/ وَتَلَّهُ/ لِلْجَبِينِ / نَجْزِي/ بِذِبْحِ/الْمُبِينِ.
Lesson 2: 12 point Start time :10:48:04 end time:10:52:34	لِيَهْتَدِي / سَعَادَتِهِم تَسِيرُ/ وَالْبِنَاءُ/ قَارِئًا/ بِمَا/ أَتَاهُ/ اقْرَأْ / مُجْتَمَعِهِ /وَكُلٍّ/ مُجْتَمَعِهِ/ تَنْتَظِرُ / لِيَهْتَدِيَ / شَرِيكَ / كَثِيرًا؛/
Lesson 3: 14 point Start time: 11:32:55 End time:11:49:45	تُقِيمُ/ تَرْفِيهِيَّةٌ/ اشْتِرَاكِهِم/ سَتَنْفُلُهُمْ/ مُنْبَهِجِينَ/ الْحَبِيبَةُ/ الطَّبِيعَةِ/ الطَّبِيعَةِ/ يَتَبَادَلاَنِ/ وَيَسْتُ تَخْتَلِفُ/ يَجْعَلُهَا/ ثَرْوَةٌ// يَقْتَصِرُ/ وَأَهَمِّيَّتِهِ اشْتِرَاكِهِم/ مُنْبَهِجِينَ/ تَخْتَلِفُ تَأْثِيرِ/ أَهَمِّيَّتِهِ/ تَنْفِيذِ/
Lesson4:18 point Start time: 11:40:35 End time: 11:46:12	اتَّفَقْنَا/ الْهَيِّنِ/ يَبْعَثُ/ وَضَيَّعْتَ/ أَسْتَفِيدَ/ إِيَّاكَ/ فَإِنَّنِي/ ثَمِينٌ/ يَحْتَرِمُ/ يَتَسَبَّبُ/ الثَّمِينَةِ/ الْمُسْتَقْبَلِ مُحَدَّدٍ/ يَنْتَظِرُهُ/ فَاسْتَقْبَلَهُ/ انْتَظَرْتُكَ/ ثَمِينًا/

Table 15.

Personal details		
Name:	Age: 10	L of ED: 5
Reading score: over 5	Eye visual : 6	
Test : (1) font size 10		
time	Start time: 10:18: 03	End time:10:30:03
Lesson 1: 10 point.	نَبِيَّهُ/ وَتَرْكِ / سَتَجِدُنِي/ رَفَتِيهِ/ وَعِنْدَئِذٍ/ وَابْنَكَ/ تُغْنِي / لِمَ / ثُمَّ / لِإِحْسَانِكُمَا/ يَهَبْ / حَلِيمًا عَاقِلاً/ وَاسْتَطَاعَ/ الْمَنَامِ / يَذْبَحُهُ/ فَقَصَّ/ فَامْتَثَلَ / لِأَبِيهِ/ وَأَضْجَعَهُ/ جَنْبِهِ، امْتِثَالاً/ يُبْدِي / تَذْبَحُ / نَفَّذْتَ/ وَسَيَخْزِيكُمُ/ الْخَلَاصَ/ الشِّدَّةِ / كَبْشًا/ يَذْبَحَهُ/ فَبَشَّرْنَاهُ / حَلِيمٍ / بَلَغَ/ إِنِّي / أَذْبَحُكَ/ وَتَلَّهُ/ لِلْجَبِينِ / نَجْزِي/ بِذِبْحٍ/الْمُبِينِ.
Lesson 2: 12 point Start time :10:48:04 end time:10:52:34	لِيَهْتَدِيَ / سَعَادَتِهِم تَسِيرُ/ وَالْبِنَاءُ/ قَارِئًا/ بِهَا/ أَتَاهُ/ اقْرَأْ / مُجْتَمَعِهِ /وَكُلٌّ/ مُجْتَمَعِهِ/ تَنْتَظِرُ / لِيَهْتَدِيَ / شَرِيكَ / كَثِيرًا؛/
Lesson 3: 14 point Start time: 11:32:55 End time:11:49:45	نُقِيمَ/ تَرْفِيهِيَّةٌ/ اشْتِرَاكِهِمْ/ مُنْتَهِجِينَ/ الْخَبِيثَةُ/ الطَّبِيعَةُ/ الطَّبِيعَةِ/ يَتَبَادَلَانِ/ وَيَبِسَتْ تَخْتَلِفُ/ يَجْعَلُهَا/ ثَرْوَةٌ// يَقْتَصِرُ/ وَأَهَمِّيَّتِهِ/ مُنْتَهِجِينَ/ اشْتِرَاكِهِمْ/ تَخْتَلِفُ تَأْثِيرٍ/ أَهَمِّيَّتِهِ/ تَنْفِيذِ/
Lesson4:18 point Start time: 11:40:35 End time: 11:46:12	اتَّفَقْنَا/ الْهَيِّنِ/ يَبْعَثُ/ وَضَيَّعْتَ/ أَسْتَفِيدَ/ إِيَّاكَ/ فَإِنَّنِي/ ثَمِينٌ/ يَحْتَرِمُ/ يَتَسَبَّبُ/ الثَّمِينَةِ/ الْمُسْتَقْبَلِ مُحَدَّدٍ/ يَنْتَظِرُهُ / فَاسْتَقْبَلَهُ/ انْتَظَرْتُكَ/ ثَمِينًا/

Table 16.

Personal details		
Name:	Age: 10	L of ED: 5
Reading score: over 5	Eye visual : 6	
Test : (1) font size		
time	Start time: 10:18: 03	End time:10:30:03
Lesson 1: 10 point.	نَبِيُّهُ/ وَتَرْكِ / سَتَجِدُنِي/ رَقَبَتِهِ/ وَعِنْدَئِذٍ/ وَابْنَكَ/ تُغْنِي / لَمْ / ثُمَّ / لِإِحْسَانِكُمَا/ يَهَبُ/ حَلِيمًا عَاقِلاً/ وَاسْتَطَاعَ/ الْمَنَامِ / يَذْبَحُهُ/ فَقَصَّ/ فَامْتَثَلَ / لِأَبِيهِ/ وَأَضْجَعَهُ/ جَنْبِهِ،/ امْتِثَالاً/ يُبْدِي / نَفَّذْتَ/ وَسَيَجْزِيكُمْ/ الْخَلَاصِ/ الشِّدَّةِ / كَبْشًا/ يَذْبَحُهُ/ فَبَشَّرْنَاهُ / حَلِيمٍ / بَلَغَ/ إِنِّي / أَذْبَحُكَ/ وَتَلَّهُ / لِلْجَبِينِ / يَجْزِي/ بِذِبْحٍ/الْمُبِينُ.
Lesson 2: 12 point Start time :10:48:04 end time:10:52:34	لِيَهْتَدِي / سَعَادَتِهِم تَسِيرُ/ وَالْبِنَاءُ/ قَارِئًا/ بِهَا/ أَتَاهُ/ اقْرَأْ / مُجْتَمَعِهِ /وَكُلٌّ/ مُجْتَمَعِهِ/ تَنْتَظِرُ / لِيَهْتَدِي / شَرِيكَ / كَثِيرًا؛/
Lesson 3: 14 point Start time: 11:32:55 End time:11:49:45	تُقِيمُ/ تَرْفِيهِيَّةٌ/ اشْتِرَاكِهِمْ سَتَشْغُلُهُمْ/ مُبْتَهِجِينَ/ الْخَبِيئَةُ/ الطَّبِيعَةُ/ الطَّبِيعَةِ/ يَتَبَادَلَانِ/ وَلَيْسَتْ تَخْتَلِفُ/ يَجْعَلُهَا/ ثَرْوَةٌ/ / يَقْتَصِرُ/ وَأَهَمِّيَّتِهِ/ اشْتِرَاكِهِمْ/ مُبْتَهِجِينَ/ تَخْتَلِفُ تَأْثِيرِ/ أَهَمِّيَّتِهِ/ تَنْفِيذِ/
Lesson4:18 point Start time: 11:40:35 End time: 11:46:12	اتَّفَقْنَا/ الْمَيِّنِ/ يَبْعَثُ/ وَضَيَّعْتَ/ أَسْتَفِيدَ/ إِيَّاكَ/ فَإِنَّنِي/ ثَمِينٌ/ يَحْتَرِمُ/ يَتَسَبَّبُ/ الثَّمِينَةِ/ الْمُسْتَقْبَلِ مُحَدَّدٍ/ يَنْتَظِرُهُ/ فَاسْتَقْبَلَهُ/ انْتَظَرْتُكَ/ ثَمِينًا/

Table 17.

Personal details		
Name: محمد	Age:12	L of ED7
Reading score: over 5	Eye visual : 6	
Test : (1) font size		
time	Start time: 02:44: 03	End time:02:52:03
Lesson 1: 10 point.	تَعَالَ / بِالْعِرَاقِ / نَبِيَّهُ / وَتَرْكَ / رَفَتِهِ/ وَابْنَكَ/ تُغْنِي / مَا تُؤْمَرُ، / لِإِحْسَانِكُمَا/ يَهَبَ/ حَلِيمًا عَاقِلًا/ إِحْرَاقِهِ / خَرَجَ / يَهَبَ/ صَابِرًا،/ وَاسْتَطَاعَ/ الْمَنَام / يَذْبَحُهُ/ فَفَصَّ/ فَامْتَثَلَ/ الْأَبِهِ/ وَأَضْجَعَهُ/ جَنْبِهِ،/ امْتِثَالًا/ يُبْدِي / تَذْبَح/ نَفَّذْتَ/ وَسَيَحْزِيكُمُ/ الْخَلَاصُ/ الشِّدَّةِ / كَبْشًا/ يَذْبَحُهُ/ فَبَشَّرْنَاهُ / حَلِيمٍ / بَلَغَ / إِنِّي / أَذْبَحُكَ/ وَتَلَّهُ/ لِلْجَبِينِ / نَجْزِي/ بِذِبْحٍ/الْمُبِينِ.
Lesson 2: 12 point Start time :10:54:04 end time:10:58:34	/ جِبْرِيلُ/اقْرَأْ/ وَالْبِنَاءُ/ قَارِئًا/ بِهَا/ أَتَاهُ/ اقْرَأْ يَكُونَ/
Lesson 3: 14 point Start time: 11:07:55 End time:11:02:45	تُقِيمُ/ تَرْفِيهِيَّةٌ/ اشْتِرَاكِهِمْ/ سَنُنْفِقُلُهُمْ/ مُنْتَهِجِينَ/ الْخَبِيئَةُ / يَتَبَادَلَانِ/ وَبَيْسَتْ نَخْتَلِفُ/ يَجْعَلُهَا/ ثَرْوَةٍ// يَقْتَصِرُ/ وَأَهَمِّيَّتِهِ/ مُنْتَهِجِينَ/ اشْتِرَاكِهِمْ/ نَخْتَلِفُ تَأْثِيرِ/ أَهَمِّيَّتِهِ/ تَنْفِيذِ/
Lesson4:18 point Start time: 11:40:35 End time: 11:46:12	اتَّفَقْنَا/ الْهَيِّنِ/ يَبْعَثُ/ وَضَيَّعْتَ/ أَسْتَفِيدَ/ إِيَّاكَ/ فَإِنَّنِي / ثَمِينٍ/ يَحْتَرِمُ/ يَتَسَبَّبُ/ الثَّمِينَةِ/ مُحَدَّدٍ/ يَنْتَظِرَهُ / فَاسْتَقْبَلَهُ/ انْتَظَرْتُكَ/ ثَمِينًا/

Table 18.

Personal details		
Name: ا عوئشة	Age: 10	L of ED: 5
Reading score: over 5	Eye visual : 6	
Test : (1) font size		
time	Start time: 11:18: 03	End time: 11:30:03
Lesson 1: 10 point.	تُغْني / أَمْ / ثُمَّ / لإِحْسانِكُمَا/ يَهَبْ/ حَلِيمًا عَاقِلاً/ وَاسْتَطَاعَ/ الْمَنَام / يَذْبَحَهُ/ فَقَصَّ/ فَامْتَثَل / لأَبِيهِ/ وَأَضْجَعَهُ/ جَبْنِهِ، امْتِثَالاً/ يُبْدِي / تَذْبَحَ/ وَسَيَجْزِيكُمُ/ الخَلاصِ/ الشَّدَّةِ / كَبْشًا/ يَذْبَحَهُ/ فَبَشَّرْنَاهُ / حَلِيمٍ / بَلَغَ/ إِنِّي / أَذْبَحُكَ/ وَتَلَّهُ/ لِلْجَبِينِ / نَجْزِي/ بِذِبْحٍ/الْمُبِينِ.
Lesson 2: 12 point Start time :11:24:04 end time:11:31:34	لِيَهْتَدِيَ / وَالْبِنَاءُ/ قَارِئًا/ بِهَا/ أَتَاهُ/ اقْرَأْ / مُجْتَمَعِهِ /وَكُلٌّ/ مُجْتَمَعِهِ/ / لِيَهْتَدِيَ /
Lesson 3: 14 point Start time: 11:32:55 End time:11:49:45	تُقِيمَ/ تَرْفِيهِيَّةً/ اشْتِرَاكِهِمْ سَتَنْقُلُهُمْ/ مُبْتَهِجِينَ/ الخَبِيثَةِ/ الطَّيِّعَةِ/ الطَّبِيعَةِ/ يَتَبَادَلاَنِ/ وَلَيْسَتْ تَخْتَلِفُ/ يَجْعَلُهَا/ ثَرْوَةٌ// يَقْتَصِرُ/ وَأَهَمِّيَّتِهِ
Lesson4:18 point Start time: 11:40:35 End time: 11:46:12	اتَّفَقْنَا/ الهَيِّنِ/ يَبْعَثُ/ وَضَيَّعْتَ/ أَسْتَفِيدَ/ إِيَّاكَ/ فَإِنَّنِي/ ثَمِينٌ/ يَحْتَرِمُ/ يَتَسَبَّبُ/ الثَّمِينَةِ/ الْمُسْتَقْبَلِ مُحَدَّدٍ

Table 19.

Personal details		
Name: محمد	Age:12	L of ED: 7
Reading score: over 5	Eye visual : 6	
Test : (1) font size		
time	Start time05:40: 03	End time: 05:45:54
Lesson 1: 10 point.	يَعْبُدُونَ / بِإِحْرَاقِهِ / لِيَتَمَكَّنَ / نَبِيُّهُ/ وَتَرْكِ / رَقَبَتِهِ/ وَابْنَكَ/ تُغْنِي / مَا تُؤْمَرُ، / يَهَبَ/ حَلِيمًا بِوِلَادَةٍ / يُسَاعِدَ / فَدَيْنَاهُ /عَاقِلًا/ وَاسْتَطَاعَ/ الْمَنَامِ / يَذْبَحُهُ/ فَقَصَّ/ فَامْتَثَلَ / لِأَبِيهِ/ وَأَضْجَعَهُ/ جَنْبِهِ،/ امْتِثَالًا/ يُبْدِي / تَذْبَحُ/ نَفَّذْتَ/ وَسَيَحْزِيكُمُ/ الْخَلَاصِ/ الشِّدَّةِ / سَيَهْدِينِ.
Lesson 2: 12 point Start time 05:47:23 end time:05:49:33	تَطْمَحُ وَالْبِنَاءُ/ قَارِئًا/ بِمَا/ أَتَاهُ/ اقْرَأْ/ كِبَ/ إِنَّا/ الْمُتَفَضِّلُ/ فَتَسْعَدَ/ / جِبْرِيلُ/اقْرَأْ/ لَهُ يَكُونَ/ وَازْدِهَارٍ /
Lesson 3: 14 point Start time: 05:49:55 End time:05:53:42	نُقِيمَ/ تَرْفِيهِيَّةً/ اشْتِرَاكِهِمْ سَنُنْفُلُهُمْ/ مُبْتَهِجِينَ/ الْخَبِيئَةُ/ يَتَبَادَلَانِ/ وَيَبِسَتْ تَخْتَلِفُ/ يَجْعَلُهَا/ ثَرْوَةٌ/ / يَقْتَصِرُ/ وَأَهَمِّيَّتِهِ/ اشْتِرَاكِهِمْ/ مُبْتَهِجِينَ/ تَخْتَلِفُ تَأْثِيرِ/ أَهَمِّيَّتِهِ/ تَنْفِيذٍ/ تَنْفِيذِهِ/ بِمَا /اوَلِكَي وَقُرَانَا/ الْخَبِيئَةُ
Lesson4:18 point Start time: 05:55:49 End time: 05:58:49	no

Table 20.

Personal details		
Name: محمد	Age:12	L of ED: 7
Reading score: over 5	Eye visual : 6	
Test : (1) font size		
time	Start time05:40: 03	End time: 05:45:54
Lesson 1: 10 point.	يَعْبُدُونَ / بِإِحْرَاقِهِ / لِيَتَمَكَّنَ / نَبِيَّهُ/ وَتَرْكِ / رَقَبَتِهِ/ وَابْنَكَ/ تُغْنِي / مَا تُؤْمَرُ، / يَهَبَ/ حَلِيمًا بِوِلَادَةٍ / يُسَاعِدَ / فَدَيْنَاهُ /عَاقِلاً/ وَاسْتَطَاعَ/ الْمَنَام / يَذْبَحُهُ/ فَقَصَّ/ فَامْتَثَلَ / لِأَبِيهِ/ وَأَضْجَعَهُ/ جَنْبِهِ،/ امْتِثَالاً/ يُبْدِي / تَذْبَحَ/ نَفَّذْتَ/ وَسَيَجْزِيكُمْ/ الخَلَاصَ/ الشِّدَّةِ / سَيَهْدِينِ.
Lesson 2: 12 point Start time 05:47:23 end time:05:49:33	تَطْمَحُ وَالْبِنَاءُ/ قَارِئًا/ بِمَا/ أَتَاهُ/ اقْرَأْ/ كِبَ/ إِنَّنَا/ الْمُتَفَضِّلُ/ فَتَسْعَدَ / جِبْرِيلُ/اقْرَأْ/ لَهُ يَكُونَ/ وَازْدِهَارٌ/
Lesson 3: 14 point Start time: 05:49:55 End time:05:53:42	تُقِيمَ/ تَرْفِيهِيَّةٌ/ اشْتِرَاكِهِمْ/ سَتَنْفُلُهُمْ/ مُنْتَهِجِينَ/ الخَبِيئَةُ / يَتَبَادَلَانِ/ وَيَسَتْ تَخْتَلِفُ/ يَجْعَلُهَا/ ثَرْوَةٌ/ يَقْتَصِرُ / وَأَهَمِّيَّتِهِ/ اشْتِرَاكِهِ/ مُنْتَهِجِينَ/ تَخْتَلِفُ تَأْثِيرٍ/ أَهَمِّيَّتِهِ/ تَنْفِيذِ/ بِمَا /اوَلكَي وَقُرْآنَا/ الخَبِيئَةُ
Lesson4:18 point Start time: 05:55:49 End time: 05:58:49	no

Table 21.

Personal details		
Name: محمد	Age:12	L of ED7
Reading score: over 5	Eye visual : 6	
Test : (1) font size		
time	Start time: 02:44: 03	End time:02:52:03
Lesson 1: 10 point.	تَعَالَى / بِالْعِرَاقِ / نَبِيُّهُ/ وَتَرْكِ / رَقَبَتِهِ/ وَابْنَكَ/ تُغْنِي / مَا تُؤْمَرُ، / لإِحْسَانِكُمَا/ يَهَبُ / حَلِيمًا عَاقِلاً/ بِإِحْرَاقِهِ / خَرَجَ / يَهَبُ/ صَابِرًا،/ وَاسْتَطَاعَ/ الْمَنَام / يَذْبَحُهُ/ فَقَصَّ/ فَامْتَثَلَ / لأَبِيهِ/ وَأَضْجَعَهُ/ جَنْبِهِ،/ امْتِثَالاً/ يُبْدِي / تَذْبَح/ نَقَذْتَ/ وَسَيَحْزِيكُمْ/ الْخَلاَصَ/ الشِّدَّةِ / كَبْشًا/ يَذْبَحُهُ/ فَبَشَّرْنَاهُ / حَلِيمٍ / بَلَغَ/ إِنِّي / أَذْبَحُكَ/ وَتَلَّهُ/ لِلْجَبِينِ / نَجْزِي / بِذِبْحٍ/الْمُبِينِ.
Lesson 2: 12 point Start time :10:54:04 end time:10:58:34	/ جِبْرِيلُ/اقْرَأْ / وَالْبِنَاءُ/ قَارِئًا/ بِهَا/ أَتَاهُ/ اقْرَأْ يَكُونَ/
Lesson 3: 14 point Start time: 11:07:55 End time:11:02:45	نُقِيم/ تَرْفِيهِيَّةً/ اشْتِرَاكِهِمْ سَتَنْفُلُهُمْ/ مُنْتَهِجِينَ/ الْخَبِيبَةَ / يَتَبَادَلاَنِ/ وَبِسَتْ تَخْتَلِفُ/ يَجْعَلُهَا/ ثَرْوَةٌ// يَقْتَصِرُ/ وَأَهَمِّيَّتِهِ/ اشْتِرَاكِهِمْ/ مُنْتَهِجِينَ/ تَخْتَلِفُ تَأْثِيرِ/ أَهَمِّيَّتِهِ/ تَنْفِيذِ/
Lesson4:18 point Start time: 11:40:35 End time: 11:46:12	اتَّفَقْنَا/ الْهَيِّنِ/ يَبْعَثُ/ وَضَيَّعْتَ/ أَسْتَفِيدَ/ إِيَّاكَ/ فَإِنَّنِي/ ثَمِينٌ/ يَحْتَرِمُ/ يَتَسَبَّبُ/ الثَّمِينَةِ/ مُحَدَّدٍ/ يَنْتَظِرَهُ / فَاسْتَقْبَلَهُ/ انْتَظَرْتُكَ/ /ثَمِينًا/

Table 22.

Personal details		
Name: محمد	Age:12	L of ED7
Reading score: over 5	Eye visual : 6	
Test : (1) font size		
time	Start time: 02:44: 03	End time:02:52:03
Lesson 1: 10 point.	تَعَالَى / بِالْعِرَاقِ / نَبِيَّهُ/ وَتَرْكِ / رَقَبَتِهِ/ وَابْنَكَ/ تُغْنِي / مَا تُؤْمَرُ ، / لِإِحْسَانِكُمَا/ يَهَبْ / حَلِيمًا عَاقِلاً/ بِإِحْرَاقِهِ / خَرَجَ / يَهَبْ/ صَابِرًا/، وَاسْتَطَاعَ/ الْمَنَام / يَذْبَحُهُ/ فَفَصَّ/ فَامْتَثَلَ / لِأَبِيهِ/ وَأَضْجَعَهُ/ جَنْبِهِ، / امْتِثَالاً/ يُبْدِي / تَذْبَح/ نَفَّذْتَ/ وَسَيَجْزِيكُمْ/ الْخَلاَصَ/ الشِّدَّةِ / كَبْشًا/ يَذْبَحُهُ/ فَبَشَّرْنَاهُ / حَلِيم / بَلَغَ/ إِنِّي / أَذْبَحُكَ/ وَتَلَّهُ/ لِلْجَبِينِ / نَجْزِي/ بِذِبْحٍ/الْمُبِينُ.
Lesson 2: 12 point Start time :10:54:04 end time:10:58:34	/ جِبْرِيلُ/اقْرَأْ/ وَالْبِنَاءُ/ قَارِئًا/ بِهَا/ أَتَاهُ/ اقْرَأْ يَكُونَ/
Lesson 3: 14 point Start time: 11:07:55 End time:11:02:45	تُقِيمُ/ تَرْفِيهِيَّةً/ اشْتِرَاكِهِمْ سَتَنْفُقُلُهُمْ/ مُنْتَهِجِينَ/ الْخَبِيئَةُ / يَتَبَادَلاَنِ/ وَيَبِسَتْ تَخْتَلِفُ/ يَجْعَلُهَا/ ثَرْوَةٍ// يَقْتَصِرُ/ وَأَهَمِّيَّتِهِ/ اشْتِرَاكِهِمْ/ مُنْتَهِجِينَ/ تَخْتَلِفُ تَأْثِيرِ/ أَهَمِّيَّتِهِ/ تَنْفِيذِ/
Lesson4:18 point Start time: 11:40:35 End time: 11:46:12	اتَّفَقْنَا/ الْهَيِّنِ/ يَبْعَثُ/ وَضَيَّعْتَ/ أَسْتَفِيدَ/ إِيَّاكَ/ فَإِنَّنِي/ ثَمِينٌ/ يَحْتَرِمُ/ يَتَسَبَّبُ/ الثَّمِينَةِ/ مُحَدَّدٍ/ يَنْتَظِرَهُ/ فَاسْتَقْبَلَهُ/ انْتَظَرْتُكَ/ ثَمِينًا/

Table 23.

Personal details		
Name: محمد	Age:12	L of ED7
Reading score: over 5	Eye visual : 6	
Test : (1) font size		
time	Start time: 02:44: 03	End time:02:52:03
Lesson 1: 10 point.	تَعَالَى / بِالْعِرَاقِ / نَبِيَّهُ / وَتَرْكِ / رَفَتِهِ/ وَابْنَكَ/ تُغْنِي / مَا تُؤْمَرُ ، / لِإِحْسَانِكُمَا/ يَهَبْ / حَلِيمًا عَاقِلًا/ بِإِحْرَاقِهِ / خَرَجَ / يَهَبْ / صَابِرًا، / وَاسْتَطَاعَ/ الْمَنَامِ / يَذْبَحُهُ / فَقَصَّ/ فَامْتَثَلَ / لِأَبِيهِ/ وَأَضْجَعَهُ/ جَنْبِهِ،/ امْتِثَالًا/ يُبْدِي / تَذْبَح/ نَفَّذْتَ/ وَسَيَجْزِيكُمْ/ الْخَلَاصَ/ الشِّدَّةِ / كَبْشًا/ يَذْبَحُهُ / فَبَشَّرْنَاهُ / حَلِيمٍ / بَلَغَ/ إِنِّي / أَذْبَحُكَ/ وَتَلَّهُ/ لِلْجَبِينِ / نَجْزِي/ بِذِبْحٍ/الْمُبِينُ.	
Lesson 2: 12 point Start time :10:54:04 end time:10:58:34	/ جِبْرِيلُ/اقْرَأْ/ وَالْبِنَاءُ/ قَارِئًا/ بِهَا/ أَتَاهُ/ اقْرَأْ يَكُونَ/	
Lesson 3: 14 point Start time: 11:07:55 End time:11:02:45	نُقِيمُ/ تَرْفِيهِيَّةً/ اشْتِرَاكِهِمْ سَتَنْفُلُهُمْ/ مُنْتَهِجِينَ/ الْخَبِيبَةِ / يَتَبَادَلَانِ/ وَيَسَتْ تَخْتَلِفُ/ يَجْعَلُهَا/ ثَرْوَةٌ/ يَقْتَصِرُ/ وَأَهَمِّيَّتِهِ/ اشْتِرَاكِهِمْ/ مُنْتَهِجِينَ/ تَخْتَلِفُ تَأْثِيرِ/ أَهَمِّيَّتِهِ/ تَنْفِيذِ/	
Lesson4:18 point Start time: 11:40:35 End time: 11:46:12	اتَّفَقْنَا/ الْهَيِّنِ/ يَبْعَثُ/ وَضَيَّعْتَ/ أَسْتَفِيدَ/ إِيَّاكَ/ فَإِنَّنِي/ ثَمِينٌ/ يَحْتَرِمُ/ يَتَسَبَّبُ/ الثَّمِينَةِ/ مُحَدَّدٍ/ يَنْتَظِرَهُ / فَاسْتَقْبَلَهُ/ انْتَظَرْتُكَ/ ثَمِينًا/	

APPENDIX 6: SATISFACTION QUESTIONNAIRE USED IN THE END OF EACH EXPERIMENT

1. How difficult was the test?
   a. Very difficult
   b. Not very difficult
   c. Very easy
2. How interesting was the text?
   a. Very interested
   b. Not very interested
   c. Very boring
3. How easy was it to trace the information needed?
   a. Very difficult
   b. Not very difficult
   c. Very easy
4. How confident were you after reading the text that you could do the assignment successfully?
   a. Confident
   b. Neutral
   c. Unconfident
5. I do not mind reading off a computer screen
   a. Yes
   b. No
6. I do not like read off a computer screen
   a. Yes
   b. No
7. When reading, I prefer hard copy to digital format
   a. Yes
   b. No
8. If I had the option, I would purchase an e- book over a traditional textbook.
   a. Yes
   b. No

APPENDIX 7: SHEET OF QUESTIONS FOR EXPERIMENT (3)

Table 24.

اجاب علي جميع الاسئلة:

س1: من ارسل ابراهيم ال قومه؟ ....

س2: ماذا كان قوم ابراهيم يعبدون؟. ....

س3: ماذا رأي ابراهيم في منامه؟ ....

س4: لماذا هاجر ابراهيم الي الشام؟. ....

س5: من أرسل كبشا عظيما الي ابراهيم ؟ (الله ـ عمه ـ جاره)

س6: من ـأمر بحرق ابراهيم؟ (الله ـ ابنه ـ قومه)

س7: يعبد ابراهيم. (الله – الاصنام – الشمس)

س8: كان قوم ابراهيم يعبدون. (الله – الاصنام – الشمس)

س9: الله ارسل ابراهيم الي قومه. نعم .... لا ....

س10: هاجر ابراهيم الي الشام ليتمكن من عبادة الله. نعم .... لا ....

س11: كان ابراهيم يعبد الاصنام. نعم .... لا ....

س12: اشتري ابراهيم كبشا من السوق. نعم .... لا ....

Compilation of References

Abdullah, N. (2007). *A Study into Usability of Tools for Searching and Browsing E-books with Particular Reference to Back-of-the-Book Index* (PhD Dissertation). Department of Computer and Information Sciences, Strathclyde.

Abdullah, N. (2007). A Study into Usability of Tools for Searching and Browsing E-books with Particular Reference to Back-of-the-Book Index.

Abdullah, Z. A. (2007). A Study into Usability of Tools for Searching and Browsing E-books with Particular Reference to Back-of-the-Book Index (PhD Dissertation). Department of Computer and Information Sciences, Strathclyde.

Abubaker, A., & Joan, L. (2011). E-reading strategy model to read E-school book in Libya. *Proceedings of the International Conference on Internet Computing ICOMP*.

Abubaker, A., & Joan, L. (2012). The optimum font size and type for students aged 9-12 reading Arabic characters on screen: A case study. Journal of Physics: Conference Series, 364. Retrieved from http://iopscience.iop.org/1742-6596/364/1/012115/

Abubaker, A., & Lu, J. (2011). Model of E-Reading Process for E-School Book in Libya. *International Journal of Information Retrieval Research*, *1*(3), 35–53. Retrieved from http://www.irma-international.org/viewtitle/64170/ doi:10.4018/ijirr.2011070103

Aburrous, M., Hossain, M. A., Keshav, D., & Fadi, T. (2010). Intelligent phishing detection system for e-banking using fuzzy data mining. *Expert Systems with Applications*, *37*(12), 7913–7921. doi:10.1016/j.eswa.2010.04.044

Adolphs, R. (2002). Trust in the brain. *Nature Neuroscience, 5*(3), 192-194.

Agarwal, R., & Venkatesh, V. (2002). Assessing a firm's web presence: A heuristic evaluation procedure for the measurement of usability. *Information Systems Research*, *13*(2), 168–186. doi:10.1287/isre.13.2.168.84

Agresti, A. (1990). Categorical data analysis.New York. Statistics and Application, 2(4), 2013-12-24.

Ajzen, I. (2011). The theory of planned behaviour: Reactions and reflections. *Psychology & Health*, *26*(9), 1113–1127. doi:10.1080/08870446.2011.613995 PMID:21929476

Alamdar, F., & Keyvanpour, M. (2011). A new color feature extraction method based on QuadHistogram. *Procedia Environmental Sciences*, *10*(1), 777–783. doi:10.1016/j.proenv.2011.09.126

Alan, C. (2001). designing computer- based learning materials, Gower Publishing Limited.

Alan, C. (2001). *Designing computer- based learning materials*. Gower Publishing Limited.

Alonso, E., Dinverno, M., Kudenko, D., Luck, M., & Noble, J. (2001). Learning in multi-agent systems. *The Knowledge Engineering Review*, *16*(03), 277–284. doi:10.1017/S0269888901000170

Alotaibi, A. Z. (2007). The effect of font size and type on reading performance with Arabic words in normally sighted and simulated cataract subjects. *Clinical & Experimental Optometry, 90*(3), 203–203. doi:10.1111/j.1444-0938.2007.00123.x PMID:17425766

Alp, Ö. S., Büyükbebeci, E., & İşcanog, A. (2011). CMARS and GAM & CQP—modern optimization methods applied to international credit default prediction. *Journal of Computational and Applied Mathematics, 235*(16), 4639–4651. doi:10.1016/j.cam.2010.04.039

Amadieu, F., Tricot, A., & Marine, C. (2009). Prior knowledge in learning from a nonlinear electronic document: Disorientation and coherence of the reading sequences. *Computers in Human Behavior, 25*(2), 381–388. doi:10.1016/j.chb.2008.12.017

American National Standard. (1988). *Human Factors Engineering of Visual Display Terminal Workstations A. H. S. N. 100-1988*. Santa Monica, CA: Author.

Amin, A. (2000). Recognition of printed Arabic text based on global features and decision tree learning techniques. *Pattern Recognition, 33*, 1309-1323.

Ani, O. E., Edem, M. B., & Ottong, E. J. (2010). Analysis of internet access and use by academic staff in the University of Calabar, Calabar, Nigeria. *Library Management, 31*(7), 535–545. doi:10.1108/01435121011071229

Anonymous, . (1999). NuvoMedia eRocket. *Information Today, 16*(9), 45.

Anonymous. (2012). *Access to computer and internet use by U.S.* Retrieved from https://www.census.gov/

Anonymous. (2012). *Computer and Internet*. U.S. Department of Commerce. Retrieved from http://census.gov/topics/population/computer-internet.html

Anuradha, K., & Usha, H. S. (2006). Use of e-books in an academic and research environment: A case study from the Indian Institute of Science. *Program, 40*(1), 48–62. doi:10.1108/00330330610646807

An, X. B., Zhang, W., & Yang, J. (2011). Research on Evaluation of Banks Ecological Culture Based on Fuzzy Mathematics. *Energy Procedia, 5*, 302–306. doi:10.1016/j.egypro.2011.03.052

Arai, M. (1989). Mapping abilities of three-layer neural networks. *Proceedings of the International Joint Conference on IEEE Neural Networks*, New York (pp. 419-423). doi:10.1109/IJCNN.1989.118598

Ashby, J., & Rayner, K. (2004). Representing syllable information during silent reading: Evidence from eye movements. *Language and Cognitive Processes, 19*(3), 391–426. doi:10.1080/01690960344000233

Asmaa, A., & Asma, A. O. (2009). Arab children are reading preferences for e-learning programs.*Proceedings of the 2009 conference on Information Science, Technology and Applications*.

Asmaa, A., & Asma, A. O. (2009). Arab children's reading preferences for e-learning programs.*Proceedings of the 2009 conference on Information Science, Technology and Applications*, Kuwait. ACM.

Asmaa, A., & Asma, A.-O. (2009). Arab children's reading preferences for e-learning programs.*Proceedings of the 2009 conference on Information Science, Technology and Applications*, Kuwait. ACM.

Association, T. T. S. (2003). *Technology update. Techniques*. Author.

Ayama, M., Ujike, H., Iwai, W., Funakawa, M., & Okajima, K. (2007). Effects of Contrast and Character Size upon Legibility of Japanese Text Stimuli Presented on Visual Display Terminal. *Optical Review, 14*(1), 48–56. doi:10.1007/s10043-007-0048-7

Aydın, D., & Uğur, A. (2011). Extraction of flower regions in color images using ant colony optimization. *Procedia Computer Science*, *3*, 530–536. doi:10.1016/j.procs.2010.12.088

Baeza-Yates, R., & Ribeiro-Neto, B. (1999). *Modern information retrieval*. Reading, MA: Addison Wesley Longman.

Balzano, W., & Del Sorbo, M. R. (2007). Genomic comparison using data mining techniques based on a possibilistic fuzzy sets model. *Bio Systems*, *88*(3), 343–349. doi:10.1016/j.biosystems.2006.07.014 PMID:17204362

Bandura, A. (1986). *Social Foundations of Thought and Action: A Social Cognitive Theory. NJ*. Englewood Cliffs: Prentice Hall.

Banerjee, J., & Majumdar, D., & Dhurjati, M. (2011). Readability, Subjective Preference and Mental Workload Studies on Young Indian Adults for Selection of Optimum Font Type and Size during Onscreen Reading. *Al Ame. en J. Medical Science*, *4*(2), 131–143.

Banerjee, J., & Majumdar, D. et al.. (2011). "Readability, Subjective Preference and Mental Workload Studies on Young Indian Adults for Selection of Optimum Font Type and Size during Onscreen Reading." Al Ame en J. *Medical Science*, *4*(2), 131–143.

Barber, K.S. & Kim, J. (2003). Soft security: Isolating unreliable agents from society. In *Trust, Reputation, and Security: Theories and Practice, LNCS* (Vol. 2631, pp. 224-234).

Barker, P. (1992). Electronic book and libraries of the future. *The Electronic Library*, *10*(3), 139–149. doi:10.1108/eb045143

Barker, P. (2005). Using e-books for knowledge management. *The Electronic Library*, 5–8.

Bates, J., Loyall, A. B., & Reilly, W. S. (1992). *An architecture for action, emotion, and social behavior*. Technical Report CMU-CS-92-144. School of Computer Science, CMU.

Bates, J. (1994). The role of emotion in believable agents. *Communications of the ACM*, *37*(7), 122–125. doi:10.1145/176789.176803

Bayro, C. E., & Eklundh, J. O. (2011). Advances in theory and applications of pattern recognition, image processing and computer vision. *Pattern Recognition Letters*, *32*(16), 2143–2144. doi:10.1016/j.patrec.2011.10.008

Bell, A. (2007). Designing and testing questionnaires for children. *Journal of Research in Nursing*, *12*(5), 461–469. doi:10.1177/1744987107079616

Bellifemine, F., Caire, G., & Greenwood, D. (2007). *Developming multi-agent systems with JADE*. John Wiley and Sons. doi:10.1002/9780470058411

Bennett, L., & Landoni, M. (2005). E-books in academic libraries. *The Electronic Library*, *23*(1), 9–16. doi:10.1108/02640470510582709

Bernard, M., Lida, B., Riley, S., Hackler, T., & Janzen, K (2002). A comparison of popular online fonts: which size and type is best? *UsabilityNews.org*.

Bernard, M. L., Chaparro, B. S., Mills, M. M., & Halcomb, C. G. (2003). Comparing the effects of text size and format on the readibility of computer-displayed Times New Roman and Arial text. *International Journal of Human-Computer Studies*, *59*(6), 823–835. doi:10.1016/S1071-5819(03)00121-6

Bhuiyan, S. M., Khan, J. F., & Adhami, R. R. (2010). A bidimensional empirical mode decomposition method for color image processing.*Proceedings of the 2010 IEEE Workshop On Signal Processing Systems*, Guangzhou (pp. 272 – 277). doi:10.1109/SIPS.2010.5624802

Biswal, B., Dash, B. K., & Panigrahi, B. K. (2009). Non-stationary power signal processing for pattern recognition using HS-transform. *Applied Soft Computing, 9*(1), 107–117. doi:10.1016/j.asoc.2008.03.004

Bobbitt, L. M., & Dabholkar, P. A. (2001). Integrating attitudinal theories to understand and predict use of technology-based self-service: The internet as an illustration. *International Journal of Service Industry Management, 12*(5), 423–450. doi:10.1108/EUM0000000006092

Bouma, H. (1971). *Visual recognition of isolated lower case letters*. Vision Research DOI.

Bouma, H. (1980). Visual reading processes and the quality of text displays. *IPO Annual Progress Report., 15*, 83–90.

Boyarski, D., Neuwirth, C., Forlizzi, J., & Regli, S.H. (1998). A study of fonts designed for screen display. *Proceedings of CHI'98*. doi:10.1145/274644.274658

Boynton, P. M., & Greenhalgh, T. (2004). Selecting, designing, and developing your questionnaire. *BMJ (Clinical Research Ed.), 328*(7451), 1312–1315. doi:10.1136/bmj.328.7451.1312 PMID:15166072

Bresciani, P., Perini, A., Giorgini, P., Giunchiglia, F., & Mylopoulos, J. (2004). Tropos an agent-oriented software de- velopment methodology. *Autonomous Agents and Multi-Agent Systems, 8*(3), 203–236. doi:10.1023/B:AGNT.0000018806.20944. ef

Briot, J. P., & Gasser, L. (1998). Agents and concurrent objects. *IEEE Concurrency, 6*(4), 74–77. doi:10.1109/4434.736431

Broadbent, D. E. (1958). *Perception and communication*. London: Pergamon Press. doi:10.1037/10037-000

Bruljn, D., Mul, S., & Oostendorp, H. (1992). The influence of screen size and text layout on the study of text. *Behaviour & Information Technology, 11*(2), 71–78. doi:10.1080/01449299208924322

Bundesen, C. (1990). A Theory of Visual Attention. *Psychological Review, 97*(4), 523–547. doi:10.1037/0033-295X.97.4.523 PMID:2247540

Büttcher, S., Clarke, C. L. A., & Cormack, G. V. (2010). *Information retrieval: Implementing and evaluating search engines*. Cambridge, MA: MIT Press.

Buzzetto-More, N. R., Sweat-Guy, R., & Elobaid, M. (2007). Reading in A Digital Age: e-Books Are Students Ready For This Learning Object? *Interdisciplinary Journal of Knowledge and Learning Objects, 3*, 239–250.

Castelfranchi, C., Dignum, F., Jonker, C. M., & Treur, J. (1999). Deliberate normative agents: Principles and architecture. *Lecture Notes in Computer Science, 1757*, 364–378. doi:10.1007/10719619_27

Castelfranchi, C., & Falcone, R. (2000). Trust is much more than subjective probability: Mental components and sources of trust. *Proc. of the 33rd Hawaii International Conference on System Sciences*. 52 doi:10.1109/HICSS.2000.926815

Cavanaugh, T. W. (2006). *The Digital Reader: Using E-books in K–12 Education*. Eugene, OR: International Society for Technology in Education.

Chan, A., & Lee, P. (2005). Effect of display factors on Chinese reading times, comprehension scores and preferences. *Behaviour & Information Technology, 24*(2), 81–91. doi:10.1080/0144929042000267073

Chaparro, B. S., & Shaikh, A. D. et al.. (2005). Reading Online Text with a Poor Layout: Is Performance Worse? *Usability News*.org.

Chau, P. Y. K., & Au, G. et al.. (2000). Impact of information presentation modes on online shopping: An empirical evaluation of broadband interactive shopping service. *Journal of Organizational Computing and Electronic Commerce, 10*, 1–22.

Chen, C.-H., & Chien, Y.-H. (2005). Effect of dynamic display and speed of display movement on reading Chinese text presented on a small screen. *Perceptual and Motor Skills*, *100*(3), 865–873. doi:10.2466/PMS.100.3.865-873 PMID:16060457

Chen, J. X., Xi, G. C., Wang, W., Zhao, H. H., & Chen, J. (2008). A comparison study of data mining algorithms in coronary heart disease clinical application. *Beijing Biomedical Engineering*, *27*(3), 249–252.

Chen, J., & Bao, Q. (2012). Digital image processing based fire flame color and oscillation frequency analysis. *Procedia Engineering*, *45*, 595–601. doi:10.1016/j.proeng.2012.08.209

Chera, P., & Wood, C. (2003). Animated multimedia talking books can promote phonological awareness in children beginning to read. *Learning and Instruction*, *13*(1), 33–52. doi:10.1016/S0959-4752(01)00035-4

Cheyne, S. M. E. (2005). can electronic textbook help children to learn. *The Electronic Library*, *23*(1), 103–115. doi:10.1108/02640470510582781

Chien, C., Chen, C. H., & Wu, H. C. (2007). *Tool, toy, telephone, or information: Children' perceptions of the Internet.* San Francisco: APA.

Chou, C., Yu, S., Chen, C., & Wu, H. (2009). Tool, Toy, Telephone, Territory, or Treasure of information: Elementary school students attitudes toward the internet. *Computers & Education*, *53*(2), 308–319. doi:10.1016/j.compedu.2009.02.003

Cofta, P. (2007). Trust, Complexity and Control: Confidence in a Convergent World. John Wiley and Sons.

Cohen, P. R. & Levesque, H. J. (1990). Intention is choice with commitment. *Artificial Intelligence, 42*(3).

Collis, J. & Hussey, R. (2009). *Business research: A practical guide for undergraduate & postgraduate students.* Academic Press.

Conklin, J. (1987). Hypertext: An introduction and survey. *Computers & Education*, 17–41.

Connaway, L. S. (2007). *The future of e- book.* New York: Marcel Dekker.

Coordinating Team. F.-O. (2012). *Fipa-os developers guide.* Retrieved from http://citeseer.ist.psu.edu/477218.html

Coulouris, G., Dollimore, J., & Kindberg, T. (2000). *Distributed systems: Concepts and design.* Addison-Wesley Longman Publishing Co., Inc.

Coyle, K. (2008). E-Reading. *Journal of Academic Librarianship*, *34*(2), 160–163. doi:10.1016/j.acalib.2008.01.001

Creed, A., Dennis, I., & Newstead, S. (1987). Proof-reading on VDUs. *Behaviour & Information Technology*, *6*(1), 3–13. doi:10.1080/01449298708901814

Cress, U., & Knabel, O. B. (2003). Previews in hypertexts: Effects on navigation and knowledge acquisition. *Journal of Computer Assisted Learning*, *19*(4), 517–527. doi:10.1046/j.0266-4909.2003.00054.x

Crestani, F., Landoni, M., & Melucci, M. (2006). Appearance and functionality of electronic books. *International Journal on Digital Libraries*, *6*(2), 192–209. doi:10.1007/s00799-004-0113-9

Creswell, J. W., & Clark, V. P. (2007). *Designing & conducting mixed methods research.* London: Sage Publications.

Cruces, A., & Arriaga, F. D. (2000). Reactive agent design for intelligent tutoring systems. *Cybernetics and Systems: An International Journal*, *31*(1), 1–47. doi:10.1080/019697200124900

Davis, J., Tierney, A., & Chang, E. (2005). A user adaptable user interface model to support ubiquitous user access to EIS style applications. *Computer Software and Applications Conference, 2005, COMPSAC 2005, 29th Annual International.*

De Boer-Schellekens, L., & Vroomen, J. (2005). Sound can improve visual search in developmental dyslexia. *Experimental Brain Research*, *216*(2), 243–248. doi:10.1007/s00221-011-2926-2 PMID:22064932

DeGroot, M., & Schervish, M. (2002). *Probability and statistics* (3rd ed.). Addison Wesley.

Dempster, A. P. (1968). A generalization of bayesian inference. *Journal of the Royal Statistical Society. Series A (General)*, *30*, 205–247.

DeStefano, D., & LeFevre, J. A. (2007). Cognitive load in hypertext reading: A review. *Computers in Human Behavior*, *23*(3), 1616–1641. doi:10.1016/j.chb.2005.08.012

Deutsch, J. A., & Deutsch, D. (1963). Attention: Some theoretical considerations. *Psychological Review*, *70*(1), 80–90. doi:10.1037/h0039515 PMID:14027390

Dillon, A. (1992). Designing usable electronic text. New York: CRC Press.

Dillon, A. (1992). Designing usable electronic text. New York: CRC PRESS.

Dillon, A. (2001). designing usable electronic text: ergonomic aspects of human information usage. London: Taylor & Francis Inc.

Dillon, A. (2001). Designing usable electronic text: ergonomic aspects of human information usage. London: Taylor & Francis Inc.

Dillon, A. (1994). *Designing usable electronic text: ergonomic aspects of human information usage*. Philadelphia, PA: Taylor & Francis. doi:10.4324/9780203470343

Dillon, A., & Kleinman, L. et al.. (2004). *Visual Search and Reading Tasks Using ClearType and Regular Screen Displays: Two Experiments*. University of Texas at Austin/ School of Information.

Dillon, A., Richardson, J., & McKnight, C. (1990). The effects of display size and text splitting on reading lengthy text from screen. *Behaviour & Information Technology*, *9*(3), 215–227. doi:10.1080/01449299008924238

Dong-Huynha, T., Jennings, N.R., & Shadbolt, N.R. (2004). Fire: An integrated trust and reputation model for open multi-agent systems. Proceedings of 16th ECAI conference (pp. 18-22).

dos Santos Lonsdale, M., & Reynolds, L. (2006). Reading in examination-type situations: the effects of text layout on performance. *Research in reading*, *29*(4), 433- 453.

dos Santos Lonsdale, M., Dyson, M.C., & Reynolds, L. (2006). Reading in examination- type situations: the effects of text layout on performance. *Research in reading*, 29(4), 433- 453.

Drexler, K.E. (1988). Incentive engineering for computational resource management. In *The Ecology of Computation* (pp. 231-266). Academic Press.

Duchnicky, J., & Kolers, P. (1983). Readability of text scrolled on visual display terminals as a function of window size. *Human Factors*, *25*, 683–692. PMID:6671649

Duta, N., Jain, A. K., & Mardia, K. (2002). Matching of palmprints. *Pattern Recognition Letters*, *23*(4), 477–485. doi:10.1016/S0167-8655(01)00179-9

Dyson, M. C. (2004). How physical text layout affects reading from screen. *Behaviour & Information Technology*, *23*(6), 377–393. doi:10.1080/01449290410001715714

Dyson, M. C., & Haselgrove, M. (2001). The influence of reading speed and line length on the effectiveness of reading from screen. *International Journal of Human-Computer Studies*, *54*(4), 585–612. doi:10.1006/ijhc.2001.0458

Dyson, M. C., & Kipping, G. J. (1997). The legibility of screen formats: Are three columns better than one? *Computers & Graphics*, *21*(6), 703–712. doi:10.1016/S0097-8493(97)00048-4

Eagleton, M. B., & Dobler, E. (2006). *Reading the Web: Strategies for Internet Inquiry*. New York, NY, USA: Guilford Press.

Easterby-Smith, M., Thorpe, R., & Lowe, A. (2002). *Management research: an introduction*. London: SAGE.

Ebay. (2012). Retrieved from http://www.ebay.com

Eberhart, R.C., & Shi, Y. (2007). Computational intelligence: concepts to implementations. Morgan Kaufmann.

Eberhart, R. C., & Shi, Y. (2007). *Computational intelligence: concepts to implementations*. Morgan Kaufmann. doi:10.1016/B978-155860759-0/50002-0

Egan, D. E., Remde, J. R., Gomez, L. M., Landauer, T. K., Eberhardt, J., & Lochbaum, C. C. (1989). Formative design evaluation of super book. *ACM Transactions on Information Systems*, *7*(1), 30–57. doi:10.1145/64789.64790

Eldabi, T., Irani, Z., Paul, J., & Love, P. E. D. (2002). Quantitative and qualitative decision-making methods in simulation modelling. *Management Decision*, *40*(1), 64–73. doi:10.1108/00251740210413370

Elgohary, A. (2008). Arab universities on the web: A webometric study. *The Electronic Library*, *26*(3), 374–386. doi:10.1108/02640470810879518

Elmabruk, R. (2009). *Using the Internet to support Libyan in-service EFL teachers' professional development* (PhD Dissertation). University of Nottingham.

Evans, A. N., & Liu, X. U. (2006). A morphological gradient approach to color edge detection. *IEEE Transactions on Image Processing*, *15*(6), 1454–1463.

Farkas-Conn, I. S. (1990). *From documentation to information science: The beginnings and early development of the American Documentation Institute*. Westport, CT: Greenwood Press.

Farzanyar, Z., Kangavari, M., & Cercone, N. (2012). Max-FISM: Mining (recently) maximal frequent itemsets over data streams using the sliding window model. *Computers & Mathematics with Applications (Oxford, England)*, *64*(6), 1706–1718. doi:10.1016/j.camwa.2012.01.045

Feely, M., Rubin, G. S., Ekstrom, K., & Perera, S. (2005). Investigation into font characteristics for optimum reading fluency in readers with sight problems. *International Congress Series*, *1282*, 530–533. doi:10.1016/j.ics.2005.05.121

Ferber, J. (1999). *Multi-Agent Systems: An Introduction to Distributed Artificial Intelligence*. Addison-Wesley.

First, U. (2005). *Usability in website and software design*. Usability First.

Fisch, S. M., Shulman, J. S., Akerman, A., & Levin, G. A. (2002). Reading Between The Pixels: Parent-Child Interaction While Reading Online Storybooks. *Early Education and Development*, *13*(4), 435–451. doi:10.1207/s15566935eed1304_7

Foltz, P. W. (1996). *Comprehension, Coherence and Strategies in Hypertext and Linear Text*. Hypertext and Cognition. Retrieved from http://www-psych.nmsu.edu/~pfoltz/reprints/Ht-Cognition.html

Fontanini, I. (2004). Reading theories and some implications for the processing of linear texts and hypertexts. *Linguagem & Ensino*, *7*(2), 165–184.

Foster, J. J. (1970). A study of the legibility of one- and two-column layouts for BPS publications. *Bulletin of the British Psychological Society*, (23): 113–114.

Frenckner, K. (1990). *Legibility of continuous text on computer screens -- a guide to the literature.* TRITA-NA.

Frey, N., & Fisher, D. (2010). Identifying instructional moves during guided learning: Expert teachers use a four-part process to scaffold student understanding during small-group guided instruction. *The Reading Teacher, 64*(2), 84–95. doi:10.1598/RT.64.2.1

Fukuyama, F. (1996). *Trust: The Social Virtues and the Creation of Prosperity.* Touchstone Books.

Gabriel-Petit, P. (2007). Applying Color Theory to Digital Displays. Retrieved from http://www.uxmatters.com/mt/archives/2007/01/applying-color-theory-to-digital-displays.phpApplying

Galigekere, R. R. (2010). Color-image processing: An introduction with some medical application-examples. *Proceedings of the 2010 IEEE International Conference on Systems in Medicine and Biology,* Washington (pp. 3-9). doi:10.1109/ICSMB.2010.5735331

Garvin, P. L. (1963). *Natural language and the computer.* New York: McGraw-Hill.

Gibson, E. J., & Levin, H. (1976). *The Psychology of Reading The Colonial Press Inc.*

Giudici P., Yuan F., Wang Y., & Wang L.J. (2004). *Applied Data Mining Statistical Methods for Business and Industry.* Electronics industry Press.

Godoy, D., Schiaffino, S., & Amandi, A. (2004). Interface agents personalizing web-based tasks – special issue on intelligent agents and data mining for cognitive systems. *Cognitive Systems Research, 5*(3), 207–222. doi:10.1016/j.cogsys.2004.03.003

Goncalves, W. N., & Bruno, O. M. (2013). Dynamic texture analysis and segmentation using deterministic partially self-avoiding walks. *Expert Systems with Applications, 40*(11), 4283–4300.

Gonçalves, W. N., & Bruno, O. M. (2013). Dynamic texture segmentation based on deterministic partially self-avoiding walks. *Computer Vision and Image Understanding, 117*(9), 1163–1174. doi:10.1016/j.cviu.2013.04.006

Grainger, J., & Jacobs, A. M. (1996). Orthographic processing in visual word recognition: A multiple read-out model. *Psychological Review, 103*(3), 228–244. doi:10.1037/0033-295X.103.3.518 PMID:8759046

Greenlee-Moore, M., & Smith, L. (1996). Interactive computer software: The effects on young childrens reading achievement. *Reading Psychology, 17*(1), 43–64. doi:10.1080/0270271960170102

Grosz, B., & Kraus, S. (1996). Collaborative plans for complex group actions. *Artificial Intelligence, 86*(2), 269–357. doi:10.1016/0004-3702(95)00103-4

Gunn, H., & Hepburn, G. (2003). Seeking information for school purposes on the Internet. *Canadian Journal of Learning and Technology, 29*(1).

Haboubi, S., Maddouri, S., & Amiri, H. (2006). *Identification of Arabic word from bilingual text using character features: Case of structural features.* Retrieved from https://arxiv.org/ftp/arxiv/papers/1103/1103.3430.pdf

Hamilton, R., Richards, C., & Sharp, C. (2001). *An examination of E- learning and E- books. SocBytes Journal.*

Hammond, N., & Allinson, L. (1989). Extending Hypertext for Learning: an Investigation of Access and Guidance Tools People and Computers. Cambridge University Press.

Hanbury, A., Kazai, G., Rauber, A., & Fuhr, N. (Eds.). (2015). *Proceedings of the advances in information retrieval, 37th European conference on IR research,* Vienna, Austria. Springer.

Hannemann, J. Kiczales, G. (2002), Design pattern implementation in java and aspect. ACM Sigplan Notices, 37(11), 161-173.

Han, S., Tao, W. B., & Wu, X. L. (2011). Texture segmentation using independent-scale component-wise Riemannian-covariance Gaussian mixture model in KL measure based multi-scale nonlinear structure tensor space. *Pattern Recognition, 44*(3), 503–518.

Haralick, R. M., & Shanmugam, K. (1973). Textural features for image classification. *IEEE Transactions on Systems, Man, and Cybernetics, 3*(6), 610–621.

Harcourt, W. (2004). The personal and political: Women using the internet. *Cyberpsychology & Behavior, 3*(5), 693–697. doi:10.1089/10949310050191692

Harrison, B.L. (2000). E-books and the future of reading. *IEEE Computer Graphics and Applications, 20*(3), 32-39.

Hartley, J., & Burnhill, P. (1977). Fifty guide-lines for improving instructional text. *Programmed Learning and Educational Technology Research and Development, 14*(1), 65–73.

Hausenblas, H. A., Carron, A. V., & Mack, D. E. (1997). Application of the theories of reasoned action and planned behavior to exercise behavior: A meta-analysis. *Journal of Sport & Exercise Psychology, 19*(1), 36–51. doi:10.1123/jsep.19.1.36

Hawkins, D. T. (2000). Electronic books: A major publishing revolution (part 1). *Online, 24*(4), 14–28.

Haykin, S. (1999). Neural Networks: A Comprehensive Foundation. Prentice-Hall.

Hedetniemi, S., M., & Hedetniemi, S.T., Liestman, A.L. (1988). A survey of gossiping and broadcasting in communication networks. *Networks, 18*(4), 319-349.

Hewitt, C. (1985). The challenge of open systems. *Byte, 10*(4), 223–242.

Hirvela, A. (1996). Reader-response theory and ELT. *ELT, 50*(2), 127–134. doi:10.1093/elt/50.2.127

Huang, D., Rau, P. P., & Liu, Y. (2009). Effects of font size, display resolution and task type on reading Chinese fonts from mobile devices. *International Journal of Industrial Ergonomics, 39*(1), 81–89. doi:10.1016/j.ergon.2008.09.004

Huberman, B. A., & Hogg, T. (1995). Communities of practice: Performance and evolution. *Computational & Mathematical Organization Theory, 1*(1), 73–92. doi:10.1007/BF01307829

Huynh, T. D. (2006). *Trust and Reputation in Open Multi-agent Systems* (PhD thesis). Schools of Electronics and Computer Science, University of Southampton.

Huynh, T. D., Jennings, N. R., & Shadbolt, N. R. (2004). *Fire: An integrated trust and reputation model for open multi-agent systems*. ECAI.

Huynh, T. D., Jennings, N. R., & Shadbolt, N. R. (2006). An integrated trust and reputation model for open multi-agent systems. *Autonomous Agents and Multi-Agent Systems, 13*(2), 119–154. doi:10.1007/s10458-005-6825-4

IBM (2005). Design basics.

Ilbeygi, M., & Hamed, S. H. (2012). A novel fuzzy facial expression recognition system based on facial feature extraction from color face images. *Engineering Applications of Artificial Intelligence, 25*(1), 130–146. doi:10.1016/j.engappai.2011.07.004

Information. (2005). *Report and recommendations of the Eighteenth Meeting of the Arab team in charge of preparations for the World Summit on the Information Society*. Author.

Iser, W. (1978). The act of reading: a theory of aesthetic response. London: Routledge and Kegan Paul.

Ismail, R., & Zainab, A. N. (2005). The pattern of e-book use amongst undergraduates in Malaysia: A case of to know is to use. *Malaysian Journal of Library and Information Science, 10*(2), 1–23.

Jacobs, P. S. (1992). *Text-based intelligent systems: Current research and practice in information extraction and retrieval.* Hoboken, NJ: Lawrence Erlbaum Associates.

Jamali, H.R., Nicholas, D. & Rowlands, I. (2009). Scholarly ebooks: the views of 16,000 academics. *New Information Perspections, 61*(1), 33-47.

Janarthanam, S., Ramalingam, M., & Narendran, P. (2010). Texture analysis on low resolution images using unsupervised segmentation algorithm with multichannel local frequency analysis. *Proceedings of the2010 IEEE International Conference on Communication and Computational Intelligence*, New York (pp. 260 – 265).

Jeng, S. C., Lin, Y. R., Liu, K. H., Liao, C. C., Wen, C. H., Chao, C. Y., & Shieh, K. K. (2005). *Legibility of electronic paper*. The 5th International Meeting on Information Display. Seoul, Korea.

Ji, F.Z., Sun, S.Y., Wang, C.L., Zuo, X.Z., & Wang, J. (2011). Applications of Fuzzy Lifting Wavelet Packet Transform in MFL Signal Processing. *Nondestructive Testing, 33*(5), 22–25.

Ji, Y., Massanari, R. M., Ager, J., Yen, J., Miller, R. E., & Ying, H. (2007). A fuzzy logic-based computational recognition-primed decision model. *Information Sciences, 177*(20), 4338–4353. doi:10.1016/j.ins.2007.02.026

Johnston, S. P., & Huczynski, A. (2006). Textbook publishers website objective question banks: Does their use improve students examination performance? *Active Learning in Higher Education, 7*(3), 257–271. doi:10.1177/1469787406069057

Josang, A., Ismail, R., & Boyd, C. (2007). A survey of trust and reputation systems for online service provision. *Decision Support Systems, 43*(2), 618–644. doi:10.1016/j.dss.2005.05.019

Josang, A., & Pope, R. S. (2005). *Semantic constraints for trust transitivity. APCCM 2005.* University of Newcastle.

Jukić, A., Kopriva, I., & Cichocki, A. (2013). Noninvasive diagnosis of melanoma with tensor decomposition-based feature extraction from clinical color image. *Biomedical Signal Processing and Control, 8*(6), 755–763. doi:10.1016/j.bspc.2013.07.001

Khalifelu, Z. A., & Gharehchopogh, F. S. (2012). Comparison and evaluation of data mining techniques with algorithmic models in software cost estimation. *Procedia Technology, 1*, 65–71. doi:10.1016/j.protcy.2012.02.013

Khatkar, A., (2014). A Comprehensive Review on WiMAX Networks. *International Journal of Innovations in Engineering and Technology, 3*(3).

Kılıç, E., & Leblebicioğlu, K. (2012). From classic observability to a simple fuzzy observability for fuzzy discrete-event systems. *Information Sciences, 187*(15), 224–232. doi:10.1016/j.ins.2011.11.008

Kinny, D., Georgeff, M., & Rao, A. (1996). A methodology and modelling technique for systems of bdi agents. *Lecture Notes in Computer Science, 1038*, 56-71.

Kinny, D., George, M., & Rao, A. (1996). A methodology and modelling technique for systems of bdi agents. *Lecture Notes in Computer Science, 1038*, 56–71. doi:10.1007/BFb0031846

Kintsch, W. (2004) The construction-integration model of text comprehension and its implications for instruction.

Kleeck, A. V. (2003). *Research on book-sharing: another critical look.* Mahwah, NJ: Lawrence Erlbaum Associates.

Koehn, D. (2003). The nature of and conditions for online trust. *Journal of Business Ethics, 43*, 3-19.

Kohonen, T. (1998). The self-organizing map. *Neurocomputing*, *21*, 1-6.

Kolers, P. A., Duchnicky, R. L., & Ferguson, D. C. (1981). Eye movement measurement of readability of CRT displays. *Human Factors*, *23*, 517–527. PMID:7319497

Kolikant, Y. B. D. (2009). Digital Students in a Book-Oriented School: Students' Perceptions of School and the Usability of Digital Technology in Schools. *Journal of Educational Technology & Society*, *12*(2), 131–143.

Kol, S., & Schcolink, M. (2000). Enhancing Screen Reading Strategies. *CALICO Journal*, *18*(1), 67–80.

Kong, A. W.-K., & Zhang, D. (2004). Feature-level fusion for effective palmprint authentication. In Biometric Authentication (pp. 761-767). Springer.

Kong, W., Zhang, D., & Kame, M. (2006). Palmprint identification using feature-level fusion. *Pattern Recognition*, *39*(3), 478–487. doi:10.1016/j.patcog.2005.08.014

Korat, O. (2010). Reading electronic books as a support for vocabulary, story comprehension and word reading in kindergarten and first grade. *Computers & Education*, *55*(1), 24–31. doi:10.1016/j.compedu.2009.11.014

Korat, O., & Shamir, A. (2004). Are electronic books for young children appropriate to support literacy development? A comparison across languages. *Journal of Computer Assisted Learning*, *20*, 257–268. doi:10.1111/j.1365-2729.2004.00078.x

Kosslyn, S. M., & Rosenberg, R. S. (2004). The Brain, The Person, The World. *Psychology (Savannah, Ga.)*.

Kotzé, J. B. P. (2007). Modelling the Factors that Influence Mobile Phone Adoption. ACM: 152- 161.

Kovesip, P., & Shiono, E. (1991). Image features from phase on gruene. *Video Journal of Computer Vision Research*, *1*(3), 1-27.

Kraus, S. (1997). Negotiation and cooperation in multi-agent environments. *Artificial Intelligence Journal*.

Kruk, R. S., & Muter, P. (1984). Reading of continuous text on video screens. *Human Factors*, *26*, 339–345.

Kudik, C. (2007). Effects of Font Size and Paper Color on Resume Review Decisions. *Stephen F. Austin State University*.

Kumar, R. (2011). *Research Methodology: a step- by- step guide for beginners*. London: SAGE.

Laarnia, J., & Simolaa, J. et al. (2004). Reading vertical text from a computer screen. *Behaviour & Information Technology*, *23*(2), 75–82. doi:10.1080/01449290310001648260

Laboratory, G. (2005). Agent system development hands-on exercise, easss-05 (7th European agent systems summer school). Technical report, Utrecht.

Labrou, Y., & Finin, T. (1997). *A proposal for a new kqml specification. TR-CS-9703*. UMBC.

Labrou, Y., Finin, T., & Peng, Y. (1999). IEEE intelligent systems and their applications. *IEEE Intelligent Systems & their Applications*, *14*(2), 45–52. doi:10.1109/5254.757631

Lam, P., Lam, S.L., Lam, J., & McNaught, C. (2009). Usability and usefulness of ebooks on PPCs. *Australasian Journal of Educational Technology*, *25*(1), 30-44.

Lam, P., Lam, S. L., & McNaught, C. (2009). Usability and usefulness of ebooks on PPCs. *Australasian Journal of Educational Technology*, *25*(1), 30–44. doi:10.14742/ajet.1179

Landoni, M. (1997). *The Visual Book system: a study of the use of visual rhetoric in the design of electronic books*. Glasgow, UK: University of Strathclyde.

Landoni, M. (2010). Ebooks children would want to read and engage with. *Proceedings of the third workshop on Research advances in large digital book repositories and complementary media,* 25-28. doi:10.1145/1871854.1871862

Landoni, M., & Diaz, P. (2003). E-education: Design and evaluation for teaching and learning. *Journal of Digital Information, 3*(4).

Landoni, M., & Gibb, F. (2000). The role of visual rhetoric in the design and production of electronic books: The visual book. *The Electronic Library, 18*(3), 190–201. doi:10.1108/02640470010337490

Landoni, M., & Wilson, R. (2002). *EBONI: Electronic Textbook Design Guidelines.* University of Strathclyde.

Landoni, M., Wilson, R., & Gibb, F. (2000). From the visual book to the web book: The importance of design. *The Electronic Library, 18*(6), 407–419. doi:10.1108/02640470010361169

Lee, D., Shieh, K., Jeng, S., & Shen, I. (2008). Effect of character size and lighting on legibility of electronic papers. *Displays, 29*(1), 10–17. doi:10.1016/j.displa.2007.06.007

Leeuw, S.D., & Rydin, I. (2007). Migrant children's digital stories. *Identity Formation and Self-Representation Through Media Production, 10*(4), 447.

Lenat, D. B., & Brown, J. S. (1984). Why am and eurisko appear to work. *Artificial Intelligence, 23*(3), 269–294. doi:10.1016/0004-3702(84)90016-X

Levesque, H. J. (1990). All i know: A study in autoepistemic logic. *Artificial Intelligence, 42*, 263–309.

Liang, X. (2006). Data mining algorithm and its application. Beijing University Press.

Liao, Z. M., & Yang, W. L. (1990). Probability theory and mathematical statistics. Beijing Normal University Press.

Lin, D. M. (2004). Evaluating older adults' retention in hypertext perusal: Impacts of presentation media as a function of text topology. *Computers in Human Behavior, 20*(4), 491–503. doi:10.1016/j.chb.2003.10.024

Linderholm, T., Virtue, S., Tzeng, Y., & van den Broek, P. (2004). Fluctuations in the availability of information during reading: Capturing cognitive processes using the landscape model. *Discourse Processes, 37*(2), 165–186. doi:10.1207/s15326950dp3702_5

Ling, J., & Schaik, P. (2006). The influence of font type and line length on visual search and information retrieval in web pages. *International Journal of Human-Computer Studies, 64*(5), 395–404. doi:10.1016/j.ijhcs.2005.08.015

Lissner, I., & Urban, P. (2012). Toward a unified color space for perception-based image processing. *IEEE Transactions on Image Processing, 21*(3), 1153–1168. doi:10.1109/TIP.2011.2163522 PMID:21824846

Liu, Z. (2005). Reading behaviour in the digital environment. *Journal of Documentation, 61*(6), 700- 712.

Liu, Z. (2005). Reading behaviour in the digital environment: changes in reading behaviour over the past ten years. *Journal of Documentation, 61*(6), 700- 712.

Liu, G., & Kreinovich, V. (2010). Fast convolution and fast Fourier transform under interval and fuzzy uncertainty. *Journal of Computer and System Sciences, 76*(1), 63–76. doi:10.1016/j.jcss.2009.05.006

Liu, Z., & Huang, X. (2007). Gender differences in the online reading environment. *The Journal of Documentation, 64*(4), 616–626. doi:10.1108/00220410810884101

Lo, E. H., Mark, R. P., Michael, R. F., & John, F. A. (2011). Image segmentation from scale and rotation invariant texture features from the double dyadic dual-tree complex wavelet transform. *Image and Vision Computing, 29*(1), 15–28. doi:10.1016/j.imavis.2010.08.004

Lo, J. T. H. (2012). A cortex-like learning machine for temporal hierarchical pattern clustering, detection, and recognition. *Neurocomputing, 78*(1), 89–103. doi:10.1016/j.neucom.2011.04.046

Longman. (2011). *Longman online dictionary*. Retrieved from http://www.ldoceonline.com/dictionary/trust2:36

Long, Z., & Younan, N. H. (2013). Multiscale texture segmentation via a contourlet contextual hidden Markov model. *Digital Signal Processing, 23*(3), 859–869.

Lonsdale, M.D.S., Dyson, M. C., & Reynolds, L. (2006). Reading in examination- type situations: the effects of text layout on performance. *Research in Reading, 29*(4), 433-453.

Lu, G., Lu, J., Yao, S., & Yip, J. (2009). *A comparison of java-based multi-agent system development platforms*. The Open Information Science Journal.

Luke, T. W. (2006). *Agent-based trust and reputation in the context of inaccurate information sources* (PhD thesis). Schools of Electronics and Computer Science, University of Southampton.

Lund, O. (1999). Knowledge Construction in Typography: the Case of Legibility Research and the Legibility of Sans Serif Typefaces [PhD]. Reading University, UK.

M, B., C. B, et al., (2003). Comparing the effects of text size and format on the readability of computer- displayed Times New Roman and Arial text. *Int. J. Human-Computer Studies, 59*(6), 823- 835.

Ma, H. (2005). Interpreting middle school students` online experiences a phenological approach. collage of education. Ohio, Ohio university. PhD: 237.

Ma, H. (2005). Interpreting middle school students` online experiences a phenological approach. Ohio university.

Mailing, A., & Cernuschi-Frías, B. (2011). A method for mixed states texture segmentation with simultaneous parameter estimation. *Pattern Recognition Letters, 32*(15), 1982–1989.

Malhotra, N. K., Birks, D. F., & Wills, P. (2003). *Marketing research: An applied approach*. Essex, UK: Prentic Hall.

Manning, C. D., Raghavan, P., & Schütze, H. (2008). *Introduction to information retrieval*. Cambridge, UK: Cambridge University Press. doi:10.1017/CBO9780511809071

Marchionini, G. (1995). *Information seeking in electronic environment*. New York: Cambridge University Press. doi:10.1017/CBO9780511626388

Marques, O. (2011). Color Image Processing, Practical image and video processing using MATLAB. John Wiley & Sons.

Marsh, S. (1994). *Formalising Trust as a Computational Concept* (PhD thesis). Department of Mathematics and Computer Science, University of Stirling.

Marsh, S. (1994). Trust in distributed artificial intelligence. *Lecture Notes in Computer Science, 830*, 94.

Marsh, S. (1994a). *Formalising Trust as a Computational Concept* (PhD thesis). Department of Mathematics and Computer Science, University of Stirling.

Marsh, S. (1994b). Trust in distributed artificial intelligence. In *Artificial Social Systems, LNCS* (Vol. 830, pp. 94-112).

Marsh, S. (1994b). Trust in distributed artificial intelligence. *Lecture Notes in Computer Science, 830*, 94–112. doi:10.1007/3-540-58266-5_6

Martínez-Prieto, M. A., Fuente, P. D. L., Vegas, J. M., Adiego, J., & Cuesta, C. E. (2008). Enhancing literary electronic books with logical structure: Electronic work. *The Electronic Library, 26*(4), 490–504. doi:10.1108/02640470810893747

Martin, J. (1990). *Hyperdocuments and how to create them*. Prentice Hall.

Mash, S. D. (2003). Libraries, books, and academic freedom. *Academe, 89*(3), 50–55. doi:10.2307/40252470

Matsumoto, K. (1985). Palm-recognition systems: An ideal means of restricting access to high security areas. *Mitsubishi Electric Advance, 131*, 31–32.

Mayer, R., Davis, J. H., & Schoorman, F. (1995). An integrative model of organizational trust. *Academy of Management Review, 20*(3), 709-734.

Maynard, S. & McKnight, C. (2001). *Electronic books for children in UK public libraries*. Academic Press.

Maynard, S., & McKnight, C. (2001). Childrens comprehension of electronic books: An empirical study. *The New Review of Childrens Literature and Librarianship, 7*(1), 29–53. doi:10.1080/13614540109510643

Maynard, S., & McKnight, C. (2001). electronic book for children in the UK public libraries. *The Electronic Library, 19*(6), 405–423. doi:10.1108/02640470110412026

McKnight, D. H., & Chervany, N. L. (1996). The meanings of trust. Technical report. University of Minnesota.

Melendez, J., Miguel, A. G., Domenec, P., & Maria, P. (2011). Unsupervised texture-based image segmentation through pattern discovery. *Computer Vision and Image Understanding, 115*(8), 1121–1133.

Merriam-Webster. (2011). *Merriam-Webster online dictionary*. Retrieved from http://www.merriamwebster.com/dictionary/trust

Miller, L. M. (2001). middle school students` technology practices and preferences: Reexamine gender difference. *Journal of Educational Multimedia and Hypermedia, 10*(2), 125–140.

Miller, L. M. S., & Gagne, D. D. (2008). Adult age differences in reading and rereading processes associated with problem solving. *International Journal of Behavioral Development, 32*(1), 34–45. doi:10.1177/0165025407084050

Miller, L., Blackstock, J., & Miller, R. (1994). An exploratory study into the use of CD-ROM storybooks. *Computers & Education, 22*(1-2), 187–204. doi:10.1016/0360-1315(94)90087-6

Mills, C. B., & Weldon, L. J. (1987). Reading text from computer screens. *ACM Computing Surveys, 19*(4), 329–358. doi:10.1145/45075.46162

Minsky, N. H., & Murata, T. (2004). On manageability and robustness of open multi-agent systems. *Lecture Notes in Computer Science, 2940*, 189–206. doi:10.1007/978-3-540-24625-1_11

Mollering, G. (2005). The trust/control duality: An integrative perspective on positive expectations of others. *Int. Sociology, 20*(3), 283-305.

Moore, R. (1990). *A formal theory of knowledge and action', In formalizing common sense*. Ablex Publishing Corporation.

Moorman, K., & Ram, A. (1994). *A Functional Theory of Creative Reading. Technical Report. G. I. o*. Georgia: Technology.

Moreno, Y., Nekovee, M., & Pacheco, A. F. (2004). Dynamics of rumor spreading in complex networks. *Physical Review Series E, 69*.

Murray, M. (2012). Amazon kindle.Back Stage, 53(39), 17.

Muter, P. (1996). *Interface design and optimization of reading of continuous text*. Cognitive Aspects of Electronic Text Processing.

Muter, P. (1996). *Interface design and optimization of reading of continuous text. In Cognitive Aspects of Electronic Text Processing.*

Muter, P., & Maurutto, P. (1991). Reading and skimming form computer screen and books: The paperless office revisited? *Behaviour & Information Technology, 10*, 257–266. doi:10.1080/01449299108924288

Nathan, R. J., & Yeow, P. H. P. (2011). Crucial web usability factors of 36 industries forÂ students: A large-scale empirical study. *Electronic Commerce Research, 11*(2), 151–180. doi:10.1007/s10660-010-9054-0

National Information Standards Organisation (NISO). (2005). Information services & use: metrics & statistics for libraries and information providers: data dictionary.

National, A. (1988). *American National Standard for Human Factors Engineering of Visual Display Terminal Workstations.*

Nel, C., & Dreyer, C. et al. (2004). An analysis of the reading profiles of first-year students at Potchefstroom University: A cross-sectional study and a case study. *South African Journal of Education, 24*(1), 95–103.

Nes, F. L. V. (1986). Space, colour and typography on visual display terminals. *Behaviour & Information Technology, 5*(2), 99–118. doi:10.1080/01449298608914504

News, S. J. M. & Foundation, K.F. (2003). *Growing Up Wired: Survey on Youth and the Internet in the Silicon Valley.* Academic Press.

Nicholas, D., Huntington, P., Hamid, R. J., Rowlands, I., Dobrowolski, T., & Tenopir, C. (2008). Viewing and reading behaviour in a virtual environment: the full-text download and what can be read into it. *ASLP Proceedings, 60*(3), 185-198.

Nicholas, D., Hamid, P. H., Rowlands, J. I., Dobrowolski, T., & Tenopir, C. (2008). Viewing and reading behaviour in a virtual environment: The full-text download and what can be read into it. *Aslib Proceedings, 60*(3), 185–198. doi:10.1108/00012530810879079

Nielsen, J. (2000). *Designing Web Usability: The Practice of Simplicity.* New York: New Riders.

Nikou, C., Nikolaos, G., & Aristidis, L. (2007). A class-adaptive spatially variant mixture model for image segmentation. *IEEE Transactions on Image Processing, 16*(4), 1121–1130.

Noorhidawati, A., & Forbes, G. (2008). Students attitudes towards e-books in a Scottish higher education institute: Part 1. *Library Review, 57*(8), 593–605. doi:10.1108/00242530810899577

Nwana, H., Ndumu, D., Lee, L., & Collis, J. (1999). Zeus: a toolkit and approach for building distributed multi-agent systems. *Proceedings of the Third International Conference on Autonomous Agents,* 360-361 doi:10.1145/301136.301234

OECD. (2005). *Are students ready for a technology-rich world? What PISA studies tell us.* Paris: OECD.

Ong, S. H., Yea, N. C., & Lee, K. H. (2002). Segmentation of color images using a two-stage self-organizing network. *Image and Vision Computing, 20*(4), 279–289.

Oppenheim, A. N. (2003). *Questionnaire design, interviewing and attitude measurement.* London: Continuum.

Ourston, D. & Mooney, R. J. (1994). Theory refinement combining analytical and empirical methods. *Artificial Intelligence, 66*(2), 273-309.

Oxford. (2011). *Oxford online dictionary.* Retrieved from http://oxforddictionaries.com/de_nition/trust

Palmer, S. B. (1993). *Proto HTML.* Retrieved 20-10-2011, from http://infomesh.net/stuff/proto

Panait, L., & Luke, S. (2005). Cooperative multi-agent learning: The state of the art. *Autonomous Agents and Multi-Agent Systems*, *11*(3), 387–434. doi:10.1007/s10458-005-2631-2

Panayiota, K., & van den Broek, P. (2007). The effects of prior knowledge and text structure on comprehension processes during reading of scientific texts. *Memory & Cognition*, *35*(7), 1567.

Panayiota, K., & Broek, P. V. E. (2007). The effects of prior knowledge and text structure on comprehension processes during reading of scientific texts. *Memory & Cognition*, *35*(7), 1567–1577. doi:10.3758/BF03193491 PMID:18062535

Pan, X., & Ruan, Q. Q. (2009). Palmprint recognition using Gabor-based local invariant features. *Neurocomputing*, *72*(7), 2040–2045. doi:10.1016/j.neucom.2008.11.019

Papacharissi, Z., & Rubin, A. M. (2000). Predictors of internet use. *Journal of Broadcasting & Electronic Media*, *44*(2), 175–197. doi:10.1207/s15506878jobem4402_2

Park, H.W. (2009). Academic internet use in Korea: Issues and lessons in e-research. Proceedings of WebSci"09: Society online, Athens, Greece.

Park, W. H. (2009). Academic internet use in Korea: Issues and lessons in e- research. WebSci09: Society on-line, Athens, Greece.

Paterson, A. (2007). Costs of information and communication technology in developing country school systems: The experience of Botswana, Namibia and Seychelles. *International Journal of Education and Development using Information and Communication Technology, 3*(4), 89-101.

Pawlak, Z. (1982). Rough sets. *International Journal of Computer & Information Sciences*, *11*(5), 341–356. doi:10.1007/BF01001956

Pazzani, M., & Kibler, D. (1991). The utility of knowledge in inductive learning. *Machine Learning*, *9*(1), 57–94. doi:10.1007/BF00993254

Pazzani, M., Merz, C., Murphy, P., Ali, K., Hume, T., & Brunk, C. (1994). Reducing misclassication costs. *Proceedings of the Eleventh International Conference on Machine Learning*, 217-225.

Perse, E. M., & Dunn, D. G. (1998). The utility of home computers and media use: Implications of multimedia and connectivity. *Journal of Broadcasting & Electronic Media*, *42*(4), 435–456. doi:10.1080/08838159809364461

Phillips, P. P., & Stawarski, C. A. (2008). *Data collection planning for and collecting all types of data*. Wiley.

Polding, R., Nunes, J. M. B., & Kingston, B. (2008). Assessing e-book model sustainability. *Journal of Librarianship and Information Science*, *40*(4), 255–268. doi:10.1177/0961000608096715

Polly, C. (2009). National: Internet generation leave parents behind: Change in communication creating divide, says study: Children spend six hours a day in front of screens. *The Guardian*.

Poole, A. (2005). *Literature Review: Which Are More Legible: Serif or Sans Serif Typefaces? Alexpoole.info.*

Powell, T. A. (2000). *Web Design: the Complete Reference*. California: McGraw Hill.

Qiu, D., & Tamhane, A. C. (2007). A comparative study of the K-means algorithm and the normal mixture model for clustering: Univariate case. *Journal of Statistical Planning and Inference*, *137*(11), 3722–3740. doi:10.1016/j.jspi.2007.03.045

Rachidi, M., Chappard, C., & Marchadier, C. (2008). Application of Laws' masks to bone texture analysis: An innovative image analysis tool in osteoporosis. *Proceedings of the 2008 5th IEEE International Symposium on Biomedical Imaging: From Nano to Macro* (pp. 1191-1194).

Ralph, A. (1999). Social cognition and the human brain. *Trends in Cognitive Sciences, 3*(12), 469-479.

Randolph, G. B., & Anuj, A. N. (2005). Optimal Line Length in Reading - A Literature Review. *Visible Language, 39*(2), 120–125.

Reimer, Y. J., Brimhall, E., Cao, C., & OReilly, K. (2009). Empirical user studies inform the design of an e- note taking and information assimilation system for students in higher education. *Computers & Education, 52*(4), 893–913. doi:10.1016/j.compedu.2008.12.013

Rello, L., Kanvinde, G., & Baeza-Yates, R. (2011). Layout Guidelines for Web Text and a Web Service to Improve Accessibility for Dyslexics. *Proceedings of the 21st International World Wide Web Conference.*

Resnick, P., Zeckhauser, R., Swanson, J. and Lockwood, K. (2006). The value of reputation on ebay: A controlled experiment. *Experimental Economics, 9*(2), 79-101.

Ritter, H. (1999). *Self-organizing maps on noneuclidean spaces*. Kohonen Maps.

Rivera-Nivar, M., & Pomales-García, C. (2010). E-training: Can young and older users be accommodated with the same interface? *Computers & Education, 55*(3), 949–960. doi:10.1016/j.compedu.2010.04.006

Robert, J. N., & Paul, H. P. Y. et al.. (2008). Key usability factors of service-oriented web sites for students: An empirical study. *Online Information Review, 32*(3), 302–324. doi:10.1108/14684520810889646

Rogers, M., & Roncevic, M. (2002). E-book aftermath: Three more publishers fold electronic imprints. *Library Journal, 127*(1), 4.

Rosenschein, J. S., & Zlotkin, G. (1994). *Rules of Encounter: Designing Conventions for Automated Negotiation among Computers*. The MIT Press.

Rothkopf, M. H. (2003). The future of e-markets. *Journal of Economic Literature, 41*(1), 214.

Rowlands, I., Nicholas, D., Jamali, H. R., & Huntington, P. (2007). What do faculty and students really think about e-books? *Aslib Proceedings: New Information Perspectives, 59*(6), 489–511. doi:10.1108/00012530710839588

Rudnicky, A. I., & Kolers, P. A. (1984). Size and case of type as stimuli in reading. *Journal of Experimental Psychology. Human Perception and Performance, 10*(2), 231–247. doi:10.1037/0096-1523.10.2.231 PMID:6232342

Russell, M. C., & Chaparro, B. S. (2001). exploring effects of speed and font size with RSVP. Human factors and ergonimics society 45th Annual meeting.

Russell-Minda, E., & Jutai, J. W., Strong, J.G., Campbell, K.A., Gold, D., Pretty, L., & Wilmot, L. (2007). The Legibility of Typefaces for Readers with Low Vision: A Research Review. *Journal of Visual Impairment & Blindness, 101*(7), 402–415.

RW, D. L., E. HL, et al., (1993). Performance differences between Times and Helvetica in a reading task. *Electronic Publishing, 6*(3), 241–248.

Sabater, J., & Sierra, C. (2002). Social regret, a reputation model based on social relations. *ACM SIGecom Exchanges - Chains of Commitment, 3*(1).

Sabater, J., & Sierra, C. (2002). Social regret, a reputation model based on social relations. *ACM SIGecom Exchanges, 3*(1), 44-56.

Sabater, J., & Sierra, C. (2001). Regret: areputation model for gregarious societies. *Fourth workshop on deception fraud and trust in agent societies*, 61-70.

Salmerón, L., & García, V. (2011). Reading skills and childrens navigation strategies in hypertext. *Computers in Human Behavior*, *27*(3), 1143–1151. doi:10.1016/j.chb.2010.12.008

Saunders, M. N. K., Thrnhill, A., & Lewis, P. (2003). *Research methods for business students*. Harlow, UK: Financial Times Prentice Hall.

Saunders, M., Lewis, P., & Thornhill, A. (2007). *Research Methods for Business Students*. Prentice Hall.

Seale, C., & Gobo, G. (Eds.). (2006). *Ethical issues*. London: SAGE.

Segal-Drori, O., O. Korat, et al. (2009). Reading electronic and printed books with and without adult instruction: effects on emergent reading. Springer Science+Business Media B.V.

Segers, E., & Verhoven, L. (2002). Multimedia support of early literacy learning. *Computers & Education*, *39*(3), 207–221. doi:10.1016/S0360-1315(02)00034-9

Sekaran, U. (2003). *Research methods for business: a skill-building approach*. New York: Wiley.

Shaffer, D. W., & Clinton, K. A. (2006). Tool for thoughts: Re-examining thinking in the digital age. *Mind, Culture, and Activity*, *13*(4), 283–300. doi:10.1207/s15327884mca1304_2

Shaikh, A. D. (2005). The Effects of Line Length on Reading Online News. *Usability News*, *7*(2), 2–4.

Shaw, L. H., & Gant, L. M. (2002). users divided? use. *Cyberpsychology & Behavior*, *5*(6), 517–527. doi:10.1089/109493102321018150 PMID:12556114

Sheedy, J. E., Subbaram, M.V., Zimmerman, A.B., & Hayes, J.R. (2005). Text legibility and the letter superiority effect. *Human Factors*, *47*(4), 797- 815.

Sheedy, J. E., Subbaram, M. V., Zimmerman, A. B., & Hayes, J. R.JE. (2005). Text legibility and the letter superiority effect. *Human Factors*, *47*(4), 797–815. doi:10.1518/001872005775570998 PMID:16553067

Shin, D.H. (2011). Understanding e-book users: Uses and gratification expectancy model. *New Media & Society, 13*(2), 260-278.

Shirali-shahreza, M. H., & Shirali-shahreza, S. (2006). Persian/ Arabic text font estimation using dots. *IEEE International Symposium on Signal Processing and Information Technology*, 420-425. doi:10.1109/ISSPIT.2006.270838

Shiratuddin, N., & Landoni, M., Gibb, F., & Hassan, S. (2003). E-book technology and its potential applications in distance education. *Journal of Digital Information*, *3*(4).

Shiratuddin, N., Landoni, M., Gibb, F., & Hassan, H. (2003). E-book technology and its potential applications in distant education. *Journal of Digital Information*, *3*(4).

Shoham, Y. (1992). Agent-oriented programming: An overview and summary of recent research. *Proc. of Artificial Intelligence*.

Shoham, Y. (1993). Agent-oriented programming. *Artificial Intelligence*, *60*, 51–92.

Shu, H., Zhou, W., Yan, M., & Kliegl, R. (2010). Font size modulates saccade- target selection in Chinese reading. *Attention, Perception & Psychophysics*, *73*(2), 482–490. doi:10.3758/s13414-010-0029-y PMID:21264735

Shurtleff, D. (1967). Studies in television legibility: A review of the literature. *Information Display*, *4*, 40–45.

Shu, W., & Zhang, D. (1998). Automated personal identification by palmprint. *Optical Engineering (Redondo Beach, Calif.)*, *37*(8), 2359–2362. doi:10.1117/1.601756

Siegenthaler, E., Wurtz, P., & Groner, R. (2010). Improving the Usability of E-Book Readers. *JUS*, *6*(1), 25–38.

Siegenthaler, E., Wurtz, P., Bergamin, P., & Groner, R. (2011). Comparing reading processes on e-ink displays and print. *Displays*, *32*(5), 268–273. doi:10.1016/j.displa.2011.05.005

Simmonds, D. R. L. (1994). *Data presentation and visual literacy in medicine and science*. Oxford: Butterworth-Heinemann.

Simon Parsons, M. W. (2002). Game theory and decision theory in multi-agent systems. *Autonomous Agents and Multi-Agent Systems*, *5*(3), 243–254. doi:10.1023/A:1015575522401

Simon, H. A. (1996). *The Science of Artificial* (3rd ed.). The MIT Press.

Singh, M. P. (1994). Multiagent systems: A theoretical framework for intention as, know how, and communications. *Lecture Notes in Artificial Intelligence, 799*.

Singhal, M. (1999). *The effects of reading strategy instruction on the reading comprehension, reading process and strategy use of adult SL readers* (PhD Thesis).

Singleton, C., & Henderson, L.-M. (2006). Visual factors in reading. *London Review of Education*, *4*(1), 89- 98.

Smith, R. G. (1980). The contract net protocol: High-level communication and control in a distributed problem solver. *IEEE Transactions on Computers*, *C-29*(12), 1104–1113. doi:10.1109/TC.1980.1675516

Smith, S. M., & Brady, J. M. (1997). SUSAN—a new approach to low level image processing. *International Journal of Computer Vision*, *23*(1), 45–78. doi:10.1023/A:1007963824710

Smith, W. J. (1996). *ISO and ANSI Ergonomic standards for computer products: a guide to implementation and compliance*. Prentice Hall.

Soh, L. K., & Tsatsoulis, C. (1999). Texture analysis of SAR sea ice imagery using gray level co-occurrence matrices. *IEEE Transactions on Geoscience and Remote Sensing*, *37*(2), 780–795.

Southall, R. (1984). First principles of typographic design for document production. *TUGboat*, *5*(2), 79–91.

Stafford, L., Kline, S. L., & Dimmick, J. (1999). Home e-mail: Relational maintenance and gratification opportunities. *Journal of Broadcasting & Electronic Media*, *43*(4), 659–669. doi:10.1080/08838159909364515

Subrahmanian, V. S., Bonatti, P., Dix, J., Eiter, T., Kraus, S., Ozcan, F., & Ross, R. (2000). *Heterogeneous Agent Systems*. The MIT Press.

Suchman, L. (1988). *Plans and Situated Action*. Cambridge, UK: Cambridge University Press.

Sun, Y. (2007). *Using the organizational and narrative thread structures in an E- book to support comprehension* (PhD Dissertation). Computing, The Robert Gordon University.

Sun, Y. C. (2003). Extensive reading online: An overview and evaluation. *Journal of Computer Assisted Learning*, *19*(4), 438–446. doi:10.1046/j.0266-4909.2003.00048.x

Swanson, H. L. (1987). Information Processing Theory and Learning Disabilities: A Commentary and Future Perspective. *Journal of Learning Disabilities*, *20*(3), 155–166. doi:10.1177/002221948702000303 PMID:3549949

Tadoz. (2010). *What the Arab state in Internet use*. Tadoz Technical Arabic.

Taobao. (2011). *Chinese taobao web site*. Retrieved from http://www.taobao.com

Tapscott, D. (1998). Educating in digital world. *Education Canada*, *41*(1), 4–7.

Teacy L, W. T., Patel, J., Jennings, N. R. & Luck, M. (2005). Coping with inaccurate reputation sources: Experimental analysis of a probabilistic trust model. *AAMAS05*.

Teacy, W.T., Patel, J., Jennings, N.R. & Luck, M. (2006). Travos: Trust and reputation in the context of inaccurate information sources. *Autonomous Agents and Multi Agent Systems*, *12*(2), 183-198.

Teacy, W. T., Patel, J., Jennings, N. R., & Luck, M. (2006). Travos: Trust and reputation in the context of inaccurate information sources. *Autonomous Agents and Multi-Agent Systems*, *12*(2), 183–198. doi:10.1007/s10458-006-5952-x

Team, F.-O. D. (2011). *Fipa-os developers guide*. Retrieved from http://citeseer.ist.psu.edu/477218.html

Tenopir, C., King, D. W., Edwards, S., & Wu, L. (2009). Electronic journals and changes in scholarly article seeking and reading patterns. *Aslib Proceedings*, *61*(1), 5-32.

Tenopir, C., Edwards, S., King, D. W., & Wu, L. (2009). Electronic journals and changes in scholarly article seeking and reading patterns. *Aslib Proceedings*, *61*(1), 5–32. doi:10.1108/00012530910932267

Terras, M. (2005). Reading the Readers: Modelling Complex Humanities Processes to Build cognitive System. *Literary and Linguistic Computing*, *20*(1), 41–59. doi:10.1093/llc/fqh042

Thissen, F., (2004). *Screen design manual: Communicating effectively through multimedia*. Springer.

Tripp, L.M. (2010). The computer is not for you to be looking around, it is for schoolwork: Challenges for digital inclusion as Latino immigrant families negotiate children access to the internet. *New media & society*, 13(4), 552-567.

Truong, Y. (2009). An Evaluation of the Theory of Planned Behaviour in Consumer Acceptance of Online Video and Television Services. *The Electronic Journal Information Systems Evaluation*, *12*(2), 177–186.

Trushell, J., Burrell, C., & Maitland, A. (2001). Year 5 pupils reading an Interactive Storybook on CD-ROM: Losing the plot? *British Journal of Educational Technology*, *32*(4), 389–401. doi:10.1111/1467-8535.00209

Usó, E., & Ruiz-Madrid, M.N. (2009). Reading printed versus online texts. A study of EFL learners strategic reading behavior. *International Journal of English Studies*, *9*(2), 59-79.

Valkensburg, P. M. & Soeters, K.E., (2001). Children`s positive and negative experience with the internet: an exploratory survey. *Communication Research, 28*(5), 652- 675.

Vassiliou, M. & Rowley, J., (2008). Theme article progressing the definition of "e- book". *Library Hi Tech, 26*(3), 355-368.

Venkatesh, V., & Davis, F. D. (2000). A theoretical extension of the technology acceptance model: Four longitudinal field studies. *Management Science*, *46*(2), 186–204. doi:10.1287/mnsc.46.2.186.11926

Vidyasagar, T. R., & Pammer, K. (1999). Impaired visual search in dyslexia relates to the role of the magnocellular pathway in attention. *Neuroreport*, *10*(6), 1283-1287.

W3C. (1999). *Web Content Accessibility Guidelines 1.0*. Retrieved from http://www.w3.org/TR/WCAG10/

Walker, R. C., Gordon, A. S., & Schloss, P. (2007). Visual-Syntactic Text-Formatting: Theoretical Basis and Empirical Evidence for Impact on Human Reading. *IEEE International Professional Communication Conference Engineering the Future of Human Communication*. doi:10.1109/IPCC.2007.4464068

Walker, R., Schloss, P., & Vogel, C. A. (2007). *Visual-Syntactic Text Formatting: Theoretical Basis and Empirical Evidence for Impact on Human Reading*.

Wastlund, E., Norlander, T., & Archer, T. (2008). The effect of page layout on mental workload: A dual-task experiment. *Computers in Human Behavior*, *24*(3), 1229–1245. doi:10.1016/j.chb.2007.05.001

Weiser, E. B. (2002). Gender differences in internet usepatterns and internet application preferences: A two sample comparison. *Cyberpsychology & Behavior, 3*(2), 167–178. doi:10.1089/109493100316012

Werger, B. B. (1999). Cooperation without deliberation: A minimal behavior-based approach to multi-robot teams. *Artificial Intelligence, 110*(2), 293–320. doi:10.1016/S0004-3702(99)00023-5

White, A. (2007). Understanding hypertext cognition: Developing mental models to aid users' comprehension. *First Monday, 1*.

Wiggins, R. H. (1977). Effects of three typographical variables on speed of reading. *Visible Language, 1*, 5–18.

Wijnholds, A. D. B. (1997). *Using type: The typographer's craftsmanship and the ergonomist's research*. The Netherlands: Utrecht University.

Wikipedia. (2012). *Belief in Wikipedia*. Retrieved from http://en.wikipedia.org/wiki/Belief

Wilson, R., Landoni, M., & Gibb, F. (2002). A user-centred approach to Ebook design. *The Electronic Library, 20*(4), 30–32. doi:10.1108/02640470210438865

Wilson, R., Landoni, M., & Gibb, F. (2003). The WEB Book experiments in electronic textbook design. *The Journal of Documentation, 59*(4), 454–476. doi:10.1108/00220410310485721

Wolf, M. (2007). Proust and squid: the story and science of the reading brain. New York: Harper Collins.

Wolff, R., Bhaduri, K., & Kargupta, H. (2009). A generic local algorithm for mining data streams in large distributed systems. *IEEE Transactions on Knowledge and Data Engineering, 21*(4), 465–478. doi:10.1109/TKDE.2008.169

Wooldridge, M., & Jennings., N. R. (1994). Towards a theory of cooperative problem solving. *Proc. of Modelling Autonomous Agent in a Multi-Agent World*.

Wooldridge, M. J. (2000). *Reasoning about rational agents*. The MIT Press.

Wooldridge, M. J. (2002). *An introduction to multiagent systems*. John Wiley and Sons.

Wright, P., & Lickorish, A. (1988). Colour cues as location aids in lengthy texts on screen and paper. *Behaviour & Information Technology, 7*(1), 11–30. doi:10.1080/01449298808901860

Wu, Q., An, J., & Lin, B. (2012). A texture segmentation algorithm based on PCA and global minimization active contour model for aerial insulator images. *IEEE Journal of Selected Topics in Applied Earth Observations and Remote Sensing, 5*(5), 1509–1518. doi:10.1109/JSTARS.2012.2197672

Xie, X. Z., Wu, J. T., & Jing, M. G. (2013). Fast two-stage segmentation via non-local active contours in multiscale texture feature space. *Pattern Recognition Letters, 34*(11), 1230–1239. doi:10.1016/j.patrec.2013.04.016

Yang, Y. L., James, A. S., & Amin, I. K. (2009). Target discovery from data mining approaches. *Drug Discovery Today, 14*(3), 147–154. doi:10.1016/j.drudis.2008.12.005 PMID:19135549

Yen, N.-S., Tsai, J.-L., Chen, P.-L., Lin, H.-Y., & Chen, A.L.P. (2011). Effects of typographic variables on eye-movement measures in reading Chinese from a screen. *Behaviour & Information Technology, 30*(6), 797–808. doi:10.1080/0144 929X.2010.523900

Yen, M., Tsai, J., Tzeng, O. J. L., & Hung, D. L. (2008). Eye movements and parafoveal word processing in reading Chinese. *Memory & Cognition, 36*(5), 1033–1045. doi:10.3758/MC.36.5.1033 PMID:18630209

Yi, W., Park, E., & Cho, K. (2011). E-Book Readability, Comprehensibility and Satisfaction. Proceedings of ICUMC`11, Seoul, Korea.

Yoh, E., Damhorst, M. L., Sapp, S., & Laczniak, R. (2003). Consumer adoption of the internet: The case of apparel shopping. *Psychology and Marketing*, *20*(12), 1095–1118. doi:10.1002/mar.10110

You, J., Li, W. X., & Zhang, D. (2002). Hierarchical palmprint identification via multiple feature extraction. *Pattern Recognition*, *35*(4), 847–859. doi:10.1016/S0031-3203(01)00100-5

Youngman, M., & Scharff, L. (1998). *Text width and margin width influences*. South Western Psychological Association.

Yu, B., & Singh, M. P. (2000). *A social mechanism of reputation management in electronic communities*. Cooperative Information Agents IV - The Future of Information. doi:10.1007/978-3-540-45012-2_15

Yue, F., Zuo, W. M., & Zhang, D. P. (2010). Survey of palm print recognition algorithms. *Acta Automatica Sinica*, *36*(3), 353–365. doi:10.3724/SP.J.1004.2010.00353

Yu, J. (2011). Texture segmentation based on FCM algorithm combined with GLCM and space information.*Proceedings of the 2011 International Conference on Electric Information and Control Engineering*, Beijing (pp. 4569 – 4572).

Yu, P., Qin, A. K., & Clausi, D. A. (2012). Unsupervised polarimetric SAR image segmentation and classification using region growing with edge penalty. *IEEE Transactions on Geoscience and Remote Sensing*, *50*(4), 1302–1317.

Zacharia, G., & Maes, P. (1999). Collaborative Reputation Mechanisms in Electroni Marketplaces.*Proc. 32nd Hawaii International Conf on System Sciences.*

Zacharia, G., & Maes, P. (1999). Collaborative Reputation Mechanisms in Electronic Marketplaces.*Proc. 32nd Hawaii International Conf on System Sciences.*

Zacharia, G., & Maes, P. (1999). Collaborative Reputation Mechanisms in Electronic Marketplaces.*Proc. 32nd Hawaii International Conf. on System Sciences.*

Zadeh, L. A. (1965). Fuzzy sets. *Information and Control*, *8*(3), 338–353. doi:10.1016/S0019-9958(65)90241-X

Zernik, U. (1991). *Lexical acquisition: Exploiting on-line resources to build a lexicon*. Hoboken, NJ: Lawrence Erlbaum Associates.

Zhang, L., Gong, Z. L, Chen, Y., & Gu, S. D. (2008). *Biomedical data mining*. Shanghai Science and technology press.

Zhang, X.-m., Shu, H., & Ran, T. (2007). Effect of computer screen back and font color on Chinese reading comprehension. *Proceedings of theInternational Conference on Intelligent Pervasive Computing*. IEEE.

Zhang, Z., Shu, W., & Rong, G. (2002). Automatic palmprint classification method based on the orientation of ridges. *Journal Tsinghua University*, *42*(9), 1222–1224.

Zhou, W.L., & Wu, X. F. (2006). Survey of P2P technologies. Retrieved from en.cnki.com.cn

About the Contributors

Joan Lu is Professor in Informatics in the University of Huddersfield. She has been working in the areas of XML database, information retrieval research, mobile computing, Internet computing, mobile learning, etc. Her research projects have been collaborated with several EU, UK and other international institutions and industrial partners. The research work has been published into public domain together with a number of researchers in the academic world. She is also a member of British Computer Society, and Fellow of Higher Education Academy, UK.

Qiang Xu is a Senior lecturer at the School of Computing and Engineering, The University of Huddersfield, UK. His research activities covers computational modelling. Previously, Dr Xu was Senior Lecturer in the School of Science and Engineering at Teesside University from 2006 to 2013. In this role, Dr Xu supervised a number of PhD research projects and completed over 15 consultancy and grant applications. Dr Xu was Visiting Professor at the Northwest Polytechnic University, China from 2007 to 2012 and co-editor of two conference proceedings, key note speakers, regular reviewer for several internal journals (reviewed over 70 papers), and several internal conference committee member; and has published more than 70 papers. Dr Xu's research work has been cited worldwide by researchers in 8 nations including China, the USA, UK, Germany, Poland, India, Iran, and Russia.

* * *

Azza A. Abubaker received her BSc in Library and information Science from department of Library and information science, Benghazi University, Libya in 1992. she has an MSc degree in Library and information Science from the same university, in 2001. She earned his PhD degree from School of Engineering and Informatics, University of Huddersfield, UK in 2014. Azza is currently employed as a lecturer in Library and information Science, Benghazi University, Libya. She has taught at Benghazi University since 1993. Her current research interests include human computer interaction, information management, E- learning, electronic text formats, technical service such as; cataloguing and classification, and information system.

QingE Wu is a Professor in Zhengzhou University of Light Industry. Her main research interests include pattern recognition, data mining, image processing, fuzzy control, rough sets, and uncertainty information processing.

Weidong Yang is an associate professor in Fudan University, Shanghai, China.

Gehao Lu is an associate professor in The Software School, Yunnan University, China. His research interests include Information Systems (Business Informatics), Artificial Intelligence, Software Engineering.

Index

Purchase Print + Free E-Book or E-Book Only*

Purchase a print book through the IGI Global Online Bookstore and receive the e-book for free or purchase the e-book only! Shipping fees apply.

www.igi-global.com

Recommended Reference Books

ISBN: 978-1-4666-7456-1
© 2015; 2,072 pp.
List Price: $1,880

ISBN: 978-1-4666-5864-6
© 2014; 570 pp.
List Price: $276

ISBN: 978-1-4666-5198-2
© 2014; 398 pp.
List Price: $164

ISBN: 978-1-4666-4679-7
© 2014; 387 pp.
List Price: $140

ISBN: 978-1-4666-6567-5
© 2015; 461 pp.
List Price: $160

ISBN: 978-1-4666-6493-7
© 2015; 643 pp.
List Price: $180

Publishing Information Science and Technology Research Since 1988

www.igi-global.com Sign up at www.igi-global.com/newsletters facebook.com/igiglobal twitter.com/igiglobal

  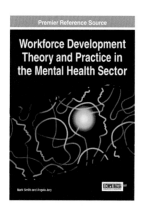 

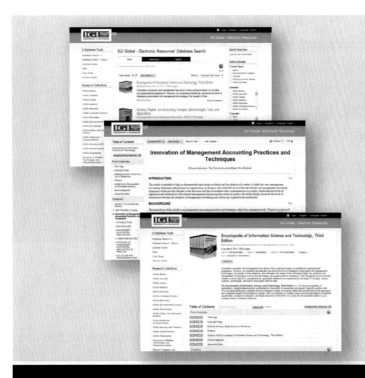

Become an IRMA Member

Members of the **Information Resources Management Association (IRMA)** understand the importance of community within their field of study. The Information Resources Management Association is an ideal venue through which professionals, students, and academicians can convene and share the latest industry innovations and scholarly research that is changing the field of information science and technology. Become a member today and enjoy the benefits of membership as well as the opportunity to collaborate and network with fellow experts in the field.

IRMA Membership Benefits:

- **One FREE Journal Subscription**

- **30% Off Additional Journal Subscriptions**

- **20% Off Book Purchases**

- Updates on the latest events and research on Information Resources Management through the IRMA-L listserv.

- Updates on new open access and downloadable content added to Research IRM.

- A copy of the Information Technology Management Newsletter twice a year.

- A certificate of membership.

IRMA Membership $195

Scan code or visit **irma-international.org** and begin by selecting your free journal subscription.

Membership is good for one full year.

Encyclopedia of Information Science and Technology, Third Edition (10 Vols.)

Mehdi Khosrow-Pour, D.B.A. (Information Resources Management Association, USA)
ISBN: 978-1-4666-5888-2; **EISBN:** 978-1-4666-5889-9; © 2015; 10,384 pages.

The **Encyclopedia of Information Science and Technology, Third Edition** is a 10-volume compilation of authoritative, previously unpublished research-based articles contributed by thousands of researchers and experts from all over the world. This discipline-defining encyclopedia will serve research needs in numerous fields that are affected by the rapid pace and substantial impact of technological change. With an emphasis on modern issues and the presentation of potential opportunities, prospective solutions, and future directions in the field, it is a relevant and essential addition to any academic library's reference collection.

Take An Extra **30% Off**[1]

[1] 30% discount offer cannot be combined with any other discount and is only valid on purchases made directly through IGI Global's Online Bookstore (www.igi-global.com/books), not intended for use by distributors or wholesalers. Offer expires December 31, 2016.

Free Lifetime E-Access with Print Purchase

Take 30% Off Retail Price:

Hardcover with <u>Free E-Access</u>:[2] **$2,765**
~~List Price: $3,950~~

E-Access with <u>Free Hardcover</u>:[2] **$2,765**
~~List Price: $3,950~~

Recommend this Title to Your Institution's Library: www.igi-global.com/books

[2] IGI Global now offers the exclusive opportunity to receive free lifetime e-access with the purchase of the publication in print, or purchase any e-access publication and receive a free print copy of the publication. You choose the format that best suits your needs. This offer is only valid on purchases made directly through IGI Global's Online Bookstore and not intended for use by book distributors or wholesalers. Shipping fees will be applied for hardcover purchases during checkout if this option is selected.

The lifetime of a publication refers to its status as the current edition. Should a new edition of any given publication become available, access will not be extended on the new edition and will only be available for the purchased publication. If a new edition becomes available, you will not lose access, but you would no longer receive new content for that publication (i.e. updates). Free Lifetime E-Access is only available to single institutions that purchase printed publications through IGI Global. Sharing the Free Lifetime E-Access is prohibited and will result in the termination of e-access.